P9-DHA-597

ALSO BY SEYMOUR MELMAN

What Else Is There to Do?

The Demilitarized Society: Disarmament and Conversion

Profits Without Production

The Permanent War Economy: American Capitalism in Decline

Managerial vs. Cooperative Decision-Making in Israel

Pentagon Capitalism: The Management of the New Imperialism

Our Depleted Society

The Peace Race

Decision-Making and Productivity

Dynamic Factors in Industrial Productivity

EDITED BY SEYMOUR MELMAN

The War Economy of the United States

Conversion of Industry from a Military to a Civilian Economy, Vols. I–VI

In the Name of America

Disarmament: Its Politics and Economics

No Place to Hide

Inspection for Disarmament

After Capitalism

After Capitalism

From Managerialism to Workplace Democracy

SEYMOUR MELMAN

ALFRED A. KNOPF

NEW YORK 2001

THIS IS A BORZOI BOOK
PUBLISHED BY ALFRED A. KNOPF

 Published in the United States by Alfred A. Knopf, a division of Random House, Inc., New York, and simultaneously in Canada by Random House of Canada Limited, Toronto. Distributed by Random House, Inc., New York.

www.aaknopf.com

Owing to limitations of space, all acknowledgments of permission to reprint previously published material will be found following the index.

Library of Congress Cataloging-in-Publication Data
Melman, Seymour.
After capitalism: from managerialism to workplace democracy / by Seymour Melman.
p. cm.
Includes bibliographical references and index.
ISBN 0-679-41859-8 (alk. paper)
1. Industrial management—Employee participation—United States.
2. Capitalism—United States. I. Title.
HD5660.U5 M45 2001
331'.01'12—dc21 2001038300

Manufactured in the United States of America
First Edition

To Lawrence Berel Cohen

Pioneer Researcher on Worker Decision-Making on Production

CONTENTS

Preface

I undertook the investigations reported in this book in order to identify the dynamics of behavior among managers and workers which, in turn, illuminate the prospect of an emerging alternative to the currently dominant economy and society of state capitalism. In particular, I have tried to map prospective changes in the employment relations while corporate and government managers pursue profit and power by deindustrialization in the United States and worldwide militarization.

I have examined the dynamics of both managerial and worker activity as these affect both the classic employment relations of business and the relations of production that are the focus of workers' decision-making.

The shape of a prospective alternative economy is defined by the disalienation response of workers to the alienations that have been long pursued by state and corporate managers.

Now, into the twenty-first century, white-collar workers, like the blues of industry, have been learning how to institute the disalienation process, to make rules among themselves for governing expanding sectors of their own work. These are new relations of production, an alternative to the long-familiar decision processes of business and state capitalism.

The workers' decision process defines the core features of workplace democracy: those who do production work of every sort are also final decision-makers—in contrast to the traditional business separation of decision-making from producing; internal democratic procedures for rule-making replace governance by hierarchy; solidarity and mutual trust replace predatory competition; countermoves to inequality and exploitation replace profit and power accumulation without limit.

The American people have been taught to believe that there is no alternative to organizing work and community by the alienated, hierarchical rule of corporate/state managers. Americans have also been asked to agree that they live in the best of possible worlds, at "the end of history," and that loyalty to state/corporate management is not only necessary for their level of living but also morally justified. Such ideas will be treated here as cover stories propagated by people and institutions that are dedicated to discouraging workplace democracy.

The education systems of America, from grade school to universities, train future employees to accept this dogma that there is no alternative to the state capitalist rule over American economy and community.

This book marshals evidence on the behavior of state/corporate managers and workers to the effect that now, in the twenty-first century, there are two decision systems on production present and unfolding in the United States: management's state capitalism, and the workers' decision processes toward workplace democracy.

I expect that younger scholars will want to explore and develop many themes of *After Capitalism.* To facilitate this work, I have organized research files (other than the materials identified in the endnotes) by chapter of *After Capitalism* and given them to the Rare Book and Manuscript Library of the Columbia University libraries, where they are accessible to researchers and writers.

This book cannot be accounted for simply as the product of a stated author. I have drawn on the published writings and generously given knowledge from many colleagues.

In particular, Lawrence B. Cohen has opened the pages of his still unpublished "Workers and Decision-Making on Production" and thereby made it possible to proceed with solid confidence to tap data and analyses that defined major elements of a new, disalienated decision process on production.

No brief statement can adequately express my intellectual debt to Zellig S. Harris, a mentor and friend for many years. Alongside his extensively published work in linguistics, he has produced *The Transformation of Capitalist Society* (Rowman and Littlefield, 1997). An archive of unpublished materials that led to that work are in the Library of the University of Pennsylvania.

Jon Rynn, a scholar in computer science and researcher in political economy, contributed early access to his studies on the development of America's capital-goods industries and their role in economic growth, and in deindustrialization, and gave valuable support for assembling and presenting data on productivity and on depletion of capital-goods industries.

David Mandel's unique investigations of Russian workers' industrial experience (Chapter 6) illuminate aspects of that economy and society that are rarely reported. His published and unpublished data, and detailed verbatim exchanges, present a notably reliable view "from below" for appreciating essential qualities of Russia's state capitalism.

Valuable contributions to this book were made by Patrick Deer (Department of English, Columbia University) and by Ashbel Green (editor at Alfred A. Knopf), who applied their considerable talents to structuring data and analyses that served clarity of statement in this many-sided book.

I am grateful beyond words to each of the colleagues who contributed knowledge and critical commentary that have enriched this book: Michael Albert, Sol Barkin, Ron Bloom, Charles Bofferding, Arie Caspi, Noam Chomsky, James L. Coen, David Ellerman, Frank Emspak, William Evan, John K. Galbraith, Carl Gersuny, Jim Haughton, Gerard Honig, Vladimir V. Kachalin, Robert Karasek, Jonathan Karp, Lou Kiefer, Karl E. Klare, Sherman Kreiner, Len Krimerman, Jesus Larranaga, Everett E. Lewis, Douglas Lummis, Staughton Lynd, David Mandel, David McCall, Tim Moody, Ken Nash, Wun Kuen Ng, Bernard Nneji, Robert S. Norris, Dan North, Mario Pianta, Sam Pizzigati, Meyer Rabban, Marcus Raskin, Michael Renner, Charles Richardson, Hugo Séguin, Harley Shaiken, Nir Shapira, Jack Sheinkman, Michael Shuman, Georgy Skorov, Yigal Stav, Louis Uchitelle, John E. Ullmann, James C. Wright, Giora Yanai, and Howard Zinn.

The research and manuscript preparation were solidly supported by a wonderful succession of assistants, for whose diligence I am grateful to the end of time: Carol Ann Luten, Jason Mandela, Ana Dopico, Kevin Chong, Wun Kuen Ng, Tawia Ansah, Jefferson Gatrall, Lead We Pang and Pooja Mehta.

After Capitalism

INTRODUCTION

Managerialism and "the Market" Are Not Forever

With strong, confident voices, the managers of American government and corporations hailed their Cold War victory over the Soviet foes of the market economy. After 1991, the celebration was joined by eager allies in the Western media and the universities. But no sooner was victory proclaimed than the Pentagon and the rest of the U.S. government installed a five-year planning and budgeting system. Not to be outdone in the quest for common ground, Moscow opened a stock exchange for the convenience of Russia's new investor class.

Meanwhile, in the face of the high-decibel trumpeting of the market system as a virtual "end of the line" for economy and society, America's workers have maintained a mostly quiet but unrelenting struggle for their own empowerment. They have responded to a great parade of alienations that have long diminished their power over their lives both within and beyond the workplace.* Largely unnoticed, they have joined workers around the world in resisting alienations that have made possible unprecedented accumulations of capital and managerial power. This ongoing struggle for workplace democracy, to invent a new kind of economy, is the focus of this book.

*I appreciate that *alienation* is a term that frequently connotes "the process of rendering a population powerless." In the usages of sociology and psychology, various feelings are also said to be linked to rendering such acts. These emotions are said to include: hopelessness, isolation, meaninglessness and estrangement.

In the present work, *alienation* is used only to describe the process that renders people powerless to affect their own work, or powerless to prevent their removal from their occupations and communities. The psychological reactions that often accompany alienation are not dealt with here.

Disalienation describes, on the other hand, workers' actions to restore power to affect their work, and their places in occupations and communities. This term was coined by Lawrence B. Cohen to encompass the procedures and results of worker decision-making on production, as detailed in Part IV.

For businessmen, the main objective has always been accumulating capital for investment and the successful growth of enterprise. If the drive toward accumulation requires alienating their workers, so be it. For state managers, notably during the latter half of the twentieth century, successive alienations, spearheaded by military power and accelerated by technologies produced on command, have opened the prospect of unrivaled hegemonic control.

Yet despite aggressive public education to induce compliance with the domestic and international programs of the state/corporate managers, workers have continued and even intensified their efforts to disalienate, to reconstruct elements of their decision power.

Since 1991, the rulers of Washington and Moscow have joined in a consensus that the managerial/hierarchical mode of organization is the best one for carrying out modern production. For every nation, the working of "free markets" has been hailed as the preferred way to set the prices of goods and the prices of work. American textbooks in economics have been translated into Russian and introduced as the last word to secondary schools and universities. In American society, the commitment within popular culture to managerialism and the market economy is so strong as to virtually exclude even the discussion of the possibility of present or future alternatives. This allegiance is bolstered by an array of "cover stories" that serve to reassure the populace about its economic prospects. Under the rubric of "globalization," U.S. state and corporate managers have constructed the ultimate worldwide cover story for their neoliberal ideology.

That central cover story proclaims that there is, above all, no alternative to managerialism, the market economy or state capitalism. This book aims to challenge that claim, and to identify an alternative that is already being shaped by economic and social developments that are under way.

There can be little doubt that the dominant ideology in matters economic is the idea that the market and market relations are the governing factors in economic function. At the heart of the idea of the market economy is the unshakable belief that prices (and wages) are set with perfect rationality—as the automatic effect of the rational decisions of many perfectly informed buyers and sellers.* In fact, "the market" is commonly referred to as though it were an object, a thing quite separate from the interactions of the people whose activity in buying and selling constitutes a market. Thus it is completely ordinary to see or hear news reports about

*Professor Yehuda Don, at Bar Ilan University, has brought my attention to the strident (and unproven) claims of the neoclassical economists' market mechanism that sets prices and wages at precisely their true value. Thereby, he said, "capitalism has expelled God!" Such perfection makes God superfluous.

"what the market is telling us," or about "what the market will (or will not) sustain."

In reality, "the market" is not a thing or an animate being; to ascribe such decision power to it is to indulge in a form of fetishism. This kind of fallacious thinking involves a displacement of categories in which human behavior is described in a way that shields the identity of the real decision-makers, whether they are individuals or social groups—like the managers of corporations or the executives of the federal government. In the process, responsibility for organizational actions and decision-making is displaced: endless numbers of decisions are imagined as stemming from an object, the market, rather than from the decision-power relations of managers, corporate and governmental.

All this is a good thing for the managerialists, as the decisions taken by government or business managers are not mentioned, and the results of their actions are ascribed to the anonymous workings of the market. There is, of course, a very large literature that describes the ways by which corporate managers have contrived to control the buying and selling of particular goods.[1] Yet, this form of displacement of categories, onto the mysterious agency of "competition," is one more version of fetishism. In reality, the conditions of the real world do not accord with the assumptions of a market economy concerning price and wages. Indeed, there is an elaborate history of collusive price-setting by managements.[2] During other times, emperors and high priests led the people in worshipping idols. Our new idols of the marketplace are the big corporate players who seem to wield occult powers or knowledge over the mysterious workings of the market. At the close of the twentieth century, decision-making by readily defined managers was displaced by the market cover stories, thereby removing accountability or responsibility from the actual decision-makers.

The gross domestic product, which is the total output of goods and services produced in the United States, valued at market prices, has a leading role in the ideology of the market. According to the cover stories, a rise in the GDP is hailed as the prime measure of increase in the nation's wealth and material well-being. In fact, the money values of weapons, research, development and investment for new nuclear warheads, training for wars, and the cost of building and operating prisons for two million people are all part of the GDP story, as are the outlays for making and broadcasting the Niagara of TV violence that affords entertaining models of destructive behavior. This all adds up to a very dubious kind of wealth.

Close cousin to the GDP myth is the idea that "money equals wealth." In fact money is a socially agreed-upon representation of value, and its relation to actual material wealth is highly variable. This mystification about the nature of money continues to foster the illusion that everyone benefits from the stock market's financial booms, when in fact the numbers show that the market bonanza significantly affects only the top 10 percent of society. The last decades of the twentieth century have seen an unprecedented concentration of wealth in the hands of a rich minority, while income levels for the majority of Americans have stagnated or even fallen. The discredited "trickle-down" economics of the 1980s have been replaced by another smokescreen: the myth of the high-tech financial boom of the 1990s, the so-called "new economy." The reality is that there is nothing new about the new economy.

These days, it seems, if you aren't "in the market," you hardly count at all.

Ironically, even if the wealth were spread around more equitably, this would not alter the social relations that underpin the vast gulf between the top 10 percent and the rest of society. As this book sets out to demonstrate, to really make a difference, the social relations that underlie the hierarchical control of economy must be changed. This would involve asking different kinds of questions: Who decides what is produced, and how are these products disposed of? By what rules? As I will argue, these social relations can be, and are in the process of being, changed. As workers all over the world have been demonstrating, there are alternatives to the endless cycle of alienation and accumulation that drives the "market."

The theory of the market economy was crucially tested as a predictive system in August–September 1998, when securities markets around the world became severely stressed. No part of "neoclassical economics," or the theory of the market economy, or any other conventional wisdom about self-correcting, perfectly rational price/money mechanisms, accounts for the government's moves with respect to the failures of Long-Term Capital Management that year. This was a straightforward political intervention—applying the government's political power to rescue the American financial superstructure, which could otherwise have been in danger of disarray and collapse triggered by the failure of this highly regarded investment-managing firm.

No textbook in economics prepared readers either for the international 1998 debacle in the value of many national currencies or for the collapse of Long-Term Capital Management. Around the world, major currency speculators moved their billions to gain short-term profits, or to minimize losses, while ordinary people of many countries watched the purchasing power of their money decline.

The fortunes of Long-Term Capital Management merited special attention by the financial press. For a moment, there was a readiness to look underneath the cover stories of the market economy. Beginning in

1973, we are told, economists tried to "correlate interest rates, prices, volatility and time," and thereby, "as would an insurance policy . . . put a price tag on uncertainty. Models had arrived." Thereupon, "trading through computer models became the hippest and most lucrative thing to do on Wall Street."[3] Nevertheless, as one banking analyst put it,

> They only model for whatever humans put into them. Are people putting in data that reflect the possibility of the financial equivalent of a nuclear meltdown? Usually not. And then they rely on computer models as if they're the word of God.

Hence, in the euphoria of the 1990s, many economists violated a very elementary rule of computer, slide rule or pencil-and-paper modeling—GIGO: Garbage Input results in Garbage Output. So the elaborate computing modeling systems of Bankers Trust, Citicorp, Chase Manhattan, Goldman Sachs, JP Morgan, Merrill Lynch and Salomon Smith Barney proved to be flawed, incompetent to make forecasts about the main elements of the market economy. Switzerland's UBS, the largest bank in Europe, suffered an unexplained $696 million loss in Long-Term Capital Management.

What lesson was learned from this financial/banking debacle? Not much. There was no lifting of the cover stories of the market economy to expose the underpinning assumptions, and the shakiness of those assumptions. The fraternity of economists did learn that

> When, instead of just trembling, the financial system threatens to come unglued, model or no model, mere worries turn to migraines. And fast action is demanded: monetary policy shifts, IMF bailouts, or in the latest case, the Federal Reserve's roping of Wall Street's biggest houses into engineering the rescue of Long-Term Capital. Then the models can settle down again, ripe for a blindsiding by the next bolt from the blue.[4]

When the crunch came, the computer models failed to anticipate the global crisis. In the United States, this crisis period was exemplified by the failure of Long-Term Capital Management.

Some financial writers did undertake a critical examination of the economic and financial models that had seemingly promised unquestioned reliability. It was noted, ruefully, that Long-Term Capital Management included as partners two Nobel laureates in economics. But in the postmortem that followed the hedge fund's collapse, nobody suggested that their Nobel awards be revoked or returned.[5]

. . .

It is a purpose of this book to demonstrate that the normal workings of corporate and government managerial control over workers have set in motion a chain reaction that has resulted in grave production weaknesses in the U.S. economy, a process that will be outlined in Part II. Alongside these effects—unanticipated by conventional wisdom—a process of change has been set in motion that promises to supplant capitalism as we have known it. But such alternative possibilities are typically excluded by the network of popular justifications that serve as cover stories.

Why are alternatives to the market economy and allied control of production by managerial hierarchies so hard to recognize? For nearly five decades, Americans were mobilized in support of the Cold War. They accepted the cover story that the alternative to the market economy was Soviet-style central planning. The grip of this story was strong enough to make it seem outlandish even to raise the prospect of alternatives to managerial hierarchical control of enterprise and the corporate/state governance of the economy. With the end of the Cold War, the marketeers declared, we have reached the end of the line.

Neoliberalism purports to be a general theory about society in which the individual is the unit of decision-making and behavior. But in actual fact, the functioning of corporate managements, government managements and workers during the latter half of the twentieth century was in each case a form of group behavior—of many people acting in concert in accordance with the accepted rules and goals of their respective endeavors or occupations. In none of these spheres is there a collection of individuals whose actions are in concert just by chance. The concert is a group process, not a collection of individually determined actions.

Independently of particular merits or demerits, the neoliberal market economy has been dubbed an "end of history." Indeed, this dogma proclaims that no new major developments should be desired or expected in economy or society. Accordingly, the agenda of cover stories includes seductive categories like the "postindustrial society," or "the information society." The postindustrial idea carries the implication that a condition has been (or is about to be) reached in which production is no longer a problem—because abundance is upon us. Accordingly, the citizens of the postindustrial society, drawing upon the full powers of "global" information technologies, are encouraged to see themselves as though natives in idyllic locations where hunger can be satisfied simply by plucking the "fruit" that is abundantly present, or by waiting for the coconut to fall while merely maintaining a prudent distance from the landing point.

But the invention of capitalism, and the subsequent rise of state capitalism, has failed to provide prospects for work-free abundance. All told, it is prudent to understand that managerialism and market economy, as systems of ideas, have standing primarily as dogma, but not by the ordinary test of predictive power that is conventional in scientific discourse.

Everyone with access to the Internet (or even TV) can see that information can now be spread at hitherto unimaginable speed. Usually overlooked, however, is the parallel concentration of control over the content of press, radio, TV and the Internet. As we will see in Parts II, III and IV of this book, vast fields of information, though nominally accessible, are usually not portrayed and explained so that a nonspecialist can use them. The much-vaunted information society then becomes an information-control society. An illusion is created: Information quantity is celebrated, even as the selective editing of information conceals the scale and quality of ideological controls and alienation operations that harness ordinary people in the service of profit/power accumulation.

In order to make sense of the status quo behind the cover stories, it is necessary to understand what is *really* new about capitalism at the beginning of the twenty-first century.

During the past three centuries, capitalism went through several major alterations, even as the core processes of alienation that served capital accumulation were kept in place. What began as a drive for profit translatable as capital was later transformed into an accumulation of profit and power over people.

The managers of business organizations have long sought advantage by disarming workers and competing managements—the better to exploit them. From the very outset of capitalism, when competing managements and hired workers were strategically weakened, larger profits could then be assembled, as capital, for further investment. Business management led the field in this phase of capitalist development, which endured to the end of the twentieth century. And throughout, despite the endless free-market rhetoric, government has moved to protect and facilitate the capital-accumulation process.

The logic of the accumulation of capital for ever-expanding investment, as a core element of business, was neatly defined by Karl Marx in *Capital.* Marx held that

> The development of capitalist production makes it constantly necessary to keep increasing the amount of the capital laid out in a given industrial undertaking, and competition makes the immanent laws of capitalist production to be felt by each individual capitalist, as external coercive laws. It compels him to keep constantly extending his capital, in order to preserve it, but extend it he cannot, except by means of progressive accumulation.

Marx did not hesitate to drive his point home with colorful language. He wrote:

> Accumulate, accumulate! That is Moses and the prophets! "Industry furnishes the material which saving accumulates." Therefore, save, save, i.e., reconvert the greatest possible portion of surplus-value, or surplus-product into capital! Accumulation for accumulation's sake, production for production's sake.[6]

During the twentieth century, even as business thrived, a major alteration in the dynamics of capitalism took place. In the new regime of state capitalism, alienation and accumulation continued and became more powerful, for these processes were, and are, managed by a collaborative business/government partnership.* This partnership has profoundly altered the accumulation process, and the militarization of the U.S. economy has been essential to its success.

After World War II, the military economy of the United States was enlarged as the primary instrument of government/business power, finally commanding more than half of federal budget funds for 2000.† This was done in ways that served both the accumulation of capital via business profit, and the accumulation of power over people—the "profit" of government.

While profits continue to be maximized by managements of business, state managers—besides lending a helpful hand to big business—have specialized in accumulating power, not only at home but abroad as well. The state managers continue to spur worldwide operations for global power extension, for hegemony over other states. Direct American capital investments that give control over foreign enterprises and resources are facilitated and encouraged by a worldwide network of specialized attachés in American embassies. Foreign aid, heavily militarized, plays a major role in this campaign of accumulating power.

*Universities explicitly train people for this collaboration. Harvard University's John F. Kennedy School of Government announced a course: Initiatives in Conflict Management: Planning for Civil-Military Cooperation, April 30–May 7, 2000 (*The Economist*, January 8, 2000).

†Career military officers play an important part in the unfolding of militarized state capitalism. Here the veterans of long military service perform a series of functionally diverse roles. Men and women imbued with the traditional values of the officer corps may find their way to military academies and think tanks. Others realize professional futures in enterprise managerial posts. Industrial firms also absorb a quota of technically skilled officers for design and evaluation/testing functions. And politically oriented officers find open doors in and around the federal Executive, and the Congress as well. The military is an invaluable training ground for the state and corporate managers of the permanent war economy.

. . .

The development of America's state capitalism is mirrored particularly in the evolving relationship between business-managed industrial capitalism and the newer, state-managed and permanent military economy, administered by the Pentagon. As I argued in an earlier study, the development has gone through three main phases.

> The World War II military economy consisted of a collaboration between business and government. War production was directed by battalions of industry managers on temporary loan to war agencies that were largely dismantled by 1946. Not surprisingly, the major firms emerged from the four-year U.S. war experience with large additions to their assets, having been favored as purchasers of government-financed plant and equipment.
>
> This function was carried out in ways that also served the enlargement of the American territorial and economic empire (for example, by trading old U.S. destroyers for British islands).
>
> The second phase in the development of American military power was the Cold War period 1950–60, from the Korean War to the close of the Eisenhower administration. . . . This decade saw rapid development of nuclear weapons. . . . Intercontinental missiles and nuclear-powered submarines were invented and put into large-scale production.
>
> By means of an intricate network of agreements, U.S. military bases were established in thirty-five countries—to "contain" the U.S.S.R. and serve as a constant threat to anti-U.S., anti-business-economy movements.
>
> This second phase of the development of military economy featured implementation of the doctrine of government-business partnership as formulated by the U.S. Army Chief of Staff, General Dwight Eisenhower, in 1946. His policy memorandum that defined this relationship was first published in my *Pentagon Capitalism.* It constituted the charter for what Eisenhower, as the outgoing President in January 1961, christened the "military-industrial complex."
>
> A third phase of development of America's war economy began in 1961. A government-based central administrative office designed by Robert McNamara was made the master of business-operated military industry. (This was accomplished by means of the managerial-control organization that I diagnosed in my *Pentagon Capitalism.*) Once the new state-managerial control system was set in motion, it exhibited the normal managerial impera-

tive for enlarging its organization, and the scope and intensity of its decision power.[7]

The latest phase of the U.S. war economy has involved a basic change in the mechanisms of capitalist economy by which capital investment is translated into power over decision-making. Under business capitalism, this decision power is accomplished by a cycle that includes investment, marketing products to regain the investment plus a profit, and ordering new investments with the enlarged capital fund that results.

The state-controlled military economy also invests capital. Here, however, it is translated directly into the instrumentalities of decision power—military organizations and their equipment. Since capital has only a one-time use in the military sphere, the application to decision power is direct.

By 2000, the government side of the corporate/state top management showed a familiar pattern. Federal cabinet members, their principal aides, and officials in key economic, national security, domestic political, military and technological commissions were drawn from among corporate and finance managers, career military officers, professors and lawyers with a mix of corporate and government administrative experience. This professional mix represents government and corporate activity across a broad spectrum of industry, politics, technology and finance. They are, functionally, the top management layers of what is touted as the "new economy."

The emergence and growth of state capitalism during the latter half of the twentieth century have been accompanied by severe alienations of populations both within the United States and abroad. Nevertheless, the calculations of American state and corporate managers did not anticipate the development of countering movements against their alienation operations. These were to become, as we shall see in this book, important components of workers' movements that effectively invented an economy after capitalism—the ongoing fruits of a struggle that creates a prospective replacement for the state/corporate-operated capitalism.

The central focus of this book is on the transformation of both the employers' and the workers' sides of employment relations (Parts II and IV). For changes in employment relations constitute changes in decision-making about production. Such moves thereby define much of the nature of economy and society; they are visible not only in the transition from feudalism to capitalism (Part I), but also in the developing mechanism of a shift from capitalism to workplace democracy (Part V).

Employment relations have been the dominant way of organizing decision-making on production during the entire three centuries of industrial capitalism. The employer decides on every major aspect of production, and workers perform as directed.

In exchange for a wage, workers acquiesce to the employer's decisions on the organization of work, division of labor, work time, standards of work performance and compensation. The employer has had great advantage for imposing his will as long as workers have been powerless to implement alternatives to the employer's preferences.

A diverse body of critical thought has developed around employment relations. The range of assessment has extended from viewing the employer as not only acting for his own profit and power, but thereby also benefitting the wider community by raising the productivity of the workforce. Employment relations have also been critiqued as the core of a system of exploitation that keeps a working class subdued.

The evolving mechanism and effects of the employer's role as a decision-maker on production is the focus of Part II. Part IV centers on the development, by workers, of a new decision process on production. Such innovations are shown to be the core of a successor economy to capitalism that is based upon workplace democracy (Part V).

Now, at the opening of the twenty-first century, it is possible to define the shape of economy and society after capitalism.

Under state capitalism, decision-making about production is guided by the rules and practices of four key institutions, which are enforced by the state: employment, property, money and capital.

Rules of *employment* link producers and decision-makers. The producers may not do their work without orders from property owners or their representatives. The rules of employment also give rise to a unique occupation: the unemployed. Within these rules, the unemployed are persons awaiting the employers' call to produce. They cannot participate in the work controlled by the employer. Thus unemployment is an occupation integral to the decision process* of state capitalism.

Rules of *property* govern who may dispose of particular objects and under what conditions that may be done. These rules facilitate control of the means of production by the employer, for the state has the power to implement the legalized rules of property and to counter infractions of these laws.

*I use here the term *decision process* as well as *decision-making*, in order to emphasize the relentless expansion of decision power that characterizes the managerialist regime of state capitalism. As I argue throughout this study, workers have struggled constantly to create and operate an alternative, a disalienated form of decision-making that is at the core of workplace democracy.

Money, though conventionally referred to as an object, actually signifies a system of social agreements. The rules of money are commonly accepted: Units of measurement should be used for stating the relative worth of goods and activities; in addition, particularly designated parties (usually a government) should be empowered to issue and circulate symbols of relative worth (coins, currency). Other socially agreed upon and legally designated symbols of relative worth may be provided by legally empowered parties (checks, credit cards). All of these representations of relative worth should be accepted for exchanges of goods and work. They are also indispensable in the presence of an intricately specialized division of labor in production and other work. These rules of money allow for the allocation of goods and services constituting the real incomes of all persons, and they also facilitate the transfer of property rights.

Last, *capital*. The rules of employment, property and money, taken together, constitute capital. From the vantage point of social relations, capital is not an object, but rather the combined system of rules under which the fabrication and operation of the means of production of goods can proceed. Whole factories and their machinery, transportation and communication facilities, dwellings and waterworks—all of these play a part in the investment and exchange mechanisms of capitalism. The rules of capital are also involved in the infrastructure—the social capital like schools and water supply—essential for the life of a community.

The rules of employment, property and money do not separately suffice to constitute capital but must operate in combination.

While these institutional arrangements have a major presence and support from the legal system, at their core they represent *social rules of behavior*—notwithstanding the fact that property and money are conventionally referred to as objects rather than as systems of rules. These rules also represent more than social consensus, for in state capitalism government plays a crucial part in interpreting, adjudicating and enforcing them.

The social rules that constitute capital are a guide to decisions on production as managerial calculation predicts acceptable profit/power for the employer. But these very rules that can command production to go forward also shape and restrain the use of physical capital, the instruments of production that multiply the production that is achievable by human hands and hand tools. Thereby the conventional businesslike, undemocratic concentration of decision power over the use of physical capital holds back the potential of the means of production. Workplace democracy, on the other hand, can enhance the productivity potential of twenty-first-century society. Democratic control over the marvelous physical capital of the economy can release productive potential that is now restrained and channeled to serve corporate and state managers' striving for profit and power.

Without such a clear understanding of the system that has transformed society and economy, and unless we know the rules underlying the hierarchical controls exercised by this partnership of government and corporate managers, we are left in the fog of illusions that masks the reality of state capitalism. If you don't see these social relations *as* social relations, you can't uncover their alteration.

After all, the state managers say to justify their ascendancy, we won the Cold War. Just what such brave words mean is not clear. In fact, as the account of state capitalism and the comparisons of the United States and Russia in the chapters of Part II suggest, we in America are much closer to the enemies of market freedom than we have been taught.

American adherents to their version of the market economy propose a very active role for what is called globalization. In their view, direct foreign investment by the United States and other forms of American influence in other countries have the inevitable effect of making for a more cohesive, and friendlier, pattern of international relations among all the states involved. Relentless enlargement of American control has been made to sound perfectly reasonable.

Finally, the agenda of cover stories has at its heart the claims of the doctrine of neoliberalism. Again, "market economy," "free trade" and "free investment" are confidently advocated as a way of bringing the peoples of the world closer together. Unstated by its advocates, the neoliberalism dogma in practice gives major advantage to the richest of the great powers. Thus they, and only they, are best able to pursue corporate/state control.

Nevertheless, as we shall see in this book, neither a global market economy nor neoliberalism can promise a smooth ride. The very concentration of state/corporate managerial efforts along those lines promises not only an unending succession of international crises, but a rough ride of wars without end. But it also ensures unceasing efforts by the already alienated to disalienate, as they struggle to reverse the historic disempowering of the worker classes out of which capitalism was born.

In sum, this book will identify:

- In Part I, the main organizing characteristics of state capitalism, inherited from the twentieth century, that dominate the American economy at the start of the twenty-first (Chapter 1);
- How the classic business-capitalist process was born in the great alienation of the feudal peasantry and the development of an employer class that introduced employment relations in place of feudal obligations, and sponsored industrialization—

as in England, the mother country of industrial capitalism (Chapter 2);

- In Part II, the way that the larger community (and workers in particular) have been alienated and weakened by the sustained deindustrialization and militarization that have served capital accumulation by business, and power accumulation by government (Chapters 3 and 4);
- How capital/power accumulation processes corrode production capability, both in Russia and the United States, even while world hegemony (globalization) is pursued (Chapters 5 and 6);
- In Part III, the effort of corporate managers, in particular, to weaken workers and unions while state capitalist accumulation processes proceed;
- In Part IV, how blue- and white-collar workers—who operate production, communication and transportation—respond to alienation by inventing rules and institutions that disalienate (reempower) their work, and herald the prospect of workplace democracy in place of managerial hierarchy;
- and finally, in Part V, the characteristics of the processes that afford a predictable exit path from state capitalism toward an alternative economy that is based on organization of production by means of workplace democracy.

PART I

From Feudalism to Capitalism, and After

From the sixteenth to the nineteenth century, Britain led a historic procession of European societies in the exit from feudalism. The lords of British manors discovered great advantage (to themselves) in converting their lands from mixed farming by communities of smallholders to more lucrative sheep-raising. Wool was a valued product, with ready buyers in Britain and on the continent. As a result, parliamentary legislation made the peasants the targets of Enclosure Acts that ordained their removal from their communities.

Faced with widespread enclosures, peasants were powerless to prevent their removal from their work, their homes, their communities. This was the earliest of a chain of alienations that has characterized capitalism from its origins.

The alienation of the British peasantry spurred direct capital accumulation by the lords and entourages of the feudal manors, and by merchants and town artisans. It also created an empty-handed, floating mass of men and women with nothing to sell but their labor. Easy targets, the dispossessed were pressed into the service of the propertied classes by laws that regulated begging and prohibited "vagabondage." Some were taken on by well-to-do farmers and townspeople, but the majority embarked on a fundamentally new way of life.

A new economy—capitalism—was being invented, as the skills of former peasants were joined with those of artisans and craftsmen and set to work, first at the command of cottage industry masters, then by employers of industrial workers. Business capitalism expanded dramatically. Capital accumulation, investment and larger markets were facilitated by the accompanying enlargement of trade—at home and abroad—and by an array of supporting financial and banking institutions.* This transformation set in motion a great dynamic in which the

*An overview of these processes can be found in Fernand Braudel, *Wheels of Commerce*,

alienation of workers spurred the accumulation of capital, making possible yet further enlargement of the industrial workforce under employer direction.

Yet all was not lost. This dynamic acted repeatedly and successfully upon workers, not inanimate objects. Thus workers struggled to regain power over their work and their homes, however defensively. They responded further with a sustained effort to disalienate, to make their own rules about their work. Indeed, as we will see throughout this book, the endless dynamic of alienation and accumulation at the heart of capitalism has proved to be, unintended, a giant engine for disalienation.

As Part IV will suggest, this struggle for disalienation has frequently focused on agreements among workers themselves and between workers and employers. Characteristically, workers undertake to agree with one another about a series of crucial subjects: worker group, work time, deployment, performance and compensation.

Over the past two centuries, the labor of this working class has created great accumulations of real wealth. In parallel, banking and other institutions have facilitated money accumulation that represented new wealth and made possible transfers of capital within and among countries.

Within capitalism, accumulation has been the main objective; indeed, in the economies of industrialized countries it has become an end in itself. The desired quantity of capital from accumulation has no defined limit. The sole objective is more profit and more power. As we shall see, this characteristic leads, finally, to irrational accumulation—an attainment that is self-destructive for economy and society.

---

vol. 2 of *Civilization and Capitalism, 15th to 18th Centuries* (Harper & Row, 1979, and later eds.).

1

The Shape of Production Under State Capitalism

Quietly—without fanfare, manifestos or plans—workers around the world have been inventing an economy that succeeds capitalism and communism as we have known them. In many different countries, workers are developing new rules for deciding about production—their own work—and for allocating the product, basing their decisions on standards that are quite different from those of capitalism and communism. These new rules offer an exit route from the militarized forms of state capitalism and state communism that dominated political economy during the latter part of the twentieth century.

What are some of the indicators of the economy after capitalism? Decision-making and producing functions are combined, as the people whose jobs lie primarily in production take an increasing part in decisions on their own work, on enterprise and on community.[1] In turn, administrators are bound by agreements with workers that represent the bulk of employees, other than managers.[2] Long-term economic viability, as against short-term profit, becomes an increasing point of emphasis for workers in the operation of enterprise. The idea of stable employment, in contrast to arbitrary downsizing, is introduced as an explicit objective for the operation of companies. Cooperation between groups of workers becomes a continuing part of working life.

All of these initiatives demonstrate a shared desire to move beyond predatory competition in the workplace. Such competition among workers is displaced, for example, when they choose seniority as a primary criterion for changes in job assignment, work time and compensation. The adoption of seemingly straightforward seniority criteria—first by workers, then concurrently by managers—alters management's sole control. In its place, unionized workers and managers install and operate a joint process of decision-making. Within the framework of competence in job performance, seniority limits the possibilities for arbitrary personnel decisions by managers, and limits favor-seeking by workers vis-à-vis managers.*

In order to live, a community must produce. A set of necessary production decisions must be made in every economy, whether feudal, tribal, merchant-capitalist, industrial-capitalist or state-capitalist. Carrying out production requires that certain key decisions be made. What and how much should be produced? How is the production to be accomplished? What is the value of the product? How should the products be shared? And finally, how should products be exchanged or distributed, bought and sold in markets?

While these decisions are necessary for production, they do not suffice. Key questions must be asked. What are the requirements that production serves in our society? What are the societal objectives that are to be served by production?

If production is organized primarily for acquiring profit and power, then prospective production activity not serving such a purpose will be either ignored or given very low priority. If, on the other hand, production is made to serve long-term economic viability, or stable employment, priority may instead be given to workplace democracy.

When there exist alternative ways of carrying out production, a selection must be made—and is made—following the requirements of the leading decision-maker. Thus, in industrial capitalism, those means of production that serve management's requirements for the enlargement of profit and power are given first priority, as against, for example, those means that would conduce to the convenience and safety of the people who will actually perform the work or use the product.

What are the rules that dominate in decision-making in industrial capitalism? They can be summarized as follows:

1. Occupations tend to be specialized into those dealing with production as against those dealing primarily with *decision-making*.

2. The decision-making occupations are organized in a hierarchy, with money and power concentrated at the top of the pyramid.

3. The rule among the decision-making occupations is that they must strive for more profit and for more control. In what follows we shall call these, together, *accumulation*.

*For a detailed discussion on seniority, see "Creating Workplace Democracy," in Chapter 9.

4. Striving for accumulation in profits or power, or both, is measured by a common rule of success: your gain is real only when it is accompanied by someone else's relative loss. That is what makes this *predatory* competition.

These rules governing relations among individuals—both deciding about work and working—go to the heart of an industrial capitalist economy. By exploring these interactions, we can uncover the changes with the most far-reaching economic effects. So, this book focuses not on political governance but rather on the rules that govern our work, how we organize and conduct our working lives, our occupations.

In capitalism, these rules, as between employer and employee, often contain an autonomous dynamic. Thus, while managers try to restrict workers to their specified production tasks,* employees either directly or through unions seek constantly to affect the conditions of their working lives. Such striving challenges the managerialist "ideal" of the total separation between production and decision-making occupations that deprives many workers of real control over their lives.

These rules about production and allocation change as employers and workers engage in a continuous process of problem-solving, albeit with fits and starts and changes of pace. This continuous problem-solving modifies the nature of successive problems. As a consequence of the drastic mechanization of work, for example, both the criteria and the array of possible solutions to the employer's problems are altered. Changes in production methods, when put in place by the employer for solving his problems, lead in turn to responses by workers that entail further negotiations about production.

By paying close attention to such changes in the rules that govern work relations, and to the struggle between managers and workers that

*Union-management agreements typically include a "management rights" clause that defines the sole rights and responsibilities of the management for governing every major aspect of production. *The Agreement Between the UAW [United Auto Workers] and the General Motors Corporation*, September 17, 1990, p. 13, specifies that

> The right to hire; promote; discharge or discipline for cause; and to maintain discipline and efficiency of employees, is the sole responsibility of the Corporation except that Union members shall not be discriminated against as such. In addition, the products to be manufactured, the location of the plants, the schedules of production, the methods, processes and means of understanding are solely and exclusively the responsibility of the Corporation.

The full, qualified meaning of "solely and exclusively" thus requires 619 pages of text in the agreement. The context of the management-workers interaction that produced such an elaboration of worker and management procedures is a central aspect of developing worker decision-making on production.

these changes reflect, we can chart the elements of an economy after capitalism. This is not the so-called "new economy" of alienated globalization. It is a new, disalienated way of organizing work that offers workers control over their work and their lives.

New problems in work relations arose throughout the twentieth century because of the continual tendency of decision-makers in both "capitalism" and "communism" to extend their power. Indeed, one of the important features of the present study is the attempt to diagnose capitalism and communism in terms of their common features. That is why a discussion of the actual as against the theoretically ideal meaning of these economies is a good place to start.

The Realities of Capitalism

From the time of Adam Smith to the latter part of the twentieth century, a common set of ideal characteristics has been used to define capitalism.

1. Property is privately owned, especially the means of production.
2. The prices of all goods and services are said to be the outcome of interaction among many buyers and many sellers—hence the product of an "unseen hand."
3. Profit from the investment of capital and the employment of labor is the purpose of management.
4. Government is restricted to political matters and laissez-faire is a thoroughgoing condition of business enterprise.
5. The share of incomes to labor and capital is proportionate to the value they contribute to production (of either goods or services).

During the twentieth century, neoliberal economists refined these elemental features and focused on market behavior as the core economic relation of capitalism, basing their theories on the rational behavior of entrepreneurs. They assume that entrepreneurs act with full knowledge of calculable consequences of their actions. So equipped, they can respond swiftly to competitive challenges.

But the actual conditions of capitalism are far removed from the ideal. Let us consider each of these ideal characteristics in turn.

Private control, or ownership, of consumer goods is common. But in the realm of capital goods, ownership is highly concentrated in government—and in the larger corporations, whose privacy consists mainly in the legal fiction by which a corporation is recognized as a person.

During the 1930s, the most important enterprise in the United States in terms of assets was the American Telephone and Telegraph Company (AT&T). By the end of the Second World War, the assets of the Atomic Energy Commission alone, wholly owned by the U.S. government, far exceeded those of AT&T.

Even in the earliest period of the Republic, government was never fully separated from the economy in the United States. During the late eighteenth and the nineteenth century, the government took a very active part in planning roads and waterways and in the regulation of shipping to promote general economic development. By the mid-twentieth century, the federal government had become the largest employer in America, and the most important regulator.

Consider the matter of subsidy, which Congress defines as "a government program designed to aid a particular industry group or type of enterprise."[3] In 1960, the Joint Economic Committee of the Congress needed 17 pages to list the various subsidies from the federal government. By 1994, the list had mushroomed to the 1,400-page *Federal Domestic Assistance Catalogue*, published annually by the Office of Management and Budget and the General Services Administration.

In American capitalism, then, the central government is deeply involved in the economy. This has great influence, of course, on the determination of prices and market positions, which in the ideal world of capitalism would be governed by the independent actions of separate buyers and sellers.

Ideally, profit is supposed to stem from the private investment of finance capital and the employment of labor. But government subsidies have a controlling influence on affected firms. Consider that the Department of Defense, even ten years *after* the Cold War, had contractual, and therefore regulatory, relationships with about 30,000 enterprises. Rather than investing privately and employing labor to keep costs down and thereby enlarge profit, the military micro-economy routinely maximizes cost. As we will see in Chapter 4, under the "cost-plus" system, introduced during World War II and fine-tuned in the 1960s by Secretary of Defense Robert MacNamara, firms bill the government based on the cost of a product plus a percentage of this cost. The greater the cost of fashioning the product, the greater the profit. Cost-plus managing and accounting, also known as "historical costing," has produced a full range of choice items, from the infamous $400 "hammer with bent nail extractor" to the B-2 stealth bomber, tagged at over $2 billion each, each plane thus worth more than its weight in gold.[4]

Economic action by individuals and enterprises is further limited by government controls. Thus banking, like the securities business and exchanges, has been subject to regulations that were installed for the purpose of restricting fraud, and as a safeguard against mixing ordinary banking with securities brokering and underwriting. These regulations, introduced during the Great Depression, have been opposed by industry lobbyists and by market-economy enthusiasts.

This brief reminder of some conditions of economic life suffices to show that real capitalism is far removed from the ideal.

Such contrasts between ideal and reality have not escaped the attention of economists. They have explained these contradictions by designating the system a market economy. This catch-all description serves several purposes at once. After all, they point out, there are markets and a lot of buying and selling. The concept of the market economy also suggests that pervasive buying and selling determines the rest of the system, including production. But once again reality challenges the ideal. As the experts well know, in the course of making decisions about production and implementing them, the chiefs of enterprises are not simply responding to external market forces. In practice, managers have developed various ways of affecting their markets within workable limits.

But none of this takes away from the political-ideological usefulness of the market economy to the advocates of state capitalism. Where the division of labor is found, they argue, the exchange of products and services is necessary for production, and thus requires a market. Since division of labor must be sensibly assumed a continuing feature, so too, the ideologues argue, must we accept the market—and market forces—as the necessary price of material progress. By identifying capitalism with "market," and by assuming, despite all the evidence to the contrary, that buying and selling control the relations of production, the advocates of the market economy justify the status quo. To be sure, that leaves many blanks in our understanding about further development of the economy. But that is not a central problem for the ideologues of capitalism; for them, market forces, and hence capitalism, are forever.

Economists have customarily understood the purpose of business in industrial capitalism to be profit. Accordingly, during the Cold War, Soviet enterprise seemed to function without accumulation in the capitalist sense. But once again there is a big difference between real and ideal.

Actually, the role of profit-maximizing as an ordinary business goal in American capitalism, especially in the larger firms, needs major qualification on at least two counts.

First, the relentless growth of administrative personnel and costs in business economy has not correlated with an increase in profits.[5] In fact, the growth of power-wielding, mirrored in top-heavy administrative costs, often has served as a brake on profit. Second, in American business great importance has been given to achieving strategic positions, as in product innovation and market control. These constitute elements of potential power that are not readily quantifiable, but no less real. The elaborate litigation against Bill Gates's Microsoft, for example, suggests exactly how much is at stake.

When firms and their chiefs attain a size and influence so that their moves (even statements) have major ripple effects within and among industries, then their actions are political. In the United States, trade associations are characteristically based in Washington, D.C., the better to coordinate with the numerous departments, boards and commissions of the federal government. They, and their lobbyists inside the Beltway, expend enormous resources on influencing legislation and regulations bearing on their industries, including export-import rules, tax law, labor relations, subsidies, foreign investment, insurance, government purchases, construction contracts and regulations on environment.

Above all, business management must contend with the Department of Defense. The DoD chiefs, led by the President, preside over programs and commitment for new weapons and related materiel expenditures planned for about 10 to 20 years, whose combined value in 1997 was $1,450 billion. This planned spending on military materiel is almost 60 percent as great as the gross stock of fixed private capital in all of U.S. manufacturing.[6] Typically, the principal firms and their chiefs are the industry leaders. Those with the strongest ties to the military budget dominate the field. Obviously, such accumulations of responsibilities and activities are political. In these ways, a political mechanism for profit and power accumulation has become an integral part of the business culture of American capitalism.

Learning from History: The Realities of Communism

As with capitalism, so too with communism. Once again, there were significant gaps between ideal and real. A consideration of the actual, historical workings of communism from a post–Cold War vantage point will allow us to see that there are many similarities between the Soviet political economy and our own.

If we use the U.S.S.R. as our baseline model, in that political economy the following characteristics were said to represent the ideal:

1. An industrial working class, after seizing political control, established a highly centralized economy with ownership and control of the means of production vested in the state.
2. The regime, subsequently established, acted as a "trustee of the working class."[7]
3. The planned economy, rather than the market, was presented as the enlightened method of overcoming the problems generated by capitalism's anarchy.[8]
4. The revolution that overthrew the ruling class of Russia and established the U.S.S.R. concluded without establishing a new ruling class in power.[9]
5. The state's primary task was to accelerate all the processes required for the accumulation of wealth, the better to escape from scarcity and economic inequality.

The realities of the Soviet Union were, as we can see with the benefit of hindsight, far removed from these formulations.

During the earliest months and years following the Russian Revolution of 1917, industrial workers who had organized themselves in enterprise- and industry-wide soviets, or workers' councils, played a certain role in government operations and policy-making.[10] This role, however, was markedly diminished as the Communist Party, during and after the years of civil war, underwent a transformation. Industrial workers were decimated and dispersed by the Civil War of 1917 to 1921. The party, notably upon Stalin's installation as its Secretary, became an organization predominantly of bureaucrats, a *Nomenklatura*.[11]

While the composition of the controlling party changed, the claim that this organization represented the workers and was the legitimate trustee of the workers as a class, acting for their welfare rather than on behalf of the power and the privilege of this new ruling class, did not correspond with reality.

Rivers of ink proclaimed that Communist Russia and its satellite states operated by means of a planned economy. In fact, the one part of the economy where a substantial correspondence existed between plan and accomplishment was the military. For that was the sphere given highest priority—the primary objective toward which all other requirements were to be subordinated. Soviet enterprises were ranked from 1 to 7, with the military firms occupying the top two places. This meant that military managers could even requisition needed materials and equipment from enterprises lower in priority, often regardless of consequences for the latter.

Meanwhile, the rest of the economy was pressed toward successively higher targets without being provided with the commensurate capital or manpower.

The life of the Soviet manager was beset by irregularities in the availability of needed materials and equipment that obstructed compliance between plan and performance. An important role in solving these difficulties was played by the Russian brand of "expediter" *(tolkatch)*. The *tolkatch*, equipped with smooth talk and bundles of unaccountable cash, was sent forth by managers to secure materials, tools and machinery without which the enterprise was bound to suffer production shortfalls.

Without a doubt, a major limitation on central planning stemmed from the sheer limits of material resources. But there is no way to dismiss the consequences that flowed from the inability of Soviet planners to put together at one national center a tight plan for the movement of materials, manpower and capital goods within the Russian economy. Thus, in the 1960s, in the heyday of central planning, Soviet mathematicians estimated that "using only desk calculators, it would take some 30 trillion man-years to produce an internally consistent plan for the Russian economy."[12] Another expert was reported as claiming that "even if one million high-speed electronic computers were harnessed to the task, optimal planning in the economy from the center would still be beyond their capacity."[13]

A crucial test of planning ability in the U.S.S.R. came when, with the end of the Cold War, the decision was made to convert the economy from military to civilian production. In reality, the central planning agency, Gosplan, proved incapable of mapping out an orderly conversion process. Following the 1991 collapse of the political economy, the Russian government embarked on a privatization program that transferred control and ownership of a major part of industry into capitalist hands. At the time, I discussed the prospects for economic conversion in Russia with a highly respected American economist. He claimed that economic conversion to civilian economy was no problem in the U.S.S.R., "since they have planning."

At the time, civilian products were assigned by Gosplan to military enterprises with no apparent rhyme or reason. For example, Ilyushin, a major aircraft producer, was directed to prepare for the production of spaghetti-packaging machines, leather-processing equipment and fur-processing machines. After a long discussion about the industrial and economic pitfalls awaiting an effort to design, manufacture and sell such a product mixture, Gosplan simply withdrew its product plan and permitted Ilyushin to proceed with its own schemes for large, long-range jet aircraft. Gosplan was unable to account for its original product-mix decree—issued without consultation with Ilyushin's engineers and managers.

In the absence of a workable plan to convert to a civilian economy, and in the absence of full-scale conversion of the military economy in the West, Russian arms manufacturers, the former backbone of the military-industrial complex, have continued to mass-produce and market arms and technology to the developing world. For this sector of the former communist economy, the Cold War has not ended. And the world continues to suffer the consequences.

Common Features of Capitalism and Communism

Both capitalism and communism have exhibited marked differences between ideal and real performance, and both have moved toward ever greater mixes of business and politics. What, then, are the ways of understanding these economies that would suggest alternative routes of development, without their authoritarian and alienating features? In order to explore further features common to both capitalism and communism, we must return to the topic set forth in the opening pages of this chapter: the basic rules for deciding about the production and allocation of goods, about work performance.

In both economies there is a powerful tendency to separate decision-making from production. An ongoing pressure for this separation comes from the managers, who strive to free themselves from any physical work. Production work is regarded as demeaning. Thus, the business schools that supply managers to the American economy, and which have trained many of the experts and consultants who manage the post-Soviet economy, do not, with rare exception, include instruction on details of production technologies and technologies for the organization of work. (One rare exception is the Deming Center, at Columbia University's School of Business, named after W. Edward Deming, the pioneer statistician and industrial engineer who played a central role in the organization of Japanese industry after World War II.)

A good example of this separation between decision-making and production is the evolution of the occupation of foreman. Early in the twentieth century, foremen were not only the first line of management in manufacturing firms, they were experts and participants in the work of the people they supervised. This arrangement, however, gave way increasingly to a supervisory specialization, so that for a time the government's

Department of Labor invented the term *working foreman* to refer to people who spent 20 percent or more of their time doing the work of those supervised. Eventually, the foreman evolved into a pure supervisor, well identified in most factories by white shirts, ties and other non–"blue collar" clothing. These days the foreman is likely to work in an office, rather than on the factory floor.

The development of the engineering occupations is also an important case in point. With the introduction of computer technology for many production functions, managers have frequently attempted to make the engineers who program the computers part of management. This has become a subject of management-labor contention, as trade unions in various industries have tried to challenge this separation by organizing engineers. Groups of production workers have also sought management agreement to train themselves in computer programming. As we will see in Chapter 9, this pattern has been repeated in automobile factories and in the larger aerospace firms where engineers have been employed in large numbers, often working with a great division of labor, in which each person performs only a minor part of a complex design process.

A second feature common to both real capitalism and real communism is the organization of decision-making. In both economies, decisions have traditionally been directed downward from the top, and position on the hierarchy's ladder is a measure of the relative power of each administrator. But in order to really understand what makes decision-makers in these hierarchies tick, we need to discuss the accumulation process common to these economies.

Managers, decision-makers or administrators accomplish their tasks in accordance with rules and procedures. But one central feature is common to all of them. Participants in the managerial occupations, apart from those engaged in routine tasks with little or no discretion or control over other people, must strive *to enlarge their decision power.* In the corporate realm this is accomplished by accumulation of profit translated into capital investing and, for the larger corporations, into power.

The corporate accumulation process can yield control over more production and people, or control over more aspects of people's lives. The first gain is enlargement of managerial decision scope. The second type of gain is enlargement of decision intensity. It may take place within the enterprise or in the relation of one enterprise to others. The government partner in state capitalism intervenes to support accumulation by corporations, even while focusing mainly on its own accumulation of power.

What is the driving force behind the accumulation process? Profit is a key requirement, and success is finally equated with an enlargement of decision power. In relations among enterprises, success is measured by the ability to control the behavior of others, while within the enterprise it is gauged by enlargement of either the scope (the number of people controlled) or the intensity of decision-making and an accompanying rise in position.

In capitalism, the mechanism of capital accumulation for managers is primarily business. In communism, it was politics. In communism, managerial success was gauged primarily by position within the enterprise hierarchy, then in the government, and supremely in the Communist Party, which oversaw the entire system. One's movement into the *Nomenklatura* and rise within it were the measure of political power, hence of success. Personal privilege of every sort accompanied political advancement.

Within the framework of business, on the other hand, success in moneymaking and in the acquisition of power over increasing material wealth, and over employees, is the proper measure of successful accumulation. All participants in the managerial occupations are expected to be constantly seeking to expand their decision power. Noncompliance with this rule is tantamount to career suicide.

Within capitalism, decision status is gauged first by the assets of a firm, and second by the role of a particular company as a condition-setter for others. Thus, the firms that produce primary metal and electronic products and chemicals, in turn, set the costs for many other enterprises. Managers in government have decision power that is gauged by their position in the executive hierarchies.

Under Soviet (and Chinese) communism, success in the political realm has been gauged by position within the hierarchy of the party and those of the national and regional ministries operating as central administrative offices over their respective economies. In these communist economies, decision power was measured not only by position in the party hierarchy but also by a manager's location in the hierarchies that control the "heavy" (including machinery-producing and military) industries, the priority industries of communist economies.

In real capitalism, as we have seen, business executives constantly cross over into government posts and thereby acquire political decision power from multiple sources. Under capitalism, profits can translate into greater political power. Under communism, political power positions were a direct objective, translatable into many forms of material gain. There the top managers of military enterprises were party members who occupied important government posts, like the membership of the controlling committee of cities or regions. Major military-industry managers also held officer rank. People holding such multiple positions in industry, party, government and army wielded enormous power over their respective regions, which took on something of the character of feudal fiefdoms.

Indeed, among ordinary Soviet citizens, such an official was often called a *fayadal* (feudal lord).

Like the decision-makers of the communist economy, our managers enjoy levels of personal consumption that far exceed the average in their societies. In capitalism, certain occupations—like entertainment, athletics and law—at their highest levels pay salaries comparable to those of top decision-makers. But these well-paid occupations are characteristically outside the managerial hierarchies. Their abundance is in consumer goods, not capital goods—hence not in decision power, the ultimate measure of success.

The profit/power accumulation processes in both real capitalism and real communism have been not only highly competitive but also predatory. What is it that makes competition truly predatory? When one person's advance in decision power is genuine only to the extent that it entails a roughly corresponding loss of decision power by someone else.

This idea is perhaps most readily grasped in a military hierarchy. Consider the unlikely case of a government decree that all officers are to be promoted one grade. In this scenario, everyone in each rank would enjoy a rise in salary and prestige, but at no one else's expense. Yet with respect to decision power, no one gets a real promotion.

Another feature common to both capitalism and communism concerns the role of the state: in both, the central government has taken a primary place for decision-making and control over the economy.

In communism, this was achieved after the 1917 revolution and the short-lived New Economic Policy, under which private business was encouraged. Thereafter, economic life was centrally controlled and the means of production were declared as government property. But how much has changed? Even after the "privatization" that followed the collapse of the Soviet regime, the government-owned and -controlled major "heavy" industries (including military industry) still continue to exercise pervasive economic decision power by means of central financial controls and management networks based upon the *Nomenklatura*. The Russian government has retained control over the heavy-industry enterprises as well as the main energy, electronics and aerospace firms.

After five years of aggressive privatization, there was a visible and definite shift to private ownership in retail trade, banking and finance. Transfer of ownership to private hands has proceeded in part of the larger industrial enterprises. Here is how the Russian labor force was proportionally distributed between private and state enterprises, first in 1992, then at the close of 1996:

	1992	1996
State-owned enterprises	68.9%	40.9%
Private enterprises	18.3	35.0
Joint enterprises and other (mixed private and state)	12.0	23.4
Social organizations and foundations	0.8	0.7[14]

The preservation of military industry in the United States has been paralleled in Russia's "postcommunist" economy, where priority has been given to government retention of high-tech industries (electronics, aerospace and various basic industries), despite the resource exhaustion that finally caused the 1991 collapse and has worsened in recent years. (See Russian industry data in Chapter 6.)

With the end of the Cold War, the process of classic communism has been altered by the addition of multiple nongovernment managements in industrial enterprises, notably in banking and finance. By introducing a capitalist version of profit-taking and profit motive, the state-controlled monopoly of power accumulation in classic communism has been modified. But like the American economy, the former Soviet Union retains all the features of a state capitalist regime.

In American capitalism, the main transformation toward large and permanent government control in the economy began in the midst of the Great Depression, when federal political power was marshaled to rescue the business economy.[15] Many regulatory agencies were established, essentially to save business from itself—by limiting forms of moneymaking by banks and the securities industries, and by regulating agriculture output in the name of soil conservation. Several large government-owned enterprises, like the Tennessee Valley Authority and the Columbia River Power developments, were followed by civilian and military projects to bolster markets for the capital- and durable-goods industries. In the name of the emergency, the government became the largest direct employer. Employment in the Works Progress Administration put several million men and women on the government payroll for a great variety of civilian public works activities throughout the country.

But it was the Second World War, and the Cold War thereafter, that spelled the major and most durable transformation of the role of the government as a manager of American economy.

To administer the Western side of the Cold War, a permanent war economy was organized in the United States. Controlled by the largest central administrative office in the industrial system, located in the Department of Defense, it dominated the affairs of more than 30,000 industrial establishments. The military operated 580 bases throughout the United States and abroad. The government became the nation's largest financier of research and development in the sciences and technologies.

By 2000, a decade after the Cold War had concluded, 2.2 million people were employed in nominally private enterprises managed by the Pentagon. The military economy has become the federal government's very own industry, whose maintenance and enlargement continued as a primary state/managerial objective. Military budgets and the pace of new weapons technologies have been kept at Cold War levels, while the Pentagon has launched weapon sales around the world to capture markets for its products, and international linkages that build political power. At the same time, the government still gives priority to maintaining its military industry, withholding the measures needed to convert from a military to a civilian economy.

In the United States and in similar economies, the institutions of industrial capitalism have continued to operate even as they were modified by the introduction of government as a management center. The profit motive for the capital-accumulation process in capitalism has been altered by the addition of political methods for power accumulation introduced by, and centrally located in, the federal government.

Real capitalism and real communism, despite different histories and cultural patterns, have now taken on a common form: state capitalism.

State Capitalism

In state capitalism, the state's dominance over the economy is accompanied by a continual enlargement of profits and power by private business. In the nominally separate and private firms of capitalism, the process of profit/power accumulation continues under the guidance of the profit motive. In the government-managed sectors of the economy, accumulation, motivated by the desire for political power, plays a continuing role. The core capitalist mechanisms for the organization of work and the enlargement of managerial control continue in real capitalism as they did in real communism.

Five-year planning of federal budgets, notably for the Pentagon, is installed in Washington even as a stock exchange is opened in Moscow. By the close of the twentieth century, the sharply opposed ideologies of "capitalism" and "communism" both served as cover stories for a common reality: state capitalism.

In real state capitalism, business and government are inseparable.

In the former communist variant, even after privatization, the power-accumulation processes continue through politics, with increasing weight given to business. In the American form developed from business capitalist roots, the accumulation of power and profit at home and abroad proceeds, even as more decision power is wielded by state managers.

Exit Paths from State Capitalism?

In both state capitalisms, the working classes—survivors of predatory competition and accumulation—have commenced a historic counter-thrust of disalienation for workplace democracy. Workers, farmers and slaves in the United States were once linked to a bourgeoisie that wrote the American Constitution; Russian workers and peasants, on the other hand, had the recent experience of feudalism, from which they were extricated by Lenin's and Stalin's managerial elite.

In both societies, blue- and white-collar workers have sought more control over their own lives, but as we shall see, their prior class-cultural experience has given them two very different clusters of resources for creating an economy after capitalism.

2

The Founding Alienation of Capitalism

The institutions of capitalism did not spring ready-made from the earth but were preceded by those of feudalism. For the workers displaced from the feudal economy, the emergence of capitalism brought profound alienation. They were rendered powerless to affect their own work, powerless to prevent their removal from their occupations and their communities. Their collective memory of this founding alienation, together with their struggle for disalienation, has had profound consequences for workers in the capitalist economy.

Workers' countermoves to powerlessness were first engendered by the great feudal evictions, and then reinforced in the twentieth century by unilateral layoffs. The mechanisms of disalienation and the struggle for workplace democracy are given full discussion in Part IV. For now, we will trace their roots in the human cost of the transition from the feudal economy to modern capitalism.

It is important to remember, of course, that the various feudal economies were as diverse in character as the economies of countries termed capitalist during the twentieth century.[1] But in order to explore the alienation from which capitalism emerged, we can trace feudalism's chief characteristics.

Feudal property relations centered on land, including rules for the transfer of control and the allocation of the products of agriculture. Ownership rights to land were usually handed down from peasant father to son (while daughters received a dowry). The same was also true for the transfer of control from the lord of the manor to his children.

The main production activity among the peasants was the work completed on their own strips of land and that performed for the lord of the manor. A tithe of about 10 percent of the land's output to the church, and the payment to the lord, had priority in the allocation of the product.

Among the peasants there were great inequalities in income, which were significantly influenced by the quality of soil and the nature of crops.

The obligations of the peasant to the lord of the manor, as well as poverty, were a powerful constraint against movement, except during periods of disease and warfare, when controls were weakened, or in the periodic outbreaks of peasant revolt. Those working the land habitually sought reductions in their obligations to the lord, as well as larger land allocations. During periods of unrest, peasants often took advantage of the relaxation of hierarchical control to flee in search of better work and payment.

Though feudalism was not static in its economic relations, it was nevertheless very slow to change, even in response to major crises. The peasant-lord relationship was modified by the annual hiring of workers to till parts of their land by the landowners or richer peasants. Such arrangements were a regular feature of annual fairs at which produce and goods could be bartered or bought and sold.

The peasants themselves performed a whole range of decision-making and production tasks needed for working the soil, caring for farm animals and processing crops for food and clothing. But this diversity of agricultural production was also characterized by a limited output capacity and a limited ability to generate surpluses that might be used for exchange or trade. The meagerness of peasant output was an important factor in the repeated revolts against the size of payments required by the church or lords of the manor. Only a small number of people, like the craftsmen in towns, were somewhat removed from the feudal system of peasant obligations, and had opportunities to accumulate property facilitated by their use of money for exchange.

In the feudal community, exchange was limited not only by the relatively small output of individual peasants but also by the modest supply of gold and silver used as money. Accordingly, beyond the towns themselves, the production of luxury goods served only a limited market consisting mainly of the lords, their families and their entourages, and the few relatively prosperous peasants.

Within the framework of feudal economic relations, then, there were few opportunities for rapid enlargement of landholdings or for the accumulation of material wealth. Exceptional opportunities were afforded, for example, by the plunder brought back from the various crusades, or from the consolidation of land through marriage alliances. Expansion of trade contributed to the accumulation of surpluses in feudal villages and towns that heralded early moves toward capitalism.

The developments in Britain are particularly interesting, because the British economy led the way in the early evolution and extension of industrial capitalism. Beginning as early as the sixteenth century, the crucial steps were as follows:

1. Peasants and smallholders were evicted from their traditional strips of land, which were then concentrated, or "enclosed," for use in the far more profitable wool trade.
2. A large number of prospective workers were made available for hire by the enclosure laws that removed them from the land, leaving them without their former means of production and livelihood.
3. Merchants and richer farmers in the wool business contracted with workers to function in small cottage industries. These were based on hand-operated equipment for processing raw wool into yarn that was used for weaving and knitting.
4. A growing market at home, and especially abroad, invited the expansion of production, which was, in turn, vastly facilitated by the invention and application of powered machinery. These were operated by working people newly grouped in factories, thereby enabling much tighter control over their activity, compared with the formerly dispersed cottage locations.
5. Exchange was facilitated by an increasing stock of silver and gold coins and by the development of occupations in finance, banking and trade.
6. The enlarged production capacity, coupled with vastly improved transportation, allowed competitive business operations to function over wider spheres.
7. Against this background, capital accumulation proceeded rapidly (more extension, more money, more investment), and hierarchy among business firms developed rapidly.

What were the consequences in human terms of these three centuries of economic development? Driving the peasants from the land destroyed the network of traditional feudal obligations, as well as the rule of the town guilds over apprentices and journeymen. Out of this process of alienation emerged the familiar combinations, specific to modern capitalism, of industrial worker, employer and market. In the case of England, these developments were spurred over the course of three centuries by the seizure of peasant-worked land, and the property of church and state. No longer able to feed themselves, the ex-peasants became a *market*.

From the point of view of the peasants themselves, land enclosure was the most disturbing and widely protested form of alienation. As they knew only too well, enclosure deprived them of control over their work and displaced them from their communities. The enclosure movement in England, begun in the 1500s, was at its peak in the eighteenth century, but it stretched on into the era of the industrial revolution. From William Lazonick, we learn that

> The enclosure movement was elevated to the level of national policy during the 18th century. The first private Enclosures Act was passed in Parliament in 1710. In the three decades between 1720 and 1750, 100 such Acts were passed. But in the decade 1750–59, 139 Acts went through Parliament; and the pace was accelerating. Between 1750 and 1850, more than 4,000 Acts were passed, with two particularly heavily-weighted periods: 1764–1780 when there were some 900 Acts and 1793–1815 when there were over 2,000 Acts. Since 70% of the Acts were passed in these two relatively short periods, the impact was bound to have been acutely felt. . . .
>
> About 6 million acres, comprising ¼ of the agricultural acreage of England, were enclosed by Act of Parliament during the whole of the enclosure period. It has been estimated that at least 4 million acres and perhaps as much as 7 million acres were enclosed by agreement in the 18th century. Even when parliamentary enclosures were widespread, enclosure by agreement retained the significant advantages of avoiding the high expense of enclosure by Act of Parliament. . . .
>
> Enclosures went on in the last decades of the 18th century and well into the 19th century. 2,000 parliamentary Enclosure Acts were passed between 1800 and 1844. By 1845, most of the open fields had been enclosed, but enclosure of some waste continued until 1876.[2]

In the absence of memoirs written by the peasants dispossessed from the feudal manor, many of whom were illiterate, we may turn to historical documents that shed light on the enclosure process.[3] They allow us to glimpse, in human terms, the cost of this alienation.

As the petition addressed to the Crown vividly suggests, enclosures irrevocably changed the face of the English countryside:

> Now, whereupon that I am so bold to trouble or disquiet your grace's majesty, your grace shall understand that I am a poor artifi-

> cer, or craftsman, which hath traveled and gone through the most part of your realm to get and earn my living. I have been in the most part of the cities and great towns in England: I have also gone through many little towns and villages: but, alas, it did pity my heart to see in every place so many monuments where that houses and habitations hath been and now nothing but bare walls standing.[4]

The enclosures were the cause of great social unrest—of robbery, murder, even fornication. As a result, the displaced peasants and their families, regarded as "rogues and vagabonds," were subjected not only to destitution but to a new battery of harsh legislation. This politely worded protest shows their awareness of how much had been lost, and more important, a strong desire to overcome this alienation:

> For if so were that every man might have in towns and villages but one little house or cottage to inhabit, and but a little garden ground withal they would so order it with their labour that they would earn their living, so should there no place untilled nor without inhabiters so that in towns or villages they should be always in a readiness at your grace's call and commandment.[5]

Much of the anger and frustration generated by the enclosure movement was directed not at the lords or Parliament but at the most visible sign of alienation: villages abandoned, and fields empty of all but sheep and the occasional shepherd.

> *Husbandman:* Marry for these inclosures do undo us all, for they make us pay dearer for our land that we occupy, and causes that we can have no land in manner for our money to put to tillage; all is taken up for pastures, either for sheep or for grazing of cattle. So that I have known of late a dozen ploughs within less compass than 6 miles about me laid down within these 7 years; and where 40 persons had their livings, now one man and his shepherd hath all.[6]

Once again, there is a plea for change:

> Which thing is not the least cause of these uproars, for by these inclosures men do lack livings and be idle; and therefore for very necessity they are desirous of change, being in hope to come thereby to somewhat; and well assured, howsoever it befall with

> them, it can not be no harder with them than it was before. Moreover all things are so dear that by their daily labour they are not able to live.[7]

As a character observes in Thomas Becon's play *The Jewel of Joy*, the consequences of enclosure affect not only the displaced peasantry but the "common weal" as a whole. Everyone lives with the consequences of alienation.

> *Philemon:* Truth it is. For I myself know many towns and villages sore decayed; so that, whereas in times past there were in some towns an hundred households, there remain not now thirty: in some fifty, there are not now ten; yea (which is more to be lamented), I know towns so wholly decayed, there is neither stick or stone standing, as they used to say. . . . And the cause of all this wretchedness and beggary in the commonweal are the greedy gentlemen, which are sheepmongers and graziers. While they study for their own private commodity, the commonweal is like to decay. . . . They are insatiable wolves. They know no measure.[8]

In his account of these processes, Karl Marx was relentless in his description, starting with the seizure of land for the more profitable commercial wool crop:

> The spoliation of the church's property, the fraudulent alienation of the State domains, the robbery of the common lands, the usurpation of feudal and clan property, and its transformation into modern private property under circumstances of reckless terrorism, were just so many idyllic methods of primitive accumulation. They conquered the field for capitalistic agriculture, made the soil part and parcel of capital, and created for the town industries the necessary supply of a "free" and outlawed proletariat.[9]

As Marx observes, the former peasants

> were turned *en masse* into beggars, robbers, vagabonds, partly from inclination, in most cases from stress of circumstances. Hence at the end of the 15th and during the whole of the 16th century, throughout Western Europe a bloody legislation against vagabondage. The fathers of the present working-class were chastised for enforced transformation into vagabonds and paupers. Legislation treated them as "voluntary" criminals, and assumed

> that it depended on their own goodwill to go on working under the old conditions that no longer existed.[10]

Marx continues with a heart-searing description of how this was enforced:

> Edward VI.: A statute of the first year of his reign, 1547, ordains that if anyone refuses to work, he shall be condemned as a slave to the person who has denounced him as an idler. . . . If the slave is absent a fortnight, he is condemned to slavery for life and is to be branded on forehead or back with the letter S; if he runs away thrice, he is to be executed as a felon. . . . All persons have the right to take away the children of the vagabonds and to keep them as apprentices, the young men until the 24th year, the girls until the 20th. If they run away, they are to become up to this age the slaves of their masters, who can put them in irons, whip them, &c., if they like.[11]

And so on, in numbing detail. Yet the *Founding Alienation*, as described here, gave rise to a "founding disalienation." Part of the dispossessed peasantry refused to even accept a new set of peasant/lord-of-the-manor obligations, or their hiring out for a season or year to a well-off farmer, or the contracting with a town artisan for some sort of unskilled labor. These refusers, vagabonds, were identified by Parliaments and subordinate guardians of the propertied interests as a menace to the status quo. To be a vagabond meant having no visible, stable source of livelihood or dwelling, hence to pose a menace to the propertied of every sort. Beggars could be viewed as prospective vagabonds if they begged without a proper license.

Altogether, these refusals on the part of the dispossessed comprised claims, if not actual attempts, to decide for themselves how they should obtain life-sustaining food, clothing, shelter. But such "independence" was not accepted by the authorities, who viewed even the prospect of such out-of-bounds behavior as intrinsically illegal and hence to be condemned, as a refusal to accede to part or all of the alienation which had been "rightfully" imposed on these candidates for vagabondage and begging.

As early as the sixteenth century in England, workers' wages also received careful attention in the House of Commons, as did the threatening prospect of any "coalition of labourers." Thus,

> A tariff of wages was fixed by law for town and country, for piecework and day-work. The agricultural labourers were to hire

> themselves out by the year, the town ones "in open market." It was forbidden, under pain of imprisonment, to pay higher wages than those fixed by the statute, but the taking of higher wages was more severely punished than the giving them. [So also in Sections 18 and 19 of the Statute of Apprentices of Elizabeth, ten days' imprisonment is decreed for him that pays the higher wages, but twenty-one days for him that receives them.][12]

Already rendered powerless by the enclosure movement, workers were threatened with legal punishment for organizing in their own defense. As Marx reports:

> Coalition of the labourers is treated as a heinous crime from the 14th century to 1825, the year of the repeal of the laws against Trades' Unions. The spirit of the Statute of Labourers of 1349 and of its offshoots, comes out clearly in the fact, that indeed a maximum of wages is dictated by the State, but on no account a minimum.[13]

As we have observed, such processes of alienation continued well into the industrial era. The British social historian E. P. Thompson offers the opinion of a laborer of that period, writing to "the Gentlemen of Ashill" in Norfolk in 1816:

> You have by this time brought us under the heaviest burden & into the hardest Yoke we ever knowed. It is too hard for us to bear, you have often times blinded us saying that the fault was all in the Place-men of Parliament, but . . . they have nothing to do with the regulation of this parish.
>
> You do as you like, you rob the poor of their Commons right, plough the grass up that God send to grow, that a poor man may feed a Cow, Pig, Horse, nor Ass; lay mulch and stones on the road to prevent the grass growing. . . .There is 5 or 6 of you have gotten all the whole of the Land in this parish in your own hands & you would wish to be rich and starve all the other part of the poor.[14]

As the anonymous writer suggested, there might be strength in numbers: "We have counted up that we have gotten about 60 of us to 1 of you: therefore should you govern, so many to 1?"[15]

The mass expulsion of peasant farmers and their families, in the absence of organization, made them helpless and often desperate. Nevertheless, essential ingredients for a new economy, an industrial capitalism, were put in place. There was more alienation to come. The landowners, who did great violence and damage to the displaced peasants, also left a model for their successors of how to deal with workingpeople, seeing them as an untutored, ignorant, dangerous rabble.

What were the ingredients for this new capitalist economy, created out of the alienation of a whole class of workers? Land seizure and wool cultivation provided valuable industrial raw material. Rich farmers and merchants supplied the finance capital for organizing the work of growing and processing wool and for the wages of workers.

Evicted peasants, on the other hand, had little to sell other than their own labor. A domestic market of landless workers unable to produce their own food or clothing was thus added to the foreign markets served by investors in the burgeoning wool and textile industries.

Government played a crucial part in every aspect of these operations. By state action, feudal controls over land were broken, and the way was paved for rich farmers and merchants to invest in wool cultivation, processing and commerce. In place of the abandoned lord-peasant relations, the conditions of employment were installed. Property rules were elaborated and enforced. The stock of money and the range of banking institutions were multiplied. As we have seen, draconian rules of employment and property were enforced by government action, enlisting the citizenry in the repressing of "vagabondage" under threat of enslavement, even execution. The ways were opened for capital investing to proceed on an ever-larger scale.

Capitalism was launched.

In the midst of this turmoil—which conferred wealth and power on the new businessmen—the farmers suffered a painful alienation that shredded their ordered lives. Once driven off the land, they lost the right to decide what and how much to produce, how to do the work, the length of the workday. The ex-peasants lost their tools, their livestock, even their homes and households and storage areas for their belongings. They lost their ability to move, to relocate to a more favorable locale where the lord of the manor might require a lesser percentage of produce as payment for tenancy. Such opportunities could only be seized by suitably equipped peasant-farmers. Once forced off the land they had worked, the peasants lost their place in both the church and civil communities. Gone were their welfare rights under parish poor laws, or their rights to the use of the common land and the forests.

No poetic imagination is really required to understand the prospective power and reach of these events on their "class memory." A founding alienation had entered the collective memory of an entire class of displaced workers. The destructive effects of the enclosure movement in England reverberated into the late nineteenth century, well within the vision and memory, however dimmed, of succeeding generations of farmers, craftsmen and industrial workers.

The peasants were rendered powerless, deprived of work, livelihood and community. Despite their protests, which took the form of vagabondage or sporadic revolts, they lacked the organization and decision power to mitigate or reverse this thorough alienation.

That alienation has been followed, of course, by a series of further alienations. In a succession of major events, by applying the force wielded by government, a ruling class has made a subordinate class powerless to prevent their removal from their occupations and communities. As we will see in the following chapters, the vulnerability of workers to alienations by corporate and state managers has markedly increased in the era of state capitalism.

In the United States, historic acts of alienation have also rendered large populations powerless in the name of economic expansion. Until the mid-1800s, Africans were enslaved and dealt with as property. As the historians Charles and Mary Beard noted in 1927:

> In the South . . . where slaves were chattels bound to their masters and not to the land, their emancipation sent them flying off into social space as [in Abraham Lincoln's words] "a laboring landless and homeless class."[16]

In the 1930s, family farms were swept up into corporate farming combines. Workers and smaller enterprise owners were wiped out by the movement of the New England textile industry to the South. More recently, "Rust Belts" and ghost towns have been created when manufacturing plants are shut down by investors, and especially major corporations, in favor of relocating factories abroad, or abandoning production in favor of moneymaking by less arduous "postindustrial" vocations.[17]

Each of these epochal events has rendered powerless millions of people, who have suffered the psychological trauma associated with the massive dislocation of their lives.

In the United States, the last half of the nineteenth and the first part of the twentieth century witnessed explosive economic growth of every sort. Farms, factories, stores, railroads, truck freight, communications and radio-TV covered the land; free elementary and high schooling became commonplace, while private and state universities flourished, as did the sciences and medical arts. New industries were invented to make the means of production for all this. American capital- and durable-goods industries took the lead in generating valued economic growth, whose extraordinary profit-taking fueled capital investing at home and abroad.

All this was the product of workers in an American population that multiplied almost fivefold in eighty-five years, from 35 million (1865) to 150 million (by 1950). More than 387,000 immigrants arrived in 1870, over a million a year from 1905 to 1914. The United States thus included a growing number of peoples who had been subjected to great alienations. The population of Native Americans, who were removed from traditional lands and consigned to pauperization on bleak reservations, grew from 25,000 men and women in 1870 to 340,000 by 1950. That of African Americans, many of whom had known the alienation of slavery, had grown from 5.3 million in 1870 to 15 million by 1950. They were mainly tenant farmers in the South, and workers restricted to low-skill jobs in the North.

Labor was invested in the farms, cities, mines and factories that produced a cornucopia of new wealth that was shared with notable inequality. For the production skills of workers were more than matched by the dexterity and relentless determination of businessmen to extract more (and more again), in profits and private wealth once visible only among royalty.

The cities and major towns of the East Coast were the earliest locations for industrial investments that employed thousands of workers. As the social historian Howard Zinn has observed, "In 1790 fewer than a million Americans lived in cities: in 1840 the figure was 11 million. New York had 130,000 people in 1820, a million by 1860."[18] His chapter "The Other Civil War" opens up a fresh view of the early American industrial workers who labored long hours at remarkably low wages. Their living conditions were abominable:

> In Philadelphia, working-class families lived fifty-five to a tenement, usually one room per family, with no garbage removal, no toilets, no fresh air or water. There was fresh water newly pumped from the Schuylkill River, but it was going to the homes of the rich. . . .
>
> In New York you could see the poor lying in the streets with garbage. There were no sewers in the slums, and filthy water drained into yards and alleys, into the cellars where the poorest of the poor lived, bringing with it a typhoid epidemic in 1837, typhus in 1842. In the cholera epidemic of 1832, the rich fled the city; the poor stayed and died.[19]

American workers, like their predecessors in Europe, struggled to remedy these alienations. Their efforts to organize unions met with similar opposition from employers and government:

> In 1835, fifty different trades organized unions in Philadelphia, and there was a successful general strike of laborers, factory workers, bookbinders, jewelers, coal heavers, butchers, cabinet workers—for the ten-hour day. Soon there were ten-hour laws in Pennsylvania and other states, but they provided that employers could have employees sign contracts for longer hours.[20]

About half a million women were part of the country's workforce by 1860. Of these, 181,000 worked in factories, half of them in textile mills. By 1864, as Zinn notes, about 200,000 women had joined trade unions. At Lynn, Massachusetts, in 1857, for example, shoemakers' wages were repeatedly cut, as machine-stitching replaced manual work, reaching $3 a week (men) and $1 (women) for sixteen-hour days. Federal troops were used to break sporadic strikes, as in Cold Springs, New York, where workers at a gunworks asked for a wage increase. In St. Louis, machinists and tailors on strike were forced back to work by the military.[21]

In the summer of 1863, "A Song of the Conscripts" circulated in New York and other cities. One stanza read:

> We're coming, Father Abraham, three hundred thousand more
> We leave our homes and firesides with bleeding hearts and sore.
> Since poverty has been our crime, we bow to thy decree;
> We are the poor and have no wealth to purchase liberty.[22]

In the great railroad strikes of 1877, 100,000 workers participated, 1,000 were arrested, and over a hundred were killed. The strike halted half the freight on the nation's 75,000 miles of railroad. From 1881 to 1885, there were on average about 500 strikes each year, involving 150,000 workers. In 1886, there were over 1,400 strikes involving 500,000 workers.[23]

A turning point in the struggle of American workers to disalienate came in the Great Depression. By the close of 1932, at its nadir, there were 330 self-help organizations in 37 states. Howard Zinn reports that

> In Seattle, the fisherman's union caught fish and exchanged them in 1931 and 1932 with people who picked fruit and vegetables, and those who cut wood exchanged that. There were twenty-two

> locals, each with a commissary where food and firewood were exchanged for other goods and services: barbers, seamstresses, and doctors gave of their skills in return for other things.

By 1934, five million tons of "bootlegged coal" was simply taken from nonworking mines by unemployed miners and sold in the cities below market price.[24]

The main continuing organization of workers had been the American Federation of Labor (AFL), which organized on a craft basis rather than an industrial basis. This was the sustaining form of America trade unionism until 1934.

By 1934–1935, the great "sit-down strikes" by workers who occupied their factories were bitterly fought and led to unionization of mass-production industries (steel, coal, auto, rubber, textile, clothing). The sit-down strike movement was preceded by a general strike in San Francisco of 130,000, who immobilized the city. In 1934, 324,000 textile workers struck in the South. During 1936, there were 48 sit-down strikes; in 1937, 477.

This wave of labor organization during the Depression years produced the unionization of workers led by the Congress of Industrial Organizations (CIO). Unionism was further boosted by the torrent of new workers into the industries that fueled World War II. But thereafter, union membership in the United States declined. American managers and government were preoccupied by another fierce international struggle—the Cold War. Ideological conformism marked the next half century. As we will see, workers were presented with a new series of alienations.

A historic transformation of the structure of the American economy was set in motion after the end of World War II, in conjuction with the onset of the Cold War. The United States was the sole major industrial economy left intact after the wartime carnage. But there was to be no disassembly of the industrial war machine: the government's very own. Served by the rest of the economy, it dwarfed every other industry. Its firms, bases, laboratories and schools, and millions of uniformed and civilian staffs, were managed by the largest central administrative office in the land—probably in the world. The war economy had a virtually unlimited supply of finance capital—based on the federal tax system. It offered inducements to engineers and scientists. The highest of high-tech was lavished without restrictions on budgets or manpower.

The war economy had begun as a grand partnership of business and government to fight World War II and then the Cold War. But in such undertakings, some partners almost inevitably become more equal than others. American state capitalism was here to stay. Even after the acknowledged close of the Cold War with the dissolution of the Soviet Union in 1991, there was no reversal. A permanent war economy was firmly installed, with the President as its Chief Executive Officer, the Congress as its Finance Committee, the Pentagon as its Central Office. To most Americans, long committed to supporting their government, state capitalism became the accustomed political-economic organization. The change was hardly noticed.

PART II

State and Corporate Managers Impose Alienation by Destroying Production Capacity

During the twentieth century, capitalism became more than a system of rules and business institutions for accumulating, investing and exchanging. Government was brought into play: first as an outside aid to business investment, then to stave off unions, and as a guarantor and rescuer of industrial managerial and finance capitalism when their system collapsed in the Great Depression of 1929–1939. Finally, as partners with business, government managers have focused on accumulating power, notably during the Cold War, while corporate managements have acted mainly to accumulate finance capital for investment. As we have seen, this partnership was the genesis of a state capitalism that has continued into the twenty-first century.

After 1945, the American business-government partnership sponsored a permanent war economy, the better to win the Cold War. While the government's R&D programs and contracts guaranteed profits and capital accumulation for business, nonmilitary parts of the economy were alienated and depleted even as foreign investing with American capital was promoted. Newly neglected industries that were targeted for disinvestment included parts of the capital-goods industries like those producing machine tools and equipment, such as civilian ships, railroad locomotives and allied technologies. Government managers and their economists saw other economies, notably Germany and Japan, as desirable alternative suppliers, while U.S. industry concentrated on military technologies. As a consequence of this government-sponsored deindustrialization, it has become unworkable to rely on domestic sources for replacing and upgrading many classes of infrastructure equipment. In other words, even as the very fabric of its economy deteriorates, the United States has lost ability to repair the damage.

Thus while the computer industries showed dramatic growth through the second half of the twentieth century, the production of machinery for making strategic components for computers became concentrated outside the United States. Of computer equipment sold in the United States, a quantity now approaching 50 percent represents imports from abroad.

The partnership between state and corporate managers has set in motion a nonstop series of alienations that has yielded profits and power for all the major players. As we will see, this has fueled income growth for the top income percentiles, even as the full record of this achievement was obscured by statistical legerdemain. Meanwhile, as a dissection of income data reveals, the living conditions and prosperity of many Americans continue to decline.

Within industrial firms over the past half century, the drive for capital accumulation required ever greater hierarchical control over the interior details of administration and production. Management enlarged the number and cost of administrative personnel. By the close of the twentieth century the sum of salaries to administrative staff in manufacturing industry equaled the wages paid to all production workers. By 1990, for every 100 people engaged primarily in producing consumer goods and services and the means for their production, the economy employed 140 others in primarily decision-making occupations.

At the same time, the growing sway of the government has been wielded to diminish the ability of workers to form independent organizations.

A major alienating feature of American state capitalism has been its military emphasis, notably its nuclear-weapons programs. Driven by the criterion that more is better, the military economy produced an overwhelming weight of nuclear weaponry (and their means of production and delivery), a quantity of weaponry far in excess of requirements for destroying prospective opponents.

What was forgone? As we will see, the cost of the *overkill part alone* of nuclear military spending was more than sufficient to replace the entire manufacturing plant and equipment of the United States—twice over—while also financing the renewal of the infrastructure. While the military industrialists got fat, not less than 30 percent of the American people were left poorly housed, poorly educated, poorly fed, with deteriorating health.

The long agenda of what has been forgone in order to execute the alienation and power-accumulation processes of state capitalism gives the lie to a major cover story: that the United States is so richly endowed as to be able to afford guns and butter without limit.

This is why the lesson of the Russian economy remains so urgent and chilling. For the evidence is overwhelming that the collapse of production and allied capability in the U.S.S.R. (the creation of a "third-rate" economy) was a direct result of the damage done by a permanent war economy, with its powerful drive toward alienation and accumulation without limit.

American state capitalism has been operating—for all its finance-capital advantages—as a replay of the Soviet scenario. In both countries, the buildup of nuclear weapons for military use was pushed beyond the bounds of rationality. The resources expended for these exercises was more than enough to modernize and rebuild each country's industry and infrastructure.

With due allowance for the differing political and cultural histories, the fact remains that powerful alienation-for-accumulation processes have dominated in both societies. In Russia, it has been the source of a full production collapse. In the United States, even after the end of the Cold War, a finance-based investment drive has spearheaded the continued growth of military institutions and their industries. Despite all the available evidence of the accompanying prospect of production collapse—the unavoidable consequence of deindustrialization and a third-rate economy—America's state and corporate managers insist that things have never been better.

3

The United States as a Third-Rate Economy

Money will get you power.
Power and money are everything.

—ANONYMOUS STATEMENT OF A YOUNG MAN CHARGED WITH ROBBERY

Unlimited accumulation of managerial profits and power is both the driving force of state-capitalist decision-making and the source of its primary problem. Two principal types of alienation are in operation in American state capitalism.

Type A is *Alienation by Design.* The alienating operations are designed to achieve a well-defined objective—profit/power accumulation. Production is shut down as facilities are moved so that a more compliant, nonunion labor force may be employed—contributing to a trend of factory relocation to cheaper wage areas with an ample reserve army of unemployed.

Similarly, large capital investments are withheld from unionized facilities in favor of acceptable nonunion profit prospects. The U.S. Steel Corporation's management declined to invest the largest part of a $6.8 billion fund to modernize its steel-producing factories, as I reported in *Profits Without Production* (1988), but chose instead to put the money into Marathon Oil, a petroleum firm whose main assets were below-ground pools.

Farmers have been evicted so that land use can be reorganized in a more profitable fashion. U.S. banks and other financial institutions foreclosed small farms in the Midwest during the Great Depression, enabling the consolidation of land holdings and the creation of "corporate farms" using machinery that required sizable investments.

The dependence of large labor forces and even whole communities on specialized work for narrowly focused government projects perpetuates alienation. The closing of military-industrial facilities has repeatedly left labor forces with useless skills and their communities in ruins. Unfortunately, the fate of those set adrift by such actions is rarely considered, and there is little systematic advance planning for economically viable alternatives. The suggestion that such contingency planning could be undertaken has been seen as a pessimistic attitude toward ongoing military projects.

Type B is *Unpremeditated Alienation.* Alienation can result from a series of actions whose result was unintended. The managers of U.S. and English machine-tool industries did not plan the collapse and disappearance of half their firms. The managers had no awareness of the role of their own conservatism and technological "backwardness." As a result, the industries became economically noncompetitive, leaving skilled labor forces unemployed and communities economically devastated.

As I observed earlier, in order to live, a community must produce. For only through production work are goods and services for consumption, as well as the means for further production, created. But these essential goods and services do not appear spontaneously. As I argued in Chapter 1, it is the primary function of every economy to organize the necessary work.

In a state-capitalist economy, such work is carried out primarily at the direction of private and government managers. But under state capitalism, production and infrastructure are shaped and operated to serve at the expense of the interests of communities as a whole; counterproductive military institutions and practices are made permanent and dominant parts of society and government; while profits and power are maximized without regard for their social cost or effects on infrastructure.

Since World War II, production workers have become a smaller part of the total U.S. manufacturing force. In 1949, they were 79 percent of all people in manufacturing firms. By 1996, they were 65 percent.

Indeed, as we will see, the triumph of the accumulation process can be seen in the creation of reserve armies of unemployed, whose very existence contradicts the essential requirements of an economy—of any economy—to organize people for work. It has become fashionable to talk of a postindustrial society. But if a society does not produce, it cannot live.

America's Disappearing Machine-Tool Industry

The competence of a country's machine-tool industry is a significant indicator of a whole industrial system. Machine tools serve as the master instruments for every kind of production, for manufacturing the equipment that, in turn, is used to fabricate other finished products.

This industry is unique in its ability to produce its own means of production: machine tools (drills, lathes, milling machines, planers, and so forth) reproduce the very same basic tools. Computers, however intricate and widely applied, cannot make other computers. Nor can a set of sewing machines fashion another set of sewing machines.

Until 1978, the U.S. machine-tool industry was a premier producer for the industrial markets of the world. Yet by 1995, it shipped $6.0 billion of machine tools, exporting $3.0 billion, but importing $4.8 billion.[1] A team of engineers and economists at MIT reported in 1989 that:

> A major problem facing American machine-tool builders is that demand by U.S. manufacturers appears to have permanently shrunk. Many metalworking companies in a broad range of industries have shut down domestic factories. Other materials, such as plastics and fiber composites, are increasingly replacing metal.

But, they observed, the military economy had also played a part in this key industry's destruction:

> There was another important barrier as well: a mismatch between the way the technology developed and the needs of most potential users. MIT's Servomechanisms Laboratory, under Air Force sponsorship, developed hardware and software suitable for precision aerospace manufacturing of very complex parts. . . . The resulting hardware and software were much too costly for most industries and for smaller users . . . the Air Force did not see its role as extending beyond the support of advanced aerospace manufacturing.

At the same time, the Pentagon and NASA were not interested in sponsoring research for developing machine tools that would advance manufacturing productivity. As a consequence, the engineering schools conformed to the defense/space agencies' interests and treated production capability as a low-status function.

Meanwhile, in Japan, industry and research and development followed very different priorities.

> Japanese machine-tool builders were urged to develop modular, standard products suitable for a wide range of users. Simple modular designs that minimized parts counts also kept costs down and cut lead time. MITI pushed each builder to specialize in a particular type of machine. Firms such as Okuma and Yamazaki emphasized lathes and machining centers, while Okamoto got

90 percent of its revenues from grinders. These specializations helped achieve economies of scale. In the 1970s MITI pushed the use of simple NC [numerical—i.e., computer—control] and CNC machines before the Europeans adopted them and at a time when American NC vendors were still finding few buyers. NC-tool production rose from about 26 percent of Japanese machine tools in 1977 to 67 percent in 1984.

These policies were part of a bold and broad commercial vision. They were aimed at improved performance of all Japanese manufacturers, especially smaller and mid-size companies. NC and CNC machines brought flexible automation to small-lot, large-variety, just-in-time suppliers to the automotive, electronics, and machinery industries. In the United States sophisticated NC machines went predominantly to giant automobile and aircraft manufacturers, but in Japan small firms were major users of the new technology.[2]

More strikingly, U.S. industry has become dependent on imported computer-controlled machine tools, the most important of the newer, sophisticated equipment in industrial production. By 1995, imports of these machines exceeded exports: imports were valued at $2.4 billion, as against $2.2 billion of shipments of these machines from the United States.[3]

The following data show the 1996 position of the U.S. industry relative to its main international competition.

	Exports (millions)	**Percentage of World Exports**
Japan	$6,549	32
Germany	$4,068	20
United States	$1,113	5
Switzerland	$1,890	9[4]

Compare this with the Hourly Compensation Costs for production workers in manufacturing, also for 1996.

Japan	$20.91
Germany	$31.20
United States	$17.70
Switzerland	$28.34[5]*

*A special reason exists for focusing on the machine-tool industries of the United States and—as we shall see in Chapter 6—of the former Soviet Union. Both countries have

In both quantity and quality of product, the U.S. machine-tool industry was, through the 1960s, the leader among industrial nations. But two basic changes were set in motion. First, the prices of American machine tools became less competitive than those in the world market and even within the United States. At the same time, during the long span of 1971–1991, prices of U.S.-produced machine tools increased far more rapidly than production wages. The prospective purchasers of machine tools found the prices from the German and Japanese industries increasingly attractive relative to U.S. wages. Worse still, other machine-tool industries, notably those of Germany and Japan, became clear leaders in technological advance.

How did the United States lose the advantage in technology? In the 1950s, the Air Force organized a major initiative, contracting with the electrical engineering department at the Massachusetts Institute of Technology, together with selected machine-tool companies, to research and actually produce equipment that could be controlled by computers.[6] These machine tools were capable of duplicating the most intricate shapes with great precision and reliability. But this technological advance was also accompanied by a pattern of cost-maximizing, so that the prices of the new tools made them inaccessible to prospective users.

It was therefore left to the Japanese and the German industries to foster the design and production of computers, linked to machine tools, that could be speedily and economically programmed and utilized by skilled machinists and even semiskilled workers. This was in striking contrast to the specialized technical training required to operate the equipment first produced by the Air Force and MIT.

The picture of decline is paralleled in the case of Russia. The Soviet machine-tool industry was once a priority of state managers, who pressed for industrial development, though with a military emphasis. In 1959, having contracted with the European Productivity Agency (a branch of the Organization for European Economic Cooperation) to conduct an investigation, I observed strategic aspects of this industry. During the course of this investigation, I studied the operations of a series of strategic production facilities in Moscow and Leningrad. My main findings on the Soviet machine-tool industry can be summarized as follows:

> The manufacture of a particular quantity-produced machine in the U.S.S.R. requires between 290 and 350 man-hours. Similar

---

suffered a dramatic decline as competent suppliers of the basic means of production. Moreover, their lowered capabilities were closely linked to the state managerial policies of each country, specifically the militarist policies that decimated industry.

> products in Western Europe call for 700 to 825 man-hours per machine. This disadvantage in man-hour productivity is consistent with, and stems directly from, the production systems prevailing in Western Europe. . . .
>
> Such major productivity differences in favor of the U.S.S.R. must correspond with major advantages in production costs for the Soviet machine-tool industry. . . .
>
> At the same time, it is important to note that a major effort, backed by the highest political support, is under way to raise the level of technological efficiency of machine-tool production in the Soviet sphere. This involves attention to the whole range of opportunities for increasing production efficiency, including the possibilities provided by modular design and the use of standardized parts. . . .
>
> A significant indicator of the future possibilities of the U.S.S.R. as a factor in the machine-tool field is given by a comparison of research efforts bearing on machine tools in the U.S.S.R. and Western Europe. The most important institute for the study of machine-tool design in Western Europe is the Technische Hochschule at Aachen, Germany. This institute has a total personnel of 150 working on matters related to machine tools. . . . the comparable institute in Czechoslovakia maintains a staff of about 400, and the ENIMS institution in Moscow has a staff of over 1,000. . . .
>
> In brief, the machine-tool industry of Western Europe shows substantial commercial strength, but also major deficiencies in its ability to supply both internal and external markets with low-cost, high-quality products. These deficiencies arise out of the essentially "handicraft" type of tradition which has guided this industry, both in the design of its products and in their production. *The technology of mass production has, in the main, not been applied* in this industry.[7]

The text of this report was translated and circulated among machine-tool firms around the world. Unbeknownst to me in 1959, Khrushchev set a second priority at that time, the space race, with consequences that became visible forty years later. (See Chapter 6.)

Following this report, I was alert to the possibilities of Soviet industry as a significant competitor, first in Western Europe and then, especially, in developing countries where the attractive pricing of Soviet machine tools would give the U.S.S.R. a significant market as well as political advantage.

Independent evidence reinforced the conclusions found in my report to the European Productivity Agency. For example, a general purpose–type lathe produced in one of the Soviet factories was sold abroad at $3,500 a copy, complete with handbook and grease gun, all neatly packaged in heavy plastic and a solid wood crate. One such machine was turned out every fifteen minutes, rolling off the end of a floor-type conveyor ready for shipment. Upon my return to the United States, I found a similar machine from an American producer costing $10,000. I asked the people at that firm the lot size in which they made this particular model; they told me, "When you order one, we make it for you."

Nevertheless, my estimate of the competitive potential of the Soviet industry was never fulfilled. I did not have reliable information to explain this outcome until the late 1980s, when many Soviet scholars visited the United States. I asked a man who knew of my earlier work on industrial economy and productivity if he could explain the evident failure of their machine-tool industry to take advantage of the production potential that was clearly theirs at one time. During my tour in 1959, for example, I had been shown a precision drawing that was produced under computer control. Surely an industry with such nascent capabilities, coupled with the development of computers as required by the Soviet missile and space programs, would have provided the technological base for computer-controlled machine tools and other equipment?

He explained that during the previous twenty years he had served as an official in a technical institute in the Moscow region. Every year, around graduation time, a committee from the Ministry of Defense would appear and review a list of prospective graduates. Top technical talent was directed to the military-industrial enterprises. Little wonder that efforts to design computer controls for machine tools were unsuccessful. The project was shifted from one civilian industry or institution to another in an effort to get the work done—in the absence of the required talent.

These developments also explained something that had puzzled me in my late-1980s visit to Moscow. I made a point of visiting an exhibit of Soviet-made machine tools offered for export by the firm Stankoimport. Among the outstanding items were several Soviet-built machine tools to which German and Japanese computer controls were attached. I asked our guide why this was so. He explained that foreign buyers were not ready to purchase machine tools with the Soviet computer controls (which, from the samples observed at this exhibit, were mainly based on unwieldy computer tape rather than the solid-state technology used in the German/Japanese equipment).

The parallels with the fate of the American machine-tool industry are too striking to miss. In the United States, the industry was rendered economically noncompetitive by its adoption of a "cost and price don't matter" approach. This was an open invitation to Germany and Japan to take over much of the American market, which they proceeded to do.

Capital Goods Production Depleted

SHIPS AND RAILWAYS

How can the economy be depleted when everyone knows that the gross domestic product has been growing, that the total United States' money-valued production has steadily increased?

Until the latter part of the twentieth century, U.S. industries were world-class producers of basic industrial equipment. Now the story is different. During the 1950s, for example, the design and fabrication of oceangoing passenger vessels came to an end in the United States, as the shipbuilding industry shifted increasingly to the production of naval craft. These days, equipment for subways in American cities also has to be purchased abroad, there being no U.S. industrial base for producing such goods.

As American economists noted, by 1985 "The shipbuilding industry was more dependent on defense expenditure than any other industry. . . . Nearly all (93 percent) of new ship construction and repair and renovation work was produced for the military."[8] Today, the greatest fear of American shipyards working for the Pentagon is that someday the military orders will run out. These institutions, and their engineers, workers and managers, are now thoroughly and exclusively trained in meeting the distinctive requirements of military productions, and so have simply lost the skills required for commercial ship production.

A similar pattern has been operative in the petroleum industry, where U.S. firms are major operators of large fleets of tankers. But these are generally not produced by U.S. shipbuilders.

Consider further that despite a boom in the cruise-ship industry, an oceangoing passenger vessel has not been built in the United States since the 1950s. Shouldn't there be an interest in investing in or building such vessels?[9] The Walt Disney Company moved into the cruise business by ordering its first two ships from Financantieri Cantieri Navali Italiani S.P.A. Disney commissioned two 85,000-ton vessels capable of carrying 2,400 passengers, each costing $300-to-400 million.

A first requirement would be to recruit designers—who would have to come from outside the United States, since the engineering schools have not been turning out civilian-oriented naval architects. Second, the equipment in a large merchant vessel is not the same as that going into a nuclear submarine, an aircraft carrier or a cruiser. Neither these ships, nor their propulsion, navigation and infrastructure, are constructed here. In effect, the design and the production capability for this class of materiel has disappeared from the United States. Materiel would have to be imported, and personnel either brought in to work with cadres of American engineers, or young American engineers sent abroad for training.

The same is true for the production of railroad equipment. The electrification of the main-line railroads in the United States, already well developed in Western Europe and Japan, would require, according to Professor John E. Ullmann, a capital outlay of about $180 billion. But the means for designing and producing the required equipment are not available in the United States. Whole new industries would have to be created to do the necessary work.*

When Los Angeles opened the first leg of its new subway, the trains put into operation were purchased from Italy. The State of Washington invested in new rail facilities between its principal cities, importing rail equipment from Spain. San Diego used German equipment for an electric trolley service to Tijuana, Mexico. The rail cars in the Washington, D.C., system were made in Japan, and the New York subways have been reequipped with cars produced mainly in Canada. The classes of equipment and the skills required for manufacturing heavy railroad equipment in the United States were unavailable; both were turned to account making military hardware.

"Light rail" is the name usually given to a sophisticated version of street railway equipment once known as trolley cars. Thus "light rail vehicle makers (LRV) in Germany, France, Belgium, Netherlands, and Italy are producing low-floor (low-ground) clearance systems that make the cars more accessible and lighter than ever before." These new vehicles are modern, sophisticated, sleek, and well appreciated by the riding public. In North America, eighteen cities have light-rail systems, and new versions are under development.

But there are no designers and builders of such equipment in the United States. Apart from the European firms indicated, light-rail vehicles for Los Angeles are to be supplied by a consortium of Sumitomo Corporation of America and Nippon Sharyo Limited. Propulsion systems

*During 1999, Amtrak received the first of several high-speed trains to be operated in the Northeast Corridor (Washington, D.C.–New York–Boston). Bombardier Inc. of Quebec, Canada, and GEC Alstom of Britain have been responsible for the design and fabrication of the new, sleek 150-mph trains (*Business Week*, September 27, 1999).

By February 2000, we learned that the first train set was marooned near Washington, D.C., for repair/redesign of the wheels, which had shown excessive wear in test runs (*New York Times*, February 3, 2000). Note that the TGV (Train à Grande Vitesse, the French high-speed train) was operated on tracks and roadbeds that were designed to be compatible with the requirements of high-speed rail equipment.

are to be manufactured by Asea Brown Boveri Ltd. (Zurich) and its subsidiary in Stamford, Connecticut. Only minor materiel items will be supplied by U.S. firms.[10]

This type of problem was confronted by the Boeing Corporation as early as the 1970s, when it attempted to build light-rail vehicles in the United States. The company dispatched a team of engineers to acquire the necessary knowledge from producers abroad. Comparable research would be required for every important capital- and durable-goods industry where the United States has lost the capability for designing, producing and marketing these commodities.

The shipbuilding and railroad industries are but two examples of the array of U.S. industries that have lost capability for civilian work. But that is not the limit of American industrial depletion.

In 1994, it emerged that the Defense Department had been trying, with little success, to acquire certain Japanese technology for a decade. "The United States has expressed interest in flat panel displays for use in cockpits, ceramics to make engines more efficient and composite materials to make lightweight airframes. Japanese expertise in these areas does not lie with its military contractors, which are relatively weak, but with its commercial technology companies, which is why the Pentagon is so interested in access to Japan's civilian technology."[11]

THE ROAD TO DEINDUSTRIALIZATION

People might like buying things cheaper. But there's a price. They're going to wake up one day and find that nothing's made here.

—A PRODUCTION WORKER IN A U.S. FACTORY BEING MOVED TO CHINA, *NEW YORK TIMES*, BUSINESS SECTION, JULY 7, 2000

During the first half of the twentieth century, the United States excelled as a supplier of capital/durable goods. As we have seen, the industries that produce the machines and principal raw materials used for fashioning capital goods—the means of production for the manufacturing industries—have a defining effect on the whole economy. Thus, the abundant supply and attractive pricing of capital goods was a major factor in the rise in output per worker that fueled economic expansion. Wages rose rapidly, which, in turn, impelled managers to seek out new methods of production to offset their growing costs.

Indeed, while industrial wages increased fivefold from 1915 to 1950, the price index of metals and metal products showed a jump of 100 percent during the same period. This was achieved by the sustained application of advances in industrial engineering and allied methods, as well as by the mechanization of particular industrial operations. During this period, the productivity of labor grew by about 170 percent for manufacturing as a whole.[12]

The table below records the considerable drop in U.S. employment of production workers (in thousands) from 1977 to 1996 in a range of machinery-producing industries.

The Road to Underdevelopment

Number of Workers (1000s)

Industry	**1977**	**1996**	**Change**
Machine tools (metal cutting)	37.2	16.2	-56%
Machine tools (forming)	16.1	8.5	-47
Power-driven hand tools	20.0	11.3	-44
Rolling mill machinery	5.4	2.4	-56
Carburetors, pistons, rings, valves	26.0	15.6	-40
Turbines and turbine generator sets	24.8	13.2	-47
Internal combustion engines	65.3	41.2	-37
Farm machinery and equipment	96.2	48.5	-50
Transformers, except electronic	32.8	22.4	-32
Motors and generators	74.1	59.9	-19
Calculators and accounting equipment	10.4	3.9	-63
Office machines, n.e.c.	22.9	8.9	-61
Ball and roller bearings	41.3	29.5	-29
Air and gas compressors	19.1	17.3	-9
Speed changers, drives and gears	17.6	12.2	-31
Construction machinery	111.2	61.1	-45
Mining machinery	20.3	8.4	-57
Oil and gas field machinery	39.8	17.0	-57
Textile machinery	18.3	10.2	-44[13]

Note: A drop in production was typically paralleled by a drop in the number of factories in the given industry, and by an increase in imports.

There is more here than meets the eye in the statistics. The decline by almost half in production employment in the machine-tool industry was accompanied by *a reduction in the number of factories by 50 percent, and a 50 percent increase in dependency on imported machine tools.* (Note as well that the period from 1977 to 1996 witnessed a 20 percent increase in the U.S. population.) The further decay of machine-tool production has been revealed by the subsequent purchase of long-standing American firms by German and Japanese companies.

Notice, for example, the catastrophic drop in production workers employed in building farm machinery and equipment in the table "The Road to Underdevelopment." While the United States has remained a leading producer of all sorts of agricultural crops and has conducted those operations with increased mechanization, the equipment for this work is increasingly drawn from abroad. Similar considerations apply in construction machinery.

What drove this depletion of the American capital-goods industries? The second part of the twentieth century saw American industrial managers increasingly seeking profits, either outside of manufacturing activity or by transferring their industrial work outside of the United States, thereby also dodging unions. A direct effect of these decisions has been the creation of relative scarcity in capital goods in the United States. Now we face a situation in which manufacturing facilities located in the United States can no longer supply the capital goods of manufacturing.

Precisely because these companies supply the means of production for all other industries, this decline in capability heralds an inability to repair the damage that could be caused by a generalized slump in manufacturing and infrastructure.

One explanation that is usually offered for these trends is the relative cost of U.S. labor. But this is mere rationalization. The fact is that when these classes of capital goods are imported to the United States, they come primarily from industrialized countries like Germany and Japan. Their compensation costs to industrial workers exceed those of the United States.

During the 1970–1997 period of decline of the U.S. machine-tool industry, foreign firms established strong positions in America. Six Japanese companies opened assembly plants in the United States to better reach the American market. German, Swiss, Scandinavian and other foreign producers also bought U.S. machine-tool companies whose plants could now assemble their former products, while also marketing the new parent companies' machines. Meanwhile, the American business press, while sympathetic to the evident plight of managements in the machine-tool industry, has not hesitated to hold them responsible for failing to conduct industrial research and development, and for neglecting product quality and new manufacturing techniques.

It is noteworthy that about 70 percent of U.S. machine tool imports come from Japan, Germany, and Switzerland.[14] These same countries by 1998 operated with hourly compensation costs for industrial workers much higher on average than in the United States.

United States	$17.70
Denmark	24.11
Finland	23.56
Germany	30.26
Japan	20.91
Sweden	24.37
Switzerland	28.34
United Kingdom	14.09[15]

There is thus no support for the claim that American managements were required to pay wages that put them at a severe cost disadvantage, thereby opening them to unmatchable price competition from abroad.

American technological and general managerial conservatism have prevented innovation in the organization of work. During the same period, the German machine-tool and other capital-goods industries retained their position. In Japan, the leading firms became the largest in the world. I have reported elsewhere on the Yamazaki machinery company and its productivity-boosting innovations in production methods and organization of work.[16] By 1994, it was clear that Japan's capital-goods industries had been undergoing a transformation. In 1981, capital goods accounted for 43 percent of Japan's industrial exports. By 1993, that number had increased to 58 percent, all told a strategic accommodation to the simultaneous rise in hourly compensation for Japanese production workers, by 1994, to $21.35 per hour, a level 26 percent higher than that of the United States.[17] Furthermore, while some part of the decline in employment in the U.S. industries may have been due to increased productivity, that is not the likely source of the massive disappearance of production activity that I reported in my study *What Else Is There to Do?*, which documents a large and rising concentration of U.S. import dependence in capital/durable goods.[18]

Such a concentration of deindustrialization in these industries is a movement toward underdevelopment. An economy is underdeveloped when it is dependent on imports for its means of production, even in the presence of the raw materials for producing them. The missing factor is the capability for doing the design and production work required: the skills and equipment of basic industry. The United States continues to lose this capacity for basic production.*

*An important set of data and analyses appears in Eamonn Fingleton, *In Praise of Hard Industries* (Houghton-Mifflin, 1999). Fingleton's subtitle states the thesis: "Why Manufacturing, Not the Information Economy, Is the Key to Future Prosperity."

COMPUTERS

The disturbing implications of this trend toward industrial depletion affect even the computer industry, a rapid-growth sector.

In advanced economies, capital- and durable-goods industries are characteristically the main location for high-tech technology. In computer production, the highest of the high-tech industries, the most recent data (1998) show the United States to be importing $72.5 billion of "computers, peripherals and parts," while exporting only $45.2 billion, as shown in the graph below.[19]

By 1996, as several American firms were making multibillion-dollar investments in new chip-producing factories, 50 percent of the required production equipment was imported.

By December 1995, about $10 billion was being invested in U.S.-located chip-manufacturing plants. At the same time, we were informed, in the newer (large and very costly) chip-manufacturing facilities, about 25 percent of the investment was taken up by the buildings themselves, and 50 percent by the manufacturing equipment. The useful life of this production equipment is only about three years, because of the rapid development of the technology for the various operations involved.[20] Thus much of the investment in capital equipment will end up outside the United States.

A Third-Rate Economy
Computers: U.S. Imports & Exports

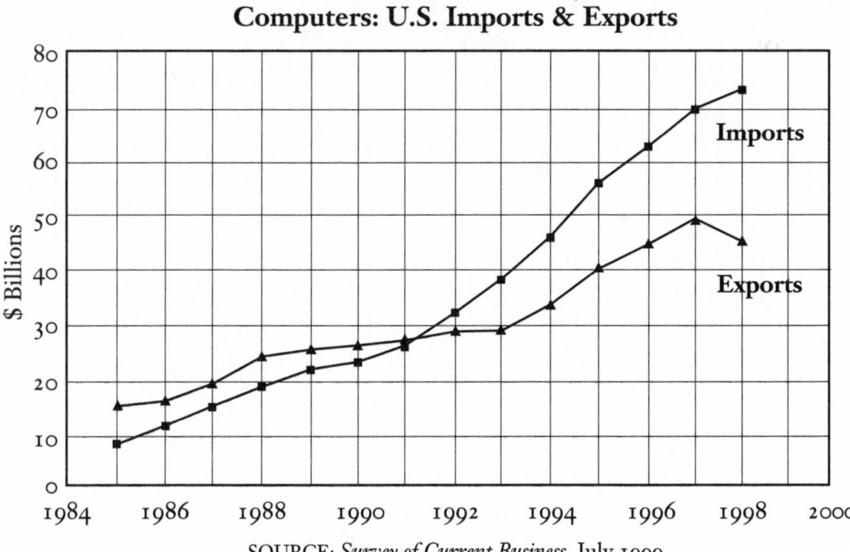

SOURCE: *Survey of Current Business*, July 1999.

Not surprisingly, American manufacturers of equipment for the chip-making field have been notably subject to sharp competition and changes in fortune. In 1982, U.S. companies accounted for 58 percent of the photo lithographic (wafer-exposure) equipment worldwide, compared with 35 percent for the Japanese. By 1989, these percentages had shifted dramatically in favor of Japan, which then had 70 percent of world markets for this equipment, while U.S. firms were left with 17 percent.[21]

In 1989, computer equipment purchased in the U.S. included 42 percent of imported components, rising to 65 percent in 1995. By 1996, most computers assembled and sold in the United States contained "disc drives from Singapore, monitors from South Korea and motherboards from Taiwan."[22]

In the electronics industry, the prognosis for U.S. manufacturing is poor. An assessment by the Berkeley Roundtable judged that these U.S. industries have become heavily dependent on imported design and manufacturing skills and materials.

Capital Goods Jobs Represented by Imports and Import Dependence, 1958–1994

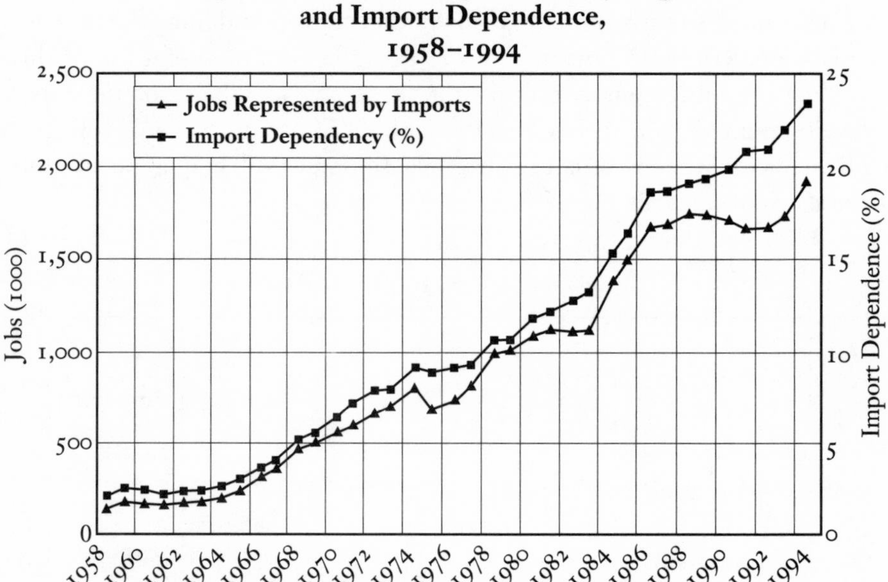

SOURCES: Eric Bartelsman and Wayne B. Gray, *Technical Working Paper* 205, *The NBER Manufacturing Productivity Database*, NBER, Oct. 1996

The trend toward deindustrialization in the shipbuilding, light-rail, and high-tech industries has also taken its toll on U.S. auto manufacturers: By 1985 it had become increasingly difficult to identify an American car, meaning one produced from materials fabricated and assembled in the United States. General Motors, for example, entered into a partnership with Toyota to manufacture the Chevrolet Nova, with about 70 percent of its materials coming from abroad. Ford and Chrysler cars also increasingly contain parts manufactured in Japan, Brazil and other countries.[23]

Importing Capital Goods, Exporting Jobs

These industries are not alone in their reliance on imported capital goods, as the graph on the facing page suggests.[24] U.S. jobs replaced by imports are shown by the line of triangles that have their scale on the left. Thus by 1958, 130,000 U.S. jobs were replaced by capital-goods imports; by 1994 that had risen to 1.9 million. In parallel, the line of small squares in the scale on the right depicts the proportion of U.S. purchases of capital goods supplied by imports: 2 percent in 1958, growing to 23 percent by 1994.

In a report titled "G.E.'s Brave New World" in 1993, *Business Week* reported on General Electric's investment plans in China, India and Mexico.[25] Besides investments in assorted consumer goods, G.E. focused priority on jet engines, major medical equipment such as magnetic resonance imaging (MRI) devices, and power systems. According to *Business Week*, "a sense of gloom hangs over General Electric Company's sprawling jet engine plant in Cincinnati, where the work force is shrinking," from 17,000 in 1991 to 8,000 in 1994. By 1999, management had been pressing the aircraft-engine division for double-digit price reductions on engine parts (this has been translated by parts suppliers as pressure for movement to Mexico). In medical electronic systems, another area of high-tech design and production, G.E. has launched major plans, especially in India. At the same time, south of the U.S. border, the company has marked Mexico as one of its major new centers for industrial investment, thereby taking advantage of wage levels that are often less than half those in the United States, while also reaping the benefits of the free trade arrangements codified in the NAFTA agreement.

General Electric has special importance in our discussion of industrial depletion, not only because of the scale and diversity of its activities but also because it is the last American firm making large generators and turbines in the United States. So, the closing of sections of its major heavy electrical machinery factories in Schenectady bespeaks a further cutback in U.S. capital-goods production. By the close of the 1990s, G.E. also owned Penske, a truck-leasing business, one of the largest leasing agencies for heavy trucks in the United States, if not the largest. With its stake in heavy trucking, G.E. will not wield its considerable weight in support of electrification of U.S. railroads.

Theoretically, a country can operate manufacturing industries while depending on imported capital goods, and machine tools are readily available to American purchasers. But the cost of paying for these goods can result in continuous negative balances of payment. The pileup of money used for buying capital and other goods to serve American needs will also finally result in a devaluation of the relative value of the dollars so employed. The exchange value of the dollar must decline under these circumstances, and consequently reduce its purchasing power. In this way what seems at first blush like the ready availability of capital goods through the global economy, albeit from foreign sources, eventually leads to a condition of relative scarcity and accompanying price penalties.

These financial costs have social ramifications, as domestic consumption has to be restricted in order to pay off the debt used to finance imported capital-goods purchases. There is also a social cost implicit in the loss of control over technology development to foreign designers and producers.

Along with the export of finance capital by U.S. firms, basic research support by corporations has diminished in recent years. An example of a move in this direction was Bell Labs' decision in 1995 to retrench the scale of its activity.[26] At about the same time, we learned that American universities were producing about 25 percent more doctorates in science and engineering than our firms and government were absorbing.[27] This is part of the same pattern whereby managers have been seeking out engineers and scientists from outside the United States. As *The Wall Street Journal* reported in 1993:

> U.S. companies are increasingly hiring highly skilled workers in Asia, the former Soviet bloc and Europe to perform jobs once reserved for American professionals. Or they are temporarily importing these professionals to tackle demanding tasks in the U.S. Texas Instruments Inc., Chase Manhattan Corp., International Business Machines Corp. and scores of other companies have contracted with Indians, Israelis and other foreigners to write computer programs. Film and TV producers increasingly bring in foreign film professionals to keep costs down. And American Telephone & Telegraph Co., Du Pont Co., Hewlett-Packard Co. and others have moved business units abroad, along with hundreds of high-paying managerial and research jobs.

This is bad news for former production workers planning to upgrade their own skills:

> The availability of low-paid professionals in Malaysia, Hungary, China, India and elsewhere calls into question the idea, popular in

the Clinton administration, that U.S. workers can raise their own wages or job prospects by acquiring more skills.

High-tech skills clearly no longer guarantee a worker's future:

> As Boeing thins the ranks of its U.S. engineers, the aerospace giant is shifting professional design and engineering work abroad. A few years ago Boeing hired, through a subcontractor, 300 Japanese engineers for its biggest airplane project, the 777. Then last year, Boeing said it planned to hire hundreds of engineers in Taiwan and Russia.[28]

The combined effects of these trends include the virtual disappearance of entire capital-goods manufacturing industries and an increasingly heavy reliance on foreign research and expertise.

According to William Lewis, a senior partner at McKinsey and Company, and an expert on competition policy, "the global system is so big, so robust, so open that anything one person denied us we could get somewhere else." And further, said Lewis, "we don't need those jobs. We're paying too much to keep them." But this form of reasoning omits reference to the specific needs of the American economy, like the expected $18 billion that will be spent, according to the American Public Transit Association, during the next decade on rail equipment, a purchase that American companies will be unable to participate in. Experts say "it will be increasingly difficult for American companies to enter the market, leaving critical technology outside the grasp of American concerns."[29]

> In electronics, U.S. producers are broadly dependent on foreign supply of a huge and growing list of essential component, materials, and machinery technologies. Indeed, most U.S. computer firms can no longer produce consumer-like products (e.g., laptop and smaller PCs) without an alliance with Japanese firms to provide the necessary components, micro-design know-how, and relevant manufacturing skills—Compaq with Citizen Watch, Apple with Sony, Sun with Fujitsu and Toshiba, and Texas Instruments with Sharp. Even IBM is not immune from this trend. The U.S. General Services Administration recently noted that IBM's RISC System 6000 model 7013-540 computer has a foreign content in excess of 88 percent. . . . A leading U.S. industrial laboratory recently reverse-engineered such products and concluded that the embodied precision mechanical skills probably no longer existed anywhere in the United States.[30]

Globalization and deindustrialization go hand in hand. In simple terms, the U.S. economy is living on borrowed technology, if not on borrowed time. Not only do these conditions of disrepair exist; more important, the capacity required to design and carry forth the necessary repair is frequently absent in the United States. In this respect, the nation displays a dramatic similarity to the condition of the former Soviet Union, which suffered a similar deterioration of capital-goods industries.

Consumer-Goods Depletion

During the same period, the workers of the largest consumer-goods manufacturing industries have also suffered blows. By 1993, the apparel and other textile industries had lost 529,100 jobs to imports, and leather and leather products industries 130,900.[31]

There was once a wide range of factories and firms that produced leather products in the United States. But by 1990, imports accounted for 60 percent of U.S. consumption. Consider the case of footwear. The most cursory survey of men's leather shoes in ordinary shops shows that they are primarily made in Portugal, Mexico, Taiwan, Korea, and Indonesia. Leather footwear of various grades from China also appeared in the 1990s, from shoes selling at middle-range prices down to those at small fractions of ordinary shoe prices.[32] Apparel of all classes is heavily imported, and imported clothing at present accounts for at least 50 percent of the clothing on sale in American shops.

No special research is required to establish the departure of the larger part of consumer electronics production from the Unites States. This is visible in the display of electronic merchandise of every sort in the principal stores of America's cities. In July 1995, for example, the last integrated TV maker in the United States, the Zenith Electronics Corporation, sold a controlling interest to a South Korean industrial conglomerate, LG Electronics. Zenith then took its place on the roster of former American producers of TV sets, reducing even *assembly* of the product in the United States (as well as Mexico) while importing the main electronic components from other countries. This is the pattern established by most of the Japanese manufacturers who also assemble sets in the United States. With this arrangement, the largest part of the value added in the product is composed of components that are fabricated outside of the United States.

The effects of such arrangements on American workers have been made clear by union officials testifying before committees in Congress. It is a tale of job scarcity created over and over again in numerous communities.[33]

But while scarcity of production employment has been widely accompanied by the abandonment of workers and their communities, the managements—especially of the larger companies—have had no difficulty finding acceptable ways of continuing their quest for profits and power. Many, for example, went into the business of selling financial services, especially during the 1970s and 1980s.

Take the experience of General Electric. "With a top notch, triple-A credit rating" and great size, the so-called new economy became an opportunity for "G.E. Capital [to] borrow more cheaply than most other companies and . . . invest in the teams of auditors and expensive computer systems needed to keep tabs on tens of thousands of loans."[34] Between 1987 and 1992, the "earnings of G.E. Capital's Equipment and Industrial Financing business had more than doubled, to about $332 million."[35] But for many other firms this did not prove to be a durably advantageous enterprise. And so by 1992 a long roster of principal firms began to liquidate their financing subsidiaries.

But do consumers really benefit from this exporting of jobs and importing of cheaper goods? One of the most striking things about consumer-goods imports is that they are frequently priced at similar levels to those produced in the United States. Where is the saving?

Here, for example, are apparel-industry hourly wage rates (including fringe benefits) in several countries in 1996:

United States	$9.56
Turkey	1.49
Slovakia	1.47
Morocco	1.38
El Salvador	1.38
Bolivia	1.34
Estonia	1.34
Romania	1.17
Mexico	1.08
Colombia	1.05
Philippines	0.62
Russia	0.58
Haiti	0.05[36]

The contrast with the U.S. wage is dramatic. Wage inequality has been a main inducement for clothing firms to move their work outside the country. Shops in New York City, Los Angeles, Detroit and Philadelphia, once leading centers of clothing manufacturing in the United States, have been dismantled in favor of the cheaper workforce, frequently working in sweatshop conditions, in other countries. As we have seen, even a cursory inspection of America's department stores shows that the prices of clothing do not correspond to the drastic differences in wages. Evidently, the wage differences were taken up in profit, as well as extravagant sales-promotion costs.

A further clue to what has been going on comes from an investigation of the Nike Corporation, which is a market leader in athletic footwear and clothing. A pair of Nike sports shoes costs about $5.60 to produce in the firm's Indonesian-contracted factories, but sells in the United States for $50 to $150. The apparent gap between production cost and final sales price is not mysterious at all, but merely a matter of lavish marketing and administrative costs and profit. "The Indonesian girls and young women who sew the shoes start at an entry level rate of $1.35 a day. . . . Overtime is often mandatory, and union protections are nearly nonexistent. If there is a strike, the military will often break it up."[37]

Nike management contracts out the performance of all production work, and so top executives—formally, at least—have no responsibility for the details of production. Even so, during the five-year period before 1994, as wages rose in various of its production sites, the company closed down operations in South Korea and Taiwan and opened up new arrangements in China, Indonesia and Thailand, "where wages are rock bottom."[38]

Indeed, it is customary for firms contracting out this type of business to hire small staffs of technicians to scour the world in search of ever-cheaper sites.

NAFTA has made Mexico increasingly attractive as " 'an enterprise zone' of 90 million people where the minimum wage is 58 cents an hour."[39] Among the managements seeking special advantage in Mexico is Smith Corona, until recently located and headquartered in Cortland, New York. As one of the big players in a small city, Smith Corona's layoff of 875 of its 1,300 workers, while it retained its general management, distribution and technical staffs, has had a powerful economic impact. In Cortland, Smith Corona had been paying manufacturing workers $11 per hour; the management estimates that labor in Mexico will cost less than $4 per hour. According to Smith Corona's senior vice president, "Labor costs accounted for a quarter of the cost of making a typewriter, and . . . moving to Mexico would allow Smith Corona to cut labor costs by four-fifths. Although moving will cost $15 million, it will save that much money every year after that, he added."[40] Whether consumers will benefit from this export of jobs remains to be seen.

The processes that lead to deindustrialization and to underproduction in capital and consumer goods in the United States are not the result of inevitable natural forces. Instead, the detailed explanation for these patterns must be found in the technological conservatism of managements, their hostility to trade unions and the availability of other money-making investment schemes in the "new economy." As we have seen, these schemes have included (despite relatively low U.S. wages) concentrated industrial investment by managements in Western Europe, as well as in the Far East and, more recently, in the Caribbean area and Mexico.

The Human Costs of Deindustrialization

For most Americans, this process of industrial depletion has occurred unseen, masked by glowing reports from Wall Street. But one human cost of the diminution of capital goods in the United States has been an all-too-visible pattern of loss of employment. These are the estimated number of jobs directly lost to imports as of 1993 in the listed industries:

Primary metal products	116,800 jobs
Fabricated metal products	113,900
Machinery, except electrical	546,400
Electrical equipment and supplies	573,600
Transportation equipment	450,600
Instruments and related products	158,400
	1,959,700

In 1993, U.S. capital-goods industries accounted for 45 percent of employment in manufacturing, but 64 percent of the total number of jobs forgone to imports.[41] This concentration of deindustrialization is a clear movement toward underdevelopment. John E. Ullmann has observed that, in the widening array of capital- and consumer-goods industries in the U.S. deindustrialization process, "rail equipment is a litmus test of sorts of industrial competence; it combines massive operating parts with sophisticated controls and has to work reliably for many years under arduous conditions."[42]

Intellectual Property

By the close of the twentieth century, producing and trading in intellectual property had also become enormously important as a way to accumulate wealth and power. By means of copyright and patent laws, knowledge is treated as property—enabling Bill Gates of Microsoft, for example, to become the world's wealthiest person. Arie Caspi has noted that,

> Software and medicine are unique in that they require most of the investment before the first product actually exists. Duplicating

> these products, by contrast, is a cheap process, whose cost has only a negligible effect on the selling price. The manufacturers claim the product is theirs because they developed it. Anyone who duplicates it, they argue, is stealing their property.[43]

But the claim to a property right on knowledge is a legal exercise that is built on sand, for the claim to identify "the inventor" of a stated piece of knowledge cannot be proven.* On the contrary, every advance in knowledge is built upon an indispensable base of prior work and knowledge that represents the heritage of humanity.

In science, the idea of "an inventor" as the source of new knowledge has been superseded by the acknowledged practice of group authorship in scientific journals that report on new knowledge. Research identified as group practice clearly acknowledges the social base of innovation. But this mode of understanding will not deter the Gateses from trying, with their considerable resources, to wield the accepted social-relational rules of property, money and employment as instruments for yet further capital accumulation by deindustrialization in the United States and investment abroad. As we have seen, these practices are based upon core rules of capitalism. They are not facts of nature.

Joblessness: Alienation

As a consequence of deindustrialization, the workers of America's depleted industries have been removed from their customary labor and communities and compelled to "take to the road" in search of employment. They are rendered powerless and alienated.

If this continues, the inability to organize work for those made jobless means the presence of a growing, deeply alienated workforce. Work is perhaps the single most important facet of ordinary life. To be without it means to be cast out of meaningful activity, without companionship, to be outside a position in which important life experiences are shared with others.

In the early 1990s, joblessness was widely acknowledged as the most depressing domestic problem in Western Europe.[44] American writers in *The Nation* noted in 1993 that with 36 million jobless amidst the twenty-four member countries of the Organization for Economic Cooperation

*See Seymour Melman, *The Impact of the Patent System on Research* (Study of the Subcommittee on Patents, Trademarks, and Copyrights of the Committee on the Judiciary, United States Senate, Eighty-Fifth Congress, Second Session, Pursuant to S. Res. 236, Study No. 11, U.S. Government Printing Office, Washington: 1958). For the possible effects of patenting on universities, see fn. 65, p. 56 of this study.

and Development (which includes the United States and Japan), or roughly 9 percent of the labor force, "unemployment beats all previous post-war records. Among the 12 European members of the EEC, the situation is even worse, the share of jobless averaging 12%, reaching 20% in Ireland and Spain."* In parts of Western Europe, joblessness has reached desperate levels, as reflected in the photographs of young men shown in August 1992 in Bristol, England, permanently unemployed. "There are no jobs and no money and there is nothing to do," said one of the unemployed youths.

This inability to organize work is characteristic of a depleted economy and a militarized state capitalism in decline. By the ordinary rules of profitability or power advantage, no justification currently exists for making productive investments that would require the employment of new workers.

Downsizing and the Miracle of the Jobless Economy

The unemployment of the Great Depression was linked to a sustained downturn in corporate sales and profits and to pessimistic forecasts of future profit. Those conditions were completely altered during the 1980s and 1990s in the United States. Now, thanks to the miracle of downsizing, countrywide poverty rates and increases in joblessness have been paralleled by a sustained rise in corporate profits.

Unemployment, as officially defined and counted, can decrease at the same time that joblessness increases. This apparent anomaly is the result of large-scale alienation of workers by design in the form of "employment at will" installed in place of ordinary full-time work. Part-time or temporary workers do their tasks for few or many hours, starting and stopping at the discretion of the employer. The workers so engaged can be dismissed without any requirement on the employer to show cause. Typically, temporary workers are paid an hourly rate, do not receive fringe benefits, such

*The International Labor Organization reported, as early as October 4, 1993, that part-time work was rising very sharply in industrialized nations. On February 9, 1995, the *New York Times* reported details of moves by major industrial firms in Western Europe to Eastern Europe for the cheaper labor found there. The firm ABB was reported as "exploring the possibility of using satellite communication system technology to move power plant engineering control operations from Mannheim, Germany, where engineers cost nearly $50 an hour, to Poland and Russia, where they cost only a fraction." The company said "with satellites you can have them online with computer operations in the West and in time you can have fewer engineers in Malheigh and more in Poland and Russia." One wonders about the feasibility of handling the power plant operation by remote control from several hundred miles away. Surely the relevant insurance company will also make its concerns known.

as medical insurance, and ordinarily earn less than they did at their previous livelihood.

David Dembo and Ward Morehouse, in their 1997 study, wrote: "Joblessness is only part of what we have termed the *Underbelly of the U.S. Economy.* Also important is the phenomenon of the pauperization of work, replacement of higher-paid jobs by those at or close to the minimum wage, often part-time and below the poverty line."[45]

From coast to coast, the legal minimum wage is a poverty wage.

In short, during the 1980s and 1990s, downsizing became big business: announcements of large layoffs by corporations have signaled reductions of costs to the stock market and, hence, increases in profits. This puts workers in a very different situation; traditional ideas about unemployment, inherited from the Great Depression, no longer apply to an increasingly jobless workforce. Dembo and Morehouse further report that "during the mid-1990s, according to Bureau of Labor Statistics, 9.4 million workers lost their jobs. Of the 4.2 million who had held those jobs for three or more years, 56.5 percent either did not find new jobs, found only part-time jobs, or found jobs paying below their previous earnings."

These data are vital to the recalculation that Dembo and Morehouse completed on the nature and amount of *joblessness* in the United States. Thus their report shows the method by which the Bureau of Labor Statistics calculated *unemployment.* The BLS unemployment count omits the part-time employee; even a person working one hour or more a week is counted as employed. Nor are discouraged workers taken into account, people who have given up on the possibility of finding a job: they are willing to work but are not formally counted in the labor force. When these factors are taken into consideration, the totals look quite different. By 1996, 14 million people, or 11 percent of the population, were jobless—almost double the official government unemployment rate.

In the past few decades, a new industry of temporary employment agencies has boomed, acting as intermediaries between workers and the firms for whom work is done. The temp agency is paid by the employer to cover the agency fee and the worker's wage.

This form of joblessness, consisting mainly of temporary and part-time workers, defines a new way of life in place of the traditional employer-worker relation. Temp jobs that typically pay only a fraction of the wage for a full week's work are therefore a form of working without livelihood. Temp workers are often driven to seek multiple part-time assignments in order to obtain something approaching an adequate livelihood.

In the United States, temporary employees do not qualify as unemployed, but they are employed "at will." They have no job rights and can be called in or sent away at the employer's convenience. They have no minimum or maximum hours per week and can be required to work as much as 70 to 80 hours per week without overtime payment. Termination need have no cause other than the employer's preference, and need not be accompanied by severance pay.

In 1997, the National Association of Temporary and Staffing Services reported handling 2.5 million workers, of whom 200,000 were "long-term temps." At Microsoft there were 5,000 temps, including 1,500 long-termers (who had been in place for more than one year). Why does a firm as prominent as Microsoft need so many temporary employees? The temps working among 17,000 Microsoft regular employees are a blessing to the firm, since, being formally ineligible for the array of benefits given the "regulars," their employment may save Microsoft up to $24 million for every 1,000 temps it uses, excluding overtime.

For all the oft-touted "advantages of flexibility," an intangible that allegedly benefits the "at-will" employee, temp jobs are a way for an employer to institute a wage cut. Recognizing this, American courts have recently ruled that Microsoft's contingent workers are in fact regular employees, and hence entitled to the benefits they have hitherto been denied on the grounds that they are independent contractors. In the words of the plaintiffs' lawyer: "They work full-time under Microsoft supervisors. They are producing Microsoft products. If it walks like a duck and quacks like a duck, it's a duck. They are undeniably Microsoft employees."[46]

Temporary employment ranges from unskilled workers to professionals like engineers, teachers, doctors and lawyers.[47] Though temporary employment is accompanied by all manner of management rationalizations, the common feature of this practice is its way to administer wage cuts, or otherwise slice labor costs by cutting out fringe payments.

"Unemployment" as reported by the U.S. Bureau of Labor Statistics for 1997 was 4.9 percent. But a "jobless" rate that accounts for 30 million part-time workers, "civilians" who want jobs, as well as the "official" unemployed, was 10 percent, again for 1997.[48]

The practice of large-scale downsizing has transformed employment into joblessness for millions. The jobless labor force is made weaker in relation to both employers and full-time workers with whom the temps have only irregular contact.

The practice of downsizing has even created a special group sometimes known as "the hit men," one of them writing a book titled *The Corporate Executioners.* In 1996, *Newsweek* ran an article titled "The Hit

Men," noting that "it used to be a mark of shame to fire workers *en masse*. . . . But the layoffs have scared the pants off the public and stirred backlash. . . . Is there a better way?"[49] "Today," reported *Newsweek*, "the more people a company fires, the more Wall Street loves it, and the higher its stock price goes."*

By 1994, a report from inside a large high-tech company revealed much about the impact of downsizing, offering the following from a middle manager: "This year, I had to downsize my area by 25%. Nothing has changed in terms of the workload. It's very emotionally draining. I find myself not wanting to go in to work because I'm going to have to push people to do more. And I look at their eyes and they're sinking into the back of their heads. People are numbing. But they are not going to complain because they don't want to be the next 25%."[50]

This trend to force larger workloads from white-collar employees is much like the measures taken during the late nineteenth and early twentieth centuries against production workers in factories. There, employers had sought to speed up worker activity and exertion. A comparable process is now being applied for the first time on a large scale to *both* production *and* salaried employees, coupled with the unspoken threat of job loss. Thus, within the loosely defined downsizing tendency, reductions in the number of administrative staff have typically not been accompanied by a reduction in the amount of work, but rather by an intensification of the workload of the remaining staff.[51] These days, everyone suffers.[52]

Simultaneously, two- and even three-tier wage systems have been instituted, meaning less pay for people employed in the same task but newly hired. As we saw in the previous section, all this has been accompanied by an ever-increasing reliance on imports from foreign-located factories. Again, unlike wage reductions and workload increases in the past, which were desperate responses to market collapses, the downsizing movement was launched in times of increasing profit.

Dismissal from workplaces entails a human cost that is not well represented by economic data. Layoffs typically are a signal to people that they are not needed, not wanted. Once sent away from their workplace, they automatically lose the fellowship they had there. Further psychological effects are unavoidable. A sense of solidarity among people in the workplace is also diminished or lost. Such psychological effects have been amplified by the international movement of factories from the United States as employers take advantage of large differences in hourly wages,

*No wonder that wits at AT&T corporation once quipped that Chairman Robert Allan would soon fire everyone but himself, and AT&T would stand for "Allan and Two Temps."

especially in classes of work where unskilled workers can be readily trained.*

Part-Time Work as Cost-Cutting

In addition to the widespread use of temporary employees, the movement toward part-time work has clearly suited employers. Like temps, the part-time workforce characteristically does not enjoy fringe benefits like unemployment and medical insurance or social security. The employer gains further advantage by effectively holding "on call" a large pool of competent workers. When a need for part-time employees arises, such a pool becomes very important.

Those not included in the official labor force who wanted full-time jobs constituted, in 1990, 5.5 million and, in 1996, 5.4 million. But the number of part-time workers, which in 1980 was 23 million, had, by 1996, increased to 31 million.[53]

Two breadwinners in a family may end up holding four or five jobs, and, in combination, delivering what had been previously available from one full-time position. The massive growth of part-time employment has accompanied the devastation of production work in U.S. industry.[54] Increasing numbers of Americans find themselves in the punishing position of being employed but effectively jobless.

An April 1996 *New York Times* report on downsizing in New York State provides a useful micro-view of the situation: "Effects of downsizing just keep on going."[55] In this snapshot from the jobless economy, it reported that Westchester County has lost 70,000 jobs in the private sector, according to a regional economist. *Reader's Digest* in Chappaqua had sent 100 workers to the unemployment lines. Prodigy Services company, an online computer operation in White Plains, laid off 115. In Yonkers, Dellwood Foods reduced the workforce by 100. Kraft General Foods announced it would cut 200 jobs to vacate a large office building in White Plains, where 1,200 are employed. Another 200 would be out of work once Stern's department store, also in White Plains, shut its doors. General Motors was closing its North Tarrytown plant, which employed nearly 2,000. The stories are all too familiar; they have become part of our lives.

Some idea of the overall scale of the problem of joblessness may be

*While managers use the sharp differences in wage levels to justify their drive for further profits, in reality they represent the spread of the alienated jobless economy beyond our borders. For, typically, these low wage levels and lack of adequate benefits, safety or environmental protection mean that foreign workers are also denied a living wage. Truly, joblessness is a global phenomenon.

gained from *The Downsizing of America*, a "Special Report" by the *New York Times*.* Big numbers conceal important features. Most striking is the way that profitable firms have repeatedly discarded workers in order to be *more* profitable. Many permanent layoffs were apparently also designed in a way that allowed the workloads to be distributed among those remaining. In the process, a large reserve army of the unemployed has been created.

There is no statistical way to assess the paralysis (as in powerlessness, alienation) that fear of job loss has induced almost everywhere among those below the very top management.

Reinforcing Joblessness: The Creation of a "Reserve Army of Unemployed"

Within the increasing scope of what I have been calling the jobless economy, the unemployed play a crucial role. As a reserve army of labor, this large pool of unemployed plays a strategic role, where they are available to checkmate the unionizing efforts of workers, or to counter demands for wage increases. The unemployed are often so numerous in one locale or industry that businesses are able to dictate terms. Once

*In 1996, the editors of the *New York Times* published a "Special Report" entitled *The Downsizing of America* (Times Books, Random House, 1996). The Introduction outlined their Report:

> Never before had layoffs persisted with such tenacity and in such magnitude in an expanding economy. The picture appeared even more discouraging than that. For two decades, people had also seen their wages level off or decline, and now dispossessed workers were frequently finding that the replacement jobs available to them paid appreciably less than their lost positions. Everywhere, people were working longer hours and feeling expendable.

Two *Times* reporters (Louis Uchitelle and N. R. Kleinfield) did a story called "The Price of Jobs Lost," saying:

> Nearly three quarters of all households have had a close encounter with layoffs since 1980, according to a new poll by the *New York Times* . . .
>
> One in 10 adults—or about 19 million people, a number matching the adult population of New York and New Jersey combined—acknowledged that a lost job in their household had precipitated a major crisis in their lives, according to the *Times* poll.
>
> While permanent layoffs have been symptomatic of most recessions, now they are occurring in the same large numbers even during an economic recovery that has lasted five years and even at companies that are doing well.

The 356-page report found that while capital accumulation was doing nicely, managements were pressing for more, with cuts in the workforce as a sure way to cut costs and grow profits.

again, the extent and degree of powerlessness and emotional disarray among the downsized cannot be gauged—except very indirectly, by the absence of visible protest or of organizing efforts.

In this respect, America handles large-scale job disappearance very differently from the way other countries handle it. Take the case of Aliquippa, Pennsylvania, which used to be a large steel town with a Jones and Laughlin Steel complex, once employing 17,000. Steel production virtually stopped, and the town and its community were thrown into turmoil.

> The Aliquippa experience is a stark contrast to that at Kamaishi, Japan, a steel town that lost its leading industry when the Nippon Steel Corporation gradually shut its steel-making operation there. Eager to preserve its lifetime employment policy, Nippon created almost any new business it could for the jobless workers.[56]

Aliquippa became a virtual ghost town.*

When a company moves to Mexico to avoid unionization, for example, it typically leaves behind a pool of employees who are unemployed or employed only part-time. A disorganized group of workers is then more than eager to pick up whatever employment might be available.

Production workers are not the only ones under pressure. As we will see in Chapter 11, even American doctors have responded to the perceived threat of a reserve army of physicians. The American Medical Association, together with other medical groups, has pressed the federal government to subsidize the reduction of training by hospitals. They claim that the number of physicians entering the workforce is excessive, as managed-care organizations have introduced nurse practitioners and physician's assistants. All the while, U.S. medical schools continue to produce MDs, and about 8,000 graduates of foreign medical schools arrive each year. So the professional medical organizations have sought to protect their own, striving for a 20 percent limit in the supply of MDs, even as rural and inner city areas are underserved.[57] By 1996, 17.6 percent of Americans were without medical insurance, but that subject has not drawn similar attention.[58]

*Rade B. Vurkmir, *The Mill* (University Press of America, 1999). See last chapter of Section VI for photographs of a "ghost town."

The Immigration Factor

The example of the widespread use of foreign doctors to reinforce a reserve army of American MDs highlights another growing trend: the importation of foreign workers. Some officials have reacted to this trend. On September 13, 1995, a bipartisan federal commission on immigration recommended " 'substantial fees' of up to $10,000" when firms hired "some skilled foreign worker." The panel making these recommendations, the U.S. Commission on Immigration Reform, stated that "paying such a fee would be a way for the company to demonstrate its need for a foreign worker as opposed to an American." No further action on this proposal has been reported.

For all the anti-immigrant rhetoric, there are powerful economic forces driving the immigration of many well-educated and highly skilled foreigners into the United States. The Center for Immigration Studies reports that 11.7 percent of American scientists and engineers in 1990 were foreign-born. Foreigners made up 49 percent of Ph.D.s in computer science in 1993, up from 35.5 percent in 1983. The influx of foreign-born workers, spurred by business interests, became a major factor in the development of U.S. manpower in the latter part of the twentieth century. The same is true for less skilled workers. We learn, for example, that "bowing to big farming interests [as in California, Florida and Texas], the House Agricultural Committee . . . approved an amendment to the House Immigration Bill that would grant temporary working visas to as many as 250,000 foreign farm workers."[59]

Stoop labor and hand work, as in vegetable farming, are often assumed to be the only available methods for the production of many parts of the country's food supply. It is argued by agribusiness that there is a need for low-paid foreign hands, working without benefits or union protection. In fact, the mechanization of agricultural work is increasingly feasible and economically successful. But smaller farmers and plantation owners are usually unable to marshal the capital required to invest in sophisticated mechanization. Nor do they necessarily possess the acreage that would justify the purchase of high-capacity agricultural machinery. As a result, the importation of agricultural labor is really a way of sustaining the operation of a considerable proportion of the medium- and smaller-size vegetable and fruit growers in the United States.

Information firms have also lobbied the Congress for special visas to admit as many as 95,000 trained foreigners for jobs in software, computer consulting and varied computer services. But these workers are typically employed at lower wages than their American counterparts.[60]

A vivid demonstration of the effect of U.S. corporate and government policy is also visible in the computer industry. By 1990, the number of exported jobs represented by net imports of computers and computer components was 118,000. By 1993, this was 139,000.[61] But in the new factories being built in the United States to produce chips, foreign designers and technicians, primarily from Japan and Germany, along with half the production equipment, are imported. Consequently, American workers of all grades are placed at a disadvantage in sharing the benefits of scientific and technological advances. Even the most high-tech of U.S. industries contributes to the "reserve army of the unemployed" in its own manufacturing activities. In the computer industry, financial prosperity is not matched by the well-being of its workforce, despite the high-profile group of Silicon Valley millionaires.

Simultaneous with the importation of skilled foreign workers, which reinforces unemployment and joblessness, is the transfer of work from the United States to skilled workers overseas. The *New York Times* reported in 1995 that while American banks already process some account statements overseas, "large accounting firms and insurance companies are looking at ways to prepare American tax returns and handle American insurance claims in East Asia." And further: "The combination of powerful personal computers and high-capacity undersea telephone cables is also subjecting millions of white-collar Americans to the same global wage-pressure that their blue-collar counterparts have long faced. As with steel and garment workers, the white-collar worker position and salary increasingly depend on whether they can justify their higher pay with higher productivity."[62]

In India, for example, which is a booming offshore software source for the U.S. industry, experienced programmers command salaries of $1,200 to $1,500 a month, compared with $4,000 or $6,000 (or even $10,000 for stars) in the United States. By 1995, 75,000 Indians were working on computer programs for the American market, as against a few thousand in the early 1980s.

Convict Labor: "The Prison-Industrial Complex"

The starkest example of the use of an increasingly large army of unemployed workers to weaken the position of the rest of the workforce comes in America's "prison industrial complex." As of 1997, inmates of both federal and state prisons supplied a labor force of over 20,000 (16 percent) out of 94,000 federal prisoners (1998) and 77,000 (7 percent) of over 1.1 million state prison inmates currently employed in prison industries.[63]

According to a survey commissioned by the AFL-CIO, the Federal Prison Industries, Inc. (FPI),

> had over $450 million in sales in 1995, projected by the General Accounting Office to have sales of $1.2 billion by the year 2000. . . . In addition, the law guarantees FPI a captured consumer base because it requires all Government agencies to give first priority to FPI over all private sector manufacturers.

FPI's product base clearly competes with major American manufacturers. Although FPI currently produces 150 different goods and services for the federal government, most of FPI's sales are focused in five major product lines.

FPI's midyear 1996 sales show that 94 percent of their sales were in the following industries: Furniture (44 percent); Electronic Cables and Components (18 percent); Clothing and Textiles (18 percent); Graphics and Services (8 percent); and Metal Products (6 percent). To take only its furniture sales:

> FPI had furniture sales of only $53 million in 1987 and projects sales of $267 million by 1998. FPI is already the largest supplier of office furniture products to the Federal government, and the ninth largest supplier of office furniture in the U.S.[64]

An array of laws and regulations since 1935 has put constraints on moving prison goods across state lines and on requirements to pay "prevailing wages" and not to "displace workers outside prisons." But the use of convict labor is clearly big business. In its 1998 annual report, UNICOR (the FPI marketing organization) reports that "Inmates . . . are paid a stipend ranging from 23 cents to $1.15 per hour, depending on their skill levels and the difficulty of their job assignments."[65]

In Oregon, for example, "Measure 17 amended the state constitution to require prisoners to spend at least 40 hours a week at work or in on-the-job training. Prison Blues, a brand of blue jeans made in Oregon state prisons, had sales of $1.5 million in 1995. Elsewhere, Oregon inmates are being put to work fighting forest fires, picking up litter, painting schools and landscaping state parks."[66]

An Arizona state official has commented, "In select industries where America has lost jobs overseas, like shoes and textiles, you could bring these jobs back."[67] In response, Peter Gilmore, the editor of *UE News*, declared: "Sounds good. But there are two problems with the employment scheme he has in mind: The jobs would still pay only 40 cents an hour. And the workers would have to be willing to go to jail." To illustrate his claim, Gilmore has assembled the following reports from the prison system:

> The San Francisco-based computer firm DPAS proved the Arizona official's claim in 1994, when the company closed its Mexico data retrieval operations. The work is now performed by inmates of San Quentin prison.
>
> "We have a captive labor force, a group of men who are dedicated. And the whole thing is very profitable," says Bob Tessler, owner of DPAS.

Gilmore notes that decades after unions won legal controls on the use of prison labor, state governments and entrepreneurs are teaming up once again to exploit convicts—ironically, often at the expense of law-abiding, working taxpayers.

- A Texas company, U.S. Technologies, left 150 workers jobless when it sold off its Austin electronics plant. Just 45 days later, the same firm opened shop in a nearby town—using prison labor.

- Inmates at the notorious Angola State Penitentiary in Louisiana have been deboning chickens for 4 cents an hour for a private firm; wealthy businessman David Miller saved himself millions of dollars in wages. An inmate who informed federal authorities of this operation was penalized by the warden.

- A Washington company "hired" prisoners to wrap software for Microsoft.

- Nevada prisoners make waterbeds for Vinyl Products, restore cars for Imperial Palace, hand-assemble $500,000 Shelby Cobra cars and build stretch limousines for Emerald Coach.

- In New Mexico, inmates take hotel reservations by telephone; California convicts took TWA airline reservations over the phone—during a flight attendants' strike.

- Prisoners in South Carolina made lingerie for Victoria's Secret.

- Hawaiian inmates pack golf balls for Spalding.

- Wisconsin enticed the Fabry Glove and Mitten Company to its Green Bay prison last June, using taxpayers' money to purchase cutting machines and industrial sewing machines worth $239,000.

- Corrections Corporation of America, the largest of the nation's eighty-eight private prison operators, teamed up with the

> work-clothes manufacturing company Apparel Safety Items. This represents the first partnership between a private prison and a private manufacturer.
>
> According to the U.S. Justice Department, more than a hundred companies have contracted out the use of thousands of prisoners in twenty-nine states. Arizona already has turned the labor of 10 percent of its inmate population over to private businesses.[68]

Further details have been made available from a "Survey of Prison Labor" (January 15, 1997), prepared by Greg Woodhead of the AFL-CIO in Washington, D.C. There we learn that in:

> Nevada—Prisoners assemble stretch limousines.
>
> Alabama—Prisoners raise cattle and swine.
>
> California—Prisoners make eyeglasses, input data, sort garbage for recycling, and take airline reservations for TWA over the phone.
>
> Washington—Prisoners shrink-wrap copies of Microsoft Office, a software program. Prisoners sew a thousand sweatshirts a week for contractor Joan Lobell.
>
> Texas—Prisoners at a private prison owned by the Wackenhut Corp. make and fix electronic circuit boards for IBM. Gov. George W. Bush has a World Wide Web site that advertises the state's inmate work programs.
>
> Colorado—Prisoners do telemarketing for AT&T.
>
> Illinois—Toys R Us used a night shift of prisoners to restock shelves in Chicago.

Through the eyes of the Pennsylvania state authorities, one can see some of the economic pressures underlying this development.

> Pennsylvania's prisons are at 152 percent of capacity; Western Penitentiary in Pittsburgh, scene of a Jan. 8 jail break, is at 162 percent of capacity.
>
> "This year, Pennsylvania taxpayers will shell out almost $1 billion for the state prison system. So why not contract prisoners out if it brings money back in?" asks Sally Kalson, a *Pittsburgh Post-Gazette* columnist.
>
> She supplies her own answer: "It's a bad deal for taxpayers, who get back far less than they spend subsidizing the profit

for private companies. And it's a bad deal for other companies and their workers trying to survive in capitalism's so-called free marketplace."

This may only be the tip of the iceberg. In September 1996, Representative Bill McCollum, Florida Republican, announced that "until now, the potential impact of prison industries has not been fully explored."

Joblessness and Poverty

As we have seen, large-scale joblessness, differing as it does from government defined "unemployment," leads to helplessness and bewilderment among a "reserve army of the unemployed," who contribute significantly to the numbers of Americans living in poverty. Again, as Dembo and Morehouse observe: "More Americans lived in poverty in 1993, 1994 and 1995 than in any year since 1963. But the official poverty line seriously understates the number of poor Americans, just as the official Unemployment Rate understates the number of jobless Americans. A more realistic calculation of the number of people living in poverty is 61 million, one out of every four Americans."[69]

This figure may seem unrealistic to people who live in middle-class circumstances and read *USA Today*. It is necessary, therefore, to discuss further some striking features of America's income distribution. Let us begin by focusing on the wealthiest 20 percent of the population, who number 54 million. After showing the percentage of the aggregate income received by each quintile (i.e., segment of 20 percent) group, we can determine the change in percentages of total income in each income grouping, from 1970 to 1995.

The lower fifth of the population, as of 1970, received 4.1 percent of the total income. By 1995, their share fell to 3.7 percent.* The highest fifth started in 1970 receiving 43 percent and had close to 49 percent of total income by 1995. The top 5 percent (the top quarter of this highest group) began at 17 percent and rose to 21 percent. The relative decreases in income for the majority of U.S. workers' families during this period can be seen in the U.S. *household* incomes, shares and changes, 1970–1995:

*To give these barren numbers more substance, note that "one half of Wal-Mart's 720,000 employees, or 'associates' as the company calls them, qualify for federal assistance under the food stamp program. Wages at Wal-Mart, now the largest private sector employer in the U.S., start as low as $5.75 an hour." (*Wal-Mart's Shirts of Misery*, A Report by the National Labor Committee, July 1999, p. 4.)

Quintile	1970	1995	Percent Change in Income Share, 1970–1995
Lowest fifth	4.1	3.7	−10
Second fifth	10.8	9.1	−16
Third fifth	17.4	15.2	−13
Fourth fifth	24.5	23.3	−5
Highest fifth	43.3	48.7	+12
Top 5 percent	16.6	21.0	+27[70]

Even as they stand, these numbers can be deceptive. A mere 20 percent of the 271 million (1998) U.S. population adds up to about 54 million, more than the population of many nations. This is a substantial market, in terms of both purchasing power and numbers of people. As a result, mass-circulation newspapers and mass-audience television are careful to target advertising at the more affluent segments of the population.

Major changes in the real income of American production workers also played an important part in all this. From 1919 to 1965, the average hourly earnings of workers rose more than fivefold (555 percent), while the Consumer Price Index didn't quite double (up 82 percent). Therefore the purchasing power of workers' wages was multiplied. But after 1970, the picture changed. From 1970 to 1993, wages to industrial workers rose threefold (349 percent), but were outpaced by the price index of consumer goods, which rose 372 percent, resulting in a decrease in real income per hour worked.[71]

Misrepresenting the Sharing of U.S. National Income

During the quarter century 1970–1995, the wealthiest 5 percent of Americans enlarged their share of the nation's income by 50 percent or more. But you cannot learn this from the Bureau of the Census's Current Population Reports, or the government's statistical compilations, such as the annually issued *Statistical Abstract of the U.S.*

Official reports on the sharing of income among *households* in the United States have been published annually since 1967. These reports have been based on measurements of consumer income collected from a national sample of 50,000 *households* visited by agents of the Bureau of the Census since 1967. They merit attention because they distort reality, notably for high-income people during the 1990s.

Prospects for distortion are built into the customary procedures and methods used by the *Current Population Reports on Consumer Income* of the

Department of Commerce. In particular, the Census Bureau, as I will show below, understates the income recently gained by the most affluent 5 percent of Americans. Similarly, the government's methods understate by far the scale of the shift in income that has favored the very rich, notably during the 1990s.

The low-income households, 80 percent, registered a 1970–1995 decline in share of total income as measured by the Commerce Department. Only the highest fifth of U.S. households showed growth in income share from 1970 to 1995. Also, the gain for the top 20 percent is concentrated in the top 5 percent, whose share grew by 27 percent: that apparent gain, however, is understated.*

In order to escape the limitations connected to the "household" as a focus of income measurement and analysis, I examined data on individual incomes from the Internal Revenue Service for 1970 and 1995. These give a more accurate picture of what happened to income sharing in the United States, especially to the highest-income group. I was influenced by the considerable evidence in the business press, after 1993, of a surge in high incomes to the top officers of American firms.

Accordingly, I focused on the top 5 percent of individual income receivers as a reasonable approximation to the top 5 percent of households in the Commerce Department report, since high-income individuals do not generate multiple incomes per family: there is no need to put other family members to work in order to cope with rent, grocery bills and leisure-time spending.

The Internal Revenue Service figures tell a different story. The *Statistics of Income* of the IRS show, for the same dates, income details from 74 million individual reports in 1970 and 118 million in 1995. Of the total, the number of individuals in the top 5 percent of IRS-reported incomes for 1970 and 1995 are readily calculated: 3.7 million (1970) and 5.9 million (1995).[72]

So, although according to the Census Bureau figures, the top 5 percent of *households* registered a 1970–1995 income growth of 27 percent, the top 5 percent of IRS *individual income receivers* registered a growth of share of 50 percent, from a 20.2 percent share (1970) to a 30.2 percent share (1995) of total individual incomes reported. This contrasts with the data of the top 5 percent "household income" group—a 1970–1995 increase of 27 percent in income group share.

*The Commerce Department's household income studies are based on a sample of 50,000. That is less than one-hundredth of one percent of a population with 102 million households. Assuming random sampling, it is rather unlikely that the 100,000 families with incomes of over $1 million would be tapped. Furthermore, there is no legal requirement to respond to the survey on money income, and the rich are reportedly reluctant to respond.

Why the glaring disparity? The understatement of top-level household income change is due to a series of methods used to prepare household income data published annually as *Money Income in the U.S.*

First, underreporting results from the guidance that the Income Statistics Branch of the Census Bureau gives its field agents. In the Earned Income part of the questionnaire that guides the agents, they are instructed to ask:

> How much did (name/you) earn from (his/her/your) business after expenses . . . ?
> FOR AMOUNTS OF $1,000,000 AND OVER ENTER $999,999.*

The staff performing these household income studies does not record particular data on respondents with over $1 million in earned income—by a procedure the staff calls top coding. Earnings above $1 million are thus recoded to $999,999 in the department's "Internal File."

By these methods, the department fulfills its pledge of confidentiality to respondents with large earnings. The same methods make large earnings individually invisible, while also shielding the location of such persons.

Moreover, I am advised, the computers used by field agents are programmed to record up to $1 million for single-person earnings. The system therefore does not report earnings from salaries and bonuses and the like with a multimillion-dollar value.

The *Statistics of Income* series from the Internal Revenue Service, on the other hand, includes a display of all the major components of individual income. "Salaries and wages" leads the field, but it is clear

*U.S. Department of Commerce, Bureau of the Census, March 1998, *CPS Field Representative/CATI Interviewer, Items Booklet*, CPS Field Representative/Interviewer Memorandum No. 98-03. On page 3, the interviewer is instructed to say:

> I am going to read a list of income categories. Which category represents the total combined income of all members of this FAMILY during the past 12 months? This includes money from jobs, net income from business, farm or rent, pensions, dividends, interest, social security payments and any other money income received by members of this FAMILY who are 15 years of age or older.

Then, the interviewer records

> <1> Less than $5,000
> [or one of the further fourteen income groupings, up to]
> <14> 75,000 or more.

On page 14 (Q49 B2), the interviewer is instructed to ask:

> How much did (name/you) earn from (his/her/your) own business after expenses?
> FOR AMOUNTS $1,000,000 OR OVER, ENTER $999,999.

that "sales of capital assets" makes the next largest contribution to total incomes of the highest-income group. But the edition of the *Current Population Report* series that presents household incomes does not include "money receipts such as capital gains" as income. Since this is a major source of top-level income, that omission casts a considerable downward bias on any comparative statement of income share to the top 5 percent of household incomes.*

Intentionally or not, the household-income mode of measurement suppresses the visibility of concentrated growth—at the top—in the sharing of national income.

This glaring disparity in fairness and accuracy requires a further comment. The earnings studies of the *Current Population Report* series were originally undertaken to measure the low end of the income and employment population, to gauge the effects of unemployment and low-income joblessness. But the consumer income reports, while detailing earnings differences among households at the lower end of the earnings range, came to be used by many writers to portray a national earnings picture. One result has been a marked understatement of the incomes growth for families and households at the multimillion annual earnings level. This understatement has masked the vast concentration of new wealth among the top managerial households in business and finance management, notably during the 1990s.

Let us consider the changing fortunes of most Americans from another angle. Average hourly money earnings define the main money income of most working Americans. What has been the purchasing power of their work time? In the following table, I show how many minutes or hours of work time are needed to purchase an array of foods and other items. By comparing average prices against average hourly earnings, we can reckon the cost in work time of each item, for 1993 and 1998.

*Elaborate attention to the securities markets in the main news media has tended to reinforce the idea that stock prices are a prime indicator of national well-being. In fact, as of 1999, "only 21 per cent of Americans [had] stock-market assets outside of retirement funds" (*Business Week*, December 27, 1999).

Purchasing Power of Work Time in
Hours-Minutes in the United States

	1993 Hrs–Mins	1998 Hrs–Mins
Milk (liter)	0–4	0–7
Meat (kilo)	0–43	0–48
Coffee (kilo)	0–33	1–18
Tea (kilo)	0–41	1–3
Sugar (kilo)	0–6	0–7
Oranges (kilo)	0–11	0–18
Bread (kilo)	0–14	0–20
Potatoes (kilo)	0–7	0–11
Man's dress shirt	1–40	2–51
Man's suit (wool)	20–51	5–7
Man's shoes	7–5	6–21
Gasoline (liter)	0–6	0–1
Television	5–5	6–56

Only three of these items could be bought for less work time in 1998 than in 1993 (gasoline and men's shoes and suits). All the others showed an increase in work time required. This is a reasonable way to view the increasing pressure on families to double and triple the number of wage earners, or double the work time put in by a single person.

Dembo and Morehouse's report on joblessness also found that during the last decades of the twentieth century, among eight leading industrial countries, the United States had the largest income difference between the highest and lowest 20 percentiles of income receivers. The U.S. largest income difference (13:1) correlated with the lowest unionization rate among industrial countries (16 percent).

Some Effects from U.S. Income Sharing

What are the social consequences of this extraordinary concentration of wealth? Some part of this accumulation in the hands of the top 5 percent of income receivers and wealth holders surely represents monies that, in other societies, would be spent on infrastructure that serves the community as a whole. In the United States, they are reserved for the private accumulation of wealth and power.

A second glance at the U.S. incomes data by 20 percent groupings (page 88), showing the changes over the twenty-five-year period, suggests a sustained drive for the preemption of wealth by those on top. By 1997, for example, the rate of growth and size of top executive compensation in American corporations had reached unheard-of levels, while increasing faster than corporate revenues.[73] Here are the 1997 data on payments to the ten highest-paid CEOs in U.S. industrial and financial firms. By comparing the CEO payment per hour (assuming a 2,000-hour work year) to average production worker hourly payment in U.S. manufacturing, we can see the contrast only too clearly. By 1997, all of these top-ranking CEOs were being paid more than a thousand times the 1997 average wage to American production workers.

Top Ten CEO Salaries, 1998

	Total CEO Compensation, in millions	**CEO Earnings per Hour (for a Work Year of 2,000 Hours)**	**Ratio of CEO: Production Worker Hourly Compensation***
Michael Eisner Walt Disney	$575.6	$287,796	15,506:1
Mel Karmazin CBS	201.9	100,967	5,440:1
Sanford Weill Citigroup	167.1	83,547	4,501:1
Stephen Case America Online	159.2	79,617	4,290:1
Craig Barrett Intel	116.5	58,256	3,139:1
John Welch General Electric	83.7	41,832	2,254:1
Henry Schacht Lucent Technologies	67.0	33,519	1,806:1
L. Dennis Kozlowski Tyco International	65.3	32,632	1,758:1
Henry Silverman Cendant	63.9	31,941	1,721:1
M. Douglas Ivester Coca-Cola	57.3	28,661	1,544:1[74]

**Compensation* is the total wage plus nonwage costs to the employer for employing a worker per hour. For 1998, the average compensation cost for production workers in the United States was $18.56.

At the top of the table, Eisner was earning well over fifteen thousand times the hourly compensation of a production worker. By 1998, the always profitable Travelers Group—owned by Sanford Weill's Citigroup—planned to cut its national work force by 8,000 jobs.[75] The concentrations of income to Eisner, Weill and other top executives are unique in the twentieth-century experience of the United States.

Princely compensation has become a characteristic not only of executives working but also of executives discharged. Companies in failing condition have frequently disposed of their top executives, but often with handsome compensatory settlements, the so-called "golden parachute." For example, it was announced that Viacom "will pay as much as $15.5 million in the next three years to its former chief executive, Frank J. Biondi Jr., who was dismissed in January after nine years with the media company."[76] It is now routine for chief executives to seek contracts that provide for a golden parachute if for any reason their services are no longer desired.

There is no escaping a special American pattern in all this. "Chief executives at the biggest American companies are paid nearly six times their counterparts in Japan and four times as much as German top executives. . . . In the U.S., more than elsewhere, executives receive bonuses and stock options that become more valuable if a company's stock price rises."[77]

When President Bush traveled to Japan in 1991, he took twenty-one businessmen with him. Recently announced executive increases touched a nerve there, and correspondents for *The Wall Street Journal* (December 30, 1991) reported the following reactions:

> "In Japan, you'd cut executive pay before eliminating jobs," one Finance Ministry official says simply. . . . The Japanese argued that overpaid American executives were preoccupied with short-term results, worsening U.S. international competitiveness. . . . Koichi Hori, representative director for the Boston Consulting Group in Tokyo, says U.S. executives should make a third or a quarter of what they earn now. "There's no logic whatsoever [for an executive to be] paid 100 times more than a secretary," he says. "All workers add value to the corporation."

The record bonuses and compensation packages of recent years suggest that it's business as usual in America.

Finally, there is the special consideration in the tax laws, put in place in recent decades, for the high-income segments of the corporate population.[78] Once again, the odds are stacked in favor of those at the top:

> Companies large and small have been signing up executives and other top employees for a generous tax break not available to other Americans. Hundreds of thousands of people have become eligible, most in the last few years, at more than 24,000 businesses. The deal is simple: Rather than take all their pay, and pay taxes on it, executives let the company hold on to some. The company invests the money, and the executives do not pay taxes on any of it until they take the money years later.
>
> . . . The amount of deferred compensation can be staggering. In 1994–95 alone, the chairman of the McDonnell Douglas Corporation, J. F. McDonnell, deferred $2.5 million in pay, and Michael H. Jordan of the Westinghouse Electric Corporation deferred $1.8 million. John L. Clendenin of the BellSouth Corporation has close to $10 million in his deferral accounts. There is no ceiling on how much money can be sheltered. One executive alone, Roberto C. Goizueta, the chief executive of the Coca-Cola Company, has accumulated $936.4 million, most of it in company stock that will not be taxed until after he retires.

Unfortunately, the government has no way of keeping track of the billions of dollars that are deferred or lost in this way.

> . . . In most cases, it requires companies to write a letter informing the Labor Department that deferred compensation is being offered. Many companies never bother to file anything with the Labor Department. And its list is riddled with inaccuracies. For example, it does not include Exxon, Ford and Wal-Mart—though they all offer deferred compensation.*

While many Americans have little sympathy for the IRS, the social cost of the loss in tax revenues involved here should give pause for thought.

The Human Cost of the "New Economy"

Accompanying this concentration of wealth has been a steady impoverishment at the other end of the scale. In the United States, during the

*"Deferred compensation is perfectly legal and always has been. . . . Deene Goodlaw, a San Francisco lawyer who teaches pension law at the University of California at Berkeley, has prepared hundreds of deferred-compensation plans. And she says that some companies are paying for these plans partly by cutting retirement benefits for the rank and file. . . . Ms. Goodlaw said she quit the tax department of a prestigious law firm after she was directed to prepare a lavish deferred-compensation plan for one company's executives on the same day she was told to draft a plan that let it cut most of its low-paid workers out of its pension plan. . . . 'If you quote me on this I'll probably never get another job drafting deferral agreements. But that's the truth, what is going on is wrong. It's immoral.' "

latter third of the past century, a group appeared that is more exploited, and worse off economically, than any other, with a larger proportion below the poverty level than the black population in the country: the Hispanic population.[79] They, and more recent arrivals from East Asia, supply a labor force for new generations of sweatshops within the United States. Attempts have been made to establish voluntary rules that might affect workers in American sweatshops, and even those employed by American firms abroad, but these measures have not been successful.

A mid-1997 report shows an increase in child labor and an enlargement of working hours, again, within the United States.[80] At the same time, the principal firms producing apparel have been expanding outside the United States. One illustration should be sufficient.

In October 1995, an inquiring U.S. reporter in San Salvador looked into one of these factories in the Progress Free-Trade zone. There, the workday ran from seven in the morning until seven in the evening. After observing and speaking to one of the women, the reporter noted: "This woman worked in the Doall plant, which makes jackets for Liz Claiborne. The jackets sell in the United States for $178 each. The garment workers who made them earned 56 cents an hour. Sources with access to data from the production line of one of the plants said a worker on that line earned about 77 cents per jacket. The dramatic difference between wages paid in these locales and U.S. wages, and the very sizable margins between product wage cost and final price, suggest very high profitability in these firms, which does not show up in reduced prices for goods made under these conditions."[81] In other words, the American trend toward extreme income inequality continues to extend beyond these shores. In the name of globalization, the United States is exporting poverty.

The consequences for consumption in society are far-reaching. The high-end effect appears, for example, in the magazine *Worth.*[82] For July 1997, it included an opulent display of homes and facilities in the richest towns of the United States. In stark contrast, for a twenty-year period up to 1997, the pay of farm workers was trailing inflation and fell 20 percent over the past two decades. A Department of Agriculture study found a 7 percent drop, to $6.17 an hour, in current dollars over that period.[83] Farm workers' wages were undercut by the steadily increasing supply of Mexican and other Latino workers to do the seasonal stoop labor of American farms. Once again, a reserve army of unemployed labor reinforces the trend toward joblessness and poverty, while the rich get still richer.

In the total U.S. working population of 1993, 8.4 million families lived in poverty. Of the white population, 9.4 percent of families were in poverty, compared with 31.3 percent of black and 27.3 percent of Hispanic families.[84]

The prodigious growth of wealth, and the accompanying concentration of control, within American corporations since World War II has spelled success by every business criterion. But the methods of their success have produced an accompanying alienation on a large scale, as workers have been uprooted from their familiar occupations and communities, and weakened by income reduction. There has been no equivalent replacement of work, for much of it has been eliminated, mechanized, or moved out of this country altogether.*

This strategy of alienation by design in the United States has entailed the technical deterioration of many industries; holding back civilian industrial R&D spending; shutting down factories while preferring investments in distant locations with new (and cheaper) labor forces; selective alienation of unionized work forces, as in the steel, clothing and machinery industries; using prison and sweatshop labor; carrying out massive layoffs through downsizing to achieve cost reduction (and profit increase) while enforcing a speedup in production and administrative work; compelling a large sector of the workforce, "employed" but jobless, to rely increasingly upon single or multiple temp jobs for their livelihood. All this while creating an American population of 31 million going hungry (a.k.a "food insecure") during 2000, including 21 percent of black and Hispanic people, and "about 17 per cent of all children."[85]

The drive for profit alone does not suffice to "explain" the behavior of private and state managers summarized here. Maximizing power is a further end-in-view for government and corporate managers in state capitalism. John Kenneth Galbraith has captured this idea, writing:

> Thus power, its pursuit and its enjoyment, is a basic and admitted motivation in all corporate organization.

He quotes Thomas J. Watson, Jr., the former head of IBM, as saying of his life in that notable enterprise:

> I learned a great deal about power, being subject to it, striving for it, inventing it, wielding it and letting it go.

As Galbraith observes, "So much for a single-minded concentration on profit."[86]

*To understand the full force of these developments, see Exhibit C of my *What Else Is There to Do?* (National Commission for Economic Conversion and Disarmament, 1996, pp. 78–82), which shows examples of IBEW job losses to Mexico.

4

State Managers Accumulate Military Power Without Limit

The deindustrialization process that gave rise to an industrially diminished American economy was not the boundary of alienation pursued by the managers of state capitalism. Their ambitions, rather, built into every part of government, included extension of their hegemony over other states and continents, without limit.

The U.S. military economy is a partnership of government and business. It is managed by a central administrative office, based in the Pentagon, which is the largest single managerial entity of the whole economy and the core of America's permanent war economy.

According to prevailing wisdom, businessmen are the nominal controllers of the enterprises listed on the main stock and bond exchanges. They also run the companies known as government contractors and the web of subcontractors and supplier firms that support them. But here the lines begin to blur.

As is often the case, partners are not necessarily equal. In the U.S. state/business partnership, it is the government that controls the bulk of the finance capital and possesses the decisive influence in extensions of government and corporate decision power, in managing the largest R&D budgets in the economy, and in deploying the armed forces worldwide.

State Managerialism

Rendering the American people powerless has not been a stated objective of the Department of Defense. But a review of the structure and functions of the defense establishment shows that the military organization, visible everywhere, has created economic dependency in every state, as long as the Pentagon's work continued. By 1999, the uniformed armed forces numbered 1,454,000, to which must be added 725,000 civilians directly employed by the Pentagon. Apart from these, 2,210,000 civilian men and women were employed in a further array of military-industrial establishments. Not accounted for in these statistics are the civilian staffs engaged in military research in the network of federally funded research and development centers, which have their top administration in the Departments of Defense and Energy and the National Aeronautics and Space Administration (NASA). In 1999, these agencies managed military-related research in locations like the Livermore, Los Alamos and Lincoln laboratories. These facilities, plus the R&D that Defense, Energy and NASA sponsor at universities across the country, accounted for $4,974 million and the activity of about 110,000 highly skilled people.[1]

This activity has brought economic privilege, even prosperity, for a lucky few, but the dependency has also left the people of whole communities, industries, and occupations stranded and quite helpless when the military's work was done. For thirty years, I led advocacy of economic conversion planning for the American military economy. I found that managers of military-serving firms and their Pentagon overseers viewed such preparations as tantamount to disloyalty to their mission.

There is no line in the federal government's budget titled "alienation" or "alienation, short-term" or "alienation, long-term." Nevertheless, the normal functioning of a military establishment requires continuing mobilizations of human activity and continuous control over behavior. These controls are enforced by a military police and military justice system with their own special legal codes.

In this chapter, I will emphasize the scale and power of the Pentagon's control system, and explore the alienation and depletion that has resulted from this partnership of government and business.

From about 1947 to 1991, the United States and the Soviet Union were involved in a standoff called the Cold War. For both societies this entailed massive militarization of their economies; it led to the establishment of the permanent war economy. Even after 1991, the U.S. economy did not collapse into a nonwarlike mode. Rather, the war economy has been maintained, at over $250 billion a year in military budgets.

From 1940 to 1996, U.S. military outlays totaled about $17 trillion, measured in dollars of 1996 purchasing power. Of this amount, $5.8 trillion was spent on nuclear weapons. This includes research, testing, production, delivery systems, command, control and early-warning networks, defense against nuclear attack, and the management and disposition of nuclear waste. Over the course of fifty years, the government produced more than 70,000 nuclear explosives. (Details on the U.S. nuclear program are in Chapter 5.)

There is surely this real limit to military power: a person or community can be destroyed only once. We need reminding that Hiroshima was ravaged on August 6, 1945, by a single nuclear explosive with a power of 15,000 tons of TNT. About 140,000 were killed by that single blast.

Consider, as purely hypothetical nuclear targets, the combined present populations of Russia and China: 1,351,000,000, or the equivalent of 9,650 Hiroshimas of 1945. Using the Hiroshima yardstick, warheads with the combined power of 144.7 million tons of TNT (9,650 × 15,000 tons) would be required to destroy these two countries. (As the nuclear planners would remind us, selection of warhead sizes and dispersion would have to take into account that blast effect does not increase proportionately with size.) If we allow for an additional 30 percent to account for possible launch and warhead failures, 188.2 million tons of TNT would be needed.

What is the size of the current nuclear arsenal? The United States now deploys warheads with the power of some 2.3 billion tons of TNT. Thus that 188.2 million tons required to destroy both Russia and China is merely 8 percent of the power of the active U.S. nuclear arsenal. The remaining 92 percent represents a vast reservoir of excess killing power and military spending, or in the language of nuclear strategy, overkill.

If $5.8 trillion was the accounted cost of America's nuclear enterprise, 1940 to 1996, then this 92 percent overkill share amounts to $5.3 trillion. *That sum is more than twice the net value of the plant and equipment in America's manufacturing industries.* What has been sacrificed in the process? The nuclear budget has cost the economy the possibility of applying the technical manpower and allied resources used up for the nuclear enterprise toward building and operating a superior manufacturing system far more sophisticated and "user-friendly" than what is now Cold War history. The Cold War may have ended, but the nuclear weapons enterprise continues at $35 billion annually in the weapons-systems contracting of the Pentagon and the Department of Energy.

A strategic way of viewing the planning of military institutions is through their commitment to new weapons and machinery spending. A Pentagon administrative report called "Selected Acquisitions Reports" reveals that, for December 1987, new weapons programs in design, development or production had a value of $732 billion. About seventy-one weapons systems were to be funded at a further cost of $705.2 billion over ten to twenty years. Surely the end of the Cold War would make a difference?

Shortly after the 1996 national elections, there was an announcement of a new weapons program named the Joint Strike Fighter, to be used by all branches of the military. Many countries would be invited to join the program, and the prospective outlay, we were told, would be $750 billion. No single weapon system of such cost had ever been seen during the half century of the Cold War. The combination of this massive project plus other planned expenditures added up to a military investing plan of $1,455 billion over ten to twenty years. Such levels of spending for new matériel were hitherto expected only at wartime peaks.

Military organizations play a prominent part in the economics and politics of state capitalism, for they are ideally suited for maximizing the extension of decision power. In the United States, the 6 million people who are employed in military organizations or in the economy that serves them thus have a twofold relation to government: as citizens and as employees. This combination constitutes a remarkably intense system of control, for hardly any aspect of their lives lies outside of one or another of the rules and regulations of the federal institutions.

One modest way of viewing the growth of state managerial controls is by noting the rise in the annual number of pages of the *Federal Register*, a government periodical that records new regulations and administrative decisions. The following are the numbers of pages for selected years:

1936	2,619 pages
1939	5,007
1942	11,134
1943	17,553
1945	15,508
1947	8,902
1951	13,175
1964	19,304
1975	60,221
1980	87,012
1994	66,431
1999	73,570

The Second World War clearly boosted the role of the state managers, but the last twenty years has seen a staggering growth in their controls.

As with other aspects of state capitalism, the control of capital in military institutions also plays an important part in facilitating the maintenance and extension of decision power. As a former Supreme Commander in World War II, Dwight Eisenhower was fully alert to the significance of this consideration, specifically targeting it in his Farewell Address to the nation in January 1961: "We annually spend on military security more than the net income of all United States corporations."[2] The Department of Defense's control of capital was a prominent feature of the Cold War period.

A confidant of Eisenhower told me (in 1963) that the President was both skeptical and fearful of America's military chiefs, and their cavalier attitude concerning the likely negative economic consequences of massive Pentagon budgets. He added that Eisenhower had tried, and failed, to convince John F. Kennedy to forgo the large increases in the armed forces that the new President's advisers had been promising. On the contrary, they sought to make up for what they saw as the feeble policies of the outgoing administration. Therefore, he said, Eisenhower welcomed the critique that several colleagues and I had prepared in *A Strategy for American Security*. He concurred with our assessment of dangers to the American economy and to society from the costs and other consequences of military overkill.[3] But little has changed.

Every year from 1952 to 1994, the new money made available to the Pentagon exceeded the combined net profits of all American corporations.[4] The federal government gave priority to the extension of control over fixed and working capital on behalf of its military enterprise.* By 1990 the Pentagon's property (weapons-related equipment and supplies, plant equipment, structures) was valued at $946 billion, of which weapons and equipment were $804 billion.[5] By comparison, the net stock of equipment and structures in U.S. manufacturing facilities was valued at $1,138 billion in the same year.[6] Hence, the Pentagon's capital assets were equivalent to 83 percent of the assets of all U.S. manufacturing industry.

By 1987, the privately owned "fixed reproducible tangible wealth in the United States," or fixed capital, amounted to $8,557.9 billion. Similar government-owned wealth (excluding the military) came to $1,978.7 billion. In total, this measure of the nation's tangible wealth added up to $10,536.6 billion (all this in dollars of "constant" 1987 value).

By way of contrast, consider the national defense outlays from 1945 to 1995 (again in dollars of 1987 value). These expenditures—which, of course, included not only fixed but also "working" capital (like wages and salaries to servicemen and women)—amounted to $12,003 billion.[7]

In other words, the combined fixed and working capital embedded in the Pentagon's budgets was great enough to finance the replacement of the largest part of what is human-made on the surface of the United States.†

*In this discussion, the term *capital* is used in the ordinary industrial-enterprise usage. Fixed capital refers to the money value of land, buildings and machinery. Working capital is the money value of all the other resources required to set an industrial enterprise in motion.

†For all the data that is produced by the various departments of the U.S. government, there is no accounting of the government's largest activity: the "war industry." Pieces of available industrial output data, purchasing information, labor-force activity statistics and federal budgets do not combine to afford an accounting of the war industry. The result is a major gap in understanding about where the wealth went and what the material potentials of the nation are. A mystery is created about the past, present and future.

Central Office Management in the Pentagon

Ultimate control over the millions of men and women who serve the military enterprises is held by the Pentagon. This organization was decisively shaped by Robert McNamara, named Secretary of Defense in 1961. As a former president of the Ford Motor Company, McNamara modeled the department administration after a corporate central office. As in any major corporation, the central office defines policy and presides over the appointment of the chiefs of subordinate units, constantly receiving and monitoring reports on their compliance with its policies.

In an industrial firm, the subordinate units typically have complete accounting and management functions. Within limits that are subject to the broad policy guidance of the central office, each of the subordinate organizations has considerable discretion. McNamara had installed this type of organization at Ford.

Acquisition of every sort of matériel and weapons is another key function of the military organization. Part of the mechanism for facilitating this is the organization within each of the military services that participates in the acquisition process.

In 1997, 288,680 employees served in acquisition and contract-management capacities for the Department of Defense. Of these, 47,500 were uniformed personnel, and the remainder were civilians. It is difficult to track the growth of these organizations that participate in military acquisition, since periodic changes have been made in the definition of *acquisition*. Thus, various armed services organizations have been added to or subtracted from this defined group. But a reasonable perspective can be obtained by comparing the growth of the staff engaged in these functions after 1981, when 83,000 were employed. By 1988, the acquisition and related staff numbered 583,131; this all-time high was reduced, in response to various reorganization reports, to 288,680 by 1997. But the latter still dwarfs the equivalent staffs of even the largest U.S. corporations.[8]

Despite the scale of these managerial control activities, as in the Pentagon's Defense Finance and Accounting Service, auditors from the General Accounting Office (GAO) told the Congress in 1995 that "at least $20 billions of expenditures could not be matched to the items they purchased. The Defense Department's Inspector General [testified] that one should not expect a turnaround until the year 2000, even though she assigned 700 auditors to clean up the accounting mess."[9]

In June 1996, the GAO (updating a 1995 audit) reported that the Defense Department's bookkeeping system could not match between $20 and $30 billion of expenditures to the items purchased. In April 1997, the Office reported that "problem disbursements" had increased to $43 billion. The department's Inspector General released a report saying it could not audit the $80+ billion Defense Business Operations Fund, owing to the absence of a sound internal control structure. This was not the only agency with problems keeping track of runaway spending. The Air Force could not verify acquisition costs of $282 billion in assets, and a $20 billion discrepancy was found between Air Force and Defense Logistics Agency values on "Government Furnished Property." The Navy could not account for $32 billion pertaining to ammunition, and the Army reported that "the values of its inventory ($38 billion), its military equipment ($81 billion) and its real property ($27 billion)" were all "misstated by an unknown but probably material amount."[10] No private corporation manager could possibly survive such lapses in accounting.*

The arm of the Pentagon's central administrative office also reaches far beyond the United States. In American embassies around the world, the Pentagon's staff includes not only representatives of the Foreign Military Sales Organization but also people assigned to train the local military in the use of weapons and in American techniques of organization. All this is distinct from instruction in managing unruly populations, and the intelligence and assorted operations of the Central Intelligence Agency. All told, these military groupings in American embassies often outnumber State Department personnel.

*Here are excerpts from the "Executive Summary" of the Inspector General's report [U.S. Department of Defense, Office of the Inspector General, *Audit Report: Internal Controls and Compliance with Laws and Regulations for the DoD Agency-Wide Financial Statements for FY 1999*, Report No. D-2000-091, February 25, 2000]:

> The DoD Agency-Wide financial statements for FY1999 are compiled from the financial statements of the DoD reporting entities: the Army, Navy, and Air Force. . . .
>
> DoD did not provide the DoD Agency-Wide financial statements for FY 1999 in time for us to perform all of the necessary audit work. Therefore, we did not verify the reported amounts. However, we identified deficiencies in internal controls and accounting systems related to $119.3 billion of general property, plant, and equipment inventory; $80 billion of environmental liabilities; $196 billion of military retirement health benefits liability. . . . We also identified $6.9 trillion in accounting entries to financial data used to prepare financial statements for the Army, Navy, and Air Force. . . . For the accounting entries, $2.3 trillion was not supported by adequate audit trails or sufficient evidence to determine their validity, $2 trillion was not reviewed because of time constraints, and $2.6 trillion were supported. . . .
>
> DoD internal controls were not adequate to ensure that resources were properly managed and accounted for, that DoD complied with applicable laws and regulations, and that the financial statements were free of material misstatements. DoD internal controls did not ensure that adjustments to financial data were fully supported and that assets and liabilities were properly accounted for and valued. . . .
>
> DoD did not fully comply with laws and regulations that had a direct and material [e]ffect on its ability to determine financial statement amounts. . . . The DoD does not expect to have systems necessary to meet these new requirements before the year 2003.

What drives this immense machine?

Pentagon policies are best understood as efforts to accumulate power and profit. The profit accrues primarily to the companies hired to perform contracted parts of the Pentagon's work. But the top officials of the military establishment, like the Joint Chiefs of Staff, do not earn anything like the extravagant incomes of corporate chiefs. Their main reward is power.

At present, their strategy for the Defense Department includes the ability to fight two wars at once, with the prospective targeted opponents being so-called "rogue" states like Cuba, Libya, Syria, Iraq, Iran and North Korea. The *combined* annual military budgets* of these states (for 1993) amounted to about $9.3 billion, not even 10 percent of the U.S. budget for this purpose.[11] But this apparently limited agenda does not account for the military and other resource commitments represented by U.S. assistance pledges for the defense of Taiwan and Israel. Pro-Taiwan military-political policy promises confrontation with China, whose twenty-first-century industrialization will make it the nation-state with the most formidable set of capabilities on earth.

The enlargement of power-wielding by the military directorate (recalling that the President is commander in chief) is visible in virtually every major activity of the Pentagon. While the number of soldiers has been reduced to reflect diminished Russian power, the elaborateness of their equipment has simultaneously been increasing. At the same time, the United States still holds a massive stockpile of nuclear weapons.

Nevertheless, by 1994 the Department of Energy was committed to building a $1.8 billion laser facility at the Lawrence Livermore National Laboratory in California. This device, the size of two football fields, is to be used to gauge the reliability of hydrogen bombs without full-scale explosive tests underground. It will also supposedly be useful for studies concerning how the stars shine and how a nuclear fire may be harnessed to generate electrical power.[12]

All this is programmed in the midst of the usual parade of spendthrift Pentagon agendas. The editors of the *New York Times* were evidently shaken in 1994 by the discovery of the "top secret spy palace" being built for the National Reconnaissance Office, which "designs, builds and operates spy satellites that photograph and overhear what other countries are up to." The "palace" is a $350 million office building used to headquarter this highly secretive agency, whose very existence was not officially disclosed until 1992. The headquarters, "designed to house some 3,000 employees and contractors," would continue "to manage . . . the agency's $8 billion program to build a fleet of satellites whose main function is to

*Defense budget figures are not available for Iraq, so estimates of "defense expenditures" have been used instead.

keep track of Russian bombers crossing the Arctic Ocean or a Russian Navy that is not going anywhere these days."[13] The new "palace" would also centralize the management of contractors' budgets of unknown billions. We will never know the exact budget of the National Reconnaissance Office: it is kept secret, or "black." Since the end of the Cold War, the expense of the secrecy has no military explanation, other than maintaining and enlarging the decision power of this part of the military apparatus.

Pentagon Capitalism

A Pentagon-serving corporation, an enterprise with its own management and profit-and-loss statements, is not autonomous. Instead, it operates like a division of a large centrally controlled firm. This central-office mode of industrial organization was introduced in private capitalism early in the twentieth century as a way of organizing multidivision enterprises. Instead of each factory being governed, in all its detail, out of the company "head office," a decentralized mode of operation was developed as a response to the problems of managing large firms with many plants.

In this new pattern, a central administrative office specializes in policy formulation. General policy is then handed down to the managers of the divisions. The managers report on operations in accordance with the requirements that the central office lays down. While the central office defines broad policy patterns, it is left to the division managers to decide on the preferred modes of detailed policy. But here there is a crucial difference from the prospects of civilian-serving firms.

In *Pentagon Capitalism*, I described the operations of the central-office system.[14] When a firm entered into a major contract with the Pentagon, it became *virtually failure-proof.* The Pentagon's managers could, through the ordinary terms of its contracts, assure the company of ample financing. Also, if required, special payments and loans could be arranged to ease the contractor's operations and forestall bankruptcy.

With an organization as large as the industrial system required to serve the Department of Defense, the Pentagon's central-office system was understandably divided into several tiers. Each industrial region of the United States thus has had its own designated central office, which in turn reports back to the Pentagon. An important part of the system has been the use of resident staffs of uniformed and civilian personnel to represent the central office on the premises of contracting firms.

These representatives serve a double purpose. They convey and interpret central-office policy directives to the local managers and can report back to the central office. All this has proceeded on a grand scale, because the policy regulations and detailed requirements of the Pentagon have been set forth in policy directives. The policy-control system covers every aspect of the contractor's operations: what should be produced; its quantities; how the production should be carried out; approvals on costs, prices and changes therein; schedules of operations; disposing of the product; the quality of contractor managerial and technical organizations.

A major step that altered an important part of U.S. industry was formalized by Robert McNamara in the 1960s. There had been a deep policy struggle among the top civilian and uniformed officials of the Pentagon, notably during the early 1960s, over procedures for costing (hence pricing) the products of industrial contractors. One side, led by an industrial engineer, A. Ernest Fitzgerald, advocated "should" costing: acceptable cost to be based on formulations of alternative designs, production methods and so forth. This approach would clearly promote economy. The other group proposed "historical" costing: price would be based upon previous costs, which had followed the "cost-plus" system widely practiced during World War II. In other words, contractors could take the previous cost of making a product for the Pentagon and simply add on an agreed-upon profit margin. The more a product cost, the more they stood to earn.

McNamara ruled in favor of "historical" costing,[15] which led to systemwide escalation. Thus, by 1980, the Defense Science Board reported that the cost of producing major weapons systems had been growing at an annual rate of 20 percent.[16] In 1996, the cost of the B-2 bomber again exceeded the value of its weight in gold.

Military contracts are not assigned on the basis of price. Characteristically, at first, the product usually exists only as a concept. In place of cheaper or cost-based decisions, the central office breaks down weapons projects into a series of functional steps. Several firms are invited to present initial proposals for design and related research work, with accompanying commitments by the Pentagon to fixed amounts for these tasks. This stage can be followed by the selection of two or three firms to compete in the design of a new weapons system. A final choice of the prime contractor can take place after that, with companies that have participated in the initial design work sharing some part of the final production contract. Everyone involved stands to gain from this top-heavy process. Except, of course, the U.S. taxpayer.

Unintended Consequences

By the close of the 1980s, twenty U.S. industrial corporations had prime contracts from the Pentagon valued at $1 billion or more. Certain industries are especially dependent on Pentagon orders. During the 1980s, as we saw in Chapter 3, machine-tool sales by American firms dropped about 60 percent—part of a worldwide collapse in orders for new machine tools. Nevertheless, U.S. military orders rose 65 percent, taking up part of the slack. But there was a hidden cost. As the machine-tool and other capital-goods industries became dependent on Pentagon orders, their ability to compete in civilian markets was seriously affected.

As we have seen, capital-goods industries, like machine tools and shipbuilding, have developed a dependency on the Pentagon.

The establishment of a state management marked the transformation of Eisenhower's military-industrial complex into a very different sort of creature. A loose collaboration of senior military officers, industrial managers and legislators has been replaced by a defined managerial control center that regulates tens of thousands of subordinate managers. The normal operation and expansion of the new state management has been based on the preemption of a large share of federal tax revenue and of the nation's finite supply of technical manpower. The state management has also become the most powerful decision-making unit in the government. The government no longer "serves" or "regulates" business, since the new management is the largest enterprise of them all. Government *is* business.

How can we explain this massive expansion?

No mere ideology can account for the colossal costs of the military machine. A drive for power has been at work here, but it is not explicable in terms of any individual impetus. Rather, state management represents an institutionalized power-lust. To see anything comparable, we have to look to the example of European imperialism in the late nineteenth and early twentieth centuries.

The operating rules of the older imperialism required the use of armed force to assure control over important investments or trade (actual or potential). Virtually none of this could be found in the case of Vietnam in the 1960s. Nevertheless, in the eyes of the managers of America's state capitalism, Vietnam was the great testing ground for direct application of the new tools available to them. The methods of the new imperialism included direct use of military, political and economic power to checkmate leftist nationalism and to take *direct political control of entire nations*—without relying on, and even in the absence of, economic mechanisms of trade and investment that were basic to the older imperialism. Accordingly, as I noted in *The Permanent War Economy*,

> The expenditure of over $150 billion of U.S. government funds and the operations of a major war that took more than fifty thou-

sand American lives and an immense toll in Indochinese lives and property is best explained in terms of the requirements for enlarging the decision power of America's state managers.[17]

The economic expenditure of the Vietnam war entailed far more than the Pentagon's direct outlays of some $150 billion. The full social cost includes interest on the war-related debt, the value of production forgone, veterans' benefits and many other economic consequences. These are estimated at $676 billion.[18] The human cost is incalculable.

The decision power of Pentagon management has reached that of a state. After all, the fiscal 2000 budget plan of the Department of Defense—about $265 billion—exceeded the economic product of entire nations. The state management has become a para-state, a state within a state.

By the measure of industrial activity governed from one central office, this organization, reporting to its CEO in the White House, is the largest industrial management in the United States, probably in the world. Never before in American experience has there been such a combination of economic, political and military decision power in the same hands.*

By 1994, the Pentagon had made prime contract awards for more than $138 billion.[19] It controlled 3.6 million of its own uniformed and civilian personnel. These do not include the employees of "defense-related" industry, which peaked at 3.6 million from 1986 through 1988, and thereafter was reduced by about 1.4 million.[20]

The number of "prime contractor enterprises" is not formally counted. In terms of "establishments,"[21] by 1996 they numbered between 25,000 and 30,000 in my estimate.

Research Controlled by the State Managers

In an industrial country, new production capability is signaled by the pattern of research-and-development spending. Since the end of World War II, the federal government has been the single most important source of research and development funds in the American economy. Plainly, the government is a meager contributor in its funding for the general advance of knowledge, while it remains, notably, the world leader in the concen-

*While a graduate student at Columbia University, I inquired into the modes of operation and the resources used by the central administrative offices of a few major firms. As many as 1,000 to 3,000 men and women were found to be functioning in their central offices. During the 1970s, while giving courses on industrial economy, I investigated further into the scale of activity of central offices in some of the very largest firms. As many as 5,000 to 10,000 people could be accounted for in the largest of such corporate units.

tration of R&D resources on military enterprises. Here are the principal "objectives" of government R&D funding in 1993–94 in the United States, Japan and Germany, as compiled by the American National Science Board:[22]

Principal Objectives	**U.S.**	**Japan**	**Germany**
Defense	55.3%	6.0%	8.5%
Health	16.5	3.0	3.3
Civil space	10.9	7.5	5.8
Energy	4.2	20.5	4.3
Advancement of knowledge*	4.0	51.2	51.4
Industrial development	0.6	3.7	12.7
Environmental protection	0.8	0.5	3.7
Total government R&D (in $millions)	68,331	18,099	14,991

Most striking is the overwhelming concentration of R&D budgets for military purposes—55 percent of the U.S. government's outlay, compared with 6 percent in Japan and 8 percent in Germany. A second outstanding fact is the funding for the "advancement of knowledge." In the United States, this was 4 percent of government R&D spending, compared with 51 percent for Japan and Germany. (The one field, outside military affairs, where the United States has been unusually active has been in health.)

With these data in hand, we see no mystery as to how Germany and Japan are able to pay their industrial workers far more than U.S. industry, while outproducing and outcompeting in an array of civilian products. The U.S. government's concentration of over half of its R&D resources on the military is a significant factor in the technological backwardness of many of its key industries. Thus, as we saw in Chapter 3, the United States, constituting the world's largest single market for computers of every sort, has been dependent on foreign labor forces for the production of computers. By 1993, imports of computer components and whole machines represented the equivalent of 139,000 industrial jobs lost in the United States.[23]

*By advancement of knowledge, I refer to freewheeling or undirected research, primarily in schools and universities.

An indication of the level of government interest in energy utilization (and the potential for energy savings or environmental protection) is the 4 percent share of government R&D that it gets in the United States, compared with 20 percent in Japan. The German expenditure for industrial development is also far greater than that of both Japan and the United States, and compares only with the intensity of activity in the smaller industrial base of Italy. This concentration of Germany's R&D on industrial development has very much to do with the leading role that its industry has had, especially since World War II, as a worldwide supplier of capital goods.

The pattern of American industrial dependence on imported capital goods is all the more interesting when one takes into account the contrast between average hourly compensation for production workers compared with the supplier countries.

As I showed in Chapter 3, the principal suppliers of imported capital goods to U.S. manufacturing firms are Japan and Germany, with Japanese industrial workers costing 18 percent more per hour, and German workers 76 percent more, than the cost of production worker hours in the United States.[24]

Obviously, the ability of Germany and Japan to find ready markets in the United States for capital goods does not derive from a labor cost advantage. Their edge has been in the concentration of R&D and allied support, not only by government but also by private firms for innovation in capital goods.

To truly appreciate the effects of striving for military power without limit, we need to examine the relationship between the amount of money devoted to military uses and the amount converted into civilian means of production in the economy as a whole (i.e., physical capital assets like machinery, tools, etc.), whether paid for out of private or out of public budgets.

The national income accounting performed by the UN provides us with the information needed to construct a ratio that illustrates the comparison described above. Specifically, its volumes of *National Account Statistics: Main Aggregates and Detailed Tables* report not only the formal budgets for defense in each country but also each country's "gross domestic fixed capital formation." This latter category is an indication, in dollars, of annual new civilian capital assets put in place in each country, whether privately or publicly financed (excluding physical assets of a military character).

The following data show the ratio of national *military* expenditure in each country for 1989–1990 to the value of new *civilian capital* assets put in place in each country. Thus:

United States	48:100
United Kingdom	25:100
France	22:100
Germany	16:100
Japan	4:100

For every $100 (or pounds, francs, marks or yen) of new civilian assets put in place in each country during 1989–1990, whoever the purchaser, the military budgets of the United States accounted for $48, compared with $4 for Japan. Plainly, the high military-budget-to-new-civilian-asset countries have not fared as well in international economic relations.

In the context of these analyses, it is important to note that even after the Cold War, military innovations of almost every sort continue in the United States, including in nuclear weapons. Thus, various treaties reducing the number of warheads and the like do not necessarily denote a freeze in the size and character of nuclear devices in stock. The current U.S. nuclear program involves the redesign of weapons to get "more bang for the buck," including, for example, a refitting of nuclear warhead–carrying bombs with special capability to destroy deep enemy bunkers. Such a job involves a new design of the bomb, its control system and its ability to penetrate the earth. The redesign would also lead to a new mission for the venerable B-52 long-range bomber.[25]

All the while, Star Wars systems are still being researched and developed, despite widely publicized doubts about their viability or effectiveness. The Pentagon proposes to spend a further $18 billion over five years after 1997 to design a system that would destroy carriers of weaponry in space, adding to the $40 billion already spent on Star Wars–type research under President Reagan.[26]

Cost and Productivity Before the Permanent War Economy

Prior to the establishment of the permanent war economy, the wages of U.S. industrial workers increased more rapidly than prices of machinery and at a much higher pace than the costs of electric power.

U.S. wages rose through a combination of factors. First, the demand for labor was such that workers were in a position of advantage, certainly until the Great Depression. The price of labor, in relation to machinery and electric power, was high compared with that in Britain, for example, where many U.S. firms sought investments. In response to this trend, American managers were inclined to invest in machinery, because technology seemed more economical in the long term than labor. That same situation played an important role in encouraging innovation in the design of machinery. In other words, rising wages promoted further mechanization, which, in turn, boosted productivity and innovation.

In my "Dynamic Factors in Industrial Productivity" (1956), I described how increases in the relative cost of labor to machinery prices had encouraged mechanization in American industry, notably during the first half of the twentieth century.

This assessment was confirmed by an analytical bulletin of the machinery-producing industries called the *Capital Goods Review* (November 1953). The analysts, published by the Machinery and Allied Products Institute, wrote that:

> The movements of hourly wages and prices in general has of course affected capital goods along with others. Their prices too declined between 1869 and 1896 in the face of substantially unchanged wage rates, and have also risen less than wages during the present century.
>
> In the case of capital goods, however, this divergence has a special significance. It arises from the fact that these goods are in some measure *competitive* with labor. They are used jointly with labor in production, but in proportions that admit in many cases of substantial variation, depending on the comparative cost of the two factors. When capital goods are relatively expensive, the "mix" tends to be shifted in favor of labor; when they are relatively cheap, the tendency runs the other way.
>
> It must be obvious, in view of this partial interchangeability or substitutibility, that the progressive cheapening of capital goods in relation to hourly wages, to which we have just referred, has had a continuously stimulating effect on the demand for these goods.[27]

This reasoning suggests the likely importance of relative changes in wages and machinery (in this case, machine-tool) prices. Under this older model of maximizing profits, innovations in mechanization thus heightened productivity sufficiently to offset rising wages. Furthermore, new technologies in the organization of work also helped to boost productivity. In all this, labor unions played a key role.

Active unions fashioned contracts with management, however hostile, while the government shielded the unions with protective rules administered by the National Labor Relations Board.* Unions could develop

*See the discussion on the Wagner Act in the Conclusion to this book.

internal solidarity and connections to the middle classes in the wider community. Within industrial firms, a tradition of change in production methods, in parallel with a weakening of Taylorist rules,* facilitated the local worker decision-making that was reflected in union-management contracts after World War II.

Cost-Maximizing

As we have seen, American state managers, through the sustained and consistent conduct of their military economy, effectively checkmated this once-important mechanism in the economy for increasing productivity.

All this, essentially, was transformed after the Second World War, as the government became the principal operator of a permanent war economy. This system grew very significantly from the pattern of cost-plus pricing. Under those conditions, additional manufacturing costs were not regarded askance, because the contracting company not only would be reimbursed for them but would actually realize an increased profit. Soon afterward, the United States became involved in the Korean War, followed by the long and costly conflict in Vietnam. During this time, the government made a decision of great importance.

In the cost-profit pattern of the permanent war economy, cost-maximizing profits could be enlarged by scoring a percentage addition on top of costs. The method by which that additional amount was levied varied substantially, because of the inventive character of contracts made by the Pentagon with the contracting firms. All such arrangements were the result of intricate negotiations, as many people moved between corporate and government positions. The revolving door between government and business became a considerable factor in institutionalizing the process. The cost-maximizing process was to have drastic consequences for American industry.

*What has been the relative importance of direct management pressures on workers for intensification of work, as against the output increases made possible by mechanization of work tasks, to reduce the production role of human labor?

In the absence of a generalized response to this question, it is worth taking note of the ways that were once formally favored by Ford engineers. Their views were discussed by David A. Hounshell, *From the American System to Mass Production* (Johns Hopkins University Press, 1984), pp. 50–253. Hounshell found that the main approach of Henry Ford and his engineers "was to eliminate labor by machinery, not, as the Taylorites customarily did, to take a given production process and improve the efficiency of the workers through time and motion study and a differential piece rate system of payment. . . . Taylor took production hardware as given and revised labor processes and the organization of work; Ford engineers mechanized work processes and found workers to feed and tend their machines."

. . .

During a period like the Cold War, when cost- and subsidy-maximizing dominated the military-industrial scene, the relationship between employers and workers is transformed. The income each receives is, effectively, less dependent on what each can take from the other and more subject to what both together can extract from the rest of society, whether it is the government or the public.

J. Ronald Fox served as Assistant Secretary of the Army (1969–71) and was an associate professor at the Harvard School of Business Administration. In his book *Arming America: How the U.S. Buys Weapons*,[28] he describes the behaviors that are here termed *cost-maximizing*. Under these conditions, the laborious and time-consuming struggle of workers and worker groups to enlarge their decision power at the point of production, as a key method for improving their position, is at least partly displaced in favor of joint action with the employer to improve the positions of both parties by seeking to profit at the expense of the rest of the community. Such collective action takes the form of joint union-and-management committees to support the C-5A, the B-2 and other weapons systems.

Thus the economic relations of employment are further altered by state capitalism. Workers engaged in state-run enterprises necessarily relate to their (government) employer as both citizen and employee. The employee's readiness to act independently vis-à-vis the employer is unavoidably altered when the latter represents the whole nation and its law enforcement agencies, rather than a management with a primary interest in profitability.

American workers thus paid a fearful price for their support of state/corporate managers through the fifty years of the Cold War. In payment for their loyalty, workers and their unions have suffered because of extensive deindustrialization and the militarization of public, and even private, life. The establishment by the Wagner Act (1935) of workers' freedom to organize unions of their choice was abridged by later legislation and by *de facto* anti-union administration of the National Labor Relations Board.

The Cold War escalation reached unprecedented proportions in the 1960s. In the name of defending the United States against the Soviet Union, state/corporate managers sent the sons of America's working people (only rarely the children of the elite) to fight a seven-year-long war in Vietnam, Laos and Cambodia, where they were defeated by peasant nationalists. During all that time, the Soviet Union was portrayed as a scientific, technological industrial giant with capabilities comparable with those of the United States. The official cover stories of the Moscow leadership were accepted uncritically by America's policy leaders and the media (a major reason why the Soviet economic collapse was a big surprise).

Entirely concealed from public view was the early effort of Ho Chi Minh and his government in Hanoi to appeal for a relationship "like the Philippines." In a letter to President Truman of February 16, 1946, Ho concluded with the proposal:

> What we ask has been graciously granted to the Philippines. Like the Philippines our goal is full independence and full cooperation with the United States. We will do our best to make this independence and cooperation profitable to the whole world.
>
> I am, Dear Mr. President,
>
> Respectfully yours
> Ho Chi Minh[29]

• • •

During the Cold War, and particularly during the Vietnam War, deindustrialization was speeded up in many American industries and regions. Evidence tells us that in the succeeding decades other, nonmilitary manufacturing industries have continued to be steadily shut down and transferred to low-wage, nonunion havens. Profits were multiplied for corporations, and the Pentagon tried to attract young men and women with promises to "be all you can be" in the armed forces.

To take one conspicuous example: The General Electric Company has long been the single most important industrial firm in the United States and a major beneficiary of the military economy. But its 1998 annual report, full of self-congratulation for billions in increased profits, also shows the consequences of breaking up and shutting down important manufacturing facilities. In the name of ever greater profits, GE cut its U.S. labor force from 1986 to 1998 "by nearly 50 percent to 163,000, while foreign employment has nearly doubled, to 130,000." There was "rapid expansion in Mexico, India, and other Asian countries. Meanwhile, GE's union workforce has shriveled by almost two-thirds since the early 1980s as work [has been] relocated to cheaper, non-union plants in the U.S. and abroad." As a spokesman for GE Aircraft Engines has indicated, "we're aggressively asking for double-digit price reductions from our suppliers. We have to do this if we're going to be part of GE."[30] The most important segment of GE by 1998 was General Electric Capital Services. This, GE's wholly owned bank, accounted for 38 percent of the firm's profit: it was by far the financially dominant part of the company.

There is far more at stake in deindustrialization than increasing profits by wage reduction, and destroying communities by eliminating corporate-controlled opportunities for gainful employment. Closing production facilities in the United States while expanding offshore production, as in Mexico or China, means unloading workforces that have made significant advances along the disalienation route in favor of employing workers who are beginners in that process.

Once upon a time, it was believed that the conventional business drive for accumulation was defined by profit-taking for use as capital. That assumption must be revised to take into account the importance given to managerial control, to blocking the struggle for disalienation among workers.

To accomplish what they desire, the most available routes for U.S. managers lie south to Mexico and beyond, or across the Pacific. The Mexico option has well-understood advantages: low wages, a vast pool of un- and underemployed, good transportation and a government committed to holding workers down. (On the other side, when U.S.-grown corn from mechanized farms is offered in Mexico, far cheaper than the "handmade" Mexican product, millions of peasants will be economically dispossessed in a latter-day version of the enclosures that once doomed feudalism in Britain.)

During the Cold War, the negotiating efforts of trade unions and the occasional pro-worker pronouncements by federal officials and members of Congress were no barrier to employers who moved production and employment from the United States to foreign locations. *This is the employers' single most powerful anti-union strategy.* (The movement of the textile and clothing industries alone removed several million Americans from jobs and trade union membership.) The deindustrialization campaign of General Electric continues, as component suppliers for aircraft engines are pressed to go to Mexico—the convenient way to cut their costs, cut their prices to GE, grow profits and disable the remaining trade unions that organize GE divisions.

During this period, the trade unions in numerous industries were weakened by their failure to see deindustrialization as a state/corporate campaign that made workers powerless and thereby facilitated both corporate and state profit/power accumulation.

The Cold War Assault on Worker Organizing

Erosion of American trade unions was a leading domestic effort of the Cold War. It was a half century of assault—direct and indirect—on the viability of independent U.S. worker organizations. One useful baseline is the alteration of workers and union "rights" once promised in the National Labor Relations (Wagner) Act of 1935.

The Wagner Act declared that:

> employees shall have the right to self-organization, to form, join, or assist labor organizations, to bargain collectively through representatives of their own choosing, and to engage in concerted activities, for the purpose of collective bargaining or other mutual aid or protection.[31]

But workers' rights* became the target of hostile employers. A legislative campaign produced the Taft-Hartley Act (1947), which enshrined a listing of "unfair practices" performed by unions. The Supreme Court saw fit to interpret parts of the Wagner Act so as to weaken whole sections of the law. Corporate attorneys declared that Senator Wagner's law was unconstitutional and "advised employers to disregard it." The media and journals of opinion were well supplied with learned tracts that condemned the act.

Conservatives were bolstered by decisions of the Supreme Court. Karl Klare (Northeastern University School of Law) reasoned that

> in shaping the nation's labor law, the Court embraced those aims of the Act most consistent with the assumptions of liberal capitalism and foreclosed those potential paths of development most threatening to the established order. Thus, the Wagner Act's goals of industrial peace, collective bargaining as therapy, a safely cabined worker free choice, and some rearrangement of relative bargaining power survived judicial construction of the Act,

*These rights were to be implemented by a National Labor Relations Board which was empowered to prohibit five "unfair practices" of employers: (1) interference with employees in the exercise of guaranteed rights; (2) financial or other support of a company union; (3) use of hiring and firing to encourage membership in a company union or discourage membership in an independent union; (4) discrimination against a worker because he complained to the board; and (5) refusal to bargain collectively with the representatives of the employees; of course this could not prevent a deadlock where a genuine effort to reach agreement had been made.

> whereas the goals of redistribution, equality of bargaining power, and industrial democracy—although abiding in rhetoric—were jettisoned as serious components of national labor policy.[32]

The employers' anti-union campaign has been waged most directly at the point of production. A former organizer of anti-union operations for management disclosed that by 1993,

> there [were] more than seven thousand attorneys and consultants across the nation who make their living busting unions, and they work almost every day. At a billing rate of $1,000 to $1,500 a day per consultant and $300 to $700 an hour for attorneys, the war on organized labor is a $1 billion-plus industry.[33]

When the Commission on the Future of Worker-Management Relations solicited a prepared statement from Klare in 1994, he formulated a wide-ranging approach to labor law reform. He judged that

> A priority for labor law reform must be, once and for all, to guarantee employees a fair chance to bargain collectively in a meaningful and effective way through representatives of their own choosing.

Klare affirmed that,

> for industrial democracy to be genuine, employees must have an independent power base and focus for collective self-organization. An independent employee power base is not only an advantage to employees themselves, but is also socially functional because it is a precondition of effective workplace cooperation. Only through power-sharing can employees elicit from and hold management to credible commitments of equitable treatment which are the foundation of workplace cooperation.[34]

Ironically, the weakening of the trade unions was facilitated by their sustained support of the Democratic Party, even as antiworker prejudice spread through the government. It comes as little surprise that industrial workers make up a major part of the nonvoting American electorate. Federal laws and administrative agencies that were installed originally to facilitate independent worker organization have been gutted by a succession of legal and administrative decisions. These anti-union measures have effectively restricted the right of workers to freely organize trade unions, as granted by the Wagner Act, and have also drastically restricted the promised role of the National Labor Relations Board.

In a 1985 report, *The Changing Situation of Workers and Their Unions*, the AFL-CIO wrote that:

> A study of organizing campaigns in the private sector shows that 95 percent of employers actively resist unionization, and 75 percent of all employers hire so-called "labor-management consultants" to guide their efforts to avoid unionization at an estimated cost of over $100,000,000 annually. . . . In 1957, the NLRB secured reinstatement for 922 workers who had been fired for union activity. By 1980, that figure had reached 10,000.
>
> . . . The Reagan Administration's handling of the air traffic controllers provided a signal to, and the model for, anti-union employers. Thereafter, the Administration turned over the labor law to an NLRB Chairman who has publicly declared that "collective bargaining frequently means . . . the destruction of individual freedom and the destruction of the market-place."[35]

This relentless assault on unions during the Cold War was underwritten by the vast accumulation of wealth that was generated by cost-maximizing in the military economy.

George Orwell's novel *1984* provided a prophetic glimpse of the qualities of militarized state capitalism. Recall the great mottoes of *1984*'s society:

War Is Peace

Ignorance Is Strength

Freedom Is Slavery[36]

The half century of Cold War indeed included a sustained series of armed conflicts—all short of a nuclear exchange, and so it was called "Peace." The manipulation of the public—including the distortion and withholding of information—was a standard pattern of Cold War politics. This included in the 1980s, for example, the falsification of U.S. records of arms shipments to Iran to fund illegal covert operations in Central America. The American public was kept in ignorance of its government's actions—the better to strengthen the hand of the state managers.[37] Finally, the Cold War sustained the freedom to conform to the wishes of the state managers. Orwell's mottoes cut too close to home for comfort.

The political ambiguities embedded in the mottoes of *1984* are a reminder of the economic ambiguities in the normal operation of militarized firms.

With respect to wages and salaries, which are important industrial costs, the cost-maximizing company is in a unique position. It is able to raise wages and salaries in a fashion that is not usually feasible for civilian industry, for military industry can draw on government subsidies to meet such increases. Cost and price go up, and the government pays. The military-industrial firm is also able to structure its workforce to emphasize higher-designated job skills, hence higher wage and salary occupations. Managements have been able to accomplish this because their incomes are insured by the federal treasury.*

In the 1970s, foreign-owned and -managed factories began to appear in the auto, steel and allied industries—with a strong anti-union bias. Even as Cold War loyalties were promoted by the government, legislation like the Taft-Hartley Act restrained more militant union tactics, like sympathy strikes. At the same time, trade unionists and even entire unions were cast out of the main labor fold, in the name of loyalty to the American side of the Cold War struggle.

Union organizing declined—as did also official Washington's sympathy and support for the unions. The attention of both the government and society at large became increasingly focused on the expanding military economy and the pursuit of objectives in Vietnam and elsewhere.

In this environment, management was encouraged by government to accommodate the needs of McNamara's state-managed industry. This could proceed without friction, as schemes of cost-maximizing that facilitated profit-maximizing dominated the preferred methods of the Pentagon. All of this suited management, as it participated wholeheartedly in the Cold War industrial enterprise, which enhanced profits and salaries.

American managers had particular advantages over the upper echelons of trade unions. The AFL-CIO chiefs had long experience with and relied on the federal government and the Democratic Party. For example, the three main "metal" unions (Auto Workers, Machinists and Steel Workers) account for a large part of military industries' skilled labor force:

*A variant of cost-maximizing is cost pass-along, without systematic government payment as in cost-maximizing on military account. In civilian firms, cost pass-along renders firms noncompetitive with imports. Inability to cost-minimize shows up even in competition with imports from high-wage economies like Germany and Japan. The main response of cost pass-along managers is to search constantly for sources of production in lower wage countries. See Byung Yoo Hong, *Inflation Under Cost Pass-Along Management* (Praeger, 1979).

aerospace; electronics; missile and heavy weapons. As a result, the unions had less of an independent position from which to influence government.

Managements have often sought ways to make their workforce more productive while also holding down labor costs by enforcing discipline on the shop floor and preventing unionization wherever possible. As we will see in Chapter 7, mechanization and computerization of machine controls afford refinements of production operations previously unavailable. Notably, Japanese and German managers enjoy definite advantages, for "only 18% of chief executives of American companies have technical training, compared with 36% for Japanese corporations."[38]

So when the Cold War subsided after 1991, the onerous work of converting people and facilities systematically from military to civilian enterprise was mainly put aside as a task not worth the trouble, while the government reorganized the core focus of its military economy and mounted lavish plans for five-year budgets and ten-to-twenty-year capital outlays.

The cost-maximizing regime of state capitalism also has corrosive effects on the reliability and quality of its products. Pentagon capitalism can often produce third-rate goods. During May 1998, for example, the U.S. Army prepared to buy a Theater High-Altitude Area Defense system. This was announced as a system with somewhat broader coverage than the Patriot system, first used during the Persian Gulf War.

Among the Congressional supporters of this program there was little suspicion that the whole idea might be inherently flawed.*

There are reliability considerations involved in the promise to intercept a bullet in outer space with another aimed "killer" projectile. But what is involved here is, by current estimates, $13 to $40 billion in public funds for an already "troubled" program.[39] This is but one example of the consequences that flow from cost-plus management, coupled with the unquestioning acceptance of the cover story that the wealth of the United States is indefinitely large.

*The reliability of a mechanism or system is indicated by the product of the reliability of the components. Thus if components have been separately tested to reliability at .998, the anticipated failure rate should be no more than 2 of each 1,000. When components of such known reliability are linked together in series, then the combined reliability of a combination of, say, three of these is .998 × .998 × .998 = .99401. . . . Hence by linking another component of this acceptable reliability to the series, the net reliability is reduced—as each added component has a reliability of less than 1.0. If linked together in series in a mechanism that relies on more than 346 such components, the reliability of the system as a whole may be expected to be less than 0.5. Hence five of ten such mechanisms will fail. A greater number of units of similar reliability, linked in series, will yield a higher failure rate (John E. Ullmann, "Managerial and Quality Constraints in SDI," IEEE, *Technology & Society*, March 1987, p. 17).

In the construction of the Trans-Alaska pipeline, to take a less exotic example, contractors were paid on a cost-plus basis, and, as a result, "the more money they spend, the more profit they make."[40] This was coupled with welding reject rates two to three times higher than in ordinary commercial practice. Similarly, in the case of Lockheed's C-5A aircraft project, multibillion-dollar cost growth was coupled with the construction of an aircraft with a spectacular record of malfunction, even the delivery of aircraft missing thousands of parts but signed off as "virtually complete."[41] In both situations, employer and employees joined to extract a maximum money-return from the rest of society. In the pipeline project, this was done by running up costs, their profits to be paid for by users of petroleum products. In the Lockheed C-5A case, costs were reimbursed by taxpayers, via the government. A. Ernest Fitzgerald has noted that "there has never been a strike over work standards in the aerospace industry." (If not never, then at least unknown.)

How do things stand now that the Cold War is over? About 2.2 million American workers were employed in "defense-related industries" in 1999, down from 3.6 million at the 1987 Cold War peak. These workers, though they are heavily unionized and concentrated in skilled, technical and engineering occupations, remain an important political instrument for state managers. For major military programs, the Pentagon continues to prepare schedules of subcontracting that are often made available to individual states or regions—the better to harness members of Congress, unions and chambers of commerce to support new contracts.

The Ripple Effect of Cost-Maximizing

As an effect of the military economy, cost and price increases "ripple out" into the outside economy in the form of precedents used to pressure the managers of civilian companies as well. At least one president, Lyndon Johnson, was so impressed with Robert McNamara that he encouraged all government departments to follow the patterns and methods McNamara laid down.

An altogether charming and symptomatic manifestation of the pattern of cost-maximizing is found in the *Pentagon Catalog.* These prices, taken from actual payments made to defense contractors, are alarming: the infamous "coffee-maker" for $7,622, designed and installed on the heavy transport aircraft C-5A; a $640 toilet seat; a $659 ashtray; and a $670 armrest pad.[42] The list goes on and on.

One of the students in my 1983 course in Industrial Economics was an engineer employed in a firm producing electronic devices for the military. As a course exercise, he explored the cost differences between manufacturing a particular product for the military as against producing it for civilian users. Two hundred units were to be manufactured, following military specifications. The same functional product was estimated for civilian use.

The military product cost $21,620 per unit, reflecting the outcome of cost-maximizing practices. With cost-minimizing, the estimated civilian unit expense was $9,389. The contrast is understated because a number of characteristic cost-maximizing practices on the military side were not factored into the analysis. Nevertheless, the comparative prices are 2.3:1. Little wonder that this approach to profit-making has had such a corrosive effect on the economy and workforce of the United States.

This pattern has not stopped at the military sector but has been adopted by other industries. Medical care follows the example of the military, while the government, again, pays the bill. *The New York Times* reported in 1997 that "a practice known as upcoding, in which hospitals received larger payments from Medicare by inflating the seriousness of illness they treat," was introduced and practiced by the Columbia Health Care Corporation.[43] Indeed, government investigators are examining whether it is legal for Columbia Health Care doctors with a financial interest in company hospitals to send patients to them.

Some of the data that have turned up are rather striking: At a Columbia Cedars medical center in Miami, 93 percent of the respiratory cases were billed for the highest-paying of the four codes of severity. At the nearby county hospital, Jackson Memorial, only 28 percent of the billings were for that code. Elsewhere, a Columbia hospital billed for 355 cases of complex respiratory infection, the costliest diagnosis, and only 28 of the three lower-paying diagnoses. Among the cases studied, the hospital did not bill for a single case of the lowest-paying illness, simple pneumonia. The *Times* also reported the striking change in billing procedure witnessed at Cedars after Columbia took it over. In 1992, when the hospital last operated independently, 31 percent of the respiratory cases were billed at the highest rate. A year later, 76 percent were billed at this rate, and in 1995, 9 of 10 cases came under the top category.

American managers sought ways to make money, other than by efficient production, and stayed committed to rates of profitability and executive salaries at standards far higher than those of other countries.

Effect of Cost-Maximizing on Productivity

As we have seen, the permanent war economy has distorted and depleted everything it touches. But perhaps the most destructive economic consequences of its cost-maximizing have been largely hidden: its effects on productivity. During the first half of the twentieth century, as we have seen, the relative cost of labor and machinery played a central role in determining the degree of mechanization of production, and thereby the productivity of labor. With many alternatives available for each particular task, the selection of production methods was decided by the least costly combination of labor time and machinery to do the work.

Wages tended to rise more rapidly than the prices of machinery, because manufacturers strove to minimize their own costs of production. They worked to offset the rise in wages in their own factories by advances in mechanization. To the extent that the manufacturers succeeded, they were not compelled to raise the prices of their own product.

Under such conditions, industrial firms had an incentive to further mechanize their own production. In turn, the wider consequence of this pattern of cause and effect included increases in the average output of production worker man-hours—that is, increases in labor productivity.[44]

The alternative cost-productivity mechanism broke down as growth in labor's wages was increasingly resisted after World War II. While wage rises were held back by managements, the chiefs of many firms shifted from cost-minimizing to cost-maximizing under the influence of the Pentagon.

No longer did changes in the relative cost of machinery as an alternative to labor's wage dominate the degree of mechanization. Managers could nevertheless try to minimize costs by stabilizing operations with more sophisticated machinery.

In the two periods 1971–1978 and 1980–1991, for example, the prices of U.S.-produced machine tools increased far more rapidly than those of Germany and Japan:

Percent Change of Labor and Machine Tool Prices in the United States, Germany and Japan[45]

	Worker Earnings/Hour	**Machine Tool Prices**
	1971–1978	
United States	+72%	+85%
Germany	+72%	+59%
Japan	+177%	+51%
	1980–1991	
United States	+55%	+58%
Germany	+61%	+37%
Japan	+45%	+7%

Within each of these periods, U.S. machine-tool prices increased more rapidly than did wages. For American cost-minimizing firms this tended to discourage purchase of new machine tools. This led to an aging stock of these basic instruments in U.S. factories, partly countered by many U.S. managers by turning to German and (mainly) Japanese suppliers for new machine tools.

The contrasting performance in Japan is dramatic: Japanese wage gains were offset by efficiencies that enabled machine-tool price increases to be held down. Indeed, this was the period when imported machine tools—notably Japanese—captured important portions of the U.S. market. Japanese firms made strong bids for holding American markets by setting up branches in the United States. (Thus the Yamazaki firm established several branches under the name Mazak.)

Nevertheless, the more favorable position of Japanese firms in U.S. markets did not necessarily mean that American companies would reequip and be more cost-competitive. In a system skewed by cost-maximizing, what would be the incentive? On the contrary, the period 1971–1991 was a time of overall decline in the metalworking industry, of the creation of the Rust Belt in the Midwestern states, of the flight of manufacturing firms away from America.

Under cost-maximizing, further productivity advance was garnered mainly by investment in new capital goods at the workplace. At the same time, employers tried to hold down, and even reduce, wages, while contracting parts of design and production work abroad. Pressure on workers was advanced by the exploitation of low-wage immigrant workers brought in to thicken a reserve army of labor whose struggle for livelihood, any livelihood, induced them to accept low wages.

The Productivity of American Workers*

Measuring productivity—of a factory, an industry, a whole economy—is important to whoever wants to gauge the record of growth. In turn, that record can be a basis for forecasting further development.

*The topic of productivity, the relation of output to input, has been clouded by the efforts of some economists, government officials, businessmen and journalists to try to attribute responsibility for increases in output to a particular input factor. It is beyond dispute that industrial production requires combined use of raw materials, production workers, machinery, engineers, electric power, management staff. Nevertheless, attempts are made to quantify the contribution that each of the factors of production makes to the finished product. But this is an inherently unresolvable problem, for industrial output is a joint product, with all of the necessary factors coming into play.

Many people have not been discouraged from formulating what they have termed "multifactor productivity," the alleged change in output owing to a set of inputs of varying

Productivity means the relation of output to input. Which output and input to measure is determined by the nature of the problem. So the fuel productivity of a vehicle is often measured as gallons of fuel (input) in relation to vehicle miles (output), or miles per gallon. In a national economy, or in industry, it is often of interest to know the changes in output that occur in relation to changes in a major (input) factor—like worker man-hours, or tons of coal, or millions of kilowatt-hours of electricity.

We are focusing on the production capability of the manufacturing industry and its labor force. Therefore, to access prospects for the future, I have assembled measures of U.S. manufacturing output for the second half of the twentieth century, as well as measures of production-worker man-hours. Both are in the form of index numbers—with 1950 as the base year for their values, hence stated as 100. The subsequent yearly values of industrial output and production-worker man-hours are then stated as percent changes as against the base year: hence a 16 percent output change is recorded as an index number value of 116; a 5 percent change in production worker man-hours is stated as 105.

The productivity of interest here is change in industrial output com-

---

quantity or quality. With standard statistical methods, it is possible to calculate the degree to which two (or more) variables correlate with each other. It is also well understood that correlation is not proof of causation. To justify a statement of cause and effect, one must show not only strength of covariation, but also evidence of direction of effect (which variable changes first) and the intervening events that link the main factors of interest.

Such requirements are amplified when several variables are involved—as in attempts to measure "multifactor productivity" with inputs of various types of labor, physical capital and administrative staff. Then differential "weights" must be applied to measure each factor. These are supposed to indicate how much output would change for a given change in labor, capital or fuel input. Such procedures can have explanatory effect, it is said, "If factor markets are assumed to be perfectly competitive, so that factors are paid their marginal product, and if the production exhibits constant returns to scale, so that a 10 percent increase in capital and labor leads to a 10 percent increase in output, then the weights equal the relative share of total income paid to capital and labor, respectively."

This means that if one assumes conditions of industrial life that are nonexistent ("perfectly competitive factor markets"), "then the weights equal the relative share of total income paid to capital and labor, respectively" (Alicia H. Munnell, "Why Has Productivity Growth Declined?: Productivity and Public Investment," *New England Economic Review*, January–February 1990). Accordingly, the multimillion-dollar annual payment to the CEO (say, 2,000 times the yearly compensation of an industrial worker) represents the value of the actual "product" of the CEO's work time—for, as assumed, "the factors are paid their marginal product."

But that assumption has not been proved. Reiteration of the statement that this would occur where "markets for labor and capital are perfectly competitive" does not make them so. Hence, reliance on the "multifactor productivity" calculation incorporates assumptions removed from reality, though still serving the ideological function of justifying the wages and salaries paid as being those that *would* be paid *if* markets were perfectly competitive (hence, not dominated by large companies, etc.).

pared with change in production-worker man-hours input. We find this value by dividing the index of output (116) by the index of worker input (105) for the same year, reflecting an average increase of just a little more than 10 percent in manufacturing per worker man-hour, then stated as the index of output per worker hours, 110.

To measure the trend of industrial output per production-worker man-hour, I have used two data series: first, the Index of Output of Manufacturing from the Federal Reserve Board;[46] second, an index of production worker man-hours, compiled from the data published by Census of Manufactures, which showed through the twentieth century the number of production-worker man-hours in industry. Together, these two indexes allow us to measure changes in average industrial output per production man-hour worked.

The chart opposite shows the result obtained by dividing the Index of Manufacturing Output by the Index of Production Worker Man-Hours, both with 1950 as a base year.*

Over the course of the twentieth century, the productivity of industrial-worker-hours increased dramatically. During the second half century, from a 1950 base, the aggregate growth in manufacturing output per production-worker man-hour was almost fivefold (4.79).

But see the components. Man-hours of production workers in manufacturing were 23.7 million (1950) and 24.5 million (1994), a modest 3 percent increase. By contrast, the output index of manufacturing industries soared from 100 (1950) to 494 (1994). This means that the output of the manufacturing industries by 1994 was almost five times as great as 1950, an immense growth.

That leap in output and worker productivity was accompanied by large increases in inputs of power and fresh capital investment. From 1950 to 1994, electric power used in industry per worker man-hour rose fivefold, from 7.6 to 37 kilowatt-hours per worker-hour.[47] Also, annual new capital expenditures in manufacturing jumped substantially, from $6.3 to $112.8 billion in the years 1950 to 1994.[48]

Where did the almost fivefold increase in output go?

It was swallowed by the military economy. In Chapter 5, I will present an estimate of national needs. As we will see, an estimated cost of repair of infrastructure needs exceeds $2,000 billion. It is unlikely that the rise in output of the manufacturing industries by a factor of 5 can be accounted for by 1950–94 investments in infrastructure facilities—which actually deteriorated during that period. The facilities of industries like auto, steel

*Before 1950, there were a number of gaps in the output data that produced a time series "joined" over the breaks—a problematic effect. From 1950 on, both indexes used here were continuous annually and without break.

and the capital-goods industries, which suffered serious depletion and disinvestment, were not the location of enlargement of manufacturing output.

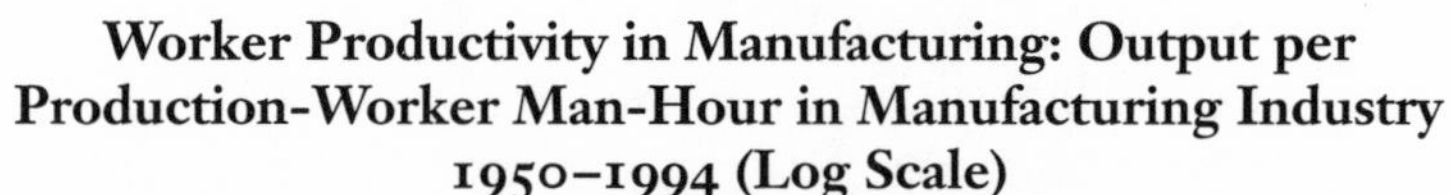

Worker Productivity in Manufacturing: Output per Production-Worker Man-Hour in Manufacturing Industry 1950–1994 (Log Scale)

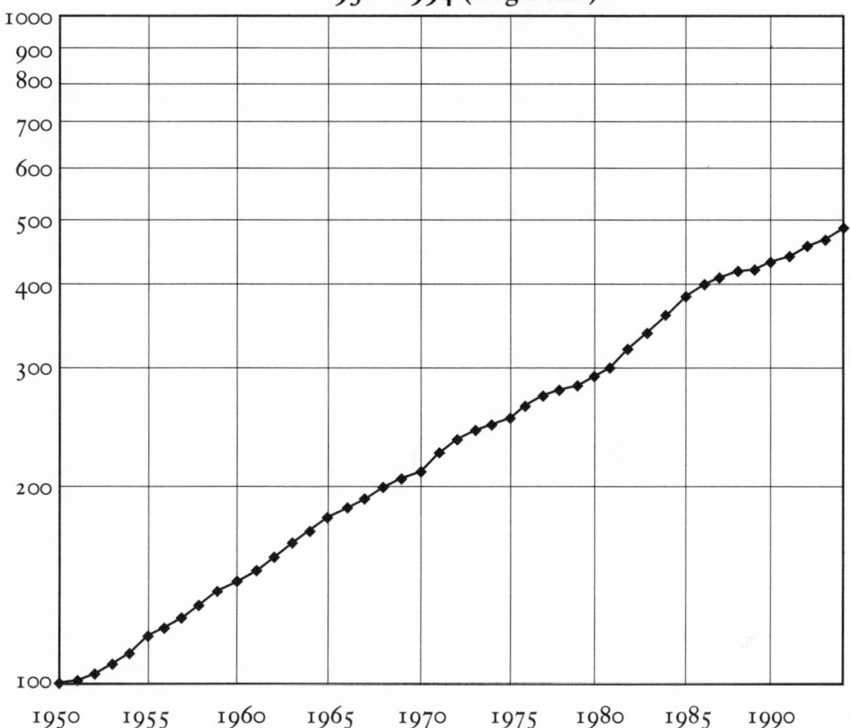

SOURCE: U.S. Federal Reserve Board, *Index of Output of Manufacturing*. Production-Worker Hours in Manufacturing from various reports of the U.S. *Census of Manufactures* and the *Survey of Manufactures*

What else could conceivably account for the consumption of manufactured physical goods at such magnitude? After 1950, the United States operated wars in Korea, Vietnam and the Persian Gulf and the largest sustained "peacetime" military buildup since World War II. Without doubt, large wars, of short or long duration, use up great quantities of metals, chemicals, machinery, fuels and nondurable goods of every sort. *But there are no systematic published records on the physical magnitudes (such as heavy ordnance and artillery shells); only the estimated money costs of what was consumed by these enormous military operations.**

*The Air Force reports dropping 6,162,000 tons of bombs during the war in Vietnam. This was three times the bomb tonnage used by the Air Force during World War II. No

. . .

Economists, even sophisticated critics of capitalism, have held that so long as the march of productivity growth continues, so long as the gross domestic product rises, then all is well with the economy, and never mind about exactly what is produced.

It is therefore interesting to see how a notably sophisticated critic of the business process could view these matters. Here is what Thorstein Veblen had to say (in 1904) in his *Theory of Business Enterprise:*

> A disproportionate growth of parasitic industries, such as most advertising and much of the other efforts that go into competitive selling, as well as warlike expenditure and other industries directed to turning out goods for conspicuously wasteful consumption, would lower the effective vitality of the community to such a degree as to jeopardize its chances of advance or even its life. . . . A persistent excess of parasitic and wasteful efforts over productive industry must bring a decline.
>
> But owing to the very high productive efficiency of the modern mechanical industry, the margin available for wasteful occupations and wasteful expenditure is very great. The requirements of the aggregate livelihood are so far short of the possible output of goods by modern methods as to leave a very wide margin for waste and parasitic income.[49]

Veblen certainly qualified as an innovative mind in matters economic, but here he places his stamp on a piece of conventional and misleading optimism. His faith in the advance of productive efficiency to high levels extended to the estimate that in a modern economy, "industrial exhaustion" cannot be expected, so large is the "margin for waste and parasitic income."

Veblen's *Theory of Business Enterprise*, published in 1904, had no way of taking into account the consequences of the nature and quantities of output that became characteristics of state capitalism, notably in its continuously militarized form. The author could not include the conditions of state capitalism that dominated the U.S. economy a half century after he completed his analysis of business enterprise. Neither could pervasive industrial collapse be predicted for England, the homeland of an empire that was once the most powerful in the world—from Veblen's thesis, that is. England in 1947 affords a lesson on limits of industrial power when

---

data could be found on Army or Navy ordnance used in the Vietnam operations. Extensive inquiries at headquarters, command centers, records centers at the Pentagon and locations at many military bases yielded no information beyond the Air Force report.

those capacities are long applied to plainly nonproductive growth—that is, contributing little to consumption goods and services and the means for their production.

I have focused on the experience of American and Russian war economies to demonstrate the consequences of deindustrialization. But I would feel remiss if I skipped the remarkable evidence of the 1947 "Snow Crisis" in post–World War II England.

Veblen's thesis was put to a test between January and March 1947 in England. A succession of snowstorms, blizzards and powerful winds swept the British Isles during that period. Coal stocks at the power plants were quickly used up and drastic rationing of electric power was in order (the National Electricity Board met in London by candlelight). Factories had to be closed, and it was soon discovered that the British economy was suffering shortages everywhere. Everywhere there were blackouts and "the most critical shortages . . . included coal, gas, electricity, steel, wood, transportation, machinery, linseed oil and of course, food, shelter, clothing, manpower and dollars. Except for linseed oil, which is important chiefly to the housing program, these things are so basic that they produce a shortage of everything else.[50]

"Britain has not enough locomotives or rolling stock to move more coal, nor enough wood to make ties to repair the railroads. Moving coal by road would be expensive and would create a shortage in the road trucking industry. There is also a shortage of ships at the shipyards, and factories for building and repairing railroad equipment. There is no margin anywhere and the bottlenecks must be overcome in a carefully planned and orderly fashion, if at all."[51]

Soon after the worst of the freezing cold paralyzed most of the country, government leaders pleaded for men and women to go into the mining, transportation and manufacturing industries.

By mid-March, a consensus was developing that "in spite of the complexity of Britain's manpower problem, the most threatening single aspect of it is the maldistribution of the available labor. In this category is the highly controversial question of the size of the nation's armed forces, which with the manpower employed to supply them, involves about 1,750,000 men and women—nearly 10% of the national working population." Military services of that size "simply cannot be carried by a country of 45,000,000 people. It is choking the life out of the national economy according to the critics."[52]

The country was short about 1,250,000 workers in its main industries. To the citizens Prime Minister Clement Attlee said, "All that can work should work." He called on the people to leave "better paid but quite useless work" for basic industries.

A succession of loans and Marshall Plan assistance helped British governments mobilize their productive resources, even while diminishing the military burden.

Veblen's prognosis fell far short of accounting for the economic crisis in England and (as we will see in Chapters 5 and 6) in the United States and Russia. He wrote, "There seems to be no tenable ground for thinking that the working of the modern business system involves a curtailment of the community's livelihood. It makes up for its wastefulness by the added strain which it throws upon those engaged in the productive work."

A militarized state capitalism introduces a quality of expansionism that is new within the realm of political economy. A firm may seek to control markets. A state management can aspire to seize control of entire continents. The appetite of state managers has no counterpart in the ambitions and achievements of the older captains of industry. Alertness to these new conditions is indispensable for responding to the new methods of alienation and profit/power accumulation.

Veblen never witnessed state capitalism in full bloom. Neither did Marx.*

*Veblen lived from 1857 to 1929, missing the Great Depression and after. Marx's lifetime extended from 1818 to 1883, mainly in England. That was also the England of Charles Dickens, 1812–1870. Marx was a contemporary of Dickens and thereby was living amid the social and material conditions made vivid in the Dickens novels. That perspective makes the array of innovations achieved by Marx the more remarkable. With the precision of a laser beam, he differentiated relations among people from the relation of people to things. Thereby changes in rules about worker and management behavior could be illuminated and their effects on design of technology, and diverse material aspects of culture, differentiated from social relations themselves.

Marx's focus on the dynamics of social relations has afforded a methodological framework that is reflected in the definition and functioning of state capitalism in the present work.

5

The Hidden Costs of Campaigning for World Hegemony

In 1999, the U.S. government participated for the first time actively in the destruction of a major American capital-goods industry. Following the 1998 financial collapse of Russia, Brazil and the "Asian Tiger" economies of East Asia, the steel industries of all those countries were spurred on by their governments to export to the United States. The dollars earned by dumping their steel would bolster the value of their currencies and allow them to keep paying the interest on loans from American banks, private investors and international institutions.

As their products reached U.S. ports in unprecedented quantities, and the market was flooded with cheap steel, the order books of American firms were full of blank spaces. Steel-plant output was cut back, while about 10,000 American workers were laid off. Several large producers shut down entire plants, and several smaller firms were forced to declare bankruptcy.

During the closing months of 1998, the steel industry trade association joined forces with the United Steel Workers of America and appealed to the government and the general public to stop a flood of steel imports at prices so low that they were below the cost of production at 80 percent of the world's steel plants.

Management and labor alike petitioned President Clinton and Treasury Secretary Rubin to take emergency measures to check the flood of steel imports. They hoped that the government would take heed as it had in previous decades: as in the job- and industry-saving Import Restraint agreements negotiated by President Reagan for 1984–1989; the emergency-loan operation that had once kept the Chrysler Corporation afloat; or the special Congressional actions that had bolstered the development of a U.S. chip and computer industry.

Until 1999, the prospect of a disappearing steel industry was unthinkable to those who viewed it as a baseline for a productive U.S. economy.

That perspective still prevails in Western Europe, Japan, India, South-East Asia and the Russian republics.

But in the United States, steel has no special economic importance for government finance chiefs and the investment managers of the leading banking and securities firms. In their view, economic growth means more money flow, never mind what goods or services are represented by the money. The finance institutions, they say—not steel- or machinery-producing industries—are the core activities of a "new" economy whose baseline measure is market exchange. Therefore, they reason, why not buy steel at the lowest price and let market competitive forces identify the seller? No matter that U.S. industries and their workers must suffer the consequences. That's life in the free-market, global economy.

As more communities and workers are eliminated and rendered powerless, the globalizers shrug their shoulders: let them adjust, take what is offered, part-time, any time, any job.

America's managers, government and corporate, are now committed to ideologies and policies that focus on moneymaking—independent of production. For them, the least 80 percent of the citizenry be damned, so long as enough of them spend (on credit, if necessary) to lubricate the finance machine.

Take the case of the Long-Term Capital Management investment fund that I discussed earlier. The finance and banking crises caused by the fund's collapse in 1998 narrowly escaped triggering a worldwide economic panic and collapse. In response, William J. McDonough, then president of the New York Federal Reserve, presided over a study of the failures of "a handful" of the largest commercial and investment banks that identified many "lapses in judgment." The report concluded that they were "blinded by the magic" of Long-Term Capital Management's reputation; in other words, blinded by its record of extravagant profit-making, regardless of the risks involved. The reported "handful" of institutions that suffered lapses in judgment included:

Chase Manhattan
Citigroup
JP Morgan
Merrill Lynch
Morgan Stanley
Goldman, Sachs
Bear Stearns
Lehman Brothers
UBS
Deutsche Bank

Credit Suisse
Société Générale

How to restrain this handful? Said the Fed report: "Any direct regulation would require a high level of political initiative and would involve consideration by political, legislative and judiciary bodies."[1] Finance rules the day.

Once the profitability of the economy's financial institutions is made the policy priority of the federal government, then dumping the U.S. steel industry becomes a consistent, even necessary, action to remove a political irritant. Seen merely as a *financial* problem, securing steel supplies for American-owned factories at attractive prices is readily managed.

What happens to American workers, their unions and their communities? They must be flexible and adjust to the changing needs of the market—that is, of the state and corporate managers.

The deception embedded in the dogma of the "new economy" is the denial that a community must produce in order to live. The banks and their political chieftains make this basic truth disappear, blinded by policies designed to ensure their profits as their first priority.

In a finance-based American economy, two kinds of activities dominate the political-economic scene: the finance institutions and the military that serves accumulation and protection for finance. That is the core combination of institutions that the state managers expect to serve them in the twenty-first century.

A Military-Political Campaign for World Hegemony

The two world wars of the twentieth century proved to government and corporate managers that military organizations are ideally suited for alienation campaigns on a world scale. As the Cold War began to unwind after 1991, the Pentagon's managers and their CEOs in the White House formulated new fashions for their military-political enterprise.

With the end of the Cold War, the military budget (always called "defense") was refashioned to wage multiple wars simultaneously, in place of a single all-out U.S.-Russian campaign. Accordingly, a whole agenda of new weapons systems, bases and military formations were devised to suit the opportunities presented by this "new world order."

The Air Force launched a program for a new F-22 fighter, with capabilities exceeding those of previous planes in terms of range, weight, versatility and destructive capability. Proponents of the F-22 claimed it would ensure U.S. air superiority into the first quarter of the twenty-first century. Early on, the cost was reckoned at $86.6 billion. That is a sum that can be compared with the fixed capital investment required to employ more than 1.3 million American workers whose jobs have been forgone, as we have seen, because of imports in the machine-tool and electrical- and transportation-equipment industries. Under 1990 production conditions and imports and consumption requirements in these capital-goods industries, $110 billion would have been required for fixed investments in modernized equipment and manufacturing plant. With these kinds of resources, whole sectors of American industry could have been regenerated. There is no evidence, however, that the managers of American state capitalism ever seriously considered trade-offs of this kind, even with the long-awaited end of the Cold War. Instead, they proceeded with a new set of military investments.[2]

Throughout the second half of the twentieth century, managers of state capitalism have been prepared to deplete capital resources as though they were "free goods," available in indefinitely large quantities and virtually costless. This drive shows no signs of slowing down. How else can a $60 billion program to construct attack submarines for the Navy be explained—in mid-1995, enemy unknown?[3] Or, for that matter, what is the justification for the program for U.S.-Russian space linkups, priced at $100 billion?[4]

Take, as another example, the Pentagon's decision to buy $18 billion worth of C-17 military transport planes, instead of the less expensive freight version of Boeing's 747 jumbo jet. But the C-17 represents a promise to the military economy of 8,500 jobs in Southern California, and 27,000 in forty-three other states, counting the plane's jet engines and the work to be performed by a large number of subcontracting firms.[5]

In a similar vein, while the government's promotion of nuclear technology after the Second World War remained in high gear, the cost of decommissioning nuclear reactor plants (the most expensive power generated by American utilities) was not taken into account. Thus in testimony before the Nuclear Regulatory Commission, utility officials disclosed that it would cost $370 million just to dismantle the Yankee Rowe facility in Massachusetts, the oldest operating nuclear reactor in the country. A significant portion of the cost of dismantling lies, of course, in the long-term security of waste nuclear fuel. These expenses are expected to be shared between higher electricity rates and special outlays for nuclear storage by the government.[6]

The huge scale and drive of the military economy has other consequences. Engineers and scientists developing new knowledge and designs, for example, are very important in the production of new capital goods. Since the Second World War, the state managers have continued using engineering and scientific talent on behalf of their military requirements.

For example, during the early 1990s, the Lincoln Laboratory in Lexington, Massachusetts, employed about 2,800 scientists, engineers and technicians in diverse fields of engineering and afforded them elaborate facilities. The lab's work has been oriented for the past two decades primarily on military operations in outer space.[7] Their gains are at the expense of the wider American economy.

By 1998, a plan began unfolding for a new Joint Strike Fighter. The program cost of the new aircraft was reckoned at $750 billion. The multifunction plane is to be used by each American military service and sold to many governments, with the United States supplying the capital investment. This plan suggests the Pentagon's exceptional capability for serving as banker for the program. Nothing on such a scale has been seen before, even at the Cold War's peak. Neither was the program included in the budgets sent to the Congress, or announced in Clinton's State of the Union address.

A campaign was launched in California to marshal political troops to secure this prospective program for firms based in the region. It was hailed as a chance to recover from the economic losses suffered by the state's firms and workers following the end of the Cold War. Both Boeing (based in Seattle) and Lockheed Martin (based in Georgia) were also competing for the prime contract. Nevertheless, it is understood that whoever wins will be sharing work with the other leading aerospace firms.

From August to December 1998, fifty-one newspaper articles on the Joint Strike Fighter appeared in the leading newspapers of California and Texas. During that period, there was virtually no discussion in Eastern newspapers on the nature of this contract and the consequences anticipated from the allocation of the work.

The scale of the problem extends beyond U.S. borders. The state/corporate partnership is also notably active as a sales-promotion organization for weaponry. Various arrangements have been institutionalized. A Defense Export Loan Guarantee program in its first year allows the Defense Department to cover 100 percent of the principal and interest for foreign arms sales, for as much as $15 billion if the recipient nation defaults. A Recycled Weapons program permits the United States to transfer billions of "surplus" weapons, mostly for free. (In the years from 1990 to 1995 this included 4,000 tanks, 125 attack helicopters, 500 bombers and 200,000 pistols and rifles.) The Pentagon is also empowered to lease equipment at little or no cost. Under an Excess Defense Articles program, for example, Pentagon stocks may be "drawn down" and given to governments in Latin America and the Caribbean to "fight narcotrafficking," and to African countries "to support participation in peace-keeping and other operations." All these arrangements are backed up by U.S. participation in air and ground weapons shows around the world.[8]

In Appendix A, I show details of 1998 U.S. military supplies to countries around the world. Until 1991, American weapons sales abroad (all of which must be approved by the Pentagon) were at approximately the same level as those of the U.S.S.R. In 1988, other countries had much smaller participation in the international arms traffic (U.K., $1.8 billion; France, 2.3; China, 2.1; Germany, 0.9 billion). But after the collapse of the Soviet state, in 1991, the U.S. government moved in to fill the vacuum, and with aggressive merchandising sold $32.4 billion in arms to other countries in 1993. In that year, Russia sold $4.5 billion, and the other countries named above, together, sold $4.1 billion.[9]

The easy-financing devices facilitated by Pentagon banking have been applied to achieve preeminence in the sale of weapons. U.S. arms transfers from 1993 to 1995 exceeded $42.8 billion, which totaled almost half of the world's shipments and was greater than the combined efforts of Russia, France, the U.K., China, Germany and Italy. The armed forces of numerous client states are thereby locked into dependence on the United States for continuing technical support.[10]

By August 1997, Washington reported that its lead in military exports was far beyond that of Britain, France and Russia. The Appendix A table illustrates the nature of the weapons, and the type of transfer—purchase, credit, bank loan, lease. Note the column explaining which branch of the armed services or government is managing it. Of further interest are the quantities and money values listed, because many of these transactions are clearly marked as gifts, which will be paid for entirely by the U.S. government.[11]

The Pentagon is also deeply involved in foreign policy analysis and formulation, and typically spends as much on foreign policy research as the Department of State, or even more.

A further—and decisive—step in this process of expansion is illustrated by the ongoing effort to enlarge NATO membership. Thereby, the governments of Eastern Europe—and others—are to be gathered into an international network of alliances that is dominated by American state and corporate managers. From 1996 to 1998, the U.S. government spent more than $1.2 billion to support NATO expansion. William D. Hartung, writing on the latter's hidden cost, has called attention to the various ways in which the U.S. government and its arms industry have been pressing for expansion of NATO membership.[12]

An unusual view of the direction of this international enterprise can be obtained from a set of authoritative (but not formally published) administrative data on the expenditures by the U.S. government in relation to major areas of the world. A report prepared by the Cato Foundation advises that NATO military operations alone have been costing U.S. taxpayers approximately $60 to $90 billion a year; U.S. commitments to Japan, South Korea and other Eastern allies cost approximately $35 to $40 billion a year; and the American commitment to the Persian Gulf region runs at least $40 billion a year.

These commitments, which total between $135 and $170 billion annually, are in place largely to preserve American "leadership." The author of this report, Barbara Conry, writes that

> today's proponents of "global leadership," however, are advocating something better described as hegemony than as leadership. Unlike moral or economic leadership, global leadership does not envision the United States leading by example or through diplomacy. Global leadership is essentially coercive, relying on "diplomacy" backed by threats or military action.[13]

The roots of this carefully calculated campaign for world hegemony lie in the Cold War era. But this drive for "global leadership" has gathered new momentum in recent years.

During the critical period of 1984–1988—before the Iraqi invasion of Kuwait and the subsequent Gulf War—the Arms Control and Disarmament Agency recorded arms shipments to Iraq from all major weapons sellers. Yet for the United States the entry for this period is "0." The falsity of this statement has been revealed by a series of bulletins published by Senator John Glenn in which articles from many principal newspapers are collated describing transfers to Iraq of military materiel and of equipment for their manufacture. Since the coverage of these compilations covers not only the United States but also much of Western Europe, there are many hundreds of entries.[14]

This cover-up of U.S. military sales evidently helped the Pentagon use the outbreak of the 1991 Gulf War as an "example" of why the government should continue its Cold War type of budgeting.

But the primary activity of the Defense Department had been the conflict with the Soviet Union. By 1987, having observed the developing character of the U.S. military establishment and government, George F. Kennan, a veteran American diplomat, stated prophetically that "the military industrial establishment has become a veritable addiction of American society, an addiction from which American society could no longer free itself without the most severe withdrawal pains."[15] He further specified that "were the Soviet Union to sink tomorrow under the waters of the ocean, the American military industrial complex would have to go on, substantially unchanged until some other adversary could be invented. Anything else would be an unacceptable shock to the American economy."[16]

By 1991, the Soviet Union did indeed "sink," whereupon the American government proceeded to define its detailed military planning for the post–Cold War era. The Defense Department instructed the military chiefs to request forces and weapons sufficient to fight at least two large regional wars simultaneously.[17]

In further war planning, the Pentagon's focus was placed on the "rogue" states (as I noted in Chapter 4). The planners also included scenarios in which Russia attacks Lithuania and Poland, a coup in the Philippines threatens 5,000 Americans, a coup in Panama menaces the Panama Canal, and a new expansionist superpower emerges.

But this retooling did not suffice to address the prospect of terrorist-type assaults on American installations. Indeed, the apparent ability of small groups, lightly armed but determined and ready to risk their lives, to attack the United States led to a crisis in U.S. military planning, whereupon the Defense Science Board was invited to inquire into this thorny subject. The Board completed a study of this set of problems, and reported on them in October 1997 as part of its study of the U.S. superpower position and the use of transnational forces by military-political opponents of the United States.[18]

Kennan had also judged that "the truth of the matter is that the greater portion of American society that lies outside the defense establishment is rapidly falling into a position resembling that of much of civilian society in Northern Europe toward the end of the Thirty Years War; reduced to trailing behind the armies as camp-followers, hoping to live off the remnants from the military stores and kitchens."

The management of the U.S. government, however, does not heed prognoses of Kennan's sort. Its planning proceeds on a long-range basis, as indicated by the scheme for spending $750 billion on the Joint Strike Fighter that will come to ultimate fruition by the mid-twenty-first century. Accordingly, it should be no surprise that General John M. Shalikashvili, former chairman of the Joint Chiefs of Staff, laid out a strategic plan for the United States called "Joint Vision 2010." The perspectives there were reaffirmed by the Secretary of Defense in a speech at the Brookings Institution in Washington, D.C., on May 12, 1997. The essence of the "Joint Vision" involves bringing about a "revolution in military affairs" and beginning "to build a future force today."

The industrial and allied decay in America's civilian economy caused by this long concentration in the service of the military economy has not induced a reversal of policy by state managers. Indeed, as Kennan had envisioned, the directorate of America's state capitalism holds fast to its methods and strategic design. But there is far more involved in military policy than is briefly summarized here, for military institutions and methods have far-reaching effects on the quality of life in the wider society.

The contribution made by militarism to social control was analyzed as early as 1904 by Thorstein Veblen. He wrote that

> The modern war-like policies are entered upon for the sake of peace with a view to the orderly pursuit of business. In their initial motive they differ from the war-like dynastic politics of the 16th, 17th and 18th centuries. But the disciplinary effects of war-like pursuits and of war-like preoccupations are much the same whatever may be their initial motive or ulterior aim. . . .
>
> Warfare with a stress on subordination and mastery and the insistence on gradations of dignity and honor incident to a militant organization has always proved an efficient school in barbarian methods of thought.
>
> In this direction, evidently, lies the hope of a corrective for "social unrest" and similar disorders of civilized life. There can, indeed, be no serious question but that a consistent return to the ancient virtues of allegiance, piety, servility, graded dignity, class prerogative, and prescriptive authority would greatly conduce to popular content and to the facile management of affairs. Such is the promise held out by a strenuous national policy.[19]

The Cost of Nuclear Weapons, and the Overkill Surprise

What is the wider context for this continued military excess after the Cold War? Since 1940 (to 1996), the United States has spent about $16.2 trillion on military operations, apart from $5.8 trillion (in 1996 dollars) on nuclear weapons, including research; testing and production; delivery systems; command, control and early-warning networks; defenses against nuclear attack; and the management and disposition of nuclear waste.[20]

Recall that $5.8 trillion has been shown as the all-inclusive cost of America's nuclear enterprise,[21] and that, as we saw in Chapter 4, the 92 percent overkill share is $5.3 trillion, or more than twice the total net value of plant and equipment in all of America's manufacturing industries. What has been forgone with this nuclear overkill extravaganza is the possible application of the vast technical manpower and allied resources toward the construction and operation of a superior manufacturing and infrastructure system, more sophisticated and "user-friendly" than what is visible today.*

The President of the United States, as top manager of the military economy, with responsibilities toward the economy as a whole, cannot escape the implications of his role, for the executive responsible for that economy, the Secretary of Defense, reports to him. As we have seen, a top manager—civilian or military—does not willingly give up decision-making power, for that would breach the inviolable code of the managerial occupations.

Accordingly, it is understandable that neither the President nor the Secretary of Defense, nor their subordinates who deal in policy alternatives, have ventured to plan for conversion of the military economy to civilian work even following the end of the Cold War.

In April 1997, the Pentagon announced a further $76.6 billion of new weapons systems commitments that were not included in the administrative report, "Selected Acquisition Report," for December 31, 1996. The earlier announced value of new weapons commitments was $716.9 billion. Soon after December 1996, the Pentagon's new weapons plans included $750 billion for the Joint Strike Fighter plane.[22]† The sum of all these

*Walter Pincus of the *Washington Post* (April 2,1998) reports that the "Los Alamos National Laboratory . . . for the first time in almost 40 years is preparing to produce plutonium triggers, key components of hydrogen bombs, as a way to keep warheads in the U.S. nuclear stockpile reliable and to prepare a reserve supply if additional weapons are built in the future." In addition, "the administration maintains a $4.5 billion annual program called 'stockpile stewardship' that is designed 'to insure a high level of confidence in the safety and reliability of nuclear weapons in the active stockpile.'

"The new program includes building new elements for existing weapons, such as plutonium triggers, replenishing decaying nuclear materials in the weapons and designing new ways to test weapons components without conducting nuclear explosive tests that are banned by agreement or treaty.

"The U.S. has seven weapons systems in its strategic nuclear stockpile, which totals about 7,000 warheads: the MX land-based ICBM, each with 10 warheads; the land-based Minuteman III ICBM with three warheads each; the Trident I and Trident II submarine-launched ICBMs with up to five warheads each; the Tomahawk cruise missile with one warhead and the B-61 and B-63 nuclear bombs.

"Another key aspect of the stockpile stewardship program is the $1.2 billion National Ignition Facility (NIF) under construction at Lawrence Livermore Laboratory. It will reproduce within a laboratory the conditions of temperature and density of matter close to those that occur in the detonation of nuclear weapons.

"The NIF will give the U.S. the ability to study the behavior of matter and the transfer of energy and radiation in order to understand the basic physics of nuclear weapons and predict their performance without underground nuclear testing."

†George Runner, "California Needs to Compete for Key Military Jet Contract," *Los Angeles Times*, November 2, 1997.

"Taxpayers in Missouri and Texas dance in the streets upon reading editorials such as *The Times* wrote Oct. 26 opposing my legislation to get California on a level playing field in the competition to win the Joint Strike Fighter contract. . . .

weapons plans amounted to $1,543.5 billion. These prospective programs for new weapons did not appear in the annual (now five-yearly) Pentagon budgets. The capital commitment to new weapons outlays far and away exceeds anything that preceded it during the Reagan administration.

Indeed, knowledgeable officials in the Defense Department have reckoned that the actual cost and price of many of these weapons systems (like the F-22) are likely to double.[23] In turn, this could induce fiscal crises in the budgets of both the Defense Department and the entire government, half of whose "discretionary accounts" are now allotted to the military. No economist has ventured to assess the possible corrosive consequences of such developments for the value of the dollar or for the viability of the United States as a productive society.

The bar graph on page 144 summarizes the main expense outlays by the government from 1940 to 1996 (in 1996 dollars). The size of the main military burden is immediately obvious: National Defense, $16.2 trillion, followed by Nuclear Weapons: $5.8 trillion. Veterans' benefits, mainly war-related, are shown separately. Half the interest payments on the national debt were included in National Defense, though as much as three-quarters may be reasonably understood as war-related. All told, as the graph makes clear, direct military outlays have dominated the activities of the government since World War II, with "National Defense" and "Nuclear Weapons and Infrastructure" accounting for 50 percent of the federal government's total outlays from 1940 to 1996.

Can there be any doubt about the nature of federal priorities during the second part of the twentieth century?[24]

The chart of U.S. expenditures for 1940–1996 is a portrait of a state with a permanent war economy. Military budgets of this scale and duration necessarily shape much of American life. The priorities that have guided the U.S. government are quite different from those of other major states.

The United Nations has compiled national income accounts from which one can readily estimate, for each country, the number of dollars

---

"During the 1990's, California lost more than 50,000 aerospace jobs and $14 billion in contracts that would have paid significant taxes for new schools and more police patrol. According to the Los Angeles Economic Development Corp., L.A. County bore the brunt of the job loss: 180,600 aerospace jobs and 361,000 related ones. . . .

"The Joint Strike Fighter contract is the greatest military contract in history, a 20- to 25-year, $750-billion to $1-trillion program. Ten thousand workers will be employed by the winning prime contractor alone, and another 10,000 by subcontractors and suppliers."

(George Runner represented the 36th Assembly District, including Lancaster, Palmdale and Santa Clarita. He was vice chair of the Assembly Select Committee on Aerospace and was Assembly Republican Caucus whip.)

(or pounds, francs, etc.) spent on the military each year in relation to each 100 dollars (pounds, francs, etc.) spent by citizens or government on civilian-use capital goods or machines of every sort. The table below gives these data for the period of 1990–93.

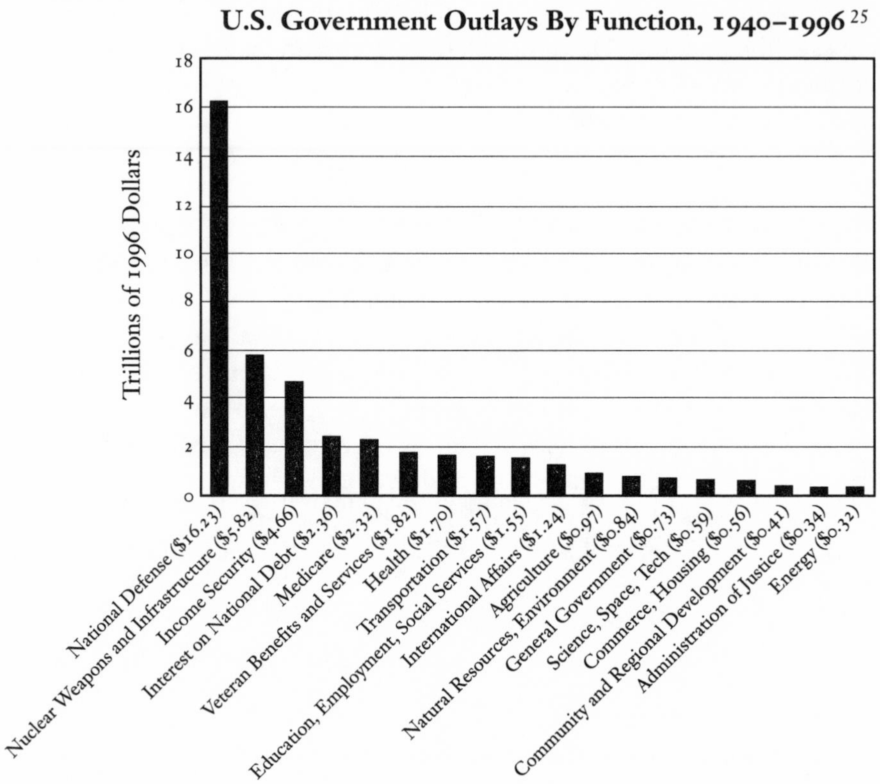

U.S. Government Outlays By Function, 1940–1996[25]

Military : Civilian Expenditure, 1990–1993

U.S.	38:100
U.K.	31
France	19
Italy	16
Japan	4[26]

These statistics throw into stark relief the attention paid to civilian capital investment in Japan, Italy and France, compared with the military focus in the United States and the United Kingdom. As we have seen, since the close of the Cold War, in 1991, the United States has sustained its preeminence in military spending. Indeed, the treatment of the military in the government's budget processes makes it a separate and unconnected function removed from the scrutiny and procedures that govern the civilian part of the government. As we have seen, in the military realm, considerations of justifiable cost in terms of what is forgone from the civilian economy are hardly operative. All this is closely linked, of course, to the conventional assumption that the real wealth of the nation is, to all practical intents and purposes, unlimited.

The Guns-and-Butter Illusion

Whether and to what degree a modern economy can enjoy an abundance of both "guns" and "butter" is a continuing problem. In the United States, this issue was dealt with by the writers of the National Security Council Memorandum, Number 68 (April 14, 1950), which laid out a broad-gauged policy blueprint for the Cold War.[27]

The authors of NSC-68 held that:

> One of the most significant lessons of our World War II experience was that the American economy, when it operates at a level approaching full efficiency, can provide enormous resources for purposes other than civilian consumption while simultaneously providing a high standard of living. After allowing for price changes, personal consumption expenditures rose by about one-fifth between 1939 and 1944, even though the economy had in the meantime increased the amount of resources going into Government use by $60–65 billion (in 1939 prices).

Their judgment was seconded by Paul A. Baran, a radical economist, who wrote in *The Political Economy of Growth* (1957):

> As is well known, in the years of the war the United States was not merely able to raise a military establishment comprising over 12 million people, to produce a prodigious quantity of armaments, to supply its allies with large quantities of food and other goods, but to *increase* simultaneously the consumption of its civilian population. The entire war, in other words—the largest and most costly war in its history—was supported by the United States by the mobilization of a *part* of its potential economic surplus.[28]

More recently, three eminent economists jointly prepared a volume titled *Beyond the Waste Land: A Democratic Alternative to Economic Decline*

(1983), tackling the same problem. In a fashion that is at once different from, but still related to, the analyses of NSC-68 and Paul Baran cited above, Samuel Bowles, David M. Gordon and Thomas E. Weisskopf together asserted that because there is so much slack in the economy as a result of unutilized or misutilized resources, *there can be such a thing as an economic free lunch* (meaning that infrastructure repair and so forth could be accomplished without taking away resources from somewhere else—like the military). Further, they stated that "this economic promise has clear historical precedent. More guns does not mean less butter unless both guns and butter are being produced efficiently and in ways which fully employ available inputs."

A vastly larger material output could certainly come from the production resources within the United States. But as the writers of *Beyond the Waste Land* make clear, that would require a real transformation in the American economy. "By changing the way we run our economic lives, it can transcend the distasteful trade-offs which insist that someone's gain must always be someone else's loss."[29] This is a very different vision from that of the state managers of the military economy. But they still do not challenge the underlying assumption.

The analysis in NSC-68 is at the heart of the matter, for the writers summed up what everyone saw with their own eyes during the Second World War: Men and women on the lower rungs of the economic ladder had more spending money during the war than they had before. But that did not make World War II into a "free lunch" for U.S. economic conditions.

Quite the contrary. During World War II, there was a major freeze in investment and in maintenance of the infrastructure. Older railroads and power stations were kept running. Everywhere, civilian production and the quality of civilian facilities and goods were characterized by a "make do with what we have" ethos. Investment in infrastructure was held up, as were investment in housing and the whole array of services to the civilian population.

The NSC analysis, the assurances of Paul Baran and the writings of later economists who promise "a free lunch" do not in fact resolve a major part of the World War II and Cold War reality: In a materially visible way, for much of the years after the war, most Americans have paid for the "guns" with shortages of civilian "butter" in many aspects of ordinary life.

Other economists have gone so far as to judge that, at least before the actual outbreak of major hostilities, Roosevelt and Hitler "benefitted similarly" from the trickle-down effects of military outlays. In this view, the price of the battleship *Missouri* was not a "negative cost" to the economy because of the numerous benefits its construction brought, in financial terms. Those could be traced directly and indirectly to the money flows occasioned by the letting of the contracts, purchases of materials, payment of wages and salaries and performance of the work in many supplier firms around the building of the *Missouri.* But the idea of assigning a positive macroeconomic worth to the money-flows occasioned by that enterprise reflects a characteristic misapprehension among many economists. Money, they believe (or assume), is wealth. If that illusion governs, then there seems hardly a better way of apparently multiplying the wealth of a community than by putting everyone to work producing military goods.

During the late 1980s, I had an opportunity to discuss economic affairs with many citizens of Moscow. I was struck by the comment of an educated young man whose affluent family derived its income from Moscow's military-serving ministries. While on a walk through the city, window-shopping, he pointed to some refrigerators and household goods on display and proclaimed, "You see, we can have guns and butter." I wonder what he would say today.

Campbell R. McConnell is the author of one of the most widely used introductory textbooks in American economics. In the 1972 edition, he noted that "there are obviously serious criticisms of the military, and therefore they deserve careful and critical review. Caught up in the divisive and emotional debate over the war in Vietnam, it is quite possible that war critics have been overzealous in laying the blame for the nation's socio-economic ills at the door of the military." He then elaborated:

> Guns and butter? Has the war industry drained the economic cupboard of resources to the extent claimed by critics? One can argue to the contrary, starting with the basic point that in a growing economy we can simultaneously have more guns *and* more butter. In fact, despite high levels of military spending, many important domestic programs have been initiated and accelerated during the past decade. For example, antipollution programs have expanded significantly, as have anti-poverty efforts.[30]

Two years after the appearance of McConnell's 1972 edition, I addressed these issues in my 1974 work *The Permanent War Economy*[31]:

> *Belief:* The United States economy can produce both "guns" and "butter" in indefinitely large amounts.
>
> Professor Walter Heller, onetime chairman of the President's Council of Economic Advisers, has said: "Economists can serve as angel's advocate [in putting at the President's disposal] the

> resources needed to achieve great societies at home and grand designs abroad . . . [and by providing] the wherewithal for foreign aid and defense efforts and for financing Vietnam on a both-guns-and-butter basis." In a comparison of two recent American wars, the "war" on poverty and the real war in Vietnam, Professor Nathan Glazer, spokesman for political conservatives, concluded: "Throughout the [Vietnam] war the United States has hardly stinted on butter to pay for guns; in fact, we have spent ever increasing amounts to cover both."[32]
>
> *Reality:* The American economy is large and wealthy, but there are limits to its wealth. There is a trade-off between military and civilian production. . . . By massive diversion of human and physical capital from economically productive to nonproductive military use, the government has been using up the "seed corn" capital that is a prime source of future productivity. In this way a policy of "no future" was followed for American society.
>
> The record of money spent on the war in Vietnam and on the ersatz "war" on poverty show that although the government spent more than before on poverty programs, the latter got only 8 percent of the combined total of government spending on these two wars . . . with the result that there was a clear failure to perform major economic development for the millions that needed it in the United States.[33]

As the previous discussion suggested, the customary social costs of the operation of America's system of political and economic governance include elements that are but rarely identified (unlike the remarkable direct military costs), and hence go largely unsuspected. These include the production losses owing to joblessness, the destruction of industrial facilities in favor of transfer of production to lower-wage locations, the loss of lives and work time owing to preventable pollution and losses caused by the prevention of education and training for skills, which are well within human reach, because of racial and gender discrimination.

Just one example: the "official" U.S. budgeted cost of the war in Vietnam is reckoned at $148.8 billion (in 1967 dollars),[34] but the overall social cost to American society has been calculated by Tom Riddell as $676 billion.[35]

The Social Opportunity Cost of the U.S. Military Establishment

What does it cost the American people to continue maintaining military organizations and the industrial-technological base that directly supports its operations? There are, of course, the annual sums voted by the Congress as part of the government's outlays.

The amounts of money, though large, do not immediately translate in terms of wealth. Therefore, we will try another approach, asking: What is forgone, what can we not afford, as a result of the allocation of funds that are readily approved for the Pentagon's operations?*

By 1990, for instance, 1,712,000 jobs once filled by Americans in the capital- and durable-goods industries were gone, replaced by imports. The imports, in turn, were generated by investments outside the United States, like those of GE, noted in Chapter 4. The fixed industrial facilities (plant and equipment) that could restore this production capability in the country would require a fixed capital outlay of about $113 billion. That deserves comparison with the scale of spending arranged by the Pentagon in pursuit of its global ambitions.

The Pentagon's projected expenditures are so large that it is difficult to convey their magnitudes. Thus, as noted, one meaningful way to express what has been planned is to imagine what is being sacrificed. Concretely, what sorts of outlays cannot be made if the Pentagon's capital-investment plan just summarized is actually implemented?

The following are a series of estimates for public expenditure on the civilian population of the United States, of what it would cost by current standards to fix or build afresh facilities that are sorely needed.

Estimated Costs for U.S. Infrastructure Repair

Schools	$112 billion
Replacing severely damaged housing	369
Radioactive waste cleanup	400
Superfund waste-sites cleanup	35
Highway, bridge and transit investment requirements, 1998–2011	517
Electrification of U.S. railroads	180
Comprehensive estimate of other infrastructure costs for U.S. based upon State of California studies—not included in above	400

*To be sure, the widespread, and firm, conviction that the United States can afford guns *and* butter, both in practically unlimited amounts, checkmates even the asking of this question, for then the unreadiness of state managers and legislators to allot money for many infrastructure purposes is seen only as a disapproval of particular items deemed not really worthwhile.

SCHOOLS

The General Accounting Office has reported that the cost of fixing or rebuilding one-third of the nation's 80,000 public schools will require $112 billion. These schools, currently classified as unsuitable or unsafe, are used by 14 million children. Among the conditions putting students at risk are asbestos and lead contamination, rotting roof beams, broken plumbing, bad lighting or ventilation systems and poor security systems.[36]

HOUSING

The 1998 American Housing Survey showed 5.32 million families in the United States, or about one-seventh of those who rent, as living in "worst-case" housing. What would it cost to fix this? From 1993 to 1996, the AFL-CIO's Housing Investment Trust financed several thousand housing units throughout the country. Their reports show an average of $69,450 for their housing units, which suggests a cost to replace severely depleted housing of $369 billion.[37]

No national survey is required to assess housing availability for the rich. The stock available to them is amply revealed in the press. For example, in the same year as the survey, a new residential condominium in Manhattan offered "room to spread out in apartments like the 6,100-square-foot, five-bedroom duplex on the 15th and 16th floors. That one will go for $12 million." The lavish description continues:

> There are servants' quarters in most of the apartments, and 10 suites on the second floor designed just for the help. Each of those will have 500 to 600 square feet, with full kitchens and baths. You could get one for $300,000 or $400,000, the management says.

There will be "15 climate-controlled private wine cellars . . . a private gymnasium, professional laundry rooms and a caterer's kitchen, where meals may be prepared for you and your guests," and on and on.[38]

Meanwhile, homelessness for families and for individuals is a continuing chronic problem in New York City, aggravated by the wipeout of about 900,000 "low-rent" apartments (1995–1998). At the same time, "the number of very-low-income families, those with incomes of less than 50 percent of the area median and who pay as much as 50 percent of their income on housing, grew by 370,000."[39]

San Francisco is one of the more civilized cities of the country. Yet, "On any night, according to the Coalition on Homelessness, there may be 16,000 people on the streets here, twice as many as 10 years ago. That means that San Francisco, the 13th largest city in the country, has the third highest population of the homeless, after New York and Los Angeles."

San Francisco's homeless, like those everywhere, are usually longtime residents. About a third are mentally ill and a third are drug addicts (or some mixture of the two), and the rest have been displaced from their homes through personal misfortunes like rising rents or loss of income. While the numbers of homeless are rising all over the nation, largely because of a decrease in federal benefits and public housing, Paul Boden, director of San Francisco's Coalition on Homelessness, said that the city's problem is exacerbated by its soaring housing prices, the highest in the country: " 'The problem is the worst I've ever seen it,' he said, 'and I've been doing this 16 years. We have 62 detox beds in the city and 1,200 people on the waiting list. We have 1,800 shelter beds and 140 families on the waiting list. The city doesn't even keep waiting lists for singles."[40]

RADIOACTIVE-WASTE CLEANUP

At Department of Defense and Department of Energy facilities across the United States, there is an urgent need to clean up and store radioactive waste safely. The outlay required for this purpose is on the order of $400 billion. Actually, this is probably a crude estimate, as the costs of coping with long-lived radioactive waste in large quantities frequently mushroom.

SUPERFUND WASTE CLEANUP

There are also about 1,232 Superfund toxic-waste sites in the United States, which will require an estimated $35 billion to clean up.

HIGHWAY, BRIDGE AND TRANSIT REQUIREMENTS

From the Department of Transportation, we have fairly detailed estimates of the investment requirements extending from 1998 to 2011 for maintaining and somewhat improving the nation's decaying highways, bridges and transit systems. An estimated $517 billion would be required for this purpose.[41]

RAILROAD ELECTRIFICATION

Electrification of about 60,000 miles of main-line railroads is a long-neglected project that would give the United States high-speed facilities comparable to those available in Western Europe and in Japan. John E. Ullmann has estimated the cost of this activity as $180 billion over a 10-year period.[42] An important part of the work would consist of new facilities to produce equipment that is not made in the United States.

OTHER INFRASTRUCTURE REQUIREMENTS

I am unable to itemize fresh national estimates for a number of infrastructure needs, like the costs of building public facilities of all sorts in cities and towns, universities and colleges and public libraries. We can, however, rely on a set of detailed studies that were completed for the state of California in January 1986, which are quite comprehensive.[43]

Comparing the size of California's population to the whole of the United States, we can derive a factor based on the state's infrastructure budget requirements. This suggests an estimate of $400 billion to meet the needs of the United States as a whole (for the items included in the California agenda, apart from the separately itemized topics shown above).

The grand total of these estimated investments required for the United States for the next ten to twenty years, extending into the twenty-first century, amounts to $2,013 billion.*

Yet none of these investment initiatives, designed to improve the quality of life of American citizens, are possible in the presence of annual military budgets of $265 billion and more, and of payments towards a military capital spending plan of $1,500 billion and more.

What will be the consequences of refraining from these civilian expenditures? The case of California is highly instructive. An elaborate 1986 report, *California and the Twenty-first Century: Foundations for a Competitive Society*, concluded that the state clearly faced major shortfalls in every major aspect of its infrastructure and environment. Each area of concern faced a potentially serious crisis unless large-scale corrective action was taken.

Having failed to follow these recommendations, by 1997 California was in fact suffering grave infrastructural problems.

> Today, California classrooms are among the most crowded in the country; many schools operate without libraries, without counselors, without nurses, without art or music, with greatly dimin-

*In March 2001, the American Society of Civil Engineers issued a *Report Card for America's Infrastructure* which rated the overall condition of that infrastructure as D+, and as requiring for its safe maintenance an investment of $1.3 trillion over five years. The ASCE's *Report Card*, we should note, does not include housing, nuclear waste cleanup or the electrification of U.S. railroads.

> ished curricular offerings. And what's true for the schools is true for other services that have no powerful constituencies: children's protective services, probation, public health.[44]

In terms of education and industry, California had simply become a dismal portrait of decay. "The tax revolt of the 1970s fractured the civic structure and ravaged support for California's universities, libraries, children's programs, and, most tragically, its public schools."[45] As of 1997, California ranked forty-third nationally in each area of education spending per capita. It had once ranked first.

What happened in California is characteristic of many states in the country. Thus, the General Accounting Office estimates that the fifty states need to spend overall an additional $112 billion just to put school buildings in reasonable working order.[46]

Other, more concrete weaknesses in infrastructure have drawn the attention of the American Iron & Steel Institute, on the grounds of its own business interest. It points out that "the U.S. would have to spend about $54.8 billion in maintenance and repair" to properly maintain the country's bridges.[47]

What happens in places that are not accessible to major cities? By March 1995, a quarter of the West Virginia population had no access to a town water supply. But the problem reaches much closer to home.

A distressing series of articles in 1996 analyzed infrastructure and governance problems in Washington, D.C. It was called "Trying to Fix the Nation's Capital, Where Inside 'Everything' Is Broken."[48] From New York City on September 16, 1996, we come upon a harrowing report in the *New York Post* titled "Rats Running Wild in the City."[49]

The federal government's Department of Education reported on September 9, 1993, that half of the nation's 191 million adults did not have the language skills needed to write a letter about a billing error or to calculate a bus trip from a published schedule.[50] These results are due partly to the deficient education given in the schools, and partly to the social cost of bringing in impoverished immigrants to work fruit and vegetable crops in states like California and Florida, and to those immigrants who arrive hoping for a better life and then find themselves in sweatshops or on the shabby fringes of the American dream.

Infrastructure Abundance: The Prison-Industrial Complex

In one area of U.S. infrastructure, spending has flourished. One of the nation's most noteworthy growth industries is the construction and operation of prisons. By the opening of the twenty-first century, the United

States, in federal, state and city prisons, was jailing more than 2 million people, thereby making the nation a world leader in the proportion of the population that is incarcerated. In 1996, Brian Ruttenbur, a securities analyst with the Equitable Securities Corporation, reported on the private prison industry, finding that the moneymaking potential was outstanding. His report was titled "Crime Can Pay." This was followed up by a January 1997 message to investors entitled "Crime Still Pays."

The securities report notes that "As stated in the book *Body Count*, by Bennett, Dilulio Jr. and Walters, the number of individuals murdered from 1990 to 1994 (119,732) was more than twice the number of soldiers killed in the Vietnam war (58,000)." An accompanying chart on prison beds in twenty-one countries shows the United States leading the way, with 1.6 million. This investment report reassures prospective investors in the principal prison industry firms: Corrections Corporation, Wackenhut Corrections, Cornell Corrections, Correctional Services, BI Incorporated.

The report calls attention to strategic factors in the American population and economy: "It is important to note that while the 15–24 population realized a 13% decline from 1980 to 1995, the incarceration rate per 100,000 individuals more than doubled. In 1994, individuals aged 15–24 accounted for over 41% of all violent crimes committed."[51]

During the 1990s, the Justice Department noted, prison building by both state and federal governments had surged nationwide. Authorities built 168 state and 45 federal prisons, to increase the number of such institutions to 1,500. Again, from California, in a dispatch from Berkeley: "New prisons cast a shadow over higher education. . . . By the fiscal year 1995–1996, the outlay for prisons exceeded the outlay for higher education." California had built and operated a world-famous network of universities, colleges and junior colleges that were the envy of the rest of the United States and of many other countries. The junior colleges prepared people for an array of skilled occupations; the state colleges provided access for further education beyond high school; and the senior universities, led by schools at Berkeley, Los Angeles and San Diego, were among the outstanding educational institutions in the United States. During the 1960s and 1970s, professors competed for appointments to California's universities. Those priorities have been replaced with prison budgets.*

*There is more to come. The Department of Justice has set up UNICOR (trade name of Federal Prison Industries), which, at the end of Fiscal Year 1998, operated 99 factories in 64 federal prisons located in 30 states, manned by 1,600 staff and over 20,000 inmates who were paid "a stipend ranging from 23 cents to $1.15 per hour" *(Unicor '98: A Revealing Look at What You Should Know About Federal Prison Industries, the 1998 Annual Report).* Note that the hourly stipends in federal prisons could qualify as "sweatshop wages."

More recently, in New York State, as in California, the fever of prison-building continues to dominate the state government's attention despite the fact that "for five straight years crime has been falling, led by a drop in murder."[52] So why are the numbers of inmates in prisons and jails around the country still going up? One important factor is a federal law that fixes mandatory sentences, notably for possession of illegal drugs, making it, along with the more serious offense of trading or trafficking drugs, a cause for multiple-year imprisonment.

New York City Infrastructure

The case of New York offers further insights into the scale of the problem. Infrastructure repair and reconstruction in New York City suffers from a long tradition of neglect of the city's physical plant.

In a pathbreaking study, the Cooper Union Infrastructure Institute analyzed data on the age of New York City's infrastructure. Drawing on city documents, city files, current and former municipal employees and studies performed by the U.S. Army Corp of Engineers, it paints a highly detailed, and depressing, portrait of disasters waiting to happen. The city's much-vaunted regeneration in "quality of life" sits on top of an infrastructure in decay. The following is a sampling:

> The useful life of sewers and water mains is estimated at 100 years. . . . By the year 2020, more than one-quarter of all mains will be centenarian. . . .
>
> Largely designed to withstand 19th century conditions, the New York water main system is failing under 20th century stresses, including vibrations from construction and heavy traffic . . .
>
> Averaging approximately 500 per year in the early 1980s, the annual number of breaks in New York City surpassed 700 in 1989. . . .
>
> . . . It is conceivable that by 2010 multiple breaks in neighborhoods will occur, leaving buildings and communities without water service for days at a time. . . .
>
> . . . The portion of the sewer system surpassing 100 years old is projected to climb to nearly one mile in five by the year 2010. . . .
>
> Twenty-five bridges are currently greater than 100 years old. . . .
>
> An estimated $250 million can be saved annually by implementing 100% preventive maintenance for all New York City bridges. . . .

> 57% of City streets have no known construction history. . . .
>
> City streets are now being repaved, on average, every 17 years. The current reconstruction cycle for City streets is 520 years.[53]

As this depressing catalogue graphically suggests, "quality of life" in the present is being enjoyed at the expense of a city's future.

An important study called *Infrastructure of New York City* was prepared in 1996 by F. H. Griffis of Columbia University. His report covers the "steel and concrete" elements, but more significant, makes reference to the major deficit in funds for infrastructure investment in New York City and the consequences of continuing only minor maintenance while withholding major capital investment.[54]

In 1998, the Comptroller of the City of New York, Alan G. Hevesi, completed an elaborate investigation of the capital-investment needs of the city government, covering all major parts of the city's public-responsibility infrastructure (hence, not including housing). It found that, all told, "it would take a minimum of $91.83 billions to bring our infrastructure to a systemic state of good repair and address new capital needs over the decade." The amounts (in billions of dollars) needed to accomplish this for each city department are in the first list of data below. The Comptroller shows the part of the estimated need expected to be covered from predictable sources of funds (the city budgets, other government funds, etc.).

	Fresh Capital Spending Needed, 1998–2007 (billions)	**Prospective Funding (% of Need)**
Board of Education	$28.43	44
Transit Authority	21.54	48
Department of Environmental Protection	12.43	64
Department of Transportation	12.16	67
Department of Sanitation	3.03	94
Department of Parks and Recreation	2.75	35
Housing Authority/ Department of Housing Preservation and Development	2.55	83

	Fresh Capital Spending Needed, 1998–2007 (billions)	Prospective Funding (% of Need)
Courts	2.37	100
City University of New York	1.66	78
Department of Citywide Administrative Services	1.13	72
Health and Hospitals Corporation	1.06	62
Fire Department	0.66	83
Department of Correction	0.54	91
Police Department	0.54	98
Department of Cultural Affairs	0.32	53
Human Resources Administration	0.25	96
Department of Homeless Services	0.22	50
New York Public Library/ Brooklyn Public Library/ Queens Public Library	0.19	47
Total	91.83	57[55]

Of the estimated $91.83 billion needed, only 57 percent has been planned for. The details of the Hevesi report are indeed specific to New York City, but the findings are also characteristic of all the other metropolitan centers of the United States. There has been deterioration in the capital assets of infrastructure in every American city.

As a former chief engineer for the city's Transportation Department observed in the *New York Times*,

> "At the turn of the century, there were 200 workers cleaning the Brooklyn Bridge. . . . By the mid-1980's, there were three."[56]

The Schools of New York City

I was a student in the public schools of New York City from 1922 to 1935. What is going on in the schools of 2000?

In March 2000, the *New York Times* reported that there remained "130 coal-burning furnaces in New York City public schools."[57] In an earlier report (1993) on the state of repair in New York City schools, Sam Dillon wrote: "some buildings are dilapidated wrecks dating to the 19th century, according to a new report."[58]

Some of the buildings where I attended school did in fact date back to the nineteenth century, but they were nevertheless well kept. A population surge, including 300,000 additional students expected in New York City by the year 2001, has put major stress on the buildings and the teachers: "More than half the buildings are over 50 years old and some are over 100 years old." To stop further physical deterioration, a Board of Education group in 1993 recommended $24 billion in school construction over the next decade. (Compare that with the General Accounting Office estimate of $112 billion required to put the 80,000 school buildings across the United States in much better shape.)

To be sure, that $24 billion only saw the light of day on the pages of the report requesting it, and in a few news stories. It was watered down to a $17 billion request, which resulted in a five-year appropriation of only $4.3 billion. As a result, "nearly half the city's elementary schools are filled beyond their capacities, as are virtually all the city's 107 high school buildings . . . the most overcrowded high school is Brooklyn's Fort Hamilton High School. Built to accommodate only about 2,000 students, the school in October 1991 was packed with more than 3,500 students."[59]

In a June 8, 1994, article entitled "A Crowded School in Queens Can Find Class Space in Unusual Places," an accompanying photograph shows an English as a Second Language class in an alcove off a corridor. Such a location is tolerable compared with the situation of the social studies teacher who had to set up an office in the men's bathroom.

In universities, tight budgets have resulted in "45% of college teaching done by part-timers, compared with 34% in 1980, and 22% in 1970."[60] This is part of a nationwide development that describes a major alienation of the professorial part-timers and adjuncts, who are not eligible for tenure appointment but must live with lower payments that do not suffice for a livelihood.

At the same time, the skills of job applicants have declined because of deteriorating schools and colleges. For example, "The New York Telephone company once tested 57,000 applicants before finding 2,100 who were qualified for any level technical jobs."[61] This reflects the worsening condition of education and, more crucially, the deficiencies in the preparation of America's young people for work.

The New York Civil Liberties Union has embarked on a lawsuit in the federal courts. The State Education Department, it charges, has

> discriminated against children in predominantly minority schools by allowing them to be taught by larger numbers of uncertified teachers, tolerating lower academic standards, relegating them to

> dilapidated and unsafe schools, supplying them with out-of-date textbooks and failing to provide sufficient remedial instruction.[62]

The children of New York City are being given a lesson in how well the larger community cares for them.

The size of the city masks impoverishment on a large scale. The Community Service Society of New York gave us a report called *Poverty in New York City in 1993: An Update.* Included are the following findings: "The poor population of New York City increased from 1.4 million in 1979 to 1.7 million in 1992. The poverty rate for New York City grew from 20% in 1979 to 24% in 1992. Impoverishment was concentrated among the city's children and among elderly." Thus, "The city's children had a poverty rate in 1992 of 39%; by contrast, the elderly have a poverty rate in 1992 of 20%." The society further reported, "Contrary to current popular opinion, many families in New York City have not benefitted from public programs aimed at assisting the poor." In the years 1992–1993, for example, only 55 percent of all poor families received any public assistance income. Notably, "the highest poverty rate for children was found among Hispanic children (57%). Their poverty rate was three times greater than that of white children (20%). . . . Nearly a quarter . . . of all poor children in 1992/1993 were not covered by Medicaid or any other health insurance."[63]

By 1999, again for New York City, a CSS analysis found that 24 percent of households were officially poor, "as many or more than in the early 1990s during the last recession."[64]

Dr. Irwin Redlener, president of the Children's Hospital at Montefiore Medical Center, reports that "an astonishing 38% of the more than 8,000 kids in the city's shelter system have asthma." Redlener reported further that this was "the highest prevalence of asthma in any child population that's ever been reported." He has concluded: "This worries me a great deal, because asthma is, first of all, life-threatening for children. But besides that, even in its milder forms, it fits into the category of chronic conditions that adversely affect the ability of a child to function at school."[65]

New York City has been making a major contribution to the alienation of the nation's children, rendering many of them powerless into a far future. During the spring of 1999, Mayor Rudolph Giuliani proposed a $41 million cut in the public library budget for the following year, 20 percent of its entire budget. "The library," Giuliani says, "should find private donors to make up the lost revenue." Juan Gonzalez, writing in *In These Times*, notes: "This is in a year when New York has a $2 billion surplus, its lowest unemployment in decades, and its main industry, Wall Street, is booming. . . . But kids whose families don't have computers at home now may have a public library system that's only open four days a week instead of six, and the waits for a terminal will grow to five hours instead of the normal three and a half."[66]

Children Who Cannot Read in New York City and Westchester County

Early in 1999, the New York State Education Department administered a test for reading ability to the fourth-grade public school students of the state. The results showed for each school the number of students tested, the number who achieved "passing" grades and a measure of the relative economic level of the students' families. (The latter was gauged by the proportion of the students who were not eligible for school-provided free lunches.)

In the public schools of New York City, 75,426 fourth-grade students were tested for reading ability and only 33 percent achieved a passing grade. In Westchester County, by contrast, of the 10,232 students tested, 62 percent passed.[67]

With the assistance of a statistician,* I took a closer look at the results for Westchester County and the New York City public schools. The relation between the proportion of fourth-grade students who passed the test in each school and their relative family income showed a correlation coefficient of 0.72 for New York City and 0.86 for Westchester County.†

While these results are statistically meaningful, we do not have detailed information on additional factors in the two public school systems that surely bear on the percentage of students with passing grades. The proportion of teachers in the Westchester schools who had completed qualifying examinations for public school teaching, for example, was higher than in New York City, as was their salary level.

Examine the charts that portray the distributions of school scores. Each dot represents one public school. Note the concentration at the lower end of the two scales in the city schools and the contrasting concentration at the highest levels of the scales in the Westchester schools. The children in the public schools of New York City are being alienated.

*Zaiying Huang, a doctoral candidate in the Department of Statistics, Columbia University.

†These results reflected a linear relation between the economic status of families and the proportion of students who received passing grades. This relationship was clearly stronger for Westchester than for New York City. Also, the square of the correlation coefficient (R^2) is meaningful in each case, as it indicates the degree to which the variability in the number passing is accounted for by the accompanying measure of economic status. Thus for New York City, R^2 was 52 percent, meaning that 52 percent of the variability of passing grades was "explained" by the accompanying variability in relative family income. For Westchester, R^2 was 74 percent.

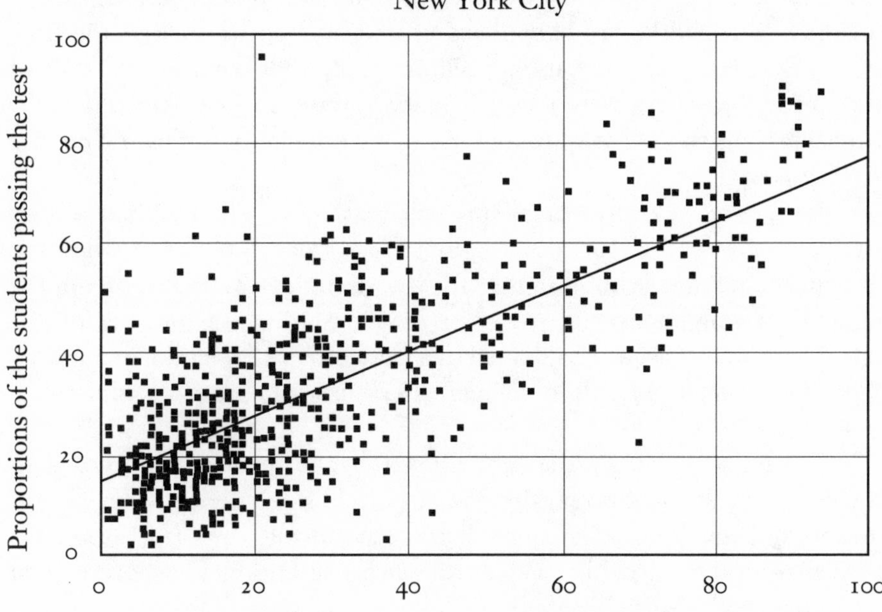
New York City
Proportions of the students passing the test
Proportions of the students not qualifying for free lunch
0
20
40
60
80
100

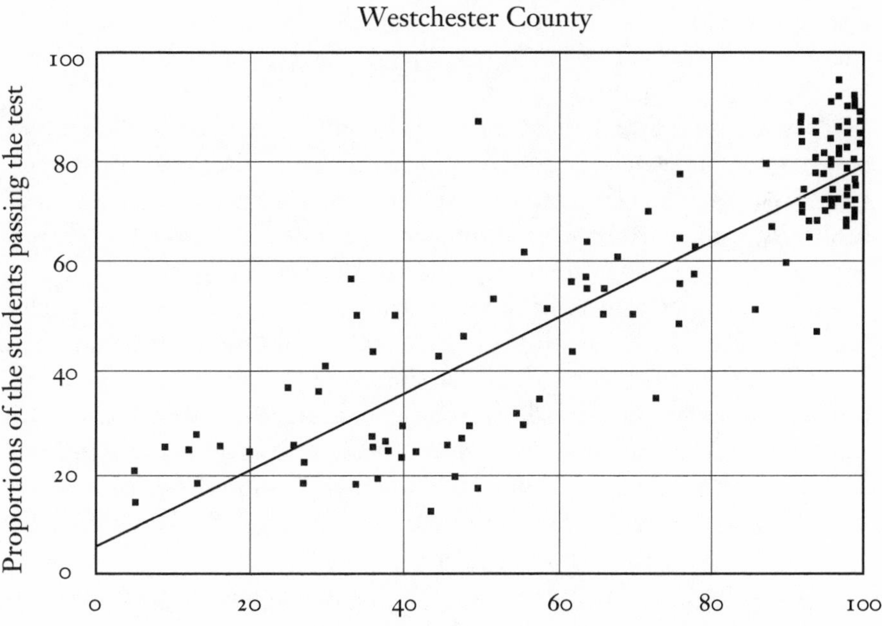
Westchester County
Proportions of the students passing the test
Proportions of the students not qualifying for free lunch
0
20
40
60
80
100

The resources of every sort needed to transform the learning capability of the city's children are being used up in government budgets that feature new aircraft carriers at $5.5 billion apiece (not counting the cost of the planes, crew, fuel, etc.), and ever larger police forces, and the additional prisons needed to warehouse growing populations of barely literate lawbreakers.

Last, note the contrasting blank spaces at the very highest end of both scales in the city schools distribution. That space surely represents the private elementary schools in the city, whose students were not part of the reading-testing population.

I view these results as a devastating portrait of what has been imposed on the city's children—all in the name of profit and power accumulation.

Until these disturbing issues are addressed, the questions are going to be raised over and over again: What is holding America's society and economy back from achieving a level of performance that is attainable and manifestly reachable? What will direct attention to where capital resources are being allocated? So long as the state managers' military agenda prevails, we will continue to suffer from the illusion that America can have both guns and butter.

Health Care

Thanks to recent federal policy, provision of medical care of every sort has been increasingly added to the business of insurance companies. Once business managements are given control of virtually every aspect of health care, they are converted into opportunities for profit-taking, and for multiplying administrative activities and costs.

The main performers of the work—doctors, nurses and other health care providers—have been introduced to the full meaning of alienation as their former traditional rights of decision are taken away and their occupations put under managerial control. (I will explore further the effects on the health-care occupations themselves in Chapter 11.) Meanwhile, I will summarize some leading conditions of the privatization of health care: the part of the population without any insurance; the care of children; care for the chronically ill; care for the enfeebled elderly.

The number of Americans who are without any health insurance has increased every year since 1987 and by mid-1998 exceeded 41 million, about one out of every six people. Millions are not covered by employers as a fringe benefit, and find themselves vulnerable to firms that charge what they believe the public will bear, or what they desire for their own profits.

Meanwhile, one of the slicker investment opportunities during the

1990s was afforded by the expansion of the nursing home industry, with its "guaranteed flow of cash consisting almost entirely of public funds." The investment bank Hambrecht & Quist advised its investor clients, "We believe nursing homes are naturally well positioned to capitalize on this growing opportunity."[68]

Beverly Enterprises, based in California, is a national chain of nursing homes.

> While Beverly executives and shareholders profited from the company's rapid growth during the 80s, many patients suffered. Across the nation, health officials filed reports on Beverly nursing homes documenting filthy living conditions, infected bedsores and painful deaths. The State of Washington banned the company from opening any new homes because of its poor track record. The chain bowed out of Maine after inspectors there cited it for substandard conditions. A Missouri Grand Jury investigated reports of Beverly patients with gaping wounds. Texas suspended Medicaid payments to 24 of the company's homes because of health hazards. California fined the firm $724,000 and put it on probation after accusing Beverly of contributing to the deaths of nine patients. At one home, inspectors found that ants had swarmed over the body of a woman, entering her respiratory system through a wound in her throat. "Something is very wrong at Beverly Enterprises," a Deputy Attorney-General in California concluded.[69]

From a strictly business standpoint, however, there's nothing wrong with Beverly Enterprises. Just examine its last annual report and read about the introduction of new computers and software, and the dedicated care that is stated as characteristic of the enterprise. The report is profusely illustrated. Everyone is smiling.

During a decade-long decline in the medically insured population, unusually heavy burdens have been placed on people who changed or lost their jobs and tried to get an assured-coverage benefit as promised by federal law (the Kassebaum-Kennedy law announced as a boon to people changing jobs). But the promises were not kept, as the all-powerful insurance companies levied charges for larger than standard rates.[70]

In 1997, the government proposed to increase the money available during the ensuing five years to assure medical care for people without coverage. Not indicated in the announcement was the fact that three-quarters of those without medical coverage would remain uncovered, even after these increases came into effect.

The Carnegie Corporation, a think tank with an interest in various community problems, conducted a three-year study of American children that "confirmed some of society's worst fears; millions of infants and toddlers are so deprived of medical care, loving supervision, intellectual stimulation, their growth into healthy and responsible adults is threatened." A variety of social developments was examined. In 1965, for instance, 17 percent of mothers returned to work within one year of a child's birth, but by 1991, this figure had jumped to 53 percent. So mothers who desired to provide care to their children at a crucial age of development were less able to do so in 1991.[71]

All told, by mid-1998, 10 million children were medically uninsured, while 4.7 million were eligible for coverage under the Medicaid program. But they, like millions of elderly citizens, are formally eligible for coverage under various "safety-net" rules that require a lawyer or accountant to understand their terms. People in need have succeeded in avoiding a series of bureaucratic quagmires by simply not applying. Implementation of safety-net programs involves "conflicts between federal and state agencies as well as a dearth of program leadership and coordination, labyrinthine red tape and demeaning application procedures." Millions have declined to be subjected to the bureaucrats' alienation nightmares. Thus health insurance safety nets "for Medicaid recipients . . . all of them based on the Federal poverty guideline . . . limit enrollees' assets, excluding a house, a car, some life insurance and a burial plot, to less than $4,000 for individuals and $6,000 for couples. Applicants must apply for coverage to state agencies that supervise welfare services."[72] We are far from hearing the last word on these programs, designed and administered in the name of health care. The *New York Times* also informs us that

> Struck by the reports of the shortfall in the programs' enrollments, many states say they are redoubling their efforts to find low-income people eligible for them.
>
> "It would be unfair to allege that Ohio has done anything to hide from these folks," said Barbara Coulter Edwards, Ohio's Medicaid director. But she said, "We are asking, 'Are there some things we could do to encourage a higher rate of participation?' "
>
> Ronald F. Pollack, executive director of Families USA, explained part of the shortfall this way: "Social Security says, 'We don't run these programs. They're run by the Health Care Financing Administration.' H.C.F.A. says, 'We have oversight, but they're administered by the states.' "[73]

On January 3, 1999, the President announced another new program in the name of health care: "The Administration says the tax credit [$1,000 a year] would benefit 1.2 million elderly people, 250,000 children and 550,000 non-elderly adults." But we are reliably informed that many people with chronic illnesses require home-care services costing tens of thousands of dollars a year. That's not all: "Five million Americans need long-term care because of illness or disability and . . . the need will grow with the aging of population."[74]

Millions in need are evidently refusing to subject themselves to the bureaucratic manipulations of the national health-care system. Though this results in continued suffering, I judge it to be a sign of sturdy mental health. For it entails, effectively, a widespread refusal of continuous managerial control and of the ever-growing, ever more complicated, alienating procedures of medical bureaucracies.*

Hunger, U.S.A.

Bob Herbert reports from Scottsdale, Arizona, on the experience of an elderly population adjacent to one of the garden spots of upper-middle-class living in the United States. Herbert writes:

> Scenes of poverty-stricken Americans standing in breadlines are standard in documentaries about the Depression, which ended more than half a century ago. What is not generally acknowledged—perhaps not widely known—is that there are breadlines all over the United States right now.
>
> Early on Thursday morning, elder residents of El Mirage began lining up at a senior citizens center for donations of food provided by the West Side Food Bank in the neighboring town of Surprise. They did not discuss their portfolios or the surging Nasdaq. The heralded free market economy had left them far behind.[75]

The Urban Institute, a research organization in Washington, found recently that "nearly two million Americans had faced at least one of two terrible dilemmas: whether to pay their rent or buy their food, or whether to pay for medicine or buy food."

Doug O'Brien, the director of public policy and research at Second Harvest, the largest nonprofit clearinghouse in the country for donations

*By way of contrast, see the dispatch by Youssef M. Ibrahim to the *New York Times*, December 20, 1995, "For the French, Solidarity Still Counts," on the benefits of the French health-care system.

Also: Jonathan E. Fielding, M.D., M.P.H., Pierre-Jean Lancry, Ph.D., "Lessons from France—'Vive la Différence': The French Health Care System and US Health System Reform," *The Journal of the American Medical Association*, 270 (August 11, 1993); Victor G. Rodwin and Simone Sandier, "Health Care Under French National Health Insurance," *Health Affairs*, Fall 1993.

to soup kitchens and food pantries, told Herbert, "We have a hunger problem. And other Western industrialized nations do not have a hunger problem. . . . [A] recent comprehensive survey showed that over the course of a year, more than 21 million sought emergency food assistance through the Second Harvest network."[76]

In New York City, the capital of stock exchanges and home of many "new economy" millionaires and billionaires, Food for Survival services foodstuffs to "1,300 soup kitchens, pantries, low income day care centers, senior centers, and other nonprofit community food programs throughout the five boroughs."*

Dolores Heuser, whose situation is typical, is resigned to her new circumstances. "I can't go to a lovely restaurant," she said. "I can't get my hair set anymore. But I am thankful for the assistance. I'll go on Monday for a food box."[77]

All this at a time when advances in genetics, chemistry and statistical analysis have allowed agricultural science to develop new solutions to the worldwide food crisis. If only their governments chose to make it a priority. The U.S. government controls millions of tons of foodstuffs, which are being shipped to various countries partly to relieve genuine hunger and partly to rescue governments that would otherwise risk being overthrown. More knowledge in agricultural sciences is surely welcome, but that is not what is holding back the governments of the United States

*From Food for Survival [1999 and budget plans for 2000] at The New York City Food Bank, Hunts Point Co-op Market, 355 Food Center Drive, Bronx, NY 10474, Phone: (718) 991-4300, Fax: (718) 893-3442:

> Approximately one quarter of New York City residents (1.8 million people) have household incomes . . . below the Federal poverty level, as many or more than during the last recession in the early 1990's. . . . The city's unemployment rate of 6% is higher than the national average of 4%. . . . [M]any low wage jobs have been dropped raising the question whether the city's labor market could sustain more low wage workers and those leaving welfare. . . .
>
> [T]here has been increased regular reliance upon private emergency food programs, especially from poor white families with children. . . . People are moving out of welfare, but not out of poverty. . . . 22% of New York City residents over age 65 live below the poverty level, one senior in four is at nutritional risk and the fastest growing part of our population is over age 85 (*Daily News* 10/17/99) . . .
>
> We have more than doubled our warehouse capacity to a total of 87,000 square feet . . . [including] 5,000 square feet of cooling space for fresh produce, meat, and dairy products. . . . More than 15,000 seniors receive daily lunches all year round.
>
> These elderly people are no longer forced to choose between filling their prescriptions and filling their plates.

For a short course on alienation: "To be destitute is to have little control over one's life. The poor and homeless are painfully aware of this hardship. All they can do is struggle to survive—to find their next meal."

from supplying obviously necessary foodstuffs in short supply to 21 million of its citizens.

Environmental Depletion

In *The Transformation of Capitalist Society*, Zellig S. Harris judges that

> perhaps the major blow to capitalist decision-making is coming from a direction which fifty years ago no one had expected: the environment.
>
> In the first place, capitalism's use of its technology is damaging human ecology in a way that is becoming increasingly obvious and unignorable: pollution, nuclear waste, global warming, ozone depletion, soil and forest depletion (with other damages that may make agribusiness and its chemical base no longer very profitable), health dangers from food additives, and the like.
>
> Secondly, the world's population growth, accelerated by medical advances in populations (especially Third World) that are retarded economically and socially, has reached the point of taxing available production.
>
> Third, the unreasoned, unplanned, unreviewed, and essentially wasteful technology of capitalism is threatening to deplete the usable material and energy resources of the planet (petroleum, rain forests, plant and animal species, etc.).

But neither the corporate nor the government managers are able to cope with the wider consequences.

> Business cannot, by its structure, consider these matters. Its decisions are essentially short-range (to reach a maximum available profit in least time), and its bottom line criterion cannot deal with these problems. . . . Within capitalism, even the governments, which might be expected to deal with such long-range problems, delay consideration of environmental problems as long as possible.

Harris held that essentially

> what makes these considerations the crucial threats to capitalism is, first, that the magnitude of capitalism's use of the planet is beginning to confront the finite magnitude of the planet, and,

> second, that manipulation, artifice, and military power, which can save rulers from their ruled population, are of no avail here.[78]

These urgent problems permeate even the air we breathe. The public has been repeatedly maltreated by refusal of the state managers to disclose the environmental hazards to which Americans are exposed. In a distressing array of public circumstances, they have found ways to manipulate and mislead the public into supporting their budgets and activities.

Starting in approximately 1994, for example, there were reports of unexplained, undiagnosed sickness among soldiers and others who participated in the Gulf War. The Department of Defense repeatedly denied any connection between these illnesses and U.S.-Iraq military operations. Panels recommended that the Pentagon and independent groups investigate further the various incidents (numbering about fifteen) in which nerve gas and other chemical agents were detected by American troops. A parade of such reports, accompanied by denials from the Pentagon, went on for about three years, and the upshot was the disclosure that emissions of toxic material did occur on a significantly large scale covering many square miles. Finally, the CIA announced on April 10, 1997, that it had failed to report the data it had possessed all along concerning the demolition of Iraqi ammunition bunkers.[79]

The public has also been put at risk by a variety of nuclear hazards at home. For many months in late 1996 and 1997, the staffs of the Brookhaven National Laboratory were subject to criticism concerning a possible leakage of radioactive water, which contained tritium, a radioactive isotope of hydrogen, that might be contaminating the groundwater of Long Island. After numerous denials and pledges to investigate, the laboratory was faced with the prospect of closing the reactor facility altogether because of the delay.

Outside the United States, the environmental hazards of nuclear power have been discussed for decades. On August 3, 1997, the *New York Times* published a photograph of a large nuclear-fuel reprocessing plant on the coast of France. Books have been written about this plant, reporting the appearance of measured pollution in the seawater off the coast and the possibility that ocean life could be carrying these materials to other locations in the area. The same sort of debate has been going on in Britain in regard to its own nuclear facilities and processing plants.

But for its part, the U.S. government took many years before it began to come forward with data explaining the unusual incidence of thyroid cancer that proved to be associated with atomic testing sites that were used in the 1950s. Two articles in the *New York Times* reported that "the releases [of radioactive material] were larger than earlier estimates, and at least 10 times larger than those caused by the 1986 explosion at the Chernobyl nuclear plant in the Ukraine."

The Chernobyl explosion alone released radioactive waste materials over northwestern Europe sufficient to require the slaughter of herds of wild animals and the removal of vast acreage in the Ukraine from agricultural use. The report from the U.S. National Cancer Institute indicated that "atmospheric nuclear bomb tests in Nevada from 1961 to 1962 exposed millions of American children to large amounts of radioactive iodine, a component of fallout that can affect the thyroid gland, the National Cancer Institute said today."[80]

As the American military knew well, these effects could be mitigated by treating exposed people with iodine. Nonradioactive iodine is ingested and taken up by the thyroid gland instead of the radioactive iodine, thereby limiting the access of the latter to the thyroid. "The National Cancer Institute did not say whether any cases of thyroid cancer were caused by the fallout, but several experts said the levels of exposure could justify special monitoring for some people—particularly those that were children in the 1950s and 1960s." The reports drew their information from a 100,000-page study by the Cancer Institute that was ordered by Congress in 1982, completed by 1994, but only finally released in 1997. "A summary of the study prepared for internal use at the Department of Energy . . . says that according to formulas in international use for calculating radiation damage, the doses were large enough to produce 25,000 to 50,000 cases of thyroid cancer around the country of which 2,500 would be expected to be fatal."

As reporters noted, "In contrast to the 50 to 160 rads those children are believed to have received, federal rules for nuclear power plant accidents call for taking protective action when the dose to human thyroid is anticipated to reach 15 rads." I cite these data not to encourage despair, but rather to focus attention on the manipulative fashion in which the leading state managerial authorities have behaved in regard to the well-being of the public when it conflicts with the pursuit of their nuclear-military ambitions. To challenge their nuclear agenda is to run up against their most deeply cherished and powerfully defended goals.

The depletion of productive capability, and of quality of life as a result of militarization (and allied nuclearization), has been experienced in many countries. In fact, this source of profound alienation has become an integral part of militarized state capitalism. In every case, governments have supported the economic, political and military technical moves that have generated powerlessness among ordinary people. We find an onset of decay in many countries of Western Europe. Even in Germany, the prospect for industrial jobs is diminished by the export of industrial factories to locations in other countries. In Japan, the lifetime employment policy has been revised to permit hiring cuts.[81]

Problems of depletion show up strongly in the prospect of energy supply. In the United States, our dependency on gasoline-powered vehicles is clearly associated with the pollution of the atmosphere, especially with nitrogen oxide and associated problems of global warming.

I was a member of a Commission on Air Pollution in New York City named by Mayor John Lindsay in 1965. I paid special attention to pollution from motor vehicles and from large boilers (hospitals, universities, power stations). The Commission's draft report was presented with no reference to air pollution from motor vehicles. A majority voted down such a recommendation.

I also called attention to the feasibility of designing an emission-monitoring system, especially for smokestacks of major fuel-burning systems, with instruments that could monitor and record the rate of emission. The panel members were skeptical of the idea, so I had a chemical engineering firm that supplied such instruments bring its equipment to our meeting. I then invited members to smoke their cigars and blow the smoke through an opening of a machine. They could see the needles in motion recording the particulate matter coming through. I recommended a fine to companies exceeding a permitted level of pollution at the rate of $100 a minute, an incentive for equipment maintenance and compliance.

Chairman Norman Cousins asked me at the last session, "How many people does this system require?"

I said, "Two. One at the central monitoring station, which is linked by special wire, radio or telephone to instruments at major smokestacks, and then someone to pitch in when the first person cannot make it." My arguments were to no avail.

Renewable alternatives to gasoline are available, most notably ethyl alcohol, made by the sophisticated chemical processing of cellulose materials like wood pulp and waste paper. Harry Gregor, until 1998 Emeritus Professor of Chemical Engineering at Columbia University, pioneered the membrane technology required and judged that such options should be commercially viable with only moderate further research. That such technologies have not yet been aggressively pursued is largely due to the very extensive government stakes, and investments by the petroleum and allied industries in oil fields, refining, distribution and the like.*

*Gregor's early work on industrially practicable membranes is reported in *Journal of General Physiology* 28, no. 179 (1945) and *Journal of Physical Chemistry* 50, no. 53 (1946).

There has also been no sustained public attention to another possible alternative: electrically powered vehicles. On November 25, 1995, a battery-powered vehicle ran 238 miles before recharge, a mileage comparable to that of many gasoline-powered cars in an electric car race in New England. But little has resulted from this remarkable technical achievement.

As I have suggested, environmental neglect is often matched by lavish subsidies from governments to industrial firms. *Time* magazine recently reported that the Louisiana legislature exempted the Exxon Corporation from $213 million it owed the state in property taxes; Shell Oil was exempted from $140 million; International Paper Company, another $103 million; and Dow Chemical Company, $96 million.[82]

Such so-called corporate welfare has very real consequences:

> When government distributes handouts to select companies, someone else pays, either in higher taxes or in reduced services. Among the nation's most innocent victims: children who attend public schools. In some Louisiana parishes (counties), 20% or more of the industrial property taxes goes to education. *So every tax break granted to a company translates into less money for schools* [my italics].
>
> Consider the consequences of that policy for the 56,000 students in the East Baton Rouge Parish school system, the state's second largest after New Orleans. Every day, many of them face some or all of these afflictions: rat bites; roofs with holes in them; buildings whose antiquated wiring will not permit more than a few computers to work at one time; walls so damaged by water leaks that paint will not adhere to the plaster; floors so rotted that children put their feet through them; long lines to use outmoded bathrooms; sewage backups in classrooms; asthma and respiratory illnesses as a result of mildew and fungus in ancient air ducts; falling ceiling tiles; condemned rooms; collapsing partitions; unusable playgrounds; broken stairs; carpets that smell from the repeated leaks and flooding. . . .
>
> [A]t the same time the state passes out tax breaks wholesale, it does not contribute one cent to building construction or other capital needs of schools, as many other states do. All of which helps explain why Louisiana ranks 45th in the nation in spending on elementary and secondary education.

A review article for the nonspecialist is in *Scientific American*, July 1978. A paper on hydrophilic membranes was in the *Journal of Applied Polymer Science* 23, no. 2611 (1979) and was followed by a series of papers in the same field.

The same companies profiting from these tax cuts are further damaging the health of children:

> As if conditions inside Baton Rouge schools were not bad enough, students and teachers must also contend with pollution alerts. Listen to assistant superintendent Christine Arab describe life amid the petrochemical plants:
>
> "Certain schools are in wind patterns from chemical plants, and they have as part of their safety drill what's called shelter-in-place, where all the windows in the building must be shut, the doors sealed in a special way. No one can go outside. They stay right there until it's cleared.
>
> "Well, we had a barge overturn up on the north end of the river last year that was about a three- or four-day emergency, and we had kids sheltered in place for hours and had to wait for the wind to shift so we would [be] permitted to take the buses in and get out as many children as we could before the wind pattern changed again. Amazing. I thought to myself, I didn't know when I took this job that I would be issued a hard hat and a gas mask."[83]

These brief glimpses of data are merely illustrations of problems of the environmental neglect and destruction that have become endemic under the guidance of America's state and corporate managers. Air, water and soil resources continue to be consumed with the tacit assumption that these are available without limit. Readers wishing to learn more may turn to a series of well-informed studies on aspects of the environment. They come from the Worldwatch Institute.[84] Especially important, however, has been the work done by Barry Commoner, who trained as a biologist and then switched fields to focus on the environment. He has written a series of notable books and articles in which he emphasizes the importance of preventing environmental problems from arising rather than focusing on fixing the damage once done.*

This discussion of infrastructure, health care and environment reflects an important, though little-considered, aspect of state/corporate capitalism. For the designers and managers of state enterprises, there are "outsides" and "afterwards" for which they are not held accountable. The "outsides"

*See Barry Commoner, *The Closing Circle: Nature, Man, and Technology* (Bantam, 1974); *Global Resources: Perspectives and Alternatives: XIV Bobel Conference*, edited by Claire McRoartie (University Park Press, 1980); *Making Peace with the Planet* (Pantheon Books, 1990).

are events and conditions beyond the formal physical and social boundaries of their enterprise. The "afterwards" are events that take place after the completion of their agendas. So, what may happen to people or places long "after" the military or nuclear programs are completed is not considered the responsibility of the corporate or state enterprise that ordered them, as the radioactive poisoning of the population of the Western United States from nuclear testing shows only too well.

If a society's future economy is shaped by the evolution of the decision-making process in and around production, then why should anyone be surprised when alienation moves on behalf of accumulating profit/power without limit are given first place and quality of life, including the environment and infrastructure, is given low priority?

There is a growing gap between what exists and what can be achieved in producing—and living—conditions in the United States. This disparity is quite different from the simpler idea of increasing misery for the underclass. But the gap between reality and what is potentially feasible is dramatic. We all see, for example, scientific and documentary programs on television that present the latest advances in modern transportation. Yet quite a difference exists between that and what exists in present urban conveyances. And there is an obvious difference between first-class medical care and the kind available to most people, between the schools that our children are attending and those they could be attending. Print and electronic media of every sort depict the possible shape of modern housing, modern health care and modern education—all achievable with available technologies and resources in more than sufficient quantities for all. But real movement toward such achievement is stalled.

This disparity represents the cost in alienation of the U.S. military and political campaign for "global leadership."

As I have suggested, the corporate managers are prevented from considering alternatives by the perceived absence of sufficient profit.

The state managers are distracted by the insatiable resources required by their drive for global military-political hegemony.

The priorities of the corporate and state managers—ever more alienation and control—are not those of the American people.

How the U.S. War Economy Was Saved from Economic Conversion

The U.S. government's activities during the Cold War included two major operations to prevent planning for converting the military economy to civilian work. The first was the work of the Kennedy and Johnson administrations in 1963–64. The second was the work of President Bush's team, with Congressional leadership by Newt Gingrich.

The methods that were used in 1963–64 and later in 1989 were demonstrations of how state managerial institutional power was applied to prevent a weakening of the state/corporate controls over the war economy. In *The Permanent War Economy* I gave an account of how proposals for economic conversion, especially from Senator George McGovern, were quashed by a battery of executive branch officials who concealed the fact that during those very days their government was planning a war in Vietnam.

At the close of the 1980s, I was afforded a personal glimpse of operations by entrenched forces committed to preventing any such meaningful process of conversion. I had several meetings with Speaker of the House of Representatives Jim Wright in 1988. At a meeting that Wright convened of congressmen who were committed to support an economic conversion bill proposed by Representative Ted Weiss, I was excited to see a genuine political initiative for economic conversion.

In my conversations with Speaker Wright, he indicated that in his view the arms race had taken on not only dangerous but also economically damaging characteristics and that spending on the military, which took about half the federal budget, was a burden that sapped the strength of the whole society in many different ways. We discussed the prospects for economic conversion offered by the end of the Cold War, particularly the legislation proposed by Congressman Weiss.

The core provision of the Weiss bill was that every military-serving factory, base and laboratory be required to set up a labor-management Alternative Use Committee charged with investigating possible civilian products for the facility, its machinery and people. Retraining of people would be supported. Surrounding this core provision, designed to ensure a decentralized planning process, came a series of supports for further research and for relocating workers and their families, if required.

On the first day of the opening of the new Congress, the Speaker convened a meeting that included members who had proposed economic conversion legislation and their aides, to ensure that various proposals be joined into one combined bill built around the Weiss proposals. Wright said that the legislation would be given priority. Accordingly, he proposed that the bill be numbered as H.R. 103, reflecting the number of the Congress then about to open. He thought that this would have both symbolic and dramatic effect.

I left Wright's office elated. This was the first time that a senior member of the Congress or the Executive Branch had committed himself to sponsoring and otherwise moving economic conversion legislation into law. The staff members of SANE (the National Committee for a Sane Nuclear Policy), the peace organization of which I was then cochairman, were excited beyond words, for they too felt that we were on the verge of a momentous development.

But the supporters of such an initiative did not reckon with the enormous power of those opposed to any such move toward economic conversion. In the weeks that followed, these vested interests waged a concerted and aggressive campaign in Congress and the national media to bring down Jim Wright over allegations of financial misconduct. Though the allegations held little substance, the insurgent House Republicans, led by Newt Gingrich, representing the headquarters district of Lockheed-Martin, got their man. Their media campaign drowned out any further discussion of economic conversion.

On May 31, 1989, Wright resigned and addressed the House. To an assembly of full attendance by the membership, he undertook to respond, in detail, to the principal "charges" that had been made against him.

It was said that his wife had received a salary of $18,000 a year for four years, and that this was a camouflage for a gift (bribe) from a friend and businessman, Mr. George Mallick. His wife, said Wright, had been engaged to look into investment opportunities on behalf of both the Wright and Mallick families, and she did that work, for which she was particularly competent.

Wright was charged with use of a car and an apartment that had been paid for by someone else.

The Ethics Committee had suggested that since the Speaker's friend Mallick was in the real estate business, with some oil and gas investments, he was a person with an interest in legislation such as the tax code. To this the Speaker responded: "Who doesn't have an interest in the tax code?"

Also, there was the book of collected letters and speeches, *Reflections of a Public Man*, that the Speaker had put together. It was the contention of the Ethics Committee that the book, which sold for $3.25 a copy, was a subterfuge for exceeding the outside earnings limitation on a Member of Congress. The Speaker responded that, "If monetary gain had been my primary interest, don't you think I would have gone to one of the big Madison Avenue publishers, the houses there that give you a big advance? People on my staff were eager to sell these books. They knew I wanted them sold. I've got to accept some responsibility for that, if it was wrong . . . but the rules expressly exempt royalty income."

The Ethics Committee suggested that there were seven cases where individuals "associated with organizations to which I made speeches bought multiple copies of the books, and distributed them among members of organizations and others." Said the Speaker, "The total amount as I figure from all these sales that are involved is about $7,700." He indicated that the seven occasions were among the seven hundred speeches that he had given during the relevant period. He had received no honoraria at all for these speeches.

The case against Speaker Jim Wright was a sham. It was a political assault by the Republicans and their supporters in the media to get rid of an influential political figure whose orientation went against the basic interests of the government and corporate managers of America's militarized politics.

A historic opportunity had been destroyed.

The Industrial and Infrastructure Opportunity Cost of America's Nuclear Overkill

Earlier in this chapter, I called attention to the idea of assessing what we have been compelled to do without as a way of measuring a society-wide "opportunity cost" in relation to military expenditures. The idea of "opportunity cost" is most frequently applied to alternatives for choices by individuals, but something is gained by extending this view to options for a larger community. Recall that the estimated cost of the overkill portion of the U.S. nuclear military spending for 1940–1996 was $5,355 billion. This measures the part of the nuclear effort that has no conceivable military use.

Now consider that the 1996 cost of all the plant and equipment of manufacturing industry in the United States is $1,481 billion.[85] Allow that its initial purchase plus full replacement after, say, twenty years of use with another complete set, would cost about $2,962 billion. In addition, a national infrastructure repair would require an outlay, as I estimated, of $2,117 billion. All told, such major industrial and other reconstruction would cost $5,079 billion.

Weighed against the price of the overkill portion of the nuclear enterprise, this would leave an unassigned block of resources of $276 billion. In other words, for less than the price of nuclear overkill, the main physical base of the U.S. economy could have been regenerated.

All that was surely not the result of a miscalculation, of the error to which humans are all too prone. A more profound causal system has been at work. For the alienation drive that is harnessed to profit/power accumulation has, without formal design or plan, shaped the purposes to which the prime (human) capacities of American society have been applied.

Manpower Limits: A Lesson from Thermodynamics

When fuel (energy) is applied to an engine, part of the energy is consumed in performing the work for which the engine is operated. Another part is used up, unproductively, in heating the engine itself and the air around it. By analogy, we can think of an economy as an engine with finite labor resources as its energy. Part of that input does the essential work for which an economy is desired, producing consumer goods and services. A second part of the labor "energy" is used up in controlling, regulating and enforcing the rules of the engine/economy, but not in contributing directly to its main task. If an ever-increasing proportion of labor "energy" is devoted to this secondary, unproductive part of the economy, its ability to meet the consumption needs of a community is constrained, then diminished.

Pursuing this line of inquiry, I was prompted to ask whether the occupations in the United States can be classified into two main groups: those that primarily contribute to the *production* of consumer goods and services—directly and indirectly; and those primarily engaged in roles of economic *decision-making*, including enforcing and supporting the laws of the business decision process. To explore this issue, it seemed essential to discover if, over time, there was a change in the relations between what I call the decision process and the production occupations.

I soon found that the U.S. Census of Population, carried out every ten years, includes detailed reports that show occupations within industries. This provided a way to count the people working primarily in decision-process occupations, in contrast to production workers and others whose work primarily contributes to consumer goods and services. Furthermore, the industry numbers showed separate reports for major decision-process areas, like banking, insurance, real estate, government, police and military operations (i.e., enforcers of decision process).

The first such retabulation of the U.S. labor force could be done for 1910, and thereafter for 1930 and 1940. (An Occupation/ Industry report for 1920 was omitted by the Census Bureau.)

The results were revealing, showing a definite growth pattern in the *whole* U.S. economy, as follows:

	Decision Process : Production Occupations
1910	22.6 : 100
1930	31.0 : 100
1940	41.9 : 100

In other words, for every 100 people primarily producing consumer goods and services there were these others: 22.6 (1910), 31.0 (1930), and 41.9 (1940). These were men and women engaged in decision-process occupations, in administration and enforcement in both private and government employment. As the table shows, between 1910 and 1940, their numbers had nearly doubled relative to those engaged primarily in consumer services and in making consumer goods and the equipment for their production.

What had been going on *within* firms that might be at the root of such a development? I examined the numbers for a specific and essential part of the economy: manufacturing industries. There I discovered the same trend toward an inflation of decision-process man-hours compared with those used for production.

I first reported this in January 1951, in "The Rise of Administrative Overhead in the Manufacturing Industries of the U.S., 1899–1947,"[86] where I found that the number of "salaried" (i.e., administrative) employees as a ratio of production workers in manufacturing industries had indeed multiplied, and that such growth was characteristic of virtually all industries. In addition, I found that this could not have been simply the result of a sustained mechanization of production work, because office operations had also been intensively mechanized. (Only those firms that had grown the most had a lesser *rate* of administrative overhead increase.)

As the Census of Manufactures figures for the entire twentieth century show, increased intensity of managerial control over production workers has been a regular feature of industrial firms. For all U.S. manufacturing, the left column, below, shows the growing number of administrative ("salaried") employees (A) per hundred production workers (P). From 1899 to 1937, there was clearly a greater growth of administrative employees, hence an A/P ratio rising from 10:100 in 1899 to 18:100 by 1937. This paralleled the trend in decision-process occupations in the economy as a whole. Total salaries for administrative work (compared with production worker wages) grew at a lesser rate.

In Manufacturing Firms

	Administration: Production (employment)	**$ Salaries:$ Wages Paid to Production Workers**
1899	10:100	$19:100
1909	14:100	28:100
1914	14:100	33:100
1919	16:100	29:100
1929	18:100	31:100
1937	18:100	27:100

After World War II, the rise of the federal government's decision power (under state capitalism) was reflected in the structure of manufacturing firms. The ratios of administrative employees to production employees in manufacturing, and administrative salaries in relation to wages of production workers, had mushroomed.* The following table makes this clear.

The Rising A/P Ratio After World War II

	Administration: Production (employment)	**$ Salaries:$ Wages Paid to Production Workers**
1947	22:100	$31:100
1958	37:100	58:100
1967	38:100	62:100
1977	43:100	68:100
1982	54:100	85:100
1987	54:100	89:100
1992	56:100	99:100
1996	53:100	99:100

Clearly, from 1947 to 1996, administrative activity within manufacturing firms more than doubled. The growth in the salaries of managerial staffs has meant that by 1992 administrative personnel payments in U.S. manufacturing virtually equaled wages to production workers.†

*A considerable literature (books, journals, government reports) has elaborated one or another aspect of the rise of administrative overhead in industrial firms. Steven Rose and Anthony Carnevale, in *Education for What?: The New Office Economy* (Education Testing Service, 1998), have tried to identify the array of occupations involved. They judge that business professionals and managers account for 37 percent of all new jobs in the United States, 1989–1998. "These are the middle-level executives, the bankers, accountants, brokers, sales account representatives, insurance agents, advertising and public relations specialists, financial officers, analysts, buyers, personnel management and data processors who occupy America's ubiquitous office towers. Their annual pay averaged a healthy $46,000 in the mid 1990's." Rose and Carnevale write: "It takes less and less to produce a product or service, but more and more to promote it, manage the process, customize it, make it consumer friendly, deal with the style and convenience. No firm feels it can cut back without losing market share." They also find that "accountants, insurance agents and brokers qualify as office professionals, but not most engineers, scientists, architects, computer system analysts and technicians. Unless they have shifted to the office environment, they are classified as production people" (Louis Uchitelle in the *New York Times*, February 10, 1998).

†Could things be different? Ken Iverson, probably the most prominent steel industry manager, has demonstrated in his firm capability for industrial growth, productivity, profits—all while managing Nucor Corporation ($3.6 billion/year steel sales), with a head-

Yet the idea that wages to production workers dominate industrial costs has long been an article of faith among various commentators on industrial affairs. Accordingly, in the mania for downsizing and restructuring during the 1990s, it seemed altogether reasonable to focus on workers' wages to find and remove excess costs and thereby increase profits. But this cover story cannot survive close scrutiny, for administrative salaries, as a group, now equal production wages.

But aren't there more engineers and technologists in management now, making for greater efficiency? Part of the folk wisdom among economists and others is the idea that managing large firms has become more expensive, while production efficiency has multiplied. This rise in administrative costs, it is believed, is due to the well-known growth in the number of engineers whose work would tend to improve manufacturing efficiency, though they add to the salary bill for administrative employees.

It could be argued that the enormous increase in administration activity for the second half of the twentieth century is a result of that activity's being somehow different from the activity of the first half. The explosion of computer technology, the wide use of the Internet, the formation of new high-tech industries, the transfer of much retailing to Internet-based operation—all have been viewed as parts of a completely different, "hi-tech" way of organizing elemental economic activities.

In these latter developments, engineers and associated technologists play a significant role. Therefore, many have understood the visible and lavish expansion of administrative operations, office and staffs as the necessary accompaniment of the exploding technologies of a high-tech economy.

But the data do not bear this out.

For the 1990 Census of Population, the Bureau of the Census assembled numbers for 446 separately identified occupations in manufacturing.[87] I proceeded to separate out the production-worker occupations from the decision-process occupations in manufacturing: engineers, scientists, technicians and administrative groups. The next step was to assemble the all-economy Census of Population occupations in the same groupings that appear in the Census of Manufactures reports—administrative, scientific, engineering and technological occupations—as salaried employees; and, separately, the production workers' occupations. This corresponded to the "Salary, Production Worker" groupings of the Census of Manufactures.

These Census of Population data showed a ratio of 56 decision-

---

quarters staff of twenty-two, himself included, located above a garage in Charlotte, North Carolina. See Ken Iverson with Tom Varian, *Plain Talk: Lesson from a Business Maverick* (John Wiley, 1998).

process employees to 100 production workers in the nation's manufacturing, a ratio that corresponds precisely to the administrative:production worker ratio (A/P) resulting from the separate data of the Census of Manufactures.

Now, return to the engineers. In 1990, the ratio of engineers to production workers was 8:100 (based on data from the 1990 Population Census). This was a small part of the 56 engineer + technician + administrative employees per 100 production occupations in the 1990 Census count of manufacturing occupations. Assume, for the moment, that there were *no engineers at all* in manufacturing as reported in the all-economy, all-population Census of 1910. Even if the engineers represented an entirely new net increase in the number of administrative employees, the 1990 *actual* count of only 8 engineers per 100 production occupations from the Census of Population could not possibly account, alone, for the much greater ratio of 56 administrative employees per 100 production workers.

As the numbers show, the century-long rise of the Administrative:Production Worker ratio resulted from a marked expansion of administrative work and occupations and not from the number of engineers involved.

With this understanding of how decision-process occupations grew in importance within manufacturing firms, I was encouraged to examine once more the development of decision-process occupations within *the economy as a whole.*

For 1980, and again for 1990, I drew upon the detailed occupations-within-industry reports of the Censuses of Population. I regrouped the total gainfully employed labor force of the United States, which I then modified to include people who were not "gainfully employed" but still had an occupational classification. These included the unemployed, people in the armed forces and prisoners in federal, state and city jails. At first sight, this new classification may seem puzzling, until we consider that none of these people produce an economic product but are instead complying with the rules and controls of the decision process. Thus, I entered the unemployed as a part of the decision-process workforce. Their occupation consists of waiting on an employer's decision to (resume) work.

These new figures showed sharp increases after World War II in decision process in relation to primarily consumer-goods-producing occupations.

1980, 131:100

1990, 140:100

By recalling the pre–World War II results of these economy-wide comparisons, I was permitted a view of the trend in the latter half of the twentieth century. *In the economy as a whole*, the primarily decision-process occupations grew explosively under the impetus of both the Cold War and continued corporate managerial growth. Accordingly, the 1940 ratio of decision-process to consumer-production occupations,

1940, 42:100

expanded sharply to

1990, 140:100.

All this is consistent with the multilayered form of militarized state capitalism that had been installed in the United States. It has resulted in the expansion of central administrative offices in private firms and in government, and in the vast networks of military-serving firms, laboratories, military bases, schools—all in the service of enlarged state and corporate managements.

As we have seen in this and previous chapters, at the opening of the twenty-first century, the United States faced a definite inability to produce a host of capital and consumer goods. They must be imported, for the technological means of producing them, including the man-hours of necessary skilled workers, are absent from this country. When this deficiency becomes endemic, then, as we have seen, the economy and the associated fabric of society are severely stressed. In the next chapter, in the case of the former Soviet Union, we will see the effects of a total collapse in production.

In order to produce, there must indeed be decision-making. But decision-making, while necessary for production, is not part of it. As we noted earlier (in Chapter 1), production requires determining what to produce: the quantity; how to perform the production; the relative price of the product; and how to distribute the product. But the multiplication of the scope and intensity of such administrative work does not necessarily contribute to the quality of these decisions.[88] Indeed, detailed studies of management costs have demonstrated that bigger management does not necessarily mean better.[89]

In the American economy of the twentieth century, decision processes expanded, both within individual enterprises and in the economy as a whole. State controls and militarization compelled the man-hours used up on the decision process and its maintenance to become a major drain on the productive competence of the whole system.* This rising proportion of decision process to production work spells a growing difference between actual and possible levels of living.

The effects of a declining production capability can be held in check for some time. But a society beset with both the relentless growth of decision-process activity that is characteristic of militarized state capitalism, and with overblown administrative loads in firms and government, is made vulnerable to the corrosive effects visible in the Soviet Union by 1991. Russia has suffered the consequence of exactly those processes that we have seen at work in the U.S. economy. The difference is merely of degree, not of kind. There is no law of nature or man that exempts the United States from the devastating effects of the processes that ultimately ran the Soviet Union into the ground.

*A conceptually similar analysis was developed by Lloyd J. Dumas in *The Overburdened Economy: Uncovering the Causes of Chronic Unemployment, Inflation and National Decline* (University of California Press, 1986).

6

The Lessons of Soviet Russia: From Alienation to Production Collapse

The Soviet experience with production has indeed been unique in several respects. Its fixed capital—the factories, power plants and infrastructure facilities of its society—were cut down by successive wars. Russia suffered major destruction of its fixed capital in World War I, again during the civil war that followed the Soviet seizure of power and again in World War II. These losses—catastrophic in each case—had a major limiting effect on what could be achieved industrially, even by heroic, often brutal, effort and prioritization of its labor force.

From the beginning, the managers of Soviet state capitalism sought to consolidate their control over economy and society by methods of alienation that were fashioned to accomplish accumulation of capital and political power—following paths that were suited to the circumstances of Russia's history.

Soon after Lenin's party seized power in 1917 and fought a civil war against the White armies, which were supported by the Allied powers, the Soviet regime sought to restore an economy that had been decimated by the wars. Leon Trotsky organized "war communism," forcing tens of thousands into industrial labor.

During the 1930s, the regime undertook to eliminate the kulaks, the better-off peasants, or render them powerless. For their reeducation, they were deported to Asian spaces. At the same time, the bulk of farmers were herded into the managerially controlled kolkhoz, or collective farms, where hierarchical local and national management took charge. Stalin meanwhile organized an enormous system of forced labor that uprooted millions and imprisoned them in work camps, especially in Siberia and Central Asia, for coal, gold and other mining, railroad construction and forestry operations. In these camps the most appalling living and working conditions prevailed.

During Stalin's long tenure as top manager of Soviet state capitalism, his police and party machine seized and deported to Siberia and Central Asia the citizens of many Soviet republics, including Meskhetians, Volga Germans, Crimean Tatars and Ukrainian nationalists. People of the Baltic lands, Chechens, Ingush, Karachai and Kalmyks were also deported, then "rehabilitated" after World War II.

These population transfers were a major contribution to rendering powerless substantial segments of the Soviet population. That excursion into powerlessness helps explain the long-delayed disalienation process among Russian workers.

In sharp contrast with the Soviet experience, the United States has suffered no military operations on its soil (apart from the wars with American Indians) since the Civil War ended in 1865. America's fixed-capital facilities lasted through ordinary use.

Even after the fall of the Soviet Union, the Russian economic experience during the last decade of the twentieth century was highlighted by an incapacity to operate a diversified industrial system. Russia's production collapse was made infinitely worse by the chaotic, predatory operations of a new financial-managerial class who plucked society clean in pursuit of their own financial gains.

The National Production Collapse

During the Russian financial crisis in September–October 1998, the relatively well-off residents of Moscow felt the sting of the fall of the ruble: from 6R:$1.00 to 21.5R:$1.00. Suddenly, they were confronted by the degree to which Russia had become dependent upon imports for the most ordinary goods. As one writer realized in August 1998:

> Suddenly, something we all knew but rarely stopped to consider became painfully apparent: we produce virtually nothing. Over seven years of reform, Russia has not managed to manufacture any noticeable consumer goods.
>
> All the abundance to which we have become accustomed in recent years was imported: today it's there, tomorrow it's gone. Everything disappeared: screens, light bulbs, mops, door handles, chairs, pillows, shampoo, wallpaper, yeast, coffee, computers, blankets and pencils. They disappeared only to return later at inaccessible prices.[1]

One-time Yeltsin administration economist Mikhail G. Delyagin became an adviser to a former prime minister, Yevgeny M. Primakov, who told an American journalist that "he was appalled that his Duma office contained nothing manufactured in Russia except the map on the wall and the flag on his desk."[2]

Russia's leaders had declared a "market" economy. But who had become the main power wielders over the labor force in industry and on the farms, where about 20 percent of Russians still live and work? The following are several incisive diagnoses of the economic and political maladies afflicting Russia. Venyamin Sokolov, a director of the Chamber of Accounts of the Russian Federation, Russia's equivalent of the General Accounting Office, suggests that:

> The main culprit is the alliance the Russian Government has formed with powerful business interests. This alliance has been raiding the public treasury and depriving the Russian people of a secure and democratic future.
>
> Item: The Finance Ministry lent $150 million to the Moscow Aviation Production Combine so it could build MIG-29 fighter planes for sale to India. An audit . . . found that not one cent of the loan reached the enterprise. At the time of the "loan," the MIGs were already finished and ready for sale outside of the plant. . . .
>
> The Russian people are paying the price. When the World Bank lent Russia $90 million, the first third of it was set aside to compensate victims of bank frauds and pyramid schemes. Several years later, audits showed that not one victim had received the money.[3]

How have the new rulers attained their wealth and positions? Informed judgment is that they stole them.

> The small group of men who have corruptly seized the assets of the state flaunt their wealth as unthinkably as any czar. These men are the oligarchs. They have also robbed the government of its sinews—the tax revenues to maintain state services and infrastructure. The taxes from natural resources—especially gold, minerals, diamonds, and timber—once provided 75 percent of state revenues under the Soviet system. . . . These resources are controlled by the tycoons. . . .
>
> With remarkable aplomb, they confused cash flow of the [country] with their own cash flows to Zurich bank accounts. They used political contacts to keep subsidies going or avoid taxes.[4]

Unfortunately, the finance institutions that the new rulers established in the name of liberalizing the economy were given unique characteristics quite unlike similar operations in major industrial economies. Thus the new Russian financiers—and businessmen large and small who mimic their ways—have not been known as financiers of manufacturing industry.

> While banks were the foundation of many fortunes in Russia in the 1990s, they engaged in relatively little "real banking." Instead of playing the textbook role of taking deposits and lending money to fuel growth, Russian banks, including Uneximbank, became sprawling, industrial Goliaths, gorging themselves on wagers made in overheated financial markets. . . .
>
> Mr. Potanin [a banker] was retained as a consultant to the Government and designed the auction process, known as loans for shares. The auctions were overseen by Anatoly Chubais, one of his sponsors in Mr. Yeltsin's administration and a leading reformer. . . .
>
> The auctions gave Uneximbank control of Norilsk Nickel, one of the world's largest nickel producers; Sidanko, Russia's fifth largest oil company, and a bevy of other industrial concerns. Uneximbank was appointed by the Government to run the Norilsk auction—and somehow won with a bid just $100,000 above the opening price of $170 million after disqualifying a competing bid of $350 million.[5]

What of the brave new world of Russian entrepreneurship?

> Almost none of the money the young entrepreneurs are making leaves the trading sector. "They put no money into productive investment," Andrei said. "It's so easy to make money. I go to Germany, buy a big consignment of cigarettes and sell them and ship the money out to a bank in England. At this level of inflation, I need huge amounts of money to live. I cannot afford to invest. I'd risk bankruptcy if I invested. Also, the tax laws and investment laws change overnight. No one's interested in production."[6]

While the new Russian financiers remain preoccupied with enriching themselves, lesser lights and ordinary people have suffered the pain of income collapse. Skilled observers compared the drop in Russian income with the U.S. experience during the Great Depression.

> The decline of Russia in the 1990s is deeper than even the Great Depression in the United States. From 1929 to 1935, American national incomes and gross domestic product fell by a third; in

> Russia, real per capita incomes are down by as much as 80 percent.[7]

The Russian experience also included a long-term decay in infrastructure. I witnessed a part of this during a visit to Moscow in 1992. The main buildings of Moscow State University—a principal Soviet institution—were literally crumbling, with classrooms, halls, floors showing gross breakdown and disrepair. This was but a fragment of a countrywide process.

> The infrastructure—electric power, nuclear plants, railroads, sewage systems—is falling apart, the result of a plunge in real capital investment of 90 percent over the past several years. Today, most industrial enterprises are losing money, unable to pay their suppliers, their workers, or their taxes. Almost three quarters of the economy operates on barter. Only 8 percent of taxes due are paid in cash, and no one pays them on time. Most of the factories provide not value added but value subtracted.[8]

The Russian regime that founded the "market economy" was, of course, headquartered in Moscow, where large capital spending on city infrastructure was undertaken by the government and the newly rich. Under their auspices, the city was prettied up. But to make the "new look" plausible, the homeless poor had to be swept away. The municipal government organized and operated street sweeps that gathered the unemployed job-seekers and homeless from various Russian republics—all of them lacking the precious permit to live in Moscow. These jobless and homeless people were held in "Social Rehabilitation Centers" to await one-way tickets to their former hometowns.*

> "We don't want our city to look like the streets of New York or the shanty towns of Latin America," Aleksandr V. Zolin, one of the mayor's legal advisors, said in an interview. "We're not saying there should be an iron curtain separating Moscow from the rest of the country, but we don't need homeless vagrants or beggars here," he said. . . .

*The Moscow rules against vagabondage resemble the laws reported by Karl Marx (*Capital*, vol. 1, chap. 18) that followed upon Enclosure Acts—laws that swept peasant farmers from the feudal manor as a service to the lord of the manor, who was making the move from agriculture to more profitable sheep-grazing. The ex–peasant farmers, wrote Marx, "were chastised for this enforced transformation into vagabonds and paupers. Legislation treated them as 'voluntary criminals,' and assumed that it depended on their own goodwill to go on working under the old conditions that no longer existed" (p. 806).

According to this report, the Moscow police estimated that 20,000 out of a city of 8 million were homeless. With few shelters available, most of them were forced to live on the streets.

> "If people can afford to live here, they are welcome," Mr. Zolin said. "If they cannot, they should stay where they are. In our view, there is no freedom without financial means."
>
> "This is terrifying," said Sergei A. Kovalyov, a human rights advocate who is also a member of Parliament. "We are all children of the Soviet era, the Stalin era. We have seen deportations before. We must raise our voices against this." But on the bustling streets here, there is little sympathy for the beggars huddling in subway stations, the vagabonds lurching past gleaming new shops and the wrinkled women pleading for rubles. . . .

One victim of the forced deportations was a man named Ryazonov, forcibly detained in Social Rehabilitation Center No. 2:

> "In Moscow at least I have a job," said Mr. Ryazanov, who loaded vegetables in a local market before he was detained. There is little work in Frolovo, the town in southern Russia where he grew up and where he will soon return, he said. "There I have no job, no family, no home," he said. "There I will be homeless and a thief. How else will I survive without stealing food?"[9]

Underlying the income and infrastructure breakdown has been the collapse of the manufacturing industries. Except for top-priority industries, like the nuclear industry and missiles, the rest have suffered various stages of decay. As Galina Strela, executive secretary of the 50-million-member Russian Federation of Independent Trade Unions, has declared,

> Russian governments have created a semblance of private economy and market institutions. Underneath, the picture is one of rot and ruin.[10]

This showed up sharply in the auto and shoe industries and in the production of machine tools, that cornerstone of modern manufacturing:

> Back in 1972, when Smirnov [a machinist] first went to work here, Avtoliniya was at its zenith, with spanking new equipment imported from Italy and a work force of 1,800, which produced 400 machine tools and about 15 automated production lines a year. With large military contracts and a specialized work force,

> an important factory like his had the best housing, resorts and shops, and workers often earned more than directors. . . .
>
> A huge painting of Lenin presides over the peeling paint, oily puddles and rows of machines in various stages of decomposition and disassembly. On a locker, a sign in indelible ink reads, "No Nonferrous Metals, So Don't Break the Lock for Nothing."[11]

The car industry has suffered a similar fate:

> After the factory was privatized, criminal gangs began collecting a $100-per-car commission from trading companies—to ensure safe delivery. Thugs muscled their way into the factory, picking cars right off the assembly line. . . .
>
> . . . Until Avtovaz cleans up its act, the company is unlikely to get the investment it sorely needs. Its creaky factory, built by Fiat, is nearly 30 years old.[12]

Consumer-goods producers, such as Russia's shoe factories, have also shared in the collapse:

> Under Soviet rule, "10 October" used to churn out up to 80,000 pairs of footwear annually, including leather boots for the military. Now the factory makes 3,000 pairs a year at most, usually for barter deals with other bankrupt factories. Yet only about 300 of the original 1,100 employees have quit.
>
> It's not until 3:30 P.M. that somebody buys a pair of heavy black boots for 228 rubles, and the money is divvied up. Stanev's share amounts to $14.52 at the day's exchange rate of 16 rubles to the dollar . . . or about a third of the minimum number of rubles needed each month to survive.[13]

All this has inevitably affected farming and food supplies. After all, Russia once not only fed itself but also supplied grains to many other countries. The Ukraine was deservedly known as "the Breadbasket of Europe." Now farms are in disrepair, casualties of a centralized "military first" priority system that continues to strangle Russian industry.

> The demise of the Soviet Union gave workers [an] opportunity to break free of the collective. No one did.
>
> All workers received a handsome certificate allowing them to take about 10 acres of tilled land and 5 acres of pasture and farm it for themselves. Instead, the workers leased their land back to the

> farm, keeping only tiny plots for themselves to grow vegetables and perhaps raise a pig or a calf.
>
> "Nobody wanted to leave," recalled Mr. Remizov, the director now as in Soviet times. "People seem to be afraid of the uncertainty and the financial difficulties." . . .

Russian farmers are caught in a vicious circle: they cannot use their land as collateral for loans; there are few programs available to train them in management and accounting; worst of all, Russia lacks the infrastructure to sustain such a vast market.

> Loans are hard to come by. The regional government in Novgorod offered the farm a two-month loan at 25 percent, but the farm cannot afford to pay it back over such a short period and turned it down; . . . instead of buying new tractors and harvesters, old ones are lined up in a muddy lot awaiting the spare parts that the farm scrambles to buy.
>
> "We don't have a chance to buy basic equipment," Mr. Remizov said. "If I could get a loan for four years, I might take it."[14]

Most of Russia has suffered from food shortages, and ordinary people are pressed to till small, family-size garden plots. Not only does their output provide insurance against empty shops, they have also become, at the opening of the twenty-first century, an essential source of foodstuffs, the baseline food supply—especially for food that, in the absence of industrial canning operations, can withstand long storage.

> Even now Russia is facing regional shortages. Russia's Agriculture Ministry has reported shortages in 22 of the nation's 89 regions. . . . Russia's disastrous harvest—the worst in 45 years—is just part of the reason. The tendency of the nation's regions to go their own way, lax government management and Russia's financial crisis have turned a difficult situation into a desperate one. . . . Before its financial crisis, Russia used to import more than 40 per cent of its food.[15]

Little wonder that food imports have become so essential. As Andrei Katargin, manager of Novgorod's top meat-packing plant, observed:

> "In most of the farms of northwest Russia, veterinary work has deteriorated. . . . The selection of forage is bad. The meat we

> bought from Australia, Canada, and Europe before the crisis was not only of high quality; it was cheaper than the meat from the St. Petersburg area, two hours away."[16]

The critical condition of Russia's food supply is reflected in the scale of such imports. The Soviet regime imported large quantities of grain from the main surplus countries: the United States, Canada, Australia, Argentina. They were paid with the gold, petroleum, diamonds and timber that the Soviets could exchange for hard currencies. By the 1990s, that trade was checkmated by Russian shortages, while domestic food production fell and the need for imports soared. During 1999, Washington agreed to supply over 300 shiploads of basic foodstuffs to Russia.

> Under today's accord, the United States will supply 3.1 million metric tons of food. That supply includes 1.5 million tons of wheat, which is being provided free. Another 1.5 million tons of feed grain, meat, dry milk, soybeans, rice, corn and other commodities is being bought by Russia under extremely favorable terms: a 20-year loan at a nominal interest rate.[17]

To add to this already dire situation, the legacy of half a century of Cold War has also included environmental destruction on a massive scale. The worst of it comes as a consequence of Russia's nuclear operations.

> Kazakhstan has been in the nuclear business for a long time and has suffered greatly from both the literal and figurative fallout. The immense Soviet testing site at Semipalatinsk, about 500 miles northeast of Alma-Ata, has left a legacy of death and doom for thousands of miles around. . . .
>
> Superfine low-level radioactive dust from the test site not only blankets the capital but has been detected, by a U.S. geologist, in the glaciers atop Tian Shan peaks, which are higher than the Alps or the Rockies. Every morning when the old men and women sweep the streets with their long brooms of wooden branches, they swirl another cloud of radioactive particles into the air.[18]
>
> • • •
>
> At the first plutonium production site, Chelyabinsk-65, beginning in late 1948 the high-level liquid radioactive wastes were discharged directly into the Techa River. After the discovery of extensive radioactive contamination and severe radiation sickness among inhabitants downstream, the liquid wastes were diverted

> to nearby Lake Karachay. Precipitation of the solid radioactive pulp from the liquid slurry and tank storage of these wastes began at Chelyabinsk-65 in 1953. This same practice—tank storage of the pulp fraction and discharging the liquid fraction into open reservoirs—was used initially at Tomsk-7, where chemical separation of plutonium began in 1956. One of the waste storage tanks at Chelyabinsk-65 exploded in 1957, resulting in severe land contamination.[19]

The high priority given by the state to its nuclear projects led to a readiness to trade off countless lives against production quotas, despite evidence that the largest part of the enormous physical efforts during the Cold War devoted to nuclear weapons programs were far in excess of any military requirements.

> Between 1948 and 1958 workers at the production reactors, the radio-chemical plant (B Plant) and the plutonium metallurgy plant (C Plant) worked under exceedingly bad radiation exposure conditions. Punishment was meted out in the early days for failure to fill the plutonium quota at Reactor A, for failure of the plan for isolating plutonium at the B Plant, and untimely delivery of plutonium to the C Plant. There were criticality accidents at B Plant, and such accidents occurred frequently at C Plant. During the initial production period job-related radiation sickness was diagnosed in 2,089 workers, while 6,000 persons received a cumulative external dose greater than 100 rems; among them were persons who received 25 rems or more in the course of one year. According to published data 17,245 persons exceeded the permissible annual exposure level (established in 1952) of 25 rems. . . .*
>
> Because plutonium production was a higher priority than worker safety, many workers received doses exceeding the administrative limits established by the Ministry of Medium Machine Building.[20]

Why the colossal scale of the collapse on all fronts? What obstacles lie in the way of conversion from a military economy and long-term economic change? How have Russia's workers responded?

*A rad is the amount of absorbed radiation that will deposit 100 ergs of energy in each gram of absorbing material. The product of an absorbed dose in rads multiplied by an appropriate "relative biological effectiveness" factor is the rem. Kosta Tsipis, *Arsenal: Understanding Weapons in the Nuclear Age* (Simon & Schuster, 1983), pp. 55–56.

Overkill: U.S.S.R.

During the twentieth century, Russia has had an economy capable of huge production and capital accumulation. Its military production systems have been a primary instrument of power at home and abroad. The Cold War fueled alienation by Soviet state managers, as it did for their U.S. counterparts, as both strove to maintain and extend their concentration of decision power. It justified and gave impetus to this imperative at home. Externally, the Cold War provided a framework for driving toward world hegemony. Soviet armed forces, notably in the nuclear realm, were an expression of this power-seeking imperative.

Viktor N. Mikhailov, Russian Minister of Atomic Energy, visited the U.S. in September 1993 and was interviewed by journalists in several cities, providing an unprecedented glimpse into the Soviet nuclear arsenal. During the Cold War, he reported, the U.S.S.R. had produced 1,200 metric tons of highly enriched (weapons-grade) uranium: "That amount is enough to make 75,000 atomic bombs of the power that destroyed Hiroshima, or to energize a host of hydrogen bombs that would be even more deadly."[21]

What was the extent of the overkill embodied in that colossal effort? If we assume, as hypothetical targets, the total populations of both the United States and China, that calculation yields 1.463 billion people, hence 10,450 Hiroshima units. Allowing for a 30 percent weapons failure rate, the requirement would then be 13,585 Hiroshima-sized weapons for the nuclear destruction of China and the United States. But 13,585 is only 18 percent of the possible Soviet stock of 75,000 Hiroshima-sized warheads.

Therefore, by this reckoning, during the Cold War, the U.S.S.R. produced a stock of nuclear weapons with about 82 percent overkill.

Readers will recall that the U.S. nuclear overkill factor was 92 percent (as 8 percent of U.S. nuclear power could overwhelm the people of Russia and China).

While there are substantial data on the dollar costs of the U.S. nuclear enterprise and its products, no such public data exist for the U.S.S.R.'s comparable nuclear production establishment. Nevertheless, orders of magnitude can be surmised. The work of the Natural Resources Defense Council, a nongovernmental group in Washington, D.C., that has specialized in collating information on the Soviet Union's nuclear arsenal is invaluable in this respect. In 1995, three of their principal staff published a report called *Making the Russian Bomb: From Stalin to Yeltsin.* This is a compilation of a massive amount of technical data on the Soviet nuclear industry: it describes in detail its principal reactors and production centers, locations, staff of the nuclear enterprise and an excellent summary history of nuclear development, with data up to 1995. This volume contains a wealth of references to materials that would previously have been accessible only to science-trained Russian-language readers.

The authors found that the Soviets essentially matched, even exceeded, the scale of the U.S. nuclear enterprise, as well as the variety of its facilities and technological approaches.

USSR: Principal Nuclear Weapon Research, Test, and Production Facilities[22]

DESIGN LABORATORIES

All-Russian Scientific Research Institute of Experimental Physics (VNIIEF)
Arzamas-16 (Kremlev) 55° 23′N 43° 50′E at Sarova, Nizhniy Novgorod Oblast

All-Russian Scientific Research Institute of Technical Physics (VNIITF)
Chelyabinsk-70 (Snezhinsk) 56° 05′N 60° 44′E 20 km north of Kasli, Urals region

TEST SITES

Novaya Zemlya (central test site)
Northern and Southern Test Areas, two islands north of the Arctic Circle

Semipalatinsk (or Kazakh) Test Site (permanently closed in 1991)

Semipalatinsk-21
Shagan River, Degelen Mountain, and Konyastan test areas—south of Semipalatinsk, Kazakhstan

WARHEAD PRODUCTION (ASSEMBLY) FACILITIES

FINAL ASSEMBLY

Sverdlovsk-45 (Lesnoy) 58° 40′N 59° 48′E
at Nizhnyaya Tura, 200 km north of Yekaterinburg, Urals region

Zlatoust-36 (Trekhgornyy) 54° 42′N 58° 25′E
at Yuryuzan, 85 km southeast of Zlatoust, Urals region

Arzamas-16 (Kremlev) Avangard see above
at Sarova, Nizhniy Novgorod Oblast

COMPONENTS

Penza-19 (Zarechnyy) 53° 08′N 46° 35′E
at Kuznetsk, 115 km east of Penza

PLUTONIUM AND/OR TRITIUM PRODUCTION REACTORS

Mayak Chemical Combine
Chelyabinsk-65 (formerly Chelyabinsk-40)
(Ozersk) 55° 44′N 60° 54′E
at Lake Kyzyltash, near Kasli and Kyshtym, Chelyabinsk Oblast,
Urals region

Siberian Chemical Combine (SKhK)
Tomsk-7 (Seversk) 56° 37′N 84° 47′E
on the Tom River 15 km northwest of Tomsk in Siberia

Mining-Chemical Combine (GKhK)
Krasnoyarsk-26 (Zheleznogorsk) 56° 20′N 93° 36′E
on the Yenisey River 10 km north of Dodonovo near
Krasnoyarsk in Siberia

URANIUM ENRICHMENT FACILITIES

Ural Electrochemical Combine (UEKhK)
Sverdlovsk-44 (Novouralsk) 57° 15′N 59° 48′E
near Verkh-Neyvinsk, near Yekaterinburg, Urals region

Siberian Chemical Combine
Tomsk-7 (Seversk) see above
on the Tom River 15 km northwest of Tomsk in Siberia

Electrochemistry Combine
Krasnoyarsk-45 (Zelenogorsk) 56° 08′N 94° 29′E
on the Kan River between Krasnoyarsk and Kansk, Siberia

Electrolyzing Chemical Combine (AEKhK) 52° 31′N 103° 55′E
at Angarsk, 30 km northwest of Irkutsk in Siberia

The writers noted, for example, that in the United States plutonium, a scarce and costly resource, was typically reworked and reused when desired for new weapons designs. By contrast, in the Soviet scheme, the old weapons were kept and new plutonium was used for new weapons. There were evidently no cost constraints in the nuclear system on the use of this expensive material. In addition, while they constructed separation processes for nuclear warheads that matched the Oak Ridge and Hanford plants in the United States, the Soviets also produced and operated centrifuges for concentrating weapons-grade uranium. I am told that there was no counterpart in the United States to that effort.

In one major respect, though, the two military enterprises were closely matched. Both operated according to the principle that more is better. Thus, a massive number of weapons were produced in each country, exceeding any possible need, as revealed in the overkill estimates for the United States and the U.S.S.R.

As in America, the Soviets made a substantial effort to marshal scientific and engineering talent for these operations.

Included in the study *Making the Russian Bomb* is the compilation of a table of data (Table D.1, entitled, "Nuclear-Powered Vessels in Russia," p. 286). Details of cost, operating characteristics and technical design data are not given in the report, but a description of the scale and sophistication of the engineering work involved is very revealing. We are told, for instance,

> By the beginning of 1994, the Soviet Union . . . (now Russia) had constructed 256 nuclear-powered vessels including: 243 nuclear-powered submarines, three nuclear-powered cruisers, one nuclear-powered communications/missile-range ship, eight nuclear-powered icebreakers, and one nuclear-powered transport ship. Some 466–481 nuclear-reactors were on board these vessels. . . .
>
> Of the nuclear submarines, at least 121 have been retired, with possibly as many as 150 out of service. Taking into account three nuclear submarines which have sunk (1970, 1986, and 1989) and not been recovered, this leaves 90 to 119 operational submarines in the fleet as of 1994.[23]

This brief enumeration informs us that the Soviet Union possessed a large-scale manufacturing system that included the principal metalworking and electrical industries that will be found in the ordinary listings of the U.S. government's Census of Manufactures. Only a large-scale and highly diversified network of metallurgical and related industries could be capable of producing such quantities of attack submarines and of ballistic-missile-launching submarines. Even in the absence of detailed industrial-statistical information, it is reasonable to conclude that the Soviets operated a vast manufacturing system with the personnel and the means of production and engineering to turn out a great variety of complex weapons systems.

In a similar vein, fragments of data have also become available on Soviet biological warfare research and production facilities. A single article published on December 28, 1998, in the *New York Times* gave important insight into the probable scale of the U.S.S.R.'s large-scale preparation of bacteriological warfare matériel. The article included an illuminating photograph and description of fermenters used for preparing anthrax disease organisms: "Six stories high and two football fields long, the central factory there is filled with 10 giant fermentation vats, each meant to brew 5,000 gallons of anthrax microbes—enough to kill every man, woman and child in America many times over. Iraq's entire germ production could have just about fit into one of these vats. And Stepnogorsk was only one of six such Soviet plants."[24]

Of course, there were differences between the U.S. and Soviet enterprises in the details of the types of warheads and their functional assignment. But this does not obscure the ultimate point that the magnitude of nuclear-weapons production, including reactors and bomb factories, was comparable for both countries.

In the previous chapter, I discussed some of the principal economic consequences of what was forgone in the United States by virtue of the expenditure on the cost of the overkill part *alone* of the nuclear enterprise. We have no comparably detailed data for the U.S.S.R. nuclear effort. But it is nonetheless reasonable to infer that its capital cost was *far more* than the equivalent capital cost of one copy of the whole U.S. manufacturing system, complete plant and equipment (at 1996 costs). I judge this from the known cost of the American-produced nuclear overkill that far exceeded the net value of American manufacturing-industry plant and equipment. (See Chapter 5.) The Soviet military economy lost more than the Cold War. It cost Russia the opportunity to avoid a national collapse in production.

Achieving the scale of military overkill probably destroyed the Soviet industrial economy.

The Scale of the Collapse of the Militarized Soviet Economy

The Soviet Union constructed and operated a large industrial system for the production of every sort of weapon for land, sea and air units. The labor force required included a vast assembly of researchers, designers, operators of test facilities, industrial engineers and industrial workers in the thousands of vertically integrated manufacturing facilities that produced the means of destruction.

After 1991, there was a sharp reduction in government orders for matériel and in the size of the military budget. Despite special loans, grants and credits, military industry enterprises suffered a financial meltdown that had disastrous consequences for the entire Russian economy.

For the interested reader, I recommend the following authoritative manuals of military matériel in the arsenals of many governments, which can be found in most major university and public libraries. They include details of all the important Soviet weapons, as well as much information about the numbers in hand. A reader can also compare the Soviet weaponry of a particular class with its counterpart manufactured in the West.[25]

Jane's Armour and Artillery

Jane's Fighting Ships

Jane's Military Communications

Jane's All the World's Aircraft

Jane's Ammunition Handbook

Jane's Military Vehicles and Logistics

I rely on two independent estimates of the scale of Russia's military industry. One is the set of observations reported to me by a Russian industrial economist. After 1991, he was directed to survey major industrial districts: the number of factories, and their scale and role for the military. He found that, on the average, 70 percent of the activity of these industrial areas was on military account. To corroborate this we have the testimony of Major Alexander A. Belkin, who in 1992 wrote an article titled "Needed: A Russian Defense Policy" in the journal *Global Affairs*:[26]

> In the last years of the Soviet Union's existence, the fact that the military consumed 20 to 25 percent of our GNP was officially acknowledged. As a result, about 80 percent of Russia's industry is associated with military production. For example, about half of the enterprise in Moscow and about three-quarters in St. Petersburg are mostly engaged in military related production. By various estimates, from 7.3 to 16.4 million people were employed in nearly 5,000 plants of the Soviet military industrial complex.*

*There are no official Soviet data on the number of factories ("establishments" in the U.S. Census of Manufactures) that produced for the military. (Such data would correspond, roughly, to the number of firms that are "contractors" to the Pentagon.) Also, Major Belkin's figure of "5,000 plants of the Soviet military industrial complex" seems very small compared with, say, 20,000 and more U.S. contractors to the Pentagon. A major factor

But the meaning of such estimates is compounded by the presence in the Soviet Union of such institutions as a network of "closed cities," such as Sverdlovsk and Krasnoyarsk. These were cities that concentrated on various classes of secret military operations and functioned with strict security controls. They could not be located on Soviet maps.

Populations of the Ten "Closed" Cities in 1999[27]

Principal Soviet/Russian Nuclear Weapon Research, Test, and Production Facilities

Design laboratories	
Arzamas-16*	83,000
Chelyabinsk-70	48,000
Test sites	
Novaya Zemlya	not operating
Semipalatinsk-21	not operating
Warhead production (assembly) facilities	
Sverdlovsk-45	58,000
Zlatoust-36	33,000
Penza-19	64,000
Plutonium and/or tritium production reactors	
Chelyabinsk-65	88,000
Krasnoyarsk-26	100,000
Uranium enrichment facilities	
Sverdlovsk-44	96,000
Tomsk-7	119,000
Krasnoyarsk-45	67,000
Total	**756,000**

accounting for this difference is the mode of organization of Soviet industry. When managers were assigned responsibility for a particular product, Soviet conditions dictated maximum self-production of critical components. Dependence on subcontractors was thereby reduced and the size of the major "contractor" facilities was enlarged; hence relatively few "plants" produced for the Soviet military.

*The name and number of each "closed city" referred to the post office box number for the "closed" facility in a nearby "ordinary" city post office.

Visitors to these towns after the Soviet Union went under confirmed that these were entire communities focused on particular military projects, as Los Alamos, New Mexico, was engaged in designing nuclear weapons. Not only the physicists, engineers and production workers doing the direct hands-on work were militarily involved, but also the supporting population providing the infrastructure and security in the surrounding towns.

Large, vertically integrated industrial facilities were a standard pattern of the military economy. An enterprise was committed to delivering a product, and it was given the people and the facilities to do the job. But under Soviet conditions, the enterprise would also include a series of workshops producing components that, in the United States, would be purchased from subcontractors. (This may be a crucial factor in explaining the relatively small number of unit enterprises working for the Soviet military.) The money cost of this military establishment can be estimated only with some difficulty. One possible approach is afforded by the U.S.S.R. State Committee for Statistics' *Economic Survey Number 9*, which reported on budgeted expenditures for the military as well as for various civilian capital purposes (covering nine months of 1991, before the U.S.S.R. was formally dissolved).[28]

These data can be used to estimate, however crudely, the ratio of the military funds budgeted for 1991 compared with the money value of new civilian capital assets put in place. The lowest estimated ratio for the U.S.S.R. in 1991 was 122:100, meaning that for every hundred rubles of new civilian assets put in place, the military were allocated 122. (The highest conceivable estimated level was 372 rubles for the military per hundred rubles of new civilian assets.)

Even if we rely on a low estimate of the new capital assets budgeted in 1991, the crushing weight of the military economy is immediately obvious. This can be compared with similar ratios for other countries in 1989–1990:

New Military:Civilian Capital Assets

U.S.S.R.	122:100 (1991)*
United States	38:100
United Kingdom	31:100
Germany	14:100
Japan	4:100

*Except for the U.S.S.R., these data come from various volumes of the reports collected and published in United Nations, *National Accounts Statistics: Main Aggregate and Detailed Tables*, various years 1990–93.

These data clearly suggest a large weight of new military compared with new civilian capital assets. It is the kind of sustained military drain on the economy that goes far to explain its collapse by 1991.

THE MILITARY APPETITE FOR MACHINERY

Military production has an enormous appetite for machinery and allied capital goods. Indeed, a critical understanding of the decline of the Soviet economy may be found in the way Moscow allocated new machinery resources. During the period 1960–1980, Soviet machinery production had been falling, even as the proportion of military durables had been sharply rising. Thus "the military share rose from 19.0 percent in 1965 to 30.1 percent in 1980 and is projected to rise to a range of 32.8 to 37.2 percent by 1985." In the same period, the share of durable goods allocated for civilian work "fell from 70.2 percent in 1965 to 60.9 percent in 1980" and was "projected to fall to a range of 46.6 to 56.8 percent by 1985."[29]

Despite the political weight given by Soviet officials to the machine-tool industry, by 1994, three years after the dissolution of the regime, "nearly one third of Russian industry's machine tools and equipment [was] worn out and need[ed] replacement, and only 16% of machine tools in use in Russia . . . [met] world standards."[30]

As a result, by 1994 Russia ended up with 43 out of 88 former Soviet machine-tool plants. The rest were located in the other newly independent states. This broke up a network among the factories that had typically specialized in particular classes of machinery. The falloff in production, even of the most important machine tools, was dramatic. Thus, output of machining centers, computer-controlled machines of great versatility, was reduced to 130 units produced in 1994, compared with 1,269 in 1991. Since 1990, there had "practically been no replacement of machine tools in the country's stock of machinery."[31]

A report on the post-1991 metalworking equipment of Russian industry was prepared for the U.S. Commerce Department by an analyst headquartered in Moscow. The Far East is essential to the industry, because "the major importer of Russian machine tools is China whose orders make up 50 to 60% of the current output (especially from those plants based in Siberia)."[32]

Russia was left with half of its previous machine-tool capability. Without its own capital resources for replacement, it was forced to rely on financing from Russian banks that were conspicuously unready to back industrial investments. This is the state of affairs that permeates, and limits the possibility of reconstructing, Russia's industry and economy.

The loss of the machine-tool industry necessarily diminishes production capability in all capital durable goods. During 1991–1996, the industry collapsed.

> Before 1991, Russia was the world's fifth large[st] producer of metal-processing tools with seven percent of total global output. In 1996 it occupied twentieth place, with only 0.6 percent. Between 1992 and 1996 Russian machine tool industry lost 140,000 specialists, about half of all human resources. World machine-tool manufacturing, in contrast, has been growing since 1994, after the slump which ended in 1992–1993. World sales in 1996 amounted to US $38 billion, up 5.4 percent from 1995. The biggest machine-tool importers were the United States (US $3.6 billion) and China ($2.3 billion).
>
> According to Interfax, output by the machine-tool industry in 1992–1996 fell . . . from US $600 million to US $120 million in value. The data provided by GOSKOMSTAT (Russian State Statistics Committee) show that in 1991, Russia produced 67,500 units of machine-tools, in 1996—12,000 units, and in the first half of 1997—5,000 units.[33]

All this was anticipated by some analysts, notably by Professor Stanley H. Cohn, who wrote early on an article called "Declining Soviet Capital Productivity and the Soviet Military Industrial Complex." The gist of his analysis was that the productivity of industry was doomed to decline because of the degree to which the military-industrial complex was taking up vital equipment.[34] A listing from the Center for International Security and Arms Control of Stanford University, *American Ventures in Russia*, as of March 1995 further accounts for the later decline. Major players in the American military-industrial complex moved to join forces with various Soviet firms. They are able to purchase Russian talent at bargain basement rates.[35]

CONSUMER GOODS

The failure of the state-capitalist directorate to deliver on its promises of consumer goods was plainly visible by the 1980s. There were lines for everything (except in the "closed" cities). Discontent with material conditions of life, plus marked loosening of political controls on speech and the press, combined to produce a population so dissatisfied with its share of a militarized state capitalism as to welcome the dissolution of the Communist Party as well as the control apparatuses of the Soviet government.

In March 1992, during a visit to Germany, Mikhail Gorbachev said of the system, "It was not only economically deformed but also incapable of solving social problems. It survived only by imposing the yoke of militarism."[36]

For ordinary people in the Soviet Union, the steady decline in production brought a decline in the level of living. I have assembled data to show the direct purchasing power of work time. An hour of work time is the wage of Russian semiskilled production workers in 1988, 1993 and 1998. In each year, the prevailing wage was compared with the price of milk and other goods in ordinary shops in Moscow. For instance, in 1988 a production worker could buy a liter of milk with 9 minutes of earnings. But by 1993, the same purchase required the money equivalent of one hour of work; in August 1998, the liter went down to 18 minutes of a worker's wage. After the financial bust in that month, the milk cost one hour and 19 minutes of work time.

Purchasing Power of Work Time
(in Hours-Minutes), Moscow

	1988–1989	**1993**	**August 1998**	**December 1998**
Milk (liter)	0–9	1–0	0–18	1–19
Beef (kilo)	8–28	8–3	2–6	5–21
Coffee (kilo)	11–28	13–3	5–6	47–16
Tea (kilo)	0–39	23–14	2–36	26–16
Sugar (kilo)	0–38	2–31	0–18	1–26
Oranges (kilo)	3–57	7–12	0–42	3–17
Potatoes (kilo)	0–3	0–19	0–12	0–28
Bread (kilo)	0–9	0–17	0–30	0–55
Man's dress shirt	10–10	14–23	8–30	14–26
Woman's dress	41–15	97–9	34–12	85–20
Man's suit (wool)	102–16	359–43	85–30	262–34
Man's shoes	8–28	103–36	25–36	78–46
Gasoline (liter)	0–15	0–32	0–12	0–21
Television	163–51	503–36	153–48	787–41

What emerges from these data is a portrait of impoverishment, a quality of life in Russia such as is normally associated with the Third World.

Where were all the managers, engineers, designers, researchers, production managers, production workers and machine operators in the labor force? To put the matter somewhat differently, in the presence of the means of production that were in place from Soviet times, why was the entire labor force incapable of producing an ordinary amount of consumer goods? No military security considerations prevent the production of these goods. Why was the assembly of skilled workers of every sort collectively incapable of undertaking production of obviously desired consumer goods?

Beyond doubt, the managers and industrial workers had become accustomed to fulfilling orders from state managers, not from ordinary citizens who might conceivably express their desire for goods by appearing in the relevant shops to purchase them. But seven years had gone by from the breakdown of the Soviet control apparatus to the occurrence of the 1998 financial collapse.

The Economic Conversion Problem

The end of the Cold War was read in many countries as a signal to turn military economies to civilian work. *Economic conversion* was the name for such a process. But whenever this became a public issue, a repeated pattern played out. Managers, most engineers and workers in the war industry objected to the conversion idea as farfetched and impractical. They liked their salaries and were fearful of mass unemployment, loss of their home values and the breakup of community.

In the United States, universities graduated a considerable number of talented and politically motivated people interested in economic conversion. They identified with the ideal of a peaceful society and were at odds with the militarization of the economy and politics that had become a staple of public life during the half century of the Cold War.

I have had considerable experience with efforts in the United States and in Russia to address the problem of conversion from a military to a civilian economy. From about 1988 to the present, I have served as chairman of the National Commission for Economic Conversion and Disarmament. This private, nongovernmental group of economists, engineers and politically concerned people has attempted to formulate analyses and workable proposals for carrying out conversion from military to civilian work in the industrial economy, especially of the United States and the Soviet Union. I wrote on aspects of these subjects in many books, scholarly articles and newspaper reports. All this knowledge was subjected to a steady flow of critical comment.

The subject of economic conversion has been a part of almost every one of the books that I have published in this country. In 1988, I published

The Demilitarized Society: Disarmament and Conversion in Montreal. By 1990, a Russian translation of this book was available in Moscow from the Mir Press of Moscow. Sadly, it was the only Western book in Russian on the subject.

All the materials I wrote on economic conversion have contained a central theme: The core requirement for successful performance of competent conversion from military to civilian economy is the organization and operation of joint labor-management conversion committees in every factory and enterprise whose activity had to be dealt with. Unfortunately, these proposals and the orientation they represent have proved to be completely unacceptable to the managers of American and Soviet states and their assorted industrial enterprises. In the U.S.S.R., a variety of approaches were attempted, but they were all based on initiatives controlled by the "economic planning" institutions of the Soviet Union, centralized in the Gosplan (the State Planning Committee).*

While pursuing a 1980 study for the United Nations on the state of economic conversion planning in major countries, I visited the Deputy Chairman of the Soviet Ministry for Electrical Machinery Production. (I was told by another senior official that this man was "comparable to the Executive Vice President of your General Electric.") During the interview, which was to focus on problems of conversion to civilian economy, I asked whether the ministry had done any such planning. He responded, "What would you have us produce, kielbasa?" With that remark he burst out in extended and vigorous laughter.

Undeterred, seeking insight into the workings of the Soviet "priority system," I asked how he coped with problems of supply for the managers in his ministry. He said that if one of them faced a shortage, the enterprise manager would turn to the ministry, whereupon the Deputy Chairman would call his opposite number in the ministry dealing with that particular material, and thereby "we would solve the problem." I asked him to describe the last such problem that arose, and he mentioned a chemical material shortage in one of his ministry's factories. I said I thought he would not be able to do the same if he were in a similar post in a ministry dealing with, say, men's clothing.

Given the tenacious character of the priority system, it is no surprise that the production of military-serving machinery and other durables

*For a fairly detailed portrait of the economic conversion problem in Russian industry, see David Mandel, "Conversion in a Russian Defence Plant: Interview with Nikolai Prostov, Union President of Arsenal, St. Petersburg," *Socialist Alternatives* 3, no. 1 (1994). This interview was done in St. Petersburg in February 1994, and was translated by David Mandel (c/o Département de science politique, Université du Québec à Montréal, C.P. 8888, succ. "centre-ville," Montréal, Qué., H3C 3P8, Canada, Tel and Fax: 514-486-1958).

should continue to advance, even after the Cold War's end, at the same time that the total output of durables, including equipment for low-priority civilian industry groups, has declined.

By 1998, after several years of reductions in Russian military budgets—without parallel arrangements for economic conversion—the unions of workers in military industries sent an open letter to Boris Yeltsin:

> Mr. Boris Yeltsin,
> President of the Russian Federation
>
> The Executive Committee of the Association of the Russian Unions of Workers in the Defence Industries has repeatedly urged you, Mr. President, as well as the Governments of Gaidar, Chernomyrdin and Kiriyenko, to take measures in order to ensure stabilisation in the defence complex, a planned implementation of conversion, and the settlement of debts for work performed under government defence order. We have also drawn your attention to the fact that workers in the defence sector have not been paid their wages for more than a year. . . .
>
> It looks like our appeals either have failed to reach you or have been sent down to some lower executives who had neither sufficient authority nor any wish to tackle the problems in question. Meanwhile, the situation in the defence sector keeps growing worse. This has made us appeal to you through the mass media. We hope that this time you may become aware of the plight in which our country, the majority of its population and its defence potential have found themselves.
>
> None of your promises to raise the living standards has ever come true. None of your messages or decrees on overcoming the crisis has ever been carried out in most of the industries. Your actual policies and deeds are a far cry from your declarations. It is particularly true of the defence sector. The laws on conversion and government defence order[s], as well as your decrees on funding and stabilising the defence industry, are not being implemented. All remains on paper. The government defence order for 1998 has failed to reach the enterprises, and has not been funded. The debts for the last year's work amounting to 19.2 billion (new) roubles have still to be paid. The schemes of restructuring defence enterprises do not provide for any measure of social protection of the workers to be discharged. They lack comprehensive planning, while references to the experience in restructuring the coal industry are quite irrelevant.

> The reforms have pushed the people to the dangerous brink, where any further steps in this direction could have irreversibly negative social consequences.
>
> We are particularly concerned about the weakening of the national defence potential. The starving Army increasingly lacks up-to-date weapons. The development of modern military technology is not being funded. Some of the most sophisticated technologies for manufacturing armaments and civilian products have been lost. We suppose you are not informed of the crisis in the defence sector. If, however, you are aware of the situation, then we ask you: who is interested in the deliberate destruction of the military-industrial complex that is taking place? Such information must be made known to the broad public.
>
> We hope this appeal will reach you, and you will finally realise the scope of the tragic situation in Russia. We hope you will be able to muster enough courage to radically change your economic course so that it serves the interests of the domestic producers and the people of Russia. Otherwise millions of Russian citizens may think this country does not need such a President.
>
> *Presidents of the trade unions of workers in the defence industries*[37]

PLANNING BY GOSPLAN

None of this happened by chance, for Gosplan contained a defense production division within which military needs were given highest priority. Gosplan planning processes were hardly "rational." Thus it is the judgment of some scholars of the Soviet economy that Ministers of Defense were rarely the decision-makers with respect to procurement of military hardware. All that, it is said, was worked out in the Politburo itself, in concert with representatives of the military-industrial complex.

One unanticipated result of such procedures was that the armed services were often required to accept unneeded or shoddy equipment. Indeed, Julian Cooper has reported that the glasnost reforms instituted by Gorbachev at last made it possible for military customers to voice dissatisfaction with "poor-quality hardware exemplified by some naval equipment and the new TU-160 'Black Jack' long-range bomber." The latter, Cooper reports, "was transferred to the Air Force in an unfinished state requiring extensive debugging to convert into a viable operational system."[38] Lest we Westerners become complacent, the parallels with the United States are striking: this report seemed to replay the American experience with the production of the C5-A transport for the Air Force. There, too, unfinished planes (with thousands of parts missing) were signed off as completed, delivered and accepted by Air Force representatives. Of course, this occasioned fresh contracts for the purchase of the necessary components and their installation—all of this part of the normal cost-escalation process.

Among American academics there have been some who judged that the Russians would have little problem with proposing and implementing the conversion from military to civilian economy, "because they have planning." In reality, managers at all grades have been preoccupied with problems of maintaining and extending their power. Moving toward the manufacture of civilian goods was obviously no way to rise in priority ranking (hence in all-around importance). Accordingly, the industrial reality following the collapse of the Communist central-control apparatus left managers to carry on in their familiar cost-maximizing mode of operations. Characteristically, economic conversion to civilian production was strongly resisted throughout the 1990s by the managers of the military-industrial complex.

In Moscow in 1989, I visited factories and design offices of the Ilyushin aircraft company. The chief engineer explained that he had just been given a new assignment from Gosplan. In detail, Gosplan had drawn up a list of desirable new products and apportioned them among various industrial ministries that, in turn, assigned them to particular firms. Ilyushin, a veteran design and production firm for military and civilian aircraft, was asked to produce equipment for packaging spaghetti and for processing fur and leather. I was given a briefing on the characteristics of the spaghetti-packaging machine, which existed at that point only in drawings obtained from the Italian firm that had pioneered that equipment.

At a meeting with the general manager, the chief engineer and a Gosplan representative, I asked how they saw themselves as producers and marketers of such machinery. Typically, a supplier of industrial equipment is expected to provide a technician to install machines (notably larger and more expensive units) and train the staff of the buying company. A maintenance manual is usually sent with a new machine. But Ilyushin had no people with such experience. An industrial-equipment vendor is also expected to stock an inventory of replacement parts. But making such an inventory requires some knowledge of the realistic reliability of components as a guide to the number that should be kept in inventory, and Ilyushin was unaccustomed to such equipment. A machinery vendor also has to make available troubleshooting staff on short notice when required by purchasers of equipment (especially more expensive units)—in order to minimize downtime and its effects on a whole production process. But Ilyushin had no experience with the new equipment and no people trained and available to do this sort of troubleshooting. Moreover, the company had no one available with knowledge of competitive designs of such equipment in other countries. All this would ordinarily be expected of a firm specializing in a class of industrial machinery with a wide market.

My queries were referred to the Gosplan representative who had brought me to this factory. He responded that the assignment of these machinery products to Ilyushin was a decision of Gosplan and the aircraft industry ministry, and the company would have to cope with this assignment for the next three years. The Gosplan representative was unable to explain the possible meaning of the three-year assignment, or of the designation of Ilyushin as designer and producer of these machinery products.

A year later, I was in Moscow, again attending a conference on conversion, and Ilyushin's general manager told me, with much enthusiasm, that after my visit a year before, Gosplan withdrew these proposals, and the company was now designing and producing an advanced four-engine jet passenger liner for intercontinental passenger/freight use. Indeed, I was shown a mock-up of this plane, which was to carry engines from Pratt and Whitney, and avionics (mainly electronic control and navigation equipment) from Rockwell.

RUSSIAN AIRCRAFT AND AEROSPACE INDUSTRY

In 1993, a conference of the Russian aircraft and aerospace industry was convened by the government for the purpose of discussing methods and problems of economic conversion. My task was to outline the main requirements for successfully converting military industry to civilian work. I emphasized the importance of advance planning, with the main responsibility in the hands of a labor-management committee of the enterprise; of selecting alternative civilian products with an eye to both producibility and marketability; of providing professional retraining for workers, engineers, and managers; and of income support for workers to ensure the feasibility of retraining.

No single person from any of the aircraft and aerospace firms made any proposal on economic conversion. The implicit, unstated policy attitude of the industry officials was this: If you want us to do something, tell us what it is; tell us what the budget is, and so on.

I sat through several sessions with aircraft producers and felt fully briefed on the scale and variety of wind tunnels, experimental equipment, size of airfields, number of engineering staffs in principal aircraft manufacturing firms. There was no apparent connection between these self-serving presentations and economic conversion.

I took the floor and outlined a particular economic conversion perspective. I noted that every country needs a reliable food supply, and that Russia was deficient in that respect. Consider the availability of potatoes, a well-appreciated part of the Russian diet.

I reminded this high-tech group of something they all surely knew. The harvesting of potatoes has been typically carried out by shutting down schools, factories and government offices and piling people onto trucks and buses which carry them to the fields where they are to help in picking and gathering potatoes in baskets, and thereby contributing to the common food supply.

I told the audience I had recently studied potato harvesting methods in the United States and other countries and had obtained detailed specifications on machinery used for this purpose. I explained that from videotapes supplied by the potato-harvester producing firms, and from their catalogues, one obtained an appreciation of the high level of productivity that is possible with the use of such equipment.

Furthermore, I noted that the machinery for potato harvesting is of a sort whose components were readily producible in the general-purpose machine shops that are surely found in every aviation-industry factory in Russia. Even if such production were at first undertaken in a less organized way, the availability of this new equipment would begin to make a considerable difference in improving the productivity of this crop and would help reduce the normal waste in harvesting, which can range from 30 to 50 percent of the crop.

The response of the engineers and managers was of two sorts. First, the chairman of these sessions, a veteran manager, stated that since Russia was a very large country, with many parts inaccessible by water or other surface transportation, a large fleet of commercial aircraft was a necessity for travel within its bounds. But the existing aviation industry, he went on, did not have the capacity to produce a sufficient number of aircraft for such internal use. Left unstated was the assumption that whatever was needed here would be in addition to, on top of, the already large industrial capacity for producing fairly complicated military aircraft.

A second respondent introduced himself as the principal designer of Russia's guided missiles. He asked me whether I had ever planted a potato. I replied that I hadn't. He then proceeded to explain "how we do it in Russia." He had a small plot of land that he cultivated himself, from which he had filled twelve sacks with potatoes during the previous year. He was greeted by a round of applause.

As my suggestion had evidently been acceptably dealt with, I was about to leave the podium, but first I turned to the assembled group and said, "Perhaps I should explain why I have never planted a potato. Within a hundred yards of my apartment on Broadway, near Columbia University, there is a well-stocked fruit-and-vegetable market that is open twenty-four hours every day of the year, so when I need a potato I can get it."

As this frustrating story suggests, there is great reluctance to plan for conversion from a military to a civilian economy, or to undergo a process of demilitarization. Instead, top managers have pursued the idea of "dual-use" technology that is supposedly applicable to both military and civilian purposes. Since such programs are typically housed under the military directorate, they tend to carry the emphasis appropriate to their chief sponsor. During the Cold War, the Soviet industrial system in its entirety was a major exercise in dual use, with military enterprises being called upon from time to time to assist in some civilian production, and civilian industry—in the size of their enterprise, product design and production methods—required to bear responsibilities for potential military uses. So much for "dual use."

Workers in the Soviet Union

The lives of workers in the Soviet Union were not well reported. Perhaps this had something to do with the political design of the Soviet state. Since the Communist Party claimed to rule in the name of the workers, it may have seemed superfluous to develop a special literature about workers, who, by definition, were being spoken for by the leaders of the Soviet state.

Given the dire state of the Russian economy, however, the role of the workers has taken on a new urgency. It is thus essential for our purposes to know whether the workers have moved toward independent organizations comparable to trade unions and other groupings found in other countries. Independent inquiries on the behavior of Soviet workers became possible only with the advent of Mikhail Gorbachev and the policies of glasnost and perestroika (openness and reform) that he sponsored. It was then possible for a scholar of Soviet labor, David Mandel of the University of Quebec, to move relatively freely among workers in the U.S.S.R., interviewing them and recording their comments.*

From 1988 to 2000, Mandel paid successive visits to the Soviet Union and interviewed workers active in trade unions and in new forms of indus-

*See David Mandel, *Petrograd Workers and the Soviet Seizure of Power: From July Days, 1917 to July, 1918* (Macmillan, 1984), two volumes. Mandel did his doctoral studies at Columbia University, completing a path-breaking study on the early development of Soviet workers.

trial organization that were formed under Gorbachev, such as the work collectives. He interviewed these men and women about aspects of their working life, and published an important collection of these interviews in a volume titled *Rabotyagi: Perestroika and After Viewed from Below: Interviews with Workers in the Soviet Union* (Monthly Review Press, 1994). In the interviews that follow, the worker's name is followed by the page in *Rabotyagi.*

VOICES OF RUSSIAN WORKERS

In order to present a portrait of Soviet workers, I begin with excerpts from interviews by Mandel. These included interviews with workers in a locomotive factory, an automobile manufacturing plant, an optical factory and the postal system; agricultural machinery workers; members of the executive of the Independent Miners Union; and members of the Kirov Factory Workers Committee. I selected comments made by workers, often in response to questions from Mandel.

Over many decades of party and state rule, the relation of Russian workers to government has discouraged the growth of confidence in their capacity to shape events. During the last decades of the twentieth century, workers began to show initiatives vis-à-vis enterprise management, even while some maintained loyalty to Boris Yeltsin. That is one reason why the repeated strike actions of Russia's miners has had a possible leading-edge quality.

Mandel's respondents were typically activists with experience in organizing strike committees and other kinds of union groups. Many were skeptical about their leaders' willingness to allow worker participation. As a postal worker observed,

> Who is Yeltsin? A former Communist Party member, a man with totalitarian inclinations. I don't want to criticize the entire Communist movement. . . . Yeltsin spent his whole life in it, was a leader there . . . and one can't expect him to change completely.
>
> My prognosis is that since some 50 percent of the Russian Supreme Soviet consists of *nomenklatura,* we couldn't expect reforms that would improve the lot of the people (Tatyana Markova, 138).
>
> The party's leadership says it should seed its social base in the middle class. But that's totally detached from reality. What kind of middle class is there with so few skilled workers and when our entrepreneurs are basically recruited from the mafia-style elite of *nomenklatura*? (Tatyana Markova, 133).

Did the government ever explain its refusal to negotiate?

. . . To put it in the crudest and most abstract terms, we are witnessing a struggle between the Communist *boyars* [as in the Russian higher aristocracy] and the new bourgeoisie, the enterprising people, who used to serve those *boyars* as their ideologues but got tired of it. This new bourgeoisie wants to rise to the top itself (Aleksandr Sergeev, 183).

I've been told that at the start of perestroika, workers began to work more conscientiously because they believed that real change was coming.

That was very noticeable. People took hope. When the old leaders made speeches, especially Brezhnev, people switched off their televisions. Whatever they said was immediately of great historical value. In institutes of higher technical education, instead of studying their own fields of specialization, people studied quotations from these speeches. And any speech . . . was considered better the . . . more times the general secretary's name appeared. But with Gorbachev, people stopped studying his speeches and began to read them, people who before would never have opened a book of a general secretary's speeches (Grigorii Artemenko, 120).

Workers pressed by long delays in wage payments became sensitive to privileged people, such as the administrators of their own enterprises. Union staffers have reported, for example, on the growth of salaried employees in city and national governments.

You said that they were laying off workers. What about management?

No way! It's frightening how their numbers have grown. And now they've set up a computing center. What do they have to compute there? But they go ahead and announce that they're laying off locomotive brigades (Volodya Fedorov, 225).

And those who manage to accumulate capital, how do they do it?

Only through illegal methods. . . . It was easy. . . . They buy cigarettes in Moscow for two rubles a pack and sell them in Kaluga for four. . . . This kind of illegal accumulation really expanded under Brezhnev. You could make big money only by stealing from the state or by robbing your own comrades (Tatyana Markova, 140).

The formation and operation of cooperatives was also often viewed with dismay by workers. The new cooperatives, first set in motion during Gorbachev's tenure, were mainly in distributive services (retail).

> Already in 1989 the crisis began to emerge. A little later, the law on Cooperatives was adopted. . . . [I]t allowed the creation of cooperatives attached to state enterprises, and it made possible the transformation of non-cash credits from the enterprise's accounts into cash sums that were paid to the cooperatives, opening the way for large-scale theft from the state (Grigorii Artemenko, 120–21).

During a visit to a leading machine-tool firm, I was told about production limitations owing to the departure of younger, skilled workers to better-paid work prospects in cooperatives.

> Think about it: a worker spends his entire working life at an enterprise, and now, on the eve of market relations, he leaves with nothing but his minimal pension. After a life's work! Meanwhile, a director who has just been appointed, on the basis of a ministerial decree . . . is personally, along with other top management, designated as owner of the basic plant and resources of the enterprise (Vera Lashch, 105–6).
>
> Is there anywhere else in the world where wages constitute only 2 to 16 percent of the total cost of production? (Vera Lashch, 109).

Yeltsin's reformers launched a broad movement to transfer ownership and control of many Russian firms and industries to "private" persons or business groups. It was initiated with much fanfare about each citizen having a "certificate" that ostensibly represented a share of national wealth. But the managers of firms found ways to acquire these "shares" in blocks that carried voting rights. With the cooperation of well-connected officers of the *nomenklatura* who occupied key ministry posts, nominal ownership rights could be transformed into rights to control. Unsurprisingly, workers, who were outside such privileged circles, viewed such maneuvers with cynicism.

> *Well, do you support this economic reform?*
>
> Is there a question here? The *nomenklatura* sat on our necks and still sit on our necks. They stole and continue to steal. Who do you think the reform is for? The pensioners who have to stand in line for their pensions? (Aleksandr Safronov, 223–24).
>
> *Do the unions have a position on privatization?*
>
> Even if the workers are guaranteed 15 or 25 percent of the shares, they will own them individually—that won't give them control.

> Besides, in Russia the shares reserved for the workers are nonvoting (Grigorii Artemenko, 279–80).

> We need closer cooperation among the workers of all countries. . . . Without worker internationalism, without worker solidarity, things will only get worse. Our newfound capitalists are exporting our raw materials even though our factories stand idle. They sell them abroad for cheap, and workers elsewhere in the resource sector are without jobs. But our resources can be sold for cheap because our workers are paid nothing; we are turning into paupers. Of course, we need international solidarity (Grigorii Artemenko, 280).

One of the traditional devices of Soviet management was making especially scarce goods available to employees via the local union. Thereby the union was made into an institution held responsible by ordinary workers for allocating privileges—such as access to an overcoat, a car or household appliances. This practice—especially during periods of marked shortages—encouraged competition among workers (about whose child would go to summer camp, etc.).

Obviously, such sustained practices discouraged the development of solidarity among workers. That suited the local managers as well as their *nomenklatura* chain of command. Little has changed. Comments from workers in diverse industries testified to the widespread continuing use of such practices.

> There can't be any discipline in these conditions. People pay no attention to work. Look, they're selling winter boots for seventy rubles when they cost 400 in the shop. Why should I work, when I can make money by selling these boots? You're right, workers on the assembly line have to work all the same. But our technologists are constantly busy with these sales, taking people off the line who have cars to go pick up chickens or whatever else. Nothing at all is organized. Someone is to leave his work to go to the central warehouse, another to load and unload the goods, someone does selling, someone deals with the papers. It's a nightmare (Kolya Naumov, 101).

> . . . We get packages of food containing buckwheat, canned goods, noodles, chicken—things you can't get anywhere in the store. I wouldn't be able to feed or dress myself without the factory, so I won't leave it. I was talking with a guy about going to work for a cooperative. He said that it made no sense, since even if you earn 700 rubles a month, you can't buy anything with the money. You

have to go to the free market and all the money disappears. Here in the factory, you can play the fool and, if you have good relations with the management, not work, and dress and feed yourself. You can even do some selling and make money (Kolya Naumov, 100–101).

. . . In the past they were forced to distribute scarce consumer goods among their members—three cars among 1,000 workers—but I firmly declared at the factory that we would distribute nothing. Our union concerns are wages, employment, collective agreements, layoffs. We won't distribute anything because it's always a source of conflict and division among workers (Natalya Kuzental, 234).

I told Olga Vakulenko, the chairwoman of the district union council, that the work we were doing wasn't suitable for a union. . . . What was I doing? I was allocating one food mixer, one refrigerator, one vacuum cleaner for 600 people. We'd get one car in six months or a year, and it was a tough job figuring out what to do with it: veterans who had served at the front had priority, but so did workers with long seniority, and people who had been in line a long time (Aleksandr Safronov, 211).

Among Stalin's many innovations, there was his invention called the collective. That was the name of the enterprise organization used to harness the efforts of workers, clerks, foremen and all levels of administrators, finally including the enterprise director as well. (In a wider context, the collective of an industry included the ministers.) In theory, the difference between rulers and ruled was formally bridged. In practice, *nomenklaturists* dressed differently, had chauffeured cars, lived in special neighborhoods and often spoke in tones of authority and *hauteur* that ordinary people recognized. How much has changed?

A reform in the early 1980s gave the "work collectives" (that is, the entire enterprise labour force, including management) broad, if vaguely defined, powers to participate in managerial decisions. In practice, however, few workers had any knowledge of these rights (until Gorbachev's liberalization, it was practically impossible for any ordinary worker even to obtain a copy of the Labour Code), and even fewer ever saw them put into practice.*

What sort of union is it where management and workers are

*David Mandel, "The Trade-Union Movement in the Community of Independent States (CIS)," October 1993 (unpublished), p. 3.

> together? It's clear that the trade unions leaders will defend the positions of the administration, because they are dependent on the administration (Aleksandr Safronov, 217).

Nikolai Prostov, reform chairman of the (old) union at the Arsenal (defense) Factory in St. Petersburg, explained:

> You know, even I have problems trying to change my shop committees. . . . I've been telling the workers for a long time that they shouldn't elect managerial personnel to their shop committees. But the workers often have their own logic. They say: "We don't know much when it comes to managing production. The bosses know better. So let them be there." I answer: "But you have different interests. Why do you refuse to see that? You still trust the administration. . . ." Well, this is the mentality of dependents, who want to believe they'll be taken care of by the higher-ups. The problem is that management nowadays isn't taking such good care of the workers.*

It is a fateful statement: " 'We don't know much when it comes to managing production. The bosses know better. So let them be there.' " Readers will recall that the Soviet rule over Russia for the last three-fourths of the twentieth century entailed a dramatic population shift from only 20 to 80 percent urban and industrial. The industrialization process was under Stalinist authoritarian rule that included iron-fisted managerial control over the factory workplace and the newly urbanized workers. A tightly defined division of labor was also a built-in feature of technology training. Such conditions did not encourage the development of a decision process among workers that was competent to organize production. (In Part IV, I discuss this very idea as a central theme of the worker decision process.)

The breakdown of Russian civil production and failures of distribution, especially after 1991, led to widespread short-time working, compulsory "vacation time" (unpaid) and full-time without work. All this while the employment relation of workers to the managements of enterprise was maintained. In this dismal array of degrees of employment and unemployment, women workers had the worst of it.

The economic position of female workers deteriorated markedly during the 1990s. Many services like health care and education were left short of funds by a central government that operated in permanent financial crisis.

*Reported in Mandel, "The Trade Union Movement" [1993], pp. 11–12.

> The textile industry is not getting enough cotton. These workers are mothers, heads of large families. In the Soviet Union a family can't live on just the husband's wage (Vera Lashch, 110).

Women suffered particular discrimination as employment collapsed in most industries.

> The Soviet pattern was that a woman first got an education, then a lifelong job and finally a pension. It was very stable and secure. Now all this pattern is smashed. Women make up 70 percent of the unemployed. And of these unemployed women, 85 percent have higher or specialized educations. Now the placement officers say they should be cleaners or nurses, the lowest-paid, least prestigious jobs. They say women under 18 or over 45 should not be trained or retrained, because there are no jobs for them.[39]

During the Yeltsin regime and various "privatization" moves, transfer of major enterprise ownership was featured as a move from state to corporate ownership and control. Among workers the move from state to enterprise ownership was ambiguously understood. Mandel asked one union activist:

> *Do you think that workers support the idea of collective ownership?*
>
> They do, although they often don't realize it or fully understand its meaning. After all, we've lived with the idea for seventy years, and before that there was Russian peasant collectivism. They know for sure that they don't want to be hired labor. They're only now realizing that they were hired labor all their lives (Natalya Kuzental, 241).

In this atmosphere of confusion and deliberate manipulation, even genuine efforts at collective action could misfire. Take, for example, the unprecedented "job action, staged by air-traffic controllers in Moscow, who stayed on the job but refused to collect their pay."[40] While this could be interpreted optimistically as an assertion of the right to strike, the controllers denied a cardinal rule of the employment relationship, that workers' pay is linked to their work performance as specified by management. By breaking that linkage between payment and work, the controllers placed themselves in a weaker, not a stronger, position. This is the hostile environment in which Russian workers struggle to assert control over their working lives.*

*Many people outside the U.S.S.R. put great importance on the relative freeing of the

COAL MINERS ON STRIKE

In 1989, the coal miners initiated a nationwide strike movement, with profound effects for both workers and government. Under the Soviet regime, strikes had been outlawed. The remarkable degree of miners' solidarity was unexpected, as was the bitterness of their statements, demonstrating the way that strike waves could roll across the vast country without elaborate organization or communication.

This was the first industry-wide strike in the U.S.S.R. since 1962, when the workers of Novocherkassk, a small industrial city in the south, organized themselves spontaneously, put down their tools and marched to the city center. The strike in Novocherkassk was crushed in bloody style with heavy penalties not only on the strikers but on their families as well.[41]

Donetsk, 1989–1990

By the close of the 1980s, the level of living for Soviet miners had become unbearable. Long-suffering workers could no longer bear deteriorated conditions that included even the unavailability of soap. The already modest standards of Russian mining communities could not be sustained. While news of the privileged populations of the "closed cities" was certainly not reported in the media, word of good living for parts of the society could not be completely suppressed. The miners also responded to ideas being floated, under Gorbachev, about new forms of industrial organizations.

In the late 1980s, American journalists reported on a rising tide of miners' demands.

> As in Siberia's Kuznetsk Basin, the miners' demands—for more financial and managerial independence from government officials, for the right to create independent trade unions and the right to sell excess coal abroad to benefit local workers—were loaded with political implications.[42]

Russian press during the Gorbachev period. Some journalists saw it differently: "The novelty of a liberated press and unfettered political debate may intoxicate the Moscow intellectuals, but in the factories and villages *glasnost* has largely served to publicize the miseries people already knew—overcrowded housing, empty stores, crime and a poisoned environment—without instilling any confidence that those problems would be solved" (Bill Keller, "Worry for Gorbachev; Workers, Resentful of His Changes, Could Topple Crippled Economy," *New York Times*, July 26, 1989).

Among miners, both the economic and political aspects of their predicament were desperately debated. So reporters were not wanting for newsworthy formulations. In Donetsk (1990), for example, one miner,

> Dena Shelopodin, showed an understanding of Gorbachev's dilemma, saying: "I realize the problem. He wants to satisfy demands, but where is the money supposed to come from? The economy is a mess for everyone. If they give us raises, isn't everyone going to want the same thing? In the end, the point of perestroika is going to have to be generation of wealth all around so that all of us can live better. Without that, we're all going to be in very bad shape."

The same *Washington Post* reporter found that not only managers and the government's top leaders, but also the Soviet trade unions, were targeted by the miners' rebellion.

> Workers have long regarded Soviet unions, which are largely instruments of government control, with suspicion and contempt. Many miners have been discussing the formation of an independent union, perhaps one modeled on Solidarity in Poland, which grew into a full-fledged political opposition movement.[43]

Years of accumulated grievances had been left unattended. The chiefs of the Soviet state, however adept at juggling shortages, were at the limit of their capability—within their bedrock priority requirements and in terms of actual supplies. The miners were left with their ultimate weapon: refusal to obey the order to work. But their animus also turned on the state and its core instrument, the Communist Party.

> Miners walked away from their jobs for 24 hours despite appeals from the Soviet government and party. . . .
>
> "We should kick the party not only out of the Ukraine, but everywhere," mine construction worker Viktor Kitenko declared, speaking at a rally in Donetsk, the center of the eastern Ukraine's Don River coal basin. . . . The rally passed a resolution demanding that the government of Prime Minister Nikolai I. Ryzhkov resign, that party cells be removed from mines, economic enterprises, the KGB, army and police, and that party property be nationalized. . . .
>
> One woman screamed: "Let them give back the 9–10 billion rubles they stole from our work!" It was not clear exactly what she

> was referring to, but the party last week set a value on its property at 4.9 billion rubles, $8.2 billion at the official exchange rate.
>
> One widow of a miner who died of black lung disease, a black scarf around her head and her voice cracking, addressed the crowd. "Miners, you all have these lungs," she said. "You breathe what no human being should breathe."[44]

All this, and on public display, was not enough to dissuade Gorbachev from exhibiting the typical top manager's public reaction to the large-scale miners' strike.

> Speaking Wednesday morning at the Communist Party congress in Moscow, Gorbachev labeled the strike a flop.

Nevertheless, reporters had little difficulty discovering what was moving the miners to commit these un-Soviet acts. They found that

> Groceries, clothing, television sets and household appliances are scarce in the working-class city of about 400,000. Clerks at a food shop in the city center said neither meat nor cheese had been sold there for nearly a month.

Furthermore, state-run television gave some clues during a news broadcast that

> The average Soviet miner has a life expectancy of 48 years. Only one in 20 reaches retirement age, 55. Due to often slipshod safety conditions, 800 miners are killed annually in accidents at work. Work conditions for miners are so strenuous and they fall ill so often that the physical condition of mine workers between the ages of 35 and 39 can be compared to men aged 55 to 59 in other professions. 365,000 Soviet miners are waiting for proper housing, a major problem in this country with a chronic housing shortage.[45]

Spokesmen for striking miners were not reluctant to define the wider economic issues involved in these unprecedented mass actions by the miners.

> "They don't want to talk about the economic future, about what we want now," said Viktor B. Shumyatsky of the strike committee. "They want to talk about the Black Sea fleet. We don't understand

> why we need it. We think Kravchuk raises it to make people forget about the price of bread.". . . Industry is so backward and uneconomic, they suggested, that much of it could not survive in a free market. This, they said, gives workers the choice of accepting a bad deal or losing their jobs. . . . If the unprofitable mines are closed, as they should be, Mr. Krylov said, there are no other jobs for miners, and the Government has not accepted union proposals to create alternatives.[46]

The technical challenges faced by the Donetsk mines were also a substantial factor in the miners' readiness to strike.

> Aleksandr Kozlov, 41, the leader of a seven-man brigade in the October Mine, said the operation had become so insolvent that little could be done to prevent the number of accidents from increasing. Ukraine's mines are among the deepest in the world, and the death rates from mine accidents are estimated to be five times higher than in Russia and 75 times higher than in the United States.*
>
> "To get to the emergency elevator, you have to crawl five kilometers in 45 minutes because that's how long the respirator lasts," Mr. Kozlov said, referring to a three-mile distance. "But given the hot temperature down there and the lack of air, there's no way you could make the distance in that time."[47]

Despite this unrest, changes in the Moscow regime from 1989 to 1996 failed to produce solutions to the coal miners' woes. By 1996, resentment toward the government boiled over into a nationwide strike. The miners' union tried to get the attention of the government by many methods: petitions, letters, pleas to the press, a continuous miners' picket outside the parliament. No response. Finally, they took action:

> "We'll make them respect us and teach them a lesson," said Ivan Mokhnachuk, deputy head of the Union of Coal Industry Workers. He estimated that in Russia, 161 pits and 32 opencast mines—88 percent of the pits and half of the collieries—

*The Soviets' labor-intensive coal industry employs 2.5 million miners, from the western Ukraine to Sakhalin Island in the Far East. They produce about 800 million tons a year [about 300 tons per man-year], while the highly mechanized industry in the United States, employing 140,000 miners, produced about a billion tons last year [about 7,000 tons per man-year]. Felicity Barringer, "U.S. and Soviet Miners Meet and Find Surprises," *New York Times*, January 22, 1990.

joined the strike on its first day. Russian independent television reported that about 75 percent of the coal industry had been closed down.

The strike began in the Far East in the morning and rolled westward. According to the Interfax, by day's end it had closed mines from Sakhalin in the Far East to Siberia, the Urals, south and central Russia and the Donetsk region in Ukraine. Some mines stopped work altogether, while others continued to dig coal but refused to ship it to customers. "The participation of workers exceeded expectations," said Vitaly Budko, chairman of the union.

Some of the strongest protests came in Vorkuta, in the icy Arctic, where thousands of miners held a demonstration and voted a resolution demanding the resignation of Yeltsin and his government "for carrying out a policy of popular impoverishment and breakup of the national economy."

They vowed not to support Yeltsin or Prime Minister Viktor Chernomyrdin if either runs for president in June. Viktor Semyonov, head of an independent union of Vorkuta miners, told Interfax that "if the Finance Ministry has managed to find money for the continuation of the war in Chechnya, let it find some for the miners."[48]

The miners' strikes were at once a sustained demand for immediate changes, like paying wages and supplying soap, but also a declaration of political resistance to the Moscow regime. As successive strike waves spent their force without producing a major change in the regime, miners were radicalized. They started talking about getting rid of the government chiefs altogether. This from one miner who took advantage of the presence of a reporter:

"First, the Government should resign and then be tried—Gorbachev, Yeltsin, that whole crowd," said Nikolai A. Volodin as he headed down the shaft for the three-mile underground train journey to the still-plentiful coal deposits.[49]

The miners were the first industrial group to mount strike actions from the time of Gorbachev and since. Why they did so was described by a close student of the miners' movement:

Miners are fed up with working and living on their knees. If it is as yet impossible to work in another way, it is worthwhile trying to at least live like human beings.

> And here to all appearances the vanguard role of miners serves a large number of reasons that are rooted both in the specifics of mining work (the constant threat of accidents and death, habituation to collective discipline and interaction, etc.), and in a number of social characteristics of miners: first, the quite high share of young educated people. Thus, among the miners we polled in the city of Donetsk at the end of January 1990, 20 percent were young people under 30, 25 percent were under 34 years, and another 21 percent were under 39. One-third of the respondents (32 percent) had secondary technical education; one-fifth (21 percent) had higher and incomplete higher education.[50]

The General Confederation of Trade Unions, headquartered in Moscow, reports on the desperation that has seized many Russian workers. Here is a verbatim account.

> **Ukraine: Hair-Raising Ultimatum**
>
> An attempt at mass suicide was made at the Barakov pit in the coal-mining town of Krasnodon in February 1999. The miners were on a hunger strike underground, protesting against the non-payment of their hard-earned money. As the miners' union puts it, 30 desperate hunger-strikers gave a terrifying ultimatum to the management. They warned that unless their demands were met, every two hours two miners would cut their veins. And they kept their word. By late afternoon on 22 February, nine participants had attempted to commit suicide. The local union leader went down to the pit-face accompanied by doctors who attended to the victims.
>
> The result was that 168 thousand hrivnyas out of the 10 million (roughly equivalent to US $3 million) were transferred to the pit where wages had not been paid for a year. The money will probably be paid to the 30 participants of the hair-raising [ultimatum] whose unpaid wages amount to 150 thousand hrivnyas.[51]

The experience of coal miners at work and in politics had a transforming effect on many of them. They no longer accepted that government officials were working, however remotely, on behalf of the workers, for a better life.

The malaise that moved miners and other industrial workers of Russia to strike was not, of course, restricted to those occupations. White-collar employees and the intelligentsia have not been able to wax enthusiastic about the installation in Russia of America's finance-capital culture. Somehow, the Dow Jones Index hitting 10,000 does not trigger a sense of joyous accomplishment.

> Mr. Khomko, a big, burly man with a thick moustache [an artist], spoke of the failings with the passion of a man betrayed. . . . "My father always believed them when they insisted it would get better. 'As soon as we break the blockade it will be good,' they said. Then, 'As soon as the war ends, we will live.' Then, 'Wait till we do this,' 'Wait till we finish that,' " Mr. Khomko declared, lacing his monologue with ever more potent curses.
>
> "After the war my father was promised an apartment, but it went to the secretary of the party leader. We got a basement with no toilet or running water—my parents, five of us, Granny. But my father still believed. 'You're a Communist,' they told him. 'You can wait. There are people who live worse than you.' " . . .
>
> "We were raised on this enthusiasm. He was of that breed of party workhorse that served the apparat. I believed it, too, I spent 18 years in the party, I worked on the Baikal-Amur Railway, I celebrated the first anniversary of the Afghan invasion. Then I got sick of enthusiasm. I got sick of being a fool. I got sick of authorities."[52]

LIMITS OF WORKERS' ORGANIZATION IN RUSSIA

Despite the conspicuous efforts of the miners, and widespread dissatisfaction throughout the Russian workforce, the prospects for genuine workplace democracy remain dim. The long regime of Stalinism did not equip workers with traditions of solidarity, mutual trust and confidence in independent organizations. So even after the formal dismantling of the Communist state apparatus in 1991, the managers of enterprises continued in place, and were generally recognized as appropriate members of the new business "collective." Workers continued to rely on their managers as available channels to the top levels of state management. The miners' union proved to be virtually the only major industrial-worker grouping with the capacity for sustained organizational cohesion and action.

Factory, enterprise and other local-level initiatives by workers have been widespread since 1991. But on the whole they did not endure as continuing organizations whose strength came "from below."

In addition to the invaluable work of David Mandel, there are the researchers and writers of "The Workers' Movement in Russia." Their recent investigations of a series of important worker initiatives in several industries led them to conclude that

> The relative consolidation of the power structure meant that management was increasingly willing to victimize worker activists, and the courts were increasingly ready to support such dismissals. . . .
>
> Where workers in the past did have channels through which they could take grievances, even if those grievances only disappeared upstairs, today there are none, apart from the courts, which are costly, tardy, and operate with little regard for the law. True, there is no gulag, nor confinement in a psychiatric hospital, to greet the protester. But, increasingly, worker activists are being threatened, beaten up, and on occasion assassinated. . . .
>
> Nevertheless . . . small groups of worker activists are still engaged in struggling for their rights in virtually every large enterprise in Russia, and the new workers' organizations have put these activists in contact with one another, at enterprise, city and even national level, whereas before 1987 even communication between activists in neighbouring shops in the same factory was rare and dangerous. Conflict is still endemic on the shop floor, with the new issues of privatization and redundancy joining the old issues of job control, the allocation of work and the distribution of benefits.[53]

Despite these pessimistic conclusions, it is reasonable to judge that at the opening of the twenty-first century, Russian workers have new opportunities for independent initiatives, even as they confront considerable obstacles in the way of achieving workplace democracy.

I have defined the economic constraints that stem from the concentration of manpower in decision-process activities of every sort, instead of in the production of consumer goods and services.

As we have seen, in the development of the Russian economy we can trace a major development of just this sort. Decision-making of both state and enterprise management was oriented toward the extension of managerial power. The workforce was mobilized in controlled "company unions" that organized workers under Communist Party supervision; their control blocked the development of any sustained process of disalienated decision-making with respect to worker group, work time, deployment, performance or compensation. This is a legacy that still haunts the Russian economy.

The scale of the Soviet control apparatus had a restraining effect on the development of labor productivity. Studies of productivity processes in the United States and England have shown a linkage between changes in the relative cost of labor to machinery, and management decisions on degree of mechanization of work. Thus managers of profit-maximizing, but also cost-minimizing, industrial firms have used increased mechanization as an offset to wage increases. In a similar vein, managers have focused on achieving stable output rates, as that tends to increase productivity both of labor and of capital (plant and equipment). Management interest in all such technologies is diminished, however, when there is no independent-worker wage pressure, or wage pressure from market conditions, or—as in military-serving industry—when profit is pursued by maximizing cost.

An Inability to Break Out of Irrational Accumulation

I have noted that the U.S. government had ordered the production of nuclear weapons in quantities that exceeded any plausible military requirement. Similar reasoning holds for the Russian nuclear stockpile.

Why were the state managers of these economies unable to abandon the pattern of irrational accumulation, even when large resources were at stake? In both societies, two mechanisms have predominated: first, the professional imperative associated with status in large military establishments; second, a much wider political-economic imperative, linked to competition for accumulating decision power in managerially controlled societies.

To illustrate the first of these mechanisms, we have only to consider the characteristic pattern that surrounds military-political decisions about ordinary weapons (see Chapter 5). Military officers declared "superiority" as their goal in nuclear weapons. But as we have seen, accumulation was never stopped for military reasons, since what was wanted was "more."

Lest we should think that this trend is confined to the military economy, we should consider the drive toward irrational accumulation in the wider economy. As we see in both the United States and Russia, pervasive competition for enlargement of decision power is a potent force in a capitalist (and state-capitalist) economy.

For Russia, like the United States, the roots of both these trends reach back to the beginning of the Cold War. We learn from Alexander Werth of the *Sunday Times* (London) of the immediate effect of Hiroshima on the Russian people: "The news had an acutely depressing effect on everybody. It was clearly realized that this was a New Fact in the world's power politics, that the bomb constituted a threat to Russia, and some Russian pessimists I talked to that day dismally remarked that Russia's desperately hard victory over Germany was now 'as good as wasted.' "[54]

Stalin issued a "call to arms" in August 1945. He summoned Boris L. Vannikov, the People's Commissar of Munitions, and his deputies to the

Kremlin. There they were met by Igor Kurchatov, a principal science adviser. Stalin reportedly said, "A single demand of you, comrades. Provide us with atomic weapons in the shortest possible time! You know that Hiroshima has shaken the whole world. The balance of power has been destroyed! Provide the bomb—it will remove a great danger from us."[55] Nor did it escape the attention of Soviet *Nomenklaturists* that the man in overall charge of the Soviet nuclear effort was Lavrenty Beria, Stalin's chief enforcer.

In combination, the military-professional imperative and the drive to accumulate economic decision power account for the otherwise irrational production and accumulation of nuclear weapons. Given the known physical scale of their Russian nuclear arsenal and its production system, we can infer that at the very least the Soviets used up resources for the overkill part of this enterprise at least equal in cost to one complete set of equivalent U.S. manufacturing industry plant and equipment. Nor can it be said that either the Soviet or American nuclear enterprise as a whole was needed for defense. They were but a product of irrational accumulation.

But the scale in both the United States and Russia in the latter half of the twentieth century reached new and unprecedented extremes. No leaders of state-capitalist economies have pursued economic conversion. The U.S. and Soviet imperatives for armed forces and weapons accumulation do not altogether account for the opposition within state management toward policies to convert from military to civilian economy. Two further considerations have surely been operative: the dogma of the affordability of guns and butter, and the usefulness of armed forces for ever-widening political-hegemonic control—hence, for attempting to accomplish alienations.

A SOVIET MANPOWER LIMIT

In the Soviet Union, the state managers believed, like their counterparts, that they could have guns and butter. In the United States, we tend to assume that the fixed capital resources of our industries will permit unlimited economic expansion, and unlimited accumulation of profits and power. As we have seen, faced with the repeated destruction of their economic fabric in war and revolution, the Soviet managers had the luxury of no such illusion. Instead, they believed their answer was unlimited manpower.

Ironically, however, the breakdown of Russian production in both producer goods and consumer goods, with parallel decay in infrastructure, is finally explainable in terms of manpower limits. Russia's economy and society are not exempt from the manpower constraints that operate in the United States.

Production activity of every sort requires a process of decision-making, and those two vital functions can be performed by alternative means. For production, the alternatives are technical in nature, and social, mainly economic, criteria determine the main technical choices. Here we find the deciding factor that has shaped the direction of the Soviet economy, for its comprehensive managerial system was driven by the imperatives for accumulating money-valued outputs, but, above all, power. In Soviet society, the main operative test of managerial achievement was not "how much profit is enough?" but, above all, "how much power is enough?" That accounts for the vast and costly accumulation process that we found in the military-nuclear realm.

Keeping in mind the inescapable manpower constraints of every large economy, we ask for the Soviets: What activity was productionally necessary for the larger community, as against the continuing pursuit of social and economic control? Readers will recall that by *production* we mean the activity required (directly and indirectly) for making every sort of life-serving consumer goods and services.* Occupations whose work time is primarily devoted to formulating, communicating, controlling and enforcing production decisions, on the other hand, are designated *decision process.* All *production* requires *decision time.* But how much?

We have seen that decision-process occupations can show large growth in both numbers and complexity. But their growth, however preferred, does not add to, and frequently detracts from, production.

What part of the U.S.S.R.'s labor force in 1980 was primarily engaged in administering and enforcing the decision processes of the government and enterprise managers, as against the labor force in occupations largely active in producing the society's consumer goods and services?

A report titled *U.S.S.R. People's Economy in 1989: Statistical Annual* gave considerable detailed data for industry groups, occupations and sectors of the economy, showing, in particular, the use of manpower in these areas.[56] With the invaluable assistance of a Russian economist, Vladimir V. Kachalin,† I was able to understand the relevant statistical tables and the Soviet statistical categories. The detailed tables of occupation and industry made it possible to estimate the number primarily engaged in decision-process occupations, on all levels, among those gainfully

*Prevailing standards and tastes are accepted without prejudice.

†Dr. Kachalin, in Moscow, had been at the Institute of World Economy and International Relations, Russian Academy of Sciences.

employed. For their classification, I applied the same criteria that were utilized for such a classification of U.S. occupations.

The number of those employed in decision process in the *Statistical Annual* was expanded to include other identifiable occupations not included in the report. Thereby, it was possible to take into account estimates for the armed forces, the militia, the KGB, KGB internal troops, prisoners, the prison staffs and the unemployed. These latter segments of the labor force accounted for 11.4 million.

In total, this produced an estimate of 77.3 million primarily engaged in decision-making and decision-process-enforcing occupations (U.S.S.R., 1980) in relation to 35.2 million people primarily engaged in consumer-goods and -services occupations.

In the form of a ratio, the economically relevant occupations in 1980 stand at 219 in the primarily decision-process and enforcing occupations per 100 of those in production occupations. This ratio of 219:100 compares to 130:100 for the U.S. economy in 1980.*

The Soviet economy and society were smothered by this huge overlay of administrative jobs. In July 1991, Georgy Skorov, a Senior Research Fellow at the Academy of Sciences of the U.S.S.R., wrote: "In 1990, it was acknowledged that the economy was going through the most 'severe crisis' comparable to the one immediately following the Second World War without, however, any destruction of the physical capital."[57]

By 1991, there were extreme shortages of consumer and capital goods and services, including—as I illustrated with machine tools—basic means of production. As in the United States, the repair of what is now in disrepair, including infrastructure and environment, is not approachable without a large-scale transfer of people and facilities to civilian work.

But what of the much vaunted liberalization of the Russian economy? Hasn't this remedied the problem? Predictably, the answer is no.

While ordinary citizens suffered the worst of hard times after 1991, a newly developed business class in Russia, centered on finance and banking operations, was heavily involved in takeover operations of existing large and valuable enterprises, like those in oil and mining of various minerals. Based on the natural wealth being exploited (and exported), those enterprises had high money value. These new elite pressed political advantage, government connections and the like to take control of such enterprises. By February 17, 1997: "In a recent interview Deputy Security Counsel Boris Berezovosky announced proudly that he and six other businessmen control 50% of the Soviet economy. 'Russia is undergoing a redistri-

*For 1980 also, I had reclassified the entire U.S. labor force, whether "gainfully employed" or not, thus taking into account unemployed, prisoners, armed forces, etc.

bution of property on a scale unprecedented in history,' he boasted." An altogether reasonable understanding, owing to the great success of the buccaneering methods used, connections with top political officials and connections with the criminal underground in Russia.

Skorov's analysis noted the following:

> Another significant factor, responsible for the failure of economic reforms, is the *resistance of all those who would like to maintain the old system.* The opponents of change simply do not see room for themselves in a new system. According to available estimates, there are altogether between 16 to 18 million people (the party *nomenklatura*, all levels of government bureaucracy, managers of the defense and heavy industries, neo-landlords in agriculture, a good deal of high and middle rank officers in the army, KGB, and militia (police), a huge apparatus of law-enforcing agencies and other important pressure groups). Together with their families they account for one-fifth to one-quarter of the total population. One could add to them, those who are as yet undecided, but getting more and more disgruntled with shortages, lines, rising crime, inflation, unemployment and whatnot, associated rightly or wrongly with a transition to a market economy. They are a formidable force resisting change.[58]

In other words, the Russian workforce remains as top-heavy as ever. The "market" has not resolved the problem.*

One of the showcases for the U.S. government's promotion of Russian "free enterprise" has been the city of Nizhni Novgorod. Stanford University was particularly involved in a project in that city to sponsor privatization. A conference on their work at Columbia University in the spring of 1995 heard a report from the team sent from the United States to encourage the privatization process of the economy. A remarkable characteristic of the team for such a project was that it included four lawyers specializing in bankruptcy but not a single engineer. The whole orientation seemed detached from any real interest in carrying out conversion to civilian products.

*Indeed, we learn that the number of staff in the "apparatus" of the Federal Russian Government was 36,600 in December 1992. Two years later it was 42,000. The number of federal ministries increased from 40 in 1992 to 75 in 1995, and staff in regional government bodies grew from 347,000 in 1991 to 520,000 in 1994 (*Ogonyok*, No. 24 [4403], June 1995, p. 18).

Quality of Life

By October 1995, the Russian grain harvest was the worst in thirty years. How was the population eating? Apparently, millions of small plots are tended by families who grow just enough potatoes and vegetables to keep them going through the year.

As many readers will no doubt be aware, the collapse of Russian industry, combined with infrastructure decay, has dramatically affected the quality of life in Russia. Some idea of the terrible scale of the problem can be gained from a 1996 *60 Minutes* segment on Russia's ever-worsening situation that included comments from Murray Feshback, a specialist on population problems. Stephen Kroft, a CBS correspondent, stated that between 1989 and 1996

> The life span of the average Russian man has plummeted from 65 to 58 years. It is a drop in life expectancy that many experts say is unparalleled in history. And the worst-case prediction of some medical experts is that if nothing drastic is done, the average life span of Russian men will decline further from 58 to 53 years of age, just below the level of Ghana. . . .
>
> FESHBACK: Down to 53, let's say by the year 2005.
>
> TOM FENTON (CBS staff): [There are now] two abortions in Russia for every live birth. It's the lowest birthrate of any country in the world. The upshot: 800,000 more Russians die every year than are born. . . . Only one in four of Russian children who are born are healthy, and if the trend continues, by the end of the century only one in ten will be in good health. Even more serious is the steadily increasing number of infants born with physical or mental defects. We met some of them at an orphanage for such children outside Moscow. The majority of the children had been cast off by their parents—considered too great a burden for the family.

Fenton added to the picture of gloom:

> FENTON: In some of the worst areas of industrial pollution, new figures show that 40 percent of the children are born mentally impaired. . . . There is a host of suspect causes for all of these appalling statistics. Heading the list: the rampant consumption of alcohol, which has now reached epidemic proportions. To quench his sorrows, the average Russian male now guzzles an

incredible half a bottle of vodka per day. And remember, that's the average.

FESHBACK: Last year 46,000 people died of drinking bad alcohol.

In the Soviet era, the five-year plans that charted industrialization featured targets in quantities of goods. Delivering the planned amounts was a primary measure of management success. For the short run, this meant monthly bonuses that fattened the salaries of the engineering and executive staff. Production workers counted on the bonus as a regular part of income. In the long run, plan fulfillment was a key factor for management promotions up the ladder of the *Nomenklatura* hierarchy. The reduction of environmental pollution effects was not a customary plan target.

FENTON: Added to alcohol there is pollution. The Russians have been ruthlessly poisoning their land and water and air for decades, from oil pipelines in the vast Siberian tundra to factories and cars that befoul their towns and cities, not to mention their reckless disregard of the dangers of nuclear radiation. And if that doesn't do it, the Russians seem intent on smoking themselves to death. Billions of Western cigarettes are flooding into Russia. . . . The fact that 50 percent of water in the country, including in Moscow itself, is polluted. Half the population is drinking polluted water?

FESHBACK: Oh, probably more.

Such conditions, reported here for the late 1990s, are not new in the Russian experience. The history of Magnitogorsk, the important steel center, affords a many-sided view of the general Soviet industrial investment pattern. Stephen Kotkin illuminates the almost savage circumstances of work and living conditions that persisted from the first five-year plan to the close of the century.[59] The human toll from hard work, terrible pollution, seriously damaged environment and difficult living conditions is incalculable. A sustained, relentless drive for more tonnage left little space for refinements like clean drinking water and careful monitoring of disease resistance. Today, the world faces the consequences. But it is the Russian people who are living them day to day.

FENTON: The threat from Russia is now seen as not only nuclear proliferation but the proliferation of killer diseases as well, like diphtheria.

FESHBACK: The drug scene has gotten so bad that they expect now that one out of every six males, young males, will become a drug addict.

FENTON: This is going to be a nation of junkies?

FESHBACK: Well, they've got a lot of other problems too.

FENTON: AIDS may turn out to be one of the worst. Once they do get a decent test, that is, for AIDS, they could find themselves in the middle of a major AIDS crisis. . . . Russia's ramshackle health system is in a sorrier state than is the country's health itself. It was already starved under the Communists and that continues under Yeltsin.

FESHBACK: The war in Chechnya, for instance, consumes far more than Russia's entire health budget.

FENTON: This hospital uses old plastic water bottles as drip containers. Bare sponge rubber serves as a mattress. Paper is stuffed in cracks in the windows to keep out the cold; wires dangle from electrical installations.

FESHBACK: Twenty percent of hospitals throughout the country, in fact, don't have any water at all, and 50 percent do not have any hot water. Now there are no later figures—this is five years ago.[60]

You might think that three-quarters of a century afforded time for major improvement in the rudiments of living suitable for an industrialized society. Nevertheless, apart from the *Nomenklaturists* and their scientific-technological entourage (like the populations of the "closed cities" of the nuclear project), the rest of the Russian people have hardly had a chance. The warmaking and war-preparing checkmated the assignment of skilled manpower and allied resources needed for seriously upgrading the general level of living.

Beyond the distant human tragedy, however, there is also a lesson that cuts close to home. The deterioration of Russian industry, economy and infrastructure is unique not in kind but only in degree, because these developments are paralleled for parts of the population in the United States. Americans are shielded from the full meaning of the great profit/power emphasis that has yielded a superabundance of decision-process activity, as in Soviet Russia.*

*Many people had hoped, even during the long Soviet rule, to see Russia evolve somehow as a bearer of a possible socialist future: an economy that could incorporate cooperative, nonpredatory relations, with a measure of economic democracy. But possible paths, if any, in that direction were cut off by the long and weary military state capitalism, with its elaborate institutions for rigid managerial controls and personal coercion.

PART III

Managing as Deindustrialization Proceeds

Beyond deindustrialization, their most potent latter-day alienation strategy, American managers have acted to advance their power position in industry by two main courses of action: by using mechanization to save money and reduce workers' power, and by conceding ownership to workers without control.

Mechanization has typically followed the pattern of replacing manual work with machine operations—wherever that could be justified by cost reduction or blocking worker organization. This process was prevalent in the colonial United States from the early decades of capitalism, as the wages to American workers were manifestly higher than those of the English in the home country. Accordingly, the mechanization of work in the United States proceeded at a much faster pace than in England—the mother country of all the principal industries and machinery that were fueling economic expansion across the Atlantic.

As long as the alternative costs of new machinery compared with workers' wages yielded a cost-effective substitution, the mechanization processes proceeded apace. And productivity rose accordingly. But in the second half of the twentieth century, these processes were altered by the sheer physical depletion of many industries formerly located in the United States, and by the pattern of cost-maximizing. Thus it has become impossible even to investigate the alternative costs of machinery to labor in commercial shipbuilding or passenger train manufacturing, because there have been virtually no such civilian industries operating in the United States. Navy warships became the principal products of American shipbuilding, and transit bus and train equipment for American cities has been produced mainly by Japanese and Canadian-British firms.

In some industrial situations, managers have traditionally pursued mechanization as a sure way to be less dependent on workers who—unlike motors or microchips—can form unions and make demands on the employer. Similarly, managements have often made reducing their dependence on workers an objective in its own right, irrespective of the costs involved.

According to the pundits of the "new economy" and the "information society," a brave new world of the mechanization of work was opened up by the invention and widespread availability of microchips and computers. But there is only qualified evidence that this has transformed the economic feasibility of mechanizing industrial work in the United States, because so much of industrial production has been stopped: factories closed completely, or work transferred to industrial locations in low-wage Third World countries.

As Chapter 7 will show, managers have frequently opted to use high technology to make workers obsolete, resulting in a new cycle of alienating Taylorist techniques. The resulting speedup and dumbing down of the workplace has exerted a relentless toll on workers in the United States or in American factories, as in Mexico. Low wages and unskilled workers plus high technology yield only further alienation and depletion. By contrast, the main European countries have retained strong industrial positions despite the fact that their wages are higher than those here in the United States.

A second form of management response to the depleting effects of state capitalism within the domestic labor force has been the development of offers of shared ownership to workers of all occupations. With much fanfare, and in various formal structures, ownership-sharing in firms has been opened to participation by employees, while control has been effectively reserved as the province of management. Nevertheless, this fundamental distinction between ownership and control, first enunciated by Adolf Berle and Gardiner Means in their classic work *The Modern Corporation and Private Property* (1933), still stands. Unfortunately, the weight of evidence about new employee stock ownership plans (ESOPs) is quite clear: management has been prepared to share in ownership, but hardly at all in control.

All told, the design of new technologies and of new shared ownership agreements have been governed first and foremost by government and business requirements—that is, they have been in the service of alienation for accumulation. Some technological developments, like the Internet, clearly do have potentially liberating characteristics—such as enabling easy communication and the flow of information across boundaries—even as much of the Web is filled with commercials of every sort. But overall, management's application of the newer technologies has been bad news for America's workers.

7

The Attempt to Make Workers and Unions Obsolete

What determines the shape of technology in production? Some have held that technology is autonomous, that the tools, machines and production organization used in industry have dynamics of their own and are therefore separate from the behavior of people. The results of my investigations, including many industrial observations, suggest this view is wrong. In an earlier study, I examined the alternative technologies for performing such basic tasks in production as measuring, moving things from one place to another and removing metal from a piece of unformed raw material.[1] Among the alternatives that were commonly available, only particular ones were employed. Nothing was inherently "advanced" or inherently "backward" about which choices were made. Rather, it became clear that the preferred technologies were those best suited to the relative cost of labor to machinery at the time. But the methods for performing metal-removing and for transporting and the measuring operations in the 1950s were, of course, different from those preferred twenty years earlier. The relative cost of labor and machinery had shifted dramatically, so that a much higher level of mechanization was appropriate in 1956 than in 1936.

This view of the matter is completely contrary to the key assumption made at the turn of the century by engineers who attempted to systematize industrial work. These were the followers of Frederick Winslow Taylor, whose belief was that there was a "single best way" for accomplishing any particular work task. A Department of Labor report of 1989 summed up the tenacious hold of the Taylorist approach:

> The key assumption is that the labor force has nothing to contribute to the production process. In effect, employees are simply appendages to machines, and therefore the most cost-effective approach is to drive skill out of work and operate with as low-cost a labor force as possible. Although few people would identify

> themselves with as crude a view as the foregoing, it seems hard to deny that these attitudes underlie much of the American production system. In both union and non-union settings, narrow job categories, strict work rules, lack of sharing of information concerning new technology and the general absence of workers in the planning of production all flow from the Tayloristic approach to planning work. . . . One firm may use automation not simply to improve quality and reduce labor input per unit but also to sharply reduce actual employment levels. Another firm will use the same technology to maintain employment. In one setting, operators receive training and learn how to use the data and control possibilities of technology to manage the production process; in another firm, control and planning is shifted to managers, and the labor force is deskilled.[2]

As the report suggests, instead of discussing "invention," with its overtones of spontaneous, heroic and indeterminate creativity, we are concerned here with the processes whereby considerations, both social and natural (in combination), determine the character of society's means of production. It is essential to differentiate between the formulation of a new idea, a new design, on the one hand, and systematic changes in the preferred character of technologies used as means of production, for the latter is controlled by management decisions based upon their effects of the changes on cost and profit. The patent offices and technology museums of the world include large numbers of designs that never came to fruition and utilization on the factory floor. Similar reasoning goes far to account for the characteristics of industrial research. The bottom line is what counts to employers.

Many of the most familiar features of production technology in the United States can be traced to business requirements. The development of the assembly line, for example, first employed on a large scale in the U.S. automobile industry, is traceable to the character of the business routine prevailing for the early carmakers. Early auto companies were small establishments and had limited funds at their disposal. In the Detroit-Cleveland area, however, there were many machine shops with unused capacity that the auto firms could call upon to supply the necessary parts for cars. These parts were brought together in the plant of the auto firm and assembled into a complete vehicle, whereupon the car was shipped to a dealer and sold to its ultimate user. Since these new firms were not regarded by bankers as good credit risks, it was of vital importance for the business managements involved to have as little of their operating money as possible tied up in inventory—completed or semi-complete vehicles.

Given this rather precarious way of doing business, the means had to be found to speed the production of vehicles, getting them out to the dealers and sold in the fastest possible time. The answer to this problem was the assembly line, which in the hands of Henry Ford, it is said, made it possible for his company to buy parts from machine shops, assemble them in a completed automobile, ship the car to a dealer and receive the sale price all before the date fell due for meeting the company's bills with the suppliers of parts. The turnover of finished cars in relation to the total fixed equipment of the company was therefore very great, making big profit margins in relation to a given investment. The assembly line was the answer to a tough economic environment.

Economic factors also determine much of the specific design of technologies used for production. John E. Ullmann once demonstrated that the big pre–World War II differences in the fuel efficiency of steam boilers used in the United States and Europe could be accounted for by contrasting the costs of fuel against the labor employed in boiler construction and operation.[3] In Europe, coal was expensive and labor cheap. In the United States, the reverse was true. So it paid off for European electric power stations to use much more labor in refining boiler designs, which could thus operate with greater fuel efficiency than in the United States. The same knowledge of boiler design was available to Americans as to the Europeans, but here we simply burned more coal to produce a pound of steam at a cost that was acceptable to the economy. The environment paid the price.

Unfortunately, the same logic applies today in the manufacture of automobile engines: In the United States, where gasoline is much cheaper, car engines burn on average twice the fuel consumed by cars in Europe or Japan. Faced with high gasoline prices, car designers in Europe and Japan have favored compactness and fuel economy. Despite dwindling supplies of fossil fuels, in the United States we continue to produce ever larger gas-guzzling minivans and sports utility vehicles.

The Rise of Computers

The use of computers to control many types of production marked a major transformation of industrial operations. In the 1950s, the Air Force sponsored a basic research program that involved the Electrical Engineering Department of the Massachusetts Institute of Technology and key firms in the machine-tool industry. The objective was to design a computer control system that would operate a milling machine. The challenge for its designers was to locate the path of a cutting tool in three dimensions.[4]

The project succeeded, but the resulting machine design was very expensive and could not be used economically by most industrial firms. It was left to the Japanese and German engineers to take advantage of the subsequent development of solid state electronics and miniaturization, and to design, produce and market compact, less expensive computer controls that could be readily used on virtually all machine tools.

The move from punched or magnetic tape for storing information to micro-electronically based computers made it possible to control the computer at the machine site and even alter the program with ease, thereby allowing suitably trained machinists to program the machines themselves. Further developments of technology enabled the direct numerical control of many different machine tools from a single central computer.

Another addition to the sophistication of automatic machine-tool operation was the development of adaptive controls. "Here the machine tool is fitted with sensors to monitor parameters, such as spindle deflection, tool deflection, and resistance to feed which are fed into the computer which then automatically changes speeds, feed rates." Thus were these building blocks for sophisticated production processes transformed by computerization, largely by engineers outside the United States.

Studies of maintenance operations in England and Germany reported that "new machine tools which incorporate diagnostic devices can reduce the time taken to locate a fault from several hours to five minutes."[5]

The work of designers and draftsmen has also been transformed by the use of computer-assisted design (CAD) technology with the capability to represent the object being designed in three dimensions on the screen before it is produced.

Virtually every aspect of industrial operations has been affected by computerization. When the capabilities of computer control are applied to the assembly line, those classes of work, utilizing computer-controlled robots, are transformed. Thus, early on in its computer manufacturing, IBM was operating a robotic assembly system at Greenock, Scotland, for making keyboards. *The Financial Times* of November 4, 1986, reported that the work was being done at speeds and with low error rates that could not be matched by human operators.

The "Old Thinking" Wins Out: Wages and Workers Held Down

Production costs, with wages rising relative to machinery prices,[6] were key variables for industry during the first half of the twentieth century.

The growing wages for industrial workers relative to prices of machines had led to the progressive mechanization of industrial work. This continued even as diversification in products and the tasks of computer-controlled machine tools made it increasingly arbitrary to calculate and assign to products the specific machine component of production cost. Along with such developments, the complexity of machines made for capital costs that came to dominate the costs of production. Thus the single hour downtime cost of a medium-size "machining center" can easily exceed the cost of an hour of labor time.* The advance of machine productivity has therefore been accompanied by the growth of capital-versus-labor costs in American manufacturing. One effect of this growth is to make the stability of operations and the minimization of downtime increasingly important for minimizing cost, and these conditions depend strongly, in turn, on the skill and diligence of production workers.

Certainly since 1970, a major change emerged: change in the relative cost of labor no longer exceeded that of the price of machinery. Management succeeded brilliantly in repressing the wages of workers. After 1975, the cost of German, Japanese, Swiss, French work hours, for example, became greater than compensation to U.S. workers.

Before, it had been typically assumed that the controlling variable in the design of mechanized work was the relative cost of labor compared with machinery. The pattern showed that wages to industrial workers rose more rapidly than the price of machinery. This was the case in the United States during the first half of the century, extending into the 1970s. By the mid-seventies things had changed. The development of this whole class of new technologies was combined with a strong managerial thrust to contain union power.

Machinery is not the only fixed charge in computer-controlled manufacturing operations. Now that wages have fallen relative to the cost of machinery, the labor force can be regarded as a fixed charge as well. In order to operate such a manufacturing system efficiently, workers must be retained as well-paid engineers and technologists. Unwilling to allow for the increased investment in a multiskilled workforce trained to make the most of the potential new technologies, American managers revived the old Taylorist approach to production. They reasoned that wages must not become a fixed cost, meaning that wages are not allowed to be independent of the quantity turned out or the exact time actually doing "hands-on" work.

*I illustrated this point in *Profits Without Production* (p. 109). A "machining center" is a computer-controlled machine with capability for an indefinitely large number of workpiece shapes and utilizing many tools—all being changed quickly by computer control. It was computer programming and control that made such machines possible.

Conventional standards for the proper allocation of production-worker time has its roots in the early-twentieth-century teachings of Frederick Winslow Taylor. He believed that the actions of direct production workers should be specified in detail and monitored. But by the 1970s, the direct production worker accounted for only a minority of the total labor and manufacturing cost in many industries. This change led to a debate about the mode of work organization appropriate under conditions where the labor cost seems no longer readily variable but takes on instead the quality of an "indirect" cost that does not vary directly with output. In the latter case, many argued that the Taylor view of workforce and production management was obsolete.

A part of American management was persuaded that a post-Taylorist approach was in order. In the Taylorist tradition, workers are to be assigned to limited-skill work under hierarchical control. A proposed alternative sees a multiskill perspective for industrial work and limited hierarchy. Instead of viewing workers as replaceable parts, they can be trained to new, broader skills. In the Taylorist tradition, the wage is set by job evaluation, in contrast to schemes of payment based on skills acquired. While incompatible interests for management and workers are a built-in feature of Taylorist labor relations, a "new look" for management would accent a common stake in the success of the company.

Some observers, by 1982, called attention to the fact that direct labor cost in much of American manufacturing amounted to only about 10 percent of total manufacturing cost. Direct labor means those workers whose work time varies directly with the production activity. It does not refer to those who may be engaged in maintenance of equipment, preparation of tooling, plant housekeeping or similar "indirect" activities.

Managements had ordinarily assumed that the regulation of production workers made the biggest difference in the cost and quality of production operations, and had been placing about 75 percent of control effort on a small portion of the total cost.

Where the cost of capital dominates the cost of production, the best productivity of a manufacturing system is reached when output rate is stabilized, which is not necessarily obtainable simply by specifying the micro-detail performance of each production worker at each task. In fact, this has become even less possible as workers take on supervision of increasingly intricate production equipment. Machines often include self-correcting equipment to measure the characteristics of what is being produced and make adjustments in their operation accordingly. The net effect is that workers are no longer engaged simply in the manipulation of hand tools or small machines.

With this change, the manufacturing process is far removed from

Taylor's earlier version of work. His basic descriptions of work concerned a one-worker, one-tool operation. He literally specified the details of shoveling coal. The principle involved there was applied to many operations—logical only if the worker's muscular effort was the main governing agent over the details of the operation. But as formerly "manual" operations have been increasingly "built into" the machine—as machinery has become self-adjusting, self-correcting, to meet the requirements set by the operator—human physical manipulative capability has also become a negligible factor.

In particular, with computer-controlled operations, an operator's knowledge and conscientiousness becomes far more important for minimizing unscheduled downtime. All of these factors contribute to the "stability of operations" factor diagnosed by Sebastian B. Littauer and explored in the work of W. Edwards Deming that has been so influential in shaping postwar Japanese manufacturing.[7]

Much of this "new thinking" proceeded while union membership was in decline and labor suffered spectacular defeats, including the Caterpillar Company strike and the Detroit newspaper lockout of the 1990s. Unfortunately, it is the "old thinking" that has won out. All the available evidence suggests that a well-educated, versatile workforce, trained to exercise a high degree of control and decision-making on the factory floor, will get more productivity and less downtime out of the new technologies. But managers remain determined to focus on and hold down labor's wage and to guard their power jealously. Taylorism has returned with a vengeance, worldwide. In GM's new high-tech plants, for example, there are separate factories for each part of the new modular assembly process, many of them outside the United States and using cheap nonunion labor. New technologies are used to build modules that will be assembled elsewhere.[8] For all their high-tech surroundings, workers often face limited tasks, unvarying work assignments and ever-faster work rates.

The result of this combination of new technologies and old-style Taylorist managerialism? Management gets less-than-optimum productivity. Workers not only suffer increased occupation stress, they become ever more discontented and alienated as well. Ironically, this new type of regime is bad for both workers and management. For as we have seen, when a workforce is discontented and worn down, the result is poorer quality and lower productivity. It is little wonder, for example, that despite U.S. car manufacturers' investment in new technologies worldwide, Japanese firms still have the edge in quality and reliability.

For U.S. industrial managers and their use of new technologies, the old saying seems regrettably true: the more things change, the more they stay the same.

The Flexible Manufacturing System: Managers Dream of a Workerless Factory

We can see all of these lessons at work in the ultimate attempt by management to make workers obsolete: the flexible manufacturing system. Despite futuristic developments in flexible manufacturing explored by Japan's Yamazaki corporation and the ICAM program of the Air Force, the FMS system has largely failed to deliver on its promises. I saw the Taylorist pattern in operation, for example, when inspecting a large aerospace manufacturing plant whose manager was considering the installation of an FMS and an accompanying reduction in workers. Since the equipment was designed to be highly automated and self-correcting, with internal checks on the quality of work, the plant's manager assumed that fewer skilled people would be required for all normal operations. I pointed out, as tactfully as possible, that he had failed to take into account the cost of downtime, when more people at the highest skill level would be needed. Under the circumstances, to have workers on the plant floor other than those of top skill level would be counterproductive.

The FMS consists of a set of various kinds of machine tools. They can be machining centers, drills, lathes, milling machines in particular sequence—determined by the nature of the metal-removing and related operations that must be performed. But the FMS has two other prime characteristics. First, it utilizes machines that are flexible, and suited for varied products or operations. A second feature is that these machines, while individually computer-controlled, are linked to a central coordinating computer. The cycle of operations on these separate machines is coordinated so that the movement of workpieces from one machine, or one station, to the next, may also be carried out in a programmed fashion. What you can visualize here is the construction of a factory in which the workpiece begins at one end of the operation and then is moved automatically from one workplace to another. An important part of the art involved is designing and carrying out the work operations so that they are coordinated. A further requirement of the FMS is an intensive effort for built-in capability for control of quality. The result is a fairly intricate array of machines that are rather different from the traditional automobile factory producing particular components with single-purpose, limited-function machines.

As we saw in Chapter 4, during the second part of the twentieth century, cost-minimizing in U.S. industry was replaced by cost-maximizing in the design and selection of technologies that the government wanted for certain military results. Neither price nor cost really mattered. The civilian tradition was disregarded in favor of cost-maximizing for the military.[9] But this entailed more than pressure to design and produce another kind of technology. It involved a very different managerial style. For the source of the new technology order was the Department of Defense, which was by far the most important management in the American economy as a purchaser of machinery.

Aside from a few larger corporations, notably those in the auto industry, the most important American management to investigate the possible operation of FMS was the U.S. Air Force. The Air Force organized a wide-ranging project centered at the Wright Aeronautical Laboratories at Wright-Patterson Air Force Base in Ohio. The project was called ICAM, Integrated Computer-Aided Manufacturing. By October 30, 1984, elaborate designs existed that, if implemented, could theoretically allow a person located anywhere to type the appropriate commands on a computer keyboard and set in motion a series of operations that would manufacture a wing. This remarkably ambitious undertaking was not finally implemented, but instead generated a considerable amount of skepticism. Still, the project went quite far: the planners laid out software, planning and blueprinting, and then proceeded to fashion designs for whole products or components of products. Typically, the practical implementation of this highly expensive innovation was left to foreign engineers.

As a demonstration of the potential of FMS, Yamazaki built a small factory at its headquarters in Nagoya, Japan. Ambition guided the company, and it received permission from Japanese authorities to shave off a mountaintop and create a large flat area for the site of an FMS facility. The factory is a showpiece of mechanization and computer-controlled integration. In a rather surreal twist, Yamazaki's plant manufactures machining centers, the key production machines used for FMS operations. Its robots build robots.

Here is a comparison of FMS compared with conventional machine tools for a particular metalworking task, producing 1,400 units per month, including varying amounts of multi-shift work.

	Conventional Machine Tools	**Flexible Manufacturing System**
Floor space	70,000 sq. ft	30,100 sq. ft.
Machines	68	18
Operators	215 (some on multiple shifts)	12
In-process time	90 days	3 days

Why would tasks with conventional machines take as long as 90 days? When a set of conventional pre–computer-controlled machine tools was used, the work was constantly being placed, then removed from one machine, put aside, transported to another part of the factory, put in place on another machine, further processed and then again removed to another part of the plant, while requiring much in-process inventory time throughout. With FMS, 90 days could be reduced to 3, the "dead time" virtually eliminated. Thus, no accumulation of inventory time and cost is involved. Transport time (and cost) between major FMS units is minimized by performing multiple operations at each machine.

The cost effects of this demonstration were dramatic. Over a five-year period, total cost would amount to $34.7 million under the conventional machines system as against the FMS outlay of $12.1 million. Yamazaki, as you would expect, made an enormous splash during the 1980s when such results were released.

I visited both Yamazaki's demonstration factory and the mountaintop plant, where observers walking around on an elevated ramp could watch the machines operate in sequential fashion. While these demonstrations were impressive and generated a tremendous surge of attention around the world, they did not, in the first years, lead many to duplicate the Yamazaki facilities. Why? My belief is, first, that managers were fearful of the enormous scale of investment required and were not certain of their ability to operate a system of this kind; and, second, they were not certain of the market prospects. It is worthwhile to focus on the first consideration.

The requirements for FMS call for much finesse, both in the design of the system and the mode of operation. One of the important things learned about these systems emerged from a study undertaken for the Army Tank Automotive Command in 1983. Its central findings are plain enough: first, competent functioning of an FMS system requires a highly trained, sophisticated workforce to control the costly equipment in optimum fashion. To train and employ such a high-tech workforce is in itself an expensive undertaking.

Therefore the Army report recommended that continuous education and training of the workforce should be an integral part of the operation: to bring each person to the highest possible level.

> Some users have found that there are significant benefits to be gained when most personnel running the system have the skills needed to do the other jobs as well, from fixturing parts to supervising the system. Aside from the obvious advantage that absentees can easily be covered by others, users find that surges can be handled better. For example, there may be a sudden need to load eight parts on their fixtures. It is very helpful if all "hands" can respond to the need. In addition, this is a method to provide job

> enrichment, especially if the FMS team is allowed to assign their work on a revolving basis by group agreement.
>
> The ability to operate in this manner depends strongly on union policies. It may require that the same job description, pay, and ranking, etc., be given to everyone.[10]

The set of machines is designed to function without human intervention from one machine to another. In this respect, FMS illustrates a more general point. Every production technology carries the stamp of the system within which it operates—the stamp of its system-of-decision criteria.

The consequence of applying computers to the control of machines in production has led to a reassessment of the possible role of workers. Many alternatives have been opened up. The managerialists have responded by assuming that "progressive" technology would deliver advances in industrial productivity even in the hands of a workforce without high educational preparation. But the weight of evidence is clear: the combination of sophisticated technology with a workforce trained up to a high standard is the path for optimum performance on all counts.*

A new set of contractions awaits the workers in U.S. automobile firms. General Motors has announced plans for redesigning the structure of its own production. The new strategic plan would have supplier firms and factories assemble significant "modules" of the vehicle and ship those units to the assembly plants. Thus, the whole set of controls and instruments that constitute the dashboard of the automobile would be assembled in a supplier plant and shipped intact to the assembly plant. Employment in the assembly plants would drop sharply, and management preference for subcontracting to nonunion suppliers would give management further benefits from the strategic design of production facilities aimed at particular modules, while those facilities employ lower-wage, non–union-organized workers—either in the United States or at locations abroad.

*Such alternatives have been defined in a conceptual model with wide applicability by Peter S. Albin, in his "Job Design, Control Technology and Technical Change," *Journal of Economic Issues*, 19, no. 3 (September 1985). (Note: This paper includes a solid bibliography covering innovative works that are relevant to alternative organizations of work.)

Managements have typically tried to reserve the programming of computers to an engineering staff that is usually not unionized. But such management preferences have been contested by "blue collar" unions. Apart from formal assignment of these responsibilities, it is well known that workers have often taught themselves or taken formal courses in computer programming.

Worker Decision-Making Means Increased Productivity

A chance encounter at an industrial exhibition of machine tools opened the way for an unusual investigation of these conclusions: an engineer for an important machine-tool company told me about two factories (let's call them Plant A and Plant B), both of them equipped by his firm with similar machine tools, although they had radically different approaches to organizing the workplace.

Both A and B performed the same classes of work for two separate divisions of a major American auto firm. A and B were similarly equipped, had similar labor forces belonging to the same union (UAW) and were paid the same wages, but they showed strikingly different productivity performances.

The manager of Plant A had, for several years, operated a program of worker training that included computer programming; methods for machine maintenance; periodic meetings where plant operations were discussed; discussions about prospective work projects expected from the parent firm; topics brought up by the workers about plant operations.

There was no counterpart training or meetings or discussions at Plant B, other than occasional individual matters brought up by workers to foremen, or grievances that were submitted to the plant manager.

Bernard Nneji investigated this situation. The following is extracted from his findings following field research and an intensive statistical analysis.[11]

> Plant A, which has the highest level of worker participation in production decision making, also reported the lowest unscheduled machine downtime for 5 percent and a machine utilization rate of 70 to 90 percent. This plant, as measured by the data collection tool of the research, had the highest level of multi-skill and performs the most multi-task. It also reported a higher productivity.
>
> Plant B, on the other hand, reported an unscheduled machine downtime rate of 10 percent and a machine utilization rate of 20 to 35 percent. This plant, when compared to Plant A, has a significantly lower level of multi-skill and multi-task performance.

The sales engineer who first called attention to these two plants had also visited them about five years following their reequipment by his firm. In Plant A, the visiting engineer found machines in excellent condition, typically wiped clean, as were the surrounding floor spaces. The equipment in Plant B was laden with the grit and grime that collects easily in major metalworking shops, and the machines showed signs of heavy wear. Work areas were littered.

> The difference in performance between Plant A and Plant B could be attributed to the method [by which] work is organized since the two plants share the same operational variables and constraints. They have similar equipment, belong to the same union, utilize the same machine technology and belong to the same parent company. They also share the same environmental conditions with respect to geography, labor pool, and governmental regulations. The major difference between the two, which has been identified and quantified, is how work is organized. Plant A practises more worker multi-tasking and participation in production decision-making than Plant B. Plant B is more restrictive as to worker job-control and decision latitude. It has a work organization structure that can be as described as being more mechanistic, rigid and Taylorite.[12]
>
> *Implications of the Study*
>
> Some quite surprising matters showed up in this study. The first and foremost is that *worker participation in production decision-making seems to be an important variable of productivity* in a computer-controlled machine tool shop.
>
> If Taylor was correct in proposing that productivity would be enhanced when workers do not participate in decision-making, could we have achieved this result? Taylor's proposition might have been adequate for the level of societal and technological sophistication at the time of his work organization theories. Labor was mostly uneducated and cheap. Also, mechanical technology was simple, inexpensive, and most production processes were driven by the operator's dexterity, manipulative skills and control.
>
> Today, the story is different. Most machinists have a high school education. Technology is very complex and expensive, and the computer-controlled machine tool environment requires sophisticated training. For such a capital intensive system to run optimally, it requires a new way of organizing work that minimizes downtime and stabilizes operations, by utilizing the comparatively higher level of worker education, skill, and experience. This can be realized by giving workers more control over their work by allowing them to participate in the production decision process.[13]

The meaning of *productivity* is strongly affected by the nature of technology that is used in production. In manufacturing operations whose pace is regulated by computer controls, the output per unit of capital dominates the scene—as against operations that rely on human physical effort. But productivity of capital translates swiftly into output per worker (or per worker-hour).

> It is true that "experience" has been shown to affect productivity directly and "multi-tasking" indirectly. . . . [But] one cannot expect a high-tech machine shop to enjoy high productivity just based on allowing the workers to perform multi-tasks. The machinist must be allowed to participate in production decision-making. . . . In addition, throwing "multi-task" and "multi-skill" at workers may not necessarily result in experienced workers. Management needs to invest and operate for the long term before the fruits of their labor can be reaped. *There is no quick way of creating experience.*
>
> The study therefore concludes that for a given level of worker experience, and character of machine technology, what is critical to productivity in a computer controlled machine tool shop or plant is the way work is organized. This implies that when machinists acquire more skills, and perform multiple tasks with a high degree of participation in production decision making, then productivity is increased.[14]

These conclusions are supported by pioneering work done in Sweden and elsewhere. An admirable study reports the experience of many Swedish employers with respect to the utilization of numerically controlled machine tools:

> At Atlas Copco MCT in Nacka, near Stockholm, there are approximately 40 numerically controlled machine tools, each equipped with its own computer (CNC: computerized numerical control) in operation. One of them is a lathe in the tool department. The operator of this machine is himself responsible for its programming. The operation is as follows:
>
> The operator receives a drawing of the component in question and inserts the proper material in the lathe. He then translates the measurements in the drawing to coordinate values. He then transmits these values to the computer's memory by punching them into a computer keyboard. By analyzing how the machining must be done and, step-by-step, feeding the proper

> values into the computer, he thus programs the machine. After that, the operator need only turn on the lathe and let it do the work. If, in making control measurements, he discovers an error, he can correct the program while the machine is running.
>
> The other departments in the company have not progressed quite so far, but it is clear that workers with extensive practical experience, and interested in progressing technically, can be given highly skilled and meaningful jobs on NC machines.[15]

It is worth noting that in Norway, engineers specializing in computer technologies have taken a lead in training production workers in computer-controlled operations, including use of computers for integrating industrial operations.

I reported these findings to several groups of engineers. At one meeting in New York City in 1990 to consider characteristics of automation technologies, I was met with skepticism and undisguised hostility from those who felt that production workers would not take on the responsibility that is being suggested here. If intricate equipment is involved, the engineers assumed, it needs a workforce of experts that is current, knowledgeable and diligent in application, something not to be expected from "ordinary" workers. Indeed, the pervasiveness of that idea, and the hostility with which it is defended, suggests that these engineers felt threatened that workers were needed who could carry out these sorts of necessary functions with equipment of a high technical order.

As I have shown, gradual mechanization and then computerization in the control of work disables Taylorism as a set of competent rules for the organization of work in modern industry. But managers and many engineers continue to defend the status quo.

A Bill of Rights for High Technology

But while American managers have resisted the implications of the new technologies, workers have not stood still. They have sought to find ways to share in the future of high-tech production. The International Association of Machinists and Aerospace Engineers (IAM), for example, has its own agenda, which was formulated in a Technology Bill of Rights. This is a set of principles to which the IAM has subscribed, and it recommended the Bill to all its divisions. It argues that new technology should be viewed as a tool that serves the needs and interests of the workers involved, as well as the wider community. The IAM wanted to participate in the formulation of technology characteristics and uses.

The concept was first formulated by Harley Shaiken as a contribution at a Scientists and Engineers Conference convened in 1982 by the IAM, and was subsequently elaborated upon by the IAM. The text is important enough to be quoted in its entirety:

A Technology Bill of Rights

Proposed by the International Association of Machinists and Aerospace Workers

Preamble

Powerful new technologies are being poured into the workplace at a record rate. Based on the expanding capabilities and decreasing cost of computers and microelectronics, new forms of automation will leave few workplaces or occupations untouched. Robots on the assembly line, word processors in the office, numerical control in the machine shop, computer-aided design in the engineering department, and electronic scanners in supermarkets are only a few examples of the widespread changes that are taking place.

While such technologies offer real promise for a better society, they are being developed in a shortsighted and dangerous direction. Instead of benefits, working people are seeing jobs threatened, working conditions undermined, and the economic viability of communities challenged. In the face of these unprecedented dangers, labor must act forcefully and quickly to safeguard the rights of workers and develop technology in a way that benefits the entire society. Key to this is proclaiming and implementing a Technology Bill of Rights. This should be a program that is both a new vision of what technology can accomplish and a specific series of demands that are meant to guide the design, introduction, and use of new technology. This approach is based on the following assumptions:

1. A community has to produce in order to live. As a result, it is the obligation of an economy to organize people to work.
2. The well-being of people and their communities must be given the highest priority in determining the way in which production is carried out.
3. Basing technological and production decisions on narrow economic grounds of profitability has made working people and communities the victims rather than the beneficiaries of change.

4. Given the widespread scope and rapid rate of introduction of new technologies, society requires a democratically determined institutional, rather than individual, response to changes taking place. Otherwise, the social cost of technological change will be borne by those least able to pay it: unemployed workers and shattered communities.

5. Those that work have a right to participate in the decisions that govern their work and shape their lives.

6. The new automation technologies and the sciences that underlie them are the product of a worldwide, centuries-long accumulation of knowledge. Accordingly, working people and their communities have a right to share in the decisions about, and the gains from, new technology.

The choice should not be new technology or no technology but the development of technology with social responsibility. Therefore, the precondition for technological change must be the compliance with a program that defines and insures the well-being of working people and the community. The following is the foundation of such a program, a Technology Bill of Rights:

1. *New technology must be used in a way that creates or maintains jobs.* A part of the productivity gains from new technology can translate into fewer working hours at the same pay or into fewer jobs. This is not a technical but a social decision. Given the pervasiveness of new forms of automation, the former approach is vital. The exact mechanisms for accomplishing this—a shorter work week, earlier retirement, longer vacations, or a combination—ought to be a prerogative of the workers involved. In addition, comprehensive training must be provided well before any change takes place to insure that workers have the maximum options to decide their future. Moreover, new industries that produce socially useful products must be created to insure the economic viability of regions that are particularly affected by technological change.

2. *New technology must be used to improve the conditions of work.* Rather than using automation to destroy skills, pace work, and monitor workers, it can be used to enhance skills and expand the responsibility workers have on the job. In addition, the hazardous and undesirable jobs should be a first priority, but at the

discretion of the workers involved and not at the expense of employment. Production processes can be designed to fully utilize the skill, talent, creativity, initiative, and experience of people—instead of production designs aimed at controlling workers as if they were robots.

3. *New technology must be used to develop the industrial base and improve the environment.* At the same time corporate America has raised the flag of industrial revitalization, jobs are being exported from communities, regions, and even countries at a record rate. The narrow economic criteria of transnational companies are causing an erosion of the nation's manufacturing base and the collapse of many communities that are dependent on it. While other countries in the world have a pressing need and legitimate right to develop new industry, it is nonetheless vital that corporations not be allowed to play workers, unions, and countries against each other, seeking the lowest bidder for wages and working conditions. Instead, close cooperation among unions throughout the world and stringent controls over plant closings and capital movement are in order. In addition, the development of technology should not be at the expense of the destruction of the environment.[16]

This Bill of Rights for the new technologies was an innovative departure for American unions as they continue to seek ways for sharing in the effects of the further mechanization of work. Once the concept was taken on by the unions, they elaborated on the basic ideas to include the following:

Unit Labor Cost Savings and Labor Productivity Gains resulting from the use of New Technology shall be shared with workers at the local enterprise level and shall not be permitted to accrue excessively or exclusively for the gain of capital, management and shareholders. Reduced work hours and increased leisure time made possible by New Technology shall result in no loss of real income or decline in living standards for workers affected at the local enterprise level.

Local Communities, the States and the Nation have a right to require employers to pay a replacement tax, on all machinery, equipment, robots and production systems that displace workers, cause unemployment and, thereby, decrease local, state and federal revenues.

New Technology Shall Be Used to Develop and Strengthen the U.S. Industrial Base, consistent with the Full Employment goal and national security requirements, before it is licensed or otherwise exported abroad.

Workers, Through Their Trade Unions and Bargaining Units, Shall Have an Absolute Right to Participate in All Phases of Management Deliberations and Decisions That Lead or Could Lead to the Introduction of New Technology or the changing of the workplace system design, work processes and procedures for doing work, including the shutdown or transfer of work, capital, plant and equipment.

When New Technology is employed in the production of military goods and services, workers, through their trade union and bargaining agent, shall have a right to bargain with management over the establishment of Alternative Production Committees, which shall design ways to adopt that technology to socially useful production and products in the civilian sector of the economy.[17]

Occupation Stress: The Human Cost of Making Workers' Skills Obsolete

There has been a renewed interest in examining the conditions that relate work characteristics to their human consequences and seeing the effects on production workers as a part of their environment. One of the pioneers in this approach is Robert Karasek, who was for several years a professor of industrial engineering at Columbia University. Thanks to his imaginative work, previously unexplored consequences of high-stress occupations have been identified. Karasek and his associates showed that jobs could be classified according to "high" or "low" decision control, with a "high" or "low" psychological demand in the occupation. People holding jobs with low decision control and high psychological demand were found to have dramatically high incidences of cardiovascular disease—the occupations in question including those of firefighter, freight handler, waiter/waitress, cashier, clerical positions such as an "information operator" whose performance is often monitored, cook, garment-stitcher, mail worker. Occupations of the opposite character, those having high decision control and low psychological demand, included those of auto repairman, peddler, skilled machinist, dentist, natural scientist, forester, architect; and these jobs correlated with relatively low incidences of cardiovascular disease.[18]

When occupations are categorized in this way, it was found, the classifications have considerable predictive power for stress and heart ailments. As a result, new sets of variables for predicting these and other ill effects on workers could be used for the design of work operations. This approach opens up the possibility of redesigning occupations with low decision latitude and high psychological demand, so as to lower the currently high incidence of heart disease associated with them.[19] Job design, in sum, is a part of the wider approach to healthy work.

Apart from technological and economic considerations that must be taken into account, the organization of work plays a crucial part. Karasek and Theorell report this illuminating experience from an unsuccessful quality-of-work life (QWL) project at a New York hospital:

> The QWL project was intended to decentralize decision making, while (management) was attempting to centralize control. The project focused on patient care, while (management) refocused the organization in the direction of better financial performance. The project attempted to foster collaboration across departmental boundaries; (management) sought to strengthen boundaries in order to (define control structures). The project strove for union-management cooperation, while (management's) financial strategy demanded an "arm's-length" and often highly adversarial stance towards the unions. In sum (management) was creating an environment that was hostile to the aims of the (QWL) project.[20]

The recent trend toward managed care in medicine, which has inflicted hardships on health care workers and patients alike, serves only to underline the urgency of these questions.

On available evidence from many industries and the experience of a range of well-developed societies, we are aware that work technologies are not given by nature. Instead, we know that the prevailing decision-makers on production cause technologies to be developed by design. The choice of design is affected by capabilities that are afforded by the great array of materials in nature and by the physical, chemical and biological mechanisms at work in nature. From these options, managerial decision-makers in capitalism selectively prefer the combinations that best serve their primary goals of accumulating profits and power.

8

Management Promotes Ownership Without Control

In about 2,000 American companies, employees own a *majority* of the outstanding stock in some type of employee stock ownership plan (ESOP). But these much-vaunted schemes, which offer workers greater participation in the running of their firms, all too often fail to deliver on their promises. Management might be prepared to share in ownership, but they are far less interested in sharing in control. The chief executives of such firms, like their counterparts generally, "almost always put corporate survival ahead of saving everyone's job." Like corporations elsewhere, ESOP corporations have also turned to layoffs as a way of reducing costs and improving profits. Indeed, about 16 percent of firms with substantial employee ownership experienced layoffs during 1996 alone, as ordered by managers whose power is not limited by worker-owners. Though they own stock, these workers do not control their boards of directors; instead, the management, or the "trust committees" named by boards that supply capital, are fully empowered to make policy.[1]

By 2000, about 8,000 companies were participants in ESOPs in which employee ownership exceeds 4 percent of total company market value. Advocates of the ESOP form of organization claim that by 1991 about 12.5 percent of the private economy workforce in the United States (about 10.8 million American workers) owned stock in companies.[2]

From longtime advocates of the ESOP scheme we learn that "employee ownership owes its current success not to utopian aspirations but to the tax code. Since ESOPs were first mentioned in the Regional Rail Reorganization Act of 1973, fifteen federal laws have been passed concerning them. The most notable was the Employee Retirement and Income Security Act of 1974 (ERISA), which established the statutory framework for ESOPs, permitted them to borrow and established the tax deductibility of employer contributions to ESOPs. Since then a number of other measures have established regulations for ESOPs and expanded their tax coverage."[3]

Yet ESOPs have been widely promoted as utopian solutions that offer the hope that ownership would, in due course, include control, thereby greatly enlarging the number of working people with decision power over the behavior of corporations.[4]

Ownership and Layoffs

How much control do employee owners really have? I have assumed that employees strongly prefer sustained employment and the avoidance of layoffs, and that, if they had voting rights with which to exercise control, they would vote against downsizing as company policy except in exceptional circumstances. A fairly direct mode of address to this issue was made possible by the appearance of a listing titled "The Employee Ownership 100."[5] These were firms with more than 30 percent of company securities owned by employees. Within that listing, the companies with more than 50 percent employee ownership were identified.

Does a high level of employee ownership make a difference in corporate behavior about downsizing? From this listing and other data, I could identify eighteen firms where a majority of securities was employee-owned through an ESOP. All of these enterprises had major downsizing.

Three other companies were also majority-owned through an ESOP but had no layoffs in 1993–1996. I inquired into the management policies and practices of these twenty-one companies and found the following similarities. Layoffs were implemented in most of them by decision of management "trustee" committees. These committees had been set up and empowered to make major decisions.

In the handful of firms that were majority employee-owned and had no downsizing, the managements and the unions confirmed the following: where the management-labor agreement stipulated no layoffs, or where a management was not prepared to do battle on this issue with the union, there were no layoffs.

A notable demonstration of this pattern is found in the contract agreement between United Airlines and District 141 of the International Association of Machinists and Aerospace Workers (IAM). In a letter to the union, the vice president of Employee Relations of United Airlines wrote explicitly:

> No employee on the payroll or on leave of absence as of January 26, 1994 and no employee currently on furlough with right of recall as of January 26, 1994 who is subsequently recalled, shall be laid off during the terms of this agreement.[6]*

*In order to convey a sense of the circumstances surrounding this agreement, I note

One of the majority-owned firms did major downsizing before it was reorganized as an ESOP and signed a union agreement. Thereafter, the management declined a profitable merger deal that would have included downsizing about a thousand employees of the subordinate firm.

What can we infer from these data, however limited in sample size? Even substantial employee ownership—30 percent to over 50 percent of stock—does not, of itself, necessarily alter the management practice of downsizing for corporate profit advantage. Employee voting rights, though attached to the stock, are typically delegated to a "voting trust," which acts as a proxy for employee owners. Conventional downsizing was ruled out, on the other hand, when corporate policies were altered as a result of explicit union-management agreements to make continuity of employment a priority.[7] In other words: workers should read the fine print on their ESOP agreements before assuming that ownership guarantees any degree of actual control.

Ownership and "Participation"

Some theorists of the ESOP movement, on the other hand, have held that ownership participation in the affairs of an enterprise should normally lead to greater participation in the conduct of work, hence a greater readiness of workers to engage in initiatives like "quality circles" and work teams. Broadly, ESOP proponents have argued that management/labor joint participation would, in due course, substitute for class struggle and the social distancing between managers and working people. Accordingly, the results of a survey sponsored by the National Center for Employee Ownership deserves some attention. In a sample of eighty-two firms, only minor participatory differences were found between companies with varying degrees of employee ownership and those without it. Financial and other operating information on new technology and business plans, which are of crucial importance for decision-making, were available to the work-

---

that the contract between IAM and United Airlines also included other safeguards for employment maintenance related to "contracting out" and "foreign repair station work." The contract states:

> No Contracting Out Under Certain Circumstances: The company's ability to contract out shall be limited to up to 20% of all maintenance work, annually. No work shall be contracted out during the term of the agreement unless the Company can demonstrate that layoffs would not result.
>
> Foreign Repair Station Work: No heavy maintenance work shall be performed in a foreign repair station without Union approval. This addresses the continuing job security issues created by the changes to FAR 145 which would allow the repair of United aircraft in foreign repair stations (*141 Messenger*, IAM District Lodge 141, January 1994, p. 6).

ers of non–employee ownership companies in about the same degree as to those in firms with employee ownership programs.[8]

Nevertheless, Joseph R. Blasi and Douglas L. Kruse have argued that employee stock ownership affords an alternative orientation to that represented by traditional hierarchies, which they call Rights or Control. They claim that "Control tries to replace the managerial hierarchy with a worker hierarchy. Control does not understand that groups in a company or an organization need to find ways to cooperate rather than solve problems of dominance. Control says now that employee shareholders finally have a chance to push other people around, let's see how they like it. Control is the French Revolution in corporations. It is interesting that the worst fear of many corporate citizens about employee ownership, control, is actually completely absent from the employee-ownership scene. The employee-ownership world is heavy on Trusteeship, well represented with Paternalism and tending towards Rights in some companies."[9]

By March 1996, Blasi, who has written widely in support of the ESOP development, judged that "most of the early examples of large employee-owned companies have failed to create a true ownership culture. . . . Management is unwilling to let employees exercise normal shareholder rights."[10] Nevertheless, some view the ESOP movement as a path entailing increased employee ownership, heralding a large change in the character of the economy and society.

ESOP Trusts and Tax Advantages

There is a considerable disparity between the various "visions" for ESOP operation. Louis Kelso, a founding father of the movement, judged revealingly that

> Under capitalism, the labor union will obviously not be needed as an instrument of power to effect a laboristic distribution of wealth. This was the function it performed in the transition from primitive to mixed capitalism and is still performing. . . . Voluntary associations of capitalist workers, operating through democratic processes of self-government, may serve their own members and the whole society by functioning as agents for the economic education of the newly made capitalists, and as instruments for the protection of their property rights.[11]

But as David Ellerman has noted, Kelso did not look forward to workers' use of ownership rights to democratically self-govern their own work. Said Kelso:

> Manager-employees should manage, and non-manager-employees should be beneficial owners, but should not interfere with management. Amateur management is the last thing such a concern needs. The difficulty with European-type codetermination plans is that they inject amateur management into business corporations, and therefore add enormous confusion to the business scene.[12]

Ellerman has further noted that

> Progressive ESOP advocates would like to dismiss these views of Kelso and others as individual idiosyncrasies—which just coincidentally are shared by all but a handful of ESOP boosters. But these ideas about the "proper" role for labor are unfortunately built into the typical ESOP design. Trusts are usually set up when someone is not "trusted" with direct ownership. The trust mechanism interposes a layer of trustees between the indirect "beneficial owners" and the exercise of ownership rights.
>
> Trusts are used, for example, when the beneficial owners are children, or are legally incompetent. Trust mechanisms have also been used to separate the control of massive pension funds from the worker-beneficiaries. As a result, the pension funds have been used to finance the export of jobs to union-free environments.

By means of the trust mechanism built into the federal law,

> The "employee-owners" are insulated from the control of their own work lives by the trustees who exercise the votes in the "best interests" of the worker-owners. For ESOP workers, as for children, the ownership is put in a "trust" because the ultimate owners are not trusted.
>
> This insulation of control from the workers underlies the ESOP vision. It is a vision of society split between an elite including top managers, industrialists, bankers and lawyers, and . . . their employees on other side. It is a "populist" vision of placating the workers by letting them in on "a piece of the action" in a manner appropriate to their station in life.
>
> In this vision, there are really two classes of ownership:
>
> (1) first-class ownership for the elite, and
>
> (2) second-class or beneficial ownership for the workers.
>
> First-class ownership is ownership with control. Second-class

> ownership is "ownership" without control. . . . ESOPS were designed to promote worker capitalism, not worker democracy.[13]

Ellerman goes on to observe that "ESOPs are usually established by corporate managers or owners who are interested in the tax benefits and who are not particularly interested in transferring any power or control to the employees." He finds still further that "the main tax advantage to the company is the ability to deduct the value of shares issued to an ESOP from the taxable corporate income." The original ESOP legislation sponsored by Senator Russell Long, as well as the Tax Reform Act of 1984, "has increased the tax favored status of ESOPs for companies, owners and banks. The taxable income to a bank is the interest paid on a bank loan. On a loan to the leveraged ESOP, 50% of the interest is now tax-free to the bank. Dividends paid on stock held in an ESOP are deductible from corporate income, whereas dividends on other shares come out of after-tax corporate income."[14]

The General Accounting Office, in its report of December 29, 1986, wrote that

> Much of this attention has focused on controversies over the use of ESOPS to save firms or prevent hostile takeovers. ESOPS are, however, employee benefit plans found in a wide variety of corporate settings. They covered over 7 million participants and held nearly $19 billion in assets in 1983.

These numbers have since been substantially enlarged. The GAO report continues:

> Congress has provided a number of tax incentives to encourage corporations to establish ESOPS as a way of broadening the base of corporate stock ownership and providing a tool for corporate finance.

Quite apart from the use of ESOPs to expand employee ownership, there is the widespread application of the ESOP mechanism to make a corporate raider's task extremely difficult, for shares representing the value of company assets are held in trust by a trustee group designated by management and the bankers who lend the money for the nominal purchase of a company's assets. These two can be counted on to enforce conditions of stability that include effective barriers to outside takeovers.[15]

There is no question that the ESOP mechanism does entail a widening participation in ownership of company stock. But the same cannot be said for control. These shares, as we have seen, are mainly held in trust and cannot be wielded by their formal owners in the form of voting rights, as in an annual meeting of company stockholders that votes on top officers and on major policy changes.

Various economists have undertaken studies of a possible connection between employee ownership and the growth of firms. Yet the most recent of these scholarly works have shown that the results are not conclusive.[16]

A LOCAL PHENOMENON: THE NORTHEAST OHIO EMPLOYEE OWNERSHIP CENTER

The ESOP movement has been notably prominent in the state of Ohio, which has offered a particularly conducive environment. Ohio is part of the industrial zone called the Rust Belt, which harbored the machinery-producing industries that were once at the core of U.S. industrialization. The Rust Belt is now an area that has experienced a high concentration of factory closures, company relocations abroad, bankruptcies unresolved by new owners and economic depression in the surrounding areas.

A considerable initiative toward reorganizing and reconstituting firms, and to sustaining continued employment and production, was the formation of the Center on Employee Ownership at Kent State University in Kent, Ohio. Its bulletin, *Owners at Work*, has reported the experiences of a series of unusually successful ESOP firms. These have been in companies of small-to-medium size located in relatively small communities where networks of personal relationships were already in place, not only among the workers in the enterprise but also among the townspeople.

Leaders of the Northeast Ohio Employee Ownership Center have found that in their considerable experience with many small and medium-size firms, the best prospects for successful ESOP operation lie where employees have long tenure and are highly skilled, and where the bankers who are called upon to do the financing have built up a body of familiarity and trust. The environment and history of the Ohio center has also made the people of the region unusually conscious of the worth of keeping communities whole, and of the need for mutual support in confronting a depleted regional economy.*

*John Logue, the veteran director of the Northeast Ohio Employee Ownership Center, emphasizes that "current law makes ESOPs beneficial to practically everyone—except taxpayers that don't have them. Employee shares are first taxable when sold, generally at retirement, when income and taxes are lower; company contributions are deductible; commercial lenders are permitted to deduct half the interest on ESOP loans from their

> The Central Ohio economy, with an unemployment rate of 2.9%, offers lots of employment opportunities. The bitter truth that this masks, however, is that this regional economy is built on low wage jobs. Columbus, Ohio, with a poverty rate of 18%, is third highest in the nation in terms of poverty, yet has one of the lowest unemployment rates.[17]

Ohio had seemed to offer a promise of locally sponsored employee ownership in smaller firms where a sense of community binds people together. However, this sense of community could not override the business decisions that had produced massive, concentrated deindustrialization and which checkmated possibilities of sharing control with workers.

ESOP Limits

As we have seen, ESOPs usually involve arrangements whereby the employees assign the management decisions to a trustee group. This group in turn is designated by parties, like the local bank, who allocate the capital used to fund the enterprise. The workers in an ESOP company typically agree to lower wages, which provides additional capital. In a fundamental sense, the workers trade wages for continued employment. Over time, the employee owners gain shares of the firm's asset. But this ownership does not entitle workers to immediate access to these assets—in contrast, for example, to the stockholders of a corporation. This is partly done to prevent the sell-off of securities, thereby allowing a constant and relatively stable body of capital from which the firm can draw to continue its operation. Upon an employee's retirement, the stock can be sold and he or she can receive its cash value, though in many cases the stock can only be sold back to the firm, which is often designated as the "preferred purchaser" of stock in the ESOP contract.

ESOPs have sometimes ensured the continuing operation of communities. But this was not the case in Akron, Ohio, where the tire industry was once dominant. Over the years, the tire companies closed their factories in and around Akron and relocated. Now, as one drives down the city's main thoroughfare, one is struck by the absence of ordinary life. Few pedestrians and very little traffic are found. Closer examination shows that over 90 percent of previous establishments—shops and the like—have been closed. Department stores that once operated are out of business.

---

income; and businessmen who sell closely held companies to their employees are permitted to defer capital gains taxes by rolling their capital gains over into other corporate equities."

Akron has become, in good part, a ghost town. A recent inquiry to the National Center for Employment Ownership in Oakland, California, confirmed this dismal picture: there have been no successful ESOP initiatives in Akron to date.

The main argument in favor of ESOP plans has been their presumed ability to avert the formation of many new ghost towns, especially in the areas where ESOPs have been pursued with some intensity, as was the case elsewhere in Ohio. That's why their proponents emphasize that ESOPs are a recognition of both employee and community rights. Communities may thus, they contend, be saved from shutdown and disarray.

Hyatt Clark in Clark, New Jersey, was once a branch of General Motors producing ball bearings. GM, for its own reasons, decided to dispense with that division, and was prepared to sell it off or otherwise shut it down, but the workers at Hyatt Clark attempted an ESOP arrangement.

The results on the shop floor were dramatic. The workers applied themselves diligently to improving productivity and reducing costs. They were very innovative. I visited the plant and saw that the large battery of heat-treating furnaces was now operating on only about half the previous fuel requirement. The heat-treating building housing these furnaces was about 150 yards long, with a high ceiling and a row of furnaces operating. They each emitted a long arc of flame and gas as the metals were being treated internally. The furnaces obviously used an immense amount of combustible material, so a 50 percent reduction represented a substantial saving.

The machine tools used to make the ball bearings were old, and replacing them would have required a large capital outlay. The maintenance department began rebuilding the existing machines at a fraction of the cost of buying new equipment. The layout of the operations on the plant floor was also fundamentally revised to allow for a more productive use of space and worker time. As a result of these worker initiatives, there was visible evidence of substantial improvements in productivity and reductions in costs.

For all that, however, Hyatt Clark did not continue operation and was shut down in August 1987. The closing was probably a result of bitter conflict over wages and top-management salaries, and between management and the organized workforce represented by the UAW over a long list of union demands that were rejected as improper infringement on management's right to manage. The plant's management consisted of some former GM executives and staff named by the bankers who had made the considerable loans under the ESOP plan. These two parties fought strenuously, even though the value of the old plant and equipment was nominal.

This was a classic demonstration of the impossibility of continuing an ESOP operation in which the workers believed that as investors through their wage reduction, they were entitled to a substantial voice in the policy of the enterprise, but where bank-designated managers remained unwilling to concede decision power to the union. The result was a class war conducted in and around the plant.

There is a considerable dispute concerning who will finally gain from the operation of the ESOP institution. Joyce Rothschild-Whitt, for example, asks, "Who Will Benefit from ESOPs?" She notes that:

> Management and small business owners were quick to grasp ESOPS, as were workers who were facing job loss. The unions took a few more years but they too seemed to be coming around to worker ownership, not out of some *a priori* ideological commitment, but out of the practical opportunities it offers for job preservation, for getting shares of stock in return for concessions that would be exacted anyway and for advancing democratic control of the workplace. The outcomes for the individual worker-owned firms and the outcome for this movement as a whole depend to a great extent on who stays involved in bringing the changes about.

She concludes with this:

> If management continues to dominate the planning of ESOPs, we can expect to see more ESOPs with minority worker ownership stakes and without any special avenues for workers' participation. In this case, ESOPs will come to be seen by all concerned as a simple supplement to wages, like a profit-sharing plan or a pension, signifying no essential alteration in the social relations of production. The future of worker ownership will be determined by those constituencies who remain actively involved.[18]

There is nothing new in all this. In *The Modern Corporation and Private Property*,[19] Berle and Means established that top-management control in corporations had come to be exercised by people with small percentage shares of the securities representing the formal ownership of corporate property. Thereby, primary control by top managers could be exercised by people without majority ownership. For all the optimism, this also applies to the ESOP under corporate control.

. . .

From the standpoint of working people with an interest in the development of workplace democracy, ESOPs, like consultation, participatory management structures, employee participation and autonomous work groups and problem-solving groups, do not address the key question: Who decides?

PART IV

Workers, White Collar and Blue, Create a Process of Disalienated Decision-Making for an Economy and Society After Capitalism

The unpleasant, sometimes nasty, qualities of ordinary life for a large part of American society are certainly discouraging. Nonetheless, alongside of capitalism's ruthlessness and exploitation, we can define the formation of a very different kind of economy and society.

Alienation and accumulation is an old story, oft retold during the long tenure of capitalism. But, as this study contends, workers have refused to stand still. Every wave of alienation during the twentieth century has spurred the struggle for disalienation.

The news here is about disalienation, about the workers' responses to the attempts to render them powerless. To disalienate means to re-empower, and much more. For workers, reempowering means much more than simply countering the employer's agenda of alienation.

Just like everybody else, workers want a voice over their lives in the workplace and beyond. This fundamental desire for freedom is not a uniform feeling, ever present with the same intensity, or to be expected from every person. But disalienation is rooted in a basic human desire for freedom. That is why industrial workers have been joined by medical doctors, nurses, psychologists, engineers, professors and young graduate assistants/instructors in colleges, in the struggle to formulate jointly agreed rules about their working lives: they are organizing themselves (in unions) to secure formal agreement from their employers in contracts that disalienate important parts of their jobs and workplaces.

Alienation and disalienation are central themes of this book. They have been present throughout the five-centuries-long history of capitalism, only to be heightened under state capitalism with its powerful drive for deindustrialization and militarism. The alienating actions by employers and corporate/state managers (Parts I, II and III) evoke the disalienating responses of workers, both blue- and white-collar (Parts III, IV and V). But these two communities do not play by the same set of rules. That is why the relation of employers to employees in state capitalism is a continuous contest in which the workers of every calling commit themselves to codes of behavior that are the obverse of managerial hierarchy and predatory competition without limit. The rules of workplace democracy are founded in solidarity and mutual trust. They are at the core of a historic process which promises to introduce a new economy, and thereby a new society, after capitalism.

The disalienation process gives rise to solidarity and to mutual trust among workers instead of predatory competition; to democratic decision-making in place of managerial hierarchy; to judgments based on equality and fairness in place of arbitrary prejudice. Above all, the disalienated quality of worker decisions about production demands that the people who formulate decisions (or proposals for action) are the same people who implement them. Thereby, the crucial occupational pattern of managerialism—the separation of decision-makers from implementors—is transformed.

I have tried to show that the primary categories of economy are readily comprehended in social-relational terms. Thus, employment, money and property—jointly present—constitute capital. Add a drive for accumulating decision power in terms of these elements, and the main features of capitalism are then accounted for. Disalienation entails core changes that define the movement toward an economy and society after capitalism.

Despite the ordinary absence of formal planning mechanisms among workers for regulating their work, there is a sustained pattern in their efforts, across occupations and across industries, to make rules about production—their work. These rules originate characteristically as rules about workers' relation to one another. Once there is agreement within the relevant worker group, the rule can be included in worker-employer agreements.

Characteristically, workers formulate rules that regulate who is part of the worker group, rules about work time, job deployment, work performance and compensation.

Taken together, these rules cover the main occupational activity of workers in the workplace. Since workers carry out the many-sided task of production, it follows that these classes of rules about their activity comprise core rules about production.

Workers are not content to conduct their lives under the alienated procedures of management that codify degrees of their powerlessness with respect to decision-making. Evidently, acting for achieving empowerment is integral to the employment relation. It is a normal, ordinary aspect of worker activity. Hence, the attempt to reverse alienation, to *disalienate*, is at its core simply a central aspect of being employed. When men and women enter into the relation of employee to employer, they are moved to attempt to disalienate, hence to undertake rule-making with respect to their own work. If a real shift toward workplace democracy is to take place, this is followed by rule-implementation, where the rules are put in force first by consensus among workers to one another, and second in relation to the employer.

Since the main elements of disalienation also involve the main aspects of production, it follows that even in the formal absence of such a designation, the combined effect of disalienation carried out by workers is to regulate the performance of production. In other words, there is no conflict between workplace democracy and productivity. Indeed, there is an abundance of evidence to suggest that disalienated workplaces are frequently more productive and more cost-effective than those governed by managerialism (Chapters 7, 9, 10).

Workers' rules are not established as a competitive replacement for managerialism, as though in a contest with the employer over who will achieve control of decision-making. Rather, as we will see, worker agreements, as codified in union contracts and a multitude of side accords, are first of all compacts among workers with one another, with respect to their activity. The achievement of mutual consensus among workers about the details of their occupational performance is at the heart of the worker decision process. Such agreements among workers are followed by efforts for negotiation and formal contracts with the employer.

There is, however, a second approach: the installation of carefully designed agreements with the employer that use arrangements in other enterprises or industries as a baseline for worker organization and for proposed relations among workers, and with management. This is what I call Disalienation by Design. In this pattern, systems of rules drawn from tried and tested precedents are used as a basis for formulating and negotiating systematic, many-sided disalienation proposals, processes and agreements.

The net effect of workplace democracy, whether growing spontaneously in piecemeal fashion or installed as a systematic pattern, is similar. It establishes a relationship of workers to employer that comprises degrees of disalienation.

While Chapters 9 and 10 concentrate on moves toward workplace democracy in industry, Chapter 11 gives attention to evidence of a widespread movement for unionization in the health care occupations, in education and in engineering. Of course, unions, like management, have not been immune to the corrosive effects of competition for personal gain, which can result in illegality and, in extremis, racketeering. But those activities are well-appreciated violations of mutual trust among workers. Nevertheless, unionization represents a major breakthrough in the disalienation process. Indeed, its importance is made all the more obvious as white-collar occupations join in union initiatives formerly the preserve of blue-collar workers.

It is noteworthy, in fact, that the union contracts that are concluded by the white-collar occupations—and hence the patterns of disalienation that are undertaken—are closely comparable with those of blue-collar employees, down to a detailed focus on the five categories of worker decision-making noted above.

As we will see, the prospects for the extension of workplace democracy are made ever more attractive and realistic as white-collar workers discover solidarity and unionism as ways to cope with the transformation of their own occupations. The alienating legacy of managerialism is fostering, despite itself, a new spirit of cooperation in those at the sharp end of the "new economy." The appearance of physicians, professors and engineers in the ranks of unions will do far more than merely raise morale. For they will be followed by the science and tech-trained workers in computer and allied firms, and universities, research institutions and R&D departments of both private firms and governments.

As white collars continue to join the blue, the promise defined by Professor Carter Goodrich of Columbia University in 1920 becomes a reality. The range of occupations in unions will correspond to the skills needed in every aspect of production, as well as technical and administrative services. Workers are defining the reality of an economy beyond domination by managerialism, the shape of workplace democracy after capitalism.

9

Creating Workplace Democracy

Workers are now, and always have been, prime targets for the employers' drive to extend their profit and power. Especially when operating on a large scale, ambitious companies have not hesitated to cast off workers they deem "redundant," thereby breaking their ties with workplace and community. Another alienation is set in motion, another trigger for evoking the "class memory" of the great alienations of the business capitalist epoch.

Yet each new wave of alienation includes the prospect of creative and active responses from workers worldwide. The twenty-first century, with its familiar litany of corporate restructurings and layoffs, has seen a continued thrust toward greater workplace democracy. Disalienation agreements are the workers' countermoves to the powerlessness first engendered by the great feudal evictions, and then reinforced in recent times by a succession of alienations like the employers' unilateral layoffs.

The struggle for disalienation begins with the workers formulating their own rules, as for example on the topic of seniority, which has been given the force of legal code among workers. Once agreed upon within the worker group, the desired procedure is taken to the employer for further implementation. Disalienation is carried out in a manner that establishes a mutual independence founded in solidarity. This solidarity includes consensus on common social goals and values, mutually agreed-upon procedures for decision-making and for resolving disputes, and mutual trust. Trust stems from a belief or confidence in the honesty, reliability and justness of other people.

Thus far, our data and analyses have centered on corporate and state management, on their main behaviors and effects. In doing so we have highlighted management's continual efforts at expanding its power and, in particular, how predatory competition has given rise to a succession of alienating effects on workers. We now move away from managerialism to identify the presence of workplace democracy and the growth of alternative ways of organizing our working lives.

In American industry, decision-making by workers, unionized or otherwise, has become a characteristic feature. When visiting a nonunionized plant, I found machinists who were programming (or modifying the programs of) the computers that controlled their milling machines. Management was emphatic that programming was the special task of "our" engineers. In fact, the machinists on the shop floor had arranged, unofficially, to learn computer programming and were applying their talents. They were avoiding the removal of decision power over their machine tools, countering a management ploy to use computers to "deskill" their jobs.

The machinists did not transfer decision-making away from the employer to the workers. Their actions were solely directed toward themselves: they had disalienated their work by making decisions over the control of machine tools.

I will discuss several illustrative examples of this ongoing thrust toward disalienation in the workplace. They demonstrate on a systematic basis the essential elements of workplace democracy, and the role of unions in this process.

For defining general features of worker disalienation, we can draw upon an as yet unpublished book called *Workers and Decision-Making on Production*, by Lawrence B. Cohen, Professor Emeritus of Industrial Engineering at Columbia University.

Cohen takes as his point of departure the recognition that sustained alienation of workers has been a core element in the organization of work, first by employers, then by the government/corporate managers of state capitalism.

> The role of the employer as the essential decision maker has so deeply permeated contemporary thinking about the organization of production that the conception of an alternative possibility seems unreal. As a corollary, the union is conceived, with respect to decision making on production, to be a passive, responsive agency, concerned primarily with the division of the product and with ameliorating the impact of the decision making employer upon the workers.[1]

This conventional approach to managing suggests a particular style of decision-making: a person placed in a decision hierarchy, appointed by people above, functioning by the hierarchy's rules, and not subject to decisions made by the workers. As Cohen notes, these are the familiar characteristics of managerialism, which has become so commonplace that it is often used as a generic term for all forms of decision-making. But this approach only serves to obscure a very different process at work in American industry.

> Without external instigation, without plan or blueprint, without benefit of ideology, the workers are becoming decision makers on production as the result of their joint, day by day actions in employment. By methods which enjoy widespread public approval, the workers have launched an autonomous social development of whose character and implications they are themselves probably not aware.[2]

The short-term reaction of workers has included frequent efforts to improve their economic position.

As Cohen notes, during the restless course of industrial relations in the past century or so, workers have tried a variety of alternatives, including abolishing the private business employer, "substituting for him some kind of state or national decision making, or the direct executing of managerial functions by the workers themselves. These programs include socialism, communism, syndicalism and workers' control of industry." Other approaches have involved workers in "some form of sharing in the managerial functions. These include the schemes of labor-management cooperation, joint production committees and the like. . . . Different from the political approach, these preserve the employer function, while affording the workers a voice in their working activities."[3] The continuous history of trade union activities represents an approach that traditionally

> has neither sought to eliminate the employer nor to share his managerial functions. Rather, it has pursued a course seeking to ameliorate the workers' position and to modify their relations with the employer. Of all the ways of dealing with the workers' situation, this one represents their own autonomous creation.[4]

Indeed, as Cohen observes, it is within the growth and functioning of the unions that we find evidence of a different kind of process of decision-making.

> External evidence of the workers' decision system is provided by the growth and expansion of unionization. Collective bargaining

> agreements, the rules and regulations promulgated by organized workers and the unceasing flow of demands and grievances, particularly at shop level, are products of worker decision making.[5]

For while their struggles for wages have been accorded primary public attention, a second, long-term response has been a sustained process of disalienation that bears upon every aspect of work and worker relations.

> The workers' decision system is a second decision making process housed within the individual business enterprise. It exists side by side with the employer's. The evidence will disclose that the workers' system is absorbing decision functions which the employer formerly exercised unilaterally. Despite this drastic change—indeed because of it—the performance of contemporary industry continues to rise to historically unprecedented levels. Production decisions continue to be made, and production flows, even though two decision systems operate within a single firm.[6]

In every sphere of their employment, workers have been making rules for their behavior toward one another and toward their employer.

> They originate in the social and occupational relations among workers, rather than in the formal organizational performances of unions. Their circuit is completed within a systematic set of effects which are decision making on production, rather than harassment of the employer.[7]

Since production is performed by them, the rules that they formulate to govern their behavior have consequences on production. For Cohen, this is the alternative process of decision-making that is obscured by our conventional assumptions about the roles of employer and union.

> It is a decision system which is dramatically different from the employer's and from other systems. In it, the people who execute the decisions also make them. There is no substitute for the employer in the arrangements of the workers' system. The employer is not replaced—he is eliminated as a function. The union or union officials are not alternative employers.[8]

Cohen asks, What kind of decision structure do workers produce? In what ways is this unique? How does it come into being? As a framework for his diagnosis of a worker decision system, he writes,

> Any production decision can be shown to possess three component elements: 1) the action which it decides; 2) the executor of the action; 3) the formulator of the decision. A decision inherently is a directive which specifies activities or conditions which are to be carried out, thereby determining what must take place in production.[9]

According to Cohen, these three components constitute the internal decision structure that governs the main aspects of the worker decision process. Consider a decision to work overtime:

> In the worker's decision structure, the formulator of this decision is also the individual worker. Indeed, the decision to work overtime is known to the employer and workers as the right to refuse.[10]

The ability of the individual worker to refuse indicates that he is the final decision-maker with respect to this matter. Who, then, is the formulator of such a decision on working overtime? On the worker's side, Cohen writes:

> the formulator is a rule. The rule is an equalization—which is one part of a code.[11]

That is to say, among the worker group that may be involved in overtime work, there shall be equal opportunity or equal penalty with respect to carrying out this activity. This means that no single person but the occupation involved was the ultimate formulator of this rule.

Cohen judged that it is useful to consider the decision to allocate, in this case, overtime, as a solution to a major problem of decision structure. Cohen reasons that

> Overtime was allocated before the decision was instituted, perhaps inequitably by the foreman. The new rule constrained the foreman.[12]

The change that was caused by the new rule was clearly intended to remove the foreman's ability to choose overtime workers. Once overtime was allocated on the basis of seniority among a worker group, then the foreman was removed as the decision-maker.

As this example suggests, there are certain conditions that workers must fulfill if they are to make this process both real and lasting.

> First, they must produce decisions which effectively determine those aspects of production to which they apply. This means that the workers' activities must be shown to result in decisions which observably shape the activities and conditions of productive operations. Not all such operations need be determined by their decisions for a decision system to be present; such systems universally evolve and extend themselves to an increasing range of decision making.[13]

Not only must real decisions be produced, they must be produced within a clear and strong framework.

> Second, the decisions must emanate from processes which have the evident characteristics of a decision system. These include continuity, systematic and responsible handling of production issues, independent criteria and methods of decision, and the special property of decision systems, an internal mechanism which continuously extends its range of decision.[14]

Last, the real key lies in changing the structure of decision-making, so that the workers have real power.

> Third, if both the preceding conditions are met, they must ultimately be shown to modify the allocation of decision functions of the employment system in such form as to constitute a significant change in decision making on production. Various kinds of reallocation of function might be made, but the critical one is the addition of decision formulating and issuing to the receiving and executing functions which the workers have always possessed.[15]

Thus, as Cohen argues, workers are learning and acting to reverse the alienation by which they were organized and controlled for centuries. An employer's production decisions derive from management's plans for profitability and power, which they hope will also lead to an extension of their decision-making. But for workers, production decisions originate from their disalienation process.

How does this fresh approach to decision-making help us understand the full scope of workers' decisions on their work? A brief anecdote will illustrate the relevance and power of Cohen's approach.

When I first visited the Standard Motor Company in England in 1955 and met with the union shop stewards, I asked about their possible role in decision-making and received no response at all. I tried putting the question in varied terms—*decision process, decision-making, deciding*—but I got nowhere. I dropped all reference to decision-making and asked them, "In the new contract that you have, what changes have taken place with respect to who is covered, working time, job deployment, work performance, compensation of every sort?"

Our meeting was transformed. With respect to each of these topics, these men could perform like Old Faithful gushing. Each man could speak in great detail on these matters. Their concerns related to the establishment of rules that have benefitted their working lives, rules dealing with disalienation. That these categories still ring true for today's workers was borne out by a similar discussions I had with workers at Harley-Davidson as recently as 1998.

If worker decision-making is as widespread as the previous discussion suggests, why did my first question bring such an indifferent response? Cohen posits an answer.

> [Some] workers understand the question but deny that they engage in decision-making on production. Partly, their denial is a matter of self-protection. They do not want the employer or the outside world to attribute to their organized activities any impermissible objectives. But there is a more fundamental reason. Decision-making on production is associated by workers with the functions of the employer. To engage in decision-making on production means in the language and categories of the workers, to act in the role of the employer. The phrase and the function convey to them exactly the opposite of what they seek through unionization—relief from the employer's decisions. To concede that they practice decision-making on production is tantamount to a betrayal of the union's functions.[16]

As my experience at Standard Motors suggests, Cohen's research has given us a systematic formulation of the workers' decision process. In the course of his study, Cohen found that the terms of employment that workers strive to alter can be encompassed in five categories: worker group, work time, deployment, performance and compensation. Union contracts lend themselves readily to classification of all their contents under these categories.

The *worker group* defines those who may perform production work or bargain or negotiate on the side of the workers. Those included in the worker group need not be limited to manual tasks. In various industrial companies, union contracts explicitly deal with engineering, office and clerical personnel as well. For example, the UAW-Chrysler agreement includes sections representing engineering, office and clerical workers, as well as production employees who make components, assemble cars and test, repair and maintain the tooling, machinery and plant.*

Work time covers all the details of the period and circumstances during which workers must be available for their tasks. This includes not only regular working hours but also special time: for example, under what conditions may an employer call its employees to work during other than regular hours? Who may be called upon to do this? What are the conditions of that particular activity? If an employee works on a Saturday or a Sunday, rather than part of the normal workweek, then the employer may be required to compensate the worker for a full day of work even though the tasks to be performed are completed in less time.

Deployment refers not only to a person's present job location but also to changes in place, grade and department within the organization, and how these changes are made. These rules pertain also to the requirements for a change in job character or location. How may that be carried out? Is it natural that this decision be solely at the discretion of the employer and his representatives to relocate a worker from one job to another, or from one department to another? In union contracts, the employer's control over deployment of workers is sharply limited by the rules of seniority.

Performance concerns the quality and the extent of the task required of

*In the United States, shortly after the Declaration of Independence was published, "First, labor felt that the employer who worked in the shop was a member of the producing class, not of the idle exploiting class of capitalists, the bankers, 'and all who now live on, or intend hereafter to live without useful labor.' " Philip S. Foner, in the first of his four-volume *History of the Labor Movement in the United States*, noted, "One of the first unions to recognize the weakness in employer membership was the New York Typographical Society. The union had approved a resolution in 1809 that said, 'Between employers and employed there are mutual interests.' Eight years later it discovered an employer member conspiring with other employers to break the union. The union expelled him and amended its constitution to exclude employers because:

> "Experience teaches us that the actions of men are influenced almost wholly by their interests, and that it is almost impossible [that] a society can be regulated and useful where its members are actuated by opposite motives and separate interests. This society is a society of journeymen printers, and as the interests of the journeymen are separate and in some respects opposite to that of the employers, we deem it improper that they should have any voice or influence in our deliberation" (Philip S. Foner, *History of the Labor Movement in the United States: From Colonial Times to the Founding of the American Federation of Labor* [International Publishers, 1947], p. 74).

On reading Foner's account of the earliest organizing efforts of colonial American workers, I recalled that David Mandel had found similar patterns in his studies of Russian workers' early organizing efforts following the 1991 collapse of the Soviet regime. There too, workers, in a "pre-solidarity" stage, convened their "Collective" to consider industrial action. In their view, the "Collective" included management.

a person in a particular job. Thus the sections of a contract dealing with performance can often involve massive detail and an array of side agreements on workload, work standards and the procedures by which they are established.

Compensation encompasses every sort of income, not only in terms of money but also in various nonwage payments. It may include bonuses or access to facilities for medical or recreational purposes. It may also involve the allocation of time for personal matters—the birth of a child, a marriage, a death in a family. Occupational training is not necessarily considered compensation to the employee, because the advantages that result will also benefit the employer.

These five categories are mutually interdependent and cover every aspect of worker decision-making. They provide a framework that makes sense of the often complex and lengthy terms of formal agreements between employees and employers. I have not seen a union contract that does not deal with each of these five terms.

How, then, do they help us understand a matter of concern to every worker, the question of job security? Job security is defined by work time and deployment rules. The terms of the occupation may be different, for example, if the work is to be performed only two months of the year, instead of year round.

Job security is also strongly affected by rules concerning layoffs, termination of employment, compensation and lengthy unemployment. Union contracts can refer to it as an objective that both management and worker organizations strive to achieve. But, of course, it is not assured. Efforts have emerged to bolster such a commitment—for example, by providing compensation close to that of the employment level even during a period of layoff—but that is not the same as job security.

Job security can also mean employment security, the status of a person in an organization, or can be related to such matters as seniority, which, in turn, plays a part in work time, deployment and compensation. But unfortunately for many American workers, security does not necessarily entail stability in employment or job performance. It can be accompanied by variations in the hours of work, a commitment to function in a particular period or continuation of a task in a particular occupation.

Union contracts, of course, may include other considerations. For example, while analyzing the union contracts of the Standard Motor Company for the 1940s and 1950s, I found clauses concerning interplant relations that also had a bearing on the wider markets for company products. These have their counterpart in the 1990s in the sections of Saturn's Memorandum of Agreement that specify, contrary to the policy of its parent company GM, a commitment to using only components made in the

United States. The implications clearly go beyond Saturn's agreed terms of deployment, at a time when U.S. corporations continue vigorously to export jobs and production.

In addition, one of the usual patterns in a union contract is the appearance of what is very often called a "management-rights clause." This section will typically state that management has the sole responsibility and obligation to design and conduct the operations of the enterprise according to accepted management criteria.

But the implications of these clauses, which may also imply that the union cannot abridge any of them, are not consistent with the pattern of agreements by which a union negotiates with management on the terms of employment.

The Widening Scope of Workplace Democracy

We have identified the presence of worker decision-making on production by the development of decisions on worker group, work time, deployment, performance and compensation. Decisions on these matters define worker performance *within* the enterprise. But, decisions about action *outside* the enterprise are also essential for sustained production *inside* the area covered by worker-management contracts, or by autonomous worker decision-making.

How do workers' decisions and actions *outside* connect with the decisions they make within the point of production or firm? Linkages to the rest of the economy and to society are readily dealt with in the framework of *performance* and *compensation.*

Performance requires the inputs of tools, machines, materials, power and information that come from people and organizations apart from the worker group covered by contract between the workers and the employer. "Management-rights" clauses are thus more political-ideological statements than terms of employment.

The range of union activity on decisions about production that connect to the wider economy has not been widely studied. But such activity is there and is likely to accelerate as managements pursue domestic disinvestment and "globalization" policies. The United Automobile Workers and the United Steel Workers, for example, have traditions of negotiating with industry managers about the sourcing of components, factory construction and maintenance for steel and autos (on whether from union or nonunion firms, domestic or foreign suppliers).

The 1990 and 1999 Ford contracts with the UAW thus include detailed procedures for transferring production work *into* Ford facilities—

called *insourcing*—as well as the reverse: *outsourcing*. National and local management-union committees are established for this purpose. The National Committee encompasses

> National Job Security, Operational Effectiveness and Sourcing Committee, comprised of Company and Union representatives including the Vice President and Director of the National Ford Department and a senior member of Employee Relations Staff.[17]

On the workers' side, the agreement specifies:

> The International Union and, where appropriate, the local union will be provided full and timely access to all appropriate data, including financial information that is pertinent to evaluate product competitiveness and contemplated sourcing.

The contract also includes specific procedures for both insourcing and outsourcing.

> The National Committee and, where appropriate, the Local Committee will discuss the practicality of insourcing, in whole or in part, work previously outsourced or new work which the Union identifies as that which might be performed competitively within the location based on [agreed] criteria.

Ford's management agreed to provide information that will facilitate discussion with the UAW.

> To assist in this process, the International Union will be furnished a complete list of work similar to that currently performed at the location that (1) has been outsourced from that location or (2) is currently performed by non-Ford-UAW suppliers for Ford Motor Company. . . . Thereafter, the parties will initiate efforts to insource particular work consistent with the aforementioned criteria to create prospects for growth and to provide jobs for . . . employees . . . on layoff.
>
> If it is established that certain work can be performed competitively, judged by the above criteria, management will adopt the Committee's proposal and, barring unique or unforeseen circumstances, bring the work in-house. The Union shall thereafter obtain any necessary approval or ratification within 30 days of the decision to bring the work inhouse.

I have included, below, the full list of criteria to be dealt with in Ford-UAW discussions on sourcing.* The scope of this discussion is wide-ranging and involves detailed knowledge about the functioning of the Ford company.

Outsourcing is carefully addressed. Thus, when

> an outsourcing decision is contemplated, the International Union and the local union will be given 120 days' written notice, or longer advance notice, when possible. The notice will include the reason for the outsourcing, a description of the work involved, the impact on the workforce, the identification of the sourcing authority, and all financial information. . . .
>
> Additionally, International Union and local union input will be sought by the company as early as possible in the outsourcing decision-making process. The intent of the evaluation period being expanded and Union input being sought as early as possible is to allow for more thorough discussion and to permit the parties to assess better the impact of outsourcing on the long-term job stability of employees and the financial viability of given Company locations. . . .
>
> . . . if it is established [in union-management discussion] that the work can be performed competitively . . . management will, barring unique and unforeseen circumstances, keep the work in-house. . . .
>
> The Company agrees to a full disclosure to the International Union of the procedures utilized in the sourcing decision-making process.

In addition to the national contract, there are typically networks of policy statements and local agreements that amplify and detail procedures

*Ford-UAW Memorandum of Understanding: Appendix P. Sourcing includes the following formulation of criteria for sourcing decisions: "The rationale for sourcing actions will consider the criteria of quality, technology, cost, timing, statutory requirements, the impact on long-term job stability, the degree to which the Company's resources can be allocated to further capital expenditures, the overall financial stability of affected facilities, and the impact on related facilities. The National parties will jointly further develop the above criteria to be used to address sourcing issues. In developing financial criteria appropriate Corporate return on investment and burden will be considered. Pertinent criteria will be applied consistently in comparisons of internal and external supply capability."

The 1999 agreement added "Occupational and related environmental health and safety issues" as a criterion. This means that effects on the workers' health and safety are formally acknowledged as decision criteria. Their application qualifies the usual managerial money cost-minimizing yardsticks.

used for considering both insourcing and outsourcing. The Ford contract declares that

> It is an objective of the Company to grow the business and to continue to rely upon its employees and facilities as the source of its products. During the term of the 1990 Agreement, data regarding work brought in-house and work outsourced will be given to the International Union in a quarterly meeting. In this manner, the parties can judge the success of mutual efforts toward improved job security.

The October 1999 national agreements between Ford and the UAW continue to pay close attention to both national and local negotiations about both *insourcing* and *outsourcing* (notably in Appendix P). To take one important point, when outsourcing is proposed by management, a local committee is to be established that is broadly representative of both local management and the local UAW, with participation by senior officials of the management and union.

The agreements further specify that with respect to procedures regarding Future Product Sourcing,

> Ford-UAW Quarterly Meetings . . . will include regularly scheduled reviews of Ford's North American vehicle cycle plans for assembly, stamping and powertrain. These will include confidential summaries of these plans which identify new or redesigned vehicles, subsystems or component parts, etc.

Future Product Development also includes the following mutual agreements:

> It is imperative that sourcing discussions and notification become an effective and trusted tool. It is recognized that early involvement by the UAW will greatly enhance the chances for mutual success and will not jeopardize the product development objectives of quality, speed to market, product innovation, and lower total cost.

The contract includes provisions for union meetings with senior operations managers of Ford:

> Upon the request of the Union, the Company will schedule subsequent meetings with Program Managers and/or Operations

> Managers or their designated representatives to discuss issues of concern to the Union. Other appropriate Management personnel, such as representatives from Purchasing and Engineering, may attend the meetings. Further follow-up meetings will be scheduled as required at the request of either party. . . . The implementation of this process should provide the parties the mechanism to take advantage of every opportunity to use internal resources.
>
> The commitments expressed in this Memorandum of Understanding are intended to contribute significantly to our cooperatively working together to provide Ford Motor Company employees in the United States improved job security by expanding business.

Compensation requires revenue from the sale of the industrial product. Accordingly, some local unions have developed detailed interest in management's selection of products and strategies for marketing. These matters had priority, for example, in the 1999 internal union elections and debates at the Saturn division of GM.

The same trend is visible in a recent union agreement with Kaiser Permanente, a not-for-profit, group practice prepayment health care program, with 60,000 employees, in 38 unions, and serving 8.5 million in seventeen states and the District of Columbia. In June 1997, management formalized a National Labor-Management Partnership Agreement with the AFL-CIO representing the Coalition of Kaiser Permanente unions. The agreement is intended to be a strategic move affecting virtually every aspect of management and worker decision-making. By April 2000, representatives of the 38 unions were meeting with management to negotiate a combined contract.

Marketing cooperation is the subject of a principal Partnership clause whereby "all parties will make their best efforts . . . to market KP to new groups and individuals and to increase KP's penetration in existing groups." The AFL-CIO "will use its influence . . . to include Kaiser Foundation Health Plan as a unionized health care option available to their members."

An "Employment and Income Security" agreement was announced November 9, 1999, that committed KP management to job/income security, as a strategic move to remove the fears of job loss that often cause reluctance to introduce or participate in worker-productivity improvements.

These sampled data from union-management agreements bear importantly on worker performance and compensation. They illustrate how these core features of worker decision-making are affected by links with the rest of the economy.

Systematic investigation about worker decision-making bearing on *performance* and *compensation* will yield important understanding of how developments toward workplace democracy include linkages with workers in the wider economy, at home and abroad.*

As the previous discussion has suggested, there is a sustained effort by workers to acquire expanded decision rights with respect to worker groups, work time, deployment, performance and compensation. What is crucial is the expanded rights of workers pertaining to their work. A vital feature of the workers' decision process is its relevance to the internal relations of the worker group. Thus, regulating performance in each of the five functional areas of worker decision-making requires methods for deciding who will have what place in each particular decision area.

Another important feature of this process of disalienation is its sustained operation. The nature of the process is such that there is no time or other limit. Control of one's work has no boundary. There is no ideology, no explicit limit to the disalienation process of workers.

A further consideration of importance is that the process moves independently of variation in personality. This doesn't suggest that individuals have no effect on the process in different ways. It simply means that the operation of the process, notably in its drive for disalienation, is a group phenomenon. It is at once formulated on a collective basis and carried out according to the standards and requirements of a worker group.

Many of these considerations will take on a more tangible quality as they are examined with respect to an important feature of the decision process of American workers, which, like job security, involves every aspect of the five categories we previously noted. That feature is seniority.

Seniority

The regulation of deployment or other worker activities on a seniority basis removes an arbitrary aspect of decisions about who works where and when. Seniority provides greater fairness in a whole host of situations: in decisions about transfers, promotions, holidays, overtime and who gets the better-paying jobs. Under an agreement to select people from the top

*See, for example, the collections of contract clauses assembled by the Bureau of National Affairs, Washington, D.C. They disclose that the topics of insourcing and outsourcing are dealt with, though variously, by a great many union-management agreements.

of a seniority roster, the only issue management can unilaterally decide on is the number of workers required in a department. Thereafter, the particular workers who are to enter into that occupation (or section, department or plant) may not be designated by management but must be chosen on the basis of seniority. These workers must usually also demonstrate their capability in the occupation.

What led to the strategic role of seniority as a way of carrying forth decisions as to who should do which work, who might change from one job to another and the like?

Negotiation of seniority rules has always been high on the agendas of American unions. Indeed, because seniority serves to remove competition among workers for the employer's favors, such agreements can even precede formal contracts with the employer. The first seniority rules with private firms in the United States were established in the railroads.[18] From the 1890s, seniority became an important issue in the printing trades as well.[19]

From her studies of the origins of job structures in the steel industry, Katherine Stone reports that the principal steel employers at the beginning of the twentieth century decided jointly to carry out a policy of internal job selection and promotion by means of a "job ladder" of their design for production workers. This, it was hoped, would arouse the ambitions of workers throughout the organization. Stone writes further:

> The other advantage of the job ladder arrangement was that it gave the employers more leverage with which to maintain discipline. The system pitted each worker against all the others in rivalry for advancement and undercut any feeling of unity which might develop among them. Instead of acting in concert with other workers, workers had to learn to curry favor with their foremen and supervisors, to play by their rules, in order to get ahead. As one steel worker described the effect this had on workers during the 1919 organizing campaign, "Naw, they won't join no union; they're all after every each other feller's job." This competition also meant that workers on different ladder rungs had different vested interests, and that those higher up had something to lose by offending their bosses or disrupting production.[20]

As might be expected, these kinds of practices aroused calls for more equitable terms of employment. Stone notes, for example, that as early as 1900, *Iron Age*, an industry journal,

> was advising employers to fill production work vacancies from inside the firm. They advocated a policy of hiring only at the low-

> est job levels and filling higher jobs by promotion—what contemporary economists refer to as limiting the ports of entry. In one article, titled "Developing Employees," a columnist sharply criticizes a specific employer who has very often failed to find the proper qualifications among his employees to promote any one of them to certain higher positions which had become vacant from various causes. . . . At such times he usually hired outsiders to fill the positions and thus engendered dissatisfaction among his helpers.

In contracts between the steel industry and the United Steel Workers, seniority agreements came to have an important place. Having decided not to compete with one another, workers adopted the seniority system, declining to fight for certificates issued by the employer that were used to obtain better jobs. They appreciated, as Stone says, "that certificates in themselves did not guarantee anything. They merely improved one's chances—so the 'loyal ones' still had to compete."

This process of disalienation gained in momentum during the Depression. Lawrence B. Cohen was once studying worker organization in a New England textile factory and learned some interesting history:

> During the thirties, before the formation of the union, workers noticed that many people were never laid off while others suffered reduced work weeks and extended periods of unemployment. They called these fated ones the "Twelve Apostles" because there were supposed to have been 12 who worked steadily. Naturally, the unfavored ones considered this allocation of work unfair and discriminatory, but they tended to blame the supervisors less and the favored ones more for this situation. They claimed that the 12 received steady work because they curried favor with the foreman. The old-timers in the union recited detailed anecdotes about the things the fully employed workers had to do for their foremen in order to win their favored treatment: washing the foremen's cars, mowing their lawns, and the like.[21]

What results in such a situation is a severe decline in solidarity and mutual trust.

> When a worker receives special treatment from a foreman, he is not an innocent, passive victim of some bounty. He earns this treatment by the explicit things he does either for the foreman personally or by his activities on the job. The individual benefici-

ary is a collaborator or an initiator of the discrimination, not its unlucky victim.

Cohen's formulation eloquently describes the conditions of industrial life that underlie the importance given historically to seniority rules, which provide a systematic way to eliminate these kinds of destructive practices. His formulation should not be understood as a simple anecdote, but rather as an illustration of behavior occurring on a scale that justifies the wide application of seniority rules in relations between workers and employers.

In the 1990 contract between Ford and the UAW, for example, about 50 pages include references to seniority, and a 27-page section of the contract deals solely with these rules. The 1990 Chrysler contract includes 10 pages of rules on seniority practice.

By way of contrast, the 1956 contract between the management of the Standard Motor Company and the Confederation of Ship Building and Engineering Unions did not include "any reference to seniority methods."[22]

For further comparison, the Ferguson tractor was produced both in Britain, at Standard's factory in Coventry, and also for the U.S. market in a plant in Detroit. Evidence of this difference in approach may be seen in the agreement between Harry Ferguson, Inc. and the American union, Local 174 (UAW-CIO). In the 1949 UAW contract of 25 pages, 7 were taken up with seniority regulations. Though there was no mention of seniority rules in the Standard Motor Company contract, it was regarded at the time as the most sophisticated, advanced and far-reaching contract between union and management in the automotive industries in Great Britain.*

*A possible clue to the source of such a difference may be contained in an analysis of the last chapters of my *Decision-Making and Productivity*.

Unlike their American counterparts, the union representatives at the Standard Motor Company were not aware of the concept of frequent changes in job grades and job positions. A person entered into a particular occupation, like tool-maker or sheet metal worker, and then went through a series of gradations within that occupation. The workers in these occupations insisted on entry into the full craftsman position solely through apprenticeship and journeyman status. One might think these terms carry the overtone of the feudal guild.

Transfer among jobs, departments and the like could not be carried out under those circumstances by rules of fairness, tantamount to a seniority rule.

The matter of layoffs was important. In the opinion of one senior shop steward, the desirable long-term action for handling layoff problems would include changes in the contract with the management: a 40-hour week instead of 42½ hours; no dismissals without alternative employment found; removal of foreign trade restrictions, notably those relating to Eastern Europe, China and the U.S.S.R., so that those markets could become available for the shipment of Standard Company products. In the view of this steward, any sacking

Beyond doubt, only a beginning has been made here in understanding the processes of alienation and disalienation that are the center of attention in this book. So it may be important to undertake specialized, concentrated explorations from the vantage point of any one of the major aspects of disalienation. For example, the rules of seniority may seem to be straightforward in meaning and effect. But we have a set of analyses by Carl Gersuny that illuminate a surprising number of problems and effects from efforts to apply diverse seniority rules, particularly in American industry (see the Gersuny papers list in the Bibliography).

This discussion of seniority serves to answer the question Why do workers attempt to disalienate? What they have done is effectively remove competition from one another. And by this absence of competition, they find themselves better able to deal not only with one another, but also with the employer. These consequences are of sufficient importance to justify elaborate and devoted attention by American workers to seniority rules and similar arrangements.

AN EARLIER VENTURE IN WORKPLACE DEMOCRACY: THE GANG SYSTEM IN COVENTRY, ENGLAND

British workers may not have accorded seniority the kind of importance given by their American counterparts, but their struggle for disalienation may nevertheless provide us with an earlier example of workplace democracy in action.

Dwight Rayton was the name (or pseudonym) of a worker in an aircraft plant in Coventry during and after World War II. His account of the formation and operation of a "gang system" in his own factory gives an unusual glimpse into an early venture in workplace democracy. The system that he described was either a precursor or a close relative to the one I discussed in my 1958 study *Decision-Making and Productivity*.[23] In the gang system, which had its origins in the British mining industry, instead of individual piecework, the gang as a whole is paid for what they produce, and it is up to them how they divide up their wages. What to produce and how much is still dictated by the employer, but as Rayton's account makes clear, the workers thus have power over how they organize their own work group, their deployment and their compensation.

---

without a search for alternative employment would require the introduction of government responsibility for the handling of layoff (also called "redundancy") problems. Indeed, that happened.

In American unions, the differentiation between temporary cessation of work and termination of connection with the company is carefully drawn.

Rayton reported on the genesis and mode of operation of the gang system in the aircraft factory in which he worked:

> We worked out between us how many men we would want and the boss agreed. We elected a ganger, and a deputy ganger to take charge on night shifts. We sorted out men, openly, to do the work they were best fitted for. We made mistakes, but they were immediately corrected. We reckoned up the various prices of jobs and proved theoretically, that we could increase our earnings. We had all the benches and other contraptions moved to suit our own way of working.[24]

This democratic workplace at first met some resistance.

> Some of the firm's officials objected that we were "infringing their rights" and the management proper insisted that *they* would appoint the ganger. We said "No! He would then be a boss and we are not having a boss. He is *our* man responsible to us, and we, individually and collectively, will be responsible for all the work done by the gang!" It wasn't put quite so explicitly as I have just written, but that was what was meant, and the managers being good chaps (we knew them personally) accepted it.

Rayton identifies the key importance of self-organization.

> This, insisting on ourselves appointing the ganger, turned out to be the key to success. The "contract" (unwritten, as is the Common Law kind of contract) was not between the firm and the ganger, but between the firm and the gang as an entity. In our case "Gang No. 3." Gangers could come and go, but Gang 3 went on. We knew of course that in a serious situation the management could abolish Gang 3—but why would they? They wanted us. Wanted the work. We had endless discussions the first few weeks. . . . And then, eventually, finding that everything was working out well we gave up worrying and concentrated on work.

The ganger took the lead in organizing compensation and deployment, but he was responsible, and accountable to his fellow workers.

> The position was that the ganger kept track of work and money and left discipline and other details to us. He was just one member of a democratic team. He saw to it that the gang was supplied with tools, materials, and information derived from design office

> memos and blueprints. Clever men helped others decipher difficult drawings, not so clever men were content to do the drudge work. *No* distinction was made on degrees of skill—that was a waste of time. Divisive.

His account provides a glimpse into a workplace run on truly democratic principles.

> Every week men joined us and were accepted at once as equals. Only the ganger and his deputy worried about money; the rest were free to concentrate on their work which was a great relief to men previously tormented by individual piecework. But it was still piecework, still gave men the urge to earn more, and earn it by brains and skill rather than by being driven. Decisions were made at gang meetings (in meal breaks) and the ganger was obliged, as in Parliament, to answer questions. He could also, in return, publicly castigate men who were at fault. Naturally he was the best man on the gang for all this, which was why the men picked him. Men working together almost always "sense" the man they want as leader. And they could sack him, at a gang meeting.

For Rayton, one of the great attractions of the gang system was its impressive lack of formality.

> All this was tacitly understood. Management also tacitly understood, and no written rules were made. Consequently there were no "orthodoxies," everything being left as fluid as possible. In this way all kinds of initiatives came from the shop floor, and these, added to brilliant design, planning and organization, pushed the firm into the lead in aircraft production.

In retrospect, however, this lack of a formal contract may have put the workers in a position of weakness. As we shall see, more recent ventures in workplace democracy have been formulated in precise agreements between employers and managers that deal with each of Cohen's five categories.

Nevertheless, Rayton's account of these evidently sensible actions hardly begins to convey the force of this innovation. It was a departure from authoritarian managerial ways, and from Frederick Winslow Taylor's technique of prescribing all the details of work performance. It was a surefire surprise to anyone convinced that proper higher education is the indispensable requirement for organizing and planning production.

Union Initiative for Major Decision-Making Change

Until this point we have focused on the changes in decision process initiated among industrial workers, "from below." As the following sections dealing with recent ventures in workplace democracy in the United States will show, there are other possible routes to the extension of worker decision-making.

In recent decades, the International Association of Machinists and Aerospace Workers (IAM) has developed a pattern of union-management contracts and relationships that includes an impressive array of departures promising major advances in decision-making by worker groups.[25]

A notable example is the Partnership Agreement between Harley-Davidson, the IAM, and the United Paperworkers International Union (UPU). Implementation of the agreement is fully the responsibility of the local unions in relation to Harley-Davidson.

Perhaps the most striking feature of the agreement is its emphasis on the importance of *consensus decision-making*. The specific procedures involved are spelled out in some detail. The only place I had seen this method described as a regular decision procedure was in the Israeli kibbutz. The top people in the kibbutz enterprise Netafim (discussed in Chapter 10) emphasized that consensus was a preferred method for ensuring workforce democracy. It's worth examining the exact text of the IAM's procedure at Harley-Davidson, whose contract is cited as an important model of the "high performance work organization" (HPWO).[26] Agreement on the use of consensus method by management and union bears upon every aspect of worker and management decision-making, for it constitutes a *recognition of the union as a co-equal partner.*

In the Milwaukee facilities of Harley-Davidson, workers (and salaried staff) are formed into work groups with defined product and service responsibilities. Management and union have moved toward making these work groups (rather than the individual worker) the defined responsibility unit. In this realm, however, all employees are trained to perform a variety of tasks. "All employees must develop an annual plan of rotation through the various jobs, which will ensure backups and employee development." A consensus approach is thus made an integral part of the terms of both deployment and performance.

An *employment security agreement* assures no loss of employment for eligible employees. When job details and numbers require change, training and reassignment will be provided in accordance with collective bargaining agreements. And "in the event of severe economic hardship, the Partners will explore alternative courses of action before considering the necessity for employment reduction." Readers will recall that job security pertains automatically to work time and deployment.

This commitment to consensus is a central part of the IAM's effort to negotiate other HPWO agreements, in which union and management will engage in "joint determination of the methods, process and means of manufacturing."[27] Indeed, one of the necessary components for bargaining is deemed to be "a co-determined definition of quality and its continuous measurement."[28] All aspects of worker decision-making are automatically affected by the "co-determined" character of what is proposed. "As we explore the potential and the challenges of worker ownership, we need to have on hand a well-defined, working model HPWO that can save and create jobs for our members while pioneering a production process that is co-determined and perfected by the workforce and its managers."[29]

In its *General Guidelines for Negotiating the High Performance Work Organization*, the IAM makes clear that this commitment extends beyond the traditional role of the union, moving by implication into financial planning and capital investment, areas often regarded as the ultimate preserve of management.

> The IAM and management will jointly explore and create new markets, brainstorm product development, and work out the methods and processes needed to offer new products and services.
>
> Financial and technical information will be shared with IAM to determine all costs from prototype to production, administration, marketing and sales, as well as units of wage and profit. This will be done in a process that effectively produces goods and services to customer specifications that are jointly predetermined.

The IAM's "model" agreement defines three classes of decision-making procedures.

> Type 1: Unilateral. Management or labor decides by themselves.
>
> Type 2: Unilateral with prior input. Management or labor decides with full input.
>
> Type 3: Joint Consensus. Management and labor agree through consensus on the decision. All who participate agree that this is the best decision that the group can make.

The partnership agreement with Harley-Davidson mentions twenty-three elements of decision-making that the management and union consider critical to the business. After identifying the elements, the partners evaluated each to determine how that decision is made, and labeled each one with a 1, a 2 or a 3. Apart from the starting classification, the partners agreed that consensus is the best procedure and expected that development of the HPWO system would move toward consensus for all the decision elements listed as follows:

1. Employee Participation
2. Education/Training
3. Employee Development
4. Production Scheduling
5. Staffing Levels Up/Down
6. Staffing Hourly and Jointly Specified Salaried Positions
7. Subcontracting
8. Technology Integration
9. Defining Customer Value
10. Work Organization and Product/Process Improvement
11. Quality Standards
12. Information Sharing

    Exceptions:

    *Legally restricted to one of the parties

    *Preliminary discussion regarding acquisition

    *Potential litigation

    *Compensation not publicly reported

    *Confidential personnel changes

    *Personnel/medical files of any employee, EXCEPT as required by law or labor agreement

13. Cost of Product and Process
14. Capital and Operating Budgets
15. Alternative Source of Funding
16. Acquisitions/Divestitures

17. Strategic Business Plan
18. Discipline/Dismissal
19. Interplant Transfers
20. Selection of Resources [for Training]
21. Design/Location of New Plant(s)
22. Internal Communications Strategy Re: Partnership
23. External Public Relations RE: Partnership[30]

As the following brief comments suggest, the HPWO system is notable for its built-in flexibility.

Production scheduling (#4) is now operated in several patterns: management currently makes an annual estimate, while scheduling by quarterly, monthly and lesser periods is done by consensus—mainly by management and workers on the plant floor.

Changes in staffing (#5): hiring is by consensus, up to final decisions, which are now made by management; reduction in staffing is now by consensus, although final staffing decisions (#6) are currently in management hands. Subcontracting decisions (which feed back to staffing #5 decisions) involve joint sourcing agreements by management and workers. Item #8 (technology integration) pertains to the production process itself and is expected to move toward type 3 (consensus) decision.

The costing of products and processes (#13) is designed by Harley-Davidson management. There is a joint interest in reducing the scope of arbitrary "overhead" costing in order to minimize expense.

At this writing, the parties agree to deal jointly with acquisition and divestiture matters (#16), a major capital decision matter. Likewise with decisions on design and location of new plants (#21). The union strongly favors excluding locations in states with so-called "right-to-work" laws, which severely restrict the functioning of unions. Joint consensus has operated in this sphere.

Finally, public relations pertaining to the partnership (#23) agreement is to be operated by consensus.

The president of the Machinists' Union, R. Thomas Buffenbarger, prepared a statement in which he defined how the IAM views the new form of contract with employers:

> On one road, we can do nothing, which is what many employers and unions are doing. They are carrying on business pretty much as they always have. Management administers and the union

> enforces the labor agreement. Management, for the most part, makes all the key decisions over design and production. Labor "punches in," picks up the job ticket, studies the "specs." For the most part, labor does just what is expected or what it is told to do. This is the prevailing system in workplaces all across North America.
>
> But there is another road we can successfully travel together. The HPWO Partnership defines a new approach to the way we design and build products and deliver services, the way we represent collective and individual interests, structure the work process, and ultimately do our jobs. Unlike prior "team concept," flavor-of-the-month programs that urged shop floor participation while maintaining top floor control, in the HPWO partners jointly decide on a strategy to stabilize and grow the business. Through consensus decision-making, the problems are jointly defined, the solutions and responsibilities are truly shared.
>
> However, I must caution you: the road to HPWO Partnerships is difficult and slow, but it should be. You cannot get there in the fast lane. And I encourage you: It is the high road and the right road, for it is lined with the inventive and creative capacity of everyone at the work site. It relies on running our engines and creative juices at full throttle—free to think and free to improvise.
>
> This approach has proven to be bold, innovative, and not without risk. It requires each member of the Partnership—hourly and salaried, labor and management—to modify their respective roles and responsibilities. It requires members and representatives of the union, management, and other salaried personnel—it calls on everyone—to modify their behavior.[31]

About thirty companies have signed on for developing partnership agreements. The IAM has established a special office in its headquarters to service and promote extended participation in this form of innovative contract relationship with the union.

USX and United Steel Workers of America

USX is currently the largest steel-producing firm in the United States. It includes about 13,000 workers belonging to the United Steelworkers of America (USWA).

Once again, this contract can be usefully analyzed for the pattern defined by the five main categories of worker decision-making.

Worker Group

Worker group includes not only production workers of all grades but also office and technical staff. (Their inclusion is also characteristic of the union agreements with the other integrated steel companies.) The present agreement with USX includes a commitment to observe neutrality in USWA organizing efforts, and (very important) to practice "cardcheck recognition" of the union. Management agreed to recognize the union as a bargaining agent without any National Labor Relations Board (NLRB) election if a majority of employees in the bargaining unit signed authorization cards.

Where a local union agrees with management to conduct a quality-improvement program in production or maintenance, the present agreement provides for plant job protection and includes clerical and technical employees in the program—and thus in virtually any payouts that may be made.

Work Time

As average hours per week have risen—attracted by time-and-a-half payment after 40 hours—some workers do more than 56 hours per week. The contract provides that $10 per hour for half of the work time over 56 hours in a payroll week should go to an Institute for Career Development that offers education courses to steelworkers. About two-thirds of USX steelworkers have opted to participate in such programs, with computer courses getting by far the most interest—about 65 percent.

The remarkably heavy workweek that many steelworkers undertake at USX is due to their eagerness to earn more—despite the strain that a 56-hour-plus workweek inevitably brings. Management has been well disposed to such long workweeks, since paying an employee at the overtime rate is much cheaper than hiring an additional worker (because of the size of the "fixed" charges for regular full-time employees, made up of fringe benefits plus the wage for a job).

Performance

An ongoing major change in the content of work has been gradual incorporation of maintenance work into production jobs. Such changes at once add a burden of responsibility to production jobs, but also add interest. This signals a considerable departure from the narrow, limited-task design of work in the Taylor tradition.

Job performance is also affected by the option, if union and management agree, to form self-directed work teams that are empowered to investigate and recommend changes in organization and methods to a joint plant leadership committee.

Work performance includes the union in true power-sharing over decisions previously off limits to union or employee influence. This new power-sharing is slated to involve "members in the full decision-making process of the company from the shop-floor to the board room." Workers get a voice in "all decisions involving new technology—including not only technology implementation" but "the actual decision on whether to install it." Once again, this affects sharing decisions on capital investment, for that is what expensive new technology entails in the capital-intensive technologies of the steel industry.

"Contracting out" in the industry has meant, especially, bringing in outside workforces to accomplish major new construction. The 1994 agreement provides that this can be done only when new construction is "of a larger or grander scale than other projects which bargaining unit forces are normally expected to do."

Job Security

What about *job security*? Employment security is provided at USX by a management commitment to a no-layoff guarantee "during the entire five and one half year term of the agreement." Exception to this assurance is provided only "in case of disaster," such as "permanent shutdown of a steel-producing plant."

Compensation. In the 29-page summary of the current contract, 15 pages are taken up with the details of wage increases, pensions, surviving spouse benefits and a variety of "improvement" changes in all manner of insurance.

Apart from this realm of ordinary worker decision considerations, the contract between the USWA and USX (which ran through the year 2000) provided for a number of innovative moves:

- Rebuilding the number and quality of craft specialist workers
- USX plus the union to form a National Policy for Steel Committee to address such matters as national trade policy, national health policy, industrial infrastructure, fiscal and monetary policy, the environment
- Participation by management and union in a steel industry strategic study.

Seniority measures are held intact.

UNITED STEELWORKERS OF AMERICA 1998 WAGE-POLICY STATEMENT

A series of important disalienation moves can also be expected for U.S. and Canadian firms in the steel industry: The International Wage Policy Committee of the USWA announced a series of key bargaining priorities on June 16, 1998. The union proposed that employers should agree to formal recognition when it "submits cards validly signed by a majority of non-represented workers" that would bypass multiple NLRB hearings and court proceedings that can delay recognition for years.

Recognizing the employer's nonstop drive to increase profitability by new technologies and new forms of work organization that are often "designed to increase control that management has over our work," the union recommends formal "partnership" agreements. These include notice of all changes and enable negotiation over them before they are implemented.

Moreover, the union proposed "continuous bargaining" with management over technological changes that affect "job security, seniority and health and safety" of workers.

The union "opposes any two-tier wage agreements," or workers' income based upon "profit sharing," for these are based "on decisions over which they have no say."

The steelworkers' wage-policy committee emphasized several "absolutely essential elements":

> One is contract language which eliminates the *successorship* clause which guarantees that in the event of a plant sale, the buyer will recognize the Union and adopt either the current agreement or an acceptable substitute. [Another "essential element" was] a program to *reduce the level of overtime.*

Job security for steelworkers required further protection:

> There is no security if the company can escape contractual wages and benefits by shipping out bargaining unit work to low-wage contractors. Similarity, absent a successorship* clause, the employer can always sell the Union and put our members on the street in favor of a new work force. Finally, massive levels of overtime will eventually erode security for all of us, even those working it.

*Upon sale of unionized steel industry facilities, the selling firm agrees to include in its sale agreement a provision that the acquiring firm shall recognize the contract in force between the union and the selling firm.

This is a primary union response to out-of-control overtime working that has led to workweeks of 60 and more hours.

Maintenance work, 20 to 30 percent of the workforce, a concentration area for excessive overtime work, is given particular attention.

> Because many companies abandoned their apprenticeship training programs in the early 1980's, there exists today a severe shortage of maintenance employees and other skilled workers. Some of these same companies then use the shortage they created as an alibi for contracting out bargaining unit work. . . . It is therefore essential that we negotiate the reestablishment of apprenticeship and training programs on an accelerated basis and insist on the replacement of departing craft workers.

New Directions in Bargaining in the American Steel Industry

The economically depressed experience of the steel industry during the 1980s formed a background to the bargaining strategy formulated by the Steel Workers Union since 1997.* The union has about 700,000 members, of whom 300,000 are employed in steel in the United States and Canada, with the remaining number in the aluminum, copper, chemical, rubber and other industries of the United States.

"From 1956 until 1985," the largest steel companies formed a coordinating committee, representing the major firms. Wages and other terms of employment were comparable in these operations, as well as smaller integrated steel and mining companies. The pattern of coordinated bargaining dissolved during the economic depression in steel of the 1980s. The industry lost a major part of its markets to imported steel producers. By 1993, the union had sought to restore a bargaining pattern. By 1998, this effort was largely successful and made possible a common "New Directions Bargaining" with steel-producing firms.[32]

This program "rests on a union belief that the task of managing is simply too important to leave to managers alone." Accordingly, the union has pursued and elaborated a series of initiatives including a Union Involvement Program. This program is designed to "bring the union and its members into the decision processes of the industries' firms from the shopfloor to boardroom."

*The union reports that "in 1985 major steel companies disbanded their coordinating committee and began to bargain with the Union one by one. The largest company (U.S. Steel) and the seventh largest each locked out their workers, for 184 days and 98 days respectively, to try to force their workers to accept pay cuts greater than the Union would recommend. Neither company succeeded."

Information-sharing is required, "subject to appropriate confidentiality," and will give union representatives "all information relevant to formulation of the companies' business plan, regular operating and financial results," as well as notification about acquisitions, sales and joint ventures and details about new technology planning.

The union proposed that "in every department of every steel mill, 'a joint area committee' be equipped to tackle work place challenges of concern to employees and supervisors." The committees must be "given the tools to jointly plan all significant technological changes." At the corporate level, "a joint strategic partner committee" will bring together union leaders and company executives to consider facilities utilization, capital expenditures, product mix, etc. The USWA expects such provisions to "encourage union representatives to move from a traditionally reactive role to a planning and initiating one."

To facilitate New Directions, union trainers would meet with union members of joint committees on all levels. Training under way "includes function and formulation of business plans and analysis of profit and loss and balance sheet statements. The union stressed that in all of this . . . its greater involvement in the business means no sacrifice of traditional trade union objectives." At the same time, the union, in most companies, agreed to increasing flexibility in the use of the workforce and to otherwise improve productivity at reduced cost.

The union has emphasized overtime work reduction. The "companies are demanding that our members work longer and longer. And our members, because of wage stagnation, are working increasing amounts of overtime simply to maintain their standard of living." The union judges that 1980s "wage reductions and 1990s wage stagnation have driven our members to overtime." All this proceeded despite "huge corporate profits and the unseemly growth of executive compensation."

As a result, employers avoided hiring new workers. Such trends were worsened by a tendency to "a mandatory 12-hour day and rapidly rotating shifts . . . [these created] a stressed out work force, too fatigued to work safely, participate in the union, or enjoy a rewarding family life." Accordingly, the reduction of overtime was made a primary union objective.

The union stressed limiting the right of companies to contract out construction work. It pointed out that "in most large Japanese manufacturing companies only about half of the work is done by permanent employees of the company. The other work is done by temporary workers of firms called 'contractors' who make contracts to perform specific tasks. Usually the contractors' employees are paid less and have few benefits." The union reported that each steel company had agreed to a landmark joint program whose goals were to promptly enlarge skilled trade and craft forces to handle maintenance needs as much as possible with bargaining-unit employees and without excess overtime.

The 1997 compacts also broke ground with management's agreement to "award the union recognition based on a card check majority." Effectively, the steelworkers' union achieved a "labor law union reform." The union has also succeeded in obtaining comparable clauses that protect its members where the sale of a plant is contemplated. Thereby a "successorship" clause "prohibits the company from selling the business unless the buyer recognizes the United Steel Workers of America and negotiates contracts with USWA."

THE BETHLEHEM COMPANY CONTRACT: A MODEL OF "NEW DIRECTIONS" POLICY

The Bethlehem Steel Corporation is the second-largest steel company in the United States. Appendix 15 of the USWA contract (1993–1999) is titled "Memorandum of Understanding on Employee and Union Participation." The memorandum opens with an agreement to establish a "strategic partnership and that this must extend from the boardroom to the shopfloor." The contract provides "for full and continuing access by appropriate union representatives to the books, records, and information" that relate to "implementation of new and innovative approaches to the way work is performed and for the establishment of a comprehensive training and educational program."

The stated objectives (13) are then detailed. They include: "Reduction of all overhead cost, including managerial, supervisory, and other none-bargaining cost." By that joint agreement, the hierarchical authority of managers is automatically qualified.

Joint partnership committees were to be established for all main functional divisions. (But union members were not permitted to participate in discussions of the company's strategy for collective bargaining and other labor-relations issues.)

Joint leadership committees would be established to discuss the general business affairs of the company, including issues and actions that have an impact on plans and performance.

The committee would establish a technology-change program to include the following major elements involved in "Workplace Redesign." Advance notice would be given of any proposed technological change, including the following:

(a) a description of the purpose and function of the technological change, and how it would fit into existing operations and processes;

(b) the estimated cost of the technology, a cost justification of it, and the proposed timetable for it;

(c) disclosure of any service or maintenance warranties or contracts provided or required by the vendor (if any);

(d) the number and the type of jobs (both inside and outside the bargaining unit) which would be changed, added, or eliminated by the technological change;

(e) the anticipated impact on the skill requirements of the work force;

(f) details of any training programs connected with the new technology (including duration, content, and who will perform the training);

(g) an outline of the other options which were considered by the Company before formulating its proposed changes; and

(h) the expected impact of the change on job content, pace of work, safety and health, training needs, and contracting out.

And further: Union representatives on the Leadership Committee may request and receive reasonable access to Company personnel knowledgeable about any proposed technological change (including outside consultants) to review, discuss, and receive follow-up information concerning any technological changes proposed by the Company or Union and their effects on the bargaining unit.

These openings for union decision-making on technology matters are consistent with the IAM Technology Bill of Rights. Also, union members on joint committees "shall be entitled to: adequate opportunities on Company time to caucus for purposes of study, preparation, consultation, and review" and shall be compensated for their work time on these matters.

In a lawyerly way, this contract section concluded with understandings "that the parties might not always agree." Accordingly, management was assigned final decision rights on a range of subjects. However, even in those cases, "the process of decision making is subject to the grievance procedure and arbitration."

By the sum of these agreements, management went far toward conceding the presence of two decision processes and two decision-makers in the enterprise. The strategic importance of the industry in the American economy multiplies the significance of these agreements. From the union's standpoint, Appendix 15 leaves the door open for new concerns. It did not represent a frozen agenda. Rather, the workers' decision rights were bound to expand with sustained bargaining.

A discussion with a senior steel-company manager suggested the following understanding of the New Directions agreement on the company-union relationship. Without any doubt, this type of agreement meant that much more information about the company would be made available to the union. The union's role in technological change is important, as is the presence of a union-nominated member on the company's board of directors.

Every steel-company management will have to change because traditional styles of confrontation are no longer viable. All that was worked through during the 1980s, and the combination of strikes and lockouts produced a disaster for the industry. *For no sooner were the domestic sources of steel cut off, than the Japanese and other foreign steel industries offered to supply the U.S. market. Their offers were accepted by American firms, which led immediately to a major and permanent loss of market for the U.S. industry.* According to senior managers, both they and the union recognized that the industry could not survive another market-loss debacle of that magnitude.

Saturn*

Saturn is a division of General Motors whose 6,700 workers produce a line of small cars in its plant near Nashville, Tennessee. It was established in 1983 following the recommendations of a joint management–United Auto Workers study team. The study group was dubbed the Committee of 99, with half the members selected by the UAW, including autoworkers from various GM factories.

Saturn has had the highest percentage of U.S.-made components of any major auto company.

*The preparation of this report was assisted by the availability of the detailed and invaluable paper by three colleagues at the University of California: Professors Harley Shaiken and Steven Lopez (UC Berkeley), and Isaac Mankita (UC San Diego). Their first-hand account of decision-making at Saturn benefitted from their direct participation in the various work groups of the Nashville plant. Their experience was a valuable supplement to the formal contract documents and related data I have obtained from the union and management.

The firm has attracted attention for the scope of its commitment to workplace democracy: "Saturn has arguably the most far-reaching worker and union involvement in production decisions of any major firm in the United States in what both the company and union refer to as 'the partnership.' "[33] The agreement between Saturn and the UAW, the 1985 "constitution" of the enterprise, defines the union's role as follows:

> As a stakeholder in the operation of Saturn, the UAW will participate in business decisions as a full partner including site selection and construction, process and product design, choice of technologies, supplier selection, make-buy decisions, retail dealer selection, pricing, business planning, training, business systems development, budgeting, quality systems, productivity improvement, job design, new product development, recruitment and hiring, maintenance, and engineering.[34]

At Saturn, decision-making by consensus is the prescribed method, from the basic work unit of about a dozen workers, all the way up to the Strategic Action Council, which addresses long-range issues and includes a representative of the international union. The president of the Saturn union local sits on the Manufacturing Action Council, which deals with shorter-term production issues.

The consensus procedure in place at Saturn requires a dissenting person to propose an alternative. Just naysaying is out of order.

THE SATURN MODEL OF DISALIENATION

Production at Saturn is organized around the "Work Unit, an integrated group of approximately 8–12 Work Unit members." Production is viewed as a group effort, not a set of individual performances.

The tasks that constitute production are dealt with in comprehensive fashion, extending from design and timing of work tasks and scheduling them for optimum performance to keeping production records, budget analysis, developing and delivering production, training and performing repairs and housekeeping.

In other organizations, of course, these and allied work tasks are the traditional province of management. Production workers may recommend, but managers, from supervisors on up, decide. By marked contrast, at Saturn the tasks for which the work unit is given authority and responsibility represent an extensive disalienation.

The force of this way of decision-making is illustrated by the range of responsibilities that must be dealt with by the work unit:

The Thirty Work-Unit Functions

1. Reach decisions by consensus
2. Self-managed work units
3. Make their own job assignments
4. Resolve conflicts
5. Plan work
6. Design jobs
7. Control scrap
8. Control material and inventory
9. Perform incidental equipment maintenance
10. Schedule direct and indirect work
11. Schedule communications within and outside the group
12. Keep their own records
13. Select new members of the unit
14. Constantly seek improvement in quality, cost and work environment
15. Perform to their own budget
16. Integrate horizontally with business unit resources
17. Reflect synergistic group growth
18. Determine methods
19. Schedule relief
20. Schedule vacation
21. Provide absentee replacements
22. Perform their own repairs
23. Perform housekeeping
24. Maintain and perform their health and safety program
25. Be responsible for producing quality products to schedule at competitive costs
26. Assist in developing and delivering training

27. Obtain supplies
28. Seek resources as needed
29. Schedule and hold their own meetings
30. Initiate the consultation process for self-corrective action, with responsibility on the individual members

This list represents, as a whole, a notable departure from managerialism. It is one thing for high officials to talk about partnership, quite another for workers to have it as part of their job. A brief glance at the items reveals exactly how much is at stake here.

At Saturn, each team of workers determines its own methods of working. The work unit designs the job of each unit member, taking into account "the necessary resources (layout, tools, equipment, ergonomics, etc.) with flexibility for continuous improvement." These functions are typically the responsibility of industrial engineers, of management, so this departure from managerialism is a basic alteration of hierarchical control over production in favor of worker decision-making. One of the effects of the Saturn decision structure is the virtual elimination of the foreman as management's first line of control.

Work pace and the length of the workday are crucial matters in the auto industry. Plant managers are pressed by their superiors for higher productivity, and Saturn is no exception. But there is this difference: the Saturn plant manager is not an autonomous decision-maker. As the list of thirty work-unit functions makes clear, at the Nashville plant individual teams are responsible for planning their work (#5), for designing jobs (#6) and for making their own job assignments (#3).

Within this agreed framework of responsibilities, workers report, "We decide how to organize new jobs, so we try to set them up so we are working smarter, not harder."[35] Indeed, in one case, "a Saturn team rebalanced their workload in their area to provide what they considered was a more livable approach to production. . . . This team developed a 'cool-down' job, loaded less intensively than others in the area, so that workers could recoup their energies as they rotated on an hourly basis through all jobs on the team. . . . A worker remarked, 'there is that one job out there that you can more or less relax on . . . then you're ready to go at the other ones.' "[36]

One veteran Saturn worker, with long experience in other GM plants, spoke approvingly of having "a lot more independence than . . . at the other GM plant. A lot of it is on trust. We get to make a lot of the decisions. We don't get to make them all, but we have a major part in them. You don't feel like you're just a number, you have input."[37]

Managing, as I have argued, suggests a particular style of decision-making: a person placed in a decision hierarchy, appointed by people above, functioning by the hierarchy's rules and not subject to decisions made by the workers. These are the familiar characteristics of managerialism, which has become so commonplace that it is often used as a generic term for all possible forms of decision-making.

The growing practice of organizing work by teams, instead of the micro-specified tasks for single workers, does not capture the essential difference between Saturn and other more conventional factories. That difference inheres in the democratic self-governing by the teams. Labeling Saturn style as another form of managing misses the point.

Let us see how this works out in terms of the now familiar five major categories of worker decision-making defined by Lawrence B. Cohen. The particulars in what follows are from the Saturn Memorandum of Agreement (MOA), 1997.[38]

Worker Group

"To insure a fully qualified work force, a majority of the full initial complement of operating and skilled technicians in Saturn will come from GM-UAW units throughout the United States."[39] The local union includes office as well as technical staff.

Not only the firm and union but "each and every member of Saturn pledge[s] to treat all persons equally without regard to their race, color, religion, age, sex, national origin or handicap."[40] And further, "The parties will actively recruit GM-UAW employees (active and inactive), including communications emphasizing the exciting and unique opportunities available in the Saturn culture. . . . To help assure Saturn's long-term viability, jointly developed competency-based training of all Saturn members is mandatory." This should include "continuous development and implementation of new tools, methods and cutting edge technology."[41]

The members of the Saturn work group are expected to comply with the firm's philosophy and mission statements:

Saturn Philosophy

> We believe that all people want to be involved in decisions that affect them, care about their job and each other, take pride in themselves and in their contributions and want to share in the success of their efforts.
>
> By creating an atmosphere of mutual trust and respect, recognizing and utilizing individual expertise and knowledge in innova-

> tive ways, providing the technologies and education for each individual, we will enjoy a successful relationship and a sense of belonging to an integrated business system capable of achieving our common goals which insures security for our people and success for our business and communities.
>
> **Saturn Mission**
>
> The mission of Saturn is to market vehicles developed and manufactured in the United States that are world leaders in quality, cost, and customer enthusiasm through the integration of people, technology and business systems.[42]

GM and the UAW agreed that because "the Saturn philosophy requires a dedicated and committed workforce," an employee's refusal of employment by Saturn will not "impact the employee's benefits under the GM-UAW National Agreements."[43] Such a person is therefore free to go elsewhere in the GM organization with the national contract's employee benefits.

Engineers at Saturn, unlike those at Chrysler, are not part of the UAW bargaining unit.

Work time. Job security is assured for the 80 percent of Saturn workers with the longest service, as well as for those who joined the firm as part of the initial full labor force and for those who were recruited while on layoff from another GM-UAW plant.

Saturn has operated with two shifts: 6:30 a.m. to 4:30 p.m., and 5:00 p.m. to 3:00 a.m. Each ten-hour daily shift includes a paid meal and two other breaks. The factory is thereby manned twenty hours a day for six days a week.

How does this highly intensive use of equipment and facilities affect the costs of running a car plant? Consider a production machine costing $200,000. Allowing for a ten-year depreciation period, if it is operated for a standard 40-hour workweek, the hourly fixed depreciation charge for the machine averages $10 per hour. At Saturn, the machine would be manned 120 hours a week, which is the total work time each week of the two 60-hour shifts. The fixed charge would be $3.30 per hour.

The actual initial investment in Saturn was $3.5 billion. If we assume that $2 billion was the outlay for machinery, then with ten years of depreciation and 120 hours of work per week, the "fixed" charge for the production equipment would be $33,333 per hour—far less than the charge of $100,000 per hour for a standard 40-hour workweek.

Unauthorized strikes, work stoppages, lockouts, slowdowns, restrictions or interference with work are deemed contrary to "the philosophy and mission of Saturn." Such actions are only allowed with "full and complete compliance with Procedure to Modify the Agreement."[44]

Deployment. As we have seen, the founding mission statement commits Saturn "to market vehicles developed and manufactured in the United States." But this objective collides with GM's current general policy, which includes transferring parts production to nonunion firms both in the United States and, particularly, in Mexico. That country now has the world's largest concentration of U.S. auto parts production as a result of the vigorous and systematic exporting of capital by all of the main U.S. auto manufacturers. At Saturn, these matters remain in dispute.

Within each Saturn work unit, the "job content . . . includes both direct and indirect work. Therefore, it is expected that Work Units will be able to handle the personal relief needs of Saturn members." In other words, planning must include arrangements for "covering" unscheduled or emergency absences.

Saturn has a simplified system of job classification. All workers, other than those in designated "skilled trades," are "operating technicians"—latter-day successors to the "semi-skilled" workers who became manifestly obsolete with the progressive complexity of production methods in the auto industry. A class of "skilled trades" includes tool and die maker, machine repairist, electrical specialist, stationary engineer and assembly layout and model maker.

Compensation. The Saturn system of work organization and decision process yields high productivity of both labor and capital.

One part of the basic wage (as agreed in 1999) is 95 percent of the GM-UAW national figure. The second part consists of the Saturn "risk/reward system" for supplementing the basic wage on the basis of achieving productivity targets, profit-sharing above a specified level and a quality bonus.[45]

During part of the 1990s, the combination of the base wage plus the risk/reward yielded a Saturn production worker an annual compensation of $50,000. But wages have had a tendency to dip significantly below that figure, pressed down by the small-car (hence small-price) output emphasis—so much so that most Saturn workers voted in 1999 to modify the wage system, giving greater weight to the nationally agreed GM hourly wage.

Like the standard contract, Saturn compensation also includes medical and disability benefits, and a pension plan.*

*Toward the end of the 1990s, a substantial debate took place among Saturn workers. The main issues pertained to the system of rotating shifts, the risk/reward wage system and

Decision-making on *performance* affects everyone at Saturn, from the single worker to the entire workforce. Moreover, as we have seen, the range and depth of what the contract calls "consensus decision-making" extends from the performance of the smallest group of workers to the organization and running of the plant as a whole. The section of the Saturn contract called "Structure and Decision-Making Process" runs to four pages, covering every aspect of performance.[46]

The last paragraph on the Strategic Action Council is a mandate to carry out the range of strategic decisions that are characteristic of the board of directors of a corporation. In the case of Saturn, the management and the union are charged, jointly, with carrying out the defined business responsibilities.

At Saturn the work units do far more than "participate," as workers do in Japan's "lean-production" systems. Unlike their Japanese counterparts, the work units are decision-making bodies. In the Japanese lean-production model, there is emphasis on tight supervision of workers. At Japanese auto plants in the United States, for instance, Nissan has a supervisor for every 20 workers, and the NUMMI factory has one for every 18. The Operations Module Adviser at Saturn, together with a union counterpart, coordinates several work units together comprising 100 to 150 workers.

The responsibilities (and authority) of Saturn's workers have no match in the lean-production model. Indeed, in the judgment of an informed observer, "Japanese lean production increases the participation of front-line workers, but not their power."[47]

The same is true with job rotation: "On some teams workers rotate jobs hourly, on others four times daily."[48] They make these kinds of decisions each week at their 47-minute team meetings: these are decision meetings, not pep rallies.

With individual engineering training widely available in the Saturn system, problems of quality control, inventory control and stabilization of output rates are dealt with by the work units and their higher-level coordinating bodies. The main technical methods that have given "lean production" its margins in productivity can all be wielded in a Saturn-type framework, with this difference: the Saturn method allows and

---

the personalities of various senior union officials. In place of shift rotation, the workers voted for relatively stable shift assignments. The workforce apparently preferred a wage system less dependent on the company's fortunes from year to year, therefore closer to the wage patterns of the GM-UAW national contract. These issues, plus an accumulation of grievances involving local union officials, led to the replacement of senior UAW officers.

A new contract ratified in 2000 reaffirmed both the previous wage and shift work systems.

indeed promotes disalienated worker performance, and "lean production" cannot.*

All production requires decision-making: what should be produced, who should do the work, the quantity, how the production should be performed and how the product should be distributed. All these topics are conventionally dealt with in schools of business and management from the vantage point of decision calculations that would best serve hierarchical management groups that are oriented to enlarging their profit and power.

In this chapter, I have shown that workers in a range of occupations have been developing decision-making on their own work while utilizing criteria that are quite different from those of management in the service of profit and power accumulation without limit.

In the following chapter, I will explore the further reach of disalienated decision-making and prospective qualities of occupational life when shaped by workplace democracy.

*Three unions—the IAM, the USWA and the UAW—have been considering a recommendation for merger, which would produce a unified metalworkers superunion resembling the German I.G. Metal. Such a strategic unification and the multiplied capabilities that such consolidation could bring would spur the further development of workplace democracy in U.S. industry.

10

White Collar Joins the Blue

At the close of the twentieth century, when doctors, nurses, technicians and other American health professionals were threatened by corporate-controlled alienation, they formed trade unions to disalienate their working lives.

When professors in American universities confronted administrations that have taken the corporate model of "managing" as the ideal, part-time faculty, graduate students and instructors also sought out formal ties with unions, including the following:

American Federation of Teachers

Federation of Nurses and Health Professionals

Union of American Physicians and Dentists

United Salaried Physicians and Dentists

Committee of Interns and Residents

Office and Professional Employees International Union

Hotel and Restaurant Workers

Service Employees International Union

International Association of Machinists and Aerospace Workers

The Doctors' Council

Hotel and Hospital Workers Union

American Federation of State, County and Municipal Employees

Communication Workers of America

United Automobiles, Agricultural and Aerospace Workers Union

National Education Association

The vital common characteristic of these different unions is not their identification and long practice of negotiation with respect to the detailed occupations of their diverse industries. The key point is that they are unions of workers who participate in a project that is common to them all: embarking on a process of empowering each of their occupations by dis-alienating the particular, detailed way of decision-making by which each worker group functions.

A common first step of these worker groups involves developing group solidarity through a buildup of mutual trust—a fundamental counterpoint to the alienating predatory competition that has been shaped by the rules and values of managerialism.

Unions have extended their organization into the high-tech human-service industries of health care and further education. These industries share an important characteristic: their activities cannot be mechanized, for the human care of human beings is not suited to mechanization. But the size, and therefore the scope, of the activities are nevertheless impressive. All told, the various sectors of the health care industries engage about 10 million people, and education over 9 million—counting public schools, colleges and universities of every sort.

By 1999, about 35,000 doctors had affiliated with unions. These were about "5% of the nation's physicians [who] belong to unions, up from about 25,000 in 1996." Observers of the medical profession estimate that physicians have been moving to unionize at the rate of about 15 percent per year.[1]

What is the cause of this? The available evidence indicates that it stems first from an accumulation of frustration, then from rising resentment at the removal of decision power from doctors by health maintenance organizations (HMOs). The HMOs are a species of private enterprise, interposed between insurance companies and government and other agencies, that guarantee various forms of money payment in return for medical care. The HMOs then deal with physicians who affiliate with them for the assignment of patients and payment of fees.

These HMOs are profit-maximizing: they do best for themselves by minimizing the cost of the medical services for which they must pay doctors and other providers. Thus, as increasing numbers of American consumers have discovered, the HMO relationship has set in motion a powerful surge of cost-cutting. Part of this was at first welcomed by a wider public, at least in principle, because of the inflated medical fees of the 1970s and 1980s, which saw ever-rising charges for physicians' fees, hospitals and tests and operations. The cost of medical care had increased at a much more rapid rate than general consumer prices.

But the HMOs attempted to minimize costs and thereby maximize their profits through a payment squeeze on doctors, on providers of specialized treatments and tests and on hospitals.

Doctors have resented the rapid growth of large and costly HMO administrative staffs, as well as the high salaries given to top officials of these new control agencies.

In sum, a new set of institutions was established in the name of reducing the average cost of health care, which had the effect, among others, of reducing income to doctors. But this was not the only or even the main source of resentment among physicians. Equal, and perhaps more important, was the impact of reductions of decision power on matters that had formerly been dealt with by them at their own discretion.

Decisions on medical treatment have been increasingly particularized by HMO regulations. A whole range of procedures can now be recommended and performed only with the formal approval of the HMO. According to these new rules, medications and allied treatment must take place within a set of preferred specifications set by the HMO. Because of fierce competition for market share and profit-maximizing by pharmaceutical companies, there has been a proliferation of different medications for a particular ailment. The HMOs have interposed themselves to make decisions about the preferred type to be prescribed by doctors. But while all of these cost-cutting measures have clearly served profits, it is generally far less clear that they have served patients.

Various types of medical treatment requiring specialist diagnosis and care must now be carried out only under terms specified by the HMO. Thus each HMO has a preferred list of specialists. If a particular physician wants to recommend examination and/or treatment by a specialist not on the list, then administrative approval has to be obtained from the HMO. The matter is further complicated when patients seek recommendations for specialist treatment by persons not on the preferred list. In that case, application would again have to be made to the HMO office for permission to carry out this recommended activity. The "nonplan" doctors would typically require some sort of conversation with an HMO medical director, or with a subordinate, who could be either a nurse or a nonmedical person authorized to examine the regulations and precedents and thereby make a recommendation. Physicians quite naturally resent a procedure that has curtailed their decision power and cast doubt on their competence.

Doctors have also been increasingly required to refer patients for second opinions by other physicians, from the pool specified by the HMO.

HMO executives have sought to specify the number of hours per week a participating physician is available to see patients. Within that time, the HMOs have also ventured to specify the number of minutes to be allotted each patient.

> One California doctor who insisted on anonymity said he was considering joining a union because his HMO wanted him to see eight patients an hour, limiting him to 7½ minutes per visit. The doctors at 46 primary care clinics in the Medalia HealthCare system in Washington State decided to unionize after the HMO ordered many of them to schedule 36 hours of appointments each week, up from 32 hours. The doctors said they did not have enough time left for essential backup work, like completing paperwork, analyzing lab results and calling HMO officials for various approvals.[2]

Even when the number of minutes per patient is not specified by the HMO, total expected work time becomes a powerful instrument for regulating the physician's work performance.

Doctors see these new rules as an imposition of industrial-type controls generally understood as a part of Taylorism. In the eyes of physicians, this has meant that they are being industrialized, treated in the same manner as industrial workers, who are not only less well paid but, most important, controlled in micro-detail by their employers.

Since the 1950s, physicians have taken note of the higher fees earned per hour of work time by specialists. This differential has led to a surge of medical training and professional practice limited to various areas of specialization. Accordingly, specialist fees have also been an important target of HMO administrative operations.

For decades, the American media have given priority of place to the American Medical Association, whose membership numbers somewhat less than half the physicians in the country. But while the AMA was pronouncing its customary conservative judgments, the occupations of doctors, nurses and other medical care specialists were being transformed.

How has the AMA responded to the changes? It has indicated its awareness of the discontent of physicians, yet it has, at the same time, remained unwilling to enter into activities that might smack of unionizing. The AMA has too long a history of opposition to unionization, its deriding of unions as strikers and raucous picketers has become too habitual, for the organization to change easily. Still, the recent show of resentment among its members has compelled at least some reconsideration, and the AMA has indicated a readiness to assist physicians in their dealings with HMOs and kindred bodies.

Physicians who have been drawn to unionization have made their views plainly known. Doctors like Brian J. Moore, an internist in Bernardsville, New Jersey, have supported the efforts of the International Association of Machinists to organize physicians in that area. "The way medicine is going right now and the way patients are being treated by managed care is just terrible," Dr. Moore has said, "and someone has to stand up for proper health care. I don't see a physicians' union particularly like unions of the past, where we're going to strike and carry placards. It's primarily to get the message out that we have to improve health care."

A sort of "final line of defense" by the AMA has been the claim that unionization by physicians necessarily entails, at some point, the withholding of medical care for the purposes of conducting a strike. That, says the AMA, is a violation of the Hippocratic Oath, which includes the commitment to "do no harm." Dr. Robert Weinmann, president of the Union of American Physicians and Dentists, headquartered in Oakland, California, has responded:

> What kind of violation is it when the employer creates conditions when you cannot take care of patients as best you can, but can only pretend to do so? . . . Does that cause doctors to violate the Hippocratic oath? And what about the insurance companies who don't take the oath and are often cutting corners on providing appropriate care?[3]

Professional Status

There can be no doubt that for physicians, who have been the key group in the functioning of health care, all these changes have been experienced as a significant reduction in their professional status. The latter is not a term that is susceptible to unambiguous, operational specification, for it involves admixtures of feelings—in this case, among both physicians and the public. Dr. Sanford Marcus, a principal founder of the Union of American Physicians and Dentists, recalls "the event that radicalized me": The administrator of the hospital to which he was affiliated announced one day that the hospital was going to establish a health maintenance organization. Dr. Marcus was outraged, writing to the administrator that he would have expected that "we would be included in the discussions, but that just had not happened. . . . My reaction was—how can they do this to us? We're doctors!" He subsequently declared that

> "If he [the modern doctor] indeed feels pride in the dignity and achievements of his profession he is being called upon for the first time in history to exemplify that pride through concrete action rather than lofty rhetoric. With nostalgia for the good old days, but imbued with the pragmatic realization that *none* of his values can otherwise be preserved, he is reluctantly entering the Age of Medical Unionization."[4]

In a further effort to formulate his conception of the doctors' objections, Dr. Marcus said, "What is most important is being able to do what is best for your patients and to have the patients know it and appreciate it."[5]

The variety of physicians' reactions to cost-reducing pressure from the HMOs includes the following reflection:

> "You know, it's really getting to be awful with the economic incentives that insurers are putting on us." She said, "When a patient with a bilateral breast cancer comes into your office you look at her and your heart sinks. Why? Not because you feel so terrible because she has breast cancer, but because she's going to ruin your cost profile." And then she said, "That is pretty depressing. They're turning us into people we don't even like."

But subtle pressure is not the only way. The heat is turned on physicians in very direct fashion too.

> The representative from the HMO said they liked her (an obstetrician) C-section rate because it was below the mean, but her length-of-stay data was above the mean. Because her C-section rate was below the mean, they were not going to deselect her. But, if she didn't get her length-of-stay data down by next year, she was out, which of course meant that she wouldn't be able to practice in that area. She said to me, "I realized it was either my patients or me."[6]

Physicians have also engaged in sharp self-criticism; Dr. Quentin D. Young, for example, has written that

> Certainly, I share the harsh criticism that is due physicians as a group and organized medicine in particular for the excesses, the abuses, the unnecessary surgery, the inappropriate testing, the exorbitant fees, and the flawed stewardship that opened the door [to] this terrible, terrible catastrophe. . . .

> There has been a degeneration of the medical profession caused by market incentives, which has resulted in two-thirds of American doctors practicing as highly priced specialists. Hyper-specialization is a curse. . . . We have, at the best estimate, 145,000 too many specialists. This disproportion was caused by paying much higher fees to "proceduralists," while diminishing the status of primary care physicians.[7]

These views are cited here because they represent the primary reasoning behind the early retirement of many doctors, the vigorous objections by "independent" practitioners to their mobilization in HMOs and the general maltreatment experienced by doctors at the hands of the HMO system. They resent being transformed into employees from what they traditionally were: independent professionals. This intense awareness of employee status is sure to spread further, since an overwhelming majority, perhaps as many as 80 percent, of the freshly minted MDs from American universities are now contemplating careers as employed, salaried doctors. Meanwhile, among the AMA staff, it is judged that by 1999 about 40 percent of doctors' practice revenue came from and through HMOs.

Alienation is at the root of the almost universal discontent among doctors and their readiness to embark on major alterations, most notably forming unions, in their occupational practice.

By 1999, it was clear that approximately half the nation's physicians were in salaried positions.[8] Many doctors are disturbed about the limitations on their capacity to make independent clinical decisions and their inability to refer patients to the appropriate specialists or prescribe the optimal drugs." Such limitations stem from financial-incentive systems that reward them for spending less. As Dr. Jerome Kassirer has written in the *New England Journal of Medicine*,

> Doctors who reluctantly accept the mantle of physician–business person can end up dispirited or in serious financial difficulty. New methods of managing capitated payments with bonuses and "withholds" can engender ill will among previously compatible and friendly colleagues. Competition for new patients between doctors or groups of doctors can destroy longstanding cordial relationships. And the necessarily narrow focus on the bottom line can force physicians to lose sight of their primary mission—namely, the care of the sick.[9]

According to some physicians, the attempt to recover some decision-making power can be translated as an effort to restore their independence.

In fact, however, the independent physician is mainly a thing of the past. Physicians have become increasingly dependent on laboratories, suppliers of equipment, specialists in particular classes of diagnosis and the availability of hospitals, at whatever distance, with the whole panoply of modern equipment. Therefore, a recovery of decision power cannot take place as a series of single-handed operations but only jointly. And an evident option for collective solidarity is a union. The same applies to doctors who find the HMO system unbearable. The profit-taking by health maintenance organizations and the extravagant salaries of many of their CEOs are gained at the expense not only of the MDs but also of their patients.

Of course there is reason to fear predatory competition between doctors. But the main safeguard against that is organization based on mutual trust and interdependence. These are the real considerations that compel physicians to seek out trade unions or union-like organizations.

From the available evidence, it is clear that during the second half of the twentieth century, doctors and their institutions have experienced substantial alienation. No aspect of their work performance—from the reduction of their decision power to its complete curtailment—has escaped the attention of the managerialists.

Hospitals Under the Knife

Doctors and other health care professionals rely heavily on hospitals, especially the teaching hospitals connected with university medical schools. These hospitals, it is well appreciated, play a critical set of roles. They are centers of sophisticated medical practice and provide about 40 percent of the nation's charitable care. These are also the places where medical students train as physicians, and these hospitals play a role in connecting the formal studies of the curriculum with the actual world of clinical practice. The same network of hospitals also serves as centers for medical research. But hospitals generally, and teaching hospitals in particular, have suffered economic blows as Washington has considered cutting Medicare payments by about $23 billion per year.[10]

For 1999 in California, "The medical center known as UCFF Stanford Health Care expects operating losses of $50 million." The same hospital sent layoff notices to 250 employees, and in the future, given the same financial constraints, a further 2,000 of the center's 12,000 staff members will probably be laid off. "Without the layoffs, UCFF Stanford would see an operating loss of $135 million next year according to the center's chief executive, Peter Van Eten."[11] Comparable pressures and comparable reactions are being felt in hospitals everywhere.

> The situation is dire. The University of Pennsylvania health system lost $90 million [1998], and the Temple University system lost nearly $25 million. [The President of Harvard indicated that he was] "not quite sure what the cumulative deficit of our four or five closely related hospitals is, but it's certainly well over $100 million so far, and we haven't even finished the year yet."[12]

Fees to hospitals are the most important and costly item in the health care agenda. How can such costs be reduced? One important element is the amount of time allotted for the patient following particular surgeries and other medical interventions. The HMOs discovered quickly enough that there was considerable variability among hospitals and physicians with respect to the appropriate time given for patient recovery after major medical interventions. With that as a starting point, they proceeded to specify possible reductions in the length of hospital stays.

It has been noted that "hospital costs in high managed care markets were approximately 19% below hospital costs in low managed care markets." But of course there's a price for these achievements. Thus, "Patient stays are significantly shorter in high managed care markets, 6.32% less than the national average, and almost 12% shorter than patient stays in medium managed care markets."[13]

To add to this burden, a noteworthy feature of the managed care system is the complete nonstandardization of people, work, forms, etc. Therefore, the millions of individuals and hospital institutions participating in managed care must learn to cope with a dizzying amount of paperwork. At the same time, solid evidence supports the finding that HMOs have frequently misstated benefit coverage. Thus the General Accounting Office found that health plans, in substantial numbers, "simply do not give out detailed benefit information. One plan provided enrollees with a prescription drug benefit that was much less than what it had promised to provide in its Medicare contract with the government." The GAO also reported, "Even though Medicare recipients have extensive rights to appeal benefit denials, health plans often fail to inform them of those rights."[14]

In the administration of hospitals, the pressure from HMOs has been met not only by limiting the number of days for each recovery but also by cutting back on some principal expenses. A first area of targeting was the number of nurses. Nursing care was cut back not only by reducing the roster of registered nurses but also by using less trained, or even formally untrained, people for certain tasks previously performed by nurses. In response to market-driven pressures, there has been a proliferation of these "nurses' aides," unlicensed, unregistered workers without the years of formal nursing education or a degree, who are assigned to perform all manner of "routine" activities like distributing medications to patients, operating equipment and the daily monitoring of patients' condition by taking and recording body temperature and blood pressure.

These are not recent developments. As far back as 1978, the *New England Journal of Medicine* concluded that a major part of the money savings that HMOs purport to show is typically gained from lower rates of hospitalization. And an article in *The Nation* has pointed out:

> Because childbirth is the number one cause of hospitalization, managed-care plans saw that if they could cut mothers' time in the hospital, they could save billions of dollars. In 1970 women having normal vaginal deliveries stayed an average of four days; those undergoing caesarian sections stayed eight days. By 1992 these numbers had been cut in half. By 1994 most HMOs were limiting stays for C-sections to two or three days and for vaginal deliveries to one day. Some California plans, like Kaiser Permanente's, were encouraging new mothers to leave the hospital after only eight hours.[15]

Since so much attention has been given to the bottom line in length of hospital stays, it's worth noting that hospitalization does not dominate the reputedly high cost of medical care in the United States:

> The United States, which has the most expensive health care system in the world—by far—is among those with the shortest hospital stays. In Germany hospitalization averages seven days long, while that country spends 10.5 percent of its GDP on health care compared to our 13.6 percent. England and Canada also have much lower overall health care costs than the United States but more generous lengths of stay.[16]

What is driving the cost of health care? The race for profits clearly does not help. Under federal regulations that govern the operation of insurance companies (and other health maintenance organizations), the companies can take 16 percent and more off the top for profit and administration costs, as well as for more-than-generous CEO salaries, some even in the multimillion-dollar class.

HMOs Plus Medicare: A Nightmare for the Elderly

The nightmarish quality of the health maintenance system includes federal medical regulations that do not cover payment for prescription drugs for elderly Medicare patients. This has generated a frequently bewildering array of ordeals for Medicare-dependent Americans: 13 million seniors must pay for drugs out of their pockets despite their small incomes. As the press has often reported, health care has become a daily battle for survival. "A lot of time we have to make a choice about what medicine we're going to take—either that, or cut down on groceries."[17] These conditions are deeply felt by physicians as the first line of caregivers for the millions dependent on HMO and federal government largesse.

The breakdown of support from the Medicare and Medicaid plans has had reverberations throughout the country. In 1997, dozens of teaching hospitals joined an effort to cut back on the number of doctors being trained, in response to Washington's call to remedy an alleged glut in the national supply of physicians. By April 1999, half of the hospitals that had gone along with this federal government scheme had dropped out of the program. They found that they could not see themselves functioning financially in the absence of the low-cost labor provided by doctors-in-training and residents.[18]

Doctors as Employees

By 1999, according to a 1997 estimate, 42 percent of doctors in the United States would be salaried employees, up from 24 percent in 1983.[19] The organizers of doctors' unions believe that this trend will only grow. They note that about a quarter of the physicians now practicing were once union members, when they were in residence.

The main union that represents newly graduated physicians is the Committee of Interns and Residents, which has been growing rapidly in recent years. "We can't keep up with the demand," says CIR director John Ronches. "Doctors feel that their ability to take care of their patients is being influenced by non-medical people who have no relationship with the patient. . . . For people who went into medicine thinking they were going to help people who are ill, it's a great shock." Ronches also judges that the visibility of doctors unionizing will spur lower-paid staff to sign union cards as well. "Any high visibility profession that's organized has a positive effect on the organizing climate. It makes people think that it must be okay." Thus in Tucson, shortly after a doctors' vote for union affiliation, 458 other hospital employees decided to unionize as well.

In Massachusetts, doctors have also begun a movement against "the industrialization of medicine," forming an ad hoc Committee to Defend Health Care. They say that this movement has spread to some twenty states.[20]

The quality of the physicians' reaction to their occupational scene is illustrated by Dr. George Makol, an employee of the Thomas-Davis Medical Centers in Tucson. "I'm a longtime conservative Republican, and here I am—a card-carrying member of the Federation of Physicians and Dentists. I joined because unions are giving doctors a voice."[21]

In March 1999, the movement of unionization among physicians got a substantial boost when about 15,000 doctors joined a new National Doctors Alliance, sponsored by the Service Employees International Union, "which vowed to spend $1 million over the next year recruiting more physicians and dentists." Dr. Barry Leibowitz, president of the New York–based, 2,500-member Doctors' Council, which joined with the Committee of Interns and Residents and the United Salaried Physicians and Dentists to form the new alliance, became president of the NDA. Other unions helping to organize physicians include the American Federation of State, County and Municipal Employees, which includes the 5,000-member Union of American Physicians and Dentists, based in Oakland, California. The International Association of Machinists and the United Food and Commercial Workers Union have also worked to recruit physician members.[22]

Dave Parker, a spokesman for the National Labor Relations Board, which rules on whether employers of physicians must bargain with them—as with other workers who petition for union recognition when a majority demands it—has said that doctors "find themselves not independent anymore, but working for hospitals or health maintenance organizations without the rights that they are used to." Parker added, "They're working more like the rest of us, as employees who have bosses, and it's an interesting phenomenon to see."[23]

Unionization has come under serious dispute as managers of hospitals and HMOs argue that doctors are independent businessmen and -women who enter into contractual relations with an HMO or a hospital. Accordingly, they argue, doctors are not employees. But the NLRB is empowered to make judgments with respect to groups of employees. "To skirt the antitrust barrier, many doctors are forming independent practice associations, essentially large group practices that allow physicians to bargain together with HMOs."[24]

Another contrarian judgment comes from the field of management consulting. "Physicians are just plain bad employees," said Kenneth S. Abramowitz, a health care analyst at Sanford C. Bernstein, a brokerage firm. "It's not a lot of fun managing 3,000 prima donnas who don't think it's the best thing to work for you." Abramowitz noted too that many hospitals were eager to buy physician practices even though they often turn out to be money losers, because the doctors provide a steady flow of patients to fill beds.[25]

Doctors have also been seeking relief from the restrictions of antitrust laws. At a hearing on Capitol Hill, Michael Connair, an orthopedic surgeon, spoke on behalf of the Tallahassee-based Federation of Physicians and Dentists. He stated, "The problem private practice physicians face today is not different than the problem miners or factory workers face when they cannot speak with a unified voice. Individually, our bargaining power is dwarfed by the bargaining power of the insurance companies."[26]

Unlike their counterparts in unions of industrial workers and service employees, the officers and main staff of doctors' unions affirm the professional quality of their memberships. But the main elements that differentiate these associations lie in the particular attention given to compensation (5 pages out of 45 in one contract), work time (6 pages of the contract) and grievance procedures (6 pages). The contract of the Committee of Interns and Residents with New York City, for example, also includes details that have no counterpart in industrial-union agreements. These include representation on the Medical Board of the hospital, which is also concerned with medical education, internship and residency programs; malpractice insurance; health and safety details; and provision of "on-call" rooms. *Deployment* and *performance* rules that are important elements for industrial workers are generally not dealt with in doctors' contracts.

The managements of thirty principal teaching hospitals in the United States have contracts covering their unionized physicians of all grades.* As we have seen, the teaching hospitals are a major part of the medical profession, as centers for training and research. The CIR describes itself as "the oldest and largest union of salaried doctors in the United States." Its

*The historical development of unionism among doctors in the United States can be readily addressed through two principal publications. The first is a paper by Robert G. Harmon, "Intern and Resident Organizations in the United States: 1934–1977," *Milbank Memorial Quarterly: Health and Society* 56, no. 4 (School of Public Health and Community Medicine, University of Washington, Seattle, 1978); the second prime source is *When Doctors Join Unions*, by Grace Budrys, Professor of Sociology at DePaul University (see endnote number 4). The book by Dr. Budrys is notable for its history of the development of the physician's union movement, but it is particularly detailed on the formation and operation of the Union of American Physicians and Dentists. Both these sources are readable and richly detailed accounts that enable one to have an appreciation of what has been done in this field.

longest-enduring contract is with the New York City Health and Hospitals Corporation. It has been an affiliate of the Service Employees International Union (AFL-CIO). Its agreement with New York City hospitals encompasses a familiar agenda of topics on workplace democracy, as well as subjects that are especially important for physicians. How does it address the five key categories that readers have encountered in Chapter 9?

The *worker group* encompasses only the salaried physicians who work as interns or residents. *Work time* is a notably important topic and gets extended attention. In hospital emergency services, postgraduate trainees and attending physicians "shall be limited to no more than twelve consecutive hours per day on duty assignment in the emergency service." But "the Commissioner [of Hospitals] may approve alternative schedule limits of up to fifteen hours for attending physicians in a hospital emergency service." Other details of work time are given for working hours for inpatient services. Thus "the scheduled work week shall not exceed an average of 80 hours per week over a four-week period, and such trainees shall not be scheduled to work for more than twenty-four consecutive hours." All this appears as an addendum to the main text of the CIR contract with the New York City hospitals, following the statement that "the parties recognize the undesirability of excessive work hours for House Staff Officers inconsistent with optimum patient care and high standards of training and will make every effort to resolve problems in furtherance of these principles."[27]

Unlike the contracts we encountered in Chapter 9, details of *deployment* are not elaborated in the CIR agreement. It is implied, however, that doctors employed as staff officers will apply their work time in accordance with the training schedule, which includes periods of responsibility for patients (varying according to areas of specialization), and time spent in learning. For example, staff officers are expected to participate in daily rounds during which supervising physicians examine patients and comment to accompanying trainees, as well as in the professional tasks that are specific to the house staff officer's area of primary professional interest. Since starting salaries for postgraduate house officers begin at $41,100 per year (with a reduction of about $3,000 in return for housing, where that is provided), there can certainly be financial pressures for many to take on moonlighting, paid activity outside the hospital. The union bargaining agreement specifies that "hospitals employing postgraduate trainees shall adopt and enforce specific policies governing dual employment." Thus not only must the trainee notify the hospital of such outside employment, but "post-graduate trainees who have worked the maximum number of hours" in the hospital "shall be prohibited from working additional hours as physicians providing professional patient care services."[28]

Compensation for interns and residents is based on the postgraduate years (or PGY levels) appropriate to each doctor. Thus the pay levels for 1999 began with PGY-1 at $41,100 and attained a salary of $54,210 for the PGY-8 level. Additional payments are made for "on-call duty"—that is, additional to each doctor's normal on-call schedule. Thus $333 for weeknights and $444 for weekends and holidays. "On-call" work is made possible by the provision of "on-call rooms" provided for the medical staff.

The importance of the CIR's contract has been magnified by its part in the national drive to unionize doctors. The National Doctors Alliance will represent a third of all unionized physicians. " 'Medicine has been infected by a big-business mentality,' said Dr. Barry Leibowitz, president of the National Doctors Alliance. 'Hospitals are merging and downsizing. Profit-driven managed-care companies and corporate administrators are dictating medical treatments to protect the bottom line.' "[29] The new combined organization embodies the Doctors Council, the CIR and the USPD. This grouping will be known initially as the Doctors Organizing Committee, Service Employees International Union (SEIU). The formation of this new national entity also marks a departure from various attempts by doctors' organizations to organize independent practice physicians for purposes of combined bargaining representation. The Doctors Organizing Committee will focus on employed, salaried physicians and allied health care workers.

It is important to note that a closely allied set of problems besets other care-giving occupations, the nursing profession most of all. Hospital administrators throughout the country have evidently made the same discovery: If nurses are given heavier job loads, then total nursing care costs can be reduced. Since there are more than 600 hospital staff for every 100 patients in U.S. hospitals, it is evident that labor costs are a large element in hospital operating expenses.[30] As we have seen, hospital managers have also been attempting to apply the cost-cutting methods promulgated by Frederick Winslow Taylor. By a combination of heavier workloads and the frequent assignment of certain registered-nurse duties to semiskilled aides of various sorts, hospital managers have attempted to reduce their labor costs. But there is a serious constraint on such methods, for the kind of mechanization that can be applied to industrial-production operations does not lend itself readily to hospital care. This difficulty supports the general principle that the human care of human beings cannot be mechanized.

Spokespersons for the nursing profession have elaborated on the wider consequences of these attempts to treat human beings as though they are inanimate objects of production performance. Claire M. Fagin,

Professor and Dean Emerita at the University of Pennsylvania Medical School, has argued that

> Caregiving is defeated when society views care as an individual obligation that does not require institutional or societal support, or as an unaffordable luxury, rather than as a vital social relationship that demands skill, social support, and education.[31]

Nurses in American hospitals and other health care institutions have been traditionally represented by both the Federation of Nurses and Health Professionals (AFL-CIO) and the Health Care Division of the American Federation of Teachers (AFL-CIO). The nursing professions are affected by the same class of institutional changes that have altered the job of physician. The literature published by the nurses' organizations places emphasis on "protecting quality standards in a bottom-line environment." The drive toward cost reduction in hospitals has led to subdividing and "deskilling" of parts of the nursing function (like special aides for particular support services).

There is, however, a definite limit to any attempt to make broad application of industrial-oriented methods to nursing care. It's out of the question for a robot to comfort a patient, or to observe multiple aspects of patient conditions and respond with appropriate interventions. I am aware of some of the interest in developing "artificial intelligence," but I know of no grounds for suggesting that "artificial caring" can ever replace the crucial role of the nursing profession.

Nurses have shared in many of the counterproductive features that are visible elsewhere in the medical profession and, indeed, in American industry. Thus the burgeoning growth of administrative activities and their costs has produced anomalies for nurses as well. As Dr. Fagin wrote in the introduction to "Abandonment of the Patient: The Impact of Profit-Driven Health Care on the Public":

> A major New York teaching hospital was threatened by a strike, and would that lead to a shortage of nurses? No; [a senior hospital administrator] explained that if the strike lasted only a week, they would actually have more RN's on the floor than on normal staffing patterns, because there were so many who were working in non-clinical care jobs in that institution that they could staff three shifts for a week more fully than when they were operating on a regular basis.[32]

Dr. Fagin also reports: "In 1994, when the American Nurses Association surveyed its members, 70 percent of all respondents said their employers were cutting back on staffing by leaving vacant positions unfilled, 66 percent said hospitals had already laid off nurses or were planning to do so, and 67 percent of registered nurses said the number of patients assigned to them had increased."[33] The increasingly difficult conditions of nursing care, like those of physicians, will probably see significant improvements as the main professions are unionized nationally and learn to speak with a combined voice about problems that are shared among the professions.

None of these considerations have made much of an impact on the proceedings of the American Medical Association, whose large, though diminishing, body of members has shown the sure signs of being "mad as hell—and they don't want to take it anymore," as the lead line noted in the dispatch from the AMA convention in Honolulu on January 4, 1999. Since this was written by its own medical news staff, it seems fair to assume that the point of view expressed accords with changes in the policy orientation of the AMA directorate. Other headlines that AMNews prepared on this release read, "Delegates Say AMA Must Do More to Foster Collective Bargaining and Unified Front: AMA Heard from Frustrated Delegates Who Want More Help for Physicians Dealing with Large Health Clients." The AMA's release included the following:

> They're sick and tired of having no power to negotiate fees and work conditions with payers, delegates told the association leaders. . . . Collective bargaining and private-sector advocacy are, "top priorities" with their medical societies and specialty groups back home, one physician after another testified in passionate pleas before the House. A local insurer just lowered fees by five percent, with virtually no advance notice giving . . . the 25 doctors in one local practice "no opportunity" for a negotiation. . . . The president of the Illinois State Medical Society judged that, "The imbalance of negotiating power between independent physicians and mammoth organizations" is a "major, major" issue in his state. Why does a group of 300 physicians in southern New Jersey who are worried about antitrust have to go to the Meatpackers and not to the AMA?" one delegate asked.
>
> AMA officials took to the floor to assure members that they took their concerns seriously. And in a speech to the House, AMA President Nancy W. Dickey, MD, pledged AMA support to members who "experience unfair practices in the private sector." Said Dr. Dickey, "We will come. We'll come with experts. With physician leaders. Lawyers. And even communications specialists. Giving you the resources and expert input you need to level the field with managed care providers, plans and other contractors."

If an organization as cautious as the American Medical Association is becoming responsive to the widespread dissatisfaction and grievances among its membership, we can assume that the unionization of doctors represents the wave of the future. Until drastic changes in the direction of workplace democracy are made in the health care industries, the white collars will continue to join the blue.

Like physicians, most psychologists, about 80 percent at the close of the twentieth century, have been formally independent professionals, while 20 percent were salaried employees. Nevertheless, the New York State Psychological Association decided in 1999 to affiliate with the American Federation of Teachers. The president of NYSPA explained why:

> I believe that with managed care, we are being deprofessionalized and we have to face that fact. We are being made into people just paid to do things. We don't have control over our work the way we should have.[34]

Psychologists, like other health care and educational professionals, have endured alienation at the hands of managed care organizations and the governments "who come between the professional and the patient." In response, the American Federation of Teachers has been alert to

> professionals, who care about the service they provide and whose first concern is the well-being of the people they serve (including children), [and] want to maximize their ability to exercise their professionalism.

Says Sandra Feldman, president of the AFT, "They can't do it alone. That's where unions come in."[35]

A similar process is at work in the world of education. The Cold War between the Soviet Union and the United States spurred the explosive postwar growth in American higher education. During the period immediately before the Second World War, 1939–1940, federal government funds to colleges and universities totaled $38.8 million. By 1949–1950, the flow of federal dollars to colleges and universities had increased to $524 million. Under the influence of the technology shock from Soviet successes in space and nuclear programs, federal funds to colleges and universities by 1959–1960 amounted to $1,037 million. Thereafter, funding to colleges and universities grew persistently, and by 1993–1994 this amounted to $22,076 million per year. These amounts were separate from funds that paid for veterans' education under the GI Bill of Rights.[36]

These funds had a transforming effect on many aspects of professional occupations in the education industry.

Federal funds to American universities for academic research alone increased from $1.4 billion in 1971 to $10.8 billion by 1997.[37] The growing availability of grants of all sorts, and especially research funds from many federal departments, set in motion a new competition in American academia. Greatest prestige was accorded to the faculty members who brought in the most grant money. Department chairmen and deans of schools saw that "overhead" charges in research grants became an ever-increasing proportion of their funding. These funds, in turn, supported not only libraries and laboratory facilities but also the growing administrative operations in virtually all universities.

Reductions in the number of teaching courses for which a faculty member was responsible became a primary indicator of academic status. Thus teaching one course per semester, or being relieved from such responsibility for half a year or more, became a sought-after perquisite. Michael D. Yates, of the University of Pittsburgh at Johnstown, has recorded:

> If, for example, my university cared, it would not be implementing a system of "differential teaching" in which those who don't publish enough or bring in enough grants will be punished by being forced to teach more. If it cared, it would not allow professors to "buy back their courses" by hiring part-timers to teach them.[38]

Despite a few decades' observation of the academic scene, I was taken aback by this report from Yates: "I was once hired to teach a course . . . by a professor who literally begged me to do it and who had never previously met me and knew nothing about my background." Given this trend, it was remarkable that at Columbia College, Polykarp Kusch, a Nobel laureate in physics, once undertook to teach the course in physics (Physics 1001-1002) designed for non–physics majors—"Physics for Poets."

The pressures to "bring in money" to the department, the school and the university have become major and unrelenting incentives, especially to younger faculty and to those seeking tenure appointment.

In the rest of this chapter, we will explore the hidden consequences of the high-profile experiments in "distance learning" by American universities. We will also see the far more insidious and destructive impact of managerialism on education, as universities have turned increasingly to exploit part-time and graduate student labor in their drive to cut costs and increase profits. Nevertheless, these processes of alienation have triggered widespread moves toward unionization such as those we have encountered in the health care industry.

These transforming pressures on faculties have taken on a new quality in recent years which, if they are allowed to proceed, may degrade both the teaching and the research qualities of American universities.

Distance Learning

In the New York metropolitan area, two of the largest schools, New York University and Columbia University, have set up formal, university-owned and -managed distance-learning divisions, separate from their academic schools and departments. Although the plans are not detailed just yet at NYU, Columbia has announced a detailed plan entitled Fathom, with five other institutions, in the April 7, 2000, issue of the *Columbia Record.* There are some obvious and straightforward issues involved in such enterprises.

In both cases, the distance-learning operations are to be based on materials created by professors. They will, however, be set within a "design" that is prepared by outside specialists to meet the visual requirements and appealing layouts suitable for Internet use. While the futuristic and supposedly democratizing possibilities of distance learning are much vaunted by university administrations, these innovations raise a whole series of troubling questions:

- Will the faculty members who prepare the texts be paid on a corporate or a university salary basis?
- Who will hire the people for this work?
- Who will own the lectures, the courses, the books and the patents?
- How will the revenue from these operations be apportioned among the author, the "visuals" designer, the university corporate owner?
- Is such activity to be part of a faculty member's normal course load?
- Is the performance of this work to be a factor in considering tenure appointment?
- Will distance-learning enterprises located at universities be subject to faculty decisions over subject matter, the workforce involved or prices and ownership of profits?

- Who will decide on the courses to be taught?
- Who will select the instructors?
- Will participation in the distance-learning enterprise be treated as an extension of the part-time "on call" teaching that has come to characterize the part-time teaching staff of American colleges and universities—more than seventy part-time professors for every hundred full-timers?

It is possible that the ultimate effects of distance learning may not be addressed by one or another answer to these questions, for what is involved here is essentially an attempt to supplant face-to-face learning and discussion. Things are made more complicated by a further series of recent trends in college education: the tendency to teach what happens to be fashionable, a growing lack of faith in the validity of the grading system, the presence of mystifying requirements that can intimidate students and the growth of a caste system that places part-time professors in positions within a permanent academic underclass.

Despite this growing sense of uncertainty about the mission of the American university, I concur with Jerry Farber that "even today, as the corporate raiders close in, when you walk onto the campus of a large . . . university . . . you find yourself in a place that's by and large—however imperfectly—under a different set of rules."

Although their traditional role has been abridged by the surrounding conditions of a society dominated by a militarized state capitalism, universities, especially the older, richer ones, can operate, at least in part, by rules that approximate an "ideal culture" of

> intellectual openness; rigorous, reflective, critical thought; scientific inquiry; historical awareness; an orientation toward public affairs; pursuit of the arts; a celebration of culture; and, above all, one overriding criterion: not utility or profit or popularity or orthodoxy, but truth. A problematic term, to say the least, but, as with the university, there is nothing to take its place.[39]

There is no reason to suppose, of course, that distance learning should not "work," if what is being taught ranges from baseline methods in mathematics and statistics, core knowledge in physical and biological sciences—to useful but straightforward skills like how to dismantle a rifle or parts of an automobile engine, or how to fill out financial forms. But distance learning can't substitute for the kind of process that entails an exchange of views, or a consideration of alternative values and their consequences for technologies and the arts, or open debate about what determines our preferences among them.[40]

A learning community cannot be replaced by a television or computer screen. But this is not the view held by those who are applying corporate strategies and the lessons of managerialism to the "business" of education.

In March 1999, Jones International University became the first completely online institution to be accredited by one of the country's six major regional accrediting associations. This decision of the Commission on Institutions of Higher Education of the North-Central Association of Colleges and Schools met with a sharp protest from the American Association of University Professors. James E. Perley, Chairman of the AAUP Accreditation Committee, sent a letter of protest to the North-Central body objecting to its decision about Jones International University. Dr. Perley indicated that the Jones organization had only two faculty members who were full-time and that it evidently put little emphasis on faculty research or scholarship. Said Dr. Perley, "I don't have problems with any institution that says, 'We do technical training.' But they shouldn't call themselves a college or university." Margaret B. Lee, chairwoman of CIHE, countered, "Jones is providing as high a quality of education as a lot of other places. To think you can limit learning to that old model is just impossible."[41]

Pamela Pease, president of Jones International, argued: "Accreditation is important in the eyes of corporations, students and other institutions of higher education—it signifies quality. For us it's especially important because it shows that as a cyber-university we are meeting all the same standards." More important, of course, is the bottom line. Accreditation will allow students to get reimbursed under federal financial aid programs or seek tuition credits from employers. It should make it easier to transfer credits as well. To date, Jones International has been offering bachelor's and master's degrees in business communications and has sixty-four admitted master's degree students. The Jones organization indicated that it offers education at about half the cost of public institutions. It also declares that its faculty is composed of leading experts in their respective fields from colleges across the nation.

The Jones group is led by cable-industry millionaire Glenn Jones. Jones himself is an unusually aggressive and financially successful organizer of business groups and is now said to be devoting himself full-time to his University of the Web. "Our concept," he said, "is to deliver high quality education, regardless of place, to make a profit and pay taxes." The *Financial Times* reports that in the United States his initial focus has been on adult working students looking to augment their education and to enhance their chances of promotion and job mobility. According to Jones, there are 15 million students in American colleges and universities, but about 100 million would welcome further education. In his perspective, the big picture extends far wider—China, for example, has 5 million college students, and probably another 80 million ambitious for college training.[42]

The Jones approach eliminates the costs of plant, equipment and full-time faculty. Despite widespread evidence to the contrary, "There are not enough professors to go around," says Jones. According to him the time is right to unveil his "Model J," an all-Internet operation, drawing on expertise within his several private companies: his TV channel, the Web university, and E-Education, which creates software to enable universities to put courses on the Internet. According to Jones, "It's silly to think you could or even want to replace the existing structure, because that's where all the talent is." Furthermore, he says, those who have opposed him in the past and who became acquainted with his software for enabling course design and his low-cost online registration service have become true believers: "Now that the Internet is so far along, they know they must come into the 21st century with 21st century tools." Jones has said that the Ford Motor Company, U.S. West and others were consulted on their needs when the courses were being designed for the new university's main initial offering, a master's degree in business communications.

At the outset, reports Jones, with only 150 students, the University of the Web expects to start a new semester each month, and there are plans for a new semester to begin every day as the student body builds. Jones recalls a graduation ceremony for pioneer students, one of whom remarked that she took a course because the cost was so reasonable. Each of their degrees had cost him personally $500,000, but he did not mention it. These were "loss leaders" for his futuristic venture. In a word, this is an ambitious business initiative, aiming at millions of prospective participants, whose fees would generate a cash flow that, at those levels, would surely yield a considerable profit.

Nevertheless, established universities and the professoriate have yet to be heard from. In his letter objecting to the accreditation action, Dr. Perley of the AAUP said that the Jones group instructors have little academic freedom, because their courses are prepared by others. This has the earmarks of an operation in which professors with formal academic qualifications might prepare drafts or notes of proposed "courses" to be put in shape for broadcast purposes on the Internet by professional writers and designers of Web displays.

Western Governors University, backed by governors in some seventeen states, began operating in 1998. This institution was determined eligible for accreditation by an interregional committee created to develop standards for schools like Western Governors University. A further expedition in online teaching is operated by the Open University of the United States, a group associated with Britain's Open University. They are seeking accreditation from the college-and-university association that covers Delaware, where the Open University group is incorporated.

It is reasonable to expect that many such groups of business investors will seek to mimic the pattern of Glenn Jones. Serious people in the education professions will have to confront fundamental questions like those outlined above: What are the limits of conveying knowledge by digital media? Above all, can the capacity for critical, innovative thought be produced by mainly one-way communication systems? But there are also other issues involved: Will the fees that are offered by digital-teaching corporations be surefire attractions to the sections of the American professoriate who are, at present, struggling to get by as part-time instructors, without a living wage despite holding advanced degrees from well-established colleges and universities?

David Noble, the historian, author of *Forces of Production* and *America by Design: Science, Technology and the Rise of Corporate Capitalism*, has undertaken a program of studies on these efforts to replace the university as we have known it with distance learning. Part of his research has focused on the question of intellectual property rights. Administrators at the University of California, for example, have tried to require its teaching faculty members to file course materials, including electronic texts, with the university administration so that these can be treated as "intellectual property" with the rights assigned to the university. Noble has also reported on the two-month strike at Canada's York University when the faculty of that institution rejected similar demands from its administration, and won its point as the university withdrew its requirement of a property right on the intellectual output of the faculty.

The Universities Go Corporate

Distance learning is only the most recent move to apply corporate strategies to university education. These have been a series of marked alterations in the working lives of the almost 16 million people, including students, who work in American colleges and universities.

First, the mushrooming administrations of American universities: Following the pattern of growth in the managerial and control occupations in American corporations and in government, there has been a parallel process visible in American universities during the past quarter of a century. In 1976, the universities and colleges spent $38 for administration in relation to every $100 spent on instruction. By 1996, this ratio had risen to 47:100.[43] During roughly the same period, from 1975 to 1995, the number of students had advanced by 28 percent, from 11.2 million to 14.3 million. The overall growth in full-time students was 19 percent, but part-time students had increased by 41 percent.[44]

The administrations of American universities during this period were alert to the possibilities of reducing the costs of operations. Accordingly, despite the expansion of the student body, the number of full-time faculty grew by only 27 percent, from 435,000 in 1975 to 551,000 in 1995. This shortfall was sharply offset by the increased use of part-time faculty, from 188,000 to 381,000 during this period. Another strategy by which universities offset the relatively modest rise in full-time faculty was the considerable enlargement of the numbers of graduate student instructors and research assistants, from 160,000 (1975) to 216,000 (1995), a 35 percent growth.

Finally, in keeping with the corporate tradition of expanding administrative overhead, the numbers of executive, managerial and administrative staffs of U.S. colleges and universities rose 46 percent during this period, from 101,000 to 147,000. These bare-bones statistics hardly begin to convey the transformation of American universities, and the response of faculty and increasingly alienated graduate assistants to these patterns.

Lest the wider economic significance of these developments be overlooked, I underscore a point first emphasized by Professor Stanley Aronowitz of the City University of New York: "Colleges and universities employed as many people in 1990 as the steel and automotive industries combined."[45]

While organized labor long ignored these developments in university occupations, the drastic transformations that they reflect have caught the attention of teachers and students.

As we have seen, expansion of part-time and graduate student instructors was a consequence of the growth in college and university enrollments from 1975 to 1995 (the last year for which data are available). The following figures, for 1975 and 1995, summarize the composition of the teaching faculty in American universities and colleges.

	1975	1995
Students		
Full-time	6,841,000	8,129,000
Part-time	4,344,000	6,133,000
Full-time faculty, including research	435,000	551,000
Part-time faculty	188,000	381,000
Instruction and research assistants	160,000	216,000
Total teaching faculty	783,000	1,148,000
Executive, managerial and administrative	101,000 (1976)	147,000[46]

About 34 percent of those who performed full-time faculty work were on tenure track, the traditional system that offers qualified professors long-term job security. Of these, 25 percent already had tenure by 1995, while 9 percent were probationary (which in the harsh conditions of the present job market is no guarantee of job security).

A crucial factor in the enlarged number of part-time faculty has been the great growth in the enrollments of community colleges, where about two-thirds of the faculty teach at hourly rates and without the benefits usually accorded to full-time teachers. The combined effect of the community college expansion, plus the resort to part-time faculty in the four-year colleges and universities, has made "higher education as a whole . . . structurally dependent on a pool of cheap labor to teach (especially) its lower level courses."[47]

Aronowitz has looked in particular at the expansion of part-time work in the colleges and universities of New York City. He notes: "In the early 1980s, New York's City University employed more than 11,000 full-time faculty members for 200,000 students; by 1996 there were only 5,300 full-time professors for 207,000 students. The gap has been filled by part-time faculty."[48] So it is that 60 percent of classes in the CUNY system are taught by part-time faculty earning an average of $2,500 per course, per semester, without benefits. It is little wonder that both teachers and students believe that the system is in need of a major overhaul.

As the *New York Times* noted in February 1998, "The savings from using part-time teachers are clear. The average pay for full-time associate professors at the senior colleges, for example, is about $61,000 a year, as well as medical and pension benefits and paid sabbaticals, and they might teach three courses a semester. Handling the same course load with adjuncts would cost about $12,000, and adjuncts get few benefits."[49]

We need to look at the system that has trained so many highly educated Ph.D.s, only to offer them little in the way of full-time employment or a living wage. Obviously, the overproduction of students completing graduate degrees and therefore aiming for full-time faculty appointments did not come about by chance. An article in the *Chronicle of Higher Education* (December 18, 1998) reported:

> If all college and university teaching were performed by full-time faculty members who held doctoral degrees, we would be facing the under-supply of PhDs predicted in 1989 by William G. Bowen and Julie Ann Sosa in "Prospects for Faculty in the Arts and Sciences: A Study of Factors Affecting Demand and Supply." Ironically, it was their predictions, widely disseminated in the popular media, that led so many current graduate students and new PhDs to abandon other careers and pursue doctoral study."[50]

The Modern Language Association has stated: "We want to make the ratio of full-time to part-time faculty members at every college or university . . . as much a part of the professional and public discourse about an institution's quality as are its students' SAT scores, faculty publications and library holdings."[51]

The situation has been worsened by the downsizing of numbers of full-time faculty posts within the universities. The jobs promised to a future generation have never materialized. Instead of filling the vacancies left by retiring faculty, the universities have left the posts open. The University of California system of nine universities, for example, was compelled by diminished state funding to encourage the early retirement of 1,996 tenured faculty between 1990 and 1994. To replace them at bargain basement rates, part-time and temporary faculty were appointed, and some retirees were "recalled" as part-time faculty. By 1998, this was the instructional staffing structure of the California University system:

58.2 percent of the instructional staff are graduate students

20 percent are full-time tenured or on tenure track

11.6 percent are part-time instructors

8.9 percent are nontenure track instructors or on short-term contracts

By the fall of 1996, student enrollment and faculty levels showed the following pattern at California State University, with its twenty-two schools (mainly community colleges, nonresidential):

Student enrollment	336,810
Tenure track faculty	10,610
Lecturer faculty	8,440[52]

Here, the nontenure-track, or part-time, faculty are 44 percent of the total.

This is a recipe for a third-rate educational system.

Similar patterns repeat around the United States. Rutgers University, for example, lost 240 full-time faculty from 1985 to 1998 (an overall reduction of 9 percent), while enrollment during that period was stable. There is clearly great variability in the way colleges and university administrations have responded. Thus at George Mason University of Virginia, 230 of the 749 full-time faculty are on nontenured-track term contracts.[53]

Ernie Benjamin, director of research for the AAUP, reports that part-time faculty "average" earnings range from $7,400 to $12,400 per year. On a per-course basis, salaries range from about $1,000 to $3,000, and one study found that community college part-time salaries average about $1,500 per course, per semester. Much of this is made possible by the fact that about half of the part-time faculty have full-time day jobs. Of the rest, 25 percent have additional part-time jobs, while another 25 percent have no additional positions. Reportedly, the great number of people struggling to construct a livelihood by teaching multiple courses in multiple schools during the same semester gave rise to the designation of "freeway fliers." In the name of cost-cutting or profitability, America's universities are flying to nowhere, reducing the working lives of the majority of their employees to a miserable grind.[54]

Tom Coffin, a part-time instructor in the Sociology Department of Georgia State University in Atlanta, has portrayed the intolerable frustration of a part-time professor's economic position as follows:

> A beginning tenure-track faculty position in the Arts & Sciences is funded at about $60,000 per year. At GSU, a "full-time" teaching load is eight courses per year, with research and other requirements resulting in reductions of teaching assignments. A new tenure-track hire thus costs the university the equivalent of $7,500 per course. . . . I, however, cost a flat fee of $2,000 (plus a small amount for office space, supplies, etc.), with no carry-over from semester to semester. . . . The subsidy to the university is immense. This year, for example, I have taught or am teaching six three-credit hour courses in sociology. I will have taught a total of 231 students, each of whom pays at $86 per student class hour, $258 in tuition alone for each of these courses. I thus bring in

> $59,598 to the university. I am paid $12,000 for my services, for a net surplus of $47,598. . . . And I am but one of several hundred part-time instructors (and graduate teaching assistants) so used . . . as "cash cows" of the system.[55]

Thomas J. Farrell underscores the fact that administrators across the country have been using temporary faculty to hold down instructional costs while they have increased administrative outlays.[56] The title of his article captures the essence of this triumph of managerialism in the universities: "How to Kill Higher Education."

Union Organization Among Part-Time University Faculty

By 1996, some 80 colleges and universities had separate bargaining units for part-time professors, this from a directory compiled by the National Center for the Study of Collective Bargaining in Higher Education and the Professions.* Of those institutions, about 30 have been organized since 1990. Some 18,000 of these part-time professors are represented by separate bargaining units solely representing part-time faculty. Many others are represented by unions that also include full-time professors. All told, about 225 institutions, as of 1996, had faculty unions that represented both full- and part-time faculty members.[57]

A newly won union contract at the University of Massachusetts, for example, defined "half-time status" as a teaching load of four courses a year, a load carried by almost two-thirds of the part-time union members. The same contract has raised the base salary for this load to $16,000 a year, and there is provision for raising that to a minimum of $18,350 by the end of the three-year contract.[58] This improvement for adjunct faculty was achieved by an independent organization, the Part-time Faculty Committee, affiliated with the National Education Association.

To take another example, from September 1, 1997, to June 30, 1999, part-time lecturers at Rutgers had negotiated an agreement following a campaign of organization and negotiation by the American Association of University Professors. Here the part-time faculty are separately organized

*The National Center for the Study of Collective Bargaining in Higher Education and the Professors (at Baruch College–CUNY, 17 Lexington Avenue, Box F-1228, New York, N.Y. 10010) has compiled a *Directory of Faculty Contracts and Bargaining Agents in Institutions of Higher Education*, 1997. The AAUP (American Association of University Professors, 1012 14th Street NW, Suite 500, Washington, D.C., 20005-3465) has prepared "Working for Academic Renewal: A Kit for Organizing on the Issues of Part-Time and Non-Tenure Track Faculty." This is a thorough briefing on all aspects of these topics, which the AAUP staff can supplement with timely data, analyses and reports on organizing in progress, and with contract data from various universities.

in their own bargaining unit. The salary schedule is worth attention, particularly because the organization and recognition of part-time faculty at Rutgers has attracted wide attention as a major step forward for this exploited and frequently neglected class of university employees. Article 4 of the contract provides that the minimum salary rate will be $750 per credit with other rates set for other parts of the university.

What does this mean in practice? If an adjunct professor teaches three courses each semester, then the total salary income is $13,500, or $18,000 if four courses are taught. Since the contract provides an additional fee of $575 for a heavily attended course, and if we then assume that this occurs twice a year, the teaching of eight courses will thereby yield an income of $19,600 for a year of work. Anyone with experience in education will recognize that eight college courses per year is a very heavy workload. Assume that class time, plus preparation time, plus grading time, plus administrative time add up to a total of 2,000 hours of work. In that case, it appears that the average income per hour would be $9.58, before tax.

Ivy League schools have not exempted themselves from the exploitation of adjunct instructors. A full-time junior professor in social science or humanities would cost around $40,000 per year, plus health insurance, pension plan and other fringe benefits. If a normal course load is four per year, then adjuncts paid around $4,000 per year (and no fringes) are a real bargain, giving the school a net gain of more than $24,000 by using part-time rather than full-time faculty.

Consider the situation of the recently graduated Ph.D. and assume an age of twenty-eight. Looking forward to providing an income for himself or herself and a family, the adjunct professor finds that this is hardly a living wage. The need to pay back student loans that frequently total tens of thousands of dollars can only add to the financial burden of part-time teaching. In that case, there would be immense pressure on a young person and spouse for both to work in order to earn a plausible income and level of living. This illustration is an optimum case, because it assumes the availability of an overflow course load for each of two semesters. Neither can new faculty members proceed on the assumption that there is a real possibility for acquiring full-time and tenure appointment. Many part-time scholars hold on in the faint hope of getting one of the dwindling numbers of full-time positions. But with each year that passes in a brutally competitive job market, their chances diminish.

I concur strongly with James Perley of the AAUP, who has declared, "We need to take away the economic advantage that comes from overusing part-time faculty. We need to pay faculty members who teach part-time a salary equivalent per course to those who teach full-time." I would also underscore the importance of according access for part-time faculty to the support services and benefits that full-time faculty enjoy.[59]

Despite the resistance and frequent hostility of university administrators to the struggle of part-time faculty to improve their working lives, many tenured faculty members have shown their support and solidarity, alert to the prospect that the increasingly heavy use of part-time faculty represents a broader business strategy to minimize pay and maximize control.[60]

Graduate-Student Organizations

Another recent trend has been what's happening to those on the lowest rung of university teaching to demand fairer treatment from their employers. In order to get a clear sense of the unionizing of graduate-student teaching assistants, I have examined the contracts or agreements drawn up between graduate student organizations and the administrations in the following schools: the University of Michigan, the State University of New York, the University of Massachusetts at Amherst and the University of Wisconsin. The existence of common problems for graduate students teaching in all these universities is revealed by the similar agendas of topics treated in these agreements.

There is one striking omission, however. Every contract includes reference to workload, but the specific details are not discussed. In other words, university administrators still have a free hand in assigning course loads to these students, many of whom are still trying to complete their own course requirements or to write their dissertations. The stipends range from $5,570 for an academic year, to $26,816 per year for an experienced dissertator (I take that to mean lecturer).* These agreements also go into great detail on matters ranging from health insurance to parking and child care, grievance and arbitration procedure, evaluations and personnel files.

Graduate students at the University of Michigan and at Yale University have compiled directories of graduate-student employee organizations.†

*According to Article 5 of the *State University Graduate Student Negotiating Unit Agreement* between the State of New York and the State University Graduate Student Employees Union, "the minimum stipend for the 1998–1999 academic year for employees on full assistantships at University Center campuses shall be $5,570 annually." According to Article X of the *Agreement Between the State of Wisconsin and the Teaching Assistants' Association*, experienced dissertators were to receive a minimum annual stipend for the 1998–1999 academic year of $26,816.

†University of Michigan, Graduate Employees Organization
Email address: *usergeo@umich.edu*
Website: *www.umich.edu/~umgeo*

Yale University, Graduate Employees and Students Organization
Website: *www.yale.edu.geso*

One striking product of this new wave of graduate student organizing is Ivana Krajcinovic, who earned her Ph.D. in economics in 1993 at Yale, but then abandoned academia for the calling of a union activist. She organizes dishwashers in Monterey, California, for Local 483 of the Hotel and Restaurant Employees Union. According to Krajcinovic, Yale is "like a bootcamp for organizing. They run a real good program there."[61]

Boeing Engineers and Technicians

> The endless dynamic of alienation and accumulation at the heart of capitalism has proved to be a giant engine for disalienation.
>
> —PART I INTRODUCTION

The managers of Boeing, the largest U.S. aerospace firm and a prototype of state capitalism, ran their alienation engine at full throttle. They produced previously unknown solidarity among 19,000 engineers and technicians who struck the company for forty days early in 2000 and won their main demands on pay, medical benefits, many contract details and—most important of all, in their judgment—respect. Asked what the strike was about, the one engineer/technician voice said, "I never thought I'd see the day when I went out on strike. But Boeing pushed me over the edge." Another: "I didn't want to be represented by a labor union. . . . But now I feel like joining a union was the only effective way to make my voice heard at this company." And another: "It takes a lot for a bunch of engineers to get up and walk out the door. The rocket scientists are literally out on the streets here. It's kind of incredible."[62]

Said Charles Bofferding, executive director of Boeing's professional union,

> we showed not only ourselves but the rest of the nation's white-collar workers what can be done, that acting collectively does have tremendous impact.

Steven Greenhouse reported on the strikers' return to work:

> The Boeing strikers were able to cripple Boeing, which is based in Seattle, because under federal law the company needed its engineers to certify new planes for delivery.
>
> The A.F.L.-C.I.O. pushed unions to donate hundreds of thousands of dollars to the strikers, and Mr. Trumka, the A.F.L.-C.I.O.'s No. 2 official, joined union negotiators at the bargaining table.

Viewing the Boeing development as a predictor,

> many workers say it is management's unimpeded flexibility to downsize, reduce benefits and redefine workers' responsibilities that convinces them they need a union to protect them.[63]

The slogan on the picket signs at Boeing was "No Nerds, No Birds."*[64]

The engineers and technicians union at Boeing, Society of Professional Engineering Employees in Aerospace (or SPEEA), confront a management that is evidently determined to pursue a strategy of short-term financial gain. How else can one understand management's goal when more than 1,000 engineers and technicians left Boeing for other employment only a few months after the March strike settlement?

Boeing has 90,000 workers in its commercial plane division, 34,000 in space and communications and 46,000 in military planes and missile systems. But the military-serving unit yields the highest profit—a rate in the double digits. Thus the commercial plane division in 1999 lost new-order position to Europe's Airbus Industries but was still the world leader in overall deliveries.

Given this trend toward deindustrialization of Boeing in favor of military production, its engineers have become extremely pessimistic about their professional prospects at the firm. The recent departure of engineers represents an annual attrition rate of 10 to 12 percent, compared with a previous yearly turnover of only 4 to 6 percent. It is even more ominous because the departures were concentrated in the generation of twenty-five to thirty-five age group, leaving a preponderance in the thirty-five to forty-five range.

SPEEA has openly criticized Boeing management for focusing on short-term financial gain at the expense of research and development. Management has also been a vigorous outsourcer, seeking advantage by assigning design and exporting production work to firms in Japan, China, Australia and Singapore.

Boeing's top management put itself on a collision course with its engineer and technician population by trying to pursue a policy of cost-cutting rather than depending on the technical and productivity advantages to be gained from an innovative workforce.

Government and business managers have proceeded without hesitation to set in motion a series of major alienations that have transformed the working lives of American doctors and other health care workers, professors and engineers. But neither the doctors nor the part-time professors

*To keep up with SPEEA, the Society of Professional Engineering Employees in Aerospace, the main Web site is *www.speea.org*. The site is well run and appears to be a principal means of communication with the membership.

enjoyed the prospect of genuflecting before their new corporate masters. The mottoes differed within each group, but they all saw in unions the same remedy. The surrender of the AMA hierarchy before their members' onslaught offered high drama. The convention majority that turned down the AMA Board's anti-union recommendations was consistent with the association's own survey, which found 88 percent of its members favoring the unionization of salaried physicians, the better to deal with hospital and HMO managers.

11

Disalienation by Design: Installing Workplace Democracy

In the wide realm of state capitalism, industrial workers and their unions are often joined by local governments and community groups that marshal different constituencies and resources in their efforts to block alienation by corporate and government managers. In addition, the industrialized world includes economic cooperatives that perform production, trade and finance services.

What all these noncorporate organizations have in common, to varying degrees, is democratic modification of the normal rules of business. In cooperatives and labor-community initiatives alike, disalienation *by design* challenges the conventional pursuit of profits and power by predatory competition and hierarchy.

The Cooperative Alternative

THE MONDRAGON NETWORK

Even the most brief survey of the range of feasible alternatives to corporate organizations must take note of the cooperative and quasi-cooperative business networks that have been set up around the world. The enterprises I am concerned with here are workers' production cooperatives organized around joint ownership and shared decision-making, in which the share is usually based on membership rather than on size of investment.

Contrary to popular wisdom, in which they are often presented as exceptional experiments, cooperatives have been highly successful as groups of enterprises. The most important of these is the Mondragon network operating in the Basque region of northwest Spain.

The Mondragon Cooperative Corporation (MCC) has assets valued at $13.8 billion, a membership of about 30,000 and annual sales (1996) in excess of $6 billion.[1] It consists of a series of enterprises, mainly industrial, that are operated under a democratic set of rules. The cooperative extends to all aspects of working life—and even to some things beyond, such as education. The formation of the network has been very dramatic. The first Mondragon enterprise, ULGOR, which made paraffin heaters and cookers, began operations in 1960. It was initiated by a parish priest, Don José Maria Arrizmendiarrieta, and a handful of students he had helped train, who laid out the main principles of its operation.

Each of the Mondragon cooperatives has a system in which members vote for a board of directors that has responsibilities for operations. Mondragon's bank and its other important agencies are second-degree cooperatives. The workers at those facilities name a minority of their board, while the majority are chosen by members of the participating co-ops.

The average annual income of Mondragon members is about $26,000. A maximum salary differential for officials has been set at 6:1 in relation to basic wage, though in recent years this ratio has been disputed, with one group claiming a need for higher salaries to top managers. The internal costing operation of a Mondragon co-op includes setting an annual wage for each member, which does not vary with the quantity of output. Hence payments to the members is a "fixed cost."[2]

One of the most striking features of Mondragon is a highly innovative solution to the problem of finance capital for investment. Each new member of a co-op is required to deposit the equivalent of a year's wages into an "internal capital account." If members lack a lump sum, they repay a loan of that amount to Mondragon's bank, the Caja Laboral Popular (CLP). This becomes a part of an internal capital and receives interest at a regular rate, plus a share of co-op profits. Crucially, the money in this account may not be withdrawn by the member until retirement. This approach to membership helps solve a continuing problem of the cooperative economy: access to adequate finance capital for investment.

Thus an important role in the Mondragon network is played by the workers' bank, the CLP. The CLP serves as a source of capital for investments by the cooperatives. The institution functions like a commercial savings and investment bank and is also prepared to accept deposits and other business from people outside the network, but it is owned solely by the cooperative. Indeed, the inflow of funds gives the bank finance resources far in excess of the financial needs of the group's enterprises, so capital flows are activated for housing cooperatives and schools. Finance capital is also available for individual credit and for additional investing by co-op enterprises. This is but one corner of a wider account of Mondragon.*

The cooperative managements, unlike their more conventional counterparts in businesses, who may come hat in hand to ask for financing to start up a firm or an ESOP organization, are on friendly terms with a bank whose function is to encourage and to oversee the competent investment and operation of the various enterprises in which it participates.

The CLP has a vital enterprise-design department. When an individual proposes an investment for a new product or service, the bank, if it has no reason to dismiss such a plan, studies the matter in detail and prepares a complete manufacturing, cost and market analysis. For example, in the early 1990s a proposal to manufacture components for hi-fi equipment went through such a process. The reports took two years or so to prepare and thoroughly analyzed manufacturing requirements, capital requirements for equipment, plants and the like.

The bank completed analyses of markets in Spain and elsewhere for such products, and of the requirements that must be served in terms of quality and distribution. Also included was an estimate of the break-even point, in terms of volume for these products. From that, the CLP made a judgment about investment, performing every aspect in the design of industrial enterprise that we, in the Department of Industrial Engineering and Operations Research at Columbia University, would teach students to do for a proposal for organizing a new venture.

If the prospects are favorable, the matter is put to a vote of the bank's directors. The CLP is not an outside holder of finance capital exercising dominion over those interested in production; it is drawn from the same people. If the go-ahead is given, a schedule is drawn up, a program of investment and timetable of activity are created, and the work proceeds. Very important: the bank names a representative who then participates, first closely and thereafter more remotely, in the investment and other planning and formative activities of the new business. The bank acts as a friendly big brother to the managers of the newly formed enterprise. This unusual set of arrangements has worked splendidly for the Mondragon cooperatives.

A study completed at Columbia's IEOR Department by a team of undergraduates working with Professor Peter Norden analyzed the Mondragon cooperatives, comparing them with Western enterprises.[3] As their study suggested, the Mondragon production practice is strongly directed

*José Maria Ormaechea, *The Mondragon Cooperative Experience* (Mondragon Cooperative Corporation, 1993). The writer, as a young man, was one of five engineers who organized ULGOR.

to investment goods (metals, construction goods, machines) and intermediate goods (like electronic and appliance components), which together constitute 48 percent of the cooperative production.

The study includes an overview of the MCC structure, which includes three major divisions: industrial, financial and retail. All told, these employ over 30,000 people.

The financial division includes the Caja Laboral Popular, the social security system, insurance companies, real estate and commercial leasing and consumer finance and employs less than 10 percent of the workforce. The retail division encompasses a large supermarket chain, food processing and consumer services, and consists of about a third of the workforce. More than half of the workforce is employed in the industrial division, which, in turn, has seven subdivisions, each with several cooperative firms:[4]

- Capital Goods I—machine tools
- Capital Goods II—industrial presses, manufacturing equipment
- Engineering and management consulting
- Auto components
- Electronic components and domestic appliances
- Industrial components and services
- Construction division
- Household goods, domestic appliances and furniture

As this summary suggests, a strong focus is placed on capital goods and machine products. In the Mondragon system, there is no production of military materiel or goods requiring processes that might pollute the environment.

The 1990 CLP Annual Report outlines the composition of the total sales of the Mondragon co-ops:

Investment goods	23%
Intermediate goods	25%
Consumer goods	24%
Trade and services	28%

Altogether, the MCC comprises 109 enterprises. These are organized into: financial groups (6), industrial groups (80), distribution groups (8), and corporate activities, including R&D and education (15).

These include thirteen subsidiary firms with varying investment participation by the Mondragon companies. The subsidiaries are located in France, Mexico, Morocco, Spain, Egypt, Argentina, Holland and China.*

The formal system of decision-making includes a board of directors named by an annual general assembly that has final power over operational plans. The board meets monthly and names the general manager, who, in turn, works with a management council of functional department heads. Built-in rules assure rotation of offices and avoidance of single candidates for major posts. A social council is empowered to function as though it were a labor union.

Wages are based upon a job-evaluation system that includes education achievement, job responsibility (as for a work team), years of seniority and work performance.

The profits of a co-op, after labor and other expenses, are typically divided, approximately:

10% to the social cultural fund

20% to the company reserve fund

70% to the worker-members' capital account.

The last item means addition to the workers' account, which is received at retirement or upon leaving the enterprise.

How, then, does Mondragon compare overall with U.S. enterprises? In the following tables are several sets of data that show MCC "by the numbers." They contrast the performance of the CLP and the Mondragon industrial co-ops with leading U.S. banks and manufacturers. The Mondragon bank analysis shows the relative scale of CLP in terms of several categories of bank assets and activity.

*Thanks to the diligence of Greg MacLeod, author of *From Mondragon to America*, we have an informative listing of 109 Mondragon enterprises, which I have included in Appendix B.

Bank Analysis (1990)

$ Millions

	Caja Laboral Popular	JP Morgan	Citicorp	Manufacturers Hanover
Revenue	425	3,191	14,535	2,841
Profit	61	775	318	139
Expenditures	85	n/a	n/a	n/a
Loans	1,817	27,582	158,550	40,843
Deposits	3,080	37,557	142,400	40,196
Assets	3,730	93,103	217,000	61,530
Common equity	281	4,695	8,190	2,849
Employees	1,250	12,968	95,000	18,571

Source: *CLP Annual Report 1991;* S&P stock data, NYSE.

As the Bank Analysis table suggests, the CLP was an outstanding performer in profit/common equity (common stock value)—21 percent, appreciably more profitable than the three U.S. banks: 16 percent, 4 percent, and 5 percent, respectively. CLP's profit/revenue of 14 percent was surpassed by the Morgan Bank (24 percent) but outperformed Citicorp by 2 percent and Manufacturers Hanover by 5 percent.

The Bank Performance Analysis table reflects major features of CLP operations. It is strong in managing its own operations to exceed the deposits/employee and revenue/employee of the U.S. banks.

Bank Performance Analysis (1990)

	Caja Laboral Popular	Selected U.S. Banks, Average
Deposits/employee	$2.5 million	$2.2 million
Revenue/employee	$0.3 million	$0.2 million
Expenditures as % of revenue	20.0	69.6
Loans as % of deposits	59.0	95.4
Profit as % of assets	1.6	0.4
Profit as % of equity	21.7	8.4

Source: *CLP Annual Report 1991*, S&P Stock Data NYSE

In the Bank Performance Analysis table, the CLP also performs well. It is obviously frugal, as its expenditures/revenue were 20 percent, compared with the U.S. banks' 69 percent. CLR showed loans/deposits of 59 percent, compared with 95 percent for the U.S. group. CLR was evidently practicing a more cautious loan policy, as befits a bank that was set up to serve co-op institutions which are steps removed from hierarchy and the range of labor-process practices at the center of state capitalism.

The next table displays an industrial analysis of the whole Mondragon system: Of the five U.S. firms, two (GE and IBM) show a much higher profit as a percentage of sales. Nevertheless, a payoff for the Mondragon system is its ability to invest more intensively than the U.S. industrial firms, all of them major multinationals.

Industrial Income Analysis (1990)

	$ Sales per Employee	**% Investment of Total Sales**	**% Profit of Total Sales**
Mondragon (over all)	125,015	9.5	3.2
U.S. Firms			
Caterpillar	200,259	9.1	1.8
IBM	184,631	9.4	8.7
GE	193,497	7.8	7.5
United Technology	111,890	5.6	3.5
Whirlpool Corporation	183,173	4.0	1.1

Source: *CLP Annual Report 1991*; S&P stock data, NYSE.

As I have mentioned, Mondragon cooperatives are involved in all aspects of working life, and even in some things beyond, like education. The MCC includes a League of Education and Culture that operates thirteen education centers with 6,300 students. Three of the League's centers are university-grade. Of these, the largest is the Polytechnical University, whose specialities include production engineering, computer technology, microelectronics and industrial electronics. A newly established Center for Industrial Design is attached to the Polytechnical University.

The MCC organization does not, however, include the household, or the provision of the home. There may be credit from a building society or the worker's bank for purchase of a dwelling, but that is as far as it goes.

Nor does the MCC include the church, but its effects in a conservative Catholic region of Spain are visible. In the traditional Basque culture, for example, women have occupied a secondary role, and they are by long-established custom frequently confined to household duties. But the co-ops have opened up a whole range of opportunities for women's employment in activity usually reserved for men. That, together with the cultural influence of a modern city, which Mondragon has become, has gone far to alter the particular mores and practices of the region.

Some writers persist in referring to the Mondragon Cooperative Corporation as an "experiment." With annual turnover exceeding $6 billion and a record of independent investment that finances production of hundreds of products with a net expanding market, Mondragon should now be recognized as one viable alternative to state capitalism.

COOPERATIVE ALTERNATIVES: KIBBUTZ INDUSTRY

It is important to understand the diversity and the scope of the activities taking place around the world that operate differently from the model business form of economic organization. In this respect, workers' initiatives in the anarchist communes of Spain during the 1930s,* and in the then state of Palestine (later Israel) from the 1930s and on, provide examples of alternative directions.[5]

I have long paid close attention to the feasibility of operating sophisticated industry in a democratic working environment.[6] I'm sure that living in Kibbutz Ein Hashofet in 1939 and 1940 had a lot to do with that interest. In 1995, I decided it was time for a second look. With introductions from Giora Yanai of Ein Hashofet, I was able to visit in 1995 and 1997 two outstanding industrial enterprises in kibbutz communities: Netafim in Kibbutz Hatzerim and Tama in Kibbutz Mishmar-Ha'emek.

Netafim (Kibbutz Hatzerim)[7]

Kibbutz Hatzerim, near the city of Beersheba in the south of Israel, has as its principal economic activity the Netafim cooperative. The kibbutz includes 420 adults and 250 children. All told, 140 adults constitute the Netafim workforce.

As befits its arid environment, Netafim specializes in low-flow irriga-

*There is Jacov Oved's fine summary paper on anarchist communes at the time of the Spanish Civil War that appeared in *Bulletin No. 29* of the journal *Kibbutz Studies.* The subject is further reviewed in Noam Chomsky's Introduction to *Anarchism*, a book on the anarchist collectives in Spain by Daniel Guérin.

tion. The history of its main product, "the dripper," goes back to about 1963, when Kibbutz Hatzerim found itself in difficult circumstances, unable to get much agricultural productivity in the arid conditions of the area. The members were attracted to an engineer's idea for a device to save water by applying it to the root zone of a plant. Experimental work was undertaken, starting with a small injection-molding machine. By 1996, Netafim and its associated kibbutzim (Magal and Iftach) also owned about thirty foreign locations, including California and Australia. In other countries, the branch units are marketing rather than manufacturing locations. In 1996, net sales were $176 million.

Netafim's drip irrigation system involves bringing water through pipes of varying gauge and permitting the water to drip through spaced emitters in the pipe so that the water is directed maximally to the roots of plants rather than to the surrounding ground surface. A fairly sophisticated set of mechanical and hydraulic technologies are involved in regulating the flow of water, including desired additives, in rather precise quantities to the root area of each plant. This is facilitated by an ingenious array of small plastic pieces that in combination, in the interior of the pipe at each external opening, regulate the flow of liquid in precise fashion. A network of low-flow irrigation pipes is finally controlled from a central pumping and pressure-regulating station that operates to apply appropriate amounts of liquid during the course of each day. This is a much more economical use of water than conventional flood or sprinkler irrigation.

The Netafim product line now also includes devices for small garden or household applications of water in controlled doses, which are marketed in the United States by Hammacher Schlemmer and Brookstone.

There are almost no outside employees at Netafim. The work is performed by members of Kibbutz Hatzerim and by workers at the two other associated kibbutzim. This policy has helped persuade Netafim to invest heavily in automation. While the outer limit is the profitability of the enterprise, they are still prepared to spend $200,000 for a coiler machine that might not be approved on economic grounds in the United States or by private firms in Israel.

All the posts holding special responsibilities in Netafim are filled by elected kibbutz members. The general manager of the enterprise (Yigal Stav when I visited) is nominated by the kibbutz. The corporate management includes the principal officers, people elected by workers and several members of the kibbutz who are not workers. The nominations go before the entire membership for ratification.

Every Netafim manager must be a member, must show ability in running a business, and must demonstrate the talent to operate the enterprise within the framework of the values and requirements of the Hatzerim community. There is no time period or fixed term for this job and no explicit set of conditions that might lead to a manager's replacement.

The task of general manager entails a commitment both to business and the community. He or she must know the language, techniques, categories and issues of business but also has to operate in a kibbutz atmosphere in which hierarchy is not sharply defined. There are, to be sure, people with major responsibilities in each functional area, but the task of each manager is to convince and persuade his colleagues of proposals he wishes to implement. Thus a decision was taken in Netafim, early on, to avoid having a board of directors. Instead, the heads of all the managing functions meet frequently to judge various enterprise moves.

In the kibbutz, there is no limitation on a member's ambition, or desire, to make a job transfer. At the same time, there is an understanding that ambition alone to be a manager does not qualify a person.

In Netafim, there is no wage or salary—indeed, no work-related material compensation. As one of them put it to me, "Satisfaction is really the only compensation." The participants share in the personal allowance budget that is voted for every member of the kibbutz. Netafim members are expected to do their best in their work. The average all-inclusive consumption outlay by the kibbutz for each working member is $150 to $160 per day, which compares favorably with income levels elsewhere in Israel.

In return, every member shares in a quality of life in accordance with the standards of the kibbutz community. The basic rule is: From each according to their ability, to each according to their needs.

A mixed career history is characteristic of the people in the most responsible posts in the Netafim organization. Here is the record of one man who arrived in Israel during the Six-Day War.

1969–71 worked on injection machines

1971–76 manager of production of Netafim

1976–77 general secretary of Kibbutz Hatzerim

1978–79 studied applied electronics

1979–82 manager of whole production department

1982–87 manager of the extrusion department

1987–91 world secretary of the youth movement of Habonim

1991–95 manager of import purchasing—raw materials, machinery, including molds.

Netafim factories and their allied operations operate seven days a week, in three shifts. The regular workforce assigned to Netafim is supplemented by a member (rotated) who performs a particularly lengthy shift in order to make possible the three-shift operation of the firm and its facilities. Every week there is a meeting of the chiefs of each production department.

Repeatedly during my visits to Hatzerim I heard from chiefs of principal departments that they are committed to involving all workers in the enterprise. Thus twice a year, the marketing people report on operations in each country. The workers vote every two years for members of the kibbutz's governing committee.

Over and over again, I heard both veteran and newer members of Netafim state their dedication to working hard for the community, and this is coupled with an internal style that entails very unclear lines of authority. In place of reliance on the sort of hierarchical system so prevalent elsewhere, Netafim members put their emphasis on trust, which one kibbutz member defined for me as "the belief in the honesty, integrity, reliability and justice of other people." Trust, as emphasized at Netafim, must be present in place of hierarchy. Thus consensus is desired for decision-making, but a majority is surely needed. The presence of trust among all engaged is crucial for generating first a majority and finally a consensus agreement. Such concord is characteristically formed by a personal process that must be agreed upon for the purpose of settling disputes.

The consensus policy in Netafim includes the understanding that for making principal decisions, it is necessary to put in the time and energy to explain and convince a majority. People thus possess a strong sense of creating something that is unique and successful.

During the 1990s, Netafim invested heavily in its business. Such a policy, of course, is linked to the baseline commitment to invest and mechanize rather than to hire nonmembers. It is understood that this attitude can expose the company to risk and that, therefore, general policy must include measures sensibly to ensure the continuity of the whole kibbutz.

Netafim production operations demonstrate high productivity in the presence of democracy rather than hierarchy in decision-making. Thus the equipment that shapes the sets of plastic inserts that regulate the flow of liquid inside the dripper pipe is fashioned on a set of forty-one machines, each of which includes a fairly intricate set of tools that are applied to the workpieces as they move on a rotary table from one operation to the next.

Each of these machines is computer-controlled and performs inspection operations on every item that is machined. This means that there is no "statistical" or sampled quality control. One hundred percent control is exercised, so that if a succession of components fails to meet specifications during operations, the machine stops, the location of unsatisfactory operation is marked, and the cutting and positioning tools are adjusted to allow the work to proceed in good order. The forty-one machines are built to special design, and these are monitored by one member of the group. When a defect is uncovered, the whole machine is stopped and a signal light shows above the unit.

Four people (all engineers) are responsible for research-and-development activity, and they call in outside specialists as required. Such arrangements have proved competent enough to produce the following record of quality control, which shows the percentage of products rejected from 1990 to 1995:

1990	5.6%
1991	4.6
1992	4.6
1993	4.1
1994	3.3
1995	3.2

For the same assembly of automated machines, the following is the record of machine-time functioning, again from 1990 to 1995:

1990	65%
1991	71
1992	78
1993	75
1994	80
1995	85

(These data include scheduled downtime due to limited orders.)

Put together, these figures make an impressive record of the productivity of capital (i.e., the value of the machines) that makes Netafim a highly competent enterprise, with a strong impact on its community.

At first, Hatzerim was a poor kibbutz, and its members lived without capital, grants or new loans. After 1968–1969, the increase in net capital was self-generating, with the first profit reserved for buying out the 50 percent partner whose technology innovation kicked off the elaboration of drip irrigation technique. Along the way, Hatzerim saw that its own resources in manpower or money were not sufficient to serve the growing market both in Israel and abroad. Hatzerim offered to share the production operations with two partners, the kibbutzim Magal and Yiftach. There was no sale of assets or fee, even as Netafim provided the necessary assets so that the two new partners could enter into production and participate. There was no written agreement. It was all put together without lawyers and legal contracts and was orchestrated by Netafim's chief financial officer. None of this, of course, is to be expected where the parties to an economic agreement each operate in accordance with the conventional roles of accumulation without limit, predatory competition and hierarchy. In this case, the parties were experienced in mutual trust, workplace democracy and solidarity.

During the 1990s, Netafim flourished famously. With coordinating headquarters at Hatzerim, production in Israel is joined with Kibbutz Magal in central Israel and Kibbutz Yiftach in the north. Netafim has a growing network of subsidiaries and representatives in thirty countries, with a manufacturing facility in California. By 1999, sales turnover was $220 million. With a strong base in continuing research and development and production investment, Netafim is a world leader in irrigation technology.*

Tama (Kibbutz Mishmar-Ha'emek)[8]

Tama is a cooperative within Kibbutz Mishmar-Ha'emek. The kibbutz and its factory are located southeast of the city of Haifa on the southern side of the valley of Jezreel. Tama specializes in plastic products, mainly for agriculture, but also for household use and for the poultry industry.

By 1997, there were 180 workers in the Tama enterprise, and sales amounted to $32 million.

Tama started in 1950 as a small shop with a few veterans in agriculture for whom new, less strenuous jobs had to be found. Mishmar-Ha'emek, a kibbutz of 500 adults and 300 children, was long distinguished for its agricultural output and flourishing forestation programs. It also played an important role as the location of a principal high school operated by the Kibbutz Artzi movement. By 1968, Tama had expanded, but it was also looking for partnerships because of the limitations of its labor force.

By 1970, Tama had reached an agreement for a 25 percent partnership with Kibbutz Gal Ed. From this period to the present, the cooperative's output and sales have flourished.

Tama also has two subsidiaries: One is a daughter company set up in

*See Netafim on the Internet at: www.netafim.com.

1991 near Los Angeles to handle a growing export market. Its staff of three or four, including one member of Kibbutz Mishmar-Ha'emek, had by 1995 supervised $3.5 to $4 million of marketing, with prospects for major expansion.

A second daughter company was set up in the United Kingdom with nine or ten workers to cope with production and marketing in Britain. Expectation is that the British branch, employing staff originating there but trained in Israel, will grow internationally and thereby relieve the organization and kibbutz from the pressure of its labor shortage. The staff at Tama has been prepared to recommend a large investment for the U.K. operation to fulfill a strategic expansion plan without having to hire considerable numbers of wage workers at Mishmar-Ha'emek itself.

Like other kibbutzim, Mishmar-Ha'emek has been prepared to spend heavily on automation and on the technical sophistication of its workforce in order to enlarge greatly its productivity and to offset pressures for hiring people from outside the kibbutz.

Considerable importance is given to sophistication in computer technology. Accordingly, twenty-five people have been put through training programs in relevant computer skills. Members are also sent regularly to educational seminars. For this purpose, there is "no limitation of labor time or budget." This commitment to education has made working at Tama increasingly popular among the people of the kibbutz. In my conversations with those at Tama, an insistent theme was the importance of emphasizing responsibility by each worker. They are persuaded that by learning more, they will all achieve more.

Strategic decisions at the cooperative are a principal responsibility of department heads. Each of these is named by a work group, except where a new person is brought in from outside, in which case the whole kibbutz must vote. In every department, there is a weekly meeting to review problems and prospects, and about once a month the marketing manager reports on conditions in the marketplace. Tama now has a marketing manager responsible for the main products for export—that was not the case in the early 1980s. The whole kibbutz votes on the designation of a general manager.

The chief operating responsibilities for Tama have been vested in the general manager, Nir Shapira, a twenty-year veteran of this enterprise in diverse jobs. He is assisted by three division managers, who manage the plants for the three main product classes: agriculture, household and poultry. Nir Shapira thought it was important for the quality of the enterprise that three former general managers of Tama continue to work there.

In Tama, as in other kibbutz-industry units, the members holding key responsibilities have passed through remarkably diverse careers. The present general manager has been in his present post for seven years. During the two decades he has worked at Mishmar-Ha'emek, he also served as production manager for five years, worked in one of the divisions and headed the economics department. Before that, he completed a degree in management at the Ruppin Institute.

Tama's chief agricultural product is a plastic "thread." This "thread" is prepared through chemical processing that delivers a "flat" extrusion. The extrusion immediately passes through a series of knives that deliver the "threads," which are processed like the thread in a textile facility. The co-op's principal product is netting material, which takes the form of an open-mesh net and is very useful as baling material, and also for wrapping palleted loads of various sizes.

One of the consumers of the netting material is the John Deere Company (the largest agricultural-machinery-producing firm in the world), which uses rolls of the net on its hay balers. Tama's netting serves to compact hay when the hay is immediately cut in a form easily transported and stored. Traditional twine is a competing raw material for baling, but plastic netting has been expanding rapidly in this line of use.

Finer netting can also be used to make a shade net for flower and vegetable growing—to protect from direct sunlight and to permit close timing control of ripening. The netting can be applied and has contributed to substantial productivity increases in farming. These product lines are in a continual process of improvement, like the inclusion of a strip in the roll of netting to tell the farmer or machine operator when to change it.

At present, the people at Tama judge that they are the leading suppliers of such products in the United States, but not in Europe. Considerable attention is given to the factors that affect market share, notably in the United States, where retention of market share is judged to be a major economic advantage and risk-reducing factor.

Marketing considerations have grown in importance during the last years, as the industries producing these products, both in Mishmar-Ha'emek and in its partner kibbutz (Gal Ed), are a primary source of livelihood for the populations of both kibbutzim. The managers of Tama pay close attention to the world market in the machines that do the plastics work, particularly the netting. These machines are produced mainly in Germany, Italy and Spain.

Some of lesser products are also based on the plastic "thread" material—twine of varying strength and dimensions, as well as heavy-load-bearing ropes up to the thickness of a hawser.

Tama's products for household use are made mainly by compression and injection molding. These include a variety of items like utensils and storage containers. The compression and injection-mold operations run primarily by automatically operating machines. To service them, Tama maintains a machine shop to prepare and maintain the quality of the necessary molds.

All the production operations are quality-controlled, with a growing demand especially for the netting products requiring three shifts to meet market demand.

During the early 1970s, there was a strong desire at Tama to be self-sufficient. This was heightened by the labor shortage that frustrated development plans. Accordingly, the consensus judgment in the kibbutz was a readiness to pay a lot to prove that labor could be saved by some investment. The commonsense understanding was that money was just a matter of "cost," and that the kibbutz could get any loan it wanted and did not have to show real collateral. It operated without an agreed profit per worker as a basis for justified investment.

One of a group of four workers dealing with research, equipment development and maintenance—the "practical and mechanical engineer"—said he found at Tama an opportunity that he judged to be "a paradise," because modifications on equipment to raise productivity had always been welcomed. In fact, new machines were often altered to generate twice the rated productivity.

The co-op's concentration on netting and extruding operations has seen that particular work become more sophisticated, easier and cheaper. Computerization is being applied virtually everywhere, on all machines. By 1997, the netting and extruding operations were fully computerized. This automation was made possible by progressively cheaper computer hardware, unlike the old-fashioned, expensive "controllers."

As part of the quality-control program of the factory, each machine has a record of its activity.

In the Tama factory, the "R" plastic extruder is a principal production machine of the enterprise. Its operation therefore reflects both on the firm's capital productivity and on its labor productivity. The 1989–1995 production record shows a substantial gain in both the scale and regularity of operations. Combined downtime for repair and maintenance attained a 1.1 percent level, while production climbed toward the maximum of 8,760 hours/year:

Production Downtime at Tama

Year	Production Downtime Hours	Production Hours	% Downtime
1989	613	7768	7.9
1990	471	6979	6.7
1991	224	8165	2.7
1992	643	6363	10.1
1993	384	7778	4.9
1994	395	8221	4.8
1995	91	8438	1.1

This is a record of rising productivity of capital, which translates into rising productivity of labor as well.

A technician in the netting department, an important post, reported that she has worked there for eleven years. During that time, she completed a course in Germany at the firm that manufactures the netting machines. She reported that as in other operations in the kibbutz when workers want a transfer, their dissatisfaction is taken seriously, as that will probably generate lower performance if not corrected. She noted that in Mishmar-Ha'emek, only women work with the children and that usually they can ask for whatever transfer they might desire. Since Tama is on shift work and people mainly do five days on a preferred shift, there is at least one person on a shift who is not "preferred."

She emphasized that the community appreciates good work and the initiatives that are for the benefit of the community. After all, in order to be happy in the kibbutz, you are best off being productive. That makes a person part of the kibbutz, and being part of the kibbutz includes responsibility for abiding by the system of rules in the community.

Another major factor in the supply and quality of work performance in Tama is the activity of the younger people who, having completed military service, are eligible for and enter various universities and other institutes of higher learning.

The arrangement at this kibbutz (which is fairly general across the country) is that the university students must work at least 120 days per annum to fulfill their obligations there in return for support the rest of the year. Of the forty younger people from Mishmar-Ha'emek attending institutions of higher learning by 1997, around thirty have been working in the Tama factory.

Work in the factory has come to be preferred by younger people.

They know it is important for their livelihood. The factory also affords an opportunity to work with friends in close promixity, certainly more so than in various of the agricultural tasks, which entail solo operation of field machines and the like.

One woman who had been responsible for the knitting operations switched to being a student in economics at the Ruppin Institute. She reported that there was a degree of competition for young people who work first in agriculture because of the law that prohibits children under fifteen from the factory. Thereafter, younger people are attracted by the presence of a population of friends in the factory. She noted, however, that since the kibbutz (like others) has changed its internal living arrangements from a community basis to more family-based activities, young people emerging from this regimen are somewhat less group-oriented and may have a lesser understanding of the meaning of kibbutz. Under the old regimen of growing up in the "children's house," the inculcated values were primarily to accomplish things that pleased the community and then give heed to one's own happiness. These changes in kibbutz culture may mean a lesser readiness to accommodate personal activities to the needs of the community.

Altogether, the Tama enterprise has managed to fulfill its main labor requirement from the internal kibbutz population. An accommodation was made, however, in terms of four long-term outside employees (one accountant, one electrical engineer and two machinists). A kibbutz general meeting that I attended also agreed to the recommendation on the hiring of six younger people for night-shift work for nine months. The kibbutz membership voted no to a proposal to set up a factory "across the road" and hire a labor force for that operation, but it did go along with local hiring for a factory being established in the United Kingdom that is wholly owned and controlled by Tama. The voting members of the kibbutz judged that if that were undertaken near Mishmar-Ha'emek, then various of the younger people might also construe it as an invitation to opt for various jobs (perhaps better-paying) in the newly established factory.

There are assorted problems for Tama managers, which are dealt with regularly. For example, possible outsourcing of sections of Tama's products has not been undertaken, though some thought has been given to it. While there are patent problems connected with some existing or prospective products, the consensus at Tama is to try to solve these matters outside the courts. Nevertheless, the decision about whether or not to patent is an ongoing problem.

By 1997, Tama had invested $100,000 in computer controls of various sorts. In parallel, however, Tama's people have been building their own software, which is viewed as a challenging job where success yields considerable satisfaction to the people in the enterprise. Changing over to the next generation of computers will require an investment of about $250,000 and the attention of Tama's own people.

All told, it is the judgment of Tama's members that their common social goals and values have stood them in very good stead. At the same time, the work group and the responsible officers have to remain open to things never done before. They are satisfied that solidarity has been strongly sustained among the working group, and that is regarded as a matter of central importance and value by the veterans of the enterprise.

The cooperatives at Netafim and Tama are far from isolated examples of democracy by design.

A Kibbutz Industries Association, headquartered in Tel Aviv, accounts for 424 enterprises in 275 kibbutzim. They had 1996 sales of $4.2 billion and a labor force of 30,100. The following shows the number of enterprises in each product group.

Product Group	**Number of Enterprises**
Plastics and rubber	87
Metal and machinery	76
Regional enterprises	47*
Food	33
Textile and leather	29
Electricity and electronics	28
Chemicals and pharmaceuticals	26
Quarries and building materials	21
Arts and crafts	19
Wood and furnitures	19
Printing and paper	18
Service	12
Optics and glass	9

This table suggests something of the scale and variety of the cooperative enterprises included in the kibbutzim. But like the network at Mondragon, they receive little public attention. During my visit in 1997, I asked the general manager and his colleagues in Netafim whether they had been visited by any members of the press or electronic media, and they replied, "None."

*Composed of ten clusters, representing related enterprises—each run by members of several kibbutzim that include a total of forty-seven different enterprises.

. . .

In this description of two kibbutz factories, I have emphasized their mutual decision-making qualities and the ability of democratically organized work groups to operate high-tech industrial production.

During the first half of the twentieth century, kibbutz cooperative communities were an important part of the public life of their society, then a part of British-mandated Palestine. The formation of the state of Israel in the late 1940s coincided with the growth of mainly business organizations in an economy with a sustained militarized, state-capitalist quality. Internally, the new state's managers were at loggerheads with the kibbutz network, viewing them as holdovers from a bygone era. Through all this, kibbutz communities retained much of their initial value system.

THE EMILIA-ROMAGNA COOPERATIVE NETWORKS

Any survey of the range of feasible alternatives to corporate organizations should also take note of the famous business networking among small and medium-sized firms and cooperatives that have been set up in the central Italian region of Emilia-Romagna.

By 1998, there was a population of 3,960,000 in the region, of whom 1,700,000 were in the labor force. Of these, industry had 619,000 workers. Private and public services used 969,000, and agriculture only 116,000, resulting in one of Italy's highest rates of employment.

Emilia-Romagna consists typically of small enterprises. Manufacturing, with 52,470 firms, and 510,586 employed all told, in 1996, has an average of 9.7 people per local unit. Firms in machinery production engage 100,028 people and operate 6,193 local units, hence with about 16 people per unit.[9]

About 58 percent of the manufacturing workers are engaged in enterprises with no more than forty-nine people. Those with fewer than nineteen employees qualify as "artisan" firms, with the employer required to work in his own business under Italian law. Emilia-Romagna includes industrial networks that have focused on machinery (agricultural and mechanical engineering), textiles, food production, furniture, ceramics and shoes. The financing of firms is provided by a mix of commercial banks, artisan banks, regional government and self-financing.[10]

Clearly, these cooperative networks, which have achieved a world reputation through their excellent export performances, give solid demonstration of the effectiveness of division of labor among specialized units. They combine this specialization with cooperative use of the special technical and administrative skills of the network as a whole. For example, accounting, inventory, tax, payroll, cost-estimating, marketing studies and the like are performed in a centralized fashion and made readily available to these firms, so that each one does not have to shoulder the full cost of these services, but is able to buy them from a facility that is linked to the whole network.

The wages paid in these enterprises are on a union scale and are sufficient for participants on the working level to save and to become, in turn, organizers and participants of new firms of this sort. These are best understood as worker-owned enterprises, but they are small.

Are they businesses or are they cooperatives? Evidently, both. They are cooperative business firms. Their ability to function over a long time is noteworthy.

Codetermination: Worker Decision-Making Enabled by Law in Germany

Codetermination is the name of a system of legally empowered rights and organization of workers under German law. The following excerpts from the Introduction to *Co-determination in the Federal Republic of Germany* outline the development.

> Under German law employees have co-determination and participation rights both on the shop floor level (work constitution) and in the decision-making bodies of the company (co-determination at the board level). There are special, weaker co-determination arrangements for the public service.
>
> . . . industrialization at the beginning of the last century decisively altered the economic and social structure of the country. The workers had to work under inconceivably bad conditions. The growing awareness of their situation made the workers fight against material want, and, moreover, they began to unite in solidarity in the framework of trade unions and demanded to have a say in shaping their working life. . . .
>
> During the First World War the "Act on Civilian War-Work Service" was passed. The setting up of workers' and salaried employees' committees was prescribed by law for establishments which were vital for the war effort and for supply and which employed over 50 persons. Yet there was no co-determination in the sense of participation in the decision-making process.

After World War I, the economic life of Germany was one of depression without end. That endured until the Nazi regime restored employment, within a permanent war economy. The Nazis paid part of their debt to industrialists and financiers for financing Hitler's party and consolidated their own rule by outlawing trade unions and revoking the laws and codetermination regulations. These were restored and modified only after Hitler's defeat in 1945.

> After co-determination at the board level had been practiced since 1947 without statutory basis in the iron and steel industry of the British Zone of Occupation, a decisive step was taken in 1951. At the insistence of the workers and their trade unions and after violent disputes and quarrels in and outside parliament the "Act on the Co-determination of Employees in the Supervisory and Management Boards of Companies in the Coal, Iron and Steel Industry" was passed.[11]

From Lawrence B. Cohen, in 1951, we learn that

> German labor's drive for Mitbestimmungsrecht started shortly after the collapse of the Hitler regime, with the reconstruction of the works-councils and the unions. From the information at hand, Mitbestimmungsrecht certainly represents a fundamental departure from pre-1933 union goals. The principal difference lies in the shift away from government to industry as the target of trade union control.[12]

Cohen underscored the role of a political consideration guiding the drive for codetermination by the German Trade Union Federation (DGB). In their view,

> "A truly democratic economic order prior to 1933 would, without doubt, have made impossible the allocation of money by decisive segments of the German economy to Hitler and his seizure of power." This repeated theme of the complete political unreliability of the German businessman is a crucial consideration in the union's drive to curtail their economic and productional control.[13]

From the official Introduction to *Co-determination*, we learn further that:

> The co-determination at the level of the establishment was considerably expanded by the new Works Constitution Act 1972 . . . apart from its provisions on the one-third representation in the

> supervisory boards. The 1974 Federal Staff Representation Act and several Acts passed by Land Governments constitute a considerable step forward in the co-determination at the level of the establishment in the public sector.

The German trade unions and pro-union political parties sought ways to expand the scope and power of codetermination law. Major advances were made in specifying worker representation on the supervisory boards of German firms. These boards appoint and review the work of the senior managers, who, as members of the full-time administrative staff, are responsible for the main functional elements of management's decision-making.

> Since the Co-determination Act of 1976 was passed, employees and shareholders have equal numbers of representatives in the supervisory boards of stock companies which employ over 2,000 persons; the one-third representation in the supervisory boards according to the 1972 Works Constitution Act continues to apply in smaller companies. The Co-determination Act included for the first time executives in the collective representation of employees' interests and reserved one of the employees' seats in the supervisory board for them. The Executives Committee Act of 1988 created the legal basis for the representation of their interests, too, at the level of the establishment.[14]

German law on codetermination (*Mitbestimmung*) has focused mainly on systems of worker representation on the supervisory boards of companies. The size and workers' proportion of board members has varied according to the industry and the size of the firm. In the most developed form, workers (plus union representatives) and administrative employees are equal in number to the supervisory board members representing management. A neutral member may occupy the chair and vote to resolve a tie.

Works councils and works committees are two more legally established parts of the codetermination structure. Detailed regulations govern their size, election procedures and voting rights of employees (including details concerning young and trainee workers).

The codetermination procedures thus exist alongside the trade unions that negotiate terms of employment with employers.

The data and commentaries on the functioning of codetermined institutions are not available in the categories of worker decision-making set forth in the relevant chapters of this book. But the legal empowerments that are the main elements of the codetermination laws and procedures surely bear on the rules of production decision-making that may originate with workers and their unions.

A full exploration of the specifics of worker decision-making under German conditions was not available to me. Neither was it feasible to undertake production-level examinations of worker decision-making in German industry with an eye to comparing that with worker decision-making in U.S. plants. A proper effort along such lines will have to await another person's initiative.

But in 1998, a German codetermination commission reported on extensive studies to which fifty experts contributed. These included "entrepreneurs and managers, trade unionists and works councillors."*

The following are excerpts from the (Summary) *Report of the Co-determination Commission*, chaired by Professor Karl-Heinz Briam, with "accompanying social-scientific work under the leadership of Professor Wolfgang Streeck, Director of the Max Planck Institute for the Study of Societies, in Cologne."

> Modern leadership in a co-determined company does not rely on orders from the top, but rather on creativity from the bottom, by incorporating employees at all levels into the firm's processes and opening up opportunities for autonomous action. . . . (1)
>
> The history of co-determination since the Federal Republic of Germany was founded is the history of its growing plant-level orientation. . . . Co-determination at plant and company level, where they have existed alongside one another, have become increasingly closely intertwined. In practice, co-determination at company level has become the "extended arm" of plant-level co-determination, whereby as a rule the leading members of the Works Council also represent the workforce on the Supervisory Board. . . . (4–5)
>
> **Statistics of the Co-determination Process**
>
> In 1996, 728 companies were co-determined on the basis of the 1976 law. . . .
>
> According to figures provided by the German trade union federation (DGB), in 1994 works councils were elected in 40,000 enterprises with a total of around 220,000 members. . . . Accord-

*Interested readers will surely wish to consult the authoritative compilation *Labour Law in Germany*, prepared by the Federal Ministry of Labour and Social Affairs.

ing to figures provided by the Institut der [D]eutschen Wirtschaft, in 1994 around 78 percent of those eligible voted in works council elections. . . . (9–10)

Co-determination and the Productivity of German Industry

The German economy has achieved an extraordinarily high level of affluence and competitiveness in international comparative terms. . . . [F]or decades the German economy has almost continuously earned export surpluses, even though in international comparative terms it has a high and relatively narrowly dispersed wage structure. One of the most important reasons for this has been the high average level of productivity which, in turn, is due to persistently high investment and the large capital stock this has generated. Also characteristic of the German economy is the high level of education of its population and high levels of investment in industrial and public research and development. . . . (12)

The following paragraph in the codetermination commission's report opens up a vital issue for American workers: how to include union representatives from Ford-Brazil, Ford-Mexico, Ford-England and so forth on the union negotiating committee with Ford management. The codetermination commission noted that

in co-determined German companies that employ a significant proportion of their total workforce in other European countries, over the medium-term the question will increasingly arise as to *the legitimacy of filling the employee block on the supervisory board exclusively with German representatives.* A simple solution to this problem is not apparent at the present time. What could be examined, however, is whether, in the context of possible changes in the electoral procedures for the internal employee representatives, the possibility of electing representatives of workforces located abroad should be opened up. (34)[15]

The globalization processes that are pursued by American corporate/state managers will certainly produce a great number of such issues. Every U.S. industry that is so engaged will be a location for this problem.

Lawrence Cohen assessed the meaning of the codetermination development, as follows:

The specific trade union economic and industrial problems to which the Mitbestimmung program is addressed have a ring of

> generality. Wage-price problems, full and continuous employment, raising workers' shares, and other economic goals are solved only partially by collective bargaining on a firm or industry basis. Occupational problems arising from unilateral employer decision-making constitute a more subtle, though more widespread source of industrial issues. These problems of the workplace are common features of 20th century industrial society, irrespective of the social or organizational housing in which they exist. . . .
>
> Mitbestimmung has erroneously been called socialism, and cold socialism. Its differences from traditional socialism turn primarily upon its direct interest in industry, rather than in the state, as the basic instrument for improving workers' conditions.[16]

Labor-Sponsored Investment Funds

The pattern of deindustrialization by plant closings and relocation outside the United States has become so extensive that unionized workers are now extremely sensitive to early warning signs of a shutdown. A particularly competent and promising way in which unions have responded to closings is by organizing labor-sponsored investment funds. These funds are made available for long-term industrial investment, on condition that they are aimed at projects that are of importance not only to the members of the trade unions but to the whole community.

Thus an economic conversion project concerned with shipbuilding and repair in the Puget Sound area of Washington was begun in 1984 with funding from the International Association of Machinists and Aerospace Workers (Local 282, District Lodge 160). The naval shipyard located there was slated for closing, so the union organized a fund to support an alternative-use committee called Realistic Employment Alternatives for Labor. This was a substantial effort by the machinists' union to look for possible ways of organizing work in shipbuilding and repair.

There have been other labor-community initiatives organized by the IAM in the Northwest, including persuading the state government of Washington to invest in railroads. That involved improving the infrastructure of the line between Vancouver and Seattle, and the projected use of a new high-speed train making the area more attractive for tourism, with accompanying enlarged employment on the railroad and in the surrounding activities.

A CANADIAN MODEL FOR U.S. UNION INVESTMENT

When American unions wish to undertake serious moves to counter the deindustrialization practiced by management, they will find it important to examine the substantial progress made by Canadian unions in this realm. Sherman Kreiner and Keith Delaney, executives of two labor-sponsored investment funds in Canada, report that

> Labour sponsored venture capital corporations are a decade old Canadian phenomenon which now account for more than one-third of all institutional venture capital in that country. What is especially impressive is that the vast majority of the funds' more than $3.1 billion in assets come from small investments made by average working people.
>
> The specific trigger for the creation of the initial funds was the 1981–83 recession and persistent levels of high Canadian unemployment. The labour sponsored venture capital corporation model was initiated by the Québec Fédération of Labour (FTQ) in the Province of Québec in 1984 to meet identified equity capital gaps for small and medium sized businesses in a manner which would address additional social policy concerns.[17]

Since 1984, "three additional funds have been created which follow the Québec model, the Working Opportunity Fund in [British Columbia], the Crocus Fund in Manitoba and the First Ontario Fund in Ontario."

The largest by far of the Canadian labor-sponsored venture-capital corporations is the Solidarity Fund of Québec, headquartered in Montreal. It reports that

> investments by the Fund in small to medium-sized businesses [SMB] in Québec during the fiscal year ended June 30 reached close to $600 million, an increase of 29%. The Fund's SMB investments now total over . . . $2.235 billion.

From its inception in 1983 until 1999,

> the Solidarity Fund (QFL) has helped to create, preserve or maintain an accumulated total of 78,525 jobs in Québec. Of these, 42,338 jobs were created directly, and 20,060 indirectly. Further spinoffs account for another 15,915 jobs, while 212 jobs have come from investments outside Québec.
>
> . . . These figures, and the financial performance they rep-

> resent, show how the Solidarity Fund (QFL) has become an indispensable financial institution in the economic growth of Québec. According to the Fund's president and CEO, Raymond Bachand . . . "The value of our job-creating investment portfolio, which is now $2.235 billion, speaks for itself."[18]

Raymond Bachand, president of the Québec Solidarity Fund, reports:

> The fund's yearly earnings have averaged close to 7% since its creation, with 8.1% in the year ended June 30—which, with the tax credits allowed our shareholders, makes our earnings, even in the long term, very competitive. As for our size, I'll say simply this: we're still small, compared to the big pools of capital that exist in Québec and the rest of North America. But at the same time, we are one of the largest venture capital institutions in Canada.

He offers the following defining details on the Solidarity Fund's activity:

> Our presence in the New Economy is impressive, and will be felt more and more. In the biotechnology and information technology sectors alone, the Fund presently has investments of some $170 million, at market value, in over 150 companies and firms, mainly in Montreal.
>
> Last spring, we went through a large-scale exercise of rethinking our strategy, and we made a major change in policy: a decision to specialize our investment sector and put the emphasis on financing of exports and high-technology.

Addressing a business group in 1998, Bachand stated that

> from now on at the Québec Solidarity Fund, you'll find groups of consultants dedicated to specific economic sectors: biotechnology, tourism and recreation, mining, agrifood, information technology and so on.
>
> Secondly, when you come to us you'll find a networked approach, a ground-level interchange between our twenty specialized funds and our regional and local funds, as well as our internal specialist teams.
>
> Thirdly, you as people in business told us you would need capital plus expert advice to deal with markets and competition outside Canada. So we've created and earmarked sizable resources for a group that specializes in export financing.

> . . . To put it simply, we feel that the era of the one-man or one-woman band, the general-practitioner "expert" who does plastics one day, kids' toys the next, genetics, furniture or hotels the day after, is pretty well over. The Québec Solidarity Fund will specialize and be sophisticated enough to follow the market as it evolves. In any event, we won't be abandoning the traditional sectors, and we'll still be helping businesses where we've developed special expertise to re-establish themselves. We'll still be a presence and will even increase our investment in any sector that is good for the economy.[19]

The fund has been notably active in both new industries and textile and transportation equipment.

Meanwhile, in the United States, the proceedings of the Industrial Heartland Labor Investment Forum reports that

> The dilemma facing workers is that their own pension funds, as owners of almost one-third of all U.S. financial capital, are . . . financing overseas plants. They agree to outrageous pay packages for corporate managements that have shown only mediocre performance. They reward the slash and burn practices of companies that serve up quarterly returns to shareholders. They finance mergers and acquisitions in the name of retirement security. They ignore investments in job-creating ventures, instead preferring to finance leveraged buyouts that mean further layoffs. Overall, workers' pension funds are part of a system that is more trading-oriented than investment-oriented.[20]

In Canada two noteworthy investment funds with major union participation have pioneered this development, attracting sums from diverse sources.* As Len Krimerman reports, though few of the Québec Soli-

*Unlike U.S. pension funds that are directed by law to strive for maximum profit, the Canadian Labor Sponsored Investment Funds operate by other criteria. The 1983 Act to Establish the Funds de Solidarité des Travailleurs du Québec (FTC) defines that "main functions of the Fund are

> 1°to invest in qualified undertakings and provide them with services in order to create, maintain and protect jobs;
> 2°to promote the training of workers in economic matters and enable them to increase their influence on Québec's economic development;
> 3°to stimulate the Québec economy by making strategic investments that will be of benefit to Québec workers and undertakings;
> 4°to promote the development of qualified undertakings by inviting workers to participate in that development by subscribing shares of the Fund."

darity Fund enterprises are co-ops, all firms assisted by the fund must have worker representatives on their boards, open accounting and other forms of workplace democracy.[21]

This Québec initiative was followed by the establishment of the Crocus Fund in Manitoba, which had created 1,200 jobs by 1994 and by the end of 1997 had investments in twenty-six companies in which workers owned from 5 to 20 percent of stock.[22] The availability of new investment funds was combined with the activity of the provincial government, which provided a tax credit in addition to an IRA-style tax deduction to encourage local investment. As a further incentive, the Canadian federal government also added a tax credit.

These initiatives have been followed by newer funds in Manitoba, British Columbia and Ontario. Canada's labor-sponsored funds can now draw on more than $2 billion in capital drawn from the pension plans of 400,000 workers. Investors receive 15 percent tax credits from national and provincial governments.[23] All of the funds focus on investment in the local economy, where "local" refers to regions the size of up to three American states. These venture-capital funds are designed to attract long-term investment. They are not geared toward a quick return, such as a daily change in securities quotations in a stock exchange. On the contrary, the history of these Canadian funds has been reassuring with respect to their feasibility and to the positive response of the local population.

In the United States, other initiatives have pursued similar lines. The AFL-CIO has been operating an Investment Trust out of Washington, D.C. It was formed initially as a Housing Investment Trust to promote building-trades employment by making mortgage money available, largely for home-building. The success of this enterprise is indicated by its assets, which, by 1996, totaled more than $1.5 billion. The capital funds for this trust originated from pension funds of the various construction unions.

The possible use of pension funds for union-sponsored industrial investment has the potential for tapping one of the largest blocks of finance capital in the American economy. By 1994, the value of equities held by private, state and local pension funds exceeded $1.5 trillion.[24] Of course such an alternative approach to investment and job creation faces serious challenges. In addition to the legal hurdles to the use of such funds for investment, there is the problem of assuring the accountability, as well

---

Under the U.S. Employee Retirement Income Security Act (ERISA), pension fund trustees, exercising their fiduciary responsibilities, must act "with the skill, care, prudence and diligence that a prudent person acting in like capacity and familiar with such matters" would. This has usually been interpreted as meaning acting, effectively if not explicitly, for short-term profit-maximizing. See the discussion on these issues in AFL-CIO, *Investment of Union Pension Funds* (August 1980), pp. iii–vii.

as democratic control, of enterprises whose functioning must include giving the highest priority to sustained employment.[25]

Community- and Cooperative-Based Development

A COOPERATIVE EXCHANGE SYSTEM: COMMUNITY ECONOMIC INITIATIVES

On a much smaller scale, one of the most imaginative devices for spurring cooperative economic activity in the community has been the formation of a local currency. In this case, which is an alternative to the conventional distribution of products rather than to production itself, everyone participating in the scheme accepts a local scale of exchange values. The local currency can mean that a certificate representing a number of hours is issued in return for work performed. The certificate is then tradable within the community—that is, within the circle of people who are committed to cooperate—for purchasing hours' worth of goods and services.

Len Krimerman at the University of Connecticut, of the *Grass Roots Economic Organizing Newsletter*, reported in November/December 1995 that about eighty "local currencies" have sprung up in North America.[26] One of the most interesting and best developed of these, according to Krimerman, is Ithaca Hours. About 3,000 individual members accept the Ithaca Hours "currency." By mid-2000, 330 enterprises accepted the "currency" in payment, including a bowling alley, a video rental store and several restaurants. Ithaca Hours has a health insurance program whose practitioners accept the scrip for at least partial payment. In *Local Currency Without Borders*, Krimerman reports that trading in the scrip has been done among currency organizations.

The value system that is built into the Hours exchange is based on the dollar value of an average hourly wage in the area. Also, your hour (as a member) is assumed to have equal worth with another's hour, though in Ithaca Hours specialists might get twice the average hourly rate.

Variants of the local currency system have been developed in several European countries, extending to development of an International Clearing House for hours-scrip in France.[27]

Clearly, the assumption underlying these schemes is that it is possible to find a circle of mutually interdependent people who are prepared to reward each other for work done and to accept payment for such work in terms of "hour" certificates. An interesting issue is involved here: If price is not to be stated in ordinary currency units, then how is it to be stated? If the unit of this new transaction system is an "hour certificate," are hours to be given equal exchange value? After all, the differential money value assigned to hours of work is in every case arbitrary. Thus it is entirely likely in such schemes for alternative currencies that both prices and the value accorded per hour of work will vary, depending on the consensus on social values of those involved.

POWER OF EMINENT DOMAIN

Staughton Lynd, a historian and an attorney among industrial unions, has pioneered the analysis of the "power of eminent domain" and its use to keep companies from moving factories. This law has traditionally been applied in cases where government needs to make a compulsory purchase of privately owned land. Lynd's original approach permits this "ancient Anglo-American legal concept" to be applied in the interest of workers and their communities.

Thus, if a government wishes to build a highway through a stretch of land and the owner refuses to sell the property, it may obtain a court ruling that orders the owner to sell the land at a fair market value. But eminent domain has also been argued as applicable to industrial facilities in efforts to retain them in place when managements planned to close or move them.[28] As Lynd observes:

> The power of eminent domain gives local communities a means to acquire abandoned industrial facilities and operate them in the public interest. . . . Just as the management-rights clause in a collective bargaining agreement is management's residual power to take action in the interest of the enterprise, so eminent domain is part of a community's residual power to do whatever is necessary to preserve itself. When this power takes the form of restrictions and prohibitions for which no compensation is required, it is considered the "police power." But when the necessary action is the acquisition of private property for a public purpose, it is done in the name of eminent domain.

Lynd notes that in colonial America, the power of eminent domain was often used to take private property for public roads. But that "this eighteenth-century procedure is perfectly applicable to the public acquisition of a modern factory that shuts down." Thus a legal intervention might be made in the interests of its workers:

> Upon preliminary showing of need a feasibility study is made. If the feasibility assessment is favorable, the input of workers is

> solicited as to exactly which products, machinery, and buildings should be appropriated. Compensation is provided, as is a process for appealing the amount fixed. Finally, the local community not only takes but operates the plant under the direction of experienced supervisors.
>
> The city of Detroit used its eminent domain power to acquire a 465-acre neighborhood known as "Peleton," destroying in the process over 1,000 homes and apartment buildings and displacing 3,500 people. The land was then reconveyed to the General Motors Corporation at a fraction of its cost to the city to be used as the site for a new Cadillac assembly plant. The Supreme Court of Michigan held that this was a proper taking for a public purpose under the eminent domain power.[29]

Of course, the eagerness with which Detroit carried the action forward is not a sufficient indicator of what may be expected when a community seeks to apply the eminent-domain right to industrial plants owned by a corporation. If the firm is an unwilling seller, then the determination of "fair market value" is not at all straightforward. When a plant is closed (or about to be closed), does it arguably have only "scrap" value? Or is "fairness" to be based on the revenue (or profit) the facility might yield if reopened? There are other alternatives for a valuation exercise. From the vantage point of a community, the main interest in keeping a production facility going may well be to assure continued employment and income for the workers, rather than achieving a "market rate of profit."

Repeatedly, what has been at issue in efforts to apply the law of eminent domain is the nature of property rights. In 1980, the steelworkers of Youngstown, Ohio, cited the Constitution on the purpose of government—"to provide for the common defense and promote the general welfare"—as a sufficient basis for recognizing a community property right in the steel mills that U.S. Steel preferred to close. While their legal battle was ultimately unsuccessful, in a hearing to rule on a requested injunction restraining the corporation, Judge Thomas D. Hambros held that

> We are not talking now about a local bakery shop, grocery store, tool and die shop or a body shop in Youngstown that is planning to close down and move out. . . .
>
> It's not just a steel company making steel. . . . Steel has become an institution in the Mahoning Valley. . . .
>
> Everything that has happened in the Mahoning Valley has been happening for many years because of steel. Schools have

> been built, roads have been built. Expansion that has taken place is because of steel. And to accommodate that industry, lives and destinies of that community were based and planned on the basis of that institution: Steel.
>
> . . . It seems to me that a property right has arisen from this lengthy, long established relationship between US Steel, the steel industry as an institution, the community in Youngstown, the people in Mahoning County and the Mahoning Valley in having given and devoted their lives to this industry. Perhaps not a property right to the extent that can be remedied by compelling US Steel to remain in Youngstown. I think the law could not possibly recognize that kind of an obligation. But I think the law can recognize the property right to the extent that US Steel cannot leave the Mahoning Valley and the Youngstown area in a state of waste, that it cannot completely abandon its obligation to that community, because certain vested rights have arisen out of this long relationship and institution.[30]

Judge Hambros finally ruled that "a new property right" was involved that is "not now in existence in the code of laws of our nation," and declined to restrain US Steel from closing its Youngstown mills.

In 1982, on the other hand, the threat of an eminent-domain procedure helped prevent the closing of a large Nabisco factory in Pittsburgh. Following public protests and the announced readiness of a Pittsburgh City Council member to propose eminent-domain action, Nabisco withdrew its proposal for plant closing. After many steel industry closings, in May 1985 the mayor and city council of Pittsburgh also endorsed a proposal to create a Steel Valley Authority that could wield eminent-domain power. Nine city councils in the Monongahela Valley and the city of Pittsburgh secured incorporation of the Steel Valley Authority in January 1986.

THE COOPERATIVE MOVEMENT IN THE UNITED STATES

There are fewer examples of large-scale cooperative enterprises in the United States, but such networks do exist. Unlike economic development in Spain and Israel, where unindustrialized economies allowed readier opportunities for industrial expansion by democratic design, U.S. economic development has overwhelmingly followed traditional business lines. Hard data are in short supply, since neither the IRS nor the Department of Labor keeps records on worker co-ops, but a survey by the Industrial Cooperative Association in Boston produced a Directory of Workers' Enterprises in North America that listed 154 U.S. co-ops with

6,545 members, two-thirds of which are estimated to have less than 25 members.[31]

The ICA was founded in Boston in 1978 to create stable, meaningful jobs for low- and moderate-income communities through the development of worker-owned companies and community-based businesses. The ICA identifies itself as one of the nation's most experienced and respected nonprofit consulting firms specializing in community-based enterprise development.[32]

The ICA assists community-development organizations, state and city governments, churches and foundations in their efforts to create and save jobs. It has helped foster new enterprises in a wide range of industries, including home health care, recycling, food processing, fishing and wood products. It has a staff of business consultants, lawyers and education specialists. It works with community-development corporations, foundations and state and local economic development organizations to devise business programs that address the economic needs of low- to moderate-income communities. It evaluates market opportunity and prepares a feasibility analysis before investments of time and money are made.[33]

As my previous discussions have suggested, the task of coordinating activities of co-ops is an important function. The importance of this consideration has been recognized in places like Mondragon, the kibbutz organizations of Israel and Emilia-Romagna, which have formed networks for purchasing and sharing manufacturing capacity.

COMMUNITY-LINKED DEVELOPMENTS

Widespread upheavals in employment have occurred in so many U.S. industries that a large number of communities have been seriously damaged. In response, various other organizations have been founded to promote efforts aimed at economic and industrial democracy. Thanks to the diligence of Charles Roch of Rollins College, there is a useful directory of groups designed to assist people who are addressing problems of creating democratic enterprise groups.[34]

The Midwest Center for Labor Research in Chicago is one such organization with a record of positive initiatives with respect to community investment and job creation. The MCLR has carried a burden of community responsibility that emphasizes cooperation between labor and community groups in order to counter the loss of manufacturing facilities and employment. To this end it has organized several important conferences, one of which was titled "Toward a New Vision of Community Economic Development."

A repeated refrain in such organizations and conferences is the idea of sustainable manufacturing, which ensures that a drop of a few profit percentage points in sales cannot result in a shutdown by either a single owner or a group of owners. In the MCLR's report on its conference "Sustainable Manufacturing,"[35] which took place in Chicago in 1989, there was an important "Industrial Retention Primer," part of which showed the startling collapse of industrial employment in the Chicago area between 1977 and 1984. Organizations like the Midwest Center, and "The Neighborhood Works," the sponsor of this meeting, called attention to the importance of constructive action to turn around the depletion of manufacturing activity in the city by focusing on community development and job-retention strategies.[36] They are concerned about, as they put it, "what works" in the city neighborhoods and what people can do to build safe, healthy and affordable communities.

In the Pennsylvania steel industry, whole communities were shattered by the epidemic closing of mills during the 1970s and 1980s. Among the varied efforts made to rally wide support for economic revitalization, a crucial role was played by the churches, which was reflected in the formation of justice ministries involved with unions and the wider community in efforts to respond constructively to the economic and social alienation suffered by the affected communities. The Institute on the Church in Urban-Industrial Society has compiled an informative collection, *Plant Closings: The Church's Response*, detailing the participation of many churches and church organizations to the waves of steel-plant closings in Pennsylvania.[37]

Community economic development takes on increasing urgency where there are identifiable communities with especially acute problems of economic development, such as in inner-city areas. A big issue is that banks and investors prefer not to make loans or investments in the inner city. In these "ghettos," notable for their severe poverty and criminality, conditions like high infant mortality and chronic respiratory disease prevail, together with large-scale unemployment. As Michael Shuman writes, by means of various devices of community economic development and investment it becomes conceivable to rally sums for investment precisely in the areas of most acute underdevelopment.[38]

In New York City, the Community Service Society (CSS) has sponsored economic-development activities and has encouraged innovative ideas. Such initiatives have been described in a paper by Rick Surpin titled "Enterprise Development and Worker Ownership: A Strategy for Community Economic Development."[39] Surpin has been the organizer and key operative in cooperative economic enterprises in the New York area.

One unexpected product of closing enterprises, and breakdown of job opportunities, has been the organization of the New York Industrial Retention Network, a database on the manufacturing companies in New York City established by Michael Locker Associates and used to identify firms "at risk." This was designed to enable timely, as opposed to crisis, intervention. A locally based network of community groups, churches, unions, economic development and professional groups was established to enable enterprise-specific interventions to help firms survive.

A VISIONARY ALTERNATIVE: "PARTICIPATORY ECONOMICS"

Michael Albert and Robin Hahnel are innovative economists who have produced a design for what they call "a participatory economy." Albert and Hahnel illustrate the potential of their conception by comparing "hypothetical participatory workplaces with capitalist and coordinator alternatives," in book publishing and the running of an airport. At the heart of their proposals is a scheme for how work should be organized, how products should be shared, and how planning can be done by worker and consumer councils that "relay their proposals to one another via 'facilitation boards.' " Those proposals go through a succession of rounds until there is "a workable match between consumption requests and production proposals." The wide availability and use of computer networks make this kind of decentralized organization a real possibility.

> In this new economy, work is carried out under the auspices of democratic workplace councils, one person one vote, with sensible delegation of responsibilities. There is no fixed workplace hierarchy. Each worker has a complex of responsibilities—some conceptual, some manual; some empowering, some rote—such that each worker's set of tasks (or "job complex") is balanced equitably with those of other workers. Each worker has a fair share of both desirable and not so desirable things to do, has comparable responsibilities and opportunities, and is equally prepared to participate in decision making.[40]

As well as imagining a disalienated system of production, the plan also envisages a radical reorganization of our habits of consumption:

> Consumers receive roughly equal shares of the social product. While they still shop, act on impulse, and borrow and save, consumers must also do a reasonable job of predicting their consumption in advance. Changes in production and consumption eliminate needless waste in packaging, advertising, product dupli-

> cation, etc. Collective goods are chosen by consumer councils with one person one vote. Equity and self management prevail, but so do respect for privacy and a positive attitude toward diversity and experimentation.

At the heart of this proposal is a sharing of information.

> Participatory planning in the new economy is a means by which worker and consumer councils negotiate and revise their proposals for what they will produce and consume. All parties relay their proposals to one another via "facilitation boards." In light of each round's new information, workers and consumers revise their proposals in a way that finally yields a workable match between consumption requests and production proposals. The system rests on a comprehensive exchange of information including a new type of "indicative prices" to help with calculations, data about supply and demand to help people create proposals, and qualitative accounts of social relations to promote better decisions and greater solidarity.[40]

Apart from these examples of alternatives for enterprise decision-making, Albert and Hahnel also elaborate an argument and method for the "participatory allocation" of products and envisage how this might feed back to detailed planning of production.

Taking their cue from the remarkable developments in computer technology and networking, Albert and Hahnel have formulated a "participatory economics" version of "The Information Society."

The purpose of these accounts is to demonstrate the variety of possibilities that have already developed with this common feature: they are all departures, by design, from the enterprise models of state capitalism. Hierarchy, inequality and rigid separation of decision-making from producing have been replaced in varied, often imaginative ways. Given the opportunity, alienation is discarded in favor of mutual decision-making according to democratic rules.

A problem of great impact faces many developing countries—countries that together contain most of the world's population, and include, most notably, China and Russia—where the state managers desire more civilian industry and the benefits that might accrue from decentralized modes of operation. But these same parties insist on a state-capitalist system as the only serious alternative to the regimes inherited from Mao and Stalin, choosing to overlook one likely alternative, workplace democracy, because that would diminish the state's control.

PART V

An Alternative Economic System in the Making

The ideologues of capitalism and the market economy tell us that there can be no alternative to state capitalism, and no alternative to its inevitable components—deindustrialization and militarism. But the ideologues have overlooked the very process whereby capitalism took shape as an alternative to feudalism. The new capitalist economic system did not appear "made whole" overnight, or as the result of a political coup.

In the transition from feudalism to capitalism, there were many near-term changes in workers' occupations, in and around production, before the overall change in the production decision-making system became visible. These changes spelled an end to the system of obligations that bound lords and peasants, replacing them with the familiar capitalist employment relation that governed production and the sharing of its products.

Over a period of several centuries, peasant workers became industrial employees, and lords of the manor became businessmen and managers. These near-term changes for controlling production yielded new profits and power for its managers and, in turn, expanded (and were supported by) an array of new occupations to handle trade, banking and the new monied wealth. A thoroughly alienated peasantry was taken up partly by cottage industry, and then, wholesale, by factories organized by businessmen. Thereby capitalism was born.

While the component changes in business-supporting occupations were visible as near-term phenomena, it was left to economists, like Adam Smith and Karl Marx, to define, as capitalism, the long-term underlying effects brought about by the mass of localized occupation changes that gradually displaced feudalism.

Now, in the twenty-first century, albeit in a period of far more rapid and accelerated change, we can see another pattern of near-term changes at work, changes that are transforming the decision processes on production within state capitalism and opening up the prospect of an exit from its endless alienations, into the alternative economic system of workplace democracy. While the alienation and profit/power process of management take on widening scope and intensity, the worker occupations become the site of disalienation moves that are modifying, ever more, the employment relation (as we saw in chapters 9, 10 and 11). Changes in both the managerial and worker occupations are going on all the time; the pace of disalienation varies. Around this central tendency, there is room for individual variation. As in the previous great shift from feudalism to capitalism the near-term changes are yielding to a profound, underlying change in the economic system as a whole. As workers' disalienated controls come to govern a growing part of production, an alternative form of economic life emerges more and more clearly into view—an exit route from the relentless deindustrialization and militarism of state capitalism into a new system based on workplace democracy.

These processes of disalienation are at the core of the historic evolution of western society toward workplace democracy. The last part of this book explores the unavoidable conclusion that the ongoing alienation and disalienation processes have both near-term effects and system effects beyond them, which define both an alternative to state capitalism and a definable exit process from capitalism.

System change into capitalism was heralded by the growing part of production that was governed by businessmen with their new rules: for organizing work under employment relation; accumulating profit without limit; setting up managements in hierarchy form. Similarly, system change toward workplace democracy from capitalism will continue to be marked by a host of occupation changes with near-term results in a widening part of production of goods and services. The disalienation process toward workplace democracy will include men and women who combine decision-making with producing, collapsing hierarchy, diminishing exploitation and inequality, and mutual decision-making as the model for governing work in place of predatory competition for profit/power accumulation without limit.

As we have seen, there are formidable obstacles to overcome. During the twentieth century, in parallel with the widening reach of disalienation processes, the successors of the earliest financiers and industrial employers arranged a managerial partnership with government. But as in all partnerships, one partner turned out to be more equal than another: in state capitalism, the U.S. government—with its vast finance capital, police powers and military organizations—has predominated. Profit/power accumulation has been pressed at the price of unchecked deindustrialization and militarism.

State capitalism uses the mechanisms of finance and the military to launch a drive for global economic/political power.* Thereby traditional business processes continue with an additional boost from the government treasury, the deepest pockets in the U.S. economy. In state capitalism, workers face their greatest obstacle to disalienation.

Independently of the location of management—corporate or government—the prospect of a successful workplace-democracy alternative for organizing work is strategically improved as white-collar workers join the blue, for these occupations together contain the organization, financial and technical skills for the procession of disalienation near-term effects that structure workplace democracy.

Writing in *The End of Utopia*, Russell Jacoby has summed up the pessimistic view of many intellectuals at the opening of the twenty-first century:

> We are increasingly asked to choose between the status quo or something worse. Other alternatives do not seem to exist. . . . Few envision the future as anything but a replica of today—sometimes better, but usually worse. . . . A new consensus has emerged: There are no alternatives. This is the wisdom of our times, an age of political exhaustion and retreat.[1]

Yet all of this does not account for the continued refusal of many people to swallow the cover stories of the state-capitalist ideologues. Those most recently identifiable as refusers include the participants and supporters of the Seattle 1999 demonstrations against the economic institutions that spearhead the global hegemony drive of America's corporate/state managers.

Nevertheless, even intellectuals committed to resisting neoliberalism, and favoring alternative visions of system change, have often been lacking in a vital perspective essential for achieving an economy and society based on workplace democracy. What is required for real systemic change is a deeply anchored understanding of the decision processes which change the relations of production, and of the limitations and possibilities that inhere in the technologies of production themselves. Only by close attention to the role of production, by defining the desired alternative in terms of the transformed relations of production afforded by workplace democracy, can advocates of change gain a solid base for critiquing the deindustrializing and militaristic practices of the corporate/state managers.

*The finance model that dominates management thinking at the start of the twenty-first century is usefully discussed in Allan Kennedy, *The End of Shareholder Value* (Perseus, 2000).

In short, the cheerleaders for U.S. state capitalism, with their mantra "there is no alternative," can be countered with a well-formulated perspective that replaces managerial hierarchy with workplace democracy as the organizing principle of production.

Systemic change toward workplace democracy has a further secret weapon. It can increase the productivity of capital without alienating it at all. This is the significance of the marked reduction in machine downtime and in the scrap rates that are achieved by kibbutz factories (in Chapter 10) and the computer-controlled machine tools described by Nneji (Chapter 7). *Where industrial operations are "knowledge-based," workers who are accustomed to working cooperatively are best suited to optimizing the production possibilities of computer-controlled manufacturing.*

High productivity of capital can be realized by the presence of a stable production system that causes a factory with many operations to function like a single machine, with little fluctuation in the rate of output; unscheduled downtime approaching zero; near-zero rates of defective products.[2] These qualities grow in importance as the capital investment for plant and equipment continues to dominate the cost of production for a given product (as we saw in chapters 7 and 10).

By combining decision-making with production, workplace democracy can deliver all these benefits in the high-tech workplace. Evidence from diverse sources confirms the importance of workers' cooperation as an increasingly important factor in productivity of capital.

These sources of gain in the productivity of capital translate automatically into gain in productivity per worker-hour. Deindustrialization supposedly "solves" managers' problem of boosting profit by undoing production altogether—by importing, outsourcing, abandoning R&D, countering unionization at all costs, and so on. But the productivity of both labor and capital can be boosted without any alienation at all.

Appreciating the capability of workplace democracy to spur the productivity of capital introduces a new dimension in industrial economics. Moving production from the United States to very-low-wage countries is no longer obviously advantageous when the cost of capital (plant and equipment) dominates the industrial economy.* As that condition predominates in industrial production, cooperative labor among knowledgeable, highly motivated, well-paid workers becomes the dominant factor which will foster industrial efficiency of every sort.

*Wages to production workers were 15 cents of each dollar of industrial shipments in 1958 and 9 cents by 1996 (U.S. Bureau of the Census, *1996 Annual Survey of Manufactures, Statistics for Industry Groups and Industries*, 1997, table 1A).

To all this, of course, management and market-economy loyalists are prone to respond: What makes you think that management will agree to such radical changes in economy and society?

What must be recalled is that managers agree to workers' disalienated rules, as in union contracts, because they want, and indeed must have, production, so that management's decision-making on production may go forward. If, for example, the workers decide to disalienate their workplace by adopting rules of seniority, the managers have to agree to these democratizing measures in order for production to take place. If production does not take place, the whole managerial function is short-circuited.

The installation of the employment relation introduced new rules for the decision-making and producing occupations, and defined much of the change from feudalism to capitalism. So, too, the introduction of worker decision-making as the guiding principle of production will be the crucial element in a transformation from capitalism to workplace democracy.

12

The Advancing Processes of Capitalism and Workplace Democracy

The course of American economy and society during the twenty-first century will be shaped by two distinct systems for deciding production, both of which have been identified in these pages. The first is state capitalism. The second is worker decision-making. We are now in a position to make confident predictions about these processes.

The Workplace-Democracy Alternative

The businessmen who hired the former peasants of the feudal manor were early managers of the employment relation—the expanding alternative to feudalism. From their commanding position, the new (capitalist) employers carried out a process of alienation that strengthened their control over, first, cottage industry hands and, later, masses of factory workers, whose labor spurred capital accumulation.

But control over successful accumulation required ever more intricate administrative organizations and control systems. Indeed, regulation of people and financial flows became a centerpiece of managerial activity in capitalism and invited corporate/state linkages that culminated in the accumulations, rational and irrational, financial and military, of state capitalism.

Meanwhile, the workers' historic response to the employers' alienation drives centered on the relations of production. As I showed in Part IV, the employees' moves toward systematic decision-making about their own work have been based in production. These alternative approaches to the way work is organized combine the technical requirements for production—which can yield higher productivity for capital—with a disalienated, democratic decision process. They offer a successor to the managerialism of state capitalism.

. . .

Every aspect of employment is in the process of change with or without national organization and formal advocates. In conjunction with the strivings of U.S. state/corporate managers, American workers have persistently responded to the alienation of the employment relationship. Temporary or part-time jobs without medical and pension benefits are on the rise. In response, as we have seen, workers have been inventing new relations of production—in effect, an economy after capitalism.

At the side of the alienation operations of state capitalism, blue- and white-collar workers and their unions have responded with moves to disalienate their relations with the employer. They have set in motion processes that contain a new system for deciding about production, hence a new form of economy. The scope and intensity of worker decision-making on production have been advancing, even without a wider public knowledge of the changes.

Describing the characteristics of these two decision processes on production is confused by the cover stories that shield a clear view of their operation. Thus the ideology of state capitalism even excludes the possibility of the appearance of any other viable system for deciding on production.

Understanding worker decision-making is made difficult by the conventional view of worker/union behavior as an array of disparate and not necessarily systemic and related acts.

As we have seen, however, it is the content of workers' disalienation practice that makes it historically meaningful. The scope of the workers' rules can encompass every major aspect of activity necessary to production, and thereby construct an alternative to the hierarchical systems of both business and government—an alternative to state capitalism.

Workers develop rules and procedures for deciding on aspects of their own activity—who is included in the worker group (the criterion: whose work is a service to production), by what rules and procedures employees can affect their work location as well as change in deployment, standards of work performance, the time for work performance and finally the focus and size of compensation.

In turn, the disalienation process extends to relations of production, the rules that guide workers in their relation to one another in the course of their work: mutual decision-making procedures in place of predatory competition, democratic decision procedures in place of hierarchy and rules for equal sharing instead of exploitive relations.

As such rules take hold among workers, they can have profound consequences. The alienating acts of state capitalism can be checkmated at least in part by worker groups with a self-interest in stable employment, and in self-government over their own work. Predatory competition yields to cooperation and mutual trust. Exploitation cannot coexist with equal sharing. In place of the anarchic conditions spurred on by predatory competition, workplace democracy encourages stable and predictable operations in economy and community.

WHITE COLLARS JOIN THE BLUE AS WORK IS TRANSFORMED

Unheralded by economists and the media institutions that they serve, formerly "independent" and employed professionals have opened a new chapter in American labor history by turning to unionization as the response to campaigns of alienation.

This is the fruit of another process at work: the ongoing attempt by workers to disalienate their working lives. Where before the struggle for workplace democracy through union organizing was considered the preserve of industrial production workers alone, at the beginning of the twenty-first century white-collar employees are creating their own processes of decision-making and even implementing disalienation by design.

To be sure, there is the ever-present matter of pace and timing. How long will it take for the people of an occupation to develop sufficient solidarity and mutual trust to organize themselves formally into groupings based on mutual decision-making over their working lives? There is no standardized formula that could predict the timing of such outcomes. But we do know that they are possible.

A new perspective for workplace democracy is opened up by the prospect of including in workers' organizations all the occupations that are a "service to production."* In his classic work "The Frontier of Control: A Study in British Workshop Politics," Carter L. Goodrich called attention to the feasibility of

> undertak[ing] in one large contract, or in two or three contracts at most, the entire business of production throughout the establishment. Granted an alliance with the organized office workers—a development which is assured so soon as the shop committees are

*In manufacturing, direct production workers fabricate, assemble, test and transport the product. Others (indirect) maintain equipment, tools, etc. Apart from the production workers, clerical/administrative occupations perform a host of necessary tasks, such as arranging supplies of materials, tools, machines; scheduling inflow of such inputs, and transportation of product; keeping records on equipment downtime, materials and product quality. All this activity is directly, materially essential for production. Hence the people doing these tasks are "part of production," a "service to production," sometimes termed "part of the workers."

> worthy of confidence and influential enough to give adequate protection—these contracts might include the work of design and purchase of raw material, as well as the operations of manufacture and construction.[1]

Goodrich's recommendation was fully implemented in the contract between the Standard Motor Company in Coventry, England, and the union.

Many have viewed the striving of workers for disalienation as equivalent to a competitive struggle against management, with both managers and workers aiming for the same thing. But closer examination of the worker decision process points to a rather different schedule of objectives.

Corporate management strives to accumulate profit (capital) for investing and thereby enlarge its sphere of control (more production, more sales—hence customer dependency). Government-based managers strive for more power (more workers, larger budgets). The worker decision system moves to disalienate, to establish systematic workers' control over their own activity. That is defined centrally, not by profit/power, or some arbitrarily desirable portion of the value of product, but rather by establishing and extending worker decisions over their own work time, deployment, performance and compensation, and over the boundary of the worker group.

In all this, white-collar unionization will play an ever more important role. While the number of engineers, technologists and research specialists multiplied after World War II, top managers made sustained efforts to include the white-collar workers as part of management. But those efforts have been countered by the ever-widening use of computers in service occupations and enterprises, which, ironically, has resulted in the dumbing down and speeding up of many so-called "high-tech" jobs. A parallel growth in technical-support occupations was created.

- In-house user support by skilled technicians is required to keep stand-alone PCs or networks of PCs in operation.
- Where computers are used in networks to record and coordinate the details of many thousands of separate accounts, infrastructure support is needed to assure reliable operations.
- Computer hardware and software are not failure-proof. Technically competent user support is made more important as both hardware and software are constantly upgraded.
- Service industries are becoming more dependent on the reliable performance of computer networks. They then rely on

> large and growing fixed costs of both machinery and required maintenance work to assure acceptable reliability. Increasing numbers of maintenance technicians are thus required.

All told, as service businesses take on these characteristics, they become more like manufacturing industries, with large and growing fixed capital and labor costs (where "fixed" means not varying with output). For example, the cost of buying and operating mobile robots used in hospitals to deliver tools, medications and food varies only slightly with distance traveled in corridors.

Wages for engineers and technicians performing this necessary work will continue to reflect both the investment needed for professional training and the rapidly growing market. Higher costs spur the usual cost-cutting strategies: management pressure on wages and the export of jobs. The supply of trained people in the United States has been sufficiently short of demand to induce companies to try long-distance control of technical staffs—many of whom actually do their work in Asian locations.

As we saw in Chapter 10, the growth of white-collar unionization means that more strategically important workers find themselves on a dis-alienation path. Unionization of the engineering-technical occupations means a strategic gain for worker decision-making. The efforts to make engineers part of management reached their limits as large numbers of technically trained people were hired by the expanding high-tech industries. This led to an employee force that has had to include both the older production worker occupations and the new engineer-technologist groupings.

The latter typically includes knowledge and skills: about the interrelation between a particular production facility and the sources of necessary equipment, processes and materials, as well as the "external" arrangements for distributing the product—hence, the market that is served. As the span of worker groups widens to include white-collar occupations that are "a service to production," the groups encompass the necessary enterprise-integrating skills, now made operative under the rules of workplace democracy.

In the 1990s, techies, M.D.s and professors continued joining unions, and worker organization enjoyed an especially eventful year in 1999. The managers of the IBM Corporation, long renowned as an anti-union employer, found themselves maintaining a large workforce that was increasingly agitated by the decision to cut many pensions by as much as 40 percent. Union educational and organizing meetings took place at IBM sites throughout the country. Marshaling their capabilities for Internet operations, unions addressed IBM's 140,000 workers of all grades (engineers, technicians and even first-level managers) in the United States and initiated a series of organizing moves that could begin to change the face of the electronics industry. IBM employees are listening more attentively to the Communication Workers of America after managers cut some health benefits and overtime pay. Big Blue workers are concerned about the increasing number of long-term temporary workers and wage increases withheld from workers after "rave performance reviews."[2]

Successful strikes of construction and service workers in California raised Latino membership to above 10 percent of the AFL-CIO total. An anti-union report to the officers of the American Medical Association was rejected in favor of unionization by doctors who are employees. The same convention gave close attention to a plan to change federal antitrust law and National Labor Relations Board procedures that would effectively permit joint bargaining with insurance companies and HMOs by doctors who are not employees.

In Los Angeles County, a union of 74,000 home-care workers represented a substantial union-organizing gain—that being a larger number than "in the auto industry immediately after the volatile sit-down strikes of 1937."

In the universities, a pro-union vote of teaching assistants in the California university system united white-collar with blue. Perhaps more important as an omen of the future, the AFL-CIO reported that a public opinion poll commissioned by the federation recorded 54 percent of young workers saying that, given the choice, they would vote to form a union, and that was up from 47 percent in 1996.[3]

Continued alienation of present and prospective university faculty (Chapter 10) will compel them to seek amelioration through unionization. The same compelling needs will put increasing numbers of faculty on a collision course with departments of economics, business and law, whose teaching focuses on accepting state/corporate rule as the best of all possible worlds, while justifying state capitalism.

Schools of business and law train men and women for business-managerial occupations. Schools of international affairs produce candidates for government positions, especially the foreign service, and for international slots within multinational corporations. Trainees for these occupations are prospectives for conducting alienation operations either within their enterprises or in relation to larger populations.

None of this is to say that trainees for, or workers in, occupations that administer alienation are themselves exempt from these controls. Indeed, high-powered jobs within the government or corporate hierarchy frequently come at a price. But such people are prone to hope for privileged managerial positions of their own. Professional dreams tend to damp down or switch off the pains of alienation.

Nevertheless, there will always be those who share the formal knowledge of these fields but prefer to see it applied, where appropriate, in a disalienation process. Business students will seek ways of altering management codes toward accommodation with worker disalienation steps, operating and financing worker cooperatives, initiating labor-sponsored investment funds and organizing worker communities along kibbutz lines.

Law students will develop ways of supporting front-line workers in the disalienation process, critiquing the texts and the administration of laws for congruence with advancing disalienation and initiating studies and interpretations that can have important effects. For example, the power of eminent domain can conceivably be a legal-administrative tool for dealing with decisions by managements to deindustrialize entire communities.

That is why disalienation initiatives among university workers are found first among graduate students in the humanities and the sciences. Those at the bottom of the hierarchy—alienated and exploited, and furthest from its promised rewards—are most willing to look for workplace democracy.

A substantial spur to white-collar unionism came from a November 1999 decision by the National Labor Relations Board. The board reversed a 1976 decision, finding that medical interns and residents were in fact employees—not students, as they had previously been classified. As a result, the Committee of Interns and Residents that represents almost all unionized hospital residents will thereby be better positioned to organize the 100,000 interns and residents employed in public and private hospitals.[4] This decision clearly has profound ramifications for other white-collar union initiatives.

During the 1990s, it was characteristic for the business press to discuss the rise of the "temp" workforce as an expression of resurgent individualism—people who preferred to be "independent" and free to come and go from one employer to another, hence not prone to unionism or collegial solidarity. The temps also were characterized by frequent change of employer. But in *Business Week* we learn: "While many temps like the flexibility of tempting offers, they earn only $329 a week on average, 35% less than regular workers, according to the Bureau of Labor Statistics. Only 7% of temps get health care insurance from their employer, and just 4% a pension."[5]

Meanwhile, the San Jose AFL-CIO has been creating modes of operation that are helpful to the temps and other contingent workers. In the heart of Silicon Valley, which houses thirty-five of the top fifty electronic companies in the world, the South Bay AFL/CIO Labor Council sponsored a landmark 1997 study on the temp workers and their role, "Shock Absorbers in the Flexible Economy." The Labor Council found that

> The Valley's economic engine is being increasingly powered by a pool of temporary and contact labor which produces a downward pressure on wages and benefits, widespread job insecurity and a growing income gap.

About 250 offices at temp agencies in Silicon Valley account for a labor force that has been growing two to four times as fast as total employment. While temp agency employment (1991–1995) grew 48 percent, total Valley industrial jobs declined by 2 percent.

The boom in temp jobs has included a full range of occupations, excepting only corporate top managers. Thus software development has often been the province of highly skilled temps known as "software gypsies." Assembly work for electronic hardware has been assigned to contract-labor assembly companies employing immigrant Asian women.

It has not escaped the attention of Silicon Valley's AFL-CIO unions that in France temp workers must be paid (by law) the same wage as "permanent workers." The vaunted "individualism" of the temps has turned toward finding a route for mitigating the alienations of their formal occupation title.

THE CONSEQUENCES OF HIGH-TECH SOPHISTICATION

The sophistication of production technologies will offer increasing opportunities for workers to enrich not only their own professional lives but the well-being of their fellows and wider communities as well.

Workers producing technically "advanced" systems need not only manual skills, but also a sophisticated understanding of machinery they are using and making. Hence an enlargement of the knowledge and skills in the hands of the workers in production may be expected. Many workers prefer to be "challenged" and to become highly skilled.

When workers can access a company's database, they can acquire knowledge about performance, inventory, rules and regulations, the composition and costs of management and all manner of financial data. In this respect, the presence of computer terminals throughout a factory, as found in many Scandinavian companies, makes it possible for workers to acquire knowledge concerning the details of an operation.

The disalienation that takes shape among blue-collar workers who are directly engaged in production operations spreads to the white-collar workers whose activity is a necessary service to production. But the effort to maintain and extend the scope of the workers' new decision rules leads to reaching out to the wider economy—as, for example, when insourcing and outsourcing are performed. Reaching out to sources of production equipment is a natural result of negotiating with managers about overtime work where the need for more hours is affected by the choice of present versus alternative production equipment. For example, Ford UAW agreements note that

> The alternatives to overtime considered by the parties may include manpower increases, innovative shift arrangements, or improvements or additions to the plant's equipment which could eliminate a bottleneck.[6]

Under workplace democracy, those who develop products and processes (primarily engineers) would have more opportunity to participate in decisions on these matters than they now possess. That could very well be to the considerable benefit of all involved, including the wider environment, because engineers are likely to think more in terms of long-term effects than managers, who are oriented to short-term profitability.

In the petroleum industry, there is a considerable history of accidents—sometimes involving pollution of groundwater and of the atmosphere and large ocean oil spills. The managers avoided reequipping their tanker fleets with double-hulled vessels, which are less prone to breaks and the related massive oil spills that foul the seas. Why? To preserve and extend the use of their considerable investments in fleets. These managements conduct their businesses in such a manner because, essentially, they can get away with it—up to a point. It is only when communities, legislatures and unions have become strong enough that many safety features have been added and unsafe situations corrected.

In a workplace democracy environment, firms may elect to open their own schools to make up for a university's lack of proper training (as the Mondragon co-ops did). If they are faced with a flood of candidates with distinguished degrees in financial engineering but with little competence in either machine design or the details of production-planning and operations, then the school would need to offer this kind of training. Such instruction has been given in Mondragon by an institution that is an arm of the workers' bank.

In contrast to technology designed for profits and power, good civilian product and process design embodies simplicity, safety, reliability and durability, and minimizes cost for a given standard of quality and volume of output. Poor design is betrayed by complexity, willingness to bear the cost of frequent breakdown, flimsiness—as in planned obsolescence—and a design with little or no consideration of cost. A worker decision process would encourage employees to be motivated to produce technology of high quality. Those standards would also entail less pollution and waste.

It is important to differentiate between the view of production as a source of wealth, and control over production as a device for power. The enlargement of authority in the hands of workers would lead to better health and higher levels of education in the workplace and the surrounding community. The engineering occupations would have more clout than they have now, and they could be expected to press for cost-minimizing rather than cost-maximizing.

Accordingly, better quality of work life and factory design is to be expected from those conditions. A minor example: It has been normal for the interior of factories to be painted a drab battleship gray. But no one would think of painting the interior of a living room or kitchen that color. Why make it dreary, and not bright and cheerful? A whole school of design in Scandinavia has given careful attention to such opportunities, which are now being called "social technical design criteria." The designers seek to combine cultural considerations of workers and the surrounding community with those required for the work itself.

Work need no longer be divided into arbitrarily simple tasks, as Taylor's management teachings specify, because it is possible and desirable for many employees to complete more intricate work. Fewer supervisors would be needed, because the principal decisions would be made by the workers themselves.

In the early history of computer-controlled machine tools, managers authorized advertisements showing a chimpanzee pressing the green button that set the machine in motion and then the red button that stopped it. Moral: Even a chimpanzee could operate such a machine tool. This view differs sharply from one that regards the programming of the machine tool's computer, as well as maintenance of the machine, as part of the machinist's task, and therefore in no sense a work assignment for a chimpanzee, however favorably a manager may look on the animal as a friend or a compliant pet.

One of the available ways of sharing increased productivity is by reducing the length of the workweek. But such reduction has not taken place in the United States since World War II, though it is in motion in Western Europe, notably in France and Germany. It is doubtful that the quality of products would diminish as their relative prices rise owing to a shorter workweek.

In the United States, insufficient attention has been paid to the prospect of not only a shorter work year but also a shorter work life. Emile Mazey, a former secretary-treasurer of the United Automobile Workers, once described a series of steps that might be taken to limit the work year and use the free time, apart from vacation, for education. As a result, he said, the people participating would have an opportunity to improve the quality not only of their extra-work time but even of their working lives.

One of the damaging features of state capitalism is the relative inattention to occupational illness, a neglect that preceded state capitalism. Consider the growing epidemic of repetitive strain injuries that have become a leading cause of occupational illness. Conventional use of computer terminals and other motion devices has often produced combinations of significant neurological-muscular impairment. Nevertheless, such injuries can be substantially reduced through ergonomically designed equipment, rest breaks and appropriate education of both employers and employees. A workplace democracy could address these matters seriously, and without public dispute.[7]

Americans can also learn something from the Scandinavian countries, where state capitalism has been held in check by trade unions. There, it is not "markets" but worker decision-making that has underpinned a democratic society. Norwegian trade unions have led the world in forging agreements with management, making computer knowledge and computer files available to the workers. This often involves placing computer terminals throughout factories and giving workers access to the detailed workings of the enterprise.

I once mentioned this idea to a factory manager, pointing out the positive effect on productivity when workers have access to information. He replied, "Oh no, we can't do that, because that information should only be available on a need-to-know basis." It is not surprising to hear this opinion from people who have been drilled in the "need-to-know" criterion that looms so large in the military.

At present, this logic dominates the use of computer technology. The new availability and wide use of computers have made the planning of large-scale investments ever more feasible. Some may say that if General Electric can be run out of a central office, then, by extension, why not the whole economy? But we know very well that computers break down and that programs are not perfect. Any such concentration of decision power would confer control by the chiefs of state capitalism. I would not put it beyond some to propose such a system, no doubt in the name of free-market competition.

UNION INNOVATIONS

Unions will find new opportunities for innovation in organization methods, like the pattern of contracting that was developed with Kaiser Permanente (Chapter 10).

A report on strategy and tactics by the steelworkers' union has identified an important set of innovations in union organization and operations. Two points have been central: continuous initiatives and broadening the boundaries of union initiatives from single plant, to firm, to industry, to community. Here is how union president George Becker formulated the first of these points: "I have a very simple theory," he explains, "Nothing stands still. You're either moving ahead or moving behind. If you're in a struggle and not getting results, you have to escalate." Evidently, that is exactly what the steelworkers have been doing with their efforts around the idea of "corporate campaign." As David Moberg has noted, in six major strike/lockout situations, the tactical innovations introduced by the steelworkers have included the following:

> *Attacking links to customers.* The steelworkers' target is then to address either individual consumers or corporate consumers who are subject to persuasion on grounds of personal convenience or distaste for being involved in a labor dispute;
>
> *Increasing financial pressure.* The steelworkers rallied unions, churches and other institutions to withdraw funds from a major bank functioning as an important lender to a steel-company management that has blocked union recognition.
>
> *Undermining investor confidence and support for management.* The steelworkers have issued reports on company financial problems to Wall Street investment firms, and have also participated in stockholder meetings of companies that refuse to negotiate with the union. By such means, the steelworkers' resistance to unfair labor practices has been instrumental even in inducing changes of ownership that would be more friendly to dealing with the union.
>
> *Applying political, legislative and regulatory pressure.* Thus, "The steelworkers have organized against local tax breaks and subsidies for companies, arguing that they are violating their promises to the community. In Natchez, the city council suspended tax abatements until a contract was negotiated." Repeatedly, the union has increased publicity about health and

safety violations in factories where replacement workers were hired to substitute for union members on strike.

Building union solidarity globally where possible. As part of its struggle against heightened international corporate cooperation, the steelworkers joined forces with the United Auto Workers, leading to "protests at Ford dealerships in 61 cities, supporting steelworker demands that Ford stop using the German-based company General Tires. Earlier, workers from Charlotte, North Carolina, had traveled to Germany, meeting with unions, protested at a stockholders' meeting and "showed union flag" at a big truck race sponsored by Continental A.G., a German tire-maker, and explained the strike to bankers.[8]

Workers' strategy obviously entails diverse actions, implies a lot of innovation and causes the union to confront recalcitrant managements with big surprises.* David Moberg further notes that, "During an economic boom unions theoretically shouldn't face such hostile bargaining. But in the supposedly fabulous nineties economy, employers have continued to downsize and lean on employees. Manufacturing workers, especially those exposed to global competition, working for big multinationals or producing basic industrial commodities, have remained under continuing pressure."

Regarding the second point—broadening the boundaries of union initiative—business management sway over information will be abridged as participation in and use of the worldwide Web expand. Paths will be opened through the Internet for regional, national and international communication, and the way will be cleared for feasible industry-wide and interindustry linkages between workers.

Such international connections will act as countermoves against the national operations that deliberately deal with one group at a time. One of the most powerful alienation strategies is encompassed by the term *globalization.* But as we have seen, multinational managerialism generates a host of new issues and opportunities for unions. The Steelworkers gave a classic demonstration of the feasibility of mobilizing international solidarity among diverse worker groups, which led to a union victory in a 1998–1999 contest with Continental A.G., a German-based multinational tire company. The USWA organized "protests at German consulates and persuaded workers at a Continental plant in South Africa to stage a sympathy

*A demonstration of union success with unorthodox methods is detailed in Tom Juravich and Kate Bronfenbrenner, *Ravenswood: The Steelworkers' Victory and the Revival of American Labor* (Cornell University Press, 1999).

strike." Churches and other unions contributed food to tide the workers over. It was a winning—and international—strategy for the Steelworkers.

None of this is intended to understate the scope and intensity of state/corporate controls. At present, I cannot identify a university department of economics that currently gives a course on workplace democracy, on self-government in work. A "Program on Participatory and Labor-Managed Systems" once had a place at Cornell University's School of Industrial and Labor Relations, but it was discontinued. While teaching at Columbia University, I gave a seminar for graduate students on "Alternatives to Managerialism." None is currently provided.

State Capitalism Advances

The widening scope of decision power of the state/corporate managers will be accelerated, not only by the corporate merger movement but most decisively by the enlarging role of government. With a history that spans two centuries, state capitalism has spawned a dual directorate of corporate-finance businessmen and government-military/political leaders. These are the decision-makers who command and support interlinked private and government enterprise, striving to accumulate profits and power. The result of concentrated corporate/state management has been an unprecedented speeding of alienation, of imposed powerlessness in all its forms, in order to spur accumulation of profits (for capital) and power (for the state).

Government managers will continue to control by far the largest portion of finance capital in the American economy. State finance controls will continue to exempt the government's own economy, the military economy, from the uncertainties that can beset even the largest private corporation. More exactly, the continued blurring line between private and governmental managerial controls makes the military-serving corporations failure-proof.

The U.S. government's annual military budget of $289 billion for 1999–2000 continued the pattern developed during the latter part of the Cold War. But the meaning of these new budgets is given by several major military-technology and political developments.

Within the United States, not only are nuclear weapons retained in quantities far in the overkill range, they are also being refined in various fashions. Toward this end, the federal government has been financing multi-billion-dollar new research facilities, as at the Livermore Laboratories in California. The plan is to perform nuclear-weapons simulation research not only at Livermore but at a network of American universities. This will have the effect of financing many faculties and graduate students, giving them a professional-economic stake in weapons technologies. The claim of the White House and the Pentagon that this development does not violate treaties prohibiting full explosions of nuclear warheads is, at the least, doubtful. A careful investigation of the new nuclear weapons planning by the National Resources Defense Council discloses that

> Research proposals submitted by the universities through the Department of Energy during the competition for *Academic Strategic Alliances Program* grants contain passages on weapons science education and training activities and interaction with the nuclear weapons laboratories. This may be the most controversial aspect of the program for members of the academic community, an issue which may be exacerbated by the substantial matching funds (or other services) universities have offered these centers.
>
> At the very time in their careers in which students are exploring and seeking to establish the dimensions of their personal and moral universe, the *Academic Strategic Alliances Program* forces an early choice between, on the one hand, involuntary utilization of one's work product for nuclear weapons work, and on the other, foregoing graduate research support in one's chosen field.[9]

The vast Pentagon investment in fresh nuclear R&D skews the production of newly trained brains toward military uses. The "high-tech" revolution turns out to have a darker side.* All this at a time when universities have been subject to a trend toward corporatization and managerialism.

Obviously, with the background of multi-billions of new research investments in nuclear and allied weaponry, it is only a short step to the biotechnological means for mass destruction purposes. Just as there is no physical protection against the blast, fire and radiation effects of nuclear weapons, so too there is no shield easily applied against biotechnical weapons of mass terror. Joshua Lederberg, a Nobel laureate at the National Academy of Sciences, has commented on bioterrorism as follows:

> There is no technical solution to the problem of biological weapons. It needs an ethical, human, and moral solution if it's going to

*On January 29, 2000, the *New York Times* reported: "After decades of denials, the government is conceding that since the dawn of the atomic age, workers making nuclear weapons have been exposed to radiation and chemicals that have produced cancer and early death."

> happen at all. Don't ask me what the odds are for an ethical solution, but there is no other solution. But would an ethical solution appeal to a sociopath?[10]

On all available evidence, Lederberg is right, but that doesn't leave us without sensible options. Research and experience with designing inspection systems include ways of addressing even that most fearsome kind of problem. Methods of inspection that invite and organize "inspection by the people" afford ways of surrounding the prospective sociopath with a multitude of reasonably trained, alert watchers and listeners.[11]

The main shape of America's near future will derive from continuation of the alienation-accumulation (and disalienation) patterns put in place during the second half of the twentieth century—not from some surprising course of behavior or single catastrophic event.

Consider the new developments in the regular process of diverting the life-serving activity of production to serve further alienation and accumulation: Accumulation of capital in the service of business management could always be used either directly, for further investment, or be held in reserve for the time when it is justified. Not so with the present practices of government managers. Capital for the military has a one-time use only. The state managers apply their enormous financial and political power to build and operate a military machine and supporting economy as their primary activity.

Thus the U.S. victory in the Cold War was taken by American state managers to indicate that the prospect of establishing hegemony over the entire globe was now a realistic one. Accordingly, it has seemed entirely sensible, from this vantage point, to maintain a military machine requiring as much as half the tax revenues from the U.S. economy. Similarly, nuclear military capability is scheduled for yet further multiplication. Indeed, separate terms have been developed for referring to the military as against the rest of the government's budgets and activity. The former is termed defense while the rest is called government spending.

The state managers use their resources to develop technologies that will serve the further accumulation of power—notwithstanding the fact that they have reached levels of irrationality, there being no definable use for the costly new nuclear weaponry, or for new nuclear attack submarines that are built to dimensions like the length of a football field but without definable attack targets, there being no known enemy subs of relevant size.

By channeling research and development resources toward yet further military production, the partnership between government and corporate managers serves both business alienation and profit accumulation, as well as the unquenchable appetite of the military for destructive power.

But there are no government statistics that chart the scale and growth of the "war industry," this expansion of military research, military production and military use of capital and manpower. There is no measurement by government of what is lost as a result of these resource allocations. A primary cover story for the military extravaganza is that with a base of indefinitely large wealth, all this is affordable. Here, as with other cover stories, the perception of reality is confused, but reality is not altered.

Senator William Fulbright did not withhold his judgment on the scale of what is entailed, not only in the economy but in political life as well.

> If we ever do confront the consequences of our militarized economy, it will not be enough to just curb the military expenditures. We will need too to transfer a vast portion of those funds into other, long-neglected sectors of the economy. But how do you get from here to there if you cannot even discuss the issues—if you cannot, without bringing all hell down on yourself, address the issue of militarization and its ideological partner, the fervent anti-Russian animus that permeates so much of our thought and action; and if we cannot face up to this arrogant sense of our own superiority, this assumption that it is our God-given role to be the dominant power in the world?[12]

While conversion of industry from the military to the civilian economy is as important in the twenty-first century as it was in 1991, this development awaits the initiatives that must come from those committed to workplace democracy at the plants, laboratories and bases that serve the military enterprise.

A WORLD HEGEMONY DRIVE CONTINUES

After the end of the Cold War, unimpeded by another superpower, the U.S. government launched, and continues, a program for accumulating power around the world, revealed by the scope and characteristics of the armed forces, their lavish equipment and the readiness of Washington to use military force.* This drive portends wars small and large, without end.

*See U.S. Navy, "Navy Fact File," *Amphibious Transport Dock-LPD, Dock Landing Ship-LSD*, and other major equipment—all data from http://www.chinfo.navy.mil/navpalib/factfile/ships/ship-lpd.html.

The corrosive influence of U.S. militarism on the rest of the world shows no signs of flagging. When another government buys weapons from the Pentagon, a network of dependency is automatically put in place (Appendix A). The buyer needs knowledge and training for using the materiel. Maintaining it is a continuous task that includes the necessity of access to spare parts, without which the weaponry, however exotic, becomes scrap. Therefore serious purchases (and gifts) of U.S. weapons lock in a system of dependency. "We've got them by the spare parts," so to speak. And it doesn't matter if the weaponry is bought in cash (rare), or by loans or grants that are underwritten by one or another branch of the U.S. government, or received as a gift.

By the close of 1998, the Security Cooperation Program of the Department of Defense had made fresh sales agreements of $8.6 billion in weaponry and related services to 137 countries and international organizations. Shipments of arms during 1998 accounted for a further $13.9 billion in actual deliveries. The pipeline of orders from prior-year sales had a value of $70 billion by 1998. All of that apart from gifts from the Pentagon consisting of "drawdowns" of materiel from the stockpiles of weapons, components, and so forth. "Grant assistance" in FY 1997–1998 amounted to $3 billion.

Supplemental to all this are the Pentagon's International Military and Education and Training efforts in 118 countries, valued at about $50 million in 1998.

The Defense Security Cooperation Agency, during 1998, was supervising an accumulation of more than 15,000 foreign military sales "cases," worth about $222 billion.

Managing these programs cost $370 million in administrative expense for FY 1999. A far-flung staff must look after all this. The Defense Security Cooperation Agency headquarters required 135 people in 1998, in addition to 168 for assorted Defense Security Cooperation Agency activities. Field agencies to handle accounting and financing operations necessitated an additional 526 staff members. But by far the largest group was the implementers: 3,451 people doing the foreign military sales support work, in addition to 698 in various Security Assistance Offices "on the ground," so to speak, that help to link foreign governments and the United States.[13]

While the experts make busy, the armed forces are being freshly equipped with linked weapons systems designed for highly flexible military intervention operations. The Marine Corps has developed vehicles that make World War II beachhead operations look like something out of the Stone Age. The new amphibious technologies include base ships that carry not only troops but fuel, all manner of supplies, substantial medical facilities and helicopters as well. The same vessels serve as housing for the new brand of landing craft, which are large tracked vehicles armored on all sides and capable of "swimming" to shore and then moving on the land. Commentators have noted that this combination of capabilities makes it possible for the United States to order up beachhead operations on any shore in the world, "like dialing 911."

The half century of the Cold War included a series of U.S. interventions in wars large and small in overlapping succession, including the Korean War, Vietnam, Laos and Cambodia, Somalia, Grenada, Guatemala, Panama, Iraq/Kuwait, Bosnia and Kosovo. The drive toward sustained militarization clearly has potential implications.

The ruling establishment can be counted on to play the nationalism and racism cards. External threats, as from "rogue" states, are not difficult to publicize. The government participated in the arming of Iraq in the name of defeating Iran, then continued the "business," as Iraq was well endowed with salable oil. Only later did Iraq insist on going into business for itself by trying to absorb Kuwaiti oil. Again, Washington armed the freedom-loving rebels in Afghanistan the better to needle the Soviets. Then the former rebels discovered the joys of their own nationalism and religious fundamentalism. But even with a slip here and there, American state managers have many alternatives to choose from in their efforts to induce the appearance of nationalist threats.*

Racism has been a central option for American rulers. "Divide and rule" depends on maintaining differences in income, housing, education and, most important, jobs among the races. Race relations are being made more complicated by the immigration of more Latino and Asian populations. The conditions of life in their home countries make America seem attractive, and U.S. state managers are ever alert to the advantages of enlarging their own reserve army of low-income wage earners.

The consequences of such calculations are not always obvious, but the availability of a low-wage labor force for many industries does more than reduce the short-term wage: it also disables the mechanism by which a rising cost of labor relative to machinery prices compels increased mechanization and productivity growth. In some countries of Western Europe, clothing is produced by workers who are paid far more than those at for-

*The American people's response to the appearance of another "rogue" state has included substantial skepticism and reluctance to endorse the shedding of American blood. That reluctance has become a factor in the calculations of the senior military. Their defeat in Vietnam and the accompanying decomposition of their armies have not been forgotten, inducing caution as the military are called upon to implement the ambitions of the political managers.

eign locations of American "runaway" clothing shops. Those countries, notably Italy and England, are important clothing exporters to the United States.

It is no mystery that American citizen efforts to promote government policies of conversion from the military to the civilian economy never had a chance, for that would mean interfering with the motives of business management and of the political managers of state capitalism.

The executive branch, led by the President and his military directorate, has made it clear that neither enterprise nor economy-wide planning for economic conversion to civilian work is desired. They supported the concept of "dual-use" technology—that is, devices or methods with both military and civilian application. That followed the tested Soviet model, in which the whole industrial system was dual-use, with military primacy. Congress tagged along, as did the nonprofit foundations and international-affairs institutes, who couldn't see any sense in encouraging a policy option that the President and the Pentagon opposed.

Washington's drive for primacy will probably continue, carrying the promise of an endless succession of international crises and wars.

Despite the termination of the Cold War, the military emphasis in American public life has continued, and every federal administration of the 1990s avoided any serious contingency planning for conversion of major parts of the military economy to civilian work. The essential economic consequence involved here was neatly summarized by William Fulbright in 1989.

> Violence has become the nation's leading industry. It is not an enthusiasm for war but simple economic self-interest that has drawn millions of workers, their labor unions, and their elected representatives into the military-industrial complex. To those who build them, weapons mean prosperity, not war. For the industrialist they mean profits; for the worker, new jobs and the prospect of higher wages; and for the politician, a new installation or defense order with which to ingratiate himself with his constituents. These benefits, once enjoyed, are not easily parted with. . . .
>
> Yet this militarization of the economy is undermining us internally. Weapons are not reproductive; they are sheer nonproductive assets. They do not contribute to the welfare of the country in any positive way. On the contrary, they drain resources—human as well as material—that could be applied to

making our consumer products competitive, or to restoring all the infrastructure that has been so rapidly deteriorating: bridges, railroads, highways, water systems, and above all, our sorely neglected public educational systems.[14]

INSTITUTIONS FOR GLOBALIZATION

The U.S. government will continue to wield unequaled power by its support of and leading participation in the great international economic institutions—all headquartered in Washington, D.C.: the World Bank, the International Monetary Fund and the World Trade Organization.

The World Trade Organization was a post–World War II invention of the leading state-capitalist governments for the purpose of facilitating international trade in raw materials, agricultural products and manufactured goods. Its operating charter and detailed procedures placed no limitations on the exploitation either of the earth or of people.* Accordingly, when unions in Western Europe and the U.S. pressed for minimum wages and rights of independent worker organization in Third World nations, the political and economic chiefs of those lands objected to such barriers to free trade in the work time of their populations and in the materials that could be extracted from their soil. The state/corporate chiefs of countries like Egypt, India and Brazil were joined by their counterparts in the United States and other industrialized states.

But the advantages seen by ruling classes were not shared by many of the organized workers of the United States and Western Europe. They realized that the state/corporate partnerships were united to protect profits for the corporate managers and power for the state managers. U.S. managers have wanted the WTO for the further protection of their rights, recognized in American law: to deindustrialize the United States

*The process of state capitalism is not contained within the boundaries of the workplace. Powerful effects fan out to affect virtually every aspect of life, even the quality and content of imagination as reflected in the arts.

When a Mobilization for Global Justice was formed in 2000 to condemn the alienations that are organized, worldwide, by the World Bank, the International Monetary Fund and the World Trade Organization, the organizing flyer identified the following as main consequences from the power-wielding of these institutions:

HUNGER, FACTORY FARMING, DEFORESTATION, INCREASING
POVERTY, GENETIC ENGINEERING, CORRUPT POLITICIANS,
PLUNDERED RESOURCES, CUTS IN SOCIAL SERVICES, THE RICH
GETTING RICHER, MILITARIZATION, WAR, POLITICAL
PRISONERS, ERODING DEMOCRACY, FAMINE, GLOBAL
WARMING, LOW WAGES, SWEATSHOPS, SEXISM, RACISM

to their advantage;* to mine the soil and the seas to their advantage; to use up limited water supplies; to deforest the land; to pollute the air and generate worldwide temperature increase; to use up irreplaceable resources; to mine the finite stock of the ocean's fish; to take property rights in knowledge.

The 1999 Seattle meeting of the WTO could not function as planned because workers, environmentalists, students and political activists recognized that they were in the presence of the Great Partnership: state/corporate managers representing capitalist economies around the world. The WTO was seen as an instrument for alienation, for rendering the workers and ordinary people powerless.

The Western nations also support, as complements to the World Trade Organization, the International Monetary Fund and the World Bank. The IMF performed as financier of the post-Soviet regime to establish and sustain the new ruling class (with the title of "market economy") that joined with the government chiefs as rulers of post-Soviet state capitalism. The World Bank has wielded its considerable weight to reorganize former Communist regimes and Third World states along Western state-capitalist lines. Its participation in China is noteworthy. The World Bank's 1997 country study on China, *China's Management of the Enterprise Assets: The State as Shareholders*, examines centrally important topics for spurring reorganization of state-owned enterprises along Western corporate lines. The fieldwork for this country study occupied a top-level World Bank staff as well as China's State Commission on Restructuring the Economic System and other important Chinese government institutions.

But this report contains no reference to workers, unions or workplace democracy—or any related concept, like codetermination. The study is an exercise in design of hierarchical controls, drawing liberally on the Western state/corporate model.

At the opening of the twenty-first century, it is not possible to describe a particular form of economy that will dominate in China. Industrial development and the structure of state-managerial controls once hewed to the Soviet model, for it was Soviet technical and managerial expertise that shaped the Chinese industrial-development model. By

*During the 1970s, one of my former students reported on his interesting work. He was employed by a firm making shoes, with factories in many countries. His task was to assess the costs of production with an eye to recommending fresh capital investments in countries with ever-lower wage costs. Then, applying considerable experience in moving factories, and designing their production systems to accommodate to new and ever-lower conditions, his superiors were equipped with the knowledge needed to plan and order expansion and contraction of capital investments in pursuit of profit-maximizing combinations. In this process, the deindustrialization of the United States by closing shoemaking factories and dismissing their workers was a first step.

the close of the twentieth century, the Chinese government had embarked on a "privatization" program that included opportunities for homegrown business as well as foreign investors.*

American reporters found that China's largest household appliance maker, the Haier Group, with $3.2 billion sales in 1999, was "ultimately controlled by the city government" of Quingdao. A useful indicator of the shape of China's economy comes from Shanghai.

> Despite its free-market facade, even Shanghai's economy is less than 10 percent private. Many of the city's chrome-and-glass storefronts contain state-owned businesses or joint ventures between state-owned and foreign companies. Collectives, businesses owned by local government organizations, make up much of the rest.[15]

ECONOMIC COSTS OF STATE CAPITALISM

Media celebration of stock market prices, rising gross domestic product and get-rich-quick performance in the core economy has shielded the economic cost of America's state capitalism from public view. But the consequences won't evaporate in response to ideological incantation. Consider: What will be the consequences of unchecked state managerialism for industrial productivity?

From 1950 to 1994, U.S. industrial productivity, measured as physical industrial output per production-worker man-hour, increased almost 500 percent. The mystery is where this enormous increase in output went. It isn't in the infrastructure, which has endured poor maintenance and net decay over this half century. It isn't in the buildings we live in or use as schools, offices, community centers, theaters. It isn't in the universities, with their aging physical plant and equipment. The only other appropriately sized end use is the military. Their wars are very costly and consume vast quantities of materials.

The production system of the United States was once the base for a

*In 2001 an unusual official Chinese government report, as the *New York Times* noted, by a "top party research group and published by a Central Committee press," described "a growing pattern of large protests sometimes involving tens of thousands of people" that were becoming increasingly confrontational. As the Chinese government report observed, participation in such protests was "expanding from farmers and retired workers to include workers still on the job, individual business owners, decommissioned soldiers and even officials, teachers and students." The report is titled *China Investigation Report 2000–2001: Studies of Contradictions Among the People Under New Conditions*, and was published by the Communist Party's Central Compilation and Translation Press in June 2001. *New York Times*, June 3, 2001.

first-rate economy that was able to use productivity growth to improve capability in the means of production as well as in the infrastructure and allied qualities of life. By the 1980s, it had become clear that a far-reaching process of industrial/technological decay had been set in motion, and many industries had decomposed and even disappeared.

Thanks to development by Jon Rynn of his analysis *Why Manufacturing Matters: A Production-Centered Path to Economic Growth and Social Justice*, we now have a formidable forecast for U.S. capital-goods industries into the first quarter of the twenty-first century. He finds that "America's production machinery and capital goods industries will disappear entirely by approximately the year 2020 if present trends continue."[16]

Rynn examined the growing dependence on imports from foreign machinery-production and capital-goods industries. He studied the development of dependence on imports for these classes of machinery from 1970 to 1994. The key findings are that import dependence increased (import dependence is the value of imports divided by the value of U.S. domestic consumption).

Rynn found that "Imports as a percentage of domestic consumption [of capital goods] have been doubling approximately every 12 years since 1970 for these categories of machinery." Thus:

1970	6.4%
1980	12.7
1994	25.7

As we can see from these data, in 1970 imports made up 6.4 percent of U.S. consumption of these classes of machinery, which doubled by 1980 to 12.7 percent. The import percentage then doubled again by 1994, to 25.7 percent. At this rate, by about 2006 imports will account for 50 percent of these critical machines, and by 2020 U.S. suppliers could completely disappear, probably to be replaced mostly by those in Japan and Germany.*

What is the prognosis as the military economy continues to dominate in the use of capital resources (while spurring cost-maximizing)?

> The second-rate economy will then become progressively less manageable and the conditions of a third-rate economy will

*The fourteen production machinery industries in Rynn's analysis are: metal-cutting machine tools, metal-forming machine tools, industrial trucks and tractors, oil- and gas-field machinery, construction machinery, mining machinery, farm machinery and equipment, turbines and turbine generator sets, internal combustion engines, food products machinery, textile machinery, printing trades machinery, paper industries machinery and special-industry machinery.

> evolve. Professors John E. Ullmann and Lloyd J. Dumas have termed such a process the creation of a "Fifth World," undevelopment: lacking resources needed for repairing even key industries, and suffering a declining level of living. . . . That condition is now found in industries ranging from trolley cars to consumer electronics to shoes. As the decay spreads, then, as in an unindustrialized country, teams of workers, technicians, and managers would have to be sent abroad to acquire needed skills, or foreign staffs imported to the U.S. to train the natives.[17]

The third-rate economy is identified by an inability to repair the damage in the production system. That is now the American condition with respect to repair of basic capital-goods industries, such as machine tools, and major aspects of infrastructure, such as railroads. Thus, for example, the repair/replacement of the right of way and the rolling stock of the Long Island Rail Road, which serves a commuter population from Long Island to New York City, can no longer be ignored by simply having it serve as the butt of jokes. The plain truth now is that there is an incapability in the United States to repair or rebuild the Long Island Rail Road. There are no industrial plants, no engineer designers, no specialists in commuter railroad operations to do the work. Despite growing demand, we can expect the situation to remain the same across the economy.

As this incapacity multiplies throughout industry, the result is a production system of a third-rate economy, marked by an inability to repair the damage done to its production base, infrastructure, economy and communities. All this while affording an extravagant military and lavish living for the top 5 percent of income receivers. A dim future prospect indeed.

An outstanding demonstration of what is involved in the state-managerial campaign toward a third-rate economy is visible in the year 2000 blitz campaign by General Electric to strong-arm supplier firms for its aircraft engines to move production operations to Mexico in order to cut their prices to GE. *Business Week* (December 6, 1999) reports on Chairman Jack Welch's methods—which earned him $97 million in 1998 and his company profits of $9.3 billion, with tens of thousands of jobs lost and communities damaged.

Welch's war against unions has been undermining whole Connecticut communities. One vendor to GE says:

> "If it works for GE, you'll see it come to Pratt and Whitney," which has separately announced continued Connecticut layoffs.

> "Typically customers look to GE to set the model," notes [another] supplier. "We're already hearing about globalization from Allied Signal. They're talking about [suppliers' moving to] central Europe."

The top GE managers have become major organizers of corporate/state policies that degrade American workers.

AN INDEX OF SYSTEM INEFFICIENCY

Corporate and government managers during the twentieth century have given abundant evidence of their desire for ever more control over subordinates in every sort of organization. The cost of control can have a smothering effect on the ability of even large and technically sophisticated economies to deliver an acceptable level of living.

As I have said, in the United States there were, by 1990, 140 people in occupations that were primarily managerial and administrative (including enforcement) for every 100 in primarily production of consumer goods and services. From the U.S.S.R. we can see that when the index of system inefficiency approaches or exceeds 200:100, that's like a signal to "Man the Lifeboats!" When the Index is held below 150:100, there still may be capacity for repairing damage. But there is no certainty of that at all, for the strength of the state-managerial institutions is very great (as in the United States during the Cold War), and it may not be possible, politically, to accomplish needed production and infrastructure repair.

An overhead ratio of 40 to every 100 doing the producing work is not an unreasonable number, but see the effect if this model were followed. With such a reckoning, the size of the workforce engaged primarily in producing the goods and services of the U.S. level of living could be doubled. In that circumstance, a great multiplication of productive work could be carried out, or some part of that capacity could be applied to reducing the average hours of work per week or per year. By either reckoning, the prospect for a major improvement in the material quality of life is immediately available when there is a readiness to consider a marked reduction in the intensity of decision-process activity in the American economy.*

*Michael H. Shuman has written persuasively about this in *Going Local*, an outline for a community self-reliant perspective that includes substantial attention to what he has called "needs-driven industries" (*Going Local: Creating Self-Reliant Communities in a Global Age* [The Free Press, 1998]). In this connection, union-based investment funds along lines that have been more well developed in Canada may be an important strategic move for assembling capital resources for productive investment guided by the needs of work-

Why does this situation exist at the end of the victorious Cold War? Why does the American Index of System Inefficiency move toward a crisis—reminiscent of the dreadful Soviet collapse of the 1990s? Sustained alienation and irrational accumulation have continued to be operative. A military economy at the heart of state capitalism has been fashioned into a highly destructive, high-tech sewer that drains production capability across the board. To be sure, all this proceeds with the strong approval and helping hand from corporate managers who are beneficiaries of federal largesse. But the government chiefs are focused on a larger prize than even control over accumulated capital and lavish personal consumption for themselves and their families. For America's state/corporate managers, the prize is world hegemony.

American workers will have to confront the fact that the price of the state/corporate managers' appetite for power is a depressed level of living for them and their families.

The relentless effects of deindustrialization may also be heightened by the substantial movement of population into the United States from Third World countries. Carl Gersuny holds that "the First and Third Worlds will not so much disappear as mingle."[18] The prospect that Gersuny has proposed seems not to be taken seriously in the United States. He writes that

> The portents for the United States of its future as an underdeveloped society can be seen in the already existing and growing pockets of underdevelopment in the inner cities, in the "savage inequities" of educational institutions and in the way in which rationing by price skews the market-driven distribution of health care services. Another portent lies in the upward redistribution of income and wealth under public policies initiated by opponents of industrial and social citizenship. Finally, the slide down the slippery slope of devolution toward underdevelopment is epitomized by the warning of public health authorities that the question is not *if* but *when* cholera will break out in the poor Hispanic colonias around El Paso, Texas.[19]

That will be another cost of state capitalism.

Note that U.S. foreign aid budgets are overwhelmingly in support of military organizations—not of economic development. In combination,

---

ing people rather than the alienation-accumulation process of corporate or government managers.

the government's push for U.S.-sponsored global militarization, together with corrupt ruling classes in the Third World, guarantees a continued flow of desperate people for whom even "the poor Hispanic colonias around El Paso" spell opportunity.

Serious action that can disalienate the millions of Americans who are victims of alienation processes depends greatly on the further development of trade unionism, and particularly on the energy and skill applied to organizing younger workers.[20]

The recent developments in the health care and the university occupations carry the promise of a multiplied disalienation effect. But let's take a closer look at the nation that won the Cold War. There is:

No reduction in workweek.

No advance in wage level commensurate with rise in productivity.

No durable increase in work opportunity for the jobless.

Little effort to rescue the ghetto underclass.

Little repair of infrastructure.

No advance in education for the largest number of people. Only the public schools of the well-off produce literate students.

No relief of decay in nursing home care.

No reliable provision of food for the hungry beyond food stamp distribution.

No major effort to reduce drug addiction both within and outside of prisons.

No attempt to multiply the productiveness of U.S. industry by converting military industry to civilian work.

No decisive actions by government to remedy the condition of homelessness.

There are solid grounds for expecting that the main tendencies in the American economy that I have reviewed will continue. Consider: the depletion of production and employment in both capital and consumer goods, a growing dependency on imports, increased importation of labor, the decline of infrastructure, rising administrative overheads and parallel mechanization of work to get along with fewer "hands."

How can the United States begin to address the social costs of irrational accumulation when it remains unable to produce the resources with which to repair the damage?

Perhaps the greatest barrier by far to overcoming these and related deficiencies of American life is the continued mass presence of racist feelings and racist practice. These are a bulwark for continuing the most lamentable economic and allied alienations. Racism, like sexism, reinforces the hold of the dogma of no alternative to capitalism by checkmating solidarity and mutual trust among workers—indispensable features of progression toward workplace democracy.*

Overcoming Resistance to Disalienation

Why is it so hard to imagine a different way of organizing the workplace along democratic and disalienated lines? The social-relational approach outlined in this book offers insights into this problem that cut through the cover stories of managerialism.

For all the appeal of the idols of the marketplace, the most disabling barrier to the struggle for workplace democracy lies in the mistaken belief that workers simply are not capable of acting in this way. That's why, the managerialists say, "you'll always need us." But there is ample evidence to the contrary.

A few years ago, I sent a number of my papers to a colleague in a school of business. I had made a case for labor/worker initiatives for investment and job creation. In reply, he noted that it hadn't happened in the past, even though there were strong reasons for such initiatives; that while things seemed urgent now, the unions were weaker; that worker individualism had always been strong, and there continued to be a problem of reconciling job protection with pursuit of efficiency; that external financing was often required, and bankers may well insist on management

*Some American employers have encouraged contest between black and white workers for employment. That competition has been a lamentable part of American industrial history—from the Emancipation Proclamation to the twenty-first century, notably in the great expansion of the steel and the related transportation industries, from railroad to autos. All that played a part in the tumultuous history of American unions. The contemporary prison industry labor force, comprised of a heavily black prisoner population, is a manifestation of such contest, paying wages of $0.23 to $1.15 per hour. By June 2000, the U.S. Bureau of Justice Statistics reported 2 million U.S. prisoners, 46 percent of them black. (www.ojp.usdoj.gov/bjs/prisons.html)

The grip of racism in the early-twenty-first century labor force is illustrated by barriers keeping black and other minority workers out of construction unions and their jobs in the midst of one of the great U.S. building booms of the last century—as in New York City. See Timothy Bates and David Howell, "The Declining Status of Minorities in the New York City Construction Industry," *Economic Development Quarterly* 12, no. 1 (February 1998), pp. 88–100; see endnotes for Chapter 3 (above), and the papers by Gersuny (Selected Bibliography).

structures and efficiency that are incompatible with true worker control. Finally, he noted that most employee pension funds were not even subject to worker control; and while employee organization of work was a good idea and was worth encouraging, he was not optimistic that it could happen here on any substantial scale.

We have already seen that during the Cold War the main announced alternatives, endlessly repeated, for the organization of economy and society were the market economy and Soviet communism. Now only the market remains, and it seems we've reached the end of history.

I hope I have avoided that simplistic and muddled understanding by focusing on the ways of decision-making on production, by which the corporate and state managerial rules are readily defined and separated from the contrasting worker rules. By this method, the social-relational core of corporate/state managerialism can be contrasted with that of worker decision-making on production.

In this framework, there is no "end of history." When we focus on managerial rules, it is clear that the false alternatives of either the market economy or communism were a form of misrepresentation: in fact, when it comes to questions of decision power, those two supposedly contradictory modes proved to have similar characteristics.

There are more obstacles to overcome. Consider a possible situation in which reindustrializaion was an important economy-wide option for the United States. In such an event, restrictions on knowledge in the name of intellectual property rights would be barriers to the conduct of both basic and applied research. Reindustrialization would require acceleration of every aspect of research and design if the handicaps caused by deindustrialization were to be overcome.

The heritage of the military economy was visible in the failed attempt by the Boeing company to build light-rail electric vehicles for Boston and San Francisco. That operation defined the technological limits that derived from military aerospace technology applied to civilian public transportation.* The grim account is an example of the need for openness rather than intellectual property restrictions if a competent industrial base is ever to be established for designing and building new means of production.

There is also a failure in what passes for scholarly literature to account for the vital role of industrial production and the centrality of the machinery-producing industries. Wherever cooperative organization of production is reported, however large and successful and sustained, it is typically put down as an "experiment." With such ideas firmly embedded, it is only a short step to believing that money equals wealth. (You ask the

*See Seymour Melman, *Profits Without Production* (Alfred Knopf, 1988), pp. 253–59.

small child, Where does our milk come from? And he/she answers, From the supermarket refrigerator.)

In December 1988, John Kenneth Galbraith addressed these kinds of failure of understanding at the annual meeting of the Association for Evolutionary Economics.

> Neoclassical economics as now taught—I do not exaggerate—comes perilously close to being a design for concealing the reality of political and social life from successive generations of students. Were the latter exposed to the reality, their later political attitudes, those of some at least, would, at a minimum, be politically inconvenient.[21]

Galbraith's point applies to the instruction given in the universities and other schools that directly or tacitly offer the market economy as the sufficient and sensible way to organize economic life. Successive generations of students are trained to adhere to the economic and political status quo of state capitalism.

The ideology of the market economy is usually recycled in the media in terms that best serve the corporate and state managers. These include reports that portray factory closures and downsizing as ordinary parts of industrial life, or huge CEO salaries justified by advancing (or declining) stock prices or profits.

Universities are the means of production for the next generations of skilled workers. They are also the location of much direct research—basic and applied—developing new knowledge from the basic sciences to elaboration of particular technologies and their application. That is why it is important, in ways that many may not suspect, that in schools America's economy is cast in the static conditions of the "market," with little discussion of economic or institutional alternatives. The emphasis in economics courses is on the characteristics of the profit-making company. They tend to ignore anything that doesn't fit this complacent picture. Omitted, for example, is the question: Why are about 50 percent of start-up companies economic failures?

Workplace Democracy Enables Stable Operations and Advances in Productivity of Capital

Labor productivity has long been the main focus of attention for gauging the "efficiency" of operations. As wages become a diminishing part of production cost, however, as against the growing weight of machinery outlays, it is the productivity of the "capital" inputs that grows as part of total cost.

Workplace democracy can be of ever greater importance in the economics of production, because worker decision-making affords the most effective conditions for productivity of capital.

Under business rule, pressing workers for greater exertion is a central idea for reducing costs. Actually, as the value of machinery tends to dominate the economics of industrial production, lowering the cost of each unit produced is heavily affected by the total time of machine working, by stabilizing the rate of working, by reducing defective output and by minimizing unscheduled interruption. This concept is best fulfilled by a disalienated workforce.

Several lines of evidence support the expectation that a workplace-democracy production system would tend to stabilize operations, not only at the plant level but for a multiplant system as a whole. Evidence of a stable production process resulting from workplace-democracy procedures comes from two directions: first, the experience of both single-worker and small-group operations, and second, the evidence from large industrial firm and plant operations.

The effects of stable production rates on the productivity of both labor and capital were spelled out early on by Sebastian B. Littauer[22] and by his student Adam Abruzzi. The cooperative environment that is an inevitable part of a mutual decision-making operation facilitates stable operation rates, which, in turn, optimize productivity of both labor and capital under a given set of conditions.

There are by now many significant demonstrations of the stability of production operations in an enterprise brought on by worker decision-making (as shown by Bernard Nneji, in Chapter 7, and the two kibbutz-located factories, in Chapter 11). What is striking is that the nature of the operations performed is unaltered, as is the design of the machines. What is changed is the maintenance attention given by the production workers to the operation of machines, the care given to the adjustment of the machines and worker attention to uncovering and correcting sources of possible defects.

Because an interest in maintaining employment and income is a fundamental characteristic of worker decision-making, the downsizings that have shattered the lives of millions could be replaced by sustained employment and orderly conversion processes, when changes are necessary. During 1993, about 42 percent of the workers at small, medium and large companies reported "they are at companies undergoing downsizing or permanent work force reductions. At large companies, more than half the workers have been in the midst of downsizing, and 40% also report cuts in the number of managers."[23]

It is pertinent to recall a set of recommendations formulated by W. Edwards Deming. Deming's fourteen points for "Improvement of

Quality and Productivity Through Action by Management" deserve careful attention. Deming is the statistician/industrial engineer whose methods have been highly regarded in Japanese industry and society, where a "Deming Award" is one of the highest honors that can be accorded an industrial management. But an examination of Deming's argument, as well as the content of "The Fourteen Obligations of Top Management," suggest that the state/corporate managers of American industry, with their commitment to profit and power, are restrained from taking advantage of Deming's recommendations for improvement of quality and productivity.[24]

Reindustrialization

Once workers and their unions realize that the government, with its powerful alliance with corporate management, is driven to alienate and accumulate power, and to pursue deindustrialization as a central policy, they will see, as a matter of urgency, that ways must be found to marshal general community support, as well as the support of trade unions, for job-creating investments in productive enterprises.

Up to the present, the carpenters' and allied building-trade unions have been the major U.S. labor organizations to pursue a significant effort to influence the finance capital of their own industry.

The AFL-CIO as a whole, however, has yet to embark on an effort along the lines, for example, of the labor-sponsored Investment Funds in Canada.

A union-initiated capital investment fund would open up new possibilities. Take the case of Springfield, Vermont, where the citizens in September 1999 voted 2,345 to 1,535 in favor of accepting a state proposal and subsidy for building a new 350-bed prison. Why? "Springfield, once an important center of machine tool manufacturing, has been economically depressed for many years, and the state's offer of $7 million in incentives for allowing the prison to be built nearby proved to be attractive."[25] Too attractive, we might say—subordinating the community's interests to those of the prison-industrial complex. Similarly attractive proposals have been fielded from coast to coast, wherever a high-quality workforce is rendered unemployed and powerless by deindustrialization in an environment without similar alternative work. That is a signal for economic decay to thrive—in this case, prison work with a future—as the United States sports the world's second-highest incarceration rate (Russia is number one).

Contributing Toward a Way Out

Both white- and blue-collar workers have a special opportunity to help extricate themselves and their communities from state capitalism. Whether so designated or not, they can be effective role models and teachers to help shape the next generation. They have responsibilities to tell the truth about the working of the American economy and society; to unravel the trained incapacities that are produced by the cover stories; to explain how conventional ideologies can warp our senses, like looking through a lens that distorts incoming images;[26] to disclose the shape of alternatives to state managerialism that has been part of the American experience; to explain how mutual trust can replace distrust and predatory competition as guideposts to behavior.

It is essential to disclose the pain and destructiveness that have been the by-product of the ever larger appetite for power that is embedded in the mechanisms that guide corporate and public policy.

Is managerialist, hierarchical decision-making made essential by technology or large human communities? Technology is what we make of it. It is inanimate. Decision-making—a social-relational matter—is what selects the criteria that govern the design of production processes and goods.

How much of the decision-making of an enterprise can workers, apart from the top managers, accomplish? I gave considerable evidence in my *Decision Making and Productivity* (1958), showing that workers and their shop stewards, technicians, engineers and office staffs were actively engaged in communication with their counterparts in other firms, and were well informed on the interactive functioning of the company, with others in their industry.

Is mutual decision-making about work feasible for white-collar and professional occupations? The American Association of University Professors has been a union agent for many professors and university staffs. Engineers, technicians and office staff are included in the workforce of the Daimler Chrysler Corporation, and a UAW membership has existed for many of them. Local unions of university faculty are part of the wider union collective-bargaining groups in diverse industries.

Because of the long history of alienated rule, it should be no surprise to find, amid the educated occupations, people who seek power-wielding careers. Some who are endowed with such ambition may even see themselves as bearing a moral right to use political power on behalf of or in the name of the workers. A part of that tradition might be inferred from what Karl Marx had to say in a section of "The Inaugural Address of the Working Man's International Association" in 1864.

> To save the industrious masses, cooperative labor ought to be developed to national dimensions, and consequently to be fostered by national means. . . . To conquer political power has therefore become the great duty of the working classes.[27]

When those who "conquer political power" take over the operation of state management, would they be other than operators of state management? Considerable evidence suggests it is not likely. State managements operate by rules of hierarchy, not democratic consensus. Competition for decision power is a core operating method, built into the job performance of the staff—far removed from the rules of cooperation, consensus and solidarity and the values of mutual trust.* Such rules are antithetical to predatory competition and to the exploitation that has been so serviceable for extension of managerial power.

The promise of seizing political power on behalf of or in the name of workers was the grand design called Bolshevism, and its consequences as Stalinism are well known.

Blue- and white-collar workers alike know that they have only a limited stock of models and experience for teaching rules of behavior that support mutual trust and democratic decision-making. And yet, and yet . . . as Noam Chomsky writes:

> I would like to believe that people have an instinct for freedom, that they really want to control their own affairs. They don't want to be pushed around, ordered, oppressed, etc., and they want a chance to do things that make sense, like constructive work in a way that they control, or maybe control together with others. I don't know any way to prove this. It's really a hope about what human beings are like—a hope that if social structures change sufficiently, those aspects of human nature will be realized.[28]

*"Trust is the belief or confidence in honesty, integrity, reliability and justice of other people" (Giora Yanai, of Kibbutz Ein Hashofet, Israel).

CONCLUSION

An Exit Path from Capitalism to Workplace Democracy

"The terrible truth [is] that there is and can be no alternative to capitalism."

—DAVID MARQUAND*

Capitalism is in the process of transformation toward an economy based on workplace democracy. That is the main finding of this investigation into the ways decision-making on production by corporate and state managers, and by workers and their unions, is evolving.

By the middle of the twentieth century, the managers of American business and American government had discovered large areas of common ground. Accordingly, the U.S. side of the half-century-long Cold War was organized and executed by an unprecedented partnership.

The new partnership of corporate and state managers created a network of institutions that redefined the U.S. economy as state capitalism. Production was geared toward the accumulation of profit and power as a joint project of the central offices of corporations and government. Indeed, government became the site of the largest business/political control center of all, the Pentagon's management of military activities and allied industrial and finance activities, reporting directly to its Chief Executive Officer in the White House.

Formal alliances of corporate/government managers in pursuit of victory in the Cold War enabled them to marshal the Congress and judiciary effectively to amend and reinterpret the Wagner Act of 1935 so as to limit the powers of unions. Thereafter, the Wagner Act grant of a right to form unions was abridged by management's refusal to agree with unions on the contents of proposed contracts (as we saw in Part IV).

**Times Literary Supplement*, July 14, 2000, "Review of Edmund Dell, *A Strange Eventful History* (HarperCollins, 2000)."

State capitalist managers thus drew, and continue to draw, upon the centuries-long experience, whereby the accumulation of profits and power has been spurred by alienating (weakening) workers and competitors. In the Introduction to this book, I state that "The psychological reactions that often accompany alienation are not dealt with here." I would be remiss, however, if I failed to note at least in general terms that alienating acts, especially when repeated, can induce depression and paralysis, and hence an inability to act that freezes powerlessness in place. Business and labor history includes a record of alienations that spurred the capital accumulation that continues to define the American economy for the twenty-first century (Part II).

American workers—blue- and white-collar—have been discovering the merits of solidarity and learning the ways of workplace democracy in their own jobs and unions. Though U.S. unions have suffered from government and managerial manipulation, and the corrosive effects of internal criminal activity, they still represent a crucial self-liberating institution.

Deindustrialization and Militarism: A Concerted Stategy

Probably the most decisive alienation practice in the U.S. managerial arsenal has been deindustrialization. Closing industrial and allied facilities in the United States, transferring capital resources and production to foreign, preferably nonunion sites, has weakened industrial employment prospects in the United States, creating many "ghost" towns and weakening unions in relation to managers who are frequently allied to powerful government institutions.

Nevertheless, both unionized workers and nonunion workers pursued disalienation by all manner of devices, so that by 1999, with some 14 percent of "private-sector" workers in unions, a further 30 percent of the nongovernment U.S. workforce declared that they wish to be represented by a union.* Who are the third of nonunionized American workers who want to be represented by a union? In their recent study, Richard B. Freeman and Joel Rogers found that

> The workers who want a union but do not have one receive lower wages, are disproportionately black, report particularly poor

*"Despite the widely publicized flaws of unions and the unease that many members feel about the role of unions on the national scene, 44 percent of private-sector American workers would like to be represented by a union, more than three times the 14 percent share of our sample who reported union membership. . . . As far as our evidence goes, the main reason these workers are not unionized is that the managements of their firms do not want them to be represented by a union" (Richard B. Freeman and Joel Rogers, *What Workers Want* [Cornell University Press, 1999], p. 89).

> labor-management relations at their workplace, and have similar attitudes toward the independence of any workplace organization as union members. In short, they seem to be just the sort of folks who could truly benefit from union representation.[1]

The deindustrialization processes that restrained unionization by American workers have been paralleled by a militarization that has been preempting technically trained parts of the labor force and uncounted quantities of material goods. So long as workers within the military economy view themselves as citizens rather than employees of an alienation machine, they remain trapped, unable to join their civilian counterparts in the struggle for disalienation. Until workers address the need for economic conversion, they stay enmeshed in the global ambitions of the state and corporate managers, with the accompanying prospect of supporting wars abroad.

America's militarized corporate/state managers have seen to it that efforts in government (and in the "civilian" economy) to sponsor planning for economic conversions were halted. Government officials who supported such moves were cashiered (notably Speaker Jim Wright, Chapter 5), and nongovernmental efforts had their budgetary support withdrawn by formally private foundations.

Meanwhile, insecurity for workers was intensified during the half century of Cold War by the alienations of downsizing. Conditions of security, secrecy and hazardous working conditions made life inside the military economy worst of all. Little has changed since. Longer hours, multiple job-holding and lower-income positions have become the lot of many downsized workers as they try desperately to maintain their incomes. The income gap between workers on the one hand and CEOs and finance professionals on the other has become larger than ever. It is against this background that we can best understand the disalienation countermoves by blue- and white-collar workers.

The same alienation strategies also held down U.S. wages, while imports from capital-intensive foreign producers of both capital and consumer goods rose, despite the fact that these producers were paying higher than U.S. wages. At the same time, consumer goods, such as clothing and shoes, that lend themselves to labor-intensive operations have often been transferred to barely developed economies where governments are committed to preventing independent unionization.

Deindustrialization has proceeded so far as to make a major repair of U.S. industry and infrastructure problematic to unfeasible. As we have seen, that is a key characteristic of a third-rate economy (Chapter 3).

Yet on the workers' side, successive waves of alienation have produced concerted moves toward disalienation and workplace democracy (chapters 9, 10, 11).

The scope of the workers' decision-rules is constantly expanding. Rules first developed to cope with work performance have led to interest in the sources and quality of machines, tools and materials from other firms and industries. Concern with income security has also caused unions to participate in the marketing function.

Workers' unions, weakened by corporate/state offensives during the Cold War, have not been able to halt the employers' alienation operations by deindustrialization and the accompanying drive for capital and power accumulation outside the United States that is called globalization.

Nevertheless, the potential of unions to lead reindustrialization in the United States has only been partly explored. Thus the possible local, regional and economy-wide applications of labor-sponsored investment funds to the U.S. scene have still to be defined.

The White Collars Respond to Alienation

By the opening of the twenty-first century, it was evident that the parade of white-collar workers joining the blues had barely begun.

America's universities and their linked research institutions became a new frontier for alienation-accumulation operations. The corporations of research-based industries sought out connections with universities and other research centers in order to obtain preferred access to new knowledge that could be the basis for fresh accumulations of profits/power. Their researchers and supporting staffs produce knowledge in the arts and sciences that has financial value when commercially exploited. That is why the chiefs of research institutes and university administrators, with solid support from the government, have developed detailed techniques for treating knowledge as property.

The corporate interest in knowledge as property is being translated swiftly into an agenda of controls over the research occupations, who are the primary creators and bearers of new knowledge and of the means of their production. Consider the functions being targeted for managerial control in various universities and other research institutions: selecting topics for research; choosing coworkers for research; securing resources (money, facilities, equipment); sharing techniques and equipment for research; discussing work in progress; publishing and otherwise announcing research findings. This new alienation campaign promises to transform university workers' occupations for the worse by early in the twenty-first century. Union representatives are notably absent from university boards of trustees.

The further effects from treating knowledge as property are far-reaching, for they tend to be ultimately counterproductive. As early as 1958, a study called *Impact of Patents on Research* found that "there is a growing disharmony between the efficient production of new technical knowledge and the effort, through the patent system, to treat that knowledge under property relations."[2]

When producers' knowledge is treated as property, as part of an investment base for accumulation of profit/power, then managerial controls are applied to regulate the production of knowledge—that is, the behavior of researchers and supporting staffs. But as in other white-collar occupations, the introduction of managerial controls over aspects of once "independent" callings will set in motion the familiar countermoves of disalienation. The new economy will bring whole new sectors of the workforce into the struggle for workplace democracy.

Cover Stories That Conceal

Cover stories conceal the characteristics of the employment relation and, above all, the alienating changes that are taking place. Textbooks, news reports, opinions of print and other media journalists treat economic events as though part of a storybook about market competition. That is why so much of the information and analyses in this study may come as a disconcerting surprise to some readers.

The social costs of state capitalism, especially deindustrialization and infrastructure decay, are unmentionable in polite society. Military sales by the state/corporate marketing and military training apparatus are rarely described. Neither is the role of the government spelled out (of the Pentagon, Treasury and State Department teams).*

The agendas of state/corporate managers are concealed from the workers who finally pay the bill. That concealment is the great service provided by the cover stories about their rule: money is wealth; economic growth equals the sum of money-valued goods and services (including nuclear overkill, the prison-industrial complex, gambling); exchange relations (a.k.a. The Market) govern production; the United States can afford guns and butter without limit; corporate managers are merely the executors of market-based decisions; people are paid according to the money value that they produce; state managers are elected and hence

*The following studies by Noam Chomsky provide sophisticated analyses of conventional cover stories for American state capitalism: *The New Military Humanism* (South End Press, 1999), *Profit Over People* (7 Stories Press, 1998), *World Orders Old and New* (Columbia University Press, 1996).

implement the people's will; only through unhindered "globalism" can the processes of foreign capital investment and trade make the blessings of market economy available to others.

All of these cover stories for generating powerlessness can be summed up in the doctrines of neoliberalism: a condensation of managerial, market-economy and capitalist values. In the neoliberal view, maximum freedom for each person can be ensured by minimizing the functions, powers and resources of community—and finally, of the state—while leaving all residual capability to the individual. Yet as we saw in Part II, the single largest function of government, the military department, has been singularly exempted from such minimalist critiques of "big" government. Neoliberalism also assigns responsibility for the vital functions of medical care, nutrition, education of children and housing to the individual. When individual resources are insufficient, then neighbors, churches and the surrounding community should take charge. But what if the whole neighborhood suffers from a lack of resources—human and other—to cope with human breakdown? That, in the neoconservative view, is the price of individual liberty—well worth paying.*

But the neoliberal does not stand alone. He/she relates to others by the most efficient mechanism and rules: The Market. Free from state controls, The Market decides on production and allocates goods with infallible efficiency—in accordance, as we have seen, with theories that have little connection with the real world. Nevertheless, the dogmas of neoliberalism have produced widespread approval for employers' resistance to worker decision-making. When successful, that has made workers unable to participate in the struggle for solidarity and mutual trust, which enables them, acting together, to disalienate, to build workplace democracy. Indeed, "the ultimate trump card for the defenders of neoliberalism . . . is that there is no alternative."[3]

As I draw on the data and logic of this book, my judgment is: not anymore. Workplace democracy is the name for a new economy that follows capitalism.

The Core Values of Workplace Democracy

What is the prospect for the types of actions discussed in this book?

I have tried to outline the linkages that bind the struggle of both

*"Neoliberal democracy, with its notion of the market *über alles*, takes dead aim at [society]. . . . Instead of citizens, it produces consumers. Instead of communities, it produces shopping malls. The net result is an atomized society of disengaged individuals who feel demoralized and socially powerless" (Robert W. McChesney, Introduction to Noam Chomsky's *Profit Over People* [7 Stories Press, 1999], p. 11).

white- and blue-collar workers for a voice in deciding the conditions of their working lives, the rules of such worker efforts and, in turn, the ways workers support workplace democracy. Four main elements are involved:

Disalienated decision-making means that whoever finally decides that something be done is also the person (or persons) who does the work (as in Chapter 9). This contrasts with the managerialist mode of decision-making on production that separates decisions from implementation and automatically installs and elaborates hierarchy.

Solidarity among workers includes having common social goals and values and having mutually agreed procedures for decision-making and for resolving disputes, while sharing mutual trust. All this in contrast to predatory competition for accumulation.

What exactly is *mutual trust*? Mutual trust among workers is a shared belief (or confidence) in the honesty, integrity, reliability and justness of the men and women with whom decision-making is shared.

Last, worker decision-making promotes *equality*. Here, equality refers to the impartiality of rules and procedures that govern decision-making relations among workers.

Make no mistake: These characteristics are not to be confused with sainthood. They are practical and feasible ways of behaving among workers of diverse industries and callings. But it does take some learning: the lessons of workplace democracy are probably most effectively grasped by engaging in some part of the worker decision process. It takes time—and patience—not only to arrive at consensus among members of a worker group but also to do some unlearning. The unlearning may well include all-too-familiar behaviors taught (and followed) in the name of "success" within a management hierarchy, and in a wider society that has taught its people that the election of candidates to government posts is the main way to affect government policies at all levels.

Actually, Americans are quite skeptical about the feasibility of getting things done by national electoral (and party) politics. By 1996, less than 50 percent of the voting population were casting votes in the election for President, and only 45.8 percent were voting for representatives to Congress.[4] Many Americans are less inclined than ever to rely on the electoral process. In contrast to this apathy is the widespread interest in unionization revealed by recent surveys of American workers (Freeman and Rogers), of whom, as we have seen, 44 percent would readily seek union representation given the opportunity.

Many readers will be familiar with the habits of mind to be unlearned on the route to workplace democracy: the insistence on primary self-identification as an "individual" rather than as part of a congenial group; holding on to the competition rule that one's gain is real only when accompanied by another's loss; insistence that ability should be recognized in the form of hierarchical rights; and the widespread suspicion of the idea of uniformly graded compensation. Most of all, prospective members of a worker decision group must learn ways of mutual trust, an indispensable part of the solidarity that is at the core of worker empowerment.

Even the design of technologies for production will begin to take on new characteristics under a disalienated worker-decision process. The organization of work is a part of production technology altered by workplace democracy, with its cooperating traditions in both decision-making and in work performance. The effects of these traditions can be seen in the improvement of product quality in the factories of Tama and Netafim (Chapter 11) and in their marked reduction in unscheduled "downtime" of their production machinery, as well as the computer-controlled machining operations diagnosed by Nneji (Chapter 7). These are benefits reaped from production carried out by cooperating workers in groups where everyone shares in decision-making.

Characteristically, a reduction in the variability of output rates is accompanied by fewer defective products, less unscheduled "downtime" and increased machine output per hour. The latter result is crucial, for it means increased productivity of capital. This is a crucial secret advantage of workplace democracy.

The "productivity of capital" has not received sufficient attention from managers, for whom the reduction of worker time per product—by downsizing or exporting jobs—has seemed to offer the most important opportunity for cost reduction. In reality, recent decades have seen steady reduction in the importance of wages as a part of the cost of manufactured goods. Thus in 1958 production worker wages were 15 cents of each dollar's worth of U.S. industrial shipments. By 1996, worker wages were 9 cents per dollar of U.S. manufactured goods. So while holding down wage growth (but not CEO salaries) is hailed as a victory against inflation at the Federal Reserve Board, the fact is that workers' wages have been a steadily diminishing part of industrial production costs. But holding down workers' wages is a recognized, twenty-first-century way of bashing both the blue and white collars.

To be sure, increasing the output per unit of machine time (capital productivity) automatically spells increased output per worker. And it makes a big difference if formal attention is given to capital productivity and to the organization of production factors that control its change.*

*Business managers who operate in the traditional hierarchical manner may try to capture the full effects of computer control of production operations. But they can't in the absence of the cooperation that is ordinarily feasible under workplace democracy controls.

In a workplace-democracy enterprise, attention is also given to comfort and safety in the industrial workplace, as is customary elsewhere, notably in Sweden. High-tech tools—machines for producing consumer and other goods—will be increasingly designed with priority to the well-being of the workers who use them, as well as serving the productivity of the enterprise. Similarly, vital community functions like the education of children will be reshaped to be consistent with the core values of workplace democracy—to foster the values of community beyond capitalism.

The Future of Workplace Democracy

Despite the relentless deindustrialization unleashed by the state/corporate managers, the scope of the workers' decision process will continue to expand as white-collar workers continue to identify with blue-collar workers. Most important, the workers' decision process is becoming increasingly interconnected with the rest of economy. In the face of the managerial pursuit of alienation and short-term financial gain, and the widespread dogma about worker limitations, workers have set standards (i.e., rules) for their own production work. Employees in the automotive industries have, for example, focused attention on the resources (tools, machines, power, materials) whose timely availability at the desired quantity and quality is essential for production operations. By reaching out to the other parts of the economy that support production, they expand the range and potential for workplace democracy.

These interlinking aspects of the worker decision-making process will expand with the inclusion of more white-collar occupations within the framework of workplace democracy. We can confidently predict that these changes in the employment relation of workers to both corporate and state managers will only accelerate in future decades.

In such an environment, many workers may want to review their long-standing reliance for livelihood on Pentagon orders and management's financial goals, with the accompanying pressures for loyalty to state/corporate policies. Despite the rhetoric of a "postindustrial" or "information" society, the United States, like any economy, still needs production. Necessary prospects for alternative production work and markets include the whole range of capital and "heavy" consumer goods such as railroads and light-rail vehicles. These are in ever greater demand in America, while there are, at most, only a handful of U.S. facilities, engineers and production workers trained for this work—which leaves these

---

Managers may try to offset this deficiency by moving production to low-wage locations where other problems may be endemic, such as an uneducated labor force.

vital goods to be "bought in."[5] Meanwhile, the state/corporate managers' deindustrialization campaign relentlessly proceeds.

I have ventured some estimates of the further course of changes in production relations and some prospective consequences for the organizing of society. Unions are central to the future of workplace democracy worldwide. American unions have begun to revise their automatic support for state and managerial policies into which they were trained during the half century of Cold War. But there is much work to be done.

New organizing departures are likely to strengthen the AFL-CIO structure: a focus on organizing the lowest-paid workers, especially in service occupations and agribusiness, and on the surge of white-collar organizing, including schoolteachers, doctors, nurses, social workers, university instructors and professors, technologists and engineers.

Unionism among the lowest-paid (often immigrant and minority workers) is crucial, especially in boom times: it relieves the pressure that holds down worker wages across the board even while formally measured unemployment is low. White-collar recruits to the workers' community should, in turn, be able to take a lead in debunking the cover stories that shield corporate/state operations.

Indeed, the surge of unionism among white-collar occupations also builds self-confidence. The victory of the newly unionized Boeing engineers opened the year 2000 (as we saw in Chapter 10). They marshaled their colleagues for a display of solidarity and drew confidence. For the larger engineering community, the message was: If the Boeing engineers can do it, why can't we?

The proposed merger of the machinist, steel and auto unions would also open up larger prospects for reversing the state/corporate deindustrialization drive of the Cold War. The strength of such a combination could encourage attention to reindustrialization initiatives in the United States—initiatives like technology training programs in community colleges, German-style apprenticeship training at the high school level, attention to training high-caliber production engineers in American colleges and the launching of U.S. versions of the highly successful labor-sponsored investment funds of Canada (see Chapter 11).

Following these leads, workers in every industry and service will increasingly formulate proposals for investment in product design and production systems that counter alienation-by-deindustrialization. They will increasingly act to modernize and improve their work and their products. For the disalienation of their working lives will encourage such attention, just as doctors and teachers have emphasized their interest and concern with improving the quality and effectiveness of their respective practices and institutions.

What can workers and their unions do when top managers press their deindustrialization policies? At that point the relationship with management is political. For the deindustrialization strategy promises not only to damage workers' families but also to demolish communities and create "ghost towns." A "political" policy is in order, with unions mobilizing entire communities to stop the deindustrialization. Union-based capital investment funds can play an important part, as would the capabilities of a combined "metal" union (auto + steel + machinists).

Capital for new and small–medium enterprises can become increasingly available from worker-controlled investment funds. The potential for production forgone because of irrational accumulation and a permanent war economy can be translatable into capital investment programs that improve the quality of life. All this can be a direct counter to the corporate/state campaign for deindustrialization.

None of these organized worker initiatives depend on transforming the top corporate managers or their organizations. Neither must worker initiatives depend on the federal government's managers or legislators undergoing a transformation: withdrawing from their partnership with business or giving up pursuit of irrational accumulation without limit by military and finance methods. (Recall that the great shift from feudalism to capitalism involved transformation of the economy "from above" as the lords of the manor became managers.) The workers' initiatives are based upon disalienation at the workplace, combined with solidarity initiatives that organize production outside of managerialism and deindustrialization. They are transforming state capitalism "from below."

What Is in Prospect?

The struggle for disalienation in manufacturing and service occupations of every sort will continue. The word will get out, everywhere. If industrial workers, doctors, psychologists, clinical social workers, engineers, schoolteachers and professors can do it, why can't we? No productive branch of the economy will be exempt from movements to empower the people doing the work. Who is eligible? Every occupation that contributes to production, transportation, communication.

Furthermore, as the disalienating moves spread, they will focus attention on a fairer distribution of the fruits now used up by the vast array of decision-process activities. This will encourage moves to deflate the corporate and military-based processes of power accumulation. Workplace democracy can best thrive in a demilitarized economy.

Economic conversion of industries and occupations currently locked into the military economy will become an increasingly important process. Conversion will accomplish two linked objectives: retraining people toward productive work, and redesigning entire enterprises so that they can themselves design and produce consumption goods and services.

From the vantage point of workplace democracy, little is gained by disalienating a workplace that is dedicated to manufactuing destruction—whether a factory, school or research facility.

Conversions of occupations and industries will be well within the scope of their worker groups. For they will be able to draw upon the willing cooperation of other industrial workers, as well as the talents of their own engineers, scientists and cooperating academic specialists.

What will happen to big government after state capitalism? As we have seen, currently the largest part of the federal government is dedicated to military priorities. Half of the vast federal budget is absorbed by the military. Economic conversion will not only release the resources needed to fix up the distressed parts of the U.S. economy and society, it will also deflate the military economy.

Income standards will also be reconsidered, as will hours of work, the work year and the length of the working life. Starting from presently agreed-upon compensation, there will be the prospect of narrowing the vast inequalities in income. By boosting the prevailing minimum wage to living wages, upward compression of compensation could also yield a feasible top-level cutoff of, say, an agreed multiple of a base income. A schedule of income changes would have to take into account not only social values but also the availability to communities of large fixed-cost facilities like hospitals or universities.

What will happen to the stores and firms that produce consumer goods and services? The main shops, stores, services, malls, banks, hotels, communication systems and transportation systems will continue, even as they are modified by extending the rule of workplace democracy within each enterprise. Some institutions, like the financial-securities industry in Wall Street, may suffer from disuse, for the personal-income anxieties fostered by state capitalism, and its costly processes of irrational accumulation, will decline. Shops and services whose style caters to the superrich will suffer contraction as part of their traditional clientele uses up their surplus cash.

These processes of disalienation will slow, and then reverse, the concentration of capital accumulation by and for the top percentiles of the population. Personal use of money and property can stand, like everything else that is part of consumption: they will not disappear, though the inequalities that I have discussed will be addressed. The key issue here is that within capitalism the property right with respect to money is a social relation, which, especially in the case of vast fortunes, can be readily used for capital investing. This ability of the super rich to control the means of production is further enabled by the employment relation, which separates the decision-making and producing occupations. Such concentrations of capital and decision power make it much easier for the very rich to accumulate further profits and power.

But workplace democracy can take the crucial step of linking decision-making with production. Under these new rules, the pressure of money alone will not allow individuals, even the very wealthy, to control the decisions of their employees, for offers of payment in return for creating the means of production—which the individual investor seeks to control under the rules of managerialism—are invalid within the rules of workplace democracy. However much money or capital they can wield, the money owners are still outside the loop of a process that connects worker decision-making with production.

During the sit-down strikes of the 1930s in the automobile industry, the auto workers turned down management's proposal of money in return for going back to work. Why, even during the Depression, did they refuse? Because the managers' offer lay outside the loop of the workers' decision process. Production began again only after management formally recognized workers' representatives, and proceeded to bargain with the union on their terms of employment.

During capitalist development there is bound to be attention paid to the splashy accumulation of homes or yachts by single people or families. (How many cars can you ride in at once? How many shoes can you wear?) In addition, the well-advertised presence of a growing number of billionaires in the United States will probably provoke proposals for a tax on assets, which could cause no personal hardship among the wealthy community. Local governments will surely confront situations requiring some infringement on private property rights in order to carry out important actions for a wider community, such as sequestering land in order to provide clean water. As we saw in Chapter 11, there is precedent for such purposes in the law on the power of eminent domain.

None of this is to say that this process of transformation to a significantly less alienated, less exploitative economy and society will proceed without friction or pain. But the gains from democratic, and less alienated, working and living are likely to outweigh—for the greatest number of people—the friction or hardships that may be entailed.

Workplace democracy will slow, then reverse, alienation processes, bringing the deindustrialization operations of the state/corporate managers to an end. The managerialist dogma that fear promotes efficiency will have had its day. As the values of workplace democracy permeate people's livelihood and the surrounding community, the wave of alienation will recede and the quality of life will begin to transform in ways appropriate for a self-governing productive community.

Redesigning Work, Rebuilding Community

Progress in workplace democracy will open ways for altering the occupations not only of production workers and engineers but also of managers themselves. To be sure, when workers make decisions about their work preferences, they are thereby making decisions on production. Thus it is conceivable that production workers be deployed to use part of their time in administrative work that is necessary for production, including "external" tasks, like marketing.

Similarly, the jobs of administrators can be modified to include a quota of time on production tasks—say, for one day of each week. These tasks could range from work in direct production to maintaining machines for office operations. There is a prospective gain here both for production and for administrative workers. They would each have a part in a range of necessary work, thereby reducing the alienating habits of hierarchy that include assigning a lower status to work that is, nevertheless, productionally necessary.

It is worth emphasizing that the coercive quality of hierarchy will be altered as administrative posts and production tasks are rotated and intermixed.

In the course of all this a discovery could be made. Despite their long training in predatory competition, many employees will seize the opportunity to contribute knowledge and time to what they see is part of the common good, for experience with mutual trust will be found to be a great healer of the scars of competition. Workers participating in joint actions for disalienation will experience a kind of mutual well-being that Hannah Arendt described as "public happiness."* Expanding on Arendt's idea, C. Douglas Lummis writes:

*Hannah Arendt, *On Revolution* (Viking Press, 1963). See Chapter 3, "The Pursuit of Happiness." Arendt includes analyses of the political philosophy of Thomas Jefferson and his associates. In particular, Arendt assesses the role of public happiness "as a desire for some kind of freedom which the 'free inhabitants' of the mother country did not enjoy. The freedom, they called later, when they had come to taste it, 'public happiness,' and it consisted in the citizen's right . . . to be a 'participator in the government of affairs' in Jefferson's telling phrase" (pp. 123–24).

> When political action succeeds in generating real power, the participants experience a kind of happiness different from the kinds of happinesses one finds in private life. . . .
>
> Public happiness is not isolating but shared. It is the happiness of being free among other free people, of having one's public faith redeemed and returned, of seeing public hope becoming public power, becoming reality itself. It is the happiness of experiencing the moment when history is no longer an alien force by which one is squeezed and buffeted about, but is what one is doing now. . . .
>
> The experience of public happiness is an exceptional one in the politics of our time, but not such a rare exception. It has been known in many countries in this century, on every continent, in societies of every kind of political, economic, and cultural configuration. It has been felt, if sometimes only momentarily, everywhere, and therefore it is possible everywhere.[6]

Such a prospect contains a promise: whoever joins in the effort for workplace democracy will be rewarded by sharing in the public happiness among all who participate.

The cover stories of neoliberalism make such a prospect seem remote. But at the close of his pioneering investigation of worker decision-making, Lawrence B. Cohen assessed the longer-term possibilities for disalienation in the United States:

> The notion of a noncoercive, nonalienating decision system is extremely attractive to people. An unending succession of Utopias have been constructed on this theme. It accords moreover with deep-felt elements of American culture, especially with the belief in democratizing as much of social life as possible. Apart from organizational difficulties and opposition, one factor has already made the notion visionary and unreal: it lacked practicality or even a clear method by which it might be realized in the complex modern production system. . . .
>
> Now, directly within the system, the notion is turning into a reality, however limited at present. What was once visionary, Utopian, unoperational and unrealistic is being given explicit and precise definition and is being put into practice. This fact alone possesses the potential of posing a new option to people—an option of profound historical consequence.[7]

Who Wants Workplace Democracy?

While my account of a disalienated society and economy may seem to draw on the utopian, there is much support for workplace democracy in the social attitudes of American workers. In the first of three surveys, in 1984 sociologists concluded a sophisticated analysis titled "The Social Bases of Support for Workplace Democracy."[8] Taking into account age, gender, occupation, union, income, stock ownership and political party, they found that "being a blue-collar worker or professional/technical worker—regardless of all else leads one to be . . . more in favor of workplace democracy than managers." These analysts reported that

> by far, the bulk of the blue-collar effect persists in spite of controlling for affluence (and other variables), affluence does not appear to greatly reduce the support of blue-collar workers for increased democracy at work. Similarly . . . for professional/technical and clerical/sales groups.

They concluded that their

> results indicate that most workers are not rendered so passive and powerless as not to want radically to change their situations and assume more power. The results of situations in which work has been democratized also are encouraging. In almost every case, productivity and/or job satisfaction has increased.*

In a further effort to identity potential supporters of economic democracy, analysis of a 1991 national attitude survey called "Social Inequality and the Politics of Production" was conducted by Ed Collum. He concluded from his analyses of prospective support for workplace democracy that

> overall, labor is strengthened through workplace democracy as issues of wages and benefits are superseded and the nature of work itself is brought into question. Transformations of the relations in production offer the most to those who are most subjugated under contemporary capitalism. While all workers will be empowered, women and people of color will gain the most.

*See also John Simmons and William Mares, "Appendix I: Participation and Productivity," *Working Together* (Alfred A. Knopf, 1983).

This investigation found further that

> in the class location analysis, 82% of respondents (1119/1367) are in the supportive coalition. Hence, a workplace democracy movement is more likely to appeal to large portions of the American population.[9]

By 1999, we could draw upon Freeman and Rogers's sophisticated examination of American worker attitudes and opinions. Their national Worker Participation and Representation Survey on "private-sector" workers in the United States reinforces the positive findings of previous studies.*

In their conclusion, they say:

> Our central finding in *What Workers Want* is that, given a choice, workers want "more"—more say in the workplace decisions that affect their lives, more employee involvement at their firms, more legal protection at the workplace, and more union representation. Most workers reported that existing institutions—from unions to EI [Employee Involvement] committees to government regulations—are either insufficiently available to them or do not go far enough to provide the workplace voice they want.

Readers of this book also recognize the importance of their finding that

> employees can specify with some precision new forms and attributes of workplace organization and ways to enforce regulations. Employee desire for additional voice and input into workplace decisions is not inchoate but well-formed and practical enough.[10]

When we combine these findings with their discovery that, as we have seen, nearly half of American workers are strongly interested in unionization, despite the overt resistance of employers, then we can be confident that there is a readiness for such action.

It is impossible, of course, to forecast either a timetable or a precise sequence of actions that would contribute to a phasing in of an economy

*Freeman and Rogers report that they used focus groups, telephone surveys of more than 2,400 workers and in-depth follow-ups of 800 case studies. Their summary of Basic Findings (pp. 4–8) is a fine, concise statement of the principal elements of the varied survey results.

based on workplace democracy in the United States. But the data and analyses given here tell us that two main lines of future development are to be expected during the twenty-first century.

First, as we saw in Parts I and II, people will understand that many deficiencies in living well are caused by the normal operation of state capitalism, with its drive for profits and power. No exit from a spiral of further alienation, deindustrialization, and successive wars and crises is visible within the unchallenged dominance of the current state/corporate regime.

At the same time, as we saw in Part IV, the institutions and practices of worker decision-making and cooperative organizations will continue to function and expand. Judging by their performance in varied firms and industries, we can expect that all people whose work is a "service to production" of necessary goods and services will tend to become "part of the workers"—in the words of British shop stewards. When this is formalized within unions, then transforming the employment relation toward workplace democracy—even in the largest firms—is more readily accomplished.

Such developments will encompass all the work that is useful to production, while omitting only the top managers and their staffs, who are remote from production and preoccupied with the politics of accumulating profits and power.

With the repeated crises that stem from managers' competitive power-wielding, like the wars produced by the state capitalist drive for worldwide hegemony, people will more readily understand that a big part of the state and corporate managers' power is not as though an object they possess, but instead stems from the readiness of workers to do their bidding.

Envisioning the myriad aspects of life after capitalism is not an essential part of the exiting process. The essential point is that the core elements of workplace democracy are defined. Every workplace is eligible. Allegiance to state capitalism offers no way to understand recurring crises in the economy and society. The "market" cover stories are roadblocks in the way of these efforts.

There is no shortcut to patiently unraveling the tangle of dogma that is embedded in state capitalism. Nevertheless, we can draw confidence from the knowledge that workplace democracy contains the core of an alternative to capitalism beyond managerialism and militarism.

It should be no surprise that even as changes in the decision process go forward, familiar economic and cultural landmarks will be retained, just as vestiges of feudal culture (like Britain's House of Lords, however modified) continue for centuries within capitalist society.

What Can Be Done?

I write all this to encourage attention to the objective of blue- and white-collar workers everywhere—to disalienate their occupations and their workplaces: joining producing with decision-making; organizing decision-making on a nonhierarchical, democratic basis; sharing the social product without inequality; achieving human solidarity in place of alienation. These are the core values of workplace democracy.

There are many possible paths and time lines for disalienation, too many to forecast. The very readiness to consider alternatives to alienating hierarchical rule in every industry and calling may well be triggered by a question about the top managers, and their staffs, openly stated:

What do we need them for?

Appendix A

Enlarging U.S. Hegemonic Power over Other Nations by Arms Sales

During 1998, the Security Cooperation Program of the Department of Defense reported new sales of weapons and related services to 137 governments valued at $8.6 billion. These are only partly accounted for by the listings below.

By law, reported sales appear in "Notifications to Congress." The reported sales can be modified subject to Congressional reaction, changes in the terms of the order, and so forth. The types of sale are quite variable. Thus:

DCS Direct Commercial Sale of military equipment involving company-to-government or company sale via Department of State.

EDA Excess Defense Article.

FMS Foreign Military Sales, government to government, all via the Pentagon.

FMF Foreign Military Financing.

Lease Payment per year.

MD Military Drawdown: discretionary extraction from existing military stocks.

The arms-transfer activity is subject to administrative controls and/or monitoring by the Departments of Defense and State. *But there is no one with independent power to verify the scale and quality of the separate transactions.*

Interested readers who wish to confirm the character of the weapons listed below can find help in Tom Gervasi, *Arsenal of Democracy—III: America's War Machine: The Pursuit of Global Dominance* (Grove Press, 1984).

REPORTED U.S. MILITARY SALES IN 1998*

RECIPIENT	DATE OF SALE	DESCRIPTION	SALE TYPE	PRICE
Algeria	10/05/98	Border air surveillance system, including four AN/TPS-70 radars	DCS	$50 million
Argentina	11/02/98	NA†	EDA	Free
	10/02/98	NA	EDA	NA
	10/01/99	NA	EDA	NA
	08/21/98	Two-tracked cargo carriers	EDA	Free
	07/21/98	25 armored recovery vehicles	EDA	Free
	03/05/98	Aviation spare and repair parts	EDA	$48,544
	01/12/98	700 light antitank weapons	EDA	Free
Bahrain	08/21/98	60 Main Battle Tanks	EDA	Free
	03/18/98	Phase III Hawk Missile System	FMS	>$1 million
	01/09/98	12,000 8" projectiles; 61,000 M2 8" propellant charges	EDA	Free
Bolivia	01/12/98	14 C-130 wings	EDA	$445,158
Bosnia-Herzegovina	10/06/98	Defense articles and services	FMF	>$100 million
	07/28/98	Technical assistance agreement to establish a formal structure for civilian control of the military, to train forces in defensive tactics, and to improve capability to deter hostile forces and defend their territory	DCS	>$50 million
Brazil	11/02/98	NA	EDA	Sale
	01/12/98	14 wings for Lockheed C-130 Hercules cargo planes	EDA	Free
Brunei	05/11/98	S-70A helicopter with training	DCS	>$14 million

*Arms Sales Monitoring Project of the Federation of American Scientists, 307 Massachusetts Avenue NE, Washington, D.C. 20002.
†Not available.

Chile	11/02/98	NA	EDA	Sale
Colombia	03/25/98	T-700-GE-700 engines	FMS	>$1 million
Ecuador	03/03/98	2 harbor tugs and one self-propelled fuel-oil barge	EDA	Sale
Egypt	11/03/98	NA	EDA	Free
	10/26/98	4 F-16 training device simulators	FMS	$26.2 million
	09/18/98	Upgrade of 40 ALQ-131 Block I to Block II pods, possible sale of 40 ALQ-131 receiver processors, parts, support and training; principal contractors, Northrop-Grumman and Lockheed Martin	FMS	$76 million
	09/16/98	Upgrade of 6 CH-47C Chinook helicopters to the newer CH-47D configuration, parts, training, equipment and support	FMS	$203 million
	09/09/98	F-16 Depot Level Maintenance Program, including depot level repair capability for landing gear, hydraulics, pneumatics, fuel, electrical; instrument and environmental/oxygen components; construction; training and training equipment; support equipment; publications and technical data; U.S. Government and contractor representatives; spare and repair parts; and other related elements of program support	FMS	$200 million
	05/20/98	68 SM-1 Standard missiles	EDA	Free
	04/28/98	Stinger RMP Type III Missiles	FMS	>$1 million
	04/22/98	5 M728 combat engineering vehicles	EDA	Free
	03/25/98	1,058 Hughes	FMS	$304 million

		vehicle-mounted Stinger RMP Type III anti-aircraft missiles; 50 Avenger systems, turrets and vehicle-mounted launchers; launch pods on Humvees; M3P machine guns; Forward Looking Infrared Range; laser range finder; interrogator; support		
	02/17/98	Onboard small arms, spare parts and fuel	EDA	$2,705,580
	02/05/98	2 Perry-class frigates; 2 "Knox"-class frigates; 42 Harpoon anti-ship missiles and containers; upgrade kits for 20 Standard naval missiles; ammunition; support	FMS	$355 million
	01/26/98	AN/TSQ-73 Raytheon Corp. Hawk missile control	EDA	Free
	01/07/98	30 mine-clearing rakes	EDA	Free
Estonia	01/09/98	40,500 M14 rifles; 380,000 5.56mm tracer ammo; 1,328,300 7.62mm ball ammo; 1,000,000 7.62mm blank ammo; 81,219 7.62mm tracer ammo	EDA	Free
FYROM (Macedonia)	06/19/98	300 M3 machine guns with accessories and various field equipment	EDA	Free
Georgia	06/12/98	Radios and assorted commo equipment	FMS	>$1 million
Greece	12/17/98	NA	Lease	
	12/17/98	NA	Lease	
	12/17/98	NA	Lease	
	12/17/98	NA	Lease	
	12/09/98	NA	EDA	Free
	12/03/98	NA	EDA	Sale
	12/03/98	NA	EDA	Sale
	11/30/98	NA	EDA	Sale
	11/30/98	NA	EDA	Free
	11/30/98	4 KIDD Class Guided	FMS,	$742 million

	Missile Destroyers, 62,000 20mm cartridges, 4,800 5"/54 projectiles, 64 anti-submarine rockets, 320 MK 36 Super Bloom Offboard Chaff, 32 Harpoon missiles, 48 MK 46 MOD 5 torpedoes, ammunition, services, equipment and support	lease/sale	
11/30/98	NA	EDA	Sale
10/23/98	NA	EDA	Free
10/19/98	Patriot PAC-3 air defense systems, T-6A trainers and upgrade of Hawk missile systems	NA	$1.4 billion
10/19/98	Manufacturing license agreement	DCS	NA
10/19/98	20 to 50 F-16H aircraft	NA	$1.6 billion
10/08/98	Remote sensing satellite technical data and a regional operations center	DCS	+$50 million
10/05/98	Up to 6 E-2C or C-130J airframes, software laboratory, technical assistance, and unique changes to the E-2C mission system	DCS	$320 million
10/05/98	6 new production E-2C Airborne Early Warning and Control (AEW&C) mission systems as part of a purchase of either E-2C or C-130J airframe for AEW and Control, plus parts, equipment, training and services	FMS	$380 million
09/22/98	18 Multiple Launch Rocket Systems (MLRS), 146 MLRS extended-range rocket pods (six rockets per pod), 81 Army Tactical Missile System guided missiles and launching assemblies,	FMS	$245 million

		11 M577 command post carriers, 162 M26 rockets, 94 SINCGARS radio systems, 60 AN/PVS-7B night vision goggles, four M984A1 and 24 M985 heavy expanded mobility tactical trucks, forklifts, production verification testing, spare and repair parts, support vehicles, publications and technical documentation, personnel training and training equipment, support and test equipment, U.S. Government and contractor technical and logistics personnel services and other related elements of program support		
Greece	9/22/98	200 AGM-65G Maverick missiles, 200 GBU-24 A/B bombs kits (without warheads), missile Greece launchers, other parts, equipment and training	FMS	$61 million
	09/21/98	919 TOW 2A Anti-Tank Missiles	DCS	$50 million
	08/03/98	1,322 STINGER-RMP Block 1 International missiles, including 1,286 complete missile rounds without gripstocks and 36 lot acceptance missiles; 188 gripstock control group guided missile launchers; battery coolant units; publications and technical data; support equipment; and other related elements of logistics support	FMS	$150 million
	06/19/98	10 T-2C trainer aircraft, 4 J-85 engines	EDA	Free
	05/18/98	160 AGM-114KBF Hellfire II missiles,	FMS	$24 million

		including lot acceptance missiles, publications and related elements of logistics support		
	05/13/98	12 M109A5 Self-Propelled Howitzers	DCS	>$14 million
	03/04/98	12 General Dynamics M60A1 tanks; 2 TA-7C aircraft, a Boeing Harpoon antiship missile command launch system; Lockheed P-3 Orion aircraft spare and repair parts; M2 machine guns and various ammunition	EDA	Free
	02/10/98	AN/APG-65 radar from Germany	DCS	>$14 million
Hungary	03/06/98	Radios—VEH and Manpack, computers	FMS	$1 million
Israel	10/05/98	Manufacture of avionics in support of the USAF T-38 Avionics upgrade program	DCS	>$50 million
	09/22/98	60 F-16C/D Block 50/52 aircraft; 60 AN/APG-68 (V)7 or AN/APG-68(V)X radar, 30 each LANTIRN navigation and targeting pods. Either F100-PW-229 or F110-GE-129 engines by DCS; support, parts and training. Prime contractor, Lockheed Martin.	FMS	$2.5 billion
	09/22/98	30 F-15I aircraft, 30 AN/APG-70 or AN/APG-63(V)1 radar and 30 each LANTIRN navigation and targeting pods, and associated equipment, parts, training and services	FMS	$2.5 billion
	08/21/98	170,000 H708 35mm subcaliber light antitank weapon rockets	EDA	Free
	07/31/98	Codevelopment of	DCS	>$50 million

		Multiple Launch Rocket System (MLRS) Trajectory Correction System		
	07/30/98	Licensed production	DCS	NA
	06/22/98	16 Harpoon missiles, containers, spare and repair parts, support and test equipment, supply support, publications, training, contractor technical assistance, and other related elements of logistics support	FMS	$26 million
	06/11/98	Patriot Missile System equipment, including 3 AN/MPQ-53 radar sets, 3 AN/MSQ-104 engagement control stations, 3 M983 tractors, 9 M931A2 trucks and other defense articles and services	FMS	$73 million
	05/19/98	Stinger RMP, Block 1	FMS	>$1 million
	04/21/98	64 AIM-120B AMRAAM, 3 test missiles, missile containers, spare and repair parts, support	FMS	>$28 million
	04/01/98	Services and technical data to support hardware deliveries for the Seahawk Torpedo System for Dolphin-class submarines	DCS	>$50 million
	03/26/98	Technical data for the manufacture of Forward Nose Landing Gear (ANLG) doors and Leading Edge Extensions (LEX) for the Boeing F/A-18 aircraft	DCS	>$50 million
Jamaica	01/12/98	YTB 778 harbor tug	EDA	$30,650
Jordan	11/03/98	NA	EDA	Free
	10/02/98	NA	EDA	NA
	03/26/98	Aviation spare and repair parts	EDA	Sale

	03/13/98	DOD stocks, defense services, military education and training	MD	$25 million
Korea (Rep.)	06/04/98	AGM-142C/D missiles	FMS	>$1 million
	11/02/98	NA	EDA	Sale
	10/09/98	Manufacture of transmissions for use on the Korean K95 howitzer and the K1A1 Main Battle Tank	DCS	$50 million
	05/13/98	500 TOW 2A missiles, eight lot acceptance missiles, spare and repair parts, support and technical equipment, technical support and documentation and other support	FMS	$19 million
	04/22/98	Licensed production	DCS	NA
	03/25/98	112 Lockheed Martin Multiple Launch RocketSystem extended range (MLRS-ER) rocket pods, one verification testing MLRS-ER rocket pod, spare and repair parts, support	FMS	$40 million
	03/25/98	4 Hawker 800XP Aircraft	DCS	>$50 million
	03/20/98	AH-1 helicopter components, spare and repair parts	EDA	Sale
	03/04/98	12 fire-control units for Standard naval missiles; U.S. Government and contractor support; spares	FMS	$214 million
	02/26/98	Automatic data-processing equipment	Lease	NA
	02/25/98	Sentry-based air defense system	DCS	>$50 million
	02/25/98	Technical data and assistance for the development and deployment of a littoral water surveillance system	DCS	>$50 million
	02/24/98	Support intermediate level maintenance	DCS	>$50 million

		training for the AN/ALQ-165 Airborne Self Protection Jammer line replacement units and system replacement units		
	02/24/98	Licensed production of 4 Landing Craft Air Cushion amphibious vessels	DCS	NA
Kuwait	11/06/98	48 M109A6 Paladin 155mm self-propelled howitzers, armored resupply vehicles, command and observation-post vehicles, spare parts, support and training	FMS	>$450 million
	10/02/98	195 AN/VRC-92E, 484 AN/VRC-90E and 378 AN/PRC-119E SINCGARS radio systems; installation kits, platforms, base stations, radios and radio systems, U.S. Government and contractor technical and logistic support, spare and repair parts, support and test equipment, personnel training and training equipment, Technical Assistance Field Team, publications and technical data, support equipment and other related elements of logistics support	FMS	$113 million
	05/20/98	Technical data, hardware and services related to thermal sight and fire control system upgrades for the Kuwaiti BMP-3 and M-84 combat vehicles	DCS	>$50 million
	03/25/98	2 fully equipped Paladin artillery battalions made by United Defense, to include 48 M109A6 self-	FMS	$496 million

		propelled howitzers; 154 M2 machine guns; 18 M88A2 recovery vehicles; 24 M113A3 battalion/battery reconnaissance vehicles; 64 M992A2 field artillery ammunition support vehicles; 136 AN/VRC and 125 AN/PRC SINCGARS radio systems; two AN/TPQ-36(V)9 Firefinder radar sets; trucks and trailers; night-vision goggles; meteorological radar station; simulators; training and support		
	02/20/98	ADD M16A2 and M4 carbines	FMS	>$1 million
Lebanon	11/25/98	M113A2 NSN 2350-01-068-4077	FMS	>$1 million
	10/14/98	NA	EDA	NA
Lithuania	10/01/98	NA	EDA	NA
	01/09/98	40,000 M14 rifles; 500,000 7.62mm blank ammunition; 1,500,000 7.62mm ball ammunition	EDA	Free
Mexico	11/02/98	NA	EDA	Sale
	10/05/98	Manufacturing license agreement	DCS	NA
	09/29/98	Manufacture of military-vehicle wiring harnesses	DCS	>$50 million
	03/18/98	M109 and M110 howitzer spare and repair parts	EDA	NA
Morocco	11/30/98	NA	EDA	Free
	10/14/98	NA	EDA	NA
	03/04/98	Vehicles and trailers	EDA	Free
	01/09/98	16,979 8-inch rocket assist projectiles; 100,000 M188A1 8-inch propellent charges; 47,920 M1 8-inch propellent charges; 2,059 M1 8-inch propellent charges; 55,000	EDA	Free

		M2 8-inch propellent charges; M106 8-inch projectiles; M106 8-inch projectiles; 30,000 8-inch flash reducers		
Oman	08/21/98	30 M60A3TTS Main Battle Tanks	EDA	Free
	05/20/98	191 MK 20 Rockeye cluster bombs	EDA	Free
	04/01/98	Ammunition C511 and C520 105mm for M60A3	FMS	>$1 million
Pakistan	02/11/98	19 T-37B aircraft	Lease	NA
Peru	01/27/98	YO 220 self-propelled fuel oil barge, YG 880 self-propelled gasoline barge, TB 785 harbor tug	EDA	Free
Philippines	05/14/98	1,000 105mm ammunitions rounds	EDA	Free
	02/25/98	Services and equipment for a structural life-extension program upgrade of the Philippine Air Force's fleet of F-5A/B fighter aircraft	DCS	>$50 million
Romania	08/31/98	C-130B cargo aircraft and delivery system	EDA	Free
	02/27/98	Shadow 600 unmanned aerial vehicles and a short-range air defense training simulator	DELG	$20,100,000
Saudi Arabia	07/16/98	Training and support services, spare parts	FMS	$831 million
	05/20/98	Defense services related to the operation, training, maintenance and system enhancements for the Peace Shield command, control and communications system	DCS	>$50 million
	04/21/98	Upgrade 1500 AIM-9L missiles to the Raytheon AIM-9M configuration; possible sale of five sets of Pathfinder/Sharpshooter navigation and targeting pods	FMS	$115 million

	03/30/98	Upgrades of 700 GBU-10 Paveway II Laser Guided Bombs	FMS	>$14 million
	03/30/98	Upgrades of 300 AIM-7M air-to-air missiles	FMS	>$14 million
Singapore	10/09/98	Support services for the T-55-L-714A engine used on CH-47 helicopters	DCS	>$50 million
	10/09/98	Manufacturing license agreement	DCS	NA
	10/08/98	110 U2 self-propelled howitzers	DCS	>$50 million
	06/23/98	88 AH-64D APACHE attack helicopters, 216 Hellfire II laser-guided missiles, 4 spare Hellfire, 2 spare T-700-GE-701C engines, 2 spare Target Acquisition Designation Sight Systems, 9,120 Hydra-70 rockets, spare and repair parts, communications equipment, miscellaneous equipment, training, support	FMS	$620 million
	05/13/98	10 F100-PW-229 engines as spares for the F-16	DCS	>$14 million
	04/21/98	Pilot training and logistics support for Lockheed Martin F-16C/D fighter aircraft program	FMS	$138 million
	01/21/98	AIM-9M for RSAFF-16 aircraft	FMS	>$1 million
Sri Lanka	10/20/98	Three Hercules C-130E aircraft from Great Britain	Re-transfer	$8.8 million
Taiwan	12/18/98	NA	EDA	Sale
	10/09/98	Three Boeing CH-47SD Chinook helicopters, plus material order for production of six more Chinooks and related support service	FMS	$235 million
	09/22/98	Knox class frigate	Lease	$8,189,089

	U.S.S. *Kirk* (FF 1087) and associated equipment		
09/15/98	58 Harpoon missiles, 8 Harpoon training missiles, containers, Harpoon interface adapter kits, parts, equipment, training and other support	FMS	$101 million
08/28/98	50 MIM-72J Chaparral guided missiles, one ARS 40 USS hoist rescue and salvage vessel	EDA	$1,621,050
08/27/98	131 MK 46 MOD 5 (A)S torpedoes, containers, support and test equipment, publications and technical documentation, engineering and technical assistance, supply support and other related elements of logistics support	FMS	$69 million
08/27/98	61 Dual Mount Stinger Missile Systems consisting of: 61 Dual Mount Stinger (DMS) launchers (includes elevation assembly, tripod assembly, and sights) with coolant units, 61 Stinger RMP (-) captive flight trainers, 728 complete Stinger RMP (-) missile rounds (less battery coolant unit), 132 AN/VRC-91 export version SINCGAR radios, spare and repair parts, support equipment, Interrogator Friend or Foe interrogator sets, interrogator programmers, utility carrier trucks, aerial flight handling and launcher trainers, gas bottles, coolant units, publications and documentation data, personnel training and	FMS	$180 million

	training equipment, U.S. Government and contractor engineering and logistics personnel services, U.S. Government Quality Assurance Teams, Mobile Training Teams, and other related elements of logistics support		
07/20/98	Licensed production, involving the transfer of 77 F124 aircraft engines to the Czech Republic for use on L-159 aircraft	DCS	NA
06/01/98	28 sets of Pathfinder/ Sharpshooter navigation and targeting pods, integration of the pods with the F-16A/B aircraft, flight testing, personnel training and training equipment, publications and technical data, U.S. government and contractor engineering and logistics personnel services, spare and repair parts, support	FMS	$160 million
04/14/98	5"/54 projectiles and other explosives	FMS	>$1 million
04/13/98	Knox-class frigate	Lease	NA
03/17/98	2 Ambient Noise Buoys	Lease	NA
03/05/98	2 harbor tugs	EDA	Sale
03/05/98	100 Hughes SM-1 "Standard" medium-range missiles	EDA	Sale
03/05/98	Chaparral system equipment and support	EDA	Sale
02/24/98	Licensed production of 40mm ammunition	DCS	NA
02/18/98	4 S-70A helicopters	DCS	>$14 million
01/28/98	3 Knox-class frigates; 15 Phalanx close-in weapons	FMS	$300 million

		systems and 30,000 rounds of 20mm ammo; one AN/SWG-1A "Harpoon" launcher		
Thailand	09/29/98	6 M88A2 Tracked Armor Recovery Vehicles, spare parts, tech manuals and operator and preventive maintenance training	DCS	>$14 million
	05/20/98	A-7 and AV-8A aircraft engines with containers, spare parts and arresting gear	EDA	Free
Trinidad and	07/22/98	NA	EDA	NA
Tobago	03/17/98	2 C-26B aircraft	EDA	Free
Tunisia	08/12/98	20 M48A3 Chaparral guided missile systems, 300 MIM-72E guided Chaparral missiles, 30 M30\guided missile trainers, other equipment	EDA	Free
	07/15/98	8 tank gunnery trainers	EDA	Free
	04/26/98	100 M85 machine guns, 3,000 infrared smoke screen rounds	EDA	Free
Turkey	11/16/98	NA	EDA	Free
	11/16/98	3 FFG-7 Perry class frigates and eight currently leased FF 1052 Knox-class frigates, also ammunition and support	FMS	$205 million
	10/19/98	Manufacturing license agreement	DCS	NA
	09/21/98	Four A70B Seahawk helicopters, spare parts, ground support equipment and logistical support	DCS	+$14 million
	09/16/98	U.S.S. *Donald Beary* (FF 1085) frigate and associated equipment	Lease	$7,125,619
	09/16/98	U.S.S. *Thomas C. Hart* (FF 1092) frigate and associated equipment	Lease	$8,061,818
	08/31/98	UH-1H utility helicopter	EDA	Free
	08/12/98	Emplacement kit, helicopter lift kit, launch rail test set	EDA	Free

	06/04/98	Licensed production of Paveway II laser-guided bomb	DCS	NA
	05/18/98	30 Harpoon missiles and other defense articles and services	FMS	$43 million
	05/11/98	Licensed production of Low-Cost Thermal Imagers	DCS	NA
	04/28/98	Licensed production	DCS	NA
	03/04/98	24 M110 8-inch howitzers and M578 armored recovery vehicles	EDA	Free
United Arab Emirates	09/16/98	491 AIM-120B Advanced Medium Range Emirates Air-to-Air Missiles (AMRAAM) and 12 AMRAAM training missiles, 267 AIM-9M 1/2 Sidewinder missiles and 80 Sidewinder training missiles, 1,163 AGM-88 High Speed Anti-Radiation Missiles (HARM) and four HARM training missiles, 1,163 AGM-65D/G Maverick missiles and 20 training missiles, 52 AGM-84 HARPOON missiles, and thousands of other bombs, ammunition and training, in support of commercial F-16 sale	FMS	$2 billion
	07/22/98	3 AN/GSA-132A Hawk launch station control boxes, eleven Hawk loader transporters Emirates	EDA	$153,092
	05/01/98	80 F-16 Block 60 aircraft, services and support	DCS	$6–8 billion
	03/30/98	Upgrades of 72 RIM-7M Seasparrow missiles	FMS	>$14 million
Various	09/30/98	Drawdown of articles and services for counternarcotics	MD	$75 million

		assistance to Bolivia, Brazil, Colombia, Dominican Republic, Ecuador, Guatemala, Honduras, Jamaica, Mexico, Peru, Trinidad and Tobago and the countries of the Eastern Caribbean		
Venezuela	11/02/98	NA	EDA	Sale
	06/12/98	Parts and services for 17 OV-10 aircraft	Sale, Ex-Im Bank gtd	NA
	03/11/98	Seasparrow missiles for frigates	FMS	>$1 million

Appendix B

List of Mondragon Enterprises (109)

The following list of enterprises of the Mondragon Corporation is from the *1996 Annual Report* of the Caja Laboral Popular. The Web site of the MCC is http://www.mondragon.mcc.es. Details on each of the MCC firms are available on this Web site and in the appendix to *From Mondragon to America,* including: addresses, phone / fax numbers, main products.

Worker-controlled enterprises in a state-capitalist environment are not among friends. The Mondragon co-op workers surveyed the scene as Spain entered the European economic sphere. They discovered that they could be economically vulnerable to price competition based on economies of scale as practiced by big multinational firms.

How to respond? The Mondragon Cooperative Corporation made adjustments to the scale of their own operations in various co-ops, cutting back some and enlarging others. They also sought to bolster the position of MCC by investing in major shares of enterprises in other countries. That accounts for the 13 "subsidiary companies" among the 109 MCC enterprises. These moves followed extended debate on the best strategy to ensure the cooperative pattern of MCC core operations that have been centered on Mondragon while bolstering MCC's position in the larger European economy and maintaining its 1997–2000 program for co-op enlargement with 8,000 new jobs. An MCC-friendly analysis of these issues is in the postscript to Greg MacLeod, *From Mondragon to America* (University of Cape Breton Press, 1997).

I. FINANCIAL GROUP (6 Enterprises)

Aro Leasing

Caja Laboral

Credit Cooperative

Lagun-Aro Voluntary Social Welfare Entity

Lagun-Aro Vida

Lainter

Seguros Lagun-Aro

II. INDUSTRIAL GROUP (80 Enterprises)

A. Machine Tool Division (12)

DANOBAT SORALUCE

Danobat

Estarta Rectificadora

Goiti

Lealde

Soraluce

Doiki

egurko

kendu

latz

ortza

zubiola

B. Engineering Division (11)

Berriola

Fagor

Diara

LKS Consultoria

LKS Ingenieria

Ondoan

Fagor Arrasate

Fagor Sistemas

Aurrenak

Ono-Pres

Batz Troqueleria

C. Automotive Components (8)

Batz Sistemas

Fagor Ederlan

Luzuriaga, V.

Mapsa

Cikautxo

FPK (50% shareholding)

Maier

Matriplast

D. Domestic Appliance and Electronic Components (7)

Copreci

Eika

Embega

Fagor Electronica

Matz-Erreka

Orkli

Tajo

E. Industrial Components and Services (15)

Dikar

Eredu

Orbea

Ederfil

Goiplast

Hertell

Irizar

Urola

Alecop

Alkargo

Coinalde

DAnona Litografia

Elkar

Oiarso

Osatu

F. Construction Division (8)

Biurrarena

Rochman

Urssa

Orona

Covimar

Etorki

Lana

Vicon

G. Household Goods-Domestic Appliances (6)

Fagor Electrodomesticos

Coinma

Danona

Herriola

Fagor Industrial

Kide

H. Subsidiary Companies (13)
(Formed as joint stock companies and not as cooperatives)

Cima

Copreci De Mexico, S.A.

Extra Electromenager

Fagor (Thailand) Ltd.

Ferroplast

Fresh Engineering

Isei, S.a.

Omico

Mc Lean, S.A.

P.I Proin, S.A.

Sei, Fagor

Switch Controls

Tianjin Irizar Coach

III. DISTRIBUTION GROUP (8)

Commercial Erein

Consum

Eroski

Erosmer

Auzo-Lagun

Barrenetxe

Behi-Alde

Miba

IV. CORPORATE ACTIVITIES (15)

Ideko

Ikerlan

M T C

Eteo

Lea-Artibai

Mondragon Eskola Politeknikoa (Polytechnical University)

Otalora

Txorierri Politeknika Ikastegia

Saiolan

Ascorp

M C C International

Fundacion MCC

M C C Inversiones

M C C

MCC Sustrai

Notes

INTRODUCTION

Managerialism and "the Market" Are Not Forever

1. Arthur R. Burns, *The Decline of Competition: A Study of the Evolution of American Industry* (McGraw-Hill, 1936). Includes reports of the Federal Trade Commission over half a century that detailed the particular techniques that have been used by management to regulate prices.

2. Ibid.

3. Timothy L. O'Brien, "When Economic Bombs Drop, Risk Models Fail," *New York Times*, Oct. 4, 1998.

4. Ibid. See also, in *Business Week*, "The Fed Steps In: Will It Work?"; "How to Reshape the World Financial System"; "A Talk with Treasury Chief Rubin . . . ," Oct. 12, 1998; "Failed Wizards of Wall Street," Sept. 21, 1998; and in *New York Times*, Timothy L. O'Brien and Stephen Sabaton, "Financiers Plan to Put Controls on Derivatives," Jan. 7, 1999; also, Louis Uchitelle, "Who You Gonna Call After the Next Bust?," Aug. 22, 1999; and "Greenspan Ties Debate on Rates to the Markets," Aug. 28, 1999.

5. For data and analysis on the August–September 1998 money and finance crisis, see particularly, *New York Times*, Oct. 4, 1998; *Business Week*, Dec. 21, 1998; *Business Week*, Oct. 12, 1998.

6. Karl Marx, *Capital: A Critique of Political Economy: The Process of Capitalist Production* (First German Edition, 1867; Modern Library, 1906), pp. 649, 652. Quotation cited to A. Smith: 1. c., bk. iii., ch. iii.

7. Seymour Melman, *The Permanent War Economy: American Capitalism in Decline* (Touchstone, 1974, 1985), pp. 262–64 (text amended).

CHAPTER ONE

The Shape of Production Under State Capitalism

1. Pioneering research on the characteristics of industrial-worker decision-making on production was done by Lawrence B. Cohen, at this writing professor emeritus of industrial engineering, Columbia University. See his Ph.D. dissertation, "Bilateral Decisioning: The Present State of Productional Relations," Columbia

University, 1950, *Dissertation Abstracts International*, vol. 11-02, p. 0230, 00240 pages; his "Workers and Decision-Making on Production," *Proceedings of the Eighth Annual Meeting of the Industrial Relations' Research Association 1955*, pp. 298–312; and "The Structure of Workers' Decisions," *Journal of Economic Issues* 10, no. 2 (June 1976). A substantial elaboration and refinement on these topics is contained in Cohen's "Workers and Decision-Making on Production" (unpublished manuscript, 1997).

2. The organization of workers at the Standard Motor Company in Coventry included, at one time, virtually everyone employed except for the most senior handful of top managers. See data and discussion in Seymour Melman, *Decision-Making and Productivity* (Basil Blackwell, 1958).

3. Joint Economic Committee, Congress of the United States, *Subsidy and Subsidy-Effect Programs of the U.S. Government* (Mar. 31, 1965), p. 3.

4. *The Pentagon Catalog: Ordinary Products at Extraordinary Prices*, compiled by Christopher Cerf and Henry Beard (Workman, 1986).

5. See Seymour Melman, *Profits Without Production* (Alfred A. Knopf, 1988).

6. U.S. Department of Commerce, *Statistical Abstract of the U.S., 1995*, p. 558.

7. Paul Sweezy, "After Capitalism—What?," in *Socialism on the Threshold of the Twenty-first Century*, ed. Milos Nicolic (Verso, 1985), p. 214.

8. Ibid., p. 220.

9. Ibid., p. 221.

10. David Mandel, *Petrograd Workers and the Soviet Seizure of Power: From the July Days 1917 to July 1918* (Macmillan, 1984).

11. Michael Voslensky, *Nomenklatura* (Doubleday, 1984).

12. *Izvestia*, Dec. 6, 1964; Leon Smolinski, "Planning Without Theory, 1917–1967," *Survey*, London, July 1967.

13. Ibid.

14. *Ekonomicheski Almanakh*, Economics Faculty, Moscow State University, Moscow, 1997.

15. Broadus Mitchell, *Depression Decade: From New Era Through New Deal, 1929–1941* (Harper and Bros., 1947).

CHAPTER TWO

The Founding Alienation of Capitalism

1. For a useful bibliography of works dealing with the transition from feudal to capitalist economies, see Robert Brenner, "Agrarian Class Structure and Economic Development in Pre-Industrial Europe," *Past and Present* 70, 2 (February 1976).

See also Douglas Cecil North, *Structure and Change in Economic History* (Norton, 1981); Peter Spufford, *Money and Its Use in Medieval Europe* (Cambridge University Press, 1988); Karl Polanyi, *The Great Transformation* (Beacon Press, 1957).

Fernand Braudel, *Wheels of Commerce*, Vol. 2 of *Civilization & Capitalism* (Harper & Row, 1982).

For the transformation of the feudal economy in Great Britain, see especially J.M.W. Bean, *The Decline of English Feudalism, 1215–1540* (Manchester University Press, 1968).

A very contrary analysis of the economy of feudalism may be found in Henri Pirenne, "The Stages in the Economic History of Capitalism," *American Historical Review* 19, no. 3 (1914). He claims that "all the essential features of capitalism—individual enterprise, advances on credit, commercial profits, speculation, etc.—are to be found from the twelfth century on in the city republics of Italy—Venice, Genoa, or

Florence." Indeed, "the beginning of the Middle Ages gives us access to a body of material sufficient for our purpose." That purpose is to show "the permanence throughout the centuries of a capitalist class, the result of a continuous development and . . . changing circumstances."

2. William Lazonick, "Karl Marx and Enclosures in England," *The Review of Radical Political Economics* 6, no. 2 (Summer 1974).

3. The following are drawn from late feudal documents and literature on the enclosure process, in *English Historical Documents* 5, 1485–1558, ed. C. H. Williams (Eyre and Spottiswoode, 1953).

4. John Bayker, "Device to Redress a Commonwealth from the State Papers" L.P. XIII.ii, 1229. Full text in F. Aydelotte, *Elizabethan Rogues and Vagabonds*, pp. 145–47.

5. Ibid.

6. *A Discourse of the Common Weal of This Realm of England*, ed. E. Lamond, pp. 15–20.

7. Ibid.

8. Ibid.

9. Karl Marx, *Capital: A Critique of Political Economy: The Process of Capitalist Production*, vol. 1 (first German edition, 1867; Modern Library, 1906), p. 805.

10. Ibid., p. 806.

11. Ibid., pp. 806–7.

12. Ibid., p. 810.

13. Ibid., p. 811.

14. E. P. Thompson, *The Making of the English Working Class* (Vintage, 1966), pp. 232–33.

15. Ibid., p. 233.

16. Charles and Mary Beard, *The Rise of American Civilization*, vol. 2 (Macmillan, 1927), p. 116.

17. A contemporary study of such alienation of industrial working people and their families is found in Seymour Melman, *What Else Is There to Do?* (National Commission for Economic Conversion and Disarmament, Washington, D.C., 1996).

18. Howard Zinn, *A People's History of the United States* (HarperCollins, 1980), p. 213. These and other data on American workers and unions, conveying a pattern of alienation operations, are cited from this study.

19. Ibid., p. 213.

20. Ibid., p. 220.

21. Ibid., pp. 224–30.

22. Ibid., p. 230.

23. Ibid., p. 267.

24. Ibid., p. 385.

CHAPTER THREE

The United States as a Third-Rate Economy

1. The Association for Manufacturing Technology, *The Economic Handbook of the Machine Tool Industry* (McLean, Virginia, 1997–1998), pp. C-6, C-8, C-17, D-4; also for 1996–97.

2. Michael L. Dertouzos, Richard K. Lester, Robert M. Solow, and The MIT Commission on Industrial Productivity, *Made in America: Regaining the Productive Edge* (MIT Press, 1989), pp. 235, 239, 241, 242.

3. The Association for Manufacturing Technology, *Economic Handbook*. op. cit.

4. Ibid.

5. U.S. Department of Labor, Bureau of Labor Statistics, Bulletin No. 00-07, *Hourly Compensation Costs for Production Workers in Manufacturing*, Washington, D.C., Jan. 11, 2000.

6. David Noble, *Forces of Production* (Alfred A. Knopf, 1984).

7. Seymour Melman, "Report on the Productivity of Operations in the Machine Tool Industry in Western Europe," for the OEEC at the European Productivity Agency, Paris, Oct. 23, 1959.

8. David K. Henry and Richard P. Oliver, "The Defense Build-up, 1977–85: Effects on Production and Employment," *Monthly Labor Review*, August 1987.

9. *Bloomberg Business News*, April 28, 1995.

10. *Mechanical Engineering*, December 1991, pp. 30 ff.

11. *New York Times*, May 10, 1994.

12. Seymour Melman, *Dynamic Factors in Industrial Productivity* (John Wiley, 1956), pp. 151, 152.

13. U.S. Department of Commerce, *Census of Manufactures, 1987; Annual Survey of Manufactures, 1996.*

14. The Association for Manufacturing Technology, *The Economic Handbook of the Machine Tool Industry, 1993–94*, p. C2.

15. U.S. Department of Labor, *Hourly Compensation Costs.*

16. Seymour Melman, *Profits Without Production* (Alfred A. Knopf, 1988), pp. 140 ff.

17. U.S. Department of Labor, *Hourly Compensation Costs*; *New York Times*, Oct. 23, 1994.

18. Seymour Melman, *What Else Is There to Do?* (National Commission for Economic Conversion and Disarmament, 1996), p. 7.

19. *Survey of Current Business*, July 1999.

20. *New York Times*, Dec. 3, 1995.

21. U.S. International Trade Commission, Report to the Committee on Finance, United States Senate, on investigation #332-303, under section 332 (G) of the tariff act of 1930, "Global Competitiveness of U.S. Advanced Technology Manufacturing Industries: Semiconductor Manufacturing and Testing Equipment," September 1991.

22. Jacqueline Warnke, "Computer Manufacturing: Change and Competition," *Monthly Labor Review*, August 1996.

23. John Holusha, "It's All or Part Foreign Made," *New York Times*, Aug. 10, 1985.

24. Data obtained from National Bureau of Economic Research on U.S. Capital Goods Industries, SIC Nos. 33–38, NBER Technical Working Paper 205, Oct. 1996.

25. *Business Week*, Nov. 8, 1993.

26. *New York Times*, June 20, 1995.

27. Ibid.

28. *Wall Street Journal*, Mar. 17, 1993.

29. *New York Times*, Apr. 4, 1995.

30. Wayne Sandholtz et al., *The Highest Stakes: The Economic Foundations of the Next Security System* (Oxford University Press, 1992), pp. 24, 25.

31. *What Else Is There to Do?*, p. 7.

32. In mass-marketing stores like Caldor and Walmart that cater to low-income Americans, I have examined shoe departments that are almost entirely served by Chinese industry in the lowest price range. But again, Chinese-made shoes are also found (at commonly acceptable prices) in department stores that cater to the middle class.

33. *What Else Is There to Do?*, pp. 65–90.

34. *New York Times*, Dec. 28, 1992.

35. Ibid.

36. Werner International, Inc., Management Consultants to the Apparel Industries (55 East 52nd Street, New York, N.Y. 10055).

37. Richard J. Barnet and John Cavanagh, *New York Times*, Feb. 13, 1994.

38. Ibid.

39. *New York Times*, Aug. 25, 1995.

40. *New York Times*, Sept. 1, 1992.

41. *What Else Is There to Do?*, p. 7.

42. John E. Ullmann, *The Prospects of American Industrial Recovery* (Quorum Books, 1985), pp. 194–95.

43. Arie Caspi, "The High Cost of Cheap Products," *Ha'Aretz Magazine*, Tel-Aviv, Dec. 10, 1999, p. 5.

44. *The Economist*, Aug. 25, 1993.

45. David Dembo and Ward Morehouse, *The Underbelly of the U.S. Economy: Joblessness and the Pauperization of Work in America* (Council on International and Public Affairs, Apex Press, 1997), pp. 5–6.

46. *New York Times*, Mar. 30, 1998.

47. Ibid., Feb. 24, 1998.

48. U.S. Department of Labor, Bureau of Labor Statistics, *Employment and Earnings*, January 1998. For discussion of the statistical comparison of joblessness with unemployment, see Dembo and Morehouse, *Underbelly of the U.S. Economy.*

49. Allan Sloan, *Newsweek*, Feb. 26, 1996.

50. *Business Week*, Oct. 17, 1994.

51. *New York Times*, *The Downsizing of America* (Times Books, 1996).

52. *New York Times*, July 26, 1993.

53. Dembo and Morehouse, *The Underbelly of the U.S. Economy*, p. 14.

54. *What Else Is There to Do?*

55. *New York Times*, Apr. 28, 1996.

56. *New York Times*, Apr. 27, 1993.

57. *New York Times*, Mar. 1, 1997.

58. *New York Times*, Feb. 12, 1998.

59. *New York Times*, Mar. 6, 1996.

60. *New York Times*, Apr. 20, 1998.

61. *What Else Is There to Do?*, pp. 6, 61–62.

62. *New York Times*, Aug. 28, 1995.

63. From a memorandum by Greg Woodhead, AFL-CIO Public Policy staff, Washington, D.C., re: Survey of Prison Labor, Jan. 15, 1997. See also UNICOR (trade name of Federal Prison Industries, a wholly owned government corporation), Federal Bureau of Prisons, U.S. Department of Justice, *1998 Annual Report. A Revealing Look at What You Should Know About Federal Prison Industries*, p. 7; also *New York Times*, Mar. 15, 1999; Eric Schlosser, "The Prison-Industrial Complex," *The Atlantic Monthly*, December 1998.

64. Woodhead, memorandum.

65. UNICOR, *1998 Annual Report*, p. 16.

66. Woodhead, memorandum.

67. *UE News*, Feb. 21, 1997.

68. Ibid.

69. Dembo and Morehouse, *Underbelly of the U.S. Economy*, p. 6.

70. Ibid., p. 29. Based on U.S. Department of Commerce, Bureau of the Census, *Current Population Reports, P 60–200*, as cited in *Statistical Abstract of the United States*, 1974, 1981, 1984; and *Current Population Reports, P 60-200*, "Income, Poverty, and Valuation of Noncash Benefits: 1995," Washington, D.C., 1996.

71. *Historical Statistics of the United States, Colonial Times to 1970*, Series E135 and D802; *Monthly Labor Review*, appendix tables, August 1999; *Statistical Abstract of the U.S.*, 1999.

72. U.S. Department of the Treasury, Internal Revenue Service, *Statistics of Income: Individual Income Tax Returns*, 1970 and 1995.

73. *New York Times*, Sept. 2, 1997.

74. *Business Week*, Apr. 19, 1999; U.S. Department of Labor, Bureau of Labor Statistics, Bulletin No. 00-07, *Hourly Compensation Costs for Production Workers in Manufacturing*, Washington, D.C., Jan. 11, 2000.

75. *New York Times*, Sept. 18, 1998.

76. *New York Times*, May 16, 1996.

77. *New York Times*, Mar. 9, 1996. It is noteworthy that CEO payments have also grown in many firms whose stocks "underperformed."

78. David Cay Johnston and Christopher Drew, "Special Tax Breaks Enrich Savings of Many in the Ranks of Management," *New York Times*, Oct. 13, 1996.

79. *New York Times*, Oct. 13, 1996.

80. *New York Times*, July 1, 1997.

81. *New York Times*, Oct. 9, 1995.

82. *Worth*, July–August 1997.

83. *New York Times*, Mar. 31, 1997.

84. U.S. Department of Commerce, *Statistical Abstract of the U.S., 1995*, p. 484.

85. *New York Times*, Sept. 10, 2000. Data from the Bureau of Labor Statistics and Department of Agriculture.

86. John K. Galbraith, "Economics in the Century Ahead," in John D. Hey, *The Future of Economics* (Blackwell, 1992), p. 42.

CHAPTER FOUR

State Managers Accumulate Military Power Without Limit

1. Department of Defense, Office of the Undersecretary of Defense (Controller), *Defense Budget Estimates for FY2000*, March 1999, table 7-5; National Science Foundation, *Survey of Federal Funds for Research and Development: Fiscal Years 1997, 1998 and 1999*.

2. Dwight D. Eisenhower's "Farewell to the Nation," *U.S. State Department Bulletin* 44, Feb. 6, 1961.

3. Seymour Melman, Terence McCarthy, Otto Feinstein, Edwin Liewen, John E. Ullmann, William Vickrey, and Benjamin Spock, *A Strategy for American Security: An Alternative to the 1964 Military Budget* (self-published, April 1963).

4. These data are found in the statistical appendixes to the annual *Economic Report of the President* 1952–1995.

5. Department of Defense, Directorate for Information Operations and Reports, *Real and Personal Property*, "Cost Summary of DoD Property Holdings, by Type and Class, According to Defense Component—September 30, 1990."

6. *Survey of Current Business*, January 1992, p. 113.

7. U.S. Department of Defense, Office of the Comptroller, *National Defense Budget Estimates for Fiscal Year 1995*, March 1994, pp. 148–49.

8. These data were obtained in part by special communications from the Manpower Data Center of the Department of Defense, from the report to the Presi-

dent on "Defense Management" by the Secretary of Defense, Dick Cheney, July 1989. In the Cheney report, see the data on p. A-2. Also, *Acquisition Management: Workforce Reductions and Contractor Oversight*, U.S. General Accounting Office, July 1998.

9. Franklin C. Spinney, "Defense Time Bomb: F-22/JSF Case Study: Hypothetical Escape Option," *Challenge*, July–August 1996.

10. Franklin C. Spinney, "The Porkbarrels and Budgeteers: What Went Wrong with the Quadrennial Defense Review?," *Strategic Review*, Fall 1997.

11. Institute for International Strategic Studies, *Military Balance, 1994–1995* (London, 1995).

12. *New York Times*, Oct. 21, 1994.

13. Editorial, *New York Times*, Aug. 10, 1994.

14. Seymour Melman, *Pentagon Capitalism* (McGraw-Hill, 1970).

15. U.S. Department of Defense, *Defense Procurement Circular*, No. 12, 1964.

16. For details, see my *Profits Without Production*, (Alfred A. Knopf, 1988), pp. 91, 211, 212, 215.

17. Seymour Melman, *The Permanent War Economy* (Simon & Schuster, 1974), pp. 264–66.

18. Tom Riddell, "The $676 Billion Quagmire," *The Progressive*, August 1973.

19. *Statistical Abstract of the United States, 1995*, table 552.

20. *Defense Budget Estimates for FY2000.*

21. "Establishment" is underlined here in the sense of this category in the Census of Manufactures. Hence a single multidivision firm can include several "establishments."

22. U.S. National Science Board, *Science and Engineering Indicators—1996*, p. 153.

23. Seymour Melman, *What Else Is There to Do?* (National Commission for Economic Conversion and Disarmament, 1996), p. 6.

24. U.S. Department of Labor, Bureau of Labor Statistics, USDL: 00-07, *Hourly Compensation Costs for Production Workers in Manufacturing*, Washington, D.C., Jan. 11, 2000.

25. *New York Times*, May 31, 1997.

26. This has been detailed in *The New York Times*, May 18, 1997, and Sept 30, 1997.

27. "Comparative Trends of Wage Rates and Capital Goods Prices," *Capital Goods Review* (Machinery and Allied Products Institute, Chicago, November 1953).

28. J. Ronald Fox, *Arming America: How the U.S. Buys Weapons* (Division of Research, Graduate School of Business Administration, Harvard University, 1974), p. 6.

29. The full text of the Ho Chi Minh letter of February 16, 1946, is produced in *Vietnam: The Definitive Documentation of Human Decisions*, ed. Gareth Porter (E. M. Coleman, 1979), vol. 1, p. 95.

30. *Business Week*, Dec. 6, 1999.

31. Broadus Mitchell, *Depression Decade* (Harper & Row, 1947), p. 278.

32. Karl E. Klare, "Judicial Deradicalization of the Wagner Act and the Origins of Modern Legal Consciousness, 1937–1941," *Minnesota Law Review* 62, no. 265 (1978): 292–93.

33. Martin Jay Levitt, with Terry Conrow, *Confessions of a Union Buster* (Crown, 1993).

34. Karl E. Klare, "A Democracy-Enhancing Approach to Labor Law Reform," submitted to the Commission on the Future of Worker-Management Relations, Professor John T. Dunlop, Chair, Washington, D.C., Jan. 19, 1994, p. 35.

35. "The Changing Situation of Workers and Their Unions," A Report by the AFL-CIO Committee on the Evolution of Work, February 1985, pp. 10–11.

36. George Orwell, *1984* (Harcourt Brace, 1949); Afterword by Erich Fromm, in 1961 New American Library edition.

37. J. William Fulbright, *The Pentagon Propaganda Machine* (Liveright, 1970).

38. *New York Times*, Sept. 5, 1993.

39. *New York Times*, Mar. 22, 2000.

40. *New York Times*, June 13, 1976.

41. Henry Durham, a former production manager for Lockheed at Marietta, Georgia. See S. Melman, *The Permanent War Economy*, p. 44.

42. Christopher Cerf and Henry Beard, *The Pentagon Catalog: Ordinary Products at Extraordinary Prices* (Workman, 1986).

43. *New York Times*, Mar. 28, 1997.

44. Seymour Melman, *Dynamic Factors in Industrial Productivity* (Wiley, 1956).

45. U.S., *Statistical Abstract of the U.S., 1992*, Tables 645 and 748; Germany, *Statistisches Jahrbuch, 1992*, Federal Statistical Office, Wiesbaden; Japan, Special Communication from the Bank of Japan.

46. For methodology of the Federal Reserve Board Index of Output of Manufacturing, see U.S. Federal Reserve Board, *Industrial Production*, 1986 edition; and *Federal Reserve Bulletin* 83, February 1997, pp. 67–92.

47. U.S. Department of Commerce, *1995 Annual Survey of Manufactures*, M95 (AS)-1, tables 1a, 4 and 5; *Historical Statistics of the U.S.: Colonial Times to 1957* (Washington, D.C., 1960), Series P24.

48. *Annual Survey of Manufactures*, ibid.

49. Thorstein Veblen, *The Theory of Business Enterprise* (Scribner's, 1904)

50. *New York Herald Tribune*, Mar. 15, 1947.

51. Ibid.

52. *New York Herald Tribune*, Mar. 8, 1947.

Chapter Five

The Hidden Costs of Campaigning for World Hegemony

1. *New York Times*, Jan. 29, 1999.

2. Seymour Melman, "Rebuilding America's Means of Production," *The New Economy*, The National Commission for Economic Conversion and Disarmament (Washington, D.C., Summer 1994).

3. *New York Times*, May 17, 1995.

4. *New York Times*, June 29, 1995.

5. *New York Times*, Nov. 4, 1995.

6. Ibid.

7. In a brochure addressed to prospective engineer and science employees, the managers of the Lincoln Laboratories include the following description of their facilities.

> To meet its challenging goals . . . the Laboratory employs approximately 2,800 men and women, including 900 professional staff members who hold degrees in the following areas:

Electrical engineering 46%
Physics 25
Mathematics 7
Mechanical engineering 5
Aeronautical/astronautical 3
Other 14

Other degrees, such as Computer Science, Materials Science, Civil Engineering, Chemistry, and Nuclear Engineering, are represented in smaller proportions.

Eighty-four percent of the professional staff have earned advanced degrees in their areas of specialty, of which two-thirds are at the doctoral level. . . . To support staff members in their further acquisition of specialized skills and knowledge, Lincoln offers a broad program of in-house technical courses. For those who choose to extend their formal education, there is also a liberal tuition-assistance program for courses taken at MIT and other schools in the Boston area.

The technical library at the Laboratory has a collection of over 106,000 books, 3,300 periodicals, and 650,000 technical reports. Other collections include an excellent archives collection of Lincoln Laboratory publications, a map collection, and an extensive microfiche collection of standards and specifications. The technically trained library staff provides timely and comprehensive services with the aid of multiple online databases.

Salaries and benefits are competitive with industry and include medical, dental, and life insurance, retirement plans, tuition assistance for employees and a college scholarship program for staff children, a credit union, child care services, relocation assistance, a liberal vacation policy, and eleven annual holidays.

8. Federation of American Scientists Fund, *Arms Sales Monitor*, No. 33, Feb. 24, 1997.

9. Data from several government departments as well as from the Swedish International Peace Research Institute are compiled by the Center for Defense Information in its bulletin *The Defense Monitor*, 1994, vol. 23, no. 7.

10. U.S. Arms Control and Disarmament Agency, *World Military Expenditures and Arms Transfers*, table III, 1996.

11. *Arms Sales Monitor*, No. 35, Aug. 6, 1997.

12. William D. Hartung, *Welfare for Weapons Dealers 1998: The Hidden Costs of NATO Expansion* (World Policy Institute, New School for Social Research, New York, 1998); see also his *Corporate Welfare for Weapons Makers: The Hidden Costs of Spending on Defense and Foreign Aid*, in "Policy Analysis" No. 350, The Cato Institute, Aug. 12, 1999.

13. Barbara Conry, "U.S. 'Global Leadership,' " *Policy Analysis*, Cato Institute, Feb. 5, 1997.

14. U.S. Arms Control and Disarmament Agency, *World Military Expenditures and Arms Transfers, 1989* (Washington, D.C., 1990). On February 10, 1994, the *New York Times* reported that Senator Riegle, Chairman of the Senate Banking Committee, announced that his committee had obtained Commerce Department records of export licenses issued to American firms for the shipment of these viruses "used in medical research or in biological warfare," Senator Riegle said. The last shipment on record took place in January 1989. The virus samples shipped to Iraq even included anthrax, which is well known as a possible bacterial warfare agent.

15. George F. Kennan, Foreword to Norman Cousins, *The Pathology of Power* (W. W. Norton, 1987).

16. Ibid.

17. *New York Times*, Feb. 17, 1992.

18. Defense Science Board, *The Defense Science Board 1997 Summer Study Task Force on DoD Responses to Transnational Threats* (Washington, D.C., U.S. Department of Defense, October 1997).

19. Thorstein Veblen, *The Theory of Business Enterprise* (Scribner's, 1904), pp. 392–93.

20. Stephen I. Schwartz, ed., *Atomic Audit: The Costs and Consequences of U.S. Nuclear Weapons Since 1940* (Brookings Institution, 1998), pp. 3, 5, 91.

21. Ibid., p. 3.

22. *Los Angeles Times*, Nov. 2, 1997.

23. Franklin Spinney, "Defense Time Bomb: F-22/JSF. Case Study Hypothetical Escape Option," *Challenge*, July–August 1996.

24. The original drafters of this chart included Social Security as a U.S. government spending category ($7.856 trillion). I deleted this entry, because it comes out of earmarked wage/salary deductions as in an insurance system, and not out of the general revenue of the government.

25. *Atomic Audit*, p. 5; Office of Management and Budget, *Budget of U.S. Government, Fiscal Year 1998, Historical Tables*, pp. 42–49; and *Analytical Perspectives*, pp. 285, 286. National Defense category has been adjusted to include nuclear-weapons and infrastructure costs; nuclear-weapons costs are a combination of actual and estimated expenditures; income security as defined by the Office of Management and Budget excludes programs such as federal employee retirement pensions and disability, unemployment compensation, housing assistance and other "welfare" programs; the *Atomic Audit* column for income security totaled $5.346 trillion, reduced by $0.651 trillion for "Military Retirement" component, transferred to National Defense; Interest on National Debt, 1940–1996, was $4.722 trillion, half of which, $2.361 trillion, has been estimated as part of National Defense, as being war-related, transferred to National Defense column; Social Security excluded from this chart as an outlay that does not derive from government general revenue and is represented by payments into Social Security accounts by employers and employees; Veterans Benefits and Services are arguably National Defense–related but are shown separately, as in the *Atomic Audit* chart.

26. United Nations, *National Accounts Statistics: Main Aggregates and Detailed Tables*, 1996.

27. NSC-68, "A Report to the National Security Council by the Executive Secretary on United States Objectives and Programs for National Security, April 14, 1950," *Naval War College Review*, May–June 1975.

28. Paul A. Baran, *The Political Economy of Growth* (Monthly Review Press, 1957), p. 41.

29. Samuel Bowles, David M. Gordon, and Thomas E. Weisskopf, *Beyond the Waste Land: A Democratic Alternative to Economic Decline* (Anchor Press/Doubleday, 1983), pp. 11–13.

30. Campbell R. McConnell, *Economics: Principles, Problems and Policies*, 5th ed. (1972), p. 707.

31. Seymour Melman, *The Permanent War Economy*, (McGraw-Hill, 1994), pp. 129, 130.

32. Nathan Glazer, "The Great Society Was Never a Casualty of the War," *Saturday Review*, December 1972.

33. Walter Heller, *New Dimensions of Political Economy* (Cambridge, Mass., 1967), pp. 10–11, cited in R. B. Du Boff and E. S. Herman, "The New Economics: Handmaiden of Inspired Truth," *The Review of Radical Political Economics* 4, No. 4 (August 1972).

34. U.S. Bureau of the Census, *Statistical Abstract of the United States: 1995*, Washington, D.C., table 559.

35. Tom Riddell, "The $676 Billion Quagmire," *The Progressive*, October 1973.

36. *New York Times*, Feb. 2, 1995.

37. U.S. Department of Housing and Urban Development, *American Housing Survey, 1998*, Washington, D.C.; AFL-CIO Housing Investment Trust, *Annual Reports*, 1993–1996, Washington, D.C. ; *New York Times*, Apr. 28, 1998.

38. "A Haven for the Super-rich," *New York Times*, Apr. 25, 1998.

39. *New York Times*, Apr. 28, 1998.

40. *New York Times*, Nov. 13, 1998.

41. U.S. Department of Transportation, Federal Highway Administration, Federal Transit Administration, *The Status of the Nation's Highways, Bridges and Transit Conditions and Performance*, 1993, p. iii.

42. John E. Ullmann, "Task for Engineers: Resuscitating the U.S. Rail System," *Technology and Society*, Winter 1993.

43. *California and the Twenty-first Century: Foundations for a Competitive Society*, Report of the State of California Senate Select Committee on Long Range Policy Planning, vol. 2, Jan. 1986, table III, p. 23.

44. *Phoenix Gazette*, Nov. 26, 1994.

45. *Daily News of Los Angeles*, Mar. 18, 1997.

46. *New York Times*, Feb. 2, 1995.

47. *American Metal Markets*, July 22 and Aug. 25, 1997.

48. *New York Times*, July 25, 1996.

49. *New York Post*, Sept. 16, 1996.

50. *New York Times*, Sept. 9, 1993.

51. Suntrust Equitable Securities, "Crime Still Pays," a research report, Jan. 2, 1997.

52. *New York Times*, July 24, 1997, and Sept. 28, 1997.

53. The Cooper Union for the Advancement of Science and Art, *The Age of New York City Infrastructure: Water Supply, Wastewater Disposal, Bridges, Transit, Streets*, August 1991.

54. F. H. Griffis, *Infrastructure of New York City: A Policymakers' Guide* (The National Infrastructure Center for Engineering Systems and Technology, 1996).

55. City of New York Office of the Comptroller [Alan G. Hevesi], *Dilemma in the Millennium*, 2 vols., August 1998.

56. *New York Times*, Aug. 25, 1998.

57. *New York Times*, Mar. 8, 2000.

58. *New York Times*, Jan. 1, 1993

59. Ibid.

60. From a review of Carey Nelson, *Manifesto of a Tenured Radical* (New York University Press, 1997), in *The Nation*, June 23, 1997.

61. *The Nation*, Dec. 1, 1993.

62. Raymond Hernandez, *New York Times*, Dec. 4, 1998.

63. Terry J. Rosenberg, *Poverty in New York City in 1993: An Update* (Community Service Society of New York, 1994).

64. *New York Times*, Oct. 7, 1999.

65. *New York Times,* June 10, 1999.

66. Juan Gonzalez, *In These Times,* June 27, 1999.

67. Ibid., May 30, 1999.

68. *The Nation,* Mar. 29, 1999.

69. Ibid.

70. *The Nation,* Aug. 9, 1998.

71. Carnegie Task Force, *Starting Points: Meeting the Needs of Our Youngest Children* (Abridged Version) (Carnegie Corporation of New York, 1994), p. 16.

72. *New York Times,* Jan. 23, 1999.

73. Ibid.

74. *New York Times,* Jan. 4, 1999.

75. Bob Herbert, "In America," *New York Times,* Apr. 11, 1999.

76. Ibid.

77. Ibid.

78. Zellig S. Harris, *The Transformation of Capitalist Society* (Rowman & Littlefield, 1997), p. 69.

79. *New York Times,* Apr. 11, 1997.

80. *New York Times,* Aug. 2, 1997, and July 29, 1997.

81. *New York Times,* June 25, 1994.

82. Special Report/Corporate Welfare, *Time,* Nov. 23, 1998.

83. Ibid.

84. Janet N. Abramovitz, *Imperiled Waters, Impoverished Future: The Decline of Freshwater Ecosystems* (Worldwatch Institute, Worldwatch Paper 128, March 1996). See also Christopher Flavin and Odil Tunali, *Climate of Hope: New Strategies for Stabilizing the World's Atmosphere* (Worldwatch Institute, Worldwatch Paper 130, June 1996); Gary Gardner, *Shrinking Fields: Cropland Loss in a World of Eight Billion* (Worldwatch Institute, Worldwatch Paper 131, July 1996); Sandra Postel, *Dividing the Waters: Food Security, Ecosystem Health, and the New Politics of Scarcity* (Worldwatch Institute, Worldwatch Paper 132, September 1996); Michael Renner, *Fighting for Survival* (W. W. Norton; Worldwatch Institute, 1996); Lester R. Brown, Christopher Flavin, and Hal Kane, *Vital Signs 1996,* ed. Linda Starke (Worldwatch Institute, 1996); Peter Weber, *Abandoned Seas: Reversing the Decline of the Oceans* (Worldwatch Institute, Worldwatch Paper 116, November 1993); Peter Weber, *Net Loss: Fish, Jobs, and the Marine Environment* (Worldwatch Institute, Worldwatch Paper 120, July 1994); "The World Resources Institute, The United Nations Environment Programme, The United Nations Development Programme, and The World Bank," *World Resources 1996–97* (Oxford University Press, 1996); John E. Young, *Mining the Earth* (Worldwatch Institute, Worldwatch Paper 109, July 1992).

An informative TV program on the greenhouse effect in the earth's atmosphere, with details on weather and climate aspects, is in *20th Century with Mike Wallace: The Sizzling Planet* (produced by CBS New Productions in association with the History Channel, 1999, program no. AH50080).

85. "Fixed Reproducible Tangible Wealth in the United States," *Survey of Current Business,* September 1998, table 5, p. 40.

86. Seymour Melman, "The Rise of Administrative Overhead in the Manufacturing Industries of the U.S., 1899–1947," *Oxford Economic Papers,* new series, vol. 3, no. 1 (January 1951).

87. U.S. Department of Commerce, Bureau of the Census, *1990 Census of Population and Housing, Occupation and Industry,* Subject Summary Tape File (SSTF) 14 (March 1995), CD90SSTF14 compact disc.

88. In the United States, Japan, England and Russia, there has been a continuing outflow from the engineering occupations to finance, business consulting and so forth,

all paying notably higher salaries than those available to engineers. This trend is visible at Columbia University. See also "Where Have All Japan's Engineers Gone?," *Science*, Feb. 7, 1992; similar data for England: *The Economist*, May 16, 1987. The U.S.S.R. has had a long drain of engineers going into "business" and government administration.

89. Richard Alan Montage, "Administrative Employees, Productivity and Output, and Administrative Intensity at the Establishment and Corporate Headquarters," Ph.D. dissertation in Industrial Engineering, Columbia University, 1983.

CHAPTER SIX

The Lessons of Soviet Russia: From Alienation to Production Collapse

1. Tatyana Tolstaya, "Russian Roulette," *New York Review of Books*, Nov. 19, 1998.

2. *Business Week*, Dec. 27, 1999.

3. Venyamin Sokolov, "The Virus in Russia," *New York Times*, June 1, 1998.

4. Mortimer Zuckerman, "Proud Russia on Its Knees: Will the West Come to the Rescue?," *U.S. News & World Report*, Feb. 8, 1999.

5. Timothy L. O'Brien, "The Shrinking Oligarchs of Russia," *New York Times*, Sept. 27, 1998.

6. Andrew Kopkind, "From Russia with Love and Squalor," *The Nation*, Jan. 18, 1993.

7. Zuckerman, "Proud Russia on Its Knees."

8. Ibid.

9. Rachel L. Swarns, *New York Times*, Oct. 15, 1996.

10. Fred Weir, "Free Fall: Russia Tumbles into Autumn After a Catastrophic Summer," *In These Times*, Oct. 4, 1998.

11. Serge Schmemann, "How Can You Have a Bust if You Never Had a Boom?: The Precapitalist Economy of the Russian Majority," *New York Times Magazine*, Dec. 27, 1998.

12. "Anatomy of a Russian Wreck," *Business Week*, Sept. 7, 1998.

13. Schmemann, "How Can You Have a Bust if You Never Had a Boom?"

14. Michael R. Gordon, *New York Times*, Nov. 30, 1998.

15. *New York Times*, Nov. 7, 1998.

16. *New York Times*, Nov. 30, 1998.

17. *New York Times*, Nov. 7, 1998.

18. Kopkind, "From Russia with Love and Squalor."

19. Thomas B. Cochran, Robert S. Norris, and Oleg A. Bukharin, *Making the Russian Bomb: From Stalin to Yeltsin* (Westview Press, 1995), p. 54.

20. Ibid., pp. 96–97. For the prime sources used in that study, see A. K. Kruglov, "On the History of Atomic Science and Industry," *The Bulletin of the Center of Public Information*, particularly no. 10, 1993.

21. William J. Broad, *New York Times*, Sept. 26, 1993.

22. Cochran et al., *Making the Russian Bomb*, p. 34.

23. Ibid., p. 285.

24. Judith Miller and William J. Broad, "Germ Weapons: In Soviet Past, or in the New Russia's Future?," *New York Times*, Dec. 28, 1998.

25. *Jane's Armour and Artillery*, Christopher F. Foss, ed. (Jane's Information Group, 1979/80–present), 19th ed., 1998–99; *Jane's Fighting Ships*, Captain Richard Sharpe, ed. (Jane's Information Group, 1898–present), 101st ed., 1998–99; *Jane's Military Communications*, John Williamson, ed. (Jane's Information Group, 1979/80—

present), 18th ed., 1998–99; *Jane's All the World's Aircraft*, Paul Jackson, ed. (Jane's Information Group, 1909–present), 89th issue, 1998–99; *Jane's Ammunition Handbook* (Jane's Information Group, 1999); *Jane's Military Vehicles and Logistics*, Christopher F. Foss and Terry J. Gander, eds. (Jane's Information Group, 1980–present), 17th ed., 1996-97.

26. Alexander A. Belkin, "Needed: A Russian Defense Policy," *Global Affairs*, Fall 1992, pp. 89ff.

27. Cochran et al., *Making the Russian Bomb*, p. 34.

28. U.S.S.R., State Committee for Statistics, *Economic Survey, No. 9, January–September, 1991*. The U.S.S.R. was formally dissolved after September 1991.

29. Stanley H. Cohn, *Declining Soviet Capital Productivity and the Soviet Military Industrial Complex*. This paper appeared as an appendix to U.S. Arms Control and Disarmament Agency, *World Military Expenditure and Arms Transfers*, 1972–1982 (April 1984).

30. U.S. Department of Commerce, STAT-USA, National Trade Data Bank and Economic Bulletin Board, *Russia–Metalworking Equipment–ISA9410*, Market Research Reports, October 1994.

31. Ibid.

32. Ibid.

33. Maria Breiter, *Overview of the Machine Tool Industry in Russia*, U.S. Department of Commerce, International Trade Administration, November 1997.

34. The following is an able analysis of the further consequences for the Russian economy from attempts to convert its former dominant military-industrial complex. Alexei Izyumov, Leonid Kosals, and Rozalina Ryvkina, "The Russian Military-Industrial Complex: The Shock of Independence," *The New Economy*, Winter 1995.

35. Andrei Baev et al., *American Ventures in Russia: Report of a Workshop on March 20–21, 1995, at Stanford University*, Stanford University: Center for International Security and Arms Control, May 1995.

36. *New York Times*, Mar. 10, 1992.

37. Published by General Confederation of Trade Unions in its periodical, *Inform-Contact*, April–June 1998, English translation courtesy of the International Department, Executive Committee, GCTU.

38. Julian Cooper, *The Soviet Defense Industry: Conversion and Economic Reform* (Council on Foreign Relations Press, 1991), p. 63.

39. David Mandel, *Rabotyagi: Perestroika and After Viewed from Below: Interviews with Workers in the Soviet Union* (Monthly Review Press, 1994), p. 110.

40. Bill Keller, "After Rash of Wildcat Moves, Soviets Admit Right to Strike," *New York Times*, May 4, 1989.

41. Petr Siuda, "Survival and Resistance: A Soviet Family's Story," in David Mandel, *Rabotyagi*.

42. David Remnick, "Soviet Miners Spurn Call to Cease Strikes," *Washington Post*, July 23, 1989.

43. David Remnick, "Gorbachev Lauds Strikes as Reform 'Breakthrough'; 'Good Reasons' for Walkout, Soviet Leader Says," *Washington Post*, July 24, 1989.

44. *Los Angeles Times*, July 11, 1990.

45. Elizabeth Shogren and John-Thor Dahlburg, "Soviet Miners Strike, Seek to End Communist Rule," *Los Angeles Times*, July 12, 1990.

46. Henry Kamm, "Struggling Ukrainian Miners Are Put Off by Diet of Nationalism," *New York Times*, Feb. 16, 1992.

47. Jane Perlez, "Ukraine's Miners Bemoan the Cost of Independence," *New York Times*, July 17, 1993.

48. David Hoffman, "1 Million Miners Go On Strike in Russia, Ukraine," *Washington Post*, Feb. 2, 1996.

49. Richard W. Stevenson, "Russian Miners Become Victims of Upheaval They Helped Start," *New York Times*, Oct. 29, 1994.

50. V. Komarovskii, "The Miners' Movement: Dynamics and Directions of Development," New Directions in Worker-Management Relations Conference: Moscow, Mar. 22, 1991.

51. "Ukraine: Hair-Raising Ultimatum," *Inform-Contact*, No. 24, January–March 1999, p. 7. (*Inform-Contact* publishes news from the General Confederation of Trade Unions, 42 Leninsky Prospekt, 117 119 Moscow, Russia. Email: iidprof@cityline. ru)

52. Serge Schmemann, "Even With a Vote, Sending a Message to Moscow Is Tricky," *New York Times*, Mar. 24, 1991.

53. Simon Clarke, Peter Fairbrother, and Vadim Borisov, *The Workers' Movement in Russia* (Edward Elgar, 1995), pp. 409, 410.

54. Alexander Werth, *Russia at War, 1941–1945* (Dutton, 1964), p. 1037.

55. Cochran et al., *Making the Russian Bomb*, p. 10.

56. State Committee of the U.S.S.R. for Statistics, "Finance and Statistics," *U.S.S.R. People's Economy in 1989: Statistical Annual* (Moscow, 1990).

57. Georgy Skorov, "Economic Reform in the USSR: What Went Wrong," a revised summary of lectures given at the University of Florence and the University of Rome, "La Sapienza," in April and May 1991 (no publisher). Georgy Skorov was then a Senior Research Fellow at the Academy of Sciences of the U.S.S.R., and Visiting Professor at the American University of Paris.

58. Ibid.

59. Stephen Kotkin, *Steeltown, USSR: Soviet Society in the Gorbachev Era* (University of California Press, 1991).

60. *60 Minutes*, CBS Television Network, May 19, 1996. Solid data on the Soviet health and environmental breakdown can be found in Murray Feshback and Alfred Friendly, Jr., *Ecocide in the USSR: Health and Nature Under Siege* (Basic Books, 1992); Toni Nelson, "Russia's Population Sink," *WorldWatch*, January–February 1996; D. J. Peterson, *Troubled Lands: The Legacy of Soviet Environmental Destruction* (Westview Press, 1993).

CHAPTER SEVEN

The Attempt to Make Workers and Unions Obsolete

1. Seymour Melman, *Dynamic Factors in Industrial Productivity* (Wiley, 1956).

2. Paul Osterman, "New Technology and the Organization of Work: A Review of the Issues," *The Challenge of New Technology to Labor-Management Relations*, U.S. Department of Labor, BLMR 135, 1989.

3. John E. Ullmann, "Criteria of Change in Machinery Design," Ph.D. dissertation, Columbia University, Industrial Engineering, 1959.

4. David Noble, *Forces of Production* (Alfred A. Knopf, 1983).

5. *The Control of New Technology: Trade Union Strategies in the Workplace*, The Joint Forum of Combine Committees, The Centre for Alternative Industrial and Technological Systems, Dagenham, Essex, 1982, p. 23.

6. Seymour Melman, *Dynamic Factors*, p. 206.

7. Sebastian B. Littauer, "Stability of Production Rates as a Determinant of Industrial Productivity Levels," *Proceedings of the Business and Economic Statistics Section*,

American Statistical Association. Washington, D.C., 1955, pp. 241–48; W. Edwards Deming, *Out of the Crisis* (MIT Press, 2000).

8. "Outsourcing Goes Inside," *UE News*, Feb. 19, 1999. A Publication of the United Electrical, Radio and Machine Workers Union.

9. See Seymour Melman, *Profits Without Production* (Alfred A. Knopf, 1983); "Who Decides Technology," *Columbia Forum*, Winter 1968; Nathan Rosenberg, *Perspectives on Technology* (Cambridge University Press, 1976).

10. The Charles Stark Draper Laboratory, Inc., *Flexible Manufacturing System Handbook, Volume III: Buyer's/User's Guide, February 1983* (Cambridge, Mass., 1983).

11. Bernard Ogbuka Nneji, "Capital Productivity in Relation to Organization of Work in Computer Controlled Machine Tool Production," Ph.D. dissertation, Columbia University, Department of Industrial Engineering and Operations Research, 1988.

12. Ibid.

13. Ibid.

14. Ibid.

15. Stephen Aguren and Jan Edgern, *New Factories: Job Design Through Factory Planning in Sweden*, Swedish Employers Confederation, Technical Department, 1980.

16. Harley Shaiken, *Work Transformed: Automation and Labor in the Computer Age* (Lexington Books, 1984), pp. 271–73.

17. International Association of Machinists and Aerospace Workers, *Let's Rebuild America* (Kelly Press, 1984).

18. Robert Karasek and Tores Theorell, *Healthy Work: Stress, Productivity and the Reconstruction of Working Life* (Basic Books, 1990), Chap. 2.

19. Ibid., p. 6.

20. Ibid., p. 238, citing M. D. Hanlon, D. A. Nadler, and D. Gladstein, *Attempting Work Reform: The Case of "Parkside" Hospital* (Wiley, 1985), p. 16.

CHAPTER EIGHT

Management Promotes Ownership Without Control

1. Louis Uchitelle, "Downsizing Comes to Employee-Owned America," *New York Times*, July 7, 1996.

2. Joseph R. Blasi and Douglas L. Kruse, *The New Owners* (Harper Business, 1991), p. 12.

3. Katherine Ivancic and John Logue, *Employee Ownership in the United States: Legislation, Implementation and Models* (Northeast Ohio Employee Ownership Center, 1986), p. 5.

4. Among leaders of the ESOP movement, it is understood that "Most of the early examples of large employee-owned companies have failed to create a true ownership culture . . . management is unwilling to let employees exercise normal shareholder rights." This is from Joseph R. Blasi. See note 2 above, and Aaron Bernstein, "Why ESOP Deals Have Slowed to a Crawl," *Business Week*, Mar. 18, 1996.

5. National Center for Employee Ownership, *Employee Ownership Report*, July–August 1997.

6. Special communication from the union.

7. Uchitelle, "Downsizing Comes to Employee-Owned America."

8. *Employee Ownership Report*, January–February 1997.

9. Joseph R. Blasi and Douglas L. Kruse, *The New Owners.*

10. *Business Week*, Mar. 18, 1996.

11. Louis O. Kelso and Mortimer Adler, *The Capitalist Manifesto* (Greenwood Press, 1975).

12. Louis O. Kelso, Testimony Before House Committee on Small Business, 1979, p. 136, cited in David Ellerman, "ESOPs and CO-OPs: Worker Capitalism and Worker Democracy," *Labor Research Review*, no. 5 (Spring 1985).

13. David P. Ellerman, "ESOPS and Co-ops."

14. Ibid.

15. A particularly informative report on this subject is in Michael Blumstein, "New Role for Employee Plans: Warding Off Takeovers," *New York Times*, Jan. 2, 1985.

16. Gorm Winther and Richard Marens, "Participatory Democracy May Go a Long Way: Comparative Growth Performance of Employee Ownership Firms in New York and Washington States," *Economic and Industrial Democracy: An International Journal* 18, no. 3 (August 1997). This paper includes a substantial bibliography.

17. *Owners at Work* (summer 1997): 2.

18. Joyce Rothschild-Whitt, "Who Will Benefit from ESOPs?," *Labor Research Review* 6 (spring 1985): 70–80.

19. Adolph A. Berle and Gardiner Means, *The Modern Corporation and Private Property* (Macmillan, 1933; Harcourt, Brace and World, 1968).

CHAPTER NINE

Creating Workplace Democracy

1. Lawrence B. Cohen, "Workers and Decision-Making on Production," unpublished manuscript, 1954, p. 3.

2. Ibid., p. 1.

3. Ibid., p. 25.

4. Ibid.

5. Ibid., p. 3.

6. Ibid., p. 6.

7. Ibid., p. 4.

8. Ibid., pp. 4, 5.

9. Lawrence B. Cohen, "The Structure of Workers' Decisions," *Journal of Economic Issues* 10, no. 2 (June 1976): 529.

10. Ibid., p. 530.

11. Ibid., p. 531.

12. Ibid., p. 533.

13. Cohen, "Workers and Decision-Making on Production," p. 25.

14. Ibid., p. 26.

15. Ibid.

16. Cohen, "Workers and Decision-Making on Production, II," unpublished manuscript, 1994, chap. 6, p. 4.

17. *Agreements Between UAW and the Ford Motor Company*, vol. 1, Oct. 7, 1990 (pp. 220–24) and Oct. 9, 1999 (pp. 242–49). Elaboration of Appendix P of this agreement also appears in volume 4, entitled *Letters of Understanding Between UAW and the Ford Motor Company*, especially pp. 223–26 containing "Sourcing—Consolidated Letter of Understanding" and "Sourcing—Standardized Financial Form."

18. Dan M. Mater, *The Railroad Seniority System* (University of Chicago Libraries, 1941).

19. Carl Gersuny, "Origins of Seniority Provisions in Collective Bargaining," *Labor Law Journal*, August 1982.

20. Katherine Stone, "The Origins of Job Structures in the Steel Industry," *Review of Radical Political Economics*, 1974.

21. Lawrence B. Cohen, "Workers and Decision-Making on Production."

22. Seymour Melman, *Decision-Making and Productivity* (Basil Blackwell, 1958).

23. Ibid.

24. Dwight Rayton, "Shop Floor Democracy in Action" (Russell Limited, London, 1972), pp. 8, 9; cited in William M. Evan, "Hierarchy, Alienation, Commitment and Organizational Effectiveness," *Human Relations* 30 (1976): 77–94.

25. International Association of Machinists and Aerospace Workers, *HPWO Field Manual: High Performance Work Organization Partnerships*, Washington, D.C., 1995.

26. Ibid.

27. Ibid.

28. Ibid.

29. Ibid.

30. Ibid.

31. Ibid.

32. The quoted materials in the following discussions are drawn from the following publications of the United Steel Workers of America: *Comparison Study of 1993–1994 Settlements: Between the United Steelworkers of America and Four of the Major Steel Companies in the U.S.*, 1994; *Workers' Contract Negotiations in the Steel Industry of the United States*, 1996; *New Directions Bargaining in the American Steel Industry*, 1997; *Statement of the International Wage Policy Committee*, 1998. Appendix 15, in *Memorandum of Understanding on Employee and Union Participation*, Agreement Between Bethlehem Steel Corporation and United Steel Workers of America, 1998.

33. Harley Shaiken, Steven Lopez, and Isaac Mankita, "Two Routes to Team Production: Saturn and Chrysler Compared," *Industrial Relations* 36, no. 1 (January 1997): 23.

34. Ibid., p. 24.

35. Ibid., p. 38

36. Ibid., pp. 32, 33.

37. Ibid., p. 31.

38. Saturn Corporation, *Memorandum of Agreement (MOA) Between the Saturn Corporation (a Wholly Owned Subsidiary of the General Motors Corporation) and the International Union, United Automobile, Aerospace and Agricultural Implement Workers of America*, 1997.

39. Ibid., p. 2.

40. Ibid., p. 9.

41. Ibid., pp. 9, 10.

42. Ibid., p. 3.

43. Ibid., p. 11.

44. Ibid., p. 17.

45. Ibid., p. 13.

46. Ibid., pp. 4–7.

47. Eileen Applebaum and Rosemary Batt, *The New American Workplace* (ILR Press, 1994), p. 35; Robert M. Marsh, "The Difference Between Participation and Power in Japanese Factories," *Industrial and Labor Relations Review* 45, no. 2, pp. 250ff.

48. Harley Shaiken et al., "Two Routes to Team Production," p. 28.

CHAPTER TEN

White Collar Joins the Blue

1. Steven Greenhouse, "Angered by HMO's Treatment, More Doctors Are Joining Unions," *New York Times*, Feb. 4, 1999.

2. Ibid.

3. Ibid.

4. Grace Budrys, *When Doctors Join Unions* (Cornell University Press, 1997), p. 32.

5. Ibid., p. 10.

6. Suzanne Gordon, "Rescuing Quality Care: Perspectives and Strategies: Introduction," in *Abandonment of the Patient: The Impact of Profit-Driven Health Care on the Public*, ed. Ellen D. Baer, Claire Fagin, and Suzanne Gordon (Springer, 1996), pp. 54–55.

7. Dr. Quentin D. Young, "The Case Against Profit-Driven Managed Care," in *Abandonment*, pp. 68–69.

8. Laura Meckler, *AP Online*, Mar. 1, 1999.

9. These judgments are part of an assessment by Jerome P. Kassirer titled "Doctor Discontent," in *The New England Journal of Medicine* (Nov. 19, 1998).

10. *New York Times*, July 17,1997.

11. Bob Herbert, "Hospitals in Crisis," *New York Times*, Apr. 15, 1999.

12. Ibid.

13. Michael S. Hamilton, *The Impact of Managed Care on U.S. Markets*, Study by KPMG Peat Marwick LLP, Managed Care Segment, 1996.

14. Editorial, *New York Times*, Apr. 14, 1999.

15. Suzanne Gordon and Timothy McCall, M.D., "Healing in a Hurry; Hospitals in the Managed-Care Age," *The Nation*, Mar. 1, 1999.

16. Ibid.

17. *USA Today*, Apr. 29, 1999.

18. *New York Times*, Apr. 1, 1999.

19. Jane Slaughter, "Union Doctors: How Corporate Excesses Have Pushed the Most Powerful and Wealthy Members of Our Work Force to Sign Union Cards," *Labor Notes*, October 1997, pp. 8–9.

20. Ibid.

21. *Health Line*, June 5, 1998.

22. Laura Meckler, *AP Online*, Mar. 1, 1999.

23. *Medical Industry Today*, Mar. 3, 1999.

24. *New York Times*, Feb. 4, 1999.

25. *New York Times*, Nov. 12, 1998.

26. *Modern HealthCare*, Aug. 3, 1998.

27. Committee of Interns and Residents, *Collective Bargaining Agreement (April 31, 1995–March 31, 2000) Between the City of New York, Health and Hospitals Corp. and the Committee of Interns and Residents, an Affiliate of the Service Employees International Union, AFL-CIO*, Oct. 14, 1997, pp. 17 and 86.

28. Ibid., p. 88

29. *New York Times*, Mar. 2, 1999.

30. U.S. Department of Commerce, *Statistical Abstract of the United States 1998*, table 200, p. 134. For 1996, the staff-to-patient ratio for all U.S. hospitals was 624:100 but was highest in "nongovernmental nonprofit" hospitals, at 715:100.

31. Claire M. Fagin, "Nurses, Patients and Managed Care," *New York Times*, Mar. 16, 1999.

32. Claire Fagin, "Introduction," *Abandonment*, p. 11.

33. Claire Fagin, "Nurses, Patients and Managed Care."

34. *New York Times*, Oct. 19, 1999.

35. Sandra Feldman, "Professionals and Unions," *New York Times*, Dec. 5, 1999.

36. U.S. Department of Education, *Digest of Education Statistics, 1996*, table 324.

37. *Science and Engineering Indicators*, 1998, appendix table 5-9.

38. Michael D. Yates, "Frederick Taylor Comes to College: Breaking Faculty Jobs into Discrete Tasks," *Z Magazine*, March 1999, pp. 49–48.

39. Jerry Farber, "The Third Circle: On Education and Distance Learning," *Sociological Perspectives* 41, no. 4, 797–814.

40. An informative collection of short papers called "Distance Education" is presented in *Academe*, 85, no. 5 (September-October 1999).

41. *New York Times*, Mar. 31, 1999.

42. *Financial Times*, Mar. 8, 1999.

43. U.S. Department of Education, *Digest of Education Statistics, 1998*, tables 342–46. Data for 1975 not published.

44. Ibid., table 174.

45. Stanley Aronowitz, "Are Unions Good for Professors?" *Academe*, Vol. 84, no. 6 (November–December 1998): 12–17.

46. U.S. Department of Education, *Digest of Education Statistics*, tables 174, 221 (data for numbers of administrative staff in 1975 not published); U.S. Department of Education, National Center for Education Statistics, *Integrated Secondary Education Data System (IPEDS)*, various yearly tables.

47. This was the judgment of Cary Nelson, editor, *Will Teach for Food: Academic Labor in Crisis* (University of Minnesota Press, 1997).

48. Stanley Aronowitz, "Are Unions Good for Professors?"

49. Karen W. Arenson, "Part-Time Faculty Is an Issue Now at CUNY," *New York Times*, Feb. 14, 1998.

50. The book cited is William G. Bowen and Julie Ann Sosa, *Prospects for Faculty in the Arts and Sciences: A Study of Factors Affecting Demand and Supply* (Princeton University Press, 1989).

51. Mark R. Kelley, William Pannapacker, and Ed Wiltse, "Scholarly Associations Must Face the True Causes of the Academic Job Crisis," *The Chronicle of Higher Education*, Dec. 18, 1998.

52. California Faculty Association, "Handbook for Lecturers," 1997.

53. Laurence Gold and Perry Robinson, *The Vanishing Professor*, American Federation of Teachers, Higher Education Department, July 1998.

54. Text of a statement by Ernie Benjamin entitled "Part-Time Teaching and the State of the [Historical] Profession: An AAUP Perspective," January 1999.

55. "This paper was originally written as a discussion document for use in a university senate subcommittee charged with investigating and evaluating the working conditions of part-time faculty in Georgia State University in Atlanta, Georgia . . ."

56. Thomas J. Farrell, "How to Kill Higher Education," *Academe*, Vol. 78 no. 6, (November–December 1992). A pointed discussion appeared in *Academe* about administrative bloat (Vol. 77, No. 6, November–December 1991), by Barbara Bergmann, who showed that over the last two decades administrative costs have increased more than instructional costs.

57. Courtney Leatherman, "Faculty Unions Move to Organize Growing Ranks of Part-Time Professors," *The Chronicle of Higher Education*, Feb. 27, 1998.

58. Harry Brill and Gary Zabel, "U. Mass Part-Time Faculty Win Benefits: From Ivory Tower to UPS: Full-Time Work for Part-Time Pay," *Labor Notes*, September 1998.

59. Letter in *Academe*, November–December, 1998, by James E. Perley, president, AAUP, 1998.

60. Karen Thompson, "Recognizing Mutual Interests," *Academe* 78, no. 6 (November–December 1992).

61. *The Chronicle of Higher Education*, Dec. 5, 1997.

62. *New York Times*, Mar. 7, 2000.

63. *New York Times*, Mar. 21, 2000.

64. The development of the engineering professions in American idustry is portrayed in David Noble, *America by Design* (Alfred A. Knopf, 1997). For an earlier treatment, see Vera Shlakman, "Unionism and Professional Organizations Among Engineers," *Science and Society*, Parts I, II, vol. 14, no. 3, p. 214, and vol. 14, no. 4, pp. 322ff.

CHAPTER ELEVEN

Disalienation by Design: Installing Workplace Democracy

1. Greg MacLeod, *From Mondragon to America: Experiments in Community Economic Development* (University College of Cape Breton Press, 1997); Jose Maria Ormaechea, *The Mondragon Cooperative Experience* (Mondragon Cooperative Corporation, 1993); William Foote Whyte and Kathleen King Whyte, *Making Mondragon: The Growth and Dynamics of the Worker Cooperative* (ILR Press, 1988).

In addition to the above, the following are good data and analysis sources on the Mondragon co-ops: The Annual Report of the Caja Laboral; David Ellerman, *Management Planning with Labor as a Fixed Cost* (Industrial Cooperative Association, 1984); Keith Bradley and Alan Gelb, *Cooperation at Work: The Mondragon Experience* (Heinemann Educational Books, 1983); Mike Long, "The Mondragon Federation: A Model for Our Times," *Libertarian Labor Review*, no. 19 (winter 1996); Sally L. Hacker, "Gender and Technology at the Mondragon System of Producer Cooperatives," manuscript, Department of Sociology, Oregon State University (undated); David Ellerman, *The Mondragon Cooperative Movement*, Harvard Business School, Case Study No. 8-384-270, HBS Case Services, Harvard Business School; Roy Morrison, *We Build the Road as We Travel* (New Society Publishers, 1991).

2. David P. Ellerman, *Management Planning with Labor as a Fixed Cost: The Mondragon Annual Business Plan Manual* (Industrial Cooperative Association, Boston), 1984.

3. Kevin Kaighn, Kamron Keshtgar, Houman Mondarres, Rich Reimer, and Ben Spitz, *Mondragon Cooperatives: Analysis and Comparisons to Western Organizations*, a 1992 report commissioned as a Columbia University course paper in industrial engineering by Prof. Peter Norden.

4. MacLeod, pp. 165-72.

5. Daniel Guerin, *Anarchism from Theory to Practice*, with Introduction by Noam Chomsky on the anarchist collectives in Spain (Monthly Review Press, 1971). The Israeli kibbutz is covered by a large literature: books, journals, and memoirs that are in most university and other large libraries.

6. Seymour Melman, *Industrial Efficiency Under Managerial vs. Cooperative Decision-Making: A Comparative Study of Industrial Enterprise in Israel*, Studies in Comparative International Development, Sage Publications, March 1969.

7. Netafim at Kibbutz Hatzerim, D.N. Hanegev 85505, Israel. Tel: 972 (7) 647-3111, Fax: 972 (7) 643-2817, 642-0098.

8. Tama at Kibbutz Mishmar-Ha'emek, 19236, Israel. Tel: 972 (04) 989-9600, Fax: 972 (04) 989-2901.

9. Istat, *Annuario Statistico Italiano*, 1999; Istat, *Censimento Intermedio*, 1996.

10. Irene Rubbin, *Italy's Industrial Renaissance: A Strategy for Developing Small Manufacturing Business*, Comitato Regionale Dell Emilia-Romagna, 1986; Sebastiano Brusco, "The Emilian Model: Productive Decentralisation and Social Integration," *Cambridge Journal of Economics*, 1982; Pyke, Becattini, and Sengerberger, eds., "Industrial Districts and Inter-firm Cooperation in Italy" (ILO, Geneva, 1990.); Marco Bellandi, "The Incentives to Decentralized Industrial Creativity in Local Systems of Small Firms," *Revue d'Economie Industrielle*, 1992, 59; Goodman, Bamford, and Saynor, eds., *Small Firms and Industrial Districts in Italy* (Routledge, 1989); see also, OECD, *Reconciling Economy and Society*, OECD, Paris, 1996.

11. German Federal Minister of Labour and Social Affairs (Der Bundesminister für Arbeit und Sozialordnung), *Co-determination in the Federal Republic of Germany*, Bonn, November 1991, pp. 15–16.

12. Lawrence B. Cohen, "German Labor Seeks Equality of Union and Capital in Industry," *Labor and Nation*, Winter 1951, pp. 61–63.

13. Ibid. Cohen cited the following: *Die Mitbestimmung der Arbeitnehmer in der Wirtschaft*, published by the Bundesvorstand des DGB, Düsseldorf (date not given). See also Günter Halbach, Norbert Paland, Rolf Schwedes, and Ofried Wlotzke, *Labour Law in Germany: An Overview*, trans. Eva-Maria Förster, Renate Kretz, Peter Meuren, Andrew D. Pidgeon, John Power, Beate Sandmann, and Birgit Strauß (Federal Ministry of Labour and Social Affairs, Bonn, 1994).

14. *Codetermination in the Federal Republic of Germany*, p. 17.

15. *Mitbestimmung und neue Unternehmenskulturen—Bilanz und Perspektiven: Bericht der Kommission Mitbestimmung* (Verlag Bertelsmann Stiftung, 1998).

16. Cohen, "German Labor Seeks Equality," p. 63.

17. Sherman Kreiner and Kenneth Delaney, "Labour-Sponsored Investment Funds in Canada," *Report of the Industrial Heartland Labor Investment Forum*, June 14–15, 1996, Pittsburgh, Pa. Sponsored by United Steelworkers of America, AFL-CIO Industrial Union Dept., AFL-CIO Public Employee Dept., Steel Valley Authority.

18. "Solidarity Fund (QFL) Shares Increase in Value Over Last Year to $22.59," *Newsletter*, Le Fonds de solidarité des travailleurs du Québec (FTQ), September 15, 1999.

19. "Jobs and Growth: Montreal and the Québec Solidarity Fund (QFL)," Le Fonds de solidarité des travailleurs du Québec (FTQ), speech by Mr. Raymond Bachand, President and CEO of the Québec Solidarity Fund (QFL), Montreal, October 6, 1998.

20. *Industrial Heartland Labor Investment Forum: Our Money, Our Jobs: Worker Saving Funds and Long-Term Investing in Manufacturing.* Sponsored by: United Steel Workers of America, AFL-CIO·CLC; AFL-CIO Industrial Union Department; AFL-CIO Public Employee Department; Steel Valley Authority; June 14–15, 1996.

21. Len Krimerman, "How to Get Capital? Canada Shows the Way," *GEO/Dollars and Sense*, no. 219 (Sept./Oct. 1998): 47.

22. Ibid.

23. Ibid.

24. U.S. Department of Commerce, *Statistical Abstract of the United States, 1995*, table 825.

25. The following are unusually useful guides to methods for implementing self-management in the workplace: *Democracy in the Workplace: Readings on the Implementa-*

tion of Self-Management in America (Strongforce, Inc., Washington, D.C., 1977); Frank T. Adams and Gary B. Hansen, *Putting Democracy to Work: A Practical Guide for Starting and Managing Worker-Owned Business* (Barrett-Koehler Publishers, 1987). Also, the Philadelphia Association for Cooperative Enterprise (PACE) at 133 S. 18 St., Philadelphia, Pa. 19103 is prepared to give continued technical assistance for worker cooperatives and employee-owned businesses.

26. Len Krimerman, "Local Currencies—Their Pitfalls and Potential," *Grassroots Economic Organizing Newsletter*, Nov./Dec. 1995 (P.O. Box 5065, New Haven, Conn., 06525).

27. A web site with links to "hours currency" systems in many countries is at www.unet.com/gmlets.html. A Canadian, Michael Linton of Comox Valley, British Columbia, has innovated a Local Economic Trading System.

28. See Staughton Lynd, "The Genesis of the Idea of a Community Right to Industrial Property in Youngstown and Pittsburgh, 1977–1987," *Journal of American History* (Dec. 1987); "The View from the Steel Country," *Democracy* (summer 1983); *The Fight Against Shutdowns: Youngstown's Steel Mill Closings* (Singlejack Books, 1982); *Living Inside Our Hope* (ILR Press, 1997). For a detailed account of a spirited (though failed) effort to apply the doctrine of eminent domain to an industry move out of New Bedford, Mass., see Peter Gilmore and Peter Knowlton, *Refuse to Lose: Eminent Domain and the J. C. Rhodes Campaign*, United Electrical Radio and Machine Workers (UE), 1997.

29. Staughton Lynd, *Living Inside Our Hope*, pp. 171–2.

30. Staughton Lynd, "Genesis of the Idea of a Community Right to Industrial Property in Youngstown and Pittsburgh," pp. 939–40.

31. Industrial Cooperative Association, *Directory of Workers' Enterprises in North America* (1991); Dick Gilbert, survey by the Southern Appalachian Cooperative Organization (1995). See also Corey Rosen and Chitra Somayaji, "Economy in Numbers: ESOPS and COOPS," *GEO/Dollars and Sense*, No. 219, Sept./Oct. 1998, 48–49.

32. ICA's Client List includes: Brooklyn Ecumenical Cooperatives, NY; City of Burlington, VT; Farmworkers Association of Central Florida; Community Service Society, New York, NY; Naugatuck Valley Project, Waterbury, CT; Jobs For People, Cincinnati, OH; Bronx 2000 Local Development Corp., NY. The ICA Group is located at 20 Park Plaza, Suite 1127, Boston, MA. 02116.

33. Howard Engelskirchen, "Worker Ownership—Time to Take Stock (unpublished paper, Western State University College of Law, Fullerton, Ca., 1992).

34. Charles Roch, "Organizations Promoting Democratic Business in the USA, Cooperative Assistance Groups: A Resource Guide," *Economic and Industrial Democracy*, May 1998, pp. 252-284.

35. Valjean McLenighan, "Sustainable Manufacturing" (Center for Neighborhood Technology, 2125 West North Ave., Chicago, Ill., 60647, 1990).

36. *The Neighborhood Works*, 2125 West North Ave., Chicago, Ill. 60647.

37. The Institute on the Church in Urban-Industrial Society is at 5700 Woodlawn Ave., Chicago, Ill. 60637.

38. Michael Shuman, *Going Local* (Free Press, 1997).

39. Rick Surpin, *Enterprise Development and Worker Ownership: A Strategy for Community Economic Development*, Community Service Society of New York, 1984.

40. Michael Albert and Robin Hahnel, *Looking Forward: Participatory Economics for the Twenty-First Century* (South End Press, 1991), pp. 12, 13. See also Michael Albert and Robin *Hahnel, The Political Economy of Participatory Economics* (Princeton University Press, 1991); Michael Albert, *Thinking Forward* (Arbeiter Ring Press, 1997).

PART FIVE

An Alternative Economic System in the Making: Introduction

1. Russell Jacoby, *The End of Utopia* (Basic Books, 1999) pp. xi, xii. Note that the index to *The End of Utopia* accounts for about three hundred writers—historians, psychologists, sociologists, philosophers, literary critics and so forth. American economists who are bearers of this sort of wisdom are in the tens of thousands.

2. Eileen Appelbaum, Thomas Bailey, Peter Berg, and Arne L. Kalleberg, *Manufacturing Advantage: Why High-Performance Work Systems Pay Off* (Cornell University Press, 2000), chap. 3; W. Edwards Deming, *Out of the Crisis* (The MIT Press, 2000). The published writing of Deming and his videotaped lectures are important for giving operational definition to the concept of stability in production operations and consequences for quality and productivity.

CHAPTER TWELVE

The Advancing Processes of Capitalism and Workplace Democracy

1. Carter L. Goodrich, *The Frontier of Control: A Study in British Workshop Politics* (Pluto Press, 1975; first published in London by G. Bell & Sons, 1920), p. 174.

2. "Look for the Union Label—at IBM?," *Business Week*, Oct. 11, 1999; *Labor Notes*, September 1999.

3. *The Nation*, Sept. 20, 1999.

4. *New York Times*, Nov. 30, 1999.

5. *Business Week*, June 21, 1999, p. 103.

6. *Letters of Understanding Between UAW and the Ford Motor Company*, vol. 4. Note: This letter of understanding has been in force since October 7, 1990.

7. Alan S. Blinder, ed., *Paying for Productivity: A Look at the Evidence* (Brookings Institution, 1990). See especially the substantial bibliographies of reports on productivity effects on pp. 194–95.

8. David Moberg, "Striking Back: The Steelworkers Won't Let Up," *In These Times*, Oct. 3, 1999.

9. N. G. McKinzie, T. B. Cochran, and C. E. Paine, *Explosive Alliances: Nuclear Weapons Simulation Research at American Universities*, National Resources Defense Council (Washington, D.C., January 1998).

10. Joshua Lederberg's statement appears in Ivan Eland's policy analysis, "Protecting the Homeland," Cato Institute (Washington, D.C., May 5, 1998), p. 32.

11. Seymour Melman, ed., *Inspection for Disarmament* (Columbia University Press, 1958). See especially: Discussion in the General Report on Inspection by the People; essay and public-opinion poll results by William Evan; the chapters on biological warfare by Vincent Groupé; and the papers disclosing methods of underground military organization and operations.

12. J. William Fulbright, *The Price of Empire*, with Seth P. Tillman (Pantheon, 1989), p. 148; U.S. Arms Control and Disarmament Agency, *World Military Expenditures and Arms Transfers, 1988*. Table III shows Value of Arms Transfers, Cumulative 1983–1987, by Major Suppliers and Recipient Country, pp. 111–14. Entries for U.S.-Iraq show 0 (zero) shipments from the United States. Senator Glenn during this period published compilations of press reports on shipments of

military-related materiel from American firms to Iraq, whose aggregate "Arms Transfer, 1983–1987" amounted to $29.9 billion from all sources.

13. Special Communication from the Defense Security Cooperation Agency, June 24, 1999.

14. Fulbright, *The Price of Empire*, p. 137.

15. Mark Landler in the *New York Times*, July 23, 2000; Craig K. Smith in the *New York Times*, July 12, 2000.

16. Jon Rynn, "A Production-Centered Path to Economic Growth: Challenging the Finance-Centered Policy System," unpublished draft, May 20, 1999.

17. Seymour Melman, *The Demilitarized Society: Disarmament and Conversion* (Harvest House, 1988), p. 6. Also published by MIR Publishers, Moscow, 1990.

18. Carl Gersuny, "Industrial Rights: A Neglected Facet of Citizenship Theory," *Economic and Industrial Democracy* 15 (1994): 211–26.

19. Ibid.

20. Steven Greenhouse, "Asking Its Views, Labor Woos the Young," *New York Times*, Sept. 1, 1999.

21. John Kenneth Galbraith, "A Look Back: Affirmation and Error," *Journal of Economic Issues*, no. 2 (June 1989).

22. Sebastian B. Littauer, "Stability of Production Rates as a Determinant of Industrial Productivity Levels," in *Proceedings of Business and Economics Statistics Section*, American Statistical Association (Sept. 10–13, 1954).

23. *New York Times*, Sept. 19, 1993; see also Tom Peters, "Why Smaller Staffs Do Better," *New York Times*, Apr. 21, 1985.

24. W. Edwards Deming, "Improvement of Quality and Productivity Through Action by Management," *National Productivity Review*, Winter 1981–82.

25. *New York Times*, Sept. 16, 1999.

26. Arthur K. Spears, ed., *Race and Ideology: Language, Symbolism, and Popular Culture* (Wayne State University Press, 1999); Manning Marable, *How Capitalism Underdeveloped Black America: Problems in Race, Political Economy and Society* (South End Press, 1983).

27. Karl Marx, "Inaugural Address of the Working Men's International Association," in *The Marx-Engels Reader*, ed. Robert C. Tucker (Norton, 1978), p. 518.

28. Noam Chomsky, *Language and Politics*, edited by C. P. Otero, Montreal, Black Rose Books, 1988, p. 512.

CONCLUSION

An Exit Path from Capitalism to Workplace Democracy

1. Richard B. Freeman and Joel Rogers, *What Workers Want* (Cornell University Press, 1999), p. 89.

2. Seymour Melman, *The Impact of the Patent System on Research*, Study of the Subcommittee on Patents, Trademarks and Copyrights of the Committee on the Judiciary, United States Senate, Eighty-fifth Congress, Second Session, Study No. 11, U.S. Government Printing Office, Washington, D.C., 1958, p. 61.

3. Robert W. McChesney, Introduction to Noam Chomsky, *Profit Over People: Neoliberalism and the Global Order* (Seven Stories Press, 1999), p. 8.

4. *Statistical Abstract of the U.S., 1998*, table 485, p. 297.

5. On light rail, see the sophisticated equipment offered by Kinkisharyo (USA) Inc., 20 Walnut Street, Wellesley Hills, MA 02481. Phone: 781-237-2075, Fax: 781-

237-2079. On high-speed rail, see the material from Bombardier Transportation, Bombardier Inc., 1101 Parent Street, Saint Bruno, Quebec J3V 6E6, Phone: 450-441-2020, Fax: 450-441-1515, http://www.transportation.bombardier.com; also see Brian Perren, *TGV Handbook*, available at Bombardier.

6. C. Douglas Lummis, *Radical Democracy* (Cornell University Press, 1996), pp. 157–58.

7. Lawrence B. Cohen, "Workers and Decision-Making on Production, II," unpublished manuscript, 1954, chap. 14, pp. 11, 12.

8. John F. Zipp, Paul Luebke, and Richard Landerman, "The Social Bases of Support for Workplace Democracy," *Sociological Perspectives* 27, no. 4 (October 1984). The paper explains the sophisticated statistical methods used in this study.

9. Ed Collum, "Social Inequality and the Politics of Production: Identifying Potential Supporters of Economic Democracy," *Sociological Forum*, Vol. 16, No. 3, Sept. 2001.

10. Freeman and Rogers, *What Workers Want*, pp. 154, 155.

Selected Bibliography

Adams, Frank T., and Gary B. Hansen. *Putting Democracy to Work: A Practical Guide for Starting Worker-Owned Business.* Hulogos'i Communications, 1987. Revised edition: Barrett-Koehler Publishers; Hulogos'i Communications, 1992.

Adler, Frank, et al., eds. *Automation and Industrial Workers: A Cross-national Comparison of Fifteen Countries*, vol. 2, parts 1 and 2.Pergamon Press, 1986.

Albert, Michael, and Robin Hahnel. *Looking Forward: Participatory Economics for the Twenty-First Century.* South End Press, 1991.

———. *The Political Economy of Participatory Economics.* Princeton University Press, 1991.

Allen, V. L. *Militant Trade Unionism: A Re-Analysis of Industrial Action in an Inflationary Situation.* The Merlin Press, 1966.

Anthony, P. D. *The Ideology of Work.* Tavistock Publications, 1977.

Antoni, A. "Worker Cooperatives in France." *Annals of Collective Economy* 3 (July–December 1957).

Argyle, Michael. *The Social Psychology of Work.* Penguin Books, 1972.

Armstrong, P. J., J.F.B. Goodman, and J. D. Hyman. *Ideology and Shop-floor Industrial Relations.* Croom Helm, 1981.

Aronowitz, Stanley, and William DiFazio. *The Jobless Future: Sci-Tech and the Dogma of Work.* University of Minnesota Press, 1994.

Ashford, Nicholas Askounes. *Crisis in the Workplace: Occupational Disease and Injury: A Report to the Ford Foundation.* The MIT Press, 1976.

Australian Bureau of Industry Economics. *Manufacturing Industry Productivity Growth: Causes, Effects and Implications*, Research Report 21. Australian Government Publishing Service, 1986.

Australian Department of Employment and Industrial Relations, Working Environment Branch. *Corporate Accountability and Access to Information by Shop Stewards: Employee Participation Research Report No. 10.* Edited by Peter Ormonde. Australian Government Publishing Service, 1986.

———. *Diversity, Change and Tradition: The Environment for Industrial Democracy in Australia: Summary of Research for the Policy Discussion Paper on Industrial Democracy and Employee Participation.* Edited by Bill Ford and Lorna Tilley. Australian Government Publishing Service, 1986.

———. *Industrial Democracy and Employee Participation: A Policy Discussion Paper.* Australian Government Publishing Service, 1986.

Australian Department of Employment and Industrial Relations, Working Environment Branch, and Gordon E. O'Brien. *Employee Participation in an Assembly Line Factory*, Research Report No. 1. Australian Government Publishing Service, 1983.

———. *Industrial Democracy and Employee Participant: Digest of Case Studies* 1. 2d ed. Australian Government Publishing Service, 1987.

———. *Japanese Employment and Employee Relations: An Annotated Bibliography*, with Bill Ford, Millicent Easther, and Ann Brewer. Australian Government Publishing Service, 1984.

Australian Department of Employment and Industrial Relations, Working Environment Branch, Gordon E. O'Brien, and Russell D. Lansbury. *Technological Change and Employee Participation (In the Australian Retail Industry): Employee Participation Research Report No. 2*. Australian Government Publishing Service, 1983.

Bahro, Rudolf. *Socialism and Survival: Articles, Essays and Talks 1979–1982*. Heretic Books, 1982.

Bain, George Sayers. *The Growth of White-Collar Unionism*. Oxford University Press, 1970.

Balfour, Campbell, ed. *Participation in Industry*. Croom Helm, 1973.

Banks, J. A. *Industrial Participation: Theory and Practice: A Case Study*. Liverpool University Press, 1963.

Barber, Benjamin R. *Strong Democracy: Participatory Politics for a New Age*. University of California Press, 1984.

Bartolke, Klaus, et al. *Participation and Control: A Comparative Study About Industrial Plants in Israeli Kibbutzim and in the Federal Republic of Germany*. Rene F. Wilfer, 1985.

Batstone, Eric, Ian Boraston, and Stephen Frenkel. *Shop Stewards in Action: The Organization of Workplace Conflict and Accommodation*. Basil Blackwell, 1977.

———. *The Social Organization of Strikes*. Basil Blackwell, 1978.

Bauer, Raymond A., ed. *Social Indicators*. The MIT Press, 1967.

Bayat, Assef. *Work, Politics and Power: An International Perspective on Workers' Control and Self-Management*. Monthly Review Press, 1991.

Bell, Daniel. *Work and Its Discontents*. Beacon Press, 1956.

Ben-Ner, Avner, Derek C. Jones. *A New Conceptual Framework for the Analysis of the Impact of Employee Participation, Profit Sharing and Ownership on Firm Performance*. University of Minnesota: Industrial Relations Center: Working Paper Series, no. 92-10, 1992.

Ben-Ner, Avner, and Derek C. Jones, and Tzu-Shian Han. "The Productivity Effects of Employee Participation in Control and in Economic Returns: A Review of Economic Studies." Hamilton College, Department of Economics, Working Paper 93/13, 1993.

Ben-Ner, Avner, Tzu-Shian Han, and Derek C. Jones. *The Productivity Effects of Employee Participation in Control and in Economic Returns: A Review of Economic Studies*. Hamilton College, Department of Economics, July 1993.

Ben-Ner, Avner, and Derek C. Jones, *A New Conceptual Framework for the Analysis of the Impact of Employee Participation, Profit-Sharing and Ownership on Firm Performance*. Industrial Relations Center, University of Minnesota, 1992.

Bendix, Reinhard. *Work and Authority in Industry: Ideologies of Management in the Course of Industrialization*. Harper & Row, 1963.

Benello, C. George. *From the Ground Up: Essays on Grassroots and Workplace Democracy*. South End Press, 1992.

Berggren, Christian. *Alternatives to Lean Production: Work Organization in the Swedish Auto Industry* 22. Cornell International Industrial and Labor Relations Report, ILR Press, 1992.

Berman, K. *Worker-Owned Plywood Companies.* Washington State University Press, 1967.

Bernstein, Paul. *Workplace Democratization: Its Internal Dynamics.* Transaction Books, 1980.

Berry, Wendell. *The Unsettling of America Culture and Agriculture.* Avon, 1977.

Beynon, Huw, and Hilary Wainwright. *The Workers' Report on Vickers.* Pluto Press, 1979.

Blair, Thomas L. *"The Land to Those Who Work It": Algeria's Experiment in Workers' Management.* Doubleday, 1969.

Blauner, Robert. *Alienation and Freedom: The Factory Worker and His Industry.* University of Chicago Press, 1964.

Blum, Fred H. *Work and Community: The Scott Bader Commonwealth and the Quest for a New Social Order.* Routledge & Kegan Paul, 1968.

Blumberg, P. *Industrial Democracy: The Sociology of Participation.* Schocken Books, 1968.

Boucher, Thomas Owen. "Industry Structure and Productivity." Ph.D. disser-tation, Columbia University, 1978, Dissertation Abstracts International, vol. 41-09B, page 3535, 00131 pages.

Boyer, Richard O., and Herbert M. Morais. *Labor's Untold Story.* United Electrical, Radio & Machine Workers of America, 1955.

Bradley, Keith, and Alan Gelb. *Cooperation at Work: The Mondragon Experience.* Heinemann Educational Books, 1983.

———. *Worker Capitalism: The New Industrial Relations.* Heinemann Educational Books, 1983.

Brandow, Karen, et al. *No Bosses Here!: A Manual on Working Collectively and Cooperatively.* Alyson Publications, 1981.

Braverman, Harry. *Labor and Monopoly Capital: The Degradation of Work in the Twentieth Century.* Monthly Review Press, 1974.

Brecher, Jeremy, and Tim Costello, eds. *Building Bridges: The Emerging Grassroots Coalition of Labor and Community.* Monthly Review Press, 1990.

Brinton, Maurice. *The Bolsheviks and Workers' Control/1917 to 1921/The State and Counter-Revolution.* Solidarity, 1970.

Brusco, Sebastiano. "The Emilian Model: Productive Decentralisation and Social Integration." *Cambridge Journal of Economics* 6 (1982).

Buck, Trevor. *Comparative Industrial Systems: Industry Under Capitalism, Central Planning and Self-Management.* Macmillan, 1982.

Burawoy, Michael. *The Politics of Production: Factory Regimes Under Capitalism and Socialism.* Verso–New Left Books, 1985.

Burawoy, Michael, and Kathryn Hendley. *Strategies of Adaptation: A Soviet Enterprise Under Perestroika and Privatization.* Edited by Gregory Grossman, Vladimir G. Treml, and Kimberley C. Neuhauser. BDOP c/o K. Neuhauser, Department of Economics, Duke University, Distributor, 1991.

Burns, Patrick, and Mel Doyle. *Democracy at Work.* Pan Books, 1981.

Buzgalin, A., ed. *Economy and Democracy.* "Third Course" Scientific Socio-Political Series, Economic Democracy, 1992.

Campbell, Alastair. *The Democratic Control of Work or a Panacea for the Ills of Society.* Plunkett Foundation for Co-Operatives Studies, 1987.

Cannon, William B. *New Class Politics: The Polarization of America and What We Can Do About It.* Institute for Policy Studies, 1986.

Carby-Hall, J. R. *Worker Participation in Europe.* Croom Helm; Rowman and Littlefield, 1977.

Carter, Michael. *Into Work.* Penguin Books, 1966.

Chenu, M. D. *The Theology of Work: An Exploration.* Translated by Lilian Soiron. Regnery Logos Edition, 1966.

Choate, Pat. *Retooling the American Work Force: Toward a National Training Strategy.* Northeast-Midwest Institute, July 1982.

Clarke, Simon, Peter Fairbrother, and Vadim Borisov. *The Workers' Movement in Russia.* Studies of Communism in Transition Series, Edward Elgar, 1995.

Clayre, Alasdair, ed. *The Political Economy of Co-Operation and Participation: A Third Sector.* Oxford University Press, 1980.

Clegg, H. A. *A New Approach to Industrial Democracy.* Basil Blackwell, 1960.

Clegg, Ian. *Workers' Self-Management in Algeria.* Monthly Review Press, 1971.

Cliff, Tony. *State Capitalism in Russia.* Pluto Press, 1974.

Coates, Ken, ed., et al. *The New Worker Co-Operatives.* Spokesman Books, 1976.

Coates, Ken, and Tony Topham. *The New Unionism: The Case for Worker's Control.* Peter Owen, 1972; Penguin Books, 1974.

Coates, Ken, and Tony Topham, eds. *Workers' Control: A Book of Readings and Witnesses for Workers' Control.* MacGibbon & Kee, 1968; revised edition, Panther, 1970.

Cohen, Lawrence. "Bilateral Decisioning: The Present State of Productional Relations." Ph.D. dissertation, Columbia University, 1950. Dissertation Abstracts International, vol. 11-02, page 0230, 00240 pages.

———. "The Structure of Workers' Decisions." *Journal of Economic Issues* 10, no. 2 (June 1976).

———. "Workers and Decision-Making on Production." *Proceedings of the Eighth Annual Meeting of the Industrial Relations' Research Association 1955*, pp. 298–312.

———. "Workers and Decision-Making on Production." Unpublished.

Cole, Robert E. *Japanese Blue Collar: The Changing Tradition.* University of California Press, 1971; first paperback edition, 1973.

———. *Work, Mobility, and Participation: A Comparative Study of American and Japanese Industry.* University of California Press, 1979.

Cooley, Mike. *Architect or Bee? The Human/Technology Relationship.* Compiled and edited by Shirley Cooley. Hand and Brain, 1980; David Noble, Introduction to American edition, South End Press, 1982.

CSE Books. *Microelectronics: Capitalist Technology and the Working Class.* CSE Books, July 1980.

Dahl, Robert A. *A Preface to Economic Democracy.* University of California Press, 1985.

David, Paul A. *Technical Choice Innovation and Economic Growth: Essays on American and British Experience in the Nineteenth Century.* Cambridge University Press, 1975.

Davis, Howard, and Richard Scase. *Western Capitalism and State Socialism: An Introduction.* Basil Blackwell, 1985.

Deem, Rosemary, and Graeme Salaman, eds. *Work, Culture and Society.* Open University Press, 1985.

Dolgoff, Sam, ed. *The Anarchist Collectives: Workers' Self-Management in the Spanish Revolution (1936-1939).* Free Life Editions, 1974.

Drulovic, Milojko. *Self-Management on Trial.* Spokesman Books, 1978.

Dunne, Paul, ed. *Quantitative Marxism.* Polity Press–Basil Blackwell, 1991.

Earle, John. *The Italian Cooperative Movement: A Portrait of the Lega Nazionale delle Cooperative e Mutue.* Allen & Unwin, 1986.

Eccles, Tony. *Under New Management: The Story of Britain's Largest Worker Cooperative—Its Successes and Failures.* Pan Books, 1981.

Ehn, Pelle, and Morten Kyng. "The Collective Resource Approach to Systems Design." In *Participation in Change: Readings on the Introduction of New Technology.* Australian Government Publishing Service, 1987, pp. 111–50.

Ehrenberg, Ronald G., and Paul L. Schumann. *Longer Hours or More Jobs?: An Investigation of Amending Hours Legislation to Create Employment.* Cornell Studies in Industrial and Labor Relations Number 22. ILR Press, 1982.

Ellerman, David P. "The Case for Workplace Democracy." *Peace Review,* 2000.

———. "Cooperative Farming Communities: A Model Based on Mondragon and Moshav Principles." Abstract, Industrial Cooperative Association, 1988.

———. "The Democratic Firm: A 'Non-economic' Approach to the Problem of Distribution Based on Property Theory and Democratic Theory." World Bank, 1998.

———. *The Democratic Worker-Owned Firm.* Unwin-Hyman Academic, 1990.

———. *Economics, Accounting, and Property Theory.* D. C. Heath, 1982.

———. "The Employment Relation, Property Rights and Organizational Democracy." In *Organizational Democracy and Political Processes* 1, edited by Colin Crouch and Frank A. Heller. Wiley, 1983.

———. "ESOPS AND CO-OPS: Worker Capitalism and Worker Democracy." *Labor Research Review,* no. 5 (spring 1985).

———. "The Human-Capitalist Firm: An Approach from Property Theory and Democratic Theory." Conference on Human Capital and the Theory of the Firm. The Brookings Institution, May 23, 1997.

———. *Intellectual Trespassing as a Way of Life: Essays in Philosophy, Economics, and Mathematics.* Rowman & Littlefield, 1995.

———. "Knowledge-Based Development Institutions." Draft. World Bank, 1998.

———. *Property and Contract in Economics: The Case in Philosophy, Economics, and Mathematics.* Basil Blackwell, 1992.

Ellerman, David P., and Peter Pitegoff. "The Democratic Corporation: The New Worker Cooperative Statute in Massachusetts." *New York University Review of Law & Social Change* 11, no. 3 (1982–1983).

Esland, Geoff, and Graeme Salaman, eds. *The Politics of Work and Occupations.* Open University Press, 1980.

Espinosa, Juan G., and Andrew S. Zimbalist. *Economic Democracy: Workers' Participation in Chilean Industry 1970–1973.* Academic Press, 1978.

Estrin, Saul. *Can Employee Owned Firms Survive?* Centre for Labour Economics, London School of Economics, 1988.

Estrin, Saul, and Derek C. Jones. *The Determinants of Investment in Employee Owned Firms: Evidence from France.* Centre for Labour Economics, London School of Economics, 1992.

———. "The Effects of Worker Participation upon Productivity in French Producer Cooperatives." Manuscript, 1983.

———. *Survivability and Degeneration in Employee-Owned Firms: Evidence from France.* Centre for Labour Economics, London School of Economics, 1991.

———. "The Viability of Employee-Owned Firms: Evidence From France." *Industrial and Labor Relations Review* 45, no. 2 (January 1992).

Estrin, Saul, Derek C. Jones, and Jan Svejnar. "The Productivity Effects of Worker Participation: Producer Cooperatives in Western Economies." *Journal of Comparative Economics* (March 11, 1987): 40–61.

Evan, William M. "Hierarchy, Alienation, Commitment, and Organizational Effectiveness." *Human Relations* 30, no. 1 (1977).

———. *Organizational Theory Research Design.* Macmillan, 1993; notably chap. 2, "Consequences of Organizational Hierarchy."

———. *Organization Theory: Structures, Systems, and Environments.* John Wiley, 1976.

Ferman, Louis A., et al., eds. *Joint Training Programs: A Union-Management Approach to Preparing Workers for the Future.* ILR Press, 1991.

Fine, Bob, et al., eds. *Capital and Class.* No. 11 (summer 1980). Conference of Socialist Economists, 1980.

Folbre, Nancy, and the Center for Popular Economics. *The New Field Guide to the U.S. Economy: A Compact and Irreverent Guide to Economic Life in America.* The New Press, 1995.

Frieden, Karl. *Workplace Democracy and Productivity.* National Center for Economic Alternatives, 1980.

Friedman, Andrew. *Industry and Labour: Class Struggle at Work and Monopoly Capitalism.* Macmillan Press, 1977.

Friedman, David. *The Misunderstood Miracle: Industrial Development and Political Change in Japan.* Cornell University Press, 1988.

Friedman, Georges. *The Anatomy of Work: The Implication of Specialization.* Translated by Wyatt Rawson. Heinemann Educational Books, 1961.

Fusfeld, Daniel R. "Labor-Managed and Participatory Firms: A Review Article." *Journal of Economic Issues* 17, no. 3 (September 1983).

Gabor, Dennis. *Innovations: Scientific, Technological, and Social.* Oxford University Press, 1970.

Galbraith, John Kenneth. *The Good Society: The Humane Agenda.* Houghton Mifflin, 1996.

———. *The New Industrial State.* New American Library, 1986.

Gallie, Duncan. *In Search of the New Working Class: Automation and Social Integration Within the Capitalist Enterprise.* Cambridge University Press, 1978.

Gans, Herbert J. *More Equality.* Vintage, 1974.

———. *The War Against the Poor: The Underclass and Antipoverty Policy.* Basic Books, 1995.

Garson, Barbara. *All the Livelong Day: The Meaning and Demeaning of Routine Work.* Penguin Books, 1972.

Germany, Federal Minister of Labour and Social Affairs (Der Bundesminister für Arbeit und Sozialordnung). *Co-determination in the Federal Republic of Germany.* Bonn, November 1991.

Gersuny, Carl. "Employment Seniority and Distributive Justice." *The Philosophical Forum* 17, no. 1 (fall 1965).

———. "Employment Seniority and Senior Citizens." *The Gerontological Society of America*, 1987.

———. "Employment Seniority: Cases From Iago to Weber." *Journal of Labor Research* 2, no. 1 (winter 1982).

———. "Erosion of Seniority Rights in the U.S. Labor Force." *Labor Studies Journal* 12, no. 1 (spring 1987).

———. "From Contract to Status: Perspectives on Employment Seniority." *Sociological Inquiry* 54 (winter 1984).

———. "Industrial Rights: A Neglected Facet of Citizenship Theory." *Economic and Industrial Democracy* 15 (1994): 211–26.

———. "Origins of Seniority Provisions in Collective Bargaining." *Labor Law Journal* 33, no. 8 (August 1982).

———. "Seniority and the Moral Economy of U.S. Automobile Workers, 1934–1946." *Journal of Social History* 16, no. 3 (spring 1985).

———. *Work Hazards and Industrial Conflict.* University Press of New England, 1981.

Gideon, Siegried. *Mechanization Takes Command: A Contribution to Anonymous History.* Norton, 1969.

Ginzberg, Eli, and Hyman Berman. *The American Worker in the Twentieth Century: A History Through Autobiographies.* Free Press, 1963.

Gomberg, William. *A Trade Union Analysis of Time Study.* Foreword by David Dubinsky. Science Research Associates, 1948.

Goodman, Edward, ed. *Non-Conforming Radicals of Europe.* Acton Society Siena Series, Duckworth, 1983.

Goodrich, Carter L. *The Frontier of Control: A Study in British Workshop Politics.* Foreword by R. H. Tawney; new Foreword by Richard Hyman. Pluto Press, 1975.

Gorni, Yosef, Yaacov Oved, and Idit Paz, eds. *Communal Life: An International Perspective.* Transaction Books, 1987.

Gorz, Andre. *Farewell to the Working Class: An Essay on Post-Industrial Socialism.* Translated by Michael Sonenscher. South End Press, 1982.

Gould, Jay M. *The Technical Elite.* Augustus M. Kelley, 1966.

Great Britain, Department of Trade. *Report of the Committee of Inquiry on Industrial Democracy.* London: HMSO, January 1977.

Greenberg, Edward S. *Workplace Democracy: The Political Effects of Participation.* Cornell University Press, 1986.

Greenwood, Davyd J., and Jose Luis Gonzalez Santos. *Industrial Democracy as Process: Participatory Action Research in the Fagor Cooperative Group of Mondragon.* Science for Social Action Series 2. The Swedish Center for Working Life, 1992.

Guérin, Daniel. *Anarchism.* Introduction by Noam Chomsky. Monthly Review Press, 1970.

Gutman, Herbert G. *Work, Culture, and Society in Industrializing America: Essays in American Working-Class and Social History.* Vintage, 1977.

Guzzo, Richard A., and Jeffrey S. Bondy. *A Guide to Worker Productivity Experiments in the United States 1976–81.* Pergamon Press, 1983.

Hacker, Sally. *Pleasure, Power, and Technology: Some Tales of Gender, Engineering and the Cooperative Workplace.* Unwin Hyman, 1989.

Hague, Douglas, and Geoffrey Wilkinson. *The IRC, an Experiment in Industrial Intervention: A History of the Industrial Reorganization Corporation.* George Allen & Unwin, 1983.

Halbach, Günter Halbach, Norbert Paland, Rolf Schwedes, and Ofried Wlotzke. *Labour Law in Germany: An Overview.* Translated by Eva-Maria Förster, Renate Kretz, Peter Meuren, Andrew D. Pidgeon, John Power, Beate Sandmann, and Birgit Strauß. Federal Ministry of Labour and Social Affairs, Bonn, 1994.

Hall, Paddy. *Work for Yourself: A Guide for Young People.* National Extension College, 1983.

Hanami, Tadashi. *Labor Relations in Japan Today.* John Martin, 1980.

Hancock, M. Donald, John Logue, and Bernt Schiller, eds. *Managing Modern Capitalism: Industrial Renewal and Workplace Democracy in the United States and Western Europe.* Greenwood Press, 1991.

Harris, Zellig S. *The Transformation of Capitalist Society.* Rowman & Littlefield, 1997.

Hirschhorn, Larry. *Beyond Mechanization: Work and Technology in a Postindustrial Age.* The MIT Press, 1984.

Hobsbawn, Eric. *Politics for a Rational Left: Political Writing 1977–1988.* Verso–New Left Books, 1989.

———. *Workers: Worlds of Labor.* Pantheon Books, 1984.

Hofstede, Geert, ed. *Futures for Work: A Book of Original Readings.* Martinus Nijhoff Social Sciences Division, 1979.

Honingsberg, Peter Jan, Bernard Kamoroff, and Jim Beatty. *We Own It: Starting and Managing Coops, Collectives, and Employee-Owned Ventures.* Bell Spring Publishing, 1982.

Horvat, Branko, et al., eds. *Self-Governing Socialism: Historical Development Social and Political Philosophy* 1, *A Reader.* International Arts and Science Press, 1975.

———. *Self-Governing Socialism: Sociology and Politics Economics* 2, *A Reader.* International Arts and Science Press, 1975.

Hugh-Jones, E. M. *Automation in Theory and Practice.* Basil Blackwell, 1956.

Hunnius, Gerry, G. David Garson, and John Case. *Workers' Control: A Reader on Labor and Social Change.* Vintage, 1973.

Hunt, E. K. *Property and Prophets: The Evolution of Economic Institutions and Ideologies.* Revised second edition. Harper & Row, 1978.

Hutson, Jack. *Penal Colony to Penal Powers.* Revised edition. Amalgamated Metals Foundry and Shipwrights' Union, 1983.

———. *Six Wage Concepts.* Amalgamated Engineering Union, 1971.

Hyman, Richard. *Industrial Relations: A Marxist Introduction.* Macmillan, 1975.

Hyman, Richard, and Robert Price, eds. *The New Working Class?: White-Collar Workers and Their Organization—A Reader.* Macmillan, 1983.

The Industrial Cooperative Association. *Directory of Workers' Enterprises in North America 1991.* Boston, 1991.

"The Internal Democratic ESOP." *International Development in Employee Ownership.* National Center for Employee Ownership, 1990, pp. C1–C14.

International Committee of Producer and Artisanal Cooperatives. *The Future of Participative and Democratic Enterprises, Third World Conference of CICOPA, Paris, February 23–26, 1988.* International Co-operative University.

Ireland, Norman J., and Peter J. Law. *The Economics of Labour-Managed Enterprises.* Croom Helm, 1982.

Jackall, Robert, and Henry M. Levin, eds. *Worker Cooperatives in America.* University of California Press, 1984.

Jacobson, Phyllis, and Julius Jacobson, eds. *Socialist Perspectives.* Karz-Cohl, 1983.

Jenkins, Clive, and Barrie Sherman. *The Collapse of Work.* Eyre Methuen, 1979.

Jenkins, David. *Beyond Job Enrichment: Workplace Democracy in Europe.* Working Papers, winter 1975.

———. *Job Power: Blue and White Collar Democracy.* Penguin Books, 1974.

Jones, Barry O. *Sleepers, Wake!: Technology and the Future of Work.* Oxford University Press, 1982.

Jones, Derek C. *Advances in the Economic Analysis of Participatory and Labor-Managed Firms: A Research Annual.* JAI Press, 1984.

———. "The Economics of British Producer Cooperatives." Ph.D. dissertation, Cornell University, 1974.

———. "The Nature and Effects of Employee Ownership and Participation: A Review of Empirical Evidence for Transitional Economies." Paper for the Conference on Democracy, Participation and Economic Development, Columbia University, April 23, 1999.

———. "U.S. Producer Cooperatives: The Record to Date." *Industrial Relations* 18, no. 3 (fall 1979).

Jones, Derek C., and Jeffrey Pliskin. *The Effects of Alternative Sharing Arrangements on Employment: Preliminary Evidence from Britain.* Jerome Levy Economics Institute of Bard College, 1988.

———. *The Effects of Worker Participation, Employee Ownership and Profit-Sharing on Economics Performance: A Partial Review.* Jerome Levy Economics Institute of Bard College, 1988.

———. *Unionization and the Incidence of Performance-Based Compensation in Canada.* Jerome Levy Economics Institute of Bard College, 1989.

Jones, Derek C., Jeffrey Pliskin, and Takao Kato. *Profit-Sharing and Gainsharing: A Review of Theory, Incidence and Effects.* Jerome Levy Economics Institute of Bard College, 1994.

Jones, Derek C., and Jan Svejnar, eds. *Participatory and Self-Managed Firms.* Lexington Books–D. C. Heath and Company, 1982.

Kanovsky, Eliyahu. "The Economy of the Israeli Kibbutz: A Study of Kibbutz Productivity and Profitability, and the Position of the Kibbutzim in the Economy of Israel." Ph.D. dissertation, Columbia University, 1961.

Kapp, K. William. *The Social Costs of Private Enterprise.* Schocken Books, 1971.

Karasek, Robert, and Tores Theorell. *Healthy Work: Stress, Productivity, and the Reconstruction of Working Life.* Basic Books, 1990.

Kasmir, Sharryn. *The Myth of Mondragon: Cooperatives, Politics, and Working-class Life in a Basque Town.* SUNY Press, 1996.

Kazis, Richard, and Richard L. Grossman. *Fear at Work: Job Blackmail, Labor and the Environment.* Pilgrim Press, 1982.

Keremetsky, Jacob, and John Logue. *Perestroika, Privatization, and Worker Ownership in the USSR.* Studies in Employee Ownership #7, Northeast Ohio Employee Ownership Center. Kent Popular Press, 1991.

Knights, David, and Hugh Willmott, eds. *Gender and the Labour Process.* Gower, 1986.

———. *Labour Process Theory, Studies in Labour Process.* Macmillan, 1990.

———. *Managing the Labor Process.* Gower, 1986.

———. *New Technology and the Labor Process.* Macmillan, 1988.

Knights, David, Hugh Willmott, and David Collinson, eds. *Job Redesign: Critical Perspectives on the Labour Process.* Gower, 1985.

Kolaja, Jiri. *A Polish Factory: A Case Study of Workers' Participation in Decision Making.* University of Kentucky Press, 1960.

———. *Workers' Councils: The Yugoslav Experience.* Tavistock, 1965.

Konrad, George, and Ivan Szelenyi. *The Intellectuals on the Road to Class Power.* Translated by Andrew Arato and Richard E. Allen. Harcourt Brace, 1979.

Kotkin, Stephen. *Steeltown, USSR: Soviet Society in the Gorbachev Era.* University of California Press, 1991.

Krimerman, Len, and Frank Lindenfeld, eds. *When Workers Decide: Workplace Democracy Takes Root in North America.* New Society Publishers, 1992.

Labor Research Review 10. *Mismanagement and What Unions Can Do About It* 6, no. 1. Midwest Center for Labor Research, spring 1987.

Labor Research Review 14. *Participating in Management: Union Organizing on a New Terrain* 8, no. 2. Midwest Center for Labor Research, fall 1989.

"Labour Relations and Workers' Participation." *Social and Labour Bulletin* 3 (September 1983), International Labour Office, Geneva, pp. 329–57.

Lafferty, W., and E. Rosenstein. "Capital Markets and Worker Ownership." In *International Handbook of Participation in Organizations III.* Oxford University Press, 1993, pp. 344–62.

Legge, David, ed. *Skills: Selected Readings.* Penguin Books, 1970.

Leon, Dan. *The Kibbutz: A Portrait from Within.* Foreword by Anthony Wedgewood Benn. Horizons and World Hashomer Hatzair, 1964.

Levison, Andrew. *The Working-Class Majority.* Coward, McCann & Geoghegan, 1974.

Lewis, Roy, and Rosemary Stewart. *The Managers: A New Examination of the English, German, and American Executive.* New American Library, 1961.

Lindenfeld, Frank, and Len Krimerman, eds. *When Workers Decide: Workplace Democracy Takes Root in North America.* New Society Publishers, 1992.

Lindenfeld, Frank, and Joyce Rothschild-Whitt, eds. *Workplace Democracy and Social Change.* Porter Sargent Publishers, 1982.

Linhart, Robert. *The Assembly Line*. Translated by Margaret Crosland. A Platform Book. John Calder, 1981.

Littauer, Sebastian B. "Stability of Production Rates as a Determinant of Industrial Productivity Levels." In *Proceedings of Business and Economics Statistics Section*, American Statistical Association, September 10–13, 1954, Montreal, pp. 241–48.

Littler, Craig R., ed. *The Experience of Work*. Gower and the Open University, 1985.

Logue, John, Richard Glass, Wendy Patton, Alex Teodosio, and Karen Thomas, eds. *Participatory Employee Ownership: How It Works—Best Practices in Employee Ownership*. Ohio Employee Ownership Center, 1998.

Louis, Raymond. *Labour Co-operatives: Retrospect and Prospects*. International Labour Office, 1983.

Lutz, Mark A., and Kenneth Lux. *Humanistic Economics: The New Challenge*. Foreword by Amitai Etzioni. The Bootstrap Press, 1988.

Lynd, Staughton. *The Fight Against Shutdowns: Youngstown's Steel Mill Closings*. Singlejack Books, 1982.

———. *Living Inside Our Hope*. ILR Press, 1997.

McCarthy, W.E.J. *The Role of Shop Stewards in British Industrial Relations: A Survey of Existing Information and Research*, Research Papers 1, Royal Commission on Trade Unions and Employers' Associations. London: HMSO, 1966.

McCarthy, W.E.J., and S. R. Parker, *Shop Stewards and Workshop Relations*, Research Papers 10, Royal Commission on Trade Unions and Employers' Associations. London: HMSO, 1968.

McDermott, John. *The Crisis in the Working Class and Some Arguments for a New Labor Movement*. South End Press, 1980.

McGaughey, Jr., William. *A Shorter Workweek in the 1980s*. Thistlerose Publications, 1981.

MacLeod, Greg. *From Mondragon to America: Experiments in Community Economic Development*. University College of Cape Breton Press, 1997.

Mandel, David. *Petrograd Workers and the Soviet Seizure of Power: From the July Days 1917 to July 1918*. Macmillan, 1984.

———. *Robatyagi: Perestroika and After Viewed from Below—Interviews with Workers in the Soviet Union*. Monthly Review Press, 1994.

Mason, Ronald M. *Participatory and Workplace Democracy: A Theoretical Development in Critique of Liberalism*. Southern Illinois University Press, 1982.

Melman, Seymour. *Decision-Making and Productivity*. Basil Blackwell, 1958.

———. *The Demilitarized Society: Disarmanent and Conversion*. Harvest House, 1988.

———. *Dynamic Factors in Industrial Productivity*. Basil Blackwell, 1956.

———. *Managerial vs. Cooperative Decision-Making in Israel*. Sage Publications, 1971.

———. *Pentagon Capitalism*. McGraw-Hill, 1970.

———. *The Permanent War Economy: American Capitalism in Decline*. Simon & Schuster, 1974, 1985.

———. *Profits Without Production*. Alfred A. Knopf, 1988.

Misha, E. J. *Technology and Growth: The Price We Pay*. Praeger, 1969.

Moberg, David. "Workplace Democracy Aboard Ship." *In These Times*, Dec. 21–27, 1997.

Monat, Jacques, and Hedva Sarfati, eds. *Workers' Participation: A Voice in Decisions, 1981-85*. Geneva: International Labour Office, 1986.

The Mondragon Cooperative Movement, Case No. 1-384-270. Harvard Business School, 1984.

Montgomery, David. *Workers' Control in America: Studies in the History of Work, Technology, and Labor Struggles*. Cambridge University Press, 1979.

Monthly Review, *Technology, the Labor Process, and the Working Class* 28, no. 3 (July–August 1976). Monthly Review Press, 1976.

Morgan, Arthur E. *Industries for Small Communities: With Cases from Yellow Spring.* Community Service, 1953.

Morrison, Roy. *Ecological Democracy.* South End Press, 1995.

———. *We Build the Road as We Travel.* Society Publishers, 1991.

Mumford, Lewis. *The Myth of the Machine: The Pentagon of Power.* Harcourt Brace, 1964.

———. *Technics and Civilization.* Harcourt, 1934.

Nakane, Chie. *Japanese Society.* University of California Press, 1970.

Nicholas, Theo, and Huw Beynon. *Living with Capitalism: Class Relations and the Modern Factory.* Routledge & Kegan Paul, 1977.

Nicolic, Milos, ed. *Socialism on the Threshold of the Twenty-first Century.* Verso–New Left Books, 1985.

Nneji, Bernard Ogbuka. "Capital Productivity in Relation to Organization of Work in Computer Controlled Machine Tool Production." Ph.D. dissertation, Columbia University, 1988, *Dissertation Abstracts International,* vol. 49–06B, page 2333, 00254 pages.

Noble, David F. *America by Design: Science, Technology, and the Rise of Corporate Capitalism.* Alfred A. Knopf, 1977.

———. *Forces of Production: A Social History of Industrial Automation.* Alfred A. Knopf, 1983.

Oakeshott, Robert. *The Case for Workers' Co-ops.* Routledge & Kegan Paul, 1978.

Ormaechea, Jose M. *The Mondragon Cooperative Experience.* Mondragon Cooperative Corporation at José Maria Arizmendiarrieta Pasalekua, n. 5, 20500 Mondragon [Guipuzcoa], Spain, 1993.

O'Toole, James, ed. *Work and the Quality of Life: Resource Papers for Work in America.* Preface by Elliot L. Richardson, Afterword by Edward M. Kennedy. The MIT Press 1974.

Oved, Ya'akov. "Anarchist Communies During the Spanish Civil War." *Kibbutz Studies* 29 (May 1989): 4–13. Yad Tabenkin, 1989.

Page, Benjamin B. *The Czechoslovak Reform Movement, 1963–1968: A Study in the Theory of Socialism.* B. R. Gruner B.V., 1973.

Papananek, Victor. *Design for the Real World: Human Ecology and Social Change.* Introduction by R. Buckminster Fuller. Pantheon, 1971.

Perrow, Charles. *Normal Accidents: Living with High-Risk Technologies.* Basic Books, 1984.

Philipson, Morris, ed. *Automation: Implications for the Future.* Vintage, 1962.

Piel, E. J., and J. G. Truxal. *Man and His Technology: Problems and Issues.* McGraw-Hill, 1973.

Piller, Charles. *The Fail-Safe Society: Community Defiance and the End of American Technological Optimism.* Basic Books, 1991.

Politics and Power Two: Problems in Labour Politics. Routledge & Kegan Paul, 1980.

Prandy, K., A. Stewart, and R. M. Blackburn. *White-Collar Unionism.* Macmillan, 1983.

Rayton, Dwight [a.k.a. Greg Glover, 1900–1977]. *Shop Floor Democracy in Action.* Industrial Common Ownership Movement, 1972. Available at University of Warwick Library, Modern Records Centre.

Resnick, Stephen, and Richard Wolff, eds. *Rethinking Marxism: Struggles in Marxist Theory.* Automedia, 1985.

Richards, Vernon, ed. *Why Work?: Arguments for the Leisure Society.* Freedom Press, 1983.

Rifkin, Jeremy. *The End of Work: The Decline of the Global Labor Force and the Dawn of the Post-Market Era.* Jeremy P. Tarcher, 1995.

———. *Own Your Own Job: Economic Democracy for Working Americans.* Bantam Books, 1977.

Roberts, Benjamin C., ed. *Towards Industrial Democracy: Europe, Japan and the United States.* Allanheld, Osmun, 1979.

Root & Branch, eds. *Root & Branch: The Rise of the Workers' Movements.* Fawcett, 1975.

Rosen, Corey, and Karen M. Young, eds. *Understanding Employee Ownership.* ILR Press, 1991.

Rothschild, Joyce, and Whitt, J. Allen. *The Cooperative Workplace: Potentials and Dilemmas of Organizational Democracy and Participation.* Cambridge University Press, 1986.

Rothschild, K. W., ed. *Power in Economics.* Penguin Books, 1971.

Rothschild-Whitt, Joyce. "Who Will Benefit from ESOPs?" *Labor Research Review* 6 (spring 1985): 70–80.

Rubin, Lillian Breslow. *Worlds of Pain: Life in the Working-Class Family.* Basic Books, 1976.

Rueschemeyer, Dietrich. *Power and the Division of Labour.* Polity Press–Basil Blackwell, 1986.

Sabel, Charles F. *Work and Politics: The Division of Labor in Industry.* Cambridge University Press, 1982.

Salaman, Graeme. *Working.* Ellis Horwood Limited; Tavistock, 1986.

Samuels, Warren J., ed. *The Economy as a System of Power: Papers from the Journal of Economic Issues* 2. Corporate Powers. Foreword by Robert Lekachman. Transaction Books, 1979.

Sandberg, Ake, ed. *Computers Dividing Man and Work: Recent Scandinavian Research on Planning and Computers from a Trade Union Perspective.* Demos Project Report no. 13. Arbetslivscentrum, March 1979.

———. *The Limits to Democratic Planning: Knowledge, Power and Methods in the Struggle for the Future.* Stockholm, n.p., 1976.

Schuller, Tom. *Democracy at Work.* Oxford University Press, 1985.

Schumacher, E. F. *Small Is Beautiful: Economics as if People Mattered.* Harper & Row, 1973.

Scientific American. *Technology and Economic Development.* Alfred A. Knopf, 1963.

Shaiken, Harley. *Mexico in the Global Economy: High Technology and Work Organization in Export Industries.* Monograph Series 33. Center for US–Mexican Studies, University of California, San Diego, 1990.

———. *Work Transformed: Automation and Labor in the Computer Age.* Holt, 1984.

Shaiken, Harley, with Stephen Herzenberg. *Automation and Global Production: Automobile Engine Production in Mexico, the United States, and Canada,* Monograph Series 26. Center for US–Mexican Studies, University of California, San Diego, 1987.

Shaiken, Harley, Steven Lopez, and Isaac Mankita. "Two Routes to Team Production: Saturn and Chrysler Compared." *Industrial Relations* 36, no. 1 (January 1997): 23.

Shanks, Michael. *The Innovators: The Economics of Technology.* Penguin Books, 1967.

Sheridan, T. *Mindful Militants: The Amalgamated Engineering Union in Australia 1920–1972.* Cambridge University Press, 1975.

Simmons, John, and William Mares. *Working Together.* Alfred A. Knopf, 1983.

Sirianni, Carmen. *Workers Control and Socialist Democracy: The Soviet Experience.* Verso–New Left Books, 1982.

Solomonides, Tony, and Les Levidow. *Compulsive Technology: Computers as Culture.* Free Association Books, 1985.

Special Task Force to the Secretary of Health, Education, and Welfare. *Work in America: Report of a Special Task Force to the Secretary of Health, Education, and Welfare.* Foreword by Elliot L. Richardson. The MIT Press, n.d.

Spiro, Herbert J. *The Politics of German Codetermination.* Harvard University Press, 1958.

Stabile, Donald. *Prophets of Order.* South End Press, 1984.

State Intervention in Industry: A Workers' Inquiry. Spokesman Books, 1982.

Stephen, Frank H., ed. *The Performance of Labour-Managed Firms.* Macmillan, 1982.

Strassmann, W. Paul. *Technological Change and Economic Development: The Manufacturing Experience of Mexico and Puerto Rico.* Cornell University Press, 1968.

Sweeney, John J., and Karen Nussbaum. *Solutions for the New Work Force: Policies for a New Social Contract.* Preface by Eli Ginzberg. Seven Locks Press, 1989.

Sweezy, Paul M., and Charles Bettelheim. *On the Transition to Socialism.* Second Edition. Monthly Review Press, 1971.

Szekely, Gabriel. *Manufacturing Across Borders and Oceans: Japan, the United States, and Mexico,* Monograph Series 36. San Diego: Center for U.S.-Mexican Studies, 1991.

Tannenbaum, Arnold S., et al. *Hierarchy in Organizations.* Foreword by Daniel Katz. The Jossey-Bass Behavioral Science Series. Jossey-Bass, 1974.

Taylor, Robert. *Workers and the New Depression.* Macmillan, 1982.

Teich, Albert H., ed. *Technology and Man's Future.* St. Martin's Press, 1972.

Terkel, Studs. *Working: People Talk About What They Do All Day and How They Feel About What They Do.* Avon, 1972.

Thomas, Henk, and Chris Logan. *Mondragon: An Economic Analysis.* George Allen & Unwin, 1982.

Thompson, Paul. *The Nature of Work: An Introduction to Debates on the Labour Process.* Macmillan, 1983.

Thornley, Jenny. *Workers' Co-Operatives: Jobs and Dreams.* Heinemann Educational Books, 1981.

Turner, Lowell. *Democracy at Work: Changing World Markets and the Future of Labor Unions.* Cornell University Press, 1991.

Union of Radical Political Economics (URPE). "Materials Relevant to Constructive Thinking About Socialist Alternatives for America: A Bibliography." Edited by Jim Campen. *Resource Materials in Radical Political Economics* 1 (spring 1974).

United States Congress, House, Committee on Science and Astronautics. *A Study of Technology Assessment: Report of the Committee on Public Engineering Policy/National Academy of Engineering.* U.S. Government Printing Office, July 1969.

———. *Technology: Processes of Assessment and Choice: Report of the National Academy of Sciences.* U.S. Government Printing Office, July 1969.

United States Congress, Office of Technology Assessment, *Computerized Manufacturing Automation. Employment, Education, and the Workplace.* U.S. Congress, Office of Technology Assessment, OTA-CIT-235, April 1984.

United States Department of Labor, Labor-Management Services Administration. *Starting Labor-Management Quality of Work Life Programs.* U.S. Department of Labor/Labor-Management Services Administration, September 1982.

Vanek, Jaroslav. *Crisis and Reform: East and West/Essays in Social Economy.* Ithaca: n.p., 1989.

———. "Decentralization Under Workers Management." *American Economic Review* 57, no. 4 (December 1969): 1006–14.

———. *The General Theory of Labor-Managed Market Economics.* Cornell University Press, 1970.

———. *The Participatory Economy: An Evolutionary Hypothesis and a Strategy for Development.* Cornell University Press, 1971.

———, ed. *Self-Management: Economic Liberation of Man.* Penguin Books, 1975.

Voslensky, Michael. *Nomenklatura: The Soviet Ruling Class.* Translated by Eric Mosbacher, Preface by Milovan Djilas. Doubleday, 1983.

Wachtel, Howard M. *Workers' Management and Workers' Wages in Yugoslavia: The Theory and Practice of Participatory Socialism.* Cornell University Press, 1973.

Wainwright, Hilary, and Dave Elliot. *The Lucas Plan: A New Trade Unionism in the Making?* Allison and Busby, 1982.

Wallick, Franklin. *The American Worker: An Endangered Species.* Ballantine Books, 1972.

Watson, Tony. *Sociology, Work and Industry.* Second edition. Routledge & Kegan Paul, 1987.

White, Michael, and Malcolm Trevor. *Under Japanese Management: The Experience of British Workers.* Policy Studies Institute. Heinemann, 1983.

Whyte, William Foote. *Making Mondragon: The Growth and Dynamics of the Worker Cooperative Complex.* ILR Press, 1988.

Whyte, William Foote, et al. *Worker Participation and Ownership: Cooperative Strategies for Strengthening Local Economies.* ILR Paperback no. 18. ILR Press, 1983.

Wilczynski, J. *The Economics of Socialism: Principles Governing the Operation of the Centrally Planned Economies in the USSR and Eastern Europe Under the New System.* Third Edition. George Allen & Unwin, 1977.

Wilkinson, Barry. *The Shopfloor Politics of New Technology.* Heinemann, 1983.

Wilson, H. B. *Democracy and the Workplace.* Second edition. Black Rose Books, 1980.

Winpisinger, William W. *Reclaiming Our Future: An Agenda for America Labor.* Edited by John Logue, Foreword by Senator Edward M. Kennedy. Westview, 1989.

Wintner, Linda. "Employee Buyouts: An Alternative to Plant Closing." *Research Bulletin No. 140*, The Conference Board, 1983.

Wisman, Jon, ed. "The Democratic Firm: A Cooperative-ESOP Model." In *Worker Empowerment: The Struggle for Workplace Democracy.* Bootstrap Press, 1991.

Witte, John F. *Democracy, Authority, and Alienation in Work: Workers' Participation in an American Corporation.* University of Chicago Press, 1980.

Womack, James P., Daniel T. Jones, and Daniel Roos. *The Machine That Changed the World.* Rawson Associates; Collier Macmillan Canada, 1990.

Wood, Stephen, ed. *The Degradation of Work?: Skill, Deskilling and the Labour Process.* Hutchinson Education, 1982.

Woodworth, Warner, Christopher Meek, and William Foote Whyte, eds. *Industrial Democracy: Strategies for Community Revitalization.* Sage Publications, 1985.

Wright, J. Patrick. *On a Clear Day You Can See General Motors.* Avon Books, 1979.

Yanowitch, Murray, ed. *Soviet Work Attitudes: The Issue of Participation in Management.* M. E. Sharpe; Martin Robinson, 1979.

Yemin, Edward, ed. *Workplace Reductions in Undertakings: Policies and Measures for the Protection of Redundant Workers in Seven Industrialized Market Economy Countries.* International Labour Office, 1982.

Yost, Edward Franklin. "The Concentration of Management in Central Offices of Industrial Firms: The Limitations of Concentrated Management Decision Making and Control." Ph.D. dissertation, Columbia University, 1969. *Dissertation Abstracts International*, vol. 31-04B, p. 1994, 00341 pages.

Yugoslavia, Council of Yugoslav Trade Unions Federation, First International Conference on Participation and Self-Management. *Parva Medunarodna Konferencija O Participaciji I Samoupravljanju* 1. Zagreb: n.p., 1972. See also, *Participation and Self-Management* 2, *Workers' Movement and Workers' Control* 3, Zagreb: n.p., 1973; *Hierarchical Organizations* 4; *Social System and Participation* 5; *Yugoslav Experiment in Self-Management* 6.

Zablocki, Benjamin David. *The Joyful Community: An Account of the Bruderhof, A Communal Movement Now in Its Third Generation.* Penguin Books, 1971.

Zwerdling, Daniel. *Workplace Democracy: A Guide to Workplace Ownership, Participation and Self-management Experiments in the United States and Europe.* Harper Colophon Books, 1978.

For a partial bibliography of literature published 1950–1978 (3,900 references, 73 countries), see Barrie Owen Pettman, ed., *Industrial Democracy: A Selected Bibliography*, MCB Publications, 1978.

Index

A portion of this work first appeared in *The Permanent War Economy* by Seymour Melman, copyright © 1974 by Seymour Melman. Reprinted by permission of Simon & Schuster.

Grateful acknowledgment is made to the following for permission to reprint previously published material:

AFL-CIO: Excerpts from an article by Greg Woodhead (*Survey of Prison Labor*, January 15, 1997). Reprinted by permission.

The Apex Press: Excerpts from *The Underbelly of the U.S. Economy: Joblessness and the Pauperization of Work in America* by David Denbo and Ward Morehouse (Council on International and Public Affairs, The Apex Press, 1997). Reprinted by permission.

The Association for Manufacturing Technology: Statistics from tables C-2, C-6, C-8, C-17, and D-4, based on data from the U.S. Bureau of the Census, from *The Economic Handbook of the Machine Tool Industry* (The Association for Manufacturing Technology, 1997–1998). Reprinted by permission.

Blackwell Publishers/Blackwell Science Ltd.: Excerpts from "Two Routes to Team Production: Saturn and Chrysler Compared" by Harley Shaiken, Steven Lopez, and Isaac Mankita (*Industrial Relations 36*, No. 1, January 1997). Reprinted by permission of Blackwell Publishers/Blackwell Science Ltd.

Brookings Institution Press: Figure 2: "U.S. Government Historical Obligations by Function, 1940–1996," from *Atomic Audit: The Cost and Consequences of U.S. Nuclear Weapons Since 1940*, edited by Stephen Schwartz (Brookings Institution Press, 1998). Reprinted by permission of Brookings Institution Press.

Ford Motor Company: Excerpts from the Collective Bargaining Agreement between UAW and Ford Motor Company (Oct. 7, 1990 and Oct. 9, 1999). Reprinted by permission.

HarperCollins Publishers, Inc., and *Howard Zinn:* Excerpts from *A People's History of the United States* by Howard Zinn, copyright © 1980 by Howard Zinn. Reprinted by permission of HarperCollins Publishers, Inc., and the author.

International Association of Machinists and Aerospace Workers: Excerpts from *HPWO Field Manual: High Performance Work Organization Partnerships*, 1995. Reprinted by permission of International Association of Machinists and Aerospace Workers.

Kelly Press Inc.: Excerpts from *Let's Rebuild America* by International Association of Machinists and Aerospace Workers (Washington, DC, 1984). Reprinted by permission of Kelly Press Inc.

Labor Research Review: Excerpts from "ESOPS and Co-ops: Worker Capitalism and Worker Democracy" by David P. Ellerman (*Labor Research Review*, No. 5, Spring 1985). Reprinted by permission.

Father Gregory MacLeod: Excerpt from *From Mondragon to America: Experiments in Community Economic Development* by Greg MacLeod, 1997. Reprinted by permission of the author.

MIT Press: Excerpts from *Made in America: Regaining the Productive Edge* by Michael L. Dertouzos et al. (1989). Reprinted by permission of the MIT Press.

Monthly Review Foundation: Excerpts from article by David Mandel interviewing Soviet workers (*Monthly Review*, 1994). Reprinted by permission of Monthly Review Foundation.

National Science Board: Material from *Science and Engineering Indicators—2000* (Arlington, VA: National Science Foundation, 2000 [NSF-00-1]). Reprinted courtesy of the National Science Board.

Dr. Bernard Nneji: Excerpts from *Capital Productivity in Relation to Organization of Work in Computer Controlled Machine Tool Production* (1988). Reprinted by permission of Dr. Bernard Nneji.

Harley Shaiken: Excerpt from *Work Transformed: Automation and Labor in the Computer Age* by Harley Shaiken (Lexington Books, 1984). Reprinted by permission of the author.

Time, Inc.: Excerpts from "Special Report/Corporate Welfare" (*Time* magazine, November 23, 1998), copyright © 1998 by Time, Inc. Reprinted by permission of Time, Inc.

Transaction Publishers: Excerpts from *The Theory of Business Enterprise* by Thorstein Veblen, copyright © 1932, 1978. All rights reserved. Reprinted by permission of Transaction Publishers.

United Electrical, Radio and Machine Workers of America (UE): Excerpts from article by Peter Gilmore (*UE News,* February 21, 1997), copyright © 1997 by Peter Gilmore. Reprinted by permission of the United Electrical, Radio and Machine Workers of America (UE).

Westview Press: Excerpts from *Making the Russian Bomb* by Thomas Cochran and Robert Norris Oleg Bukharin, copyright © 1995 by Westview Press, Member of Perseus Books Group. Reprinted by permission of Westview Press, a member of Perseus Books, L.L.C.

A NOTE ABOUT THE AUTHOR

Seymour Melman is Emeritus Professor of Industrial Engineering at Columbia University's School of Engineering and Applied Science.

A NOTE ON THE TYPE

This book was set in Janson, a typeface long thought to have been made by the Dutchman Anton Janson, who was a practicing typefounder in Leipzig during the years 1668–1687. However, it has been conclusively demonstrated that these types are actually the work of Nicholas Kis (1650–1702), a Hungarian, who most probably learned his trade from the master Dutch typefounder Dirk Voskens. The type is an excellent example of the influential and sturdy Dutch types that prevailed in England up to the time William Caslon (1692–1766) developed his own incomparable designs from them.

Composed by
Creative Graphics,
Allentown, Pennsylvania

Printed and bound by
Berryville Graphics
Berryville, Virginia